THE BOSS

J. Edgar Hoover and the Great American Inquisition

*Athan G. Theoharis
and John Stuart Cox*

This edition published in Great Britain in 1993 by
Virgin Books
an imprint of Virgin Publishing Ltd
332 Ladbroke Grove
London W10 5AH

First published in the United States of America
in 1988 by Temple University Press,
Philadelphia

First published in Great Britain in 1989 by
Harrap Books Ltd, London

A catalogue record for this book is available
from the British Library

ISBN 0 86369 775 5

Typeset by Avocet Typesetters, Bicester, Oxon
Printed and bound in Great Britain by
Cox & Wyman Ltd, Reading, Berks

For Nancy and Martha
and our children,
Jeanne, George, and Elizabeth
Theoharis
and Giulia and Will Cox

Politics need not always have to do with legal government. It is a process. It exists in sports, in science, in the world of folk-rock, in religious organizations, in business, among fashion designers and their publicists. There is also a demi-monde of politics which has not received due attention from students of political process in particular and social action in general. I refer to secret societies.

Lionel Tiger, *Men in Groups*

ACKNOWLEDGMENTS

The most complete and accurate record of J. Edgar Hoover's conduct as director of the Federal Bureau of Investigation, including his transactions with presidents and attorneys general, is contained in the files of the FBI. While presidential libraries and other depositories house ample documents pertaining to Hoover, their resources are all of limited value either because the most important are still classified or, as in the case of the presidential libraries, the documentary record is incomplete, 'sanitized', and often quite misleading. Presidents were not apt to record their most sensitive requests to the Director in writing, or, in cases in which they did, would have sought later to hide the fact, but the Director, for his own protection, *did* record such requests in memos for the file. However, because FBI records for the forty-eight years of Hoover's tenure have not yet been deposited at the National Archives, they must be obtained from the Bureau itself, a process that in the nature of things is time-consuming and costly, requiring as it does in almost every case resort to a Freedom of Information Act request.

The research for this biography began in 1976, with a careful scrutiny of the FBI documents reprinted in the hearings of the Senate Select Committee on Intelligence Activities (the so-called Church Committee) and, subsequent to that, submission of a series of FOIA requests to the Bureau — a number of which were still pending when this book went to press. We wish to express our appreciation to James Hall and Emil Moschella, the heads of the Records Management Division of the Bureau, and their able staffs for processing our numerous requests; and also to Susan

Rosenfeld Falb, the official historian of the FBI, for her informed assistance. For their help in expediting the FBI's processing of our FOIA requests, we particularly thank Chairman Glenn English and Congressman Gerald Kleczka of the House Government Information Subcommittee and Committee Counsel Robert Gellman.

For support in funding our research at the Bureau, we are indebted to several foundations, namely the Field Foundation, the Warsh-Mott Funds, the C.S. Fund, the Youth Project, the Fund for Investigative Journalism, the Webster Woodmansee Fund, the American Historical Association—Albert Beveridge Research Grant, and Marquette University.

A number of individuals and organizations shared their FBI files with us or otherwise aided our research into FBI files. For their cooperation, we thank Congressman Don Edwards, Harrison Salisbury, Tony Mauro, Anthony Marro, John Henry Faulk, Morton Halperin, Alger Hiss, Kai Bird, Kenneth O'Reilly, Susan Dion, Douglas Cassel, Harold Weisberg, M. Wesley Swearingen, David Luce, Richard Criley, Percival Bailey, Kenneth Waltzer, Steven Rosswurm, David Garrow, Charles Martin, Jon Weiner, John Fuegi, Dan Simoniski, Theodore Kornweibel, Sam Walker, W. H. and Carol Bernstein Ferry, John Studer and Holbrook Mahn, Socialist Workers Party, Women's International League for Peace and Freedom, Committee for Public Justice, War Resisters League, American Labor Party, National Lawyers Guild, *The Nation*, American Civil Liberties Union, and National Committee to Abolish HUAC.

Our understanding of Hoover was greatly enriched by the testimony of Hoover family members, Bureau associates and acquaintances who kindly granted us interviews, most importantly Margaret Hoover Fennell, Mr. and Mrs. Dickerson Hoover, Jr., and Fred Robinette; also Ramsey Clark, Cartha DeLoach, Don Edwards, Anthony Marro, Harrison Salisbury, John Henry Faulk, George Reedy, Joseph Bryan III, Alger Hiss, M. Wesley Swearingen, and Allan Witwer. Two former associates of Hoover who asked not to be identified were also greatly helpful. But undoubtedly the greatest single assistance we received in understanding Hoover's character was given by Michael Sheard, professor of psychiatry at Yale University Medical School, who, together with his wife, Wendy Stedman Sheard, a writer and art historian, read the first draft of our manuscript, commented on it in detail and initiated a computer search into the pertinent clinical literature at Yale's medical school library.

We also wish to thank Mr. and Mrs. Thomas Catlin for their hospitality in showing us around the house that Hoover lived in on Thirtieth Place, Northwest, for more than thirty years.

And, finally, we thank our editor, Michael Ames, and our agent, Laura Fillmore, both of whom provided strong editorial and moral support.

CONTENTS

INTRODUCTION

IN HIS BEST-SELLING MYSTERY *The Chancellor Manuscript*, the adventure novelist Robert Ludlum intricately explored the blackmail potential of the files that J. Edgar Hoover, the Director of the Federal Bureau of Investigation from 1924 until his death in May 1972, secretly maintained in his office. In a complicated plot involving conspirators and double agents, Ludlum's characters vie either to destroy the 'Hoover files' or to retrieve what remains of them for purposes of subverting the federal government. Ludlum's fictional Hoover maintained a 'cabinet of filth,' consisting of dossiers on 'the most influential people in the country, in the House, the Senate, the Pentagon, the White House, Presidential and Congressional advisors, leading authorities in a dozen fields.' In this account, Hoover's mere possession of such files empowered him to 'shape the government, alter the laws and attitudes of the country.' Describing the scope and blackmail potential of the 'Hoover files,' one of Ludlum's characters pointedly observes that 'every paper, every insert, every addendum related to Security crossed Hoover's desk. And as we know, 'Security' took on the widest possible range. Sexual activities, drinking habits, marriage and family confidences, the most personal details of the subjects' lives – none were too remote or insignificant. Hoover pored over these dossiers like Croesus with his gold. Three Presidents wanted to replace him. None did.'

Ludlum's fictional Hoover and fictional Hoover files struck a responsive chord among a large number of Americans, who viewed the book not as a fictional account but as historically accurate. For by the late 1970s, when *The*

1

Chancellor Manuscript came out, many Americans were convinced that Hoover *had* blackmailed presidents and members of Congress in order to maintain his power and that of the Bureau he headed. Ludlum's reference to the 'Hoover files,' moreover, was by then not mere speculation. For in February 1975 Attorney General Edward Levi, describing Hoover's top-secret Official and Confidential office file during public testimony before a House subcommittee, had disclosed that its contents included 'derogatory' personal information on presidents, congressmen, cabinet officials, and prominent citizens. Building on these revelations, House and Senate intelligence committees later that year and in 1976, with the assistance of one of the present authors, recounted other examples of Hoover's efforts to use the resources of the government to discredit his adversaries and extend the FBI's influence, including efforts, under the code-named COINTELPRO (i.e., counterintelligence program), to destabilize domestic organizations and individuals legally opposing racial segregation, U.S. escalation of the Vietnam War, and the Nixon administration's unauthorized military incursion into neutral Cambodia.

These revelations of the mid-1970s occasioned no surprise among Washington's politicians, who had long suspected that Hoover maintained files on his adversaries, in Congress and elsewhere. But whether or not their worst fears were substantiated, none of these political leaders had earlier demanded an investigation of allegations that such files existed or sought to have the files themselves destroyed on the ground that they had no legitimate law enforcement purpose. It was simply accepted, as a fact of life, that Hoover commanded unassailable leverage.

Thus, when meeting with White House aide John W. Dean III in February 1973, President Nixon responded to Dean's remark that the Watergate-threatened Nixon White House would be better off if Hoover were still alive by saying: 'Well, Hoover performed. He would have fought. That was the point. He would have defied a few people. He would have scared them to death. He had a file on everybody.'

2

Much later, in a 1985 press interview, then-White House aide Fred Fielding jocularly attributed his long tenure on the Reagan staff, ridden by factional rivalries as it was, to the fact that 'I have their [other White House staff members'] FBI files.'

In the same vein, the former powerful chairman of the House Judiciary Committee, Emanuel Celler, attributed Hoover's power to 'the fact that he was the head of an agency that in turn had tremendous power, power of surveillance, power of control over the lives and destinies of every man in the nation. He had a dossier on every member of Congress and every member of the Senate.' Asked whether congressmen were aware of this, Celler replied unhesitatingly, 'The members of the House certainly were. He had no right to have such dossiers. But he had them, no question about it.'

Celler's assertion that Hoover maintained dossiers on congressmen was entirely accurate. Yet Celler could not have substantiated his charges even if he or some other member of Congress had seriously tried to do so. A master politician and bureaucrat, Hoover had taken steps to ensure that the practice could not be discovered if a formal congressional inquiry was begun. The FBI maintained no 'file' on any member of Congress, nor any report of anything of the kind in its central records system. Instead, Hoover had his aides prepare 'summary memoranda' on every congressman, based on information acquired by FBI agents, whose original reports were then destroyed. These 'summary memoranda' (not 'files,' mind) were maintained in the FBI's Administrative Review Unit apart from other FBI files.

Nixon's belief that Hoover maintained files on everyone likewise was no idle speculation. But, unlike Celler, Nixon had every reason to know. For, as president, he had regularly turned to Hoover for 'derogatory' information (on, for instance, Supreme Court Justices Abe Fortas and William O. Douglas and members of the Washington press corps), and Hoover had readily accommodated the president's wishes. Nixon erred only in remarking that

3

Hoover had files on 'everyone' – the FBI's personal files in fact extended only to 25 million.

Unknown to Nixon and Celler, and the rest of the nation's politicians, beginning in 1925, the year after his appointment as Director, Hoover had begun amassing yet another file to be maintained separately from the FBI's central records system – the 'Obscene File.' The Director's audacity in doing so, in brazen defiance of written orders from Attorney General Harlan Fiske Stone to limit Bureau investigations to breaches of federal statutes and in clear violation of constitutional restraints, raises questions about the man's basic character. Was he, as many believed, a great patriot in a time of danger or, as others felt, from the beginning a self-serving destroyer of God-given liberties? What emboldened him to circumvent the law and the oversight authority of the attorney general, Congress, and the courts – all three branches of the federal government? Was it confidence in his superior rectitude? Or perhaps an inkling of the opposite? Was it ambition to build an all-powerful agency or an inordinate fear of real and imagined enemies? Was the support he received from the general public and the establishment throughout half a century, in short, justified? By the time of his death in office at the age of seventy-seven, it appeared to many that it was. The Bureau he had created, after all, was viewed as a highly professional organization, efficient and accountable, wherefore its imposing new headquarters on Pennsylvania Avenue is called the J. Edgar Hoover Building.

The answers to these questions require a more careful look at the background than has been attempted heretofore. They necessitate not only an examination of the secret activities of Hoover himself, requiring a minute analysis of FBI files, but also a simultaneous consideration of the historical context: the emergence of the United States as a world power (with powerful potential enemies) at the start of this century, the shock of two world wars in a single generation, the immense growth of the federal government and the power of the state, the effect of the diaspora of Europe's Jews,

4

and the impact of new immigrant groups generally on native-born Americans.

Until the twentieth century, law enforcement in the United States was exclusively a state responsibility; both liberals and conservatives feared that a federal police role would threaten constitutional government. At the time of its creation in July 1908, the Bureau of Investigation was a minor division of a relatively minor federal department subject to the direct supervision of the attorney general.

By 1972, in contrast, the FBI was ubiquitous, and its intrusive investigations of radical activities were defended as necessary. By then, the traditional belief that a national police force could undermine individual rights and constitutional government had been abandoned. Furthermore, although theoretically subject to the attorney general's direct control, the Director himself defined the scope of his and the Bureau's increasingly independent authority.

What facilitated this remarkable transformation of the FBI's role and of Hoover's power? How was it that Hoover succeeded in undercutting the fears and constitutional limitations that until the 1940s had relegated the Bureau to the status of a mere functionary organization? The answer, quite simply, is Hoover's successful promulgation of the belief that a strong FBI was needed to safeguard the nation's security from the threat of subversion at home.

The degree of Hoover's success is indicated by statistics on the growth of the Bureau's personnel. When created, the Bureau had twenty-four operatives, a director, and twenty-three agents authorized to investigate interstate commerce and antitrust cases only. Enactment of the White Slave Traffic (Mann) Act in 1910 and the Motor Vehicles (Dyer) Act in 1919, by extending the list of interstate commerce crimes, slightly expanded the Bureau's responsibilities and personnel. U.S. involvement in World War I after April 1917 and attendant concerns about espionage also contributed to the Bureau's early growth, and the number of agents increased from 300 to 580 at war's end. The modesty of that increase is somewhat misleading, as the Bureau's enlarged wartime surveillance activities were facilitated by a cooperative relationship with a private citizens' organization, the American Protective League (APL), formed with the Justice Department's blessing in February 1917. APL members investigated and reported to the Bureau on 'subversive' activities while Bureau agents focused on major cases, provided guidance to the APL, and closely monitored radical publications (under the direction of the newly appointed head of the General Intelligence Division, J. Edgar Hoover).

Bureau interest in radical activities did not cease with the end of the war, even though the authority for such continued investigations had abruptly ended. On the contrary, spying on dissident Americans greatly increased. Still, during the budget-conscious 1920s, personnel were pared to the prewar level of approximately 300. In 1932 the Bureau employed only 326 agents.

The sharp rise in kidnappings and bank robberies during the early years of the Great Depression provided a second impetus to the Bureau's expansion. Convinced that local and state police could not effectively handle these crimes, Congress between 1932 and 1934 enacted ten laws to expand the definition of an interstate crime and thereby the Bureau's mandated investigative responsibilities. Partly in consequence, the number of FBI agents almost doubled, to 609, by 1936.

But World War II and the Cold War provided by far the greatest stimulus to the Bureau's permanent growth. From an annual appropriation of $6.3 million in 1939, the FBI's budget burgeoned sixfold to $35.9 million in 1947. By 1945 the Bureau employed 4,886 agents. This number fell to 3,559 in 1946 (a decrease stemming from the termination of the agency's World War II foreign intelligence responsibilities in Central and South America), but by 1952, kindled by fears of Cold War subversion, many of them broadcast by the Bureau itself, Bureau employment of agents had rebounded to 7,029, where it stabilized.

At the time of this last, crucial spurt of growth, no concerted effort was made to ascertain how Hoover directed

6

his Bureau. Although the rationale for Bureau enlargement was the need to monitor 'subversive' activities, responsible public officials had no direct knowledge of how Hoover defined this nebulous, legally meaningless term. Were FBI investigations confined to ascertaining foreign control of 'subversive' citizens and organizations? Or did the FBI focus without restraint on any radicals who challenged conventional political beliefs and the economic status quo?

The prevailing belief, sedulously cultivated by Hoover, was that the FBI operated with constitutional restraint and sought evidence of foreign control before involving itself. But, in reality, Hoover's philosophic and emotional antipathy toward radical dissent provided the main impetus to FBI surveillance priorities. Agents were instructed that it was 'not possible to formulate any hard-and-fast standards' for measuring 'dangerousness' and accordingly were told to investigate individuals 'espousing the line' of 'revolutionary movements.' Furthermore, whenever there was any 'doubt an individual may be a current threat to the internal security of the nation, the question should be resolved in the interest of security and investigation continued.' FBI agents were to report any protest activity *possibly* involving Communists and were to interpret 'the term "communist" . . . in its broad sense as including persons not only adhering to the principles of the CPUSA [Communist Party USA] itself, but also to such splinter and offshoot groups as the Socialist Workers Party, Progressive Labor Party, and the like.'

Not surprisingly, FBI agents continued to investigate local chapters of the National Association for the Advancement of Colored People (NAACP) long after having established that few Communists if any were involved. Hoover at one time chastised the New York field office for having concluded in a report on civil rights leader Bayard Rustin that no evidence had been uncovered to suggest that Rustin was a subversive. Because no evidence had been uncovered that Rustin was 'anti-Communist,' Hoover ordered the Bureau's investigation continued, pointing out that the completed investigation was inadequate as long as anything remained to be learned about Rustin's civil rights activities.'

Nor was it the case that Hoover demanded FBI antiradical investigations only to confirm or deny Communist associations. Convinced that the nation confronted an unprecedented peril, the Director, whenever assured that the FBI's activities could not become publicly known, discreetly used such information to purge, or try to purge, supposed radicals of every stripe from positions of power.

For example, in January 1965, alarmed by the appearance of the Free Speech Movement at the University of California at Berkeley and convinced that 'the University of California at Berkeley is, of course, infiltrated with a lot of communists, both in the student body and the faculty,' Hoover discussed the problem with former CIA director John McCone. A Berkely graduate and substantial contributor to the university, McCone advised Hoover that a close personal friend of his was a member of the University of California Board of Regents. (The FBI deleted this individual's name in releasing the memo in response to our Freedom of Information Act request, but he was either State Superintendent of Instruction Max Rafferty or Lockheed executive John Canaday.) McCone added that his friend had confided an interest in obtaining information 'on any persons who are communists or have communist associations either on the faculty or in the student body and then at a Board of Regents level handle it without disclosing his source.' Hoover seized this opportunity, directing Wesley Grapp, the head of the FBI's Los Angeles office, to provide to this regent 'public source information on some of these individuals causing trouble at Berkeley' on the assurance that he would not disclose having received it from the FBI.

The Rustin and University of California—Berkeley cases were by no means exceptional.

Although all 25 million FBI case files obviously cannot and need not be reviewed, an examination of just three FBI files, none of them known to earlier biographers of Hoover, suggests the scope of and political criteria determining Hoover's obsession with the American left. These three sensitive FBI files are the record destruction file, the Symbol

Number Sensitive Source Index, and the Surreptitious Entries file.

On Hoover's orders, FBI agents over the years collected every radical pamphlet, periodical, and newspaper they could lay their hands on as well as articles about radical activities in the popular press. This massive accumulation of unusable material (unusable for prosecutive purposes, because these publications disclosed no violation of federal statutes) in time posed a major housekeeping problem. Concluding that not all of these publications needed to be maintained, Hoover in 1971 authorized the transfer of 200 five-drawer cabinets containing some of them to the Library of Congress, on condition that agents could contact the Library should they need to research them. Then, in 1976, an additional 30 six-drawer, legal-size cabinets containing approximately 32,000 radical publications were transferred to the Library of Congress.

A second means of demonstrating Hoover's political commitment to spying on American dissenters generally is a search of the Symbol Number Sensitive Source Index (now known as the National Security Electronic Surveillance Card File), a directory of the code numbers assigned to those FBI wiretaps and bugs that were frequently cited in FBI reports. This index identifies the principal targets of FBI taps and bugs and illustrates Hoover's interest in using information so obtained for nonprosecutive, political purposes — when such use could be hidden.

Fully aware of the illegality of FBI wiretapping and bugging, Hoover required his prior authorization for each electronic installation. His main concern, however, was not to limit these practices but to maintain tight discipline and to prevent discovery of them. By formulating the Do Not File, Personal and Confidential, June Mail, and Administrative Pages procedures discussed hereafter, the Director ensured that the FBI's frequent resort to illegal investigative techniques would not be found out. Then, through the use of 'symbol numbers' and the creation of the Symbol Number Sensitive Source Index, he saw to it that information obtained from these sources could be disseminated without disclosing how it had been obtained. Instead of specifying that such information had been obtained from a tap or bug, agents' reports would cite only the assigned symbol numbers. Should FBI officials need for their own purposes to identify the source, they could consult the index.

Although the index was intended to serve as a finding aid, it now ironically allows us to identify whom the FBI tapped and bugged and the date of installation and duration of each tap/bug. The 13,500 index cards in the inactive (nonpending) section of this catalogue list the names of the individuals and organizations who, beginning in 1941, were the targets of FBI taps and bugs. When releasing this file to the authors, the FBI withheld all cards on individuals — ostensibly on personal privacy grounds — but the released cards on organizations document that virtually every American radical group active in the 1940s and thereafter was the target of an FBI tap, bug, or both. More specifically, virtually every left-of-center civil rights organization and labor union was tapped and bugged.

Despite the Director's protestations of neutrality in labor union matters, left-wing unions were extensively tapped and bugged (ostensibly to ascertain possible Communist influence). The FBI tapped the Congress of Industrial Organizations (CIO) Council, the CIO Maritime Committee, the Food, Tobacco, Agricultural & Allied Workers of America (CIO), the International Longshoremen's and Warehousemen's Union, the National Maritime Union, the National Union of Marine Cooks & Stewards, and the United Public Workers of America (formerly the United Federal Workers of America). It also bugged the United Automobile Workers, the United Electrical Radio & Machine Workers of America, and the United Mine Workers.

Hoover privately justified the FBI's tapping and bugging of unions thought to have Communist or radical leaders as essential to establishing whether they were subject to Soviet control. The scope and intensity of this coverage strongly suggest, however, that he had concluded that efforts to transform the American economy were themselves

10

subversive, whether or not directed by Soviet leaders. The targets of FBI wiretapping and bugging in the civil rights field also document Hoover's essentially political definition of subversion.[1]

Although virtually no left-wing organization, no matter how small, escaped FBI tapping or bugging, right-wing organizations almost entirely eluded Hoover's scrutiny, the principal exceptions being the Ku Klux Klan and, within carefully defined limits, six pro-fascist organizations in the period 1940–1941. (Recognizing that continued wiretapping would foreclose espionage and sabotage prosecutions, Hoover discontinued taps producing information on 'Fascist and Italian matters' in June 1941 and on 'Nazi and German matters' in December 1941.)[2]

Another indication that FBI surveillance was politically motivated – one confirming Hoover's indifference to legal restraints and his ability to surmount the oversight roles of Congress, the courts, and the Department of Justice – is contained in the FBI's file on break-ins (once termed 'black bag jobs,' now 'surreptitious entries').

Conceding that break-ins were 'clearly illegal,' Hoover nevertheless pressured his agents to use them to obtain subscription and membership lists, financial records, and correspondence of targeted individuals and organizations. At the same time, seeking to ensure that this illegal practice would not be discovered, the Director required his prior authorization before agents attempted break-ins so that they would not engage in a 'fishing expedition' and would undertake 'proper planning . . . in that the individual in the field who is making this recommendation is fully assured of complete security.'

Hoover's carefully formulated safeguards necessitated the creation of written records – records documenting both a request to commit an illegal act and the Director's authorization to proceed. To ensure that such records would not be incorporated into the FBI's case files on the targeted individual/organization – because the FBI might be required to produce these files in response to a court-ordered discovery motion or a congressional subpoena – Hoover in 1942 devised a special filing procedure for break-in documents. Memoranda requesting the Director's permission to conduct break-ins were to be captioned 'Do Not File,' and, thus captioned, were to be neither serialized nor indexed in the FBI's central records system. Following the Director's approval of a break-in, such Do Not File memoranda were then *filed* in the office of the assistant director having supervisory responsibility. These office files were in turn destroyed every six months. Heads of FBI field offices were not to make copies of their break-in requests but instead to prepare an 'informal' memorandum (again not to be serialized or indexed in the central records system), which was to be filed in the office safe 'until the next semi-annual inspection by Bureau Inspectors, at which time it is destroyed.'

Hoover's meticulous attention to detail was intended to create a fail-safe system; and, indeed, despite their frequency, FBI break-ins dating from the early 1940s went undiscovered. Ironically, it was Hoover's caution in the waning years of his directorship that subverted this careful planning.

In October 1971 the Director decided to preserve a written record of an earlier order banning domestic security break-ins. Because this order, dated July 1966, was penned on a summary memorandum describing his Do Not File procedure, Hoover inadvertently preserved a record of his break-in authorization policy. Specifically, he ordered his administrative assistant Helen Gandy, to transfer the summary memorandum from his Personal and Confidential File to his second office file, the Official and Confidential File. Had Hoover not ordered this transfer, the memorandum describing the Do Not File procedure would have been destroyed in 1972 along with the other contents of his Personal and Confidential File – as was done by Miss Gandy in the weeks following the Director's death and pursuant to his instructions. And because Hoover's Official and Confidential File was subsequently incorporated into the FBI's central records system, the 1966 memorandum afforded a retrievable record of the Director's break-in policy.

After reviewing this file in 1975 and thereby discovering this practice, the Senate Select Committee on Intelligence Activities (the so-called Church Committee) demanded information on the number of FBI break-ins conducted between 1942 and 1966. The requested statistical information could not be provided, FBI officials claimed, because the relevant records, which would have been maintained in the office files of assistant directors, had been routinely destroyed every six months.

Once again, however, Hoover's fail-safe system broke down. All break-in documents had *not* been destroyed. Included among the eighty-six folders in Assistant Director Louis Nichols's extant office file are three recording break-ins. In addition, the 'black bag job' folder of the special agent in charge (SAC) of the New York field office, containing break-in documents for the period 1954 through 1973, inexplicably was not destroyed, and this massive file now makes up the bulk of the FBI's 'Surreptitious Entries' file.

These records of FBI break-ins are not complete, but they do document the scope and political purposes of the FBI's monitoring of the American left. They confirm Hoover's interest in learning about the membership, sources of financial support, and politics of American radical organizations generally. And although the Director had conceded that break-ins were 'clearly illegal,' they reveal that in time he authorized break-ins during FBI investigations of individuals actually under suspicion of violating federal statutes, including crime syndicate leaders targeted under Hoover's Top Hoodlum program of the late 1950s – notwithstanding the fact that any information so obtained would be tainted and, technically, could not be used for prosecutive purposes. Having by the late 1950s successfully immunized FBI operations against external scrutiny, Hoover no longer worried about questions of legality.

Created in October 1941 on Hoover's order, Nichols's office file was in effect an extension of the Director's own two office files. Used to maintain especially sensitive documents of particular interest to the Director, Nichols's

Official and Confidential File, or that part of it still extant, contains three folders recording three extremely sensitive FBI break-ins.

The most sensitive of these was a January 1942 raid on the New York office of the American Youth Congress (AYC). During their photocopying of AYC documents, agents came across correspondence between AYC officials and Eleanor Roosevelt. The two copies of this intercepted correspondence, because they involved the wife of the president of the United States, were thereupon hand-delivered to Hoover's office. Keenly interested in the First Lady's liberal political activities, Hoover ordered his aides to analyze and prepare a report on this illegally obtained correspondence. No mention of the purloined letters was confided to the White House.

The second Nichols folder records that in either 1940 or 1941 FBI agents burglarized the Washington, D.C., offices of the American Peace Mobilization and those of the Washington Committee for Democratic Action to obtain these organizations' membership lists. Hoover thereupon learned that among the members of these quite reputable organizations were certain Justice Department employees or their wives. The Director immediately pressured Assistant to the Attorney General Matthew McGuire to dismiss them, thereby demonstrating his equation of membership in radical organizations with disloyalty. Among those to be purged from the Department were then Assistant Solicitor General Charles Fahy (later a federal judge) and departmental attorneys Thomas Emerson (later a Yale University law professor) and Herbert Wechsler (later a Columbia University law professor).

The third case involved a matter of great concern to the Director — namely, the attempt by liberal activists in 1940 and 1941 to publicly question his leadership of the FBI (which Hoover revealingly dubbed the 'smear campaign'). At first the Director's critics concentrated on the Bureau's February 1940 dragnet raid against recruiters for the International Abraham Lincoln Brigade (which had fought on the Loyalist side in the Spanish Civil War), depicting it as confirmation that the FBI had become an 'American OGPU.' Subsequent publicity about the FBI's investigation of the West Coast longshoremen's union leader Harry Bridges, including monitoring his trips around the country and bugging his hotel room during a visit to New York, precipitated demands that the Roosevelt administration drop deportation proceedings against Bridges (an Australian national) and instead investigate Hoover's directorship of the FBI.

Goaded by these charges, Hoover sought information about his critics' political strategies and backgrounds. In March 1942 he authorized a break-in at the office of the New York attorney Carol King, who had played a prominent role in defending Bridges and in lobbying civil libertarians, trade unionists, and radical activists to support the Bridges defense effort. Agents photocopied, and dutifully transmitted to Hoover, three volumes of 'material' and 'various items.' Summary memoranda were thereupon compiled on individuals identified from the seized documents as active in this 'smear campaign.' These included Herbert Wechsler, the CIO attorney and later Supreme Court Justice Arthur Goldberg, and the prominent civil liberties attorneys Edward Lamb and Louis McCabe. The political activities and associations of each were recounted, as well as their responses to King's invitation to have their organizations pressure Congress to stop the Bridges deportation proceedings and instead initiate an investigation of the FBI. What use, if any, was made of these accounts is not known.

In contrast, the Surreptitious Entries file — consisting primarily of 'informal' break-in memoranda maintained since 1954 in the New York SAC's personal folder — provides a nearly full record of FBI break-in targets and affords insights into Hoover's purpose in obtaining information about radical political activities. Apparently, no radical or left-liberal organization escaped the Director's surveillance interest, and when it came to the American left, the Bureau's illegal break-ins were not used with restraint. The targets of FBI break-ins included:

Civil Rights Congress

Jewish Young Fraternalists

Washington office of the Jewish Culture Society

National Committee to Secure Justice for Morton Sobell

Johnson Forest Group (a splinter faction of the Socialist Workers party)

Vietnam Veterans Against the War in Vietnam

Washington office of the National Lawyers Guild

Independent Citizens Committee of the Arts, Sciences and Professions

Veterans of the Abraham Lincoln Brigade

Student Non-Violent Coordinating Committee

Hellenic American Brotherhood

Socialist Workers party and its youth affiliate, the Young Socialist Alliance

Emma Lazarus Federation

Negro Labor Victory Committee

Joint Anti-Fascist Refugee Committee

Chicago headquarters of the National Mobilization Committee to End the War in Vietnam

Chicago Committee to Defend the Bill of Rights

Business office of Stanley Levison, an associate of the civil rights leader Martin Luther King, Jr.

Russian War Relief

League of American Writers

American Slav Congress

Nationalist party of Puerto Rico

Muslim Cult of Islam (Black Muslims)

Emergency Civil Liberties Committee (later renamed the National Emergency Civil Liberties Committee)

Office of the journal *Africa Latin America Asia Revolution*

Fair Play for Cuba Committee

Office of the magazine *Progressive Labor*

Local 1730 of the International Longshoremen's Association

Proletarian party

Chinese Hand Laundry Alliance

American Association for Democratic Germany

International Workers Order

Hoover's success in ensuring that FBI agents could monitor American radical political activities without risk of discovery that they regularly employed illegal investigative techniques in doing so left a heritage of fear and distrust. The chilled atmosphere that resulted served to silence dissent, inhibit democratic discussion, and move American politics towards an unresponsive, authoritarian right. Most disturbing, by immunizing FBI operations to critical scrutiny, Hoover made a mockery of the American Constitution and its system of checks and balances. And yet, as former Attorney General Ramsey Clark said in an interview for this book in 1985, events shaped Hoover quite as much as he shaped them.

The truth is not simple, and assessing the life of this enormously influential man is problematical indeed. For Mr. Hoover, as opposed to the Director, or 'the Boss,' as he was affectionately called at his self-styled 'Seat of Government' in Washington, was a recluse, a loner who lived with his widowed mother until her death when he was forty-three and thereafter lived alone until his own death thirty-four years later. He kept no journal, maintained no personal correspondence to speak of, and had only one close (apparently not sexually intimate) friend, his amanuensis and Bureau second-in-command, Clyde Tolson, himself a lifelong bachelor and social introvert. At the same time, Hoover, as head of one of the most powerful agencies of the federal government, used the ample resources of his office to manufacture a public persona quite imposing enough to discourage hostile inquiries into the labyrinthine evasions of his official conduct and the dreary details of his hermetic private life. (Likewise, *all* of the resources of the Bureau were used to counteract those few attacks that nevertheless did develop.) Indeed, so total was Hoover's impersonation of the incorruptible G-Man that even after his death a would-be biographer could accurately claim that the entire published record of the Director's childhood and youth could be contained in a single printed page.

The public persona is well known, almost a staple of the nation's mythology. It has been promulgated in a number of best-selling volumes, pre-eminently Don Whitehead's Bureau-authorized and Bureau-edited *The FBI Story*, and debunked in several others. But none of these books has come close to capturing the real John Edgar Hoover, so thorough was his effort to expunge from the record the extreme modesty of his beginnings, the extraordinary poverty of his personal life, and the profound abuse of his office.

The Hoover the public knows was a man of mettle and character, a God-fearing crusader and former Sunday school teacher who, curiously, did not go to church. As fledgling Director, aged twenty-nine, he cleaned out the Bureau after the scandals of Teapot Dome, dismissing those who had spied on members of Congress investigating, among other things, young Hoover's overzealous pursuit of radicals during the first Red Scare. (Years later he untruthfully denied under oath any responsibility for the Justice Department's antiradical excesses of 1919–1920.). As the foremost gangbuster during the national crime wave of the 1930s, he personally took part in apprehending several most-wanted hoodlums in carefully orchestrated and well-publicized shootouts. Propelled by this celebrity, he emerged as the bulwark of the nation's security in World War II, thwarting the espionage and sabotage designs of the Axis powers. And as the nation's Cold Warrior par excellence, he stoutly upheld the goodness of 'Americanism' against the second onslaught of international 'Commonism,' as he called it.

The private Hoover, who is just now beginning to come into view, thanks to the thousands of hitherto unpublished FBI documents cited herein and the willingness of several Hoover family members to try to set the record straight, appears to have been a fearful and compulsive maverick, who suffered torments of insecurity and had his toilet in northwest Washington built on a platform to protect him from the menace of microorganic invasion. The son of an ineffectual father who was institutionalized for depression and then forced out of a minor government clerkship without a pension and of a domineering mother who seethed with ambition for her son, he exhibited an obsession with power throughout his life.

Deeply, probably totally repressed – he never seriously courted any woman, as far as is known – he identified political radicalism with filth and licentiousness, neither of which ever failed to arouse in him almost hysteric loathing. Obliged to win his stern Calvinist mother's approbation through feats of self-denial and gaudy accomplishment, he suffered from a painful stomach ulcer most of his life.

There is nevertheless a heroic dimension to this sad, impoverished man, one that lies somewhere between his controversial public dimension and the largely impenetrable one that he kept secret, perhaps, partly, even from himself. Hoover had a remarkable capacity to discern and articulate beliefs, to bond to belief systems, and thereby to identify himself with them. The force of his convictions carried great weight with his conservative constituency, which afforded him a network of eager informers in every agency of the government, in the nation's media, and in even the remotest community and thus helped to disarm the criticisms of those who challenged him. He was, in short, a natural leader, the very sort of person every organization is looking for, the member of the team who best exemplifies its common values. Nor did he shirk his responsibilities to his colleagues. He made it clear from the beginning that any criticism of the Bureau was a criticism of himself, and he personally defended the Bureau before sometimes hostile congressional investigating committees. He was, to some, preposterously self-important, and he could be extremely cruel to loyal subordinates, but he was always the FBI agent's first line of defense. As one of his assistant directors said, he 'was the engine that pulled the train. Everyone understood that . . .'

That his beliefs were parochial to a degree in no way alters the basic fact that he resolutely entered the field of responsibility, took the heat of the most intense controversy, and repeatedly overwhelmed the Bureau's critics. That he abused his office for his own advantage in doing so was no more an offense to his aides and his right-wing constituency

19

than it was to himself. (Barry Goldwater doubtless expressed this credo most eloquently when he declared, 'Extremism in defense of liberty is no vice.')

Hoover had more to do with undermining American constitutional guarantees than any political leader before or since. Moreover, he dissembled flagrantly in denying the subversive mischief that he was doing – most notably in denying the unauthorized dissemination of Bureau file information to Senator Joseph McCarthy and his Permanent Subcommittee on Investigations, here detailed and documented for the first time. Yet in view of the success of his unparalleled, lengthy career, there seems to be no gainsaying the fact that J. Edgar Hoover was in certain crucial respects a representative American of his time.

Notes to Introduction

1. The FBI tapped and bugged virtually every civil rights organization challenging racial segregation or seeking to promote equal rights for black Americans. These included the Alabama Peoples Educational Association, Gandhi Society for Human Rights, Committee to Aid the Monroe Defendants, Southern Conference for Human Welfare, Black Panther party, Nation of Islam, Universal Negro Improvement Association, Southern Christian Leadership Conference, National Association for the Advancement of Colored People (NAACP), (World War II) March on Washington movement, African Liberation Day Coordinating Committee, and the Student Non-Violent Coordinating Committee. The FBI both tapped and bugged the March on Washington movement in March and June 1943, at the time of this *ad hoc* organization's announced challenge to the policy of racial segregation in the military and in the defense industries. Six months later, in December 1943, the FBI tapped the NAACP.

2. Hoover also authorized the bugging of the America First party (because of its suspected pro-German orientation) and of the Peace Now Movement (because of its advocacy of an immediate negotiated peace with Germany), and the tapping of Jehovah's Witnesses (because of their opposition to conscription and refusal to salute the American flag).

20

CHAPTER ONE

(1895–1913)
CHILDHOOD AND YOUTH

ANNIE HOOVER was thirty-four when she bore her fourth and last child, John Edgar, at 413 Seward Square in southeast Washington on New Year's Day, 1895. Fifteen years had elapsed since the birth of her first child, Dickerson Naylor Hoover, Jr., now a strapping, athletic, gregarious Eastern High School freshman, and fourteen since the birth of her second, her tomboyish, somewhat rebellious daughter, Lillian. A third and beloved child, Marguerite, born after the family moved from a rented house on Fifth Street, northeast, to the present two-story, semidetached frame house on Seward Square, had died at three of diphtheria during the family's annual summer vacation at Atlantic City, New Jersey, in 1893, and Annie had not recovered from her grief until the promise of this, her fourth. After Marguerite's death she had wanted to die herself, or had said so to family and friends – she later said that she had had Edgar hoping she would die in childbirth – but now she was radiant, as she had been when Dick was born, given, as she said to the end of her long life, a new reason for being.

The baby was frail like his father, which may have troubled Annie because her husband's frailty, both physical and emotional, clearly had compromised his determined efforts to gain advancement beyond a mere clerk's foothold at the United States Coast and Geodetic Survey, in which his father, John Thomas Hoover, had served as a clerk before him.[1] On the other hand, the infant had her dark eyes and dark complexion and something of the look of grim determination that some observers had professed to find in the studio photographs taken of her when she was a girl. Her other children seemed incapable of meeting her

21

expectations. Dick wanted only to be a minister of the church — the Presbyterian Church — for which, at least, he appeared well suited by temperament, and Lillian, in any case, was a girl. But John Edgar, like Annie's maternal grandfather, Hans Hitz, the capital's first Swiss consul general, who with his wife, Graitli Kohler, had emigrated to America in the early 1800s, and John Hitz, Hans's son and successor as Swiss plenipotentiary, was going to make a mark in the world. John Edgar was going to redeem the promises that she had made to herself when she had so improvidently married handsome, gentle, ineffectual Dickerson Hoover when she was a girl.

Annie was a romantic, and a determined one. Educated in the District of Columbia and in Switzerland, where her only sibling, her younger brother John Scheitlin, also attended school, she had refused to forgo her planned tour of the Continent simply because her father had died inopportunely. Notified by letter that her father was dead and that she was to return home immediately, she had withdrawn Johnny from his school and taken him with her on a leisurely cruise down the Rhine.

In those days, before 1880, the family had lived well and entertained lavishly. Jacob Scheitlin, Annie's father, the descendant of several Swiss mercenary soldiers in colonial America, had prospered in the growing capital, the population of which had expanded from 130,000 in 1868 to more than 220,000 at the end of the century. His wife, Margaret, had come to their marriage with a dowry.

But now on the day of John Edgar's birth, seventeen years after Jacob's death, none of them could afford even one servant — only 'help,' the occasional hourly wage-earner, usually a black woman who came in to assist on Sundays when Annie invited a small circle of family and friends home after services at a neighborhood Presbyterian church on Fourth Street.

Annie loved to entertain, even though she found her Sunday midday receptions something of an ongoing rebuke. For reasons that had everything to do with lack of money, she and her children were consigned to what the Georgetown brahmins and their cohorts in the lavish new mansions around Dupont Circle called the 'demimonde.' In Washington everything seemed to depend on wealth. As one historian of the District observed, 'Any well-mannered white person . . . who could afford servants and who meticulously followed the "cast-iron" rules about making calls could be a part [of] or hover on the fringes of society.' But Annie could not afford servants, and she was surrounded by neighbors without pretensions. Deeply conscious of her exclusion, she was determined to improve her situation if she could.

The bed in which she lay was the same one in which Dick and Lillian had been born, the one in which all of her children had been conceived, the one she and 'Papa' had shared almost from the day of their marriage. It occupied most of the bedroom, one of three in a row adjoining a narrow hall and bath on the second floor of the semidetached house. Beyond it, at the rear, overlooking a narrow, fenced garden, was a sunporch that she kept well stocked with houseplants, especially in winter.

At the back of the garden, abutting the property, she could see the yard of the Ebeneezer Methodist Episcopal Church, a recent red-brick Romanesque-revival building, successor to the white frame 'Little Ebeneezer' that had stood on the site before she and Papa had moved into the neighborhood and that had housed the first public school for blacks in the District of Columbia. Beyond the church, several blocks to the south, sprawled the Negro and poor-white shantytown known as Pipetown and, past it, the old Navy Yard on the Anacostia River mud-flats.

The day of John Edgar's birth was like a day in late Indian summer, crisp and clear and, now that the sun was up, suffused with warm, slanting light. From the windows of the front parlor downstairs, where Papa and the older children awaited neighbors and relatives — and where, incidentally, Annie banned all activities except on special occasions — one could almost imagine that the cannas in the round and triangular flowerbeds of Seward Square were ready to burst into bloom. Indeed, the last blooms had died only a few weeks earlier.

Beyond the front hedge, itself only three or four feet past the gloom of the front verandah, occasional hackneys passed diagonally on dusty, rutted Maryland Avenue and clattered across the paving stones of Pennsylvania Avenue in the center of Pierre L'Enfant's gigantic and forlorn square a block and a half east of the stuccoed-over frame house at 413. From time to time one of the new electric-cable streetcars called tractioncars proceeded northwest on Pennsylvania toward the Capitol and White House, disappearing from view at the corner of Fourth Street opposite the Hoovers' front windows. Others, returning, passed southeastward toward the Washington & Georgetown Street Railway Company's terminal at Seventeenth Street and the Anacostia River. The cars were shiny green with cream trim, their sides emblazoned with the name of the railroad. Some carried open trailers in which could be seen gaily dressed passengers perhaps heading home from the morning's New Year's celebration at the White House.

The *Evening Star*, the politically conservative daily that was Annie's favorite paper and would remain so, reported that afternoon on the gala for those who had missed it:

The reception commenced on time — at 11. When the great burst came from the band the President and Mrs. Cleveland and the cabinet officers and their ladies came down the west stairway and passed into the blue room. After the cabinet officers and their ladies had paid their respects to Mr. and Mrs. Cleveland, the diplomatic corps passed through, headed by Sir Julian Pauncefote, its dean. The Secretary of State made the presentation to the President, who repeated each name for Mrs. Cleveland. The diplomatic reception did not occupy more than twenty minutes, when the scene again shifted and the reception of the great American public commenced.

The two-column front-page story went on to describe, devoting a paragraph to each, the costumes of the several dozen ladies present in the receiving line.

The Washington Board of Trade meanwhile was reported to have recommended that the Norfolk & Western Railroad be authorized to enter the city, that the Potomac flats be turned into a park (ultimately Hains Point and the Tidal Basin), and that all railroad grade crossings in the city be eliminated. The Board of Trade also approved a bill for a free public library that year and discussed work on the new Post Office building (now the landmark Old Post Office on Pennsylvania Avenue in which for many years the Washington field office of the Federal Bureau of Investigation was housed). Commenting on the effects of an extension of the city limits, the summary noted:

> During the year the map for the extension of the streets throughout a portion of the northern suburbs [i.e., Cleveland Park] was completed and submitted for the approval of Frederick Law Olmstead, the landscape engineer . . . A syndicate secured a long lease on the property occupied by the late ex-Secretary Blaine as a home, and a permit was taken out for the erection of a theater building on this site [the National Theater]. The corner-stone of the new building of the Corcoran Art Gallery, at 17th street and New York avenue [west of the Old State Department Building; it formerly was directly across Pennsylvania from the State Department], was laid, and good progress was made in the construction.

Meanwhile, outside the capital, the nation was consolidating the gains and growing pains of the longest boom in its history, beginning in the 1870s with a binge of foreign borrowing to finance its industrialization and ending with the bust of '93. In the interval large fortunes had been made in railroads, mining, land speculation, petroleum, steel, and banking, and the power of one American magnate, John D. Rockefeller, had so increased that only the central government, always the ordinary citizen's friend of last resort, stood between him and the Almighty. In the name of justice, the people had turned to Congress, which in 1890, responding to the popular outcry but without laying down specific guidelines, had enacted the Sherman Anti-Trust Act, prohibiting combinations 'in restraint of trade or commerce' or any attempt to 'monopolize any part of trade or commerce.'

Not for the first time had Washington legislated approved conduct in an imperfect world. As early as 1798, in the Alien and Sedition Acts, Congress had authorized the president to expel any alien whose presence he deemed dangerous to the national security and to deport or arrest alien enemies; in addition it criminalized 'combining and conspiring to oppose the execution of the laws or publishing false, scandalous, or malicious writings against the President, Congress or the government of the United States.' More recently, in 1873, Anthony Comstock, one of the founders of the Society for the Prevention of Vice, had prevailed on Congress to bar from the mails certain specified 'obscene' publications, including medical literature concerning contraception.

But even as late as the 1890s federal laws against unpopular behavior had very little practical effect. The Department of Justice did not have an investigative division with which to enforce order and in extreme situations was compelled either to borrow personnel from the Treasury or resort to the hired guns of private detective agencies, a dubious practice, as the detectives had a deserved reputation for siding with whoever paid their bills.

The most famous of these agencies by far was that headed by Allen Pinkerton, which had distinguished itself in 1877 by killing several striking Reading Railroad employees and thereby persuading the rest to return to work. Mr. Pinkerton had then written a book, *Strikers, Communists, Tramps and Detectives*, published in 1878, in which he laid this early effort of American labor to organize at Karl Marx's door.

The Marxist bugbear was trotted out again in 1886. As strikers demonstrated in Chicago's Haymarket Square against police brutality in the death of one of their number, someone threw a bomb at the police, killing seven and injuring more than sixty. The by-then familiar accusation was predictably repeated in the Pullman Strike of 1894.

That anarchists, syndicalists, and self-styled socialists — radicals all — were involved in nineteenth-century labor disputes is incontestable. Most made no secret of their allegiances and their quests. On the other hand, that all of organized labor, or organizing labor, should have been tarred with the same communist brush, as it frequently was by management and most of the press, says a good deal less about the character of American labor than about the conformity Tocqueville had commented on a half-century earlier. In supporting the feudal prerogatives of management at that time — what A. A. Berle called 'the absolutist power of property' — the Hoovers and Scheitlins and millions like them were simply defending the status quo, one that benefited them marginally to the exclusion of others, against what they perceived as a barbarian flood. Troubled by abrupt social changes and economic dissent, conservative white Protestant America, like Colonel Custer, was of a mind to make its stand.

From the beginning Annie called the new baby Edgar. The talismanic charm of the name John (Hans Hitz, John Hitz, John Thomas Hoover) had been diminished no doubt by the incipient alcoholism of her brother Johnny, whose drunken escapades she could hardly fail to notice as he staggered past her front door from the saloons on southeast Pennsylvania Avenue to the house he shared with their widowed mother just around the corner on Fourth Street to the south. Moreover, the magic of a name that was both new to the family and of her own choosing reinforced her feeling that Edgar, unlike his brother, would give his allegiance to the presumptive matriarch. Dick, on the contrary, had belonged to his father from the start, and had been so committed to male activities all his life that there seemed no hope of influencing him in the slightest.

The cold weather kept Annie and the baby confined for several weeks, not because the weather was so wintry but because the baby was so weak. But with the advent of spring,

Annie launched John Edgar abroad in a new high-wheeled, curtained pram. Notwithstanding her disdain for many of her neighbors, many of them low-level civil service families like her own, she loved the neighborhood dearly — its friendliness, its security, its unbelievable convenience — and she must have been curious to see what kind of progress had been made on the new Library of Congress building.

From the corner of Pennsylvania and Fourth, nearly opposite her house, she could see Benjamin Latrobe's majestic Capitol dome with Horatio Greenough's bronze statue of George Washington atop it. Nearer by, just three blocks away on the right-hand side of the avenue's vast *allée*, she could see the walls of the new library rising. The miracle was that such modest dwellings as the house on Seward Square and the other houses in the neighborhood should have been tucked into something so huge as Pierre L'Enfant's grandiose plan. Like the slum on the other side of the Capitol, the Chinese community that overhung the maze of railroad tracks criss-crossing L'Enfant's plundered Capitol Mall, the domestic architecture of the capital seemed to have grown like a fungus on the stones of a temple. Annie might not have approved, but she enjoyed her proximity to Capitol Hill, recently replanted, as it had been, by the masterly hand of Frederick Law Olmstead.

A block west of Seward Square, on the left-hand side of Pennsylvania Avenue at Third Street, Annie and the baby approached a whole cluster of neighborhood stores — a newsstand, Caswell's Bakery, a German penny-candy shop, a dry goods store, and the pharmacy at the corner of Pennsylvania and Third. Around the corner on Third was one of the original Hahn's shoe stores, a tailor shop, and an ice cream parlor that would introduce little Edgar to one of his abiding passions. From there, one could walk further south on Third to Maryland Avenue, and return by that avenue to Seward Square, the corner of which was just fifty steps from the Hoovers' front door — as Annie often said to her younger son much later, very convenient.

As spring progressed and the plants in her garden came into bloom, Annie found other things to tend besides Edgar, and to fill the breach she dragooned Dick into pushing the pram on Capitol Hill. Still a boy of fifteen, Dick must have found the chore onerous, although he later recalled having performed it without objection. Still, the requirement may have contributed to what one of Dick's children eventually perceived as distance or friction between the brothers.

The chore became a regular beat – Dick was nothing if not conscientious – but from time to time the youth escaped to a friend's house in Virginia. At that time northern Virginia was garlanded with rail lines, and a young man willing to walk a few miles might get from the District to Delaplane, near Warrenton in Faukier County, in a few hours. Dick had become acquainted with a boy named Ben McCarty whose family had a place at Delaplane, and the McCartys became a refuge for the pent-up would-be farm boy from the city. Years later, Dick's son and namesake, a successful farmer in Charles Town, West Virginia, said that his father fell in love at that time with country living.

There was, however, no Hoover money to invest in a farm, and Dick dutifully turned his attention to other things. First came the ministry, a prospective calling inspired by the Reverend Donald Campbell MacLeod, rector of the Old First Presbyterian Church, a parish in northwest Washington near the present Judiciary Square, to which the family had transferred its allegiance. Mr. MacLeod was 'a hearty, virile chap, much given to promoting sports and social activities as adjuncts to the teaching of religion.' Edgar at a later date insisted repeatedly that it was he who had flirted with a career in the ministry, and that the Reverend Mr. MacLeod had been his inspiration and not his brother's, but Dickerson's offspring are adamant that it was their father who was the epigone, and Edgar's selective memory where his origins and youth were concerned tends to support them.[2]

In June 1899, when Edgar was four, Dick graduated from Eastern High School, where his sister, Lillian, was two years behind him. During the course of his high school career he had played on the football team, commanded a company of ROTC cadets, won the warm approbation of most of his classmates, and graduated as the president of the senior class. Persuaded that his family could not bear the cost of his theological education, he went to work as the stenographic secretary to the District's chief of police and, that fall, began night law-school classes at George Washington University. Much later, observers commented on the similarities between Dick's and Edgar's educations, but, whatever the similarities, Dick did what he felt he had to do and Edgar, obeying a different compulsion, followed in his brother's footsteps, determined to go him one better.

Considering Dick's strapping good looks and athletic prowess, it is a wonder Annie didn't throw out the baby with the bath water. For, according to several accounts, John Edgar was skinny, high-strung, sickly, and excessively fearful, clinging to his mother whenever he could. He himself admitted much later that he was terrified of snakes, and his phobias about germs and insects stayed with him the length of his life. With all the will in the world, he could not conquer his habit of stuttering until he was a grown man.

But he was bright, alert, and active. And although a loner all his life, he persevered from the moment he entered the Brent School at Seventh Street and Pennsylvania Avenue, southeast, in September 1901. According to one Hoover commentator whose sources remain obscure but whose other early data conform to those in the known record, 'Playmates recall that he was a serious-minded youngster who dourly refused to participate in the friendly gang battles between Pipetown boys and those from neighboring areas . . . Young John Edgar minded his own business and read his Bible.'

He was an achiever almost from the start, inspired by his mother's zeal for him to excel. His report cards, initially a mixed bag of 'goods' and 'excellents,' improved steadily toward a strong finish. Although he betrayed no intellectual passion throughout his life, he was apparently captivated by the adversarial process he created in the classroom. Nor was he without winsome ways to blunt criticism of his aggressive behavior. From quite early days he was successful in keeping the opposition on the defensive, if not always in winning it over to his side.

30

Meanwhile Dickerson, Sr., provided a kind of benign backdrop to the events unfolding in his family. Almost to the end of his days, his job at the Coast and Geodetic Survey, from 1903 an agency of the Department of Commerce, was to oversee the printing of the papers that were the end product of the survey's work: nautical charts and maps based on the explorations conducted at the agency's regional stations. From all accounts, he was diligent and responsible in discharging his duties, and his kindliness and patience were legendary.

At home he played second fiddle to his wife but offered a haven to his children in a sometimes hostile world. Annie did not drink and for understandable reasons disapproved of drinking, but Papa enjoyed an occasional ale. He liked the ceremony of drinking it while a child or grandchild joined him in a glass of Herman's ginger ale.

Lillian, called 'Sister,' by 1901 played a smaller and smaller role in the family. She had graduated from Eastern the June before Edgar entered Brent and now was teaching school herself. Her interests lay outside the home, although financial constraints obliged her to continue living there.

The same was true for Dick. He had earned his bachelor of laws degree that same June, passed his bar exam in July, and hung out his shingle to practice law later that summer. Strictly speaking, he could afford a place of his own, but only by throwing rent money into a landlord's bottomless pit. He aspired to proprietorship instead.

Thus, even though his siblings were still living at home, Edgar by the time he was six was an only child. In 1905 Dick moved out — into the house, which he had bought for $1,200, next door at 411 Seward Square. Annie thereupon had both properties fenced as one and expanded her garden to twice its size. Dick, as always, was accommodating.

That fall, after the regular family holiday at Atlantic City, in which the Hoovers were probably joined by Annie's mother, Margaret Scheitlin, Papa and Mama, leaving Edgar in the care of Sister, took themselves away on a trip of their own. Papa traveled occasionally in connection with his work, but for Annie the trip was a rare adventure, and one that she was eager to share with Edgar. On 6 October 1905 she wrote him from New York City:

My Dear little Edgar,

While Mama is writing you this letter the Steam Cars are flying past my window. The elevated road passes right by the window, the streetcars in front of the door — New York is a very busy place. Yesterday afternoon we took a ride on the sightseeing Automobile, all through Central Park along Riverside Park and Fifth Avenue, such beautiful houses, it seemed like 'Fairyland' to see such lovely places. Hope some day when you are older you may be able to see all the wonderful sights in New York.

Was so glad to hear you were perfect in your spelling and arithmetic. Study hard both your lessons and your music, and try to be a very good boy . . .

With love and kisses,
Yours lovingly,
Mama

Four days later Papa wrote from Boston, on the stationery of the Thorndike Hotel:

My dear old man,

I got up early to write this letter to you. Well this [is] a big place but not anything like New York, the people are different in fact it [sic] more on the order of Washington . . . Yesterday saw the business part of the city and in the afternoon we saw the residences and the beautiful suburbs the cottages were the prettiest I ever saw one little town called Brookline was like fairyland and is the wealthiest place for it [sic] size in the world. Today we go down on the bay side to see some of [illegible word] scenery for which this section is noted we will be gone all day as the guest of Mr.

Holden . . . Love to all with hugs and kisses to your
own dear self,

                    From Papa and Mama
Will write once more before we leave.

The same inattention to grammar and punctuation,
mingled with sadness, is evident in two other letters written
from St. Louis the year before, when Papa was on temporary
duty in the West during that city's centenary exposition.

                    St. Louis, Mo. April 29/04
My dear Edgar,

   I know you would like to hear from Papa, so this
morning I will write you a short letter.
   This is a big city and it is full of people, some parts
are very pretty but I don't think you or Mama would
like it. Everybody is in a rush, but as yet I have not
seen any bad people and the police is as scarce as they
can be. The Mississippi River is very high and the water
is like clay. The drinking water here has to be filtered
when it comes out of the spigot it is very dark –
   Take good care of Mama and when I come home will
bring you something nice . . . Love to all with a kiss
for yourself. I have a big favor to ask you – it is give
Mama a hug and a long sweet kiss.

                            Good Bye
                            Papa

The premonition that is hinted at in the letter's plangeant
exhortation to look after Mama, something John Edgar at
nine apparently was already disposed to do, yields to
something more strongly felt in the other letter:

                        Sunday evening 7 o'clock
My dear Edgar,

   This morning I wrote dear Mama a letter and this
evening I am thinking of Mama and the rest, and it

makes me somewhat homesick, so will write a few lines to you which will bring me closer to home. Yesterday I saw lots of little boys like you at the fair . . .

I wrote [sic] out in the country today but got caught in a storm while out the [sic] I dug up a pretty wild flower which I have mailed you — you can plant it and will grow.

Tell Dick that there is some very handsome stone churches out in the suburbs.

I had hoped to have a letter from you but I guess you have been very busy with school. Don't answer this, for I hope to leave for home anytime. Give Mama a hug and kiss for me and l will pay you when I come back.

> Good night — with love to all
> From
> Papa

Quite possibly Papa was leaning on Edgar to support Mama not only then but in the future because he suspected that Dick — who, after all, still lived at home — had other plans. If so, he was right. Dick, who was more ecumenical than other family members throughout his life (he ended up an Episcopalian), had begun attending services at the neighborhood Lutheran Church of the Reformation, where he met a gentle, adoring young woman six years his junior. Named Theodora Louisa Hanft, she was one of six children and five daughters.

Theo's father had moved to Washington from Ashville, Illinois, in 1894, seeking employment in the growing government bureaucracy in the wake of the crash the year before. Bearing a letter from his congressman, he had found work at the Bureau of Printing and Engraving and was easily as prosperous as the Hoovers when his daughter married Dickerson Hoover, Jr., in the Hanfts' house at 59 Quincy Place, northeast, at eight in the evening on 4 September 1907.

Still, Annie opposed the marriage, on the ground the Hanfts were parvenus. From the beginning she also seems to have found Theo's demure passivity a goad to her own aggressiveness. But Dick was a young man of independent means as well as ideas and the marriage was a fait accompli before Annie could stop it.

The following 30 June Lillian was wed. In Annie's estimation, Lillian made a better match than Dick. Fred Robinette, a classmate of Lillian's at Eastern High and a year younger than she, was a good-looking civil engineer with the Coast and Geodetic Survey. His Robinette forebears were Huguenots who had emigrated to America in the eighteenth century, eventually settling in Reading, Pennsylvania. Fred's father, Augustine Robinette had moved from Reading to Washington in the nineteenth century and there reared five sons and a daughter.

While Fred and Lillian were getting settled in their new home, Ann took a giant step toward securing her matriarchy. As Edgar noted in his childish hand in a 'pocket diary' that he kept for three years, 'On Friday July 17, 1908, at nine forty-five o'clock pm. Margaret Hoover was born at her father's home, 411 Seward Square.' Theo may have been a mouse in Annie's estimation, but Annie felt no compunction about laying claim to the baby, her first grandchild.

From the beginning Margaret exhibited exceptional spirit and intelligence, and both Annie and Edgar adored her. For Edgar, she was the nearest thing he had to a sibling, closer to him in age than his married sister and brother. For Annie, she may have replaced Marguerite. Moreover, with two birds already flown from the nest, there was now ample room for another.

In all of this Dick deferred to his mother, perhaps because he simply did not want the bother of opposing her. By 1909 he was carrying heavy responsibilities as chief clerk of the Steamboat Inspection Service in Washington. Before his marriage he had taken the civil service examination and been assigned briefly to the staff of the Steamboat Inspector at Marquette, Michigan, before being assigned permanently to the capital. Now he left Annie and Theo to work things out by themselves.

Things did not work out well for Theo. Confronted with a domineering mother-in-law and next-door neighbor, she virtually surrendered. 'Nanny considered that Father had married beneath himself,' Margaret said of her grandmother. 'Nanny bullied Mother and took advantage of her.' And Dick not only let her do it but on at least one occasion supported her.

'Mother had taken me to visit my Hanft grandparents,' Margaret recalled. 'And while we were there I bumped my head – it was an accident. But Father refused to permit further visits.' On another occasion Annie so terrorized Theo that Theo abruptly retired from the field – or rather, as Margaret recalled, was banished. Throughout, whatever the tensions, Annie was prepared to care for Margaret, who, now that there was a spare bedroom, occasionally spent the night in the middle bedroom at 413. Edgar, by virtue of seniority, now occupied the front bedroom.

Two years after Margaret's arrival, Lillian gave birth to a daughter, Dorothy, born on 23 June 1910 at 413 Seward Square. Lillian had come home to have her baby because her own place on Tenth Street was too spartan for safety's sake and because Annie wanted to manage things in her own way. The occasion proved prophetic, as hardship dogged Lillian all the rest of her life.

Meanwhile Edgar was growing up. About the time of Margaret's birth, when he was thirteen, he had begun a penny newspaper, the *Weekly Review*, with himself as sole reporter and editor and Dick, charmingly, as 'printer.' He generally led with neighborhood news, followed by news briefs from all over, and concluded with advice and homilies. In volume 1, number 4, he offered the following rules for good health: 'Eat slowly. Don't eat adulterated food. Don't eat too much. Don't eat between meals. Clean your teeth.' Under the heading 'Proverbs,' he entered, 'Where there is a will, there is a way,' and 'Whatever is worth doing at all is worth doing well.' The sole 'help wanted' ad read: 'If anybody wants any work done, call at room 4 on first floor of 413 Seward Sq., S.E. Wages 30 and 50 cents. $1.00 and $2.00. Any kind of work can be done.'

Years later Hoover liked to recall that he picked up lots of small change delivering groceries. He would hang around outside the market on Third Street and offer to carry customers' groceries home. At first he walked, but then he discovered that he could make more money running, a circumstance that may have had something to do with his acquiring the nickname 'Speed.' On the other hand, the sobriquet may have been owing simply to the fact that he appeared to be a young man in a hurry. He also spoke rapidly and gave an appearance of haste with his mincing, some thought effeminate, step.

In June 1909 Edgar graduated from the Brent School and the following September entered Central High, at O Street between Sixth and Seventh Streets, northwest. Central was a competitive school with citywide enrollment,[3] and Edgar traveled three miles each way to attend. In addition to the students from the District, Central drew heavily from neighboring counties in Maryland and Virginia and presented a slice of social life several cuts above that at Eastern.

Edgar adored it from the start. Its competitive atmosphere suited his temperament perfectly, and he enjoyed the cachet of having an uncle on the faculty. Papa's bachelor brother, Halstead, known in the family as Uncle Hal, taught music and directed the choir, of which Edgar was an enthusiastic participant. From the beginning he was involved with the Cadets, a high school ROTC program leading to a commission in the army reserve. So enamored was he of the drill and the associated male bonding that he regularly wore his uniform to church, where he taught Sunday school and sang in the choir.

At Central he also immediately hit his stride as an achiever. Nor did his pre-emptive overkill create in him the slightest false sense of security. He consistently applied himself to all his courses and was rewarded with gratifying results. His year-end report card for 1909–1910 showed all Es (for 'excellent'), except in Latin and Spelling, in both of which he got Gs (for 'good'). Thereafter his only Gs were in Spelling (1910–1911) and French (1911–1912). A brilliant

37

record in math foreshadowed his later remarkable facility with statistics.

He seems not to have had the slightest doubt about his ability. He was an aggressive and confident member of Central's four-man debate team during his last two years and, in his senior year, a tough, no-nonsense captain of the Cadets' Company A, which he commanded in Woodrow Wilson's first inaugural parade. Moreover, he made his assumption of authority stick. Although one classmate later recalled that John Edgar 'chastised us with his morality,' others took the young martinet entirely seriously. The Central yearbook of 1913 described him, in the usual somewhat stilted manner, as 'gentleman of dauntless courage and stainless honor.'

In only two respects did Edgar fail to measure up to his peers. There is no record of his ever having played on any of Central's athletic teams (his niece Margaret maintains that his famous flattened nose was caused by a boil, not a baseball), and apparently his fancy never turned to thoughts of love. A high school dance program that turned up posthumously among his personal effects contained not a single name of a female classmate. (Likewise, his copy of *The Brecky*, Central's yearbook, while containing the signatures of fifty male classmates, boasts the autographs of only eleven girls, although girls were about as numerous as boys. Thus, even given the likelihood that Edgar did not know how to dance, it is fair to say that his social interests were overwhelmingly male-oriented.) Hoover, moreover, was already embarked on a classic trajectory. For, as Harold Lasswell observed, 'Political life seems to sublimate many homosexual trends. Politicians characteristically work together in little cliques and clubs, and many of them show marked difficulties in reaching a stable heterosexual adjustment.'

Hoover seems to have had that insight, for among the effects preserved from an early period is a horoscope that reads:

Capricorn was powerfully felt in your chart when you were born, which indicates that you will live a long time,

38

be disinclined to marry, and, if you do, have few or no children. Business and politics are the strong points of a Capricorn person, but no matter what he undertakes to do, he persists in a most domineering manner until accomplishment is reached. The ancient tale in connection with this sign is that Bacchus was feasting with other gods when a frightful storm arose and, in order to escape it, he quickly changed himself into a goat and leaped into the stream. The part of him which was under water became a fish. So the sea goat was born. Sometimes the sign is depicted as a goat, or external nature, and as a crocodile, or internal nature, the interpretation being the death of the lower mind and the birth of the spiritual.

The horoscope accords with a tendency that Edgar showed then and later to attach grandiose significance to his quite ordinary activities — a significant trait, as one of the blind correlates with authoritarianism uncovered in the field work for Theodore Adorno's *The Authoritarian Personality* was precisely this givenness to self-glorification (and also glorification of certain other men).

Eventually Hoover's success in allying himself with other men for purposes of advancement would be demonstrated in his membership in three college fraternities and myriad voluntary fraternal organizations: the 'network' that some observers referred to in connection with his transactions on Capitol Hill. But for the present he was just building a base, and using his idealized virtue to keep his competitors off balance.

In reality he was very much alone. His pocket diaries from this period record frequent solitary trips throughout the District and neighboring counties on the area's streetcars and railways. Other entries cover visits, some by bike, to bathing beaches in the area, where he indulged his lifelong enthusiasm for swimming. (Later, when he undertook his FBI inspection tours cum holidays with his young associates Clyde Tolson and Guy Hottel, he invariably headed with them for the beach, even though by then he had developed a passion for the racetrack.)

But notwithstanding Edgar's dearth of friends, there was one person to whom his devotion was unequivocal and never-ending. His concern for his mother seemed to grow in direct proportion to the decline in his father's emotional health.

Shortly after returning to Central in the fall of 1912 to begin his senior year, Edgar became what he and apparently everyone else in the family had groomed him to be — the man of the house. Papa, long afflicted by depressions and anxieties, went over the edge into what young Dick's family called a nervous breakdown. He was hospitalized at Laurel, Maryland, in a sanatorium not too conveniently located at the end of a streetcar line (the town is approximately midway between Washington and Baltimore). There he mouldered, undergoing therapies one can only imagine, for months on end, his only comfort the occasional visits of his wife and younger son.

The year that ensued nevertheless was Edgar's best. Concerned he may have felt about Papa, but he heaped honors on himself. Company A was a leading competitor in the region, and Central's undefeated debating team capped its season by unanimously defeating Baltimore City College (actually a high school).

In the spring Edgar's classmates elected him class valedictorian in acknowledgment of his academic achievement, and that June he was offered a scholarship to the University of Virginia. His response to the latter was of a kind that shaped his future all along. In declining the scholarship on the grounds that he could not afford to accept it, he missed his best chance to move outside the District. Instead, he stayed home with Mama — and remained with her until the day she died.

Notes to Chapter One

1. John Thomas Hoover was the son of William Hoover and Elizabeth Huff. John Thomas Hoover married Cecilia Naylor of

Round Hill in northern Virginia. Their sons were Dickerson Naylor Hoover, William Hoover, and Halstead Hoover. The Hoovers had lived in Washington since the early nineteenth century.

2. Edgar used to tell a story about how he practiced delivering sermons in his mother's front parlor, but again, the testimony of Dickerson Hoover's daughter Margaret, who lived at 413 Seward Square, seems more convincing. She recalls hearing her uncle practice political speeches after he became a successful bureaucrat.

3. For whites only: the District's schools were not integrated until after the Supreme Court's *Brown* decision in 1954.

CHAPTER TWO

(1914–1918)

WARTIME'S FLEDGLING BUREAUCRAT

IN OCTOBER 1913, four months after his graduation from high school, Edgar went to work as a file clerk at the Library of Congress, cataloging new acquisitions at thirty dollars a month, a job obtained with the help of his Uncle William Hitz, a Justice Department attorney and future District judge. Earlier he had enrolled as a summer law student at George Washington University, attending classes there from seven till nine in the morning and working the rest of the day. At night he returned home only to eat dinner and closet himself with his casebooks and class notes before turning in. (His schedule during the academic year, from September to June, was reversed, although just as heavy – he worked at the Library from nine till four-thirty and at the University from five until seven.)

The logistics of this strenuous life were mercifully simple. The Library was a fast five-minute walk from the Hoovers' Seward Square house, and one that took Edgar past the ice cream and other shops at Pennsylvania and Third Street. The University was about a mile and a half further on, just off Pennsylvania Avenue several blocks from the White House. On a pleasant day Edgar could walk the distance in less than half an hour, straight over Capitol Hill, and on especially busy days or in inclement weather he could take the old Georgetown streetcar.

The classes themselves were organized around the case-study method – that is, the study of actual court cases to divine the legal precedents governing matters of civil and criminal procedure, criminal law, torts, contracts, and business law. There were only two departures from this basic routine of memorization and selective retrieval: constitutional law, which was taught as a term course in English and American constitutional history, and the school's mock court, in which students were given hypothetical cases and hypothetical clients to represent, using their class experience and exhaustive case-abstract research to decide what legal precedents to cite.

The prerequisite for success at the law school was respect for the law — not law-abidingness but a reverence for the accumulated statutes and decisions that underlay the requirement of *stare decisis*, settled opinion. If the result of applying this law with clever legerdemain was palpable injustice, then so be it. The law is a seamless web, as Edgar's professors were wont to tell him. And Edgar agreed.

The school itself made no pretense to being first rate. It was designed to provide its students with ammunition for the District bar exam and no more. But in at least two respects it was unusual. Its graduates did in fact pass the local bar exam in great numbers, and friendships made at George Washington had a way of carrying over into preferred positions in the government bureaucracy.

Edgar from the beginning was an outstanding, although not brilliant student.[1] His class notebooks, which he preserved until the end of his life, testify to the thoroughness that impressed his professors. Moreover, he felt comfortable with the quintessentially reductionist process of case study, although he lacked the intellect and training to become a legal scholar.

In one area, however, he excelled. He was a skillful contender in the adversarial proceedings of the mock court. Notwithstanding his residual stutter and the nervous intensity of his delivery, he knew how to identify the main ingredients of an argument and, always prompted by his defensiveness, to make a thoroughgoing case. Furthermore, by temperament he was perfectly suited to the encounter; he reveled in argument as another youth might in a wrestling match or a foot race.

In short, Edgar had become a specialist, a technician. His skills were finely honed and his attention sharply focused.

43

He had little patience with those better educated than he who lacked his powers of concentration. Combativeness was his chief distinction.

Outside the arena, he entertained no serious interests, and he fairly exulted in his homely tastes. His favorite poet, he liked to say, was Edgar Guest, the syndicated verse writer from Detroit of whom Dorothy Parker quipped, 'I'd rather flunk my Wasserman test / than read a poem by Eddie Guest,' and whose first collection, *A Heap o' Livin'*, appeared in 1916. His favorite newspaper was the Washington *Evening Star*, followed by the *New York Daily News*. At a slightly later date he fancied the *Readers' Digest* above other periodicals and journals of opinion. Throughout his life the major thinkers of his time simply passed him by (as witness his penned comment on an FBI routing slip attached to a *Washington Post* story of June 1964 to the effect that 'Author Jean Paul Sartre promised to take an active part in the French "Who Killed Kennedy Committee" — Find out who Sartre is'). Edgar read no fiction to speak of and was impervious to the appeals of great art.

He was, nevertheless, a child of his time and place. His parochialism was to a degree America's parochialism. His xenophobia reflected America's xenophobia. And the country's search for scapegoats after it became embroiled in the First World War and then in the Bolshevik revolution by way of the Russian Civil War prefigured his own life-long career as a hunter of subversives. The country, unlike himself, however, was deeply divided.

President Wilson owed his election in 1912 to a split in the Republican party, which with the single exception of Grover Cleveland's presidency had controlled the executive office since before the Civil War. Dissatisfied with President William Howard Taft's conservative term following his own progressive administration and foreclosed by party machinery from obtaining the presidential nomination himself, Theodore Roosevelt had bolted from the Republicans and organized his own Progressive party. His defection, and the candidacy of the Socialist Eugene V.

Debs, who polled 6 percent of the vote, enabled the Democratic Wilson to win the presidency with a plurality of only 42 percent.

Moreover, the Progressives were themselves of two minds.[2] There were those — settlement house founder Jane Addams and Wisconsin Senator Robert La Follette among them — who, influenced by the Social Gospel, felt an egalitarian commitment to improving the lot of the disadvantaged. Humanitarian and idealistic, these reformers acted on the belief that men have a moral responsibility to fulfill God's work on earth, and their Christian activism was captured in their selection of the Protestant hymn 'Onward Christian Soldiers' as the campaign song at the Progressive Party Convention of 1912.

A second, more conservative side of early twentieth-century progressivism identified with the muscular Christianity of Theodore Roosevelt. Moralistic and intolerant, these activists sought the eradication of evil — whether by curbing gambling, drinking, and prostitution or by limiting immigration through the requirement of a literacy test and excluding anarchists and revolutionaries.

In his political philosophy, Edgar identified with this more conservative wing of Progressivism and not its humanitarian side. A stern believer in self-improvement and self-reliance, he was intolerant of human frailty. Although wary of government interference in private business activity, he believed that government had a responsibility to regulate morals and punish offenders against the conventional morality.

Paradoxically, though, Edgar, by his own account, did not seek government employment in the first place because of a commitment to public service or to purifying American society. His subsequent career as Director of the Bureau of Investigation might seem to suggest that, but it wasn't so. Rather, he sought public employment in 1913 simply because it afforded him an opportunity to help support his family while subsidizing four years of part-time law school. A child of the District's bureaucracy, he could safely rely on his numerous relatives to secure entree for him in one or another of the executive departments or in the select legislative support system on Capitol Hill; no fewer than five of his kinsmen were then ensconced in government jobs or had recently retired from them. Although his experience at the Library of Congress was to prove valuable to him, his aspirations were bound up with the law school.

There, he felt comfortable in the company of his companions. Like himself, they were ambitious, mostly from modest circumstances, and drawn from the dominant culture of White Anglo-Saxon Protestant America. Many were recent arrivals in the capital, farm boys from the South and West who were training for advancement in one or another of the government's hierarchies while already holding down a job.

Edgar was not altogether likable, but he found to his satisfaction that he was eminently acceptable in certain quarters. In his first year he went knocking at the door of Kappa Alpha fraternity, of which he later became house manager and president while continuing to live at home. Letters of congratulation preserved from a still later date testify to the strength of his affiliation with fraternity brothers, which he in turn honored by surrounding himself with Kappa Alphas after his appointment as Director in 1924.

Edgar's leadership qualities were already apparent. Although his close and unbreakable bond with his mother evidently excluded any real bond to anyone else, male or female, he fastened himself easily onto the value systems of his peers and defended those systems with sincerity and occasional eloquence. His fraternity brothers, duly impressed, saw in him a person of unassailable steadfastness and loyalty to the band. Probably it was Edgar's intense devotion to the fraternity itself that earned him the honor of its presidency.

That Edgar by this time had developed an overriding preference for male companionship is clear. Recalling his young adulthood, his niece Margaret Fennell said, 'I think he regarded women as a kind of hindrance. You know, they sort of got in your way when you were going places. I think this is the difference between him and Father. Father married, he had a family, he had other considerations. In many ways, they were quite alike, but I think that early in his career, J. E. decided that he was going to achieve something big, and I don't think he let himself be distracted from that.'

The only photograph Edgar preserved from his law school days shows him with four unidentified male friends, all smartly dressed in suits and ties and all looking exceedingly grim. At this time he stood five feet, ten inches tall and no longer looked as thin as a rail.[3]

In addition to his law school friends, Edgar had a growing circle of companions at home. On 3 January 1912, two days after his seventeenth birthday, Theo, Dick's wife, had given birth to another child, a son, named Dickerson Naylor Hoover III and called Buster by his grandmother and subsequently Bus by everyone else in the family. Bus was a robust and attractive boy and extraordinarily equable, and Dick made no bones about it: the lad was his father's child. Two years later, on 2 March 1914, a second Robinette child was born, another daughter, named Marjorie, and a year after her, on 20 July 1915, the Dick Hoovers too had a second daughter, Anna Marie. As the Robinettes were by then hard-pressed for space, Annie's expanded garden became a family communal nursery.

At that time the family was still close, and apparently Edgar liked all the activity. The little nieces and nephews later recalled that he was invariably kind to them, buying them treats of ice cream or, some years later, when he enjoyed the perquisite of a government limousine with driver, occasionally giving them lifts to school. The younger Hoovers also recalled that their uncle was a workaholic, an indication that he may have preferred the feeling of proximity to others to the responsibility of caring for them.

There was, however, always the exception of his mother. Everything he did, he did in pursuit of Annie's approbation, which she shrewdly withheld save on the most important occasions, an aspect, it was said, of her 'stern Calvinism.' As his circumstances improved and his father's declined, he bought Annie inexpensive and then expensive gifts, artworks

47

and antiques, a practice that infuriated Dick, who from the onset of his father's illness had had to assume partial responsibility for his parents' upkeep. Both Margaret Fennell and Dickerson Hoover III recall tension between the brothers, and Mrs. Fennell guessed that it was at least partly owing to money.

Whatever Edgar's feelings about his brother, though, he continued to dote on Dick's older daughter. By the time Edgar entered law school, Margaret was old enough to go to school herself, and she was articulate and enterprising too. Given his exacting work and academic routine and his limited resources, Edgar could afford two rather prosaic indulgences, both of which he shared with Margaret. The first was walking – Edgar took her on walks as many as three nights a week; the other, somewhat later, was cigarette smoking, which he gave up after getting her hooked because by then he had an ulcer. Meanwhile they covered in the aggregate hundreds of miles of residential Washington. 'He loved to walk,' she recalled. 'We used to do a lot of walking.'

A favorite pilgrimage took them to an ice cream parlor at the corner of Eighteenth Street and Columbia Road, northwest, in the vicinity of the Rock Creek Park zoo, a good five miles from Seward Square. Normally they took the streetcar out, which was generally uphill, and walked home, starting with their ice cream cones in hand. The Capital Transit's 700 went from the Navy Yard, south of Pipetown, up Eighth Street to Florida Avenue, northeast, then northwest on Florida to U Street, northwest, and across U Street to Eighteenth Street. Thereafter it went north on Eighteenth, which climbs a steep ridge overlooking the northeastern quadrant of the city, to Columbia Road.

On other occasions Edgar took Margaret to the movies at the Fox theater on F Street. However, that activity soon ceased. According to Margaret, 'He took me once when he was about eighteen' – she could not remember to what, perhaps William S. Hart or *The Perils of Pauline* – 'and I cried and cried and he took me home and he wouldn't take me again.'

48

Margaret does not recall ever having seen Edgar with a girl his own age. 'Edgar would never have been able to get married,' she said. 'Nanny was truly the matriarch, a woman with a very independent streak — she would have stopped anything rumored.' Moreover, Annie took a dim view of most of the girls in the neighborhood. Margaret recalls that the family's neighbors 'the Stultzes — he was with the Fire Department — had a daughter who wore a fur coat, and Nanny said she was "no better than she should be." '[4]

Papa meanwhile was in and out of the picture. Margaret recalled that after his return from Laurel he was 'very changed — short-tempered and irritable.' He seems to have become altogether demoralized, inconsolably sad. His physical health, too, rapidly deteriorated, so that he frequently was absent from work. Margaret supposed that it was his inability to provide the standard of living Annie had been accustomed to, and constantly alluded to, that eventually broke his health. In any case, his problems with his work could not go on indefinitely. The outcome is recorded in a 6 April 1917 document from the Appointment Division of the Department of Commerce, which Edgar preserved: 'The Department is in receipt of your resignation, dated April 5, 1917, as plate printer at $2000 per annum in the Coast and Geodetic Survey, and has accepted the same, upon recommendation of the Superintendent, to take effect at the close of business on April 11, 1917.'

Resignation at that time was tantamount to relinquishing all title to a pension, even though Papa had served the government for forty-two years. The outcome was devastating to him and Annie alike, as now they had only their children to support them.

Moreover, one of the children was more depending than supporting. That year the Robinettes, fed up with their Tenth Street apartment, moved to Lanham, Maryland, a rural community in Prince Georges County, to a large colonial semi-ruin they had bought on Whitfield Chapel Road. Their intention was to restore the house, but in fact it simply drained them financially without becoming livable. In winters they had to close the place entirely and seek shelter

49

with such disparate family members as Rosalie Robinette, Fred's aunt in Chevy Chase, and Annie. When all was said and done, the bond with Annie was the only bulwark Edgar had at home.

In 1916 Edgar joined the Masons, which brought him into yet another ready-made circle of companions, among them numerous members of Congress. Committed to good works of various kinds, the secret fraternal order also reinforced common values and, of course, excluded those who did not share them. Its secretiveness foreshadowed Edgar's experience several years later when he joined the Justice Department's Bureau of Investigation, which in its early days, at least, conformed closely to the anthropologist Lionel Tiger's perception of the all-male secret society 'as oddly primitive, with a potential for so-called "anti-social" behavior.'[5]

From the time of Theodore Roosevelt's accession to the presidency, American presidents of the twentieth century had begun to assert unprecedented claims to centralize power in the executive office. As part of this new federalism, President Roosevelt's attorney general, Charles Bonaparte, by executive order had created the Bureau of Investigation in 1908 as a full-time investigative division of the Justice Department. The origins of the department itself were recent; it had been created by an act of Congress in 1870 in response to the extended federal law enforcement role occasioned by Military Reconstruction after the Civil War. Headed by the attorney general (a cabinet member since 1790), the Department of Justice was specifically authorized by this 1870 statute to prosecute violations of federal laws, to represent the federal government in civil suits, and to assist the president and other federal officials in fulfilling their lawful duties. The 1870 act creating the Department of Justice and appropriations legislation of 1871 granting it $50,000 annually authorized the department to employ individuals for investigative purposes.

Until 1908 attorneys general had not employed professional investigators on a full-time basis. Instead, they hired temporary personnel either through the Pinkerton Detective Agency (until they were explicitly forbidden to do so by Congress in 1892) or the Secret Service Division of the Treasury whenever investigative personnel were needed. Then, in 1907 and again in 1908, Attorney General Bonaparte formally requested congressional approval to establish an independent investigative division within the Department of Justice, emphasizing the department's inability to meet its increasing caseload and the complexity of antitrust and interstate commerce laws.

Congress not only refused these requests but, responding to revelations of Secret Service involvement in uncovering evidence leading to the indictment of two Oregon congressmen for land fraud, adopted riders to appropriation bills explicitly forbidding the attorney general to use appropriated funds to hire Secret Service agents, temporarily or otherwise. Reflecting the strong states' rights and libertarian sentiments of an earlier day, congressional leaders justified their actions as essential to safeguard representative government and prevent the evolution of 'a Federal secret police.'

When creating the Bureau of Investigation in 1908, Bonaparte may have acted lawfully with the goal of improving the department's effectiveness. His decision nevertheless contravened the spirit of Congress's appropriations restrictions as well as that body's underlying antipathy toward any federal investigative role as inviting abuse, and possibly undermining representative self-government. To disarm these objections, in February 1909, in testimony before the House Appropriations Committee, the outgoing attorney general (Taft, having won the presidency in 1908, was to be inaugurated in March 1909) outlined the safeguards he had devised to prevent any abuses. First, particular care would be taken to recruit high-quality professional investigators. Second, the attorney general would personally assume supervisory responsibility over the initiation and operation of investigations. And, third, the newly created investigative division would not investigate political beliefs and affiliations or strictly personal matters; its investigations would be confined to violations of antitrust and interstate commerce laws.

Bonaparte's testimony ultimately dissuaded the House from attempting to reverse his unilateral 1908 action. Instead, the Appropriations Committee recommended full funding for the Bureau, although Congress put on record its intention to monitor this inevitably secretive new agency.

While appreciating the potential for abuse in any federal secret police force, however, Congress inadvertently undermined Bonaparte's self-imposed restrictive guidelines a year later, when, yielding to another wave of moralistic frenzy, it passed the Mann Act, also known as the White Slave Traffic Act, outlawing the interstate transportation of any woman for 'immoral purposes.' Directed at organized prostitution, the Mann Act was intended, as its principal congressional sponsor, Congressman James Mann (R.-Ill.), argued, to redress a state and local deficiency: 'most of these girls are enticed away from their homes in the country to large cities. The police power exercised by the State and municipal governments is inadequate to prevent this — particularly when girls are enticed from one State to another.'

The Bureau, then staffed by some thirty-five investigators under the direction of Inspector Stanley W. Finch, was thus thrust into a new, less mundane area of interstate commerce investigation. To meet this additional responsibility, given the distinctiveness of 'white slave' from antitrust investigations, Bureau agents were for the first time assigned outside Washington. (The first Bureau field office was opened in Baltimore in 1911.) As a result, despite Bonaparte's 1909 assurances, attorneys general could no longer determine the inception, scope, or direction of Bureau investigations.

At the same time, the Bureau's new responsibility virtually assured that its officials would acquire damaging information on prominent persons. For when seeking information about 'every prostitute in every public house of ill fame,' Bureau officials inevitably learned about their clients. The Mann Act, moreover, could be a powerful weapon — amply demonstrated by its use in 1912-1913 against black prizefighter Jack Johnson, who was convicted for his 'immoral' relationship with an unmarried white companion, Belle Schrieber. The growing federal police force, furthermore, soon acquired other responsibilities — in 1912, when Congress outlawed the interstate transportation of prize fight films, and again in 1919, when Congress, in the Dyer Act, made it a federal crime to transport stolen motor vehicles across state lines.

Events in the larger world were also helping to shape Edgar's future career. Committed to an activist role in world affairs, President Theodore Roosevelt radically expanded the nation's involvement overseas — in the process expanding the presidency. Although Roosevelt's successor, President Taft, pursued a more conservative course overseas as at home, with Woodrow Wilson's inauguration in 1913 interventionism once again increased. Wilson's New Freedom program, like Roosevelt's assertion of power in Latin America and the Far East, both involved the country in costly activities abroad and precipitated domestic dissent over this departure from traditional isolationism. Unexamined good intentions led to U.S. military occupations of Haiti and Santo Domingo in 1915 and 1916 respectively, while the administration's benign interventionism in Mexico brought the two nations to the brink of war. The outbreak of fighting in Europe in 1914 presented another temptation to intervene, irresistible, as it turned out.

This expanded international role occurred at the very time when the country was beset by sharpened domestic divisions — occasioned by industrialization and unprecedented increases in immigration (after the 1880s from Eastern Europe, the Balkans, and Italy). Industrialization and immigration intersected to alarm the nation's predominantly middle-class Anglo-Saxon Protestants. Fearful of a more militant and numerically larger trade union movement[6] many of whose members were immigrants from Eastern European and Mediterranean countries, and the competition for jobs generated by a tide of low-paid laborers, a nativist, antiradical reaction erupted. Responding to demands for legislation restricting immigration, Congress approved a bill in February 1917, over President Wilson's veto, excluding immigrants who were illiterate or believed in radical change (and also authorizing deportation of alien anarchists and revolutionists). The literacy test masked a racialist belief in the inherent inferiority of the 'new' immigrants from eastern and southern Europe.

This ethnocentrism expressed itself in a variety of other ways. In Georgia a young Jew, Leo Frank, was convicted in 1915 of the murder of a fourteen-year-old white girl, Mary Phagan, on the sole testimony of a black man, Jim Conley, who was in fact the killer. When the governor of Georgia commuted Frank's death sentence, such a furor arose that seventy-five men calling themselves the Knights of Mary Phagan abducted Frank from a prison work camp and hanged him from an oak tree at the murdered girl's former home. In the aftermath of this act of terrorism, about half of Georgia's 3,000 Jews fled from the state.

Likewise the increased migration of blacks from the rural South to the urban North and the first stirrings of opposition to racial segregation provoked an angry reaction in those cities, Washington not least among them, that found themselves host to the destitute multitude. White Americans gravely distrusted challenges by the recently founded NAACP and the National Urban League to racial segregation and the by-then entrenched color line. Underscoring the respectability of this racialist sentiment, the membership of a revived Ku Klux Klan, reconstituted in 1915, began an increase that catapulted the Klan to national prominence in the 1920s. This general conviction that the nation was imperiled by alien subversive forces predated U.S. involvement in World War I and provided the catalyst to demands to expand federal surveillance activities to include radical trade unionists and political activists.

Edgar's concern over these developments was submerged at first in official duties as a lowly government clerk. For he had earned his bachelor of laws degree in 1916 and a master of laws in 1917, and on 26 July 1917, sixteen weeks after Congress declared war against imperial Germany, he secured what became his lifetime employment. In the words of one commentator, 'Shortly after the United States entered the war in 1917, John Edgar's chance came, not as a doughboy, for Hoover never served in the armed forces during World War I (he was listed, however, for years on reserve status as a major and delighted in being called by that rank), but in the Department of Justice.' To be precise, the twenty-two-year-old bachelor, of sound body and mind, was given an intelligence clerkship – and an indefinite deferment – at $1,200 a year.

Edgar's extreme fearfulness of physical danger and extraordinary thoroughness in protecting himself may have motivated the recent graduate to escape wartime military service by joining the Justice Department. Certainly in view of the low esteem in which the department was then held and its narrow resources – law enforcement was a state responsibility, and until the New Deal era the federal government's regulatory role was decidedly limited – the job was not a plum.

But other concerns influenced Edgar's decision, his social insecurity and dread of poverty among them. Many years later, when the Director's public persona was being manufactured by the FBI's Crime Records Division (a euphemism for the Bureau's formidable publicity department), Rex Collier a feature writer for the Washington *Evening Star* and an early Hoover ally, reported:

> He had no thoughts of detective work when he came to the department in 1917 . . . His ambition at the time was to become a government attorney and possibly later to open a law office of his own . . . Attorney General T. W. Gregory assigned Clerk Hoover to the newly formed war division of the department . . . the war division co-operated with military and naval intelligence agencies in preparing evidence for deportation of suspected and avowed anarchists.

Within a short time Hoover was the best-versed man

in the department on these deportation cases. His aptitude and tireless devotion to duty soon attracted the attention of Attorney General Gregory, and a promotion to Special Assistant to the Attorney General followed.

According to this view, pure happenstance accounted for the near-perfect fit that virtually ensured Edgar's meteoric rise in the department, although, to be sure, the clerk's position, whatever its indignities, would have exerted a powerful attraction over a young man of Edgar's severely repressed disposition. For the department, or at least Edgar's part of it, was, after all, a police force, the most visible mechanism of the state's authority, an unrivaled symbol of law and order.

Here the biographer enters a realm of unavoidable conjecture. Practically no record of a personal nature survives from Edgar's early years with the Justice Department or of his private life at that time. One recent author, in an effort to demonstrate Hoover's supposed loyalty to the values of the Old Order of Protestant America, has extrapolated a multifaceted character from the history of the early twentieth-century Sunday school movement. But the fact remains that the record shows only that Edgar taught Sunday school, not *what* he taught or what he believed.

A more likely description in the view of the present authors (and one that does not necessarily exclude the one cited above) is that Edgar was, and would remain, what the clinical literature calls a 'defended' person. Deeply, in some cases totally, repressed, the defended person manages his repressed strivings through a system of bonding, so as never to be free. Edgar, as we have seen, was bonded to his mother and to a set of largely negative belief systems, systems based not on clear philosophical or theoretical foundations, but on hostility to supposed alien traditions, defined as 'un-American,' 'subversive,' and 'communistic.' He also evidently relied on the mechanism of projection – that is, externalizing the threat of chaos caused by his suppressed and anarchic feelings by identifying the forbidden feelings with other persons and thereby keeping anxiety at bay. (If anxiety still leaks out, the severely repressed person will then deal with it through phobias and other forms of avoidance behavior — in Edgar's case through his morbid fear of snakes and germs and dimly perceived threats of consequent penetration and other violence.[7]) In short, Edgar had created a whole apparatus to take care of his fearfulness. He had become, in Bruno Bettelheim's arresting phrase, an 'empty fortress,' the entire structure of his life designed to hide his own unacceptable impulses and turn them into external threats.

In the case of the Justice Department's alien enemy registration section — the unit with authority to seek deportation of alien anarchists and revolutionists — Edgar had stumbled onto another apparatus for dealing with the chaotic forces that he perceived on every side: radical unionists, anarchists, war resisters, expropriation-minded socialists, black nationalists, and even liberal reformers. Yet while he exhibited throughout his adult life many of the rigidities associated with the authoritarian character disorder, the near future demonstrated that he also brought to his new vocation an array of positive attributes: a very efficient way of promulgating beliefs, a powerful capacity for bonding to belief systems, and an emotional conviction that carried across his message, no matter how commonplace. In the frenzied atmosphere of the day, he seized the opportunity to enforce his prejudices without risk and with the assurance of public and official approbation. He was a natural leader from this standpoint, and it soon became quite evident, as was reported by his superiors at the time, that he was destined for success. Most organizations, after all, are looking for just this kind of person.[8] Hoover, in short, had found an ideal niche that offered both fortification and opportunity.

There can be no dispute about the young bureaucrat's assiduity, nor the occasion for it. The alien registration section was formed to meet the department's vastly increased responsibilities following the passage in February of the

Immigration Act (authorizing deportation of alien anarchists and revolutionists) and that in June of the Espionage Act, which, while primarily directed at treason, came to be used by Justice Department officials to cover political dissent. The latter act defined the person guilty of espionage broadly: 'Whoever, when the United States is at war, shall willfully make or convey false reports or false statements with intent to interfere with the operation or success of the military or naval forces of the United States or to promote the success of its enemies; (2) . . . shall willfully cause or attempt to cause insubordination, disloyalty, mutiny, or refusal of duty in the military or naval forces of the United States; (3) or shall willfully obstruct the recruiting or enlistment service of the United States.'

Ostensibly directed at spying and sabotage by the enemy − that is, Imperial Germany − it was vigorously redirected at various home-grown radicals and pacifists, especially after the Bolsheviks took over the six-month-old Russian Revolution in November 1917. Acting on this antipathy to indigenous radicalism, in September 1917 Bureau officials launched a series of raids to arrest the leaders of the radical Industrial Workers of the World (IWW), a union that drew its strength mostly from otherwise non-unionized miners, lumberjacks, and migratory farm workers in the West. Prosecuted for violating the Selective Service and Espionage acts, the IWW leadership was eventually convicted and imprisoned.

Extremely attentive to these events, Hoover closely supervised the investigations, receiving Bureau agents' confidential reports of disloyal activities and filing them for prosecutive action. He despised and feared the 'Wobblies,' as the IWW were contemptuously called, and regarded their wartime propaganda − their hymns 'Dump the Bosses Off Your Back' and 'Hallelujah! I'm a Bum' and their poster slogan 'Don't Be a Soldier, Be a Man' − as treason, plain and simple. Thus native radicals as well as those refugees from Czarist Russia who quite understandably identified with the Russian Revolution commanded young Hoover's attention while other Americans his age were fighting

Germans and dying at Chateau Thierry and along the Marne.

In the meantime, while Edgar was safely ensconced in the enemy alien registration section studying the activities of the enemy within, the Bureau, its strength increased by almost one half for the duration, was also involved in tracking down draft dodgers. Aided and abetted by the volunteer-cum-vigilante American Protective League (APL), Bureau agents conducted a series of dragnet raids of 'slackers,' in the phrase of the day, from April to September 1918. Most of those arrested were quite innocent of draft evasion, by reason of old age, youth, or infirmity; many turned out simply to have forgotten to carry their draft cards. Because respected citizens were among those arrested, the ensuing furor obliged A. Bruce Bielaski, the Bureau's too-zealous director, to step down. However, the zealotry went on.

In fact, other, more dangerous forms had already appeared, most notably the lynching of Frank Little, a member of the IWW's executive committee. But potentially the most serious extremism of all was that encouraged by congressional passage of two further wartime emergency laws. An amendment to the Espionage Act of 1917, the Sedition Act of 1918, forbade anyone 'under pain of $10,000 and twenty years' imprisonment, to . . . utter, print, write, or publish any disloyal, profane, scurrilous, or abusive language about the form of government of the United States, or the Constitution of the United States, or the uniform of the Army or Navy of the United States, or any language intended to . . . encourage resistance to the United States, or to promote the cause of its enemies.'

The second act involved alien radicals, thought by patriotic citizens to constitute a particular threat to the nation. Passed in October 1918, this law amended the Immigration Act of 1917 to expedite deportation of alien anarchists and revolutionists. Under the 1918 act, deportation need no longer be based on proving individual belief in anarchism or violent overthrow of the government; mere membership in organizations judged to be anarchist or revolutionary would suffice. The law provided that 'any alien who, at any time after entering the United States, is found to have been at the time of entry, or to have become thereafter, a member of any one of the classes of aliens [above mentioned] . . . shall upon warrant of the Secretary of Labor, be taken into custody and deported.' Although enforcement was the exclusive responsibility of the Immigration Bureau of the Labor Department, Hoover and the Bureau of Investigation soon entered this field.

The law's ex post facto provision later occasioned bitter dispute, as civil libertarians argued that it abrogated the Constitution's guarantee of free speech. But as far as John Edgar Hoover was concerned, the penalty of banishment at the sole discretion of the secretary of labor set the stage for a welcome purge.

Notes to Chapter Two

1. He received his bachelor of laws degree with honors.

2. The split occurred at the height of the so-called Progressive Era, a period marked by an activist and optimistic faith that the federal government should help solve society's problems, and foreshadowed a temporary realignment of the nation's political parties. For the hallmark of the Progressive movement, of which Wilson too was a part, was not simple reformism but the belief that government and business procedures needed to be rationalized. Rejecting an earlier laissez-faire tradition and committed to a more scientific approach to public administration, increasing numbers of Americans demanded that the government regulate business and reduce anachronistic barriers to economic expansion.

3. An undated medical examination report, drawn up sometime after he entered the Bureau and preserved with effects taken from Seward Square to Thirtieth Place in 1939, gives his height as five-ten and his weight as 170 pounds. The report is in the Hoover memorabilia at the Freedom Foundation in Valley Forge, Pa.

4. Annie's judgmental streak is confirmed by a letter she wrote to Edgar (now in the Hoover memorabilia) describing how she had punished an 'insolent' day-servant by withholding her pay.

5. Tiger's generalizations seem strikingly pertinent to Hoover's career: 'secret societies . . . may emerge to defend a way of life

from threats to cultural patterns, values, etc., implied by groups living in the same territory but defined as aliens' (*Men in Groups* (New York: Random House, 1969), p. 132). Tiger's basic premise is that Homo sapiens is a herd-animal species the male of which acquired the trait of 'bonding' to other males during the 'hunter-gatherer' phase of its evolution. The leader of the herd presumably is that male who most effectively reinforces the conservative bonding trait in all the others, partly by associating himself closely with a common belief system.

6. Because of the labor leaders' more concerted organizational efforts and in part because of increased export opportunities stemming from the outbreak of war in Europe in 1914, restraints on labor organizing were considerably eased. Working men and women in America organized by the millions and won major wage and hours concessions from management, although the bosses still refused to accept the legitimacy of collective bargaining. For the first time since the Civil War, real wages materially increased, and trade unionism acquired a tenuous foothold in national life. Robert Murray, *Red Scare* (Minneapolis University of Minnesota Press, 1955), p. 8, notes that membership in the American Federation of Labor (AFL) 'skyrocketed from about 500,000 in 1900 to 4,169,000 in 1919.'

7. In discussing the authoritarian personality, the German psychologist Hans-Joachim Wilke observes: 'Experience shows that character disorder due to over-submissiveness and latent sadism represents only one possibility in the expression of the authority complex. Here escape takes a downward direction into the chthonic and anal realm, that of the *prima materia*, the prominence of which accounts for the anal and compulsive personality characteristic so often connected with it.' See 'The Authority Complex and the Authoritarian Personality,' *Journal of Analytical Psychology* (July 1977): 246.

8. Like most successful politicians, Hoover was closely in touch with the collective consciousness, in whose structure the German psychologist Hans Dieckman delimits three categories:

1. Religious authority, based either on the canonized traditions of the cult or on the numinous evocation of a god in a prophet or a reformer
2. The authority of the state, based on its constitution and laws
3. The authority of parents and teachers over children, based on the differences between generations and the degree of experience

Dreams of authority may involve brutal authority or ineffectual authority (perceived as chaos). Dreamers of the first type rebel against the authority figure outside themselves and build repressions within. 'The second possibility,' Dieckman writes, 'is to build up a strong authority outside oneself. That was what the other patient [i.e., one with an ineffectual father] had done. He had a strong persona on the outside, a supporter of law and order in the world about him. [This] patient . . . was actually a police officer.' See 'Some Aspects of the Development of Authority,' *Journal of Analytical Psychology* (July 1977): 233.

CHAPTER THREE

EMMA GOLDMAN AND THE SCOURGE OF THE INFIDEL

THE ARMISTICE OF 11 November 1918 and the abrupt demobilization that followed in the United States brought with them runaway inflation and simultaneous recession. In their train came increased political radicalism and broad-scale labor unrest. To many working Americans the sacrifices made for the war effort seemed to have been institutionalized by managements determined to reverse the limited organizational and collective-bargaining gains achieved by labor during the war years. Labor union membership had increased from 10 percent of the workforce in 1910 to 19 percent in 1919, while membership in the AFL alone had increased by almost 25 percent between 1916 and 1919. The sharp increase in wartime profits was paralleled by an increase of 42 percent in the weekly wages of union members.

Workers had not profited from these apparent gains, however. Owing to wartime inflation, real wages in the manufacturing sector had been approximately halved. Thus, with the end of the war, many of the newly organized member unions of the AFL were determined to try their wings in a showdown on collective bargaining. The militance of the workers and of a handful of left-wing intellectuals, in turn, represented to other Americans the threat of revolution then menacing the prostrate countries of central and eastern Europe. The architects of the bloody catastrophe had been discredited, and an ugly confrontation between management and labor loomed at the very moment, it seemed, when worldwide revolution was threatening private property and supposedly settled arrangements of every kind.

Although the stresses afflicting the American workingman provoked a wave of strikes in 1919–1920 on the docks of the coasts and also in such basic industries as steel, coal, and the still government-administered railroads in between – 3,600 strikes involving 4 million workers in the year 1919 alone – the hardships suffered by labor during the war years were not so apparent in white-collar Washington, where a generation of progressivism and wartime centralization had created a seller's market for clerical skills. By late 1918 the twenty-three-year-old Hoover, raised to the rank of Justice Department attorney, was already making $2,000 a year, the salary his father had been making when forced to retire a year earlier at the age of fifty-nine.

Stresses there were, to be sure – pressures of work and ambition combined with Papa's deteriorating health and the brothers' conflicts over their parents' support – but both Dick and Edgar were rising in the federal bureaucracy, and both were hankering after the perquisites of success. Shortly after Edgar's promotion at the Department of Justice, Dick was made deputy inspector general of the Commerce Department's Steamboat Inspection Service, so that in the badinage of family and friends he still had his little brother outranked – his 'General' to Edgar's 'Major.' Even Lillian and Fred Robinette, sustained by the upward trend of government salaries, felt expansive enough in their large house in Lanham to make room for a third and last child, a son, whom they named for his father.

Edgar had marked his first professional advance – his elevation to attorney at Justice – by assuming a substantial part of his parents' support. Now he required a standard of living appropriate to his new rank. An electric footbell was installed in the dining room and, in the kitchen, a black cook, named Delie, to answer it. One of the first private telephones in Pipetown was placed in the back parlor – next to a partly opened window that afforded Dick and his family access to the instrument although no longer to the house itself, which Edgar ruled as his own. Indeed, Edgar deferred to no one in the family except his mother, with whom he maintained a steady if silent contest of wills. Margaret

Fennell recalls that her uncle used to come home from work at night and open the front parlor curtains, whereupon Annie regularly rose from her chair at the rear of the house and without a word retired upstairs. This routine went on for years. But Edgar and his mother never quarreled, never disagreed. Their hopes and expectations were too much the same.

The same cannot be said of Edgar's relations with his brother. Whether because of jealousy or sincere disdain, Dickerson belittled his younger brother's precocious success. A campaign of teasing ensued, beginning with mock-respectful greetings such as 'How is the attorney tonight?' and continuing in a war of nerves directed against Edgar's too-obvious ambition. Remarking that her father and her uncle Edgar were not altogether unlike, Margaret Fennell recalled that Edgar nevertheless 'could be hard-bitten.'

Meanwhile at his office on K Street, northwest, Edgar assiduously prepared his dossiers on the activities of alien radicals for action by the Justice Department's alien enemy registration section. He did so notwithstanding the termination of the war with Germany, although not of hostilities with Russia, where U.S. and other Allied troops had been sent to reactivate the Eastern Front and had remained after the armistice to assist the counterrevolutionary White Russians in their civil war with the Reds. By January 1919, when a Senate Judiciary subcommittee began hearings into allegations that Bolshevik agents had been subsidizing radical organizations and that the Bureau had been investigating 'pro-Germanism' among prominent Americans, especially Americans on the left, on the apparent ground in most cases that they had opposed U.S. entry into the war, Hoover was working closely with A. Mitchell Palmer, the department's alien property custodian.

Palmer was a gregarious operator and former Democratic congressman from Stroudsburg, Pennsylvania. He had helped Woodrow Wilson gain the presidential nomination at the Democratic National Convention of 1912 and had recently made a large public splash by 'Americanizing' the property of German nationals, as he said. (The expropriations, undertaken with the president's knowledge and consent, were calculated to protect American industry from German domination, although German investment in the United States was miniscule compared with that of Japan in the 1980s.) Now, despite the adverse reaction of a minority of the Senate to disclosures of unwarranted wartime surveillance of syndicalists, socialists, and members of the IWW, all of whose meetings had been monitored and whose membership lists had been seized, Hoover and Palmer were flirting with the idea of launching yet another antiradical crusade.

The prospects for repressive action increased on 26 February 1919, when President Wilson named Palmer, over the opposition of Attorney General Thomas Gregory, who regarded the alien property custodian as an opportunist and hack politician, to fill the position that Gregory had insisted on resigning at the war's end. But Attorney General Palmer did not attack immediately. Indeed, he proceeded cautiously at first — perhaps because of his track record as a northern Democratic liberal (for which reason Democratic National Committee Chairman Homer Cummings had insisted that he be promoted in preference to Gregory's conservative Southern nominee) and lingering reservations as to the seriousness of the menace urgently described by his assistant Hoover.

Still, the progress of the next few months seems to have been inexorable. For the men whom Palmer chose to inform him on the nature and extent of the radical menace were themselves, as the historian Stanley Coben concluded, 'extraordinarily susceptible to the fear and extravagant patriotism so prevalent in 1919.' Those advisers included Francis P. Garvan, a veteran of the Manhattan district attorney's office, chosen by Palmer to be assistant attorney general in charge of investigating and prosecuting radicals; William J. Flynn, former head of the Secret Service, chosen to replace Bielaski as head of the Bureau; and Frank Burke, manager of the Secret Service's New York office and a self-proclaimed Russian expert, appointed Flynn's assistant.

Most significantly, Palmer retained Hoover, who was by then recognized as the department's resident expert on foreign-inspired radicalism.

Palmer himself shared his appointees' nativist and antiradical prejudices, firmly believing that the Bolshevik Revolution had been managed by 'a small clique of outcasts from the East Side of New York . . . Because a disreputable alien — Leon Bronstein, the man who now calls himself Trotsky — can inaugurate a reign of terror from his throne room in the Kremlin; because this lowest of all types known to New York can sleep in the czar's bed . . . should America be swayed by such doctrines?' Not for the last time was Hoover blessed in the president's choice of an attorney general.

The next month, on 10 March 1919, the Supreme Court upheld the conviction of Eugene Debs for violating the wartime Espionage Act. Debs, the leader of the Socialist party, had been sentenced to ten years in prison for a speech in Canton, Ohio, denouncing the government's prosecution of prominent Socialists who opposed U.S. involvement in World War I and exhorting continued opposition to the war. At the same session the Court upheld the conviction, also under the Espionage Act, of Socialist party General Secretary Charles Schenck for counseling opposition to the Conscription Act of 1917. Denying that Schenck's First Amendment rights were violated, Justice Oliver Wendell Holmes, Jr., affirmed that 'the question in every case is whether the words used . . . create a clear and present danger.'[1]

Hoover applauded both decisions, subsequently expanding Holmes's more narrow dictum into his own yardstick for prosecuting radical activists. Palmer, however, continued to have second thoughts, questioning whether the political climate would change and today's justice become tomorrow's miscarriage. He even considered recommending that President Wilson grant executive clemency for Debs; Wilson, however, had already left for Paris to win the peace, a goal that eluded him at every turn.[2]

That same month the Third International was founded

in Moscow. Its pronouncements, including its requirement of obedience to Comintern decisions, split Marxist parties throughout the world, and its proclamation of the inevitability of violent revolutionary change offended both conservatives and proponents of evolutionary socialism. Germany and Hungary were already racked by revolution, and now the leaders in the Kremlin were calling for world revolution. Although most Americans had never met a Marxist in their lives and although the American radical movement was minuscule and had been decimated by the war, who could be sure the United States was not next? Surely not Hoover and Palmer.

President Wilson, consumed by the negotiations leading to Versailles, withdrew the last U.S. troops from European Russia while he still could. But those sent via Vladivostok, numbering some 8,500, remained in Russian Siberia, where fierce fighting continued, and the government soon abandoned any pretense that they were not actually there to defend world capitalism from the Bolshevist menace. To withdraw them, Secretary of War Newton D. Baker said, 'would leave Siberia open to anarchy, bloodshed and Bolshevism.' Pax Americana had been declared, and Baker had a strapping young secretary from Iowa named Clyde Tolson (soon to make a name for himself in Hoover's FBI) urging him on.

Then, on 1 May 1919, postal inspectors in New York City uncovered a plot to assassinate a number of prominent Americans, Palmer among them. The case was quickly 'solved' and attributed to anarchists and the IWW, whose officers were all in jail. But still Palmer equivocated, unwilling to cut ties to his liberal constituency yet tormented by agonies of ambition. For there was little doubt that there was political mileage to be made in a public campaign against radicalism – the press was already dramatizing the menace of foreign-inspired radicals, and in full-page advertisements and alarmist press releases, captains of industry were pinning the Marxist tail on organized labor's donkey.

The matter was settled in the early morning of 2 June

when a bomb exploded on the front porch of Palmer's house in Washington, spewing fragments of the unfortunate bomber, who evidently had stumbled on his approach, across the neighbors' front lawns. Assistant Secretary of the Navy Franklin Delano Roosevelt, who rushed from his own house across the street to the Palmers' assistance, subsequently reported that the attorney general, a lifelong Quaker, was so shaken that he had regressed many years: 'He was "theeing" and "thouing" me all over the place – "thank thee, Franklin" and all that.'

Palmer's reaction was swift. He authorized a massive antiradical campaign and ordered a nationwide search for the bombers, who had detonated bombs simultaneously in twelve cities. Hardly had the ink dried on the Treaty of Versailles – signed by the Central Powers and the Allies on 28 June 1919 – and the last troops been withdrawn from European Russia when Palmer named John Edgar Hoover to be special assistant to the attorney general, charged with developing and coordinating information to be used to prosecute radicals, both alien and native-born. The next month, on 1 August, Hoover was empowered to establish under his own direction a General Intelligence Division (GID) in the Bureau of Investigation, the core of Palmer's planned antiradical campaign.

Hoover celebrated this new professional dignity by styling himself for the first time 'J. Edgar Hoover,' rather than 'John Edgar Hoover' or 'J. E. Hoover.' The importance of the change would have been apparent to the author of 'The Love Song of J. Alfred Prufrock.'[3] In a word, it imparted grandeur.

Hoover was then twenty-four and in almost every respect a naïf. But he had demonstrated stamina, ability, and, especially, a capacity to seize the initiative. The very lack of a capacity for bonding other men enabled him to be ruthlessly manipulative if need be to get a job done. And for him, the means were always subordinate to the end.

Moreover, he had mastered the mammoth card catalogue at the Library of Congress and was thereby equipped to master the gargantuan task collating the information to be gathered on the country's estimated 10,000 Communists. (The estimate proved too low, according to Hoover, whose division amassed files on some 60,000 Americans in its first hundred days, eventually compiling dossiers on more than 200,000 individuals and organizations, primarily radical but including the American Civil Liberties Union and such prominent liberals as Senator Robert La Follette, settlement house reformer Jane Addams, Assistant Secretary of Labor Louis Post, and Federal Judge George Anderson.)

Also included in Hoover's file was a special category: 'Negro Activities.' Early in 1919 he had begun to monitor the activities of Marcus Garvey and others in the burgeoning black nationalist movement. Always uneasy about assertive blacks, Hoover was concerned about Garvey's role as 'one of the most prominent negro agitators in New York' and concluded from a review of the Garveyite paper *Negro World* that it 'upheld' 'Soviet Russian rule' and engaged in 'open advocation [*sic*] of Bolshevism.' Nor was Hoover exercised solely about the black nationalists; black proponents of mere racial equality also commanded his interest. His fears led him to recommend to his superiors in the Justice Department that 'something must be done to the editors of these publications as they are beyond doubt exciting the negro elements of this country to riot and to the committing of outrages of all sorts.'

Hoover was no mere card cataloguer. A true believer, he was dedicated and obsessed, a tenacious and tireless adherent of postwar antiradicalism. He was, by common consent of his associates in the Bureau, the perfect man to nail the reds, even though, as Coben points out, there was not 'even a remote possibility of a serious uprising in 1919 – 1920.'

Still, Hoover succeeded in convincing Palmer of the threat, with evidence consisting of scores of newly started foreign-language journals collected by his agents. In this effort he capitalized on the unrealistic optimism of American Communists, who, captivated by the Bolshevik triumph in Russia, confidently predicted a similar success in the United States. The thinness of Hoover's evidence did not deter the ambitious Palmer. The antiradical militants were champing at the bit, and the attorney general, who by then had acquired presidential ambitions, readily promoted his youthful underling's antiradical crusade.

President Wilson meanwhile was concentrating almost all of his declining energies on winning the peace — specifically, on drumming up support for Senate ratification of the Versailles Treaty and U.S. membership in the League of Nations. In two crucial respects he proved unequal to the task. The Senate Foreign Relations Committee, under the chairmanship of Henry Cabot Lodge of Massachusetts, twice reported out a treaty containing crippling reservations (forty-five in September and fourteen in November), thereby forcing the president to pressure the Democratic senators to reject ratification. And on 2 October, following a grueling speaking tour begun in the summer, the president suffered a stroke, disabling, but not sufficiently to force him from office. His wife assumed the task of governing, scrutinizing all communications to the president and acting on them as she and her advisers saw fit. An interregnum, in effect, had begun, with the leadership vacuum at the top feeding the nation's sense of vulnerability while encouraging adventurers in the ranks to take matters into their own hands.

A month after Wilson's collapse, Palmer himself became ill. His efforts to make the Justice Department the juggernaut of administration action to deal with the manifold dislocations of the peace — the revolutionary threat of Bolshevism, militant trade unionism, the actionable activities of labor and, in one instance, management — had driven him to the brink of exhaustion, and in November his doctor ordered him to rest. In consequence, the planning for the ensuing mass dragnet raids of alien radicals descended on the shoulders of his ambitious assistant, J. Edgar Hoover.

Before deciding to focus their antiradical crusade on alien radicals, Palmer and Hoover had tried unsuccessfully to use a Civil War-era statute as the basis for prosecution of both native and alien radicals, as the Espionage Act of 1917 authorized prosecution only during wartime. Enacted in 1861, the statute, section six of the federal criminal code,

71

had been drafted to meet the real threat of civil war and thus was directed at those seeking to overthrow by violence the government of the United States. In 1919, however, Judge John Raymond Hazel foreclosed this line of attack, ruling that when passing this measure Congress 'did not have in mind . . . the overthrow of the government . . . by the use of propaganda.' Momentarily stymied by this ruling, Palmer and Hoover soon shifted the focus of their antiradical strategy to the alien deportation provisions of the 1917 Immigration Act as amended in 1918. While conceding that 'administration' of this law 'is entirely within the jurisdiction of the Department of Labor,' Palmer nevertheless concluded that 'under existing conditions of our laws it seemed to be the only means at my disposal of attacking the radical movement.'

Undaunted by the lack of any enforcement authority, Palmer in September sought and obtained Labor Secretary William B. Wilson's consent to proceed jointly to enforce the immigration statute. Immediately Hoover and other Justice Department officials met with three Labor Department counterparts – Commissioner General of Immigration Anthony Caminetti, Labor Department Solicitor General John W. Abercrombie, and Immigration Bureau Counsel A. W. Parker – to coordinate strategy.

Hoover and the Immigration officials anticipated different results from the ensuing mass dragnet raids to arrest alien radicals. For Caminetti, dragnet raids could expedite the apprehension and deportation of alien radicals if the detainees could be interrogated without benefit of counsel and possibly intimidate into admitting membership in proscribed organizations. Hoover's objective was to generate support for congressional enactment of peacetime sedition legislation. The publicity following the arrests of thousands of alien radicals, he hoped, could achieve this result by documenting the magnitude of the Red Menace. Moreover, Hoover, it was clear, was the moving force in planning and publicizing the raids. By then armed with Bureau informants' reports on alien radical organizations and their leaders, he designated the Union of Russian Workers, an avowed anarchist group of approximately 4,000 Russian immigrants, the first target.

Unfortunately, he and his antiradical cadre in the GID had confined their attentions to the published positions of Union leaders and to the literature distributed rather casually by Union affiliates, discounting the possibility that any of the members of the Union might have joined locals for purely social reasons. One such local, in New York City, is described at first hand in Kim Chernin's memoir *In My Mother's House*, in which her Russian immigrant mother recalled:

> I can't tell you what it was like for me to see this place. It was not like anything I had ever seen before. The walls were all painted in bright colors; there were slogans and posters everywhere. On Fridays there were lectures, on Saturdays dancing, there were literary evenings and in one corner of the room there was a buffet, where women were serving tea and cakes. And there was also a little stage someone had built, where the poets could read or someone could give a talk about the Soviet Union. When they would hold dances the people would just spill out of the club into the street outside.

The possibility that quite innocent people might frequent these clubhouses, in search of community or the free courses given in English and other skills, seems not to have occurred to Hoover. Nor can there be doubt that he regarded the foreign-born leaders of the Union, Emma Goldman and Alexander Berkman, as deserving no consideration at all. For both were outspoken anarchists of the nonpacific kind – Goldman's oratory was reputed to have fired up President McKinley's assassin, Leon Czolgosz – and both had celebrated their passionate adherence to the doctrine of free love in a longstanding open affair. To a young man of no sexual experience and fanatical loyalty to a late Victorian code of honor, Goldman must have appeared a witch and a whore all wrapped in one.

73

Hoover's roundup was conducted – by Bureau agents working with local police in twelve cities – without regard to constitutional niceties. Despite having obtained only 27 arrest warrants in New York City, Hoover's agents apprehended about 200 men and women in its raid there, some of whom proved to be citizens and others members of neither the Russian Workers Union nor any other radical organization. Others were dragged from their beds or snatched from their families without formal charge in the middle of the night, leaving distraught spouses and children to fend for themselves.

Yet aside from isolated criticisms, the raids were greeted with enthusiastic nationwide applause, greatly amplified by the press. Delighted to find his own prejudices confirmed by millions of Americans (he began keeping a scrapbook of newspaper reports at this time), Hoover turned his attention to impressing his superiors. In one of a series of weekly GID reports distributed confidentially to a select group of government officials, the familiar voice of the moralist condemned the literature seized at the Union's meeting halls:

> In the great bulk of material taken in the raids of November 7, 1919, when members of the Union of Russian Workers were apprehended, 99 percent of the same was wholly anarchistic in tendency. There could be submitted dozens of copies of literature typical of the anarchistic propaganda, but all of it is similar in content to the end that it is atheistic in tendency and immoral and vicious in purpose.

Responding to criticism of one of the arrests in Philadelphia, Hoover displayed the combativeness and vengefulness that were to become his trade marks:

> Immediately following his arrest, certain influences were brought to work in his behalf, it being claimed that he had tuberculosis and that he had but one lung . . .

The merit of his case so far as physical condition is concerned is unknown to me, but I do know that even though he had but one lung it was sufficiently strong enough [*sic*] for him to deliver to a group of Russians, non-citizens of the United States, a lecture upon anarchy.

The ostensible cause of these arrests was all but forgotten in the excitement – to find those responsible for the bombings at Attorney General Palmer's house and elsewhere on 2 June.

Concurrently with this dragnet raid, Hoover initiated an even more intensive investigation of American radicalism, poring over radical publications and interviewing radical activists. For Edgar, time was of the essence, as he needed to document both the anarchism and commitment to violent revolution of those arrested. To achieve this, he focused on their leaders, Goldman and Berkman, poring over their ample Bureau dossiers with particular attention – and growing contempt. For Goldman, although past fifty, was still carrying on like a girl of the streets, and both she and Berkman, who was several years her junior, treated respectable society with unvarnished disdain.

At this time Hoover also pored over the writings of Marx and Engels, Lenin and Trotsky. That he should have found 'Commonism' the greatest evil in the history of the world is not surprising when one considers that it advocated violent expropriation from the owners of the means of production and rejected religion as the opiate of the masses. This, to one who reportedly said grace at the dining table both morning and night and who, according to one longtime acquaintance, had a 'wealth reverence,' was clearly intolerable. Moreover, Hoover's definition of Communism was all-encompassing, extending even to those who argued the need for socialism, whether achieved through violence or the democratic process. Convinced that radicalism was a monstrous threat to America, Hoover, who saw himself as in some way the savior chosen to carry the light to the gentiles, could act with conviction.

The means to do so were at hand — the provisions of the 1918 Immigration Act — and he seized them. By documenting Goldman's and Berkman's sins, he might facilitate the deportation of the other detained Russian Workers as well. His involvement extended beyond the execution of a well-crafted strategy; it was deeply emotional. For Goldman and Berkman combined with their lust outspoken anarchism, the external projection of his own inner fear of disorder. His vengefulness knew no bounds.

Scenes that unfortunately cannot be reconstructed from the record of this time are Hoover's confrontation with Goldman and his later confrontation with Berkman, after their arrest in the 7 November dragnet. Hoover ever after let it be known that he had engaged in lengthy debate with both of them and that the fervor of his anti-Communism was the result of objective inquiry — he had learned about it from the horse's mouth. He must in fact have given very little thought to what Goldman and Berkman had to say, as his pursuit of their enforced exile was remorseless right up to the moment of their departure.

Hoover went about this project with his customary energy and attention to detail. First and foremost, a means had to be found to transport the hated radicals from Ellis Island, where they were being held, to Russia. He discovered the means in an old steamer, launched in Belfast in 1890 as the British transport *Mississippi*, which the Army had purchased in 1898 to bring home troops from the Spanish-American war. Second, as prosecutor, he argued the government's case against the radicals. At the same time, he made his debut as a propagandist, finding space in his hectic schedule to write and sign several Bureau reports on the subject of Communism. His dismissive but historically illiterate anti-Communism can be conveyed in a single excerpt:

From the days of Marx, when there was first enunciated in concrete form a Communist manifesto, there has been from time to time certain communistic movements appearing in the political life of Europe. These movements have usually been short lived and have been sponsored by a few intellectual perverts blinded by the thought of achievement of a utopian political commonwealth.

Hoover's efforts to make sense of another manifesto, issued by the Third International in March 1919, proved even less successful. Noting at the outset that the authors of the document 'advocate force and violence in acquiring the ultimate aim of the proletarian dictatorship,' he concluded in prose both tortuous and redolent of his deficiencies as a political philosopher:

> There is no effort to accomplish in this instance the ultimate aim by parliamentary action, but it is conclusive that in order to attain the aim desired that force and violence will be resorted to as a means of acquiring the desire . . .
>   Thus we come to the close of the communist international manifesto, and find that parliamentarism [sic] is to be considered victory in the drive of the Communists for world-wide control and that it openly advocates mass action which will result in direct conflict with the governmental machinery in open conflict.

Hoover's confusions notwithstanding, as the defendants were unarguably both avowed anarchists and aliens, the proceedings were mercifully brief. The day of reckoning came on 21 December, when 249 anarchists, attended by a host of newspaper reporters and congressmen whom Hoover had invited to the sailing, boarded the rechristened steamship *Buford* to be returned to the land of their birth.

The press response was overwhelming, delightedly referring to the *Buford* as the 'Soviet Ark.' For the first time in his stewardship at the Department of Justice, Palmer found general favor, enjoying the approval even of those on the right who had criticized him for not moving fast enough. Moved by passionate antiradicalism, even the organized bar abandoned any concern for due process and constitutional niceties. As *Bench and Bar*, a national law journal, remarked: 'There is only one way to deal with anarchy, and *that is to crush it.*' It urged 'not a slap on the wrist, but a broad-axe on the neck.' The *Cleveland Plain Dealer* concurred: 'It is hoped and expected that other vessels, larger, more commodious, carrying similar cargoes, will follow in her wake.'

By then riding a popular wave, Palmer was content to leave in the capable hands of his subordinate the orchestration of still further raids. A second roundup of alien radicals, this time Communist and Communist Labor party members, was secretly planned for the second day of January 1920, and Hoover, who had moved to the fore so effectively in the November raid and its aftermath, was put in charge.

Hoover had already taken steps to eliminate one problem which heretofore had limited the effectiveness of deportation proceedings and which he had encountered after the November raids. Under rule 22 of the immigration regulations, detainees had been accorded certain rights: 'At the beginning of the hearing under the warrant of arrest the alien shall be allowed to inspect the warrant of arrest and all the evidence on which it was issued, and shall be apprised that he may be represented by counsel.'

The right to counsel invariably meant that detainees did not volunteer the fact of their membership in proscribed organizations. Having concluded that this rule undermined the kind of mass dragnet raid that could ensure the deportation of thousands of alien radicals, Hoover wrote to Caminetti suggesting a change and continued to press him when the immigration commissioner did not respond, concluding: 'In view of the difficulty in proving the cases against persons known to be members of the Union of Russian Workers, due to the arbitrary tactics of persons [legal counsel] employed by such members, I would appreciate an early reply to my letter of the nineteenth, in order that the same condition may not arise when future arrests are made of undesirable aliens.' Ultimately convinced by this argument, Caminetti petitioned Abercrombie, the acting secretary of labor during Secretary Wilson's temporary illness, to modify rule 22. Abercrombie agreed and, in addition, signed 3,000 blank warrants for the planned January raid.

On the basis of these blank warrants (the prospective arrestee's name was not listed), that same day a letter almost certainly drafted by Hoover but signed by the Bureau's Assistant Director Frank Burke was sent to agents in thirty-three major cities (including New York, Boston, Detroit, and Chicago), covering twenty-three states, instructing them how to proceed against the Communist and Communist Labor party members who were the targets of the 2 January raid. The letter announced the planned raid and its time and date, and then declared, 'You should arrange with your undercover informants to have meetings of the Communist party and the Communist Labor party on the night set. I have been informed by some of the Bureau chiefs that such arrangements will be made. This, of course, would facilitate the making of arrests.'

Bureau agents were further instructed that Mr. Hoover was in charge of the planned dragnet and could be reached at any hour of the night at a special number at the Bureau of Investigation. Agents were to effect the arrests between 7 p.m. on Friday the second, and 7 a.m. the next morning, using local police personnel as needed. All party members not present at the meetings were to be arrested at their homes, places of business, social clubs, or elsewhere.

In the event, about 10,000 persons were arrested nationwide in the roundup. Of these, some 6,500 were released after questioning either because they were citizens and thus not liable to deportation or because they were friends or relatives who were originally arrested to ensure maximum secrecy during the conduct of the raids. Of the 3,500 held for deportation, only 556 were eventually ordered deported by the secretary of labor.

The operation had gone smoothly and according to plan. Moreover, the initial press response was enthusiastic. As the *New York Times* editorially commented: 'If any or some of us . . . have ever doubted the alacrity, resolute will, and fruitful intelligence of the Department of Justice in hunting down the enemies of the United States, the questioners and doubters now have cause to approve and applaud.' *Bench and Bar* echoed this praise, asserting that 'the need for repression is great, and the time for repression is now.'

In time, however, praise gave way to doubt, then criticism. The day after the roundup, the U.S. attorney in Philadelphia, Francis Fisher Kane, resigned in protest. A few newspapers and liberal magazines, most notably the *Nation* and the *New Republic*, took up the cry, and before long the wall of silence was breached. Then, on 28 May 1920, the National Public Government League (NPGL) published a pamphlet, 'We the American People: Report Upon the Illegal Practices of the United States Department of Justice,' written by twelve of the nation's most eminent law professors, including Felix Frankfurter, Roscoe Pound, Ernst Freund, and Zechariah Chafee, Jr. This report documented the wholesale arrests and detentions of citizens against whom there was not a ghost of a case, numerous instances of police and GID brutality, and the deplorable conditions of the improvised jails in which the victims were held.

At first Hoover to brazen it out. Defending the conduct of his Division, he renewed the rhetoric of the Scare. Seeking to capitalize on the raids to effect the deportation of those arrested and thereby generate a climate compelling enactment of peacetime sedition legislation, he declared in an indirect but attributed quotation: 'Forty thousand American citizens are working for overthrow by force of the Government, through the Communist and Communist Labor parties.'

At the same time, having learned of the proposed NPGL study prior to its release, Hoover on 8 May 1920 ordered a 'discreet and thorough investigation of all essential facts (pertaining to the NPGL)' – the first known probe of this kind. Astute bureaucrat that he was and appreciating the adverse fallout should his investigation become known, he emphasized the need for secrecy.

In his order, Hoover specifically demanded 'to know who they [League members] are and to obtain full information concerning the NPGL. The inquiry should be directed as soon as possible, without precipitating issue.' Detailed reports were prepared describing the purpose of the NPGL, its officers and financial supporters, and, as well, background information on the report's twelve distinguished authors.

Hoover's practice of soliciting derogatory information with which to discredit his critics failed to stem the rising tide of protest. His problems were compounded in March, when Assistant Secretary of Labor Louis Post joined the fray. Owing to a number of fortuitous circumstances — Abercrombie's departure to run for the Senate in Alabama and Secretary Wilson's physical indisposition, among them — Post, a lawyer and former assistant U.S. attorney in New York City, became acting secretary of labor, in charge of deportation matters. Without ceremony he quickly set about undoing the cozy arrangement between Justice and Labor that Hoover had so laboriously set up the previous fall. Post restored rule 22 and then refused to allow the presentation during deportation proceedings of information extracted from the terrified arrestees, unrepresented, as they all had been, by counsel. As a result, thousands of those arrested were released. Post's action, in turn, precipitated an avalanche of right-wing congressional criticism. At seventy-one, nearing the end of his public career, Post pressed on, releasing score after score of the prisoners and reducing the excessively high bail of most of the others.

Both Hoover and Palmer were outraged, but for the moment there was nothing they could do. As in the case of NPGL, Hoover ordered his agents to report any 'information linking Post to the IWW.' But although responding with zeal, the agents could not come up with hard evidence to confirm Hoover's suspicions.

Failing in this, Hoover was soon forced to confront the changing political reality of declining public interest in antiradical charges. By the spring of 1920, popular fears of the Red Menace had ebbed; not only was there no threat of a Bolshevik Revolution in the United States, but the revolutionary threat in Europe had been confined to Russia.

Moreover, many Americans had begun to fear for their own constitutional liberties.

Then, at the very time when Post was throwing out case after case against the radicals, and doing so with Secretary Wilson's approval, Hoover was summoned to Boston to testify in *Colyer* v. *Skeffington*, a habeas corpus proceeding initiated by a married couple arrested in January in Wellesley, Massachusetts, and seeking to avoid deportation. After hearing Hoover's testimony on the conduct of the Boston-area raids, in which 400 persons were arrested on 300 warrants, and after questioning him on the role of informers in arranging simultaneous Communist party meetings on the night of 2 January, Judge George W. Anderson declared that the government apparently 'operates some part of the Communist party in this country.' Ordering the release of the defendants, Anderson sharply condemned Hoover's use of informers and agents provocateurs, pointedly refusing to 'adopt the contention that government spies are more trustworthy or less disposed to make trouble in order to profit therefrom than are spies in the private industry . . . The spy system destroys trust and confidence and propagates hate.'

Hoover retaliated characteristically, declaring that Judge Anderson's statement was 'an unjustified misconception of the facts,' an extreme reaction dictated by the young man's extreme sensitivity to criticism. His denial, however, was carefully qualified: The GID director 'knew of no agent of the Department of Justice who had ever acted as agent provocateur.' At the same time he privately ordered the Boston office to investigate Anderson, particularly his 'well known sympathy . . . with the "liberal movement." '

Questioning Anderson's ability and integrity, the resulting Bureau reports cited the judge's earlier refusal, when a U.S. attorney, to prosecute participants in wartime 'German spy plots,' doubted Anderson's impartiality to judge the 'facts' relating to the international Communist conspiracy, claimed that his 'name is a household word among the reds,' and characterized his decision not to grant writs of habeas corpus as 'evidently intended for propaganda.' The same report said that Anderson's decision 'has been seized upon by radical papers and organizations both here and abroad.'

Unfortunately, Hoover could not use this information publicly to discredit Anderson, as it had been unlawfully obtained. Besides, the cat was already out of the bag. Swinburne Hale, a New York attorney appearing on behalf of the arrested Communists at a hearing before Secretary Wilson in January 1920, after questioning Hoover on the matter of agents provocateurs, had offered as evidence against Hoover's protestations of innocence Frank Burke's signed letter of 27 December to the Boston field office. The letter, with its damning instruction to have informers arrange meetings for the night of 2 January so as to 'facilitate' arrests, was thereupon given to the press, with catastrophic consequences for Hoover's Red Scare strategy. As a result, not only did most of the 10,000 avoid deportation, but Congress eventually lost interest in proposed peacetime sedition legislation, even going so far as to repeal the Sedition Act of 1918.

Not surprisingly, Hale too became an object of Hoover's investigative zeal. Because of Hale's conduct, which Hoover archly characterized as displaying 'somewhat peculiar attitudes,' Hoover directed Bureau agents to investigate the eminent attorney. Indeed, the GID director even asked military intelligence to forward any information it had about Hale's 'past history and connections.'

Palmer continued to do battle, driven by his ambition for the presidency and a conviction of his own rightness. But he had the bad judgment to believe — and, worse yet, to broadcast — the partisan intelligence he was getting from Hoover, which documented the Red Menace merely by recapitulating Marxist rhetoric. The crowning blow was occasioned by Palmer's unqualified forecast of riots and a general strike on the approaching May Day, which passed without more serious violence than that visited on peaceful Marxist demonstrators by angry right-wing patriots.

To Hoover's and Palmer's chagrin, the Red Scare then quickly dissipated. The denouement began in late April 1920, when a House Rules subcommittee initiated preliminary impeachment hearings against Assistant Secretary Post for his role in countermanding the Hoover-Palmer deportation strategy. By persuading Labor Secretary Wilson that rule 22 had been improperly rescinded, that information obtained from detained aliens without the presence of counsel should not be used during deportation proceedings, that mere membership in the Communist party was not sufficient grounds for deportation, and that it was time to end the 'gigantic and cruel hoax' of the 'deportation delirium,' Post had become the target of Palmer's and Hoover's ire. Palmer's ensuing tirade to the effect that Post's action aided and abetted Bolshevism had then encouraged the attorney general's congressional allies to demand the assistant labor secretary's impeachment.

The impeachment hearings proved to be a debacle for Palmer and Hoover. Post's witty and informed defense of his actions was invincible; his emphasis on the need to respect due process and the rule of law effectively turned the tables, and the proceedings fell of their own weight. The aura of Post's triumph and the fizzle of the well-advertised May Day revolution combined to turn the tide.

Hoover, lacking any independent political base, was forced for the time being to abandon the field of public anti-radicalism. But before abandoning the cause, although obviously wounded and frightened, he characteristically directed a discreet Bureau investigation of Congressman Phillip Campbell, the chairman of the House Rules sub-committee that had conducted the Post impeachment inquiry.

After Post's vindication, an abortive Senate counterattack on the redhunters began under the eloquent leadership of Thomas Walsh of Montana. The catalyst to this inquiry was the NPGL report prepared by the four Harvard law professors and the eight other distinguished jurists of their group condemning the Bureau of Investigation and the GID for illegal actions and abuse of authority. Hoover once again waged secret battle against these new critics, his Machiavellian ingenuity growing to meet each new challenge. In fact, his stratagems, not known until years later, included a secret letter to Under Secretary of State William Hurley impugning Frankfurter's loyalty.[4] He also covertly assisted Harvard University overseer Austen Fox's efforts to have Zachariah Chafee dismissed from the Harvard faculty. Hoover provided Fox with information to support the overseer's allegations that Chafee's criticisms of the Bureau's role in the January 1920 raids had been reckless and untrue and, further, ordered GID agents to monitor press coverage of Harvard's investigation of Chafee. But his efforts were to no avail. The university ultimately concluded that Fox's allegations were inaccurate, and thus no action was taken.

The Senate hearings began on 19 January and lasted until 3 March 1921. Chaired by Walsh, the committee invited legal scholars as well as those Justice Department officials involved in executing the January 1920 raids, including Palmer and Hoover, to testify. Minutely examining Hoover's 27 December instruction letter, Walsh observed that 'it is difficult to conceive how one bred in the law could ever have promulgated such an order.' The committee's case against the department ultimately turned on the department's decision to issue telegraphic warrants. The ensuing comic opera scene in the Capitol found both Palmer and Hoover eagerly evading responsibility for the raids they had earlier championed and planned:

Senator Walsh: 'How many search warrants were issued?'

Attorney General Palmer: 'I cannot tell you . . . If you would like to ask Mr. Hoover, who was in charge of this matter, he can tell you.'

Senator Walsh: 'Yes.'

Mr. Hoover: 'The search warrants were entirely a matter which the agents in charge of local offices handled.'

Senator Walsh: 'And you know nothing at all about it?'

Mr. Hoover: 'No, sir.'

Senator Walsh: 'Do you know how many searches were made without a search warrant?'

Mr. Hoover: 'I do not.'

And so it went, with Hoover and Palmer stonewalling and passing the buck. Senator Walsh reminded both of them that 'there is no warrant in the law for entering a man's house, rifling his drawers, peering into his private papers, and walking off with any documents that are his, for any purpose, much less to use them as evidence against him.' He concluded that the searches and seizures conducted by the Bureau under Hoover's direction on the night of 2 January were 'the lawless acts of a mob.'

Walsh proposed to rectify the problem, although not by drafting legislation to codify the Bureau's investigative authority. Instead, the senator shortly drafted a bill to ensure due process in deportation proceedings and specifically to exclude the Department of Justice and the Bureau of Investigation from future involvement in the administration of the immigration law. Walsh's bill was never debated, however, let alone enacted, as it was lost in the congressional uproar over immigration legislation intended to limit the admission of undesirable ethnic groups (the Emergency Quota Act of 1921 and the National Origins Act of 1924, both of which adopted the principle of ethnic quotas).

The remaining problem of what to do about Palmer's misfeasance meanwhile had proved to be self-liquidating; he failed even to receive his party's presidential nomination. Then, in the 1920 presidential election, the majority gave its votes to Warren Gamaliel Harding, the Republican candidate, over Palmer's successful opponent in the Democratic primaries, James M. Cox. As H. L. Mencken observed, the people had chosen an older Americanism instead of 'the imitations put forward by the Prohibitionists, the Palmer White Guard, the Wilson mail openers and the press agents of the American Legion.'

Palmer was on his way out. The question remained: Could Hoover long survive him?

1. In defense of this restriction of First Amendment rights, Holmes offered the example of the shout of 'Fire!' in a crowded theater.

2. President Warren Harding eventually pardoned Debs in 1921.

3. Years later, in February 1955, Francis Walter, the chairman of the House Committee on Un-American Activities and a coeval of Hoover's at George Washington University, recalled why John Edgar had changed his name. Walter recounted that young Hoover had attempted to open a charge account at Garfinckel's (a prestigious department store), but 'the credit man came out with a credit card for John E. Hoover and told the Director his credit was not good. The Director explained that there was another [John] Hoover and from that time on the Director started signing J. Edgar Hoover.' Whatever the merits of Walter's account, Hoover's only comment was a terse 'It was Woodward & Lothrop.' (Memo, Nichols to Tolson, 10 February 1955, FBI 61-7582-2614.)

4. In early 1961 Harold Arrowsmith, Jr., an associate of George Lincoln Rockwell in the American Nazi Party and a researcher for the right-wing, anti-Semitic Liberty Lobby, came across Hoover's letter to Hurley, dated 23 February 1921, in the records of the Department of Justice deposited at the National Archives. In his letter Hoover cited the 'communistic propaganda activities' of Felix Frankfurter. Arrowsmith thereupon proposed that the Liberty Lobby circulate copies of Hoover's letter in an attempt to discredit Frankfurter, who in 1961 was a Supreme Court Justice and the target of a Liberty Lobby attack because of his Jewishness and liberal philosophy. Liberty Lobby officials accordingly contacted Senator Strom Thurmond of South Carolina and Representative James Davis of Georgia for assistance in obtaining copies of the reports that Hoover had relied on in making this charge. Both congressmen cooperated promptly, but, rather than act on their requests, National Archives officials referred the matter to Hoover, who denied access 'under existing regulations.' Thereafter, Hoover had his aides advise the congressmen that 'it is not possible to make a Photostat of the letter in question available.'

Publicity about the letter, however, had come to Frankfurter's attention, and he called Hoover on 25 September. Flatly denying the authenticity of the letter, Hoover claimed, as he recorded in a memo to the FBI files, that it 'was written by an attorney in my division and my name was signed to it, but not by me. I stated I sign my name "J. Edgar Hoover" and this letter was signed "J. E. Hoover," and I had never seen the letter until this "crank" of "fanatic" began writing in demanding confirmation . . . I stated it was an erroneous letter . . . I gave orders that I wanted a memorandum prepared and placed with that letter pointing out there is no basis in fact.' That same day Frankfurter wrote to Hoover, saying acidly that 'I'm glad somebody is "protecting" me.'

Arrowsmith's discovery of Hoover's letter and the publicity given to the matter by the Liberty Lobby deeply troubled the Director, however. Not only did Hoover's letter identify his position with that of the extreme anti-Semitic Liberty Lobby, but it also blurred the image he had tried to cultivate of the Bureau as a highly professional, apolitical organization. Hoover's 1921 reference to Frankfurter underscored that the Director's definition of 'communistic propaganda activities' derived from his political conservatism. (Memo, DeLoach to Mohr, 7 September 1961; Memo, Jones to DeLoach 19 October 1961; Memo, Hoover to Tolson, Mohr, and DeLoach 25 September 1961; all in FBI 62-37356.)

CHAPTER FOUR

(1921–1923)

RETRENCHMENT

THERE WERE a number of junctures in J. Edgar Hoover's career when his seemingly charmed life might have taken a different turn. The inauguration of Warren Gamaliel Harding as president was one. On that day Harry Micajah Daugherty became attorney general. Daugherty, a card-playing crony of the president and fellow Ohio Republican, had managed Harding's successful primary campaign in 1920. Although manifestly devoid of intellectual distinction, he had been rewarded with the attorney generalship, and the new Republican Senate, despite misgivings about Daugherty's reputation as a political manipulator, went along.

The appointment, although it may not have appeared to Hoover a sign of the times, was symptomatic of a pattern of cronyism that characterized the entire Harding administration. In any case, given the history of the Bureau of Investigation, Hoover realized that with a change in the party in power, a game of musical chairs would begin. For many of the agents' positions had been filled over the years not by men of ability but by the beneficiaries of political patronage.

The excitement of the Red Scare had died down by 1921, moreover, and although antiradicalism remained a powerful force, association with the Palmer raids could be a liability. The debacle of Palmer's career was a case in point, and Hoover was not uninstructed by it.[1] On the other hand, the very immensity of Palmer's ambition provided a shelter of sorts for Hoover to hide behind. Palmer's outrageous effort to exploit the publicity from the raids to promote his presidential candidacy had served to minimize any adverse spillover to Hoover's own reputation.

The House hearings of April–May 1920 had also alerted Hoover to the importance of having a base in Congress. Acting on this knowledge, he began to cultivate key members, especially on those committees – Ways and Means, Appropriations, and the Judiciary, among them – that had occasional oversight of Bureau affairs. There would be resistance there to firing him, as there might not be to firing Director William F. Flynn, Bielaski's successor, because his position in the Justice Department, improved though it was, was not a patronage one.

Furthermore, Hoover was superior to most of his colleagues, many of whom had no legal background. He was known to be a hard worker, while many of his cohorts, the beneficiaries of political payoffs, were clearly enjoying a free ride. Like a draft private in the regular army, he covered for the brass and allowed it to take the credit, but he exacted a price in return. He knew where the bodies were buried, and as long as Flynn was in charge he was safe. Better, should Flynn be fired, his own stock would rise because of the need for continuity. At the same time, given the furor precipitated by the announcement of Daugherty's appointment, Hoover could anticipate that the new attorney general might very well resume his backroom political manipulations, and that he himself would have early opportunities to cover for him and thereby to secure his own position.

So the first order of business was to conform to the new scheme of things, to shake the discredited antiradical baggage as fast as he could. While letting it be known that he was at heart a Republican – although as a resident of the District he could not vote – he flatly disclaimed any responsibility for the Palmer raids and the excesses that had attended them. To the charge that he was a principal architect of the raids, he staunchly protested that he had simply carried out orders, and the earnestness of his denial (combined with Palmer's previous all-too-eager efforts to take credit when seeking the Democratic presidential nomination) convinced all but the most mean-spirited that this was the case. (Hoover repeated his disclaimers, just as

90

untruthfully and just as successfully, in 1940, when questions surfaced about the FBI's arrests of recruiters for the Abraham Lincoln Brigade.)

Sharing the main tenets of the new administration — its commitment to rationalized, expert decision making and its definition of problems as essentially technical and procedural in nature — Hoover projected himself as the indispensable scientific administrator. In this he captured the essence of New Era politics, personified in the career of then-Secretary of Commerce and later President Herbert Clark Hoover.

For the time being, then, Hoover could only protest his innocence and establish his indispensability as a knowledgeable insider. Driven by his ambition, but insecure in his newly acquired status as senior bureaucrat, he found no relief in female companionship or outside hobbies. To compensate, he walked, smoked, and listened to his new Victrola into the wee hours of the night. His niece Margaret Fennell remembers that he had a number of Enrico Caruso recordings — probably the immensely popular all-star renditions of the quartet from *Rigoletto* and the sextet from *Lucia* and maybe the haunting tenor-baritone duet from Bizet's *Les Pecheurs des Perles* that Caruso recorded with Mario Ancona.

Whatever they were, the songs seem to have provided solace and comfort to the lonely young man. So apparently also did a darkly handsome, fastidiously dressed young associate, Frank Baughman, whom he had brought into the Bureau in 1919. A twenty-two-year-old Army lieutenant at the time, Frank anticipated the wholesome G-Man of the 1930s with his short, well-groomed hair, impeccable suits, and courtly manner. On and off the job, the two soon became inveterate traveling companions and each other's closest friend until Frank's marriage about ten years later. On Sunday nights they went together to the new Fox movie theater on F Street, northwest, and must have made a very conspicuous pair. For Edgar was himself fastidious to a degree, always turned out in serge or tweed from his boiled collar to the tops of his spectator shoes. Frank was a gentleman, self-styled, and Edgar was too.

Edgar must have known that Frank was a luxury too. Suave, clean-cut, attractive to women – and attracted to them as well – he was everything that Edgar was not. To be sure, Edgar had the callow young man mesmerized. But there was a danger that this agreeable reliance, with its provision of strong physical support, would blow up in his face, that Frank, despite his transparent adulation, would do the usual thing and get married. On the other hand, if Edgar could keep Frank in the department, then he could maintain the relationship on a businesslike footing. Frank was a major concern.

But Edgar did not linger only on Frank. Another preoccupation had temporarily taken firmer hold of his mind. The whole family had become alarmed about Papa's health, and now Papa's long illness, although never named, appeared near its end. Margaret Fennell recalls that her grandfather died of pneumonia. The official cause of death, recorded at Congressional Cemetery, was 'melancholia.' In any case, on 30 March 1921 Dickerson Hoover succumbed, leaving his son Edgar the man of the house. Always ceremonious, Edgar submerged his grief in the business of getting things done. Characteristically, he took charge of the funeral arrangements and dealt with his bereavement, as he did with his fraternal associations, by getting out front and contending.

With Papa gone and Annie made tragic by her loss, however, Edgar soon confronted the hardest choice of his life: whether to assume the responsibility of caring for his mother, with the permanent entanglement that responsibility entailed, or to plan the steps he must take to ensure his ultimate independence. In any case he must share with Dick the financial burden of their mother's support; but no duty compelled him, at twenty-six, to make a sacrifice of his life.

One can sympathize with Edgar's predicament. But Edgar probably did not see the question as a question. The factors militating against choosing his mother were weak. Not only would he be forsaking a comfortable home and – aside from Margaret – the only sustained female companionship he ever had; he would be relinquishing the most convincing excuse for his bachelorhood. Moreover, in choosing his mother, Edgar was not only following his instincts but also giving scope to his love of the florid deed. He would make a burnt offering of himself and do it with style. For the rest of his life he made a fetish of his self-sacrifice to his mother.

Finally, Edgar must have considered the question of social security. The country was then entering a recession, the short but severe slump of 1921–1922, and the uncertainties in the outside world could only have impressed the son of a minor government clerk who had labored forty-two years for the meagerest of wages and then been cashiered without a pension. Edgar's lifelong dread of poverty, inculcated by his mother and occasioned by his father's ineffectuality, manifested itself in many ways, ranging from mere parsimoniousness and hoarding to demanding and getting gifts and gratuities and ultimately misappropriating government property and services. True, he developed a taste for betting on the horses, but given his intimacy with racing's wealthy patrons – Sid Richardson, Clint Murchison, and the proprietors of Pimlico, Laurel, and Bowie – he arguably was not gambling so much as he was simply making money. So he stayed with Annie.

Another consideration, this one having to do with his work, also impressed him at the time. Although indiscriminate antiradicalism was currently out of fashion, the recent red baiting had aroused a stirring chorus of approval, mostly from powerful interests on the right, a wealth of invaluable support when and if the fashion should change again. Edgar had discovered his true constituency during the Palmer era, and everything about his subsequent career indicates that he never forgot it. He had tasted glory. What other vocation could promise so much?

The new administration meanwhile proposed, in President Harding's indelible term, a 'return to normalcy.' But beating a retreat from the heavy regulation of the World War I period, it also favored a new deal for business – an abandonment of the Progressive agenda of social justice and regulation of business activity. The rules of the game, first enacted with the Sherman Anti-Trust Act of 1890, were quietly set aside. As President Wilson had foreseen, American entanglement in the Great War spelled the doom of his New Freedom program.

On 27 May 1921 the new Republican Congress hurriedly passed the so-called Emergency Tariff Act, propelling the nation toward the highest tariff levels in its history. At the same time, Congress granted tax relief, removing the wartime excess-profits tax and substantially reducing estate and income taxes, especially in the higher brackets. More important, as demonstrated by the Budget and Accounting Act of 1921, the Rogers Act of 1924, and the creation of the Bureau of Standards and the Bureau of Domestic and Foreign Commerce within the Department of Commerce, social and economic problems came to be defined as the product of inefficiency and incompetence. The road to success required the ambitious Hoover to identify with the principles of 'scientific management' and to hone his skills as an insider bureaucrat.

On the whole, young Hoover was pleased with the political drift if not with the manifest signs of discontent it ignored. Anything that tended to destabilize the established order offended him, and he was glad to have the nation's government again in reliable hands. He indicated later that he was so upset with the incompetence of Harry Daugherty and his gang that he seriously considered resigning from the department, but the careerist in him prevailed when on 18 August 1921 Daugherty fired Flynn by telegram and hired William J. Burns, in his stead.

Burns, like Flynn, had formerly headed the Treasury's Secret Service. Resigning in 1909, he had set up a private detective agency in New York. He enjoyed a reputation for success of a kind. (One of his achievements was servicing both British and German intelligence in America after the outbreak of World War I.) But what commended him to Daugherty most, one can only suppose with the wisdom of hindsight, was the opportunism of a scoundrel in scoundrel times. Both left office in disgrace, one of them under indictment, having disgraced both the department and the Bureau.

In any case, Hoover's initial reservations were easily overcome four days later when Daugherty named the young GID head assistant director of the Bureau at $4,000 a year. Daugherty and Burns recognized Hoover's exceptional administrative skill and happily placed on him the main burden of running the Bureau. They had correctly discerned the young man's marked capacity for loyalty. Again the traits of the herd animal, both in himself and in his senior colleagues, seemed to decide his fate. He was one of them after all.

A wholesale renovation of the Bureau ensued. Burns abruptly fired the time servers and replaced them with agents whose main qualification in most cases was a bill coming due to a Republican politician. The entire agency was radically politicized. The result was predictable.

At Burns's request, Bureau agents in September 1922 burglarized the office of Congressman Oscar Kellar (who had introduced a resolution calling for the attorney general's impeachment because of an injunction Daugherty sought against the railworkers' union). Bureau agents also scrutinized the activities (and burglarized the offices) of Senators Robert La Follette and William Borah, outspoken critics of the Harding administration's foreign and defense policies. According to one newsman of the era, the Bureau became 'a private hole in the corner goon squad for the attorney general. Its arts were the arts of snooping, bribery and blackmail.' The scholar Alpheus Mason similarly commented, 'Included among the special agents were some with criminal records. Bureau badges and property [were] issued to persons not employed by the government' and to others who posed 'as confidential agents and informers to 'frame' evidence against personal enemies of the Harding administration.'

The following October Burns hired Gaston B. Means, a notorious con man who had been narrowly acquitted of murdering a North Carolina woman and later was convicted of swindling a Washington housewife by pretending to negotiate the safe return of the kidnapped Lindbergh baby.

Burns purportedly hired Means to avail himself of Means's contacts in the underworld, but according to one account, 'No sooner had Means become a 'special employee' of the Justice Department, for ninety days at seven dollars a day, than he was selling copies of department reports to underworld figures and offering to 'fix' federal prosecutions for an appropriate price.' Suspended from his post by Daugherty, he was mysteriously rehired on the regular payroll by Burns himself.

Hoover later maintained that he had been responsible for putting Means behind bars more than once, and, indeed, the assiduous assistant director, with his fastidious self-regard, did find the garrulous Means repulsive. But the claim 'that Burns shunted [Hoover] into a side office where he handled routine paper work,' as one report had it, or that Hoover lay low for a time, as he himself said, simply does not square with the letters of congratulation that he received from former colleagues on the occasion of his being appointed Director in 1924 and that he carefully preserved until the end of his life. The consensus of his peers was that the title belatedly went with the job, and the warmest of the congratulations came from William J. Burns.

Another indication of Hoover's influence at the Bureau was the appointment shortly thereafter, and before his promotion to Director, of Frank Baughman as a special agent. Patronage was still in control, but apparently Hoover was allowed at least one assistant of his own choosing. Moreover, when business took him out of the capital, Hoover took his sturdy young associate along with him, perhaps for security. For by then, notwithstanding the location of the Fifth Precinct police station on Fifth Street right around the corner from the Hoovers' Seward Square house, security had become a problem, at least in Edgar's mind. With Frank, he felt safe, and he and Frank continued to come and go between Annie's dinner table and the Fox movie theater on F Street. But Edgar by this time regarded his role at the Bureau as sufficiently consequential – or controversial – to warrant a greater concern for his own safety.

To be sure, Hoover was not responsible at that time for policy, which was determined by Daugherty in consultation with Burns. He did not, however, disapprove of their official conduct. His state of mind, in fact, was clearly shown later when an employee of the Bureau, summoned to testify under oath before a Senate investigating committee, confirmed allegations that the Bureau had been spying on witnesses before that committee a well as on congressional critics, including burglarizing their offices and opening their mail. The next morning Hoover, by then the acting director, sent the employee a letter curtly demanding her resignation.

In practice, the Department of Justice abandoned all fraud prosecutions of war contractors and cut back on antitrust activities, while the Federal Trade Commission sought to promote rather than regulate business activity. In effect, the Justice Department had declared a holiday for business, and when organized labor undertook to counteract the antilabor drift and restore its eroding wage base by means of a series of strikes, Daugherty went to court to enjoin the unions from striking. Indeed, Justice Department officials made no secret of their allegiance, and most of the country, beguiled by the signs of an impending technological advance spearheaded by the automobile and consumer electronics industries, went along. Armed with an injunction obtained by Daugherty and furnished with detailed Bureau reports on union strategy, the reinfranchised managers of the nation's railroads broke a nationwide trainmen's strike in 1922, foreshadowing a general crackdown on labor.

The repressive climate that followed the war demoralized liberals, but there was nothing they could do about it. The entire organism of American society seemed to have contracted, as if itself wounded in the war. The siren songs of the Progressives had been drowned out by the guns, and even their leader, Wilson, was a casualty. Unburdened of much of its radical tinge by zealots during and after the war, America simply pulled in and regrouped around the collective consciousness of an earlier era.

Opportunity there was, for many — for manufacturers, salesmen, evangelists of the traditional faith. But the field of aspiration, as opposed to crass desire, had narrowed to a dangerous path.

The voices of resistance were not wholly stilled, however. Sinclair Lewis's acid *Main Street* appeared in 1920, and his bitterly satiric *Babbitt* two years later. *The Great Gatsby*, F. Scott Fitzgerald's travesty of the American dream, appeared three years after that, the first full year in which the 'petty inquisitions' of small-town America, as Nick Carraway called them, were enshrined on the national stage in the person of J. Edgar Hoover. Even the popular culture of the era betrayed a disenchantment with the quality of American life, fixated as it was on material success and moral laxness.

By the beginning of 1922 the country's immune system had begun to react. Rumors of official corruption were rife, and there was even talk of a massive looting of public petroleum reserves at a place called Teapot Dome. The chorus of rising objections was directed at the Departments of Interior and Justice, and with the advent of spring, members of Congress were calling for an investigation. All the while Hoover and his agents were drawing up a secret congressional enemies list, the better to silence their critics.

Attorney General Daugherty was the first to take up the cudgels in the department's defense. In an address to the American Bar Association, he appealed to the legal fraternity to join him in 'combatting heresy and unsound notions of government that seek to undermine and destroy the work that the [Founding] Fathers and those who succeeded them have transmitted to us.' In words echoing Palmer's, he cunningly sought to deflect criticism by mounting a familiar counterattack. 'The enemies of law and order and more active than ever before,' he declared, 'in sowing the poisons of lawlessness and unsound and experimental theories of government . . . scattering and propagating their vicious theories of government and casting unjustifiable reflections on men holding public office with the intent to undermine the confidence of the people in them. These forces must be met and combatted.'

In a similar vein Burns, testifying before the House

Appropriations Committee that spring, sought to make a case for an increased budget by breathing new life into the moribund Red Scare:

> Chief Burns: '. . . the radical activities have increased wonderfully.'
>
> Congressman Tinkham (Massachusetts): 'Do you think it is increasing from week to week and from month to month?'
>
> Chief Burns: 'I think it is . . .'
>
> Congressman Husted (New York): 'Would you say that those radical activities are particularly dangerous or of a violent character at the present time?'
>
> Chief Burns: 'Very. I cannot impress upon you too much how dangerous they are at the present moment.'

Pressed by the congressmen for hard evidence of radical activity, Burns responded that the radicals had changed their methods and gone underground and had forged their bombs into propaganda. Queried about the nature of the propaganda, Burns, invoking both fears of strikes and the menace of a subversive form of Little League baseball, replied that it

> principally consists of urging the working man to strike, with the ultimate purpose of bringing about a revolution in this country . . . Radicalism is becoming stronger every day in this country. They are going about it in a very subtle manner. For instance, they have schools all over the country where they are teaching children 4 and 5 years old, and they are organizing athletic clubs through the country. I dare say that unless the country becomes aroused concerning the danger of this radical element in this country, we will have a very serious situation.

Hoover had helped prepare Burns's data on the radical threat. (His concern for innocent youth throughout his career recalled that of Prime Minister Gladstone for young female prostitutes, whom he picked up after church and took home with his wife for Sunday dinner.) And the data were effective. As usual, Congress increased the Bureau's budget on the strength of what conservatives considered the Bureau's demonstrated need. Strong Democratic gains in the 1922 congressional elections potentially threatened to reverse these gains, but did not.

More ominously, one of the Democratic senators elected that year, Burton K. Wheeler of Montana, inaugurated his legislative career by launching an investigation of the disposition of federal oil leases by the Secretary of the Interior and the Department of Justice's unwillingness to pursue evidence of official corruption.

The department's automatic response was to investigate Wheeler. Assistant Director Hoover took charge. With characteristic zeal, he completed a case against Wheeler — in the form of an indictment — demonstrating that the senator, while a U.S. prosecutor in Montana during the war, had declined to prosecute war resisters and others singled out for their unpopular beliefs. Hoover had dug up an old bone of contention and now, for the sake of the department, he brandished it, characteristically portraying Wheeler as a red. The Bureau also tried to nail Wheeler on alleged conflicts of interest during the war, but both a Senate investigating committee and a jury in Montana subsequently exonerated him.

Edgar, meanwhile, was embroiled in other controversies at home. Relations with Dick, never easy, were particularly strained. Dick was never a compromiser — his daughter Margaret believes that he may have resigned as chief inspector of the Steamboat Inspection Service in 1936, relinquishing a pension, over a point of honor — and the spectacle of his little brother aggrandizing himself in what Dick considered a den of thieves may have been more than he could bear. To the taunt of 'How is the attorney?' he now added another game, which enraged Edgar even more.

It all began one night as Edgar was returning home — without Frank Baughman to protect him, as it happened.

As he passed the row of houses on the south side of Seward Square, he caught a glimpse of a figure moving in the shadows behind him. Frightened but reluctant to make a fool himself, Edgar pretended to be unaware of the stranger and quickened his pace. The figure came closer, and as Edgar glanced back to see what was happening, it darted behind a bush, advanced through the shadows, and reappeared with a shout. White with terror, Edgar confronted the towering figure of his brother. 'You damn fool!' he screamed. But unable to give further voice to his anger, he wheeled and dashed into the house, pursued by Dick's uproarious laughter.

Edgar retaliated in his own manner and enlisted his mother, who redoubled her cruelties to Theo. But Dick had already had enough. In January 1923 he announced to his family that they were moving to a rented house in Glendale, Maryland. Having just entered Eastern High School the previous September, Margaret was reluctant to make the move. But Dick was adamant and, enlisting Bus as his helper, moved everything, lock, stock, and barrel, in his Model T Ford. The house at 411 was sold for $3,000, and half of Annie's garden went with it. The bad feelings were pasted over, at least as far as the younger generation was concerned, but Annie apparently never once condescended to pay a call on the folks in Glendale, although, to be sure, neither she nor Edgar ever learned to drive a car.[2]

The move, incidentally, placed the Dick Hoovers only a few miles from Lillian Robinette and her family. But that connection too was soon strained. Bus remembered that the family went over to Lanham one day to pay a call, that he and his cousin Dorothy Robinette, who was two years his elder, got into a disagreement, and when Dorothy complained to her mother, Lillian irritably shouted, 'Hit him!' As Bus's wife, Virginia, later recalled, 'There was a lot of friction in the family.' In fact, the two families in Maryland eventually became permanently estranged.

The family gift for contentiousness was most productively used by Edgar, however, who filled his days framing cases to be brought against the Justice Department's numerous detractors. And as the Senate proceeded to investigate the department's response to the emerging Teapot Dome scandal, the Bureau's pursuit of its critics knew no bounds. Senator James Heflin of Alabama summarized its activities:

> These detectives went through the office of the Senator from Arkansas [Thaddeus Caraway] and they read his correspondence; they went through the office of the Senator from Wisconsin [Robert La Follette]; and God only knows how many other offices they went through. That was a 'general fishing expedition'; it was fishing in the night, when Senators were at home asleep; but the Department of Justice was awake, and its smooth and alert detectives were quietly going though the offices of United States Senators.

The stone wall began to crumble on 2 August 1923, when the president, having taken himself on a cross-country tour beginning in Alaska in order to avoid suggestions of complicity in the rumored corruption, suddenly died in a hotel room in San Francisco. (The exact cause of his death was never established.) Calvin Coolidge succeeded to the presidency, and the Senate began its inquiries in earnest, publicizing allegations of huge bribes paid to Attorney General Daugherty and Interior Secretary Albert Fall, the custodian of the Teapot Dome oil reserve. Conspicuous in the hearings, because seated at the attorney general's right hand like a defense counsel, was the Bureau's young man on the make, J. Edgar Hoover.

Notes to Chapter Four

1. The Bureau, and Hoover, nonetheless continued to monitor radical and liberal political activities, albeit more circumspectly and with a conscious avoidance of publicity. Bureau agents investigated individuals and organizations ranging from the Communist party, college students and faculty members active in radical activities,

anyone who taught or believed in anarchism, subscribers to the *Nation*; congressional critics of the Palmer raids; and congressional advocates of recognition of the Svoiet Union; to the American Civil Liberties Union. This despite the fact that William Burns, Flynn's successor, privately conceded the absence of any legal authority to act on this information. See David Williams, ' "Without Understanding": The FBI and Political Surveillance, 1908–1941' (Ph.D. diss., University of New Hampshire, 1981), pp. 220–22; Donald Johnson, The Challenge to *American Freedom: The Life of the American Civil Liberties Union* (Lexington: University of Kentucky Press, 1963), p. 165.

2. Glendale was, however, on a commuter rail line, which Dick used every weekday for years, and Edgar within a year enjoyed the perquisite of a government car and driver.

CHAPTER FIVE

(1924–1925)

THE NEW DIRECTOR CLEANS HOUSE

BY THE SPRING OF 1924, President Coolidge, facing his first election campaign for the presidency, had decided that the findings of the Senate committee investigating the Department of Justice were sufficiently conclusive to warrant his ridding himself of Attorney General Daugherty. On March 28 the president demanded Daugherty's resignation, and four days later the attorney general left office, bleating, as had his predecessor, that he had been hounded by the reds.[1] On 2 April the President named Harlan Fiske Stone attorney general.

The scandals of the Harding administration were fast coming to light, thanks to the Senate investigation initiated by Burton Wheeler, and Coolidge and the Republicans were earnestly trying to limit the damage before the badly divided Democrats, hag-ridden by the white-hooded spooks of the Ku Klux Klan, could capitalize on the Republicans' thievery. Stone was offered to the untrusting Senate – and to an uncannily unconcerned public – as a talisman, a living monument of Republican integrity. A hulking, taciturn New Hampshire Yankee, graduate of Amherst College and Columbia Law School, he had practiced law in New York City while teaching at the law school, of which he became dean in 1910. Although a conservative even by Republican standards, Stone eventually enjoyed so lofty a reputation for independence that in 1941 that most partisan Democrat, Franklin Delano Roosevelt, named him chief justice of the United States.

Stone had been an early critic of Daugherty's Justice Department and one of the first Republicans to call for reform. Once appointed, he immediately set about cleansing the department, beginning with the corrupt Bureau and its disgraced director, William J. Burns. Initially, Burns's twenty-nine-year-old assistant did not figure in the planning for a successor, as Stone looked to agencies other than the scandal-ridden Bureau. Hoover's name came up by chance when Stone, casting his net as far as other executive departments after having vainly trawled the less murky divisions of Justice, asked then Secretary of Commerce Herbert Hoover if he knew of a good lawyer-administrator to run the Bureau. Secretary Hoover in turn inquired of his street-wise assistant Lawrence Richey, who, recalling an earlier encounter with J. Edgar Hoover, said that Stone could not find a better candidate than he.

Acting on Secretary Hoover's recommendation, Stone invited Edgar, who was not related to the secretary, to his office. Forewarned of this opportunity, Edgar disarmed Stone's most serious suspicions. The relationship between Stone, who was fifty at the time, and Hoover, who was barely twenty-nine, remains something of a mystery, although Edgar clearly had the measure of the other man.[2]

The essence of what Hoover had to explain away, and did, was summarized later by Senator Wheeler:

When I first came to Washington [in 1923] and began the investigation of the Department of Justice, Mr. Hoover was present at the investigation and hearings, and sat through them during the time the charges against Mr. Daugherty were being heard. Agents of the Department raided my offices; they broke into my offices . . . they stationed men at my house, surrounded my house, and shadowed my wife . . . During all that time there were in the Department of Justice . . . Burns and Mr. Hoover.

The purpose of these activities, as Burns subsequently conceded, was to discredit the senator before he could carry through his investigation. Moreover, Hoover had personally

105

traveled to Montana to gather evidence for that state's ill-advised criminal proceeding against Wheeler.

In any case, Hoover convinced Stone of his innocence, with the result that the attorney general invited the assistant director back to his office on 10 May, the day after Burns was forced out. And there began the surrogate father and son relationship that was to last to the end of Stone's life (the only attorney general's likeness that ever graced the Director's office was Stone's). At the end of the meeting, Hoover was offered the job, although only on a provisional basis.

Tradition has it that Hoover accepted conditionally as well:

Hoover: 'I'll take the job, Mr. Stone, on certain conditions.'

Stone: 'What are they?'

Hoover: 'The Bureau must be divorced from politics and not be a catch-all for political hacks. Appointments must be based on merit. Second, promotions will be made on proved ability and the Bureau will be responsible only to the Attorney General.'

Stone: 'I wouldn't give it to you under any other conditions. That's all. Good day.'

Harlan Stone entertained a quaint trust in the honor of 'gentlemen.' At the same time, believing that most problems derive from a lack of mastery of technical detail, he placed high value on the services of disinterested professionals. Stone unhesitatingly trusted men of high moral character, gentlemen, not to do certain things, like lie and cheat, and was equally confident that professionals could both identify and resolve problems. Expert administrators, not political operators, could be relied on to enforce the law fairly and efficiently. And Edgar shared those beliefs.

But while a self-styled gentleman and an efficient bureaucrat, Hoover did not entirely fit Stone's formula. He lacked the appropriate education (having attended George Washington University night school, not an Ivy League college) and family background. But he presented the correct image, although it masked an unacknowledged belief that the end justifies the means. Willing to dissemble to achieve his ambitions so long as he was confident that this could be safely done, Hoover deceived Stone that day, as he did Roger Baldwin, director of the American Civil Liberties Union (ACLU), several months later. His genius as an administrator explains why he never got caught.

That same day Stone detailed the policies that were to govern Bureau operations. The attorney general had already dissolved Hoover's radical-hunting General Intelligence Division and prohibited any Bureau wiretapping. Now he stipulated that 'the activities of the Bureau are to be limited strictly to investigations of violations of law, under my direction or under the direction of an Assistant Attorney General regularly conducting the work of the Department of Justice.'

Stone repeated this restriction in a statement to the press intended to allay concerns about the Bureau's recently publicized political surveillance activities. 'A secret police may become a menace to free government . . .,' he said, 'because it carries with it the possibility of abuses of power which are not always quickly apprehended or understood.' Thus, beginning that day, he declared, the 'Bureau of Investigation is not concerned with political or other opinions of individuals. It is concerned only with their conduct and then only such conduct as is forbidden by the laws of the United States. When a police system passes beyond these limits, it is dangerous to the proper administration of justice and to human liberty, which it should be our first concern to cherish. Within them it should rightly be a terror to the wrongdoer.'

In addition to restricting the Bureau's mission to investigating violations of law and prohibiting investigations into political activities, Stone early sought to recruit a more professional breed of agents and to reduce the Bureau's size to one commensurate with its more restricted role. To those ends he directed that the 'personnel be reduced so far as is consistent with the proper performance of its duties' and that the acting director discontinue the services of the 'so-called "dollar a year men" ' (i.e., individuals not formally appointed as agents but possessing Bureau badges and claiming to act as consultants). No new appointments were to be made without his express approval, and nominations for approval were to go to men 'of known character and ability, giving preference to men who have some legal training.'

In response to Stone's order, Hoover sent to 'every person [other than Bureau agents] holding any official property of the Bureau of Investigation . . . letters requesting the return of such property and cancelling any official designation or connection which they may have had with the Bureau.' He also initiated an evaluation of all current employees, recommending the termination of a number of agents 'for the best interests of the service,' as he reported to Stone. Specifically addressing Stone's prohibition against politically motivated snooping, he admonished 'the heads of the respective Divisions of the Bureau that the activities of the Bureau are to be limited strictly to investigations of violations of the federal statutes . . . And I am causing to have sent to the fifty-four field offices of the Bureau similar instructions.'

In the meantime, Hoover appeared before the Senate investigating committee, which required reassurance that no repetition of the Bureau's recent political intelligence activities would occur. Responding to a question from Senator Wheeler, he cited the recent ironclad directive of the attorney general.

Then he attempted to reassure the others:

Senator Jones [Washington]: 'Are you not contemplating contracting the work of the Bureau?'

Mr. Hoover: 'Most certainly. Instructions have been sent to officers in the field to limit their investigations in the field to violations of the statutes . . .'

Senator Jones: 'As I understood, the new Attorney General contemplated restricting very materially the

scope of the work of this Bureau. Is not that a fact?'
Mr. Hoover: 'That is correct . . .'

Senator Jones: '. . . You have not been curtailing the scope of your investigations until lately, have you?'
Mr. Hoover: 'Just within the last month.'

Hoover's efforts seemed to allay the senators' suspicions. His evident scrupulousness and loyalty to his superiors seemed to exclude any possibility that the young subaltern would ever consider disregarding a direct order from the attorney general of the United States. Moreover, unlike Daugherty and Burns, Hoover gave every evidence of being a dedicated professional, which point had been repeatedly emphasized by Attorney General Stone. The senators let the unresolved matter of Hoover's past excesses rest, and at the end of the day the witness was dismissed, to return to his management of the Bureau's affairs.

Hoover's masterful performance had not silenced all doubt, however. Shortly after Stone's statement to the press, the ACLU wrote to the attorney general condemning the Bureau and claiming that in the recent past its agents had spied on political activists and labor union organizers and had disseminated antiradical propaganda. Stone forwarded the letter to Hoover, as the former head of the GID, for comment. In a detailed response, Hoover characterized the ACLU's allegations as 'untrue and misleading.' A 'small portion' of the Bureau's work had involved 'ultra-radicals,' he conceded but these investigations 'are made (only) when there is indication of a possible violation of a federal statute.' Hoover admitted that the Bureau's files contained reports on radical activities that were not criminal. But this information had been volunteered by private citizens, he said, and in the tortured syntax that subsequently became his hallmark and smokescreen, he added that Bureau agents 'are not instructed to investigate the activities of any person or persons who do not engage in activities of a character that involves a violation of the federal law.'

The newly appointed acting director did not confine his

defense to reassuring the attorney general. Operating on the premise that the best defense is a good offense, he sought a meeting with ACLU Director Roger Baldwin to defend the Bureau's work. At the meeting Hoover apparently turned on what some commentators called southern charm and a later assistant director called deviousness (the wiles of 'a master con man'), for Baldwin left the meeting, as Hoover reported to Stone, 'in a particularly friendly state of mind.' Hoover also reported that Baldwin had agreed to communicate promptly to Bureau officials any information he obtained involving 'improper' actions by the Bureau or Bureau agents, and stressed that Baldwin 'seemed to be fully satisfied with the reorganization that has been effected and I believe that the Bureau of Investigation will no longer be the subject of attacks either by himself or his organization.' (Baldwin, for his part, had not been the unwitting victim of Hoover's alleged charm. The newly appointed acting director had assured the ACLU official that he had played only an 'unwilling part' in the activities of Palmer, Daugherty, and Burns, had regretted their tactics, but had been in no position to stop them. Accepting on faith Hoover's truthfulness, Baldwin wrote to Stone that the ACLU had been 'wrong in our estimate of his attitude' toward radicals and civil liberties.)

Not only had Hoover convinced Stone of the Bureau's improved professionalism and the groundlessness of charges that the Bureau was still investigating radical political activities; he also categorically denied that the Bureau was monitoring political activities of any kind — assurances that Stone accepted on faith, as the department, as one later attorney general observed, was aware of only about 10 percent of what Hoover's Bureau was doing.

Stone's trust also stemmed in part from his belief that the Bureau's recently disclosed abuses had arisen from the character deficiencies of past Bureau personnel, and he was completely reassured by his belief in Hoover's personal loyalty, which Hoover missed no opportunity to demonstrate. For example, in June, responding to an invitation to address a police convention in Montreal, he declined, pleading the press of work. To Stone, he explained his refusal on the ground that members of the Bureau should shun publicity and seek credit only when credit was due, for work done. Stone, evidently feeling that Hoover, like Tartuffe, might be foregoing an opportunity out of an exaggerated scrupulosity, sent the acting director a memo on 26 June giving him carte blanche to attend the Montreal convention 'if you think it well to do so,' adding: 'I am inclined to think, however, that your view with relation to publicity is the sound one.'

Replying in a memo of 30 June, Hoover recapitulated:

As I stated to you a few days ago I personally believe that the officials of the Bureau of Investigation should refrain as much as possible from any public appearance, as I believe that the work of the Bureau should be conducted quietly but effectively so that the results will be the criterion by which the Bureau will be judged. Therefore, I do not believe it desirable for me to attend the Montreal convention.

Sensitive to political realities − another factor in Hoover's unaccustomed reticence − the young Director, so confident of his ability in most respects, probably did not yet dare address such an important gathering. As his nephew Dick recalled much later, 'Uncle Edgar could talk your leg off, but put him in front of a crowd and he'd have lockjaw.'

Margaret Fennell preserved the same impression, although in regard to the years 1926−1930, when she was again living with Edgar and her grandmother:

Those were busy years for him. And he worked very hard, always bringing home a briefcase full of work. I remember he had a problem with stuttering, and there were many evenings − his bedroom was next to mine − this was at the beginning of his career when he was just beginning to be asked to speak to groups − and I can remember him practicing whatever it was he was going to say. He had quite a problem there, which he overcame.

111

An astute politician cum bureaucrat, Hoover was not yet ready to reach for more authority than he had. As Berle coolly observed, 'Many in subordinate office seek to avoid power; some seek to have the power but avoid public knowledge of it; some, by force of personality, by idealist motivation, by personal capacity, or from ambition, assume as much power as they can, intending to hold and extend it.' In terms of his interaction with events at this time, Hoover was a power holder of the second degree, one who sought power but without public knowledge of it.

Hoover's hesitancy also stemmed from his constricted political values. Confident of his own superiority, he was no democrat and disdained the give and take and compromises required by public life. He could never have succeeded in electoral politics; indeed, even as a bureaucrat he derived his success from the particular character of the agency he headed. Law enforcement required a degree of secrecy, shielding the office-holder from intensive public scrutiny — so long as the public retained faith in the integrity and professionalism of the Director. Given the strong and widespread anti-government attitudes of the 1920s, Hoover's low profile made eminent sense. The impact of the Great Depression and the New Deal created new opportunities and dilemmas, but even then Hoover operated as a bureaucrat, relying on the Bureau's Crime Records Division to shield his actions from public scrutiny and craft an image of the superefficient G-Man.

In any case, Hoover had made his point so far as Harlan Stone was concerned: the servant knew his place and meant to stay there. Moreover, he had scored twice — simultaneously disarming the master and appealing to him for advice. In later years, long after Stone had joined the Supreme Court as an associate justice, the ever-obsequious Hoover continued to appeal to the older man for guidance, and Stone continued to give it. The pattern was already established in 1924.

At the same time, Hoover sought to curry favor by catering to the attorney general's personal needs. Under Hoover's careful supervision, Bureau agents provided a string of services more in keeping with the duties of personal aides than with those of professionally trained investigators.

On 2 June, for instance, one month after Hoover's interim appointment, two Bureau agents met Stone at the Columbia University Club in New York City and informed him, as they later reported to Hoover, that 'we had been assigned to him for the evening for the purpose of assisting him in any manner he might desire and to accompany him to the [railroad] depot after the dinner and speechmaking . . . was [*sic*] complete.' After escorting Stone to Penn Station in a Bureau automobile, they met another agent 'who had accompanied Mrs. Stone to the train and who had the railroad tickets in his possession.' Numerous other favors followed.

Five days later, Hoover ordered the head of the Bureau's Cleveland office to assign an agent to 'be subject to [Special Assistant to the Attorney General Warren] Martin's call at any time during the stay of Attorney General and Mr. Martin in Cleveland.' Hoover insisted that 'every courtesy and attention' be given Stone and Martin, but also that 'I do not wish the Agent assigned to the detail or any other Agent of your office by any action to cause annoyance through any attention that may be rendered.'

A month after that, again at Hoover's direction, the New York SAC made reservations and purchased railroad tickets for Attorney General and Mrs. Stone from New York City to Rockland, Maine, and arranged to have an agent 'accompany [Stone] and remain with him in Maine.' Hoover later commended the SAC for the 'prompt and efficient way in which this matter was handled' and expressed his appreciation and that of the attorney general for this assistance. The next month Hoover arranged for train and hotel reservations to be made for Special Assistant Martin, who was going to Quebec on vacation.

Hoover had anticipated Stone's wants fairly well. Indeed, he had probably *created* them, as advertisers are supposed to do. Moreover, he showed a fine appreciation of Stone's anxiety threshold, correctly estimating the amount of coddling the attorney general could accept.

113

In any case there was by fall a thorough meeting of the minds. Given Hoover's selective but meticulous briefings, and Stone's satisfaction that his specific administrative reforms were now flesh, the attorney general not surprisingly judged Hoover's brief tenure a success. Although his own tenure as attorney general was almost as brief as Hoover's apprenticeship – on 5 January 1925 President Coolidge submitted Stone's name to the Senate for confirmation as associate Justice of the Supreme Court, and Stone was appointed to the Court on 2 March 1925 – Stone acted to secure Hoover's hold as Director. On 19 December 1924, he ended Hoover's probationary period, appointing him permanent Director of the Bureau at $7,500 a year,[3] having concluded that Hoover was 'a man of exceptional intelligence, alertness and executive ability.' Moreover, on 5 January he rescinded his earlier requirement that Hoover operate under the supervision of the assistant attorney general in charge of administration by making the Director responsible only to the attorney general himself.

Describing the background of this decision, Stone recalled his determination on becoming attorney general to ensure that the Bureau 'should be essentially a fact-finding agency [whose] primary duty was that of gathering information and facts upon which the legal forces of the Department might proceed with either criminal prosecutions or civil suits.' To achieve that end, he had considered it necessary to improve the 'efficiency' of the Bureau and to recruit agents who 'should know what legal evidence is.' This essential reform had been accomplished by amending the rules of appointment 'so as to require the person under consideration for appointment to have either had legal training or a knowledge of accountancy.' Hoover, Stone added, had

> removed from the Bureau every man as to whose character there was any ground for suspicion. He refused to yield to any kind of political pressure; he appointed to the Bureau men of intelligence and education, and strove to build up a morale such as should control such an organization. He withdrew it

114

wholly from extra-legal activities and made it an efficient organization for investigation of criminal offenses against the United States.

Stone then recounted statistics on the educational backgrounds of the agents and declared that each new appointee was 'now being thoroughly investigated before appointment, with particular attention being given to the general character, personality and integrity of the applicant.' After appointment, he continued, each agent was subjected to rigorous and continuous inspection of his performance and was given a 'course of instruction' in which it was impressed on him that 'the first essential in his work as a Special Agent is that he conduct himself as a gentleman. I am firmly of the opinion,' he added, 'that officials of the Department of Justice can more effectively perform their duties by acting the part of gentlemen than by resorting to tactics of a different character. The work of gathering evidence and of conducting litigation should be done in a gentlemanly way. Agents of the Bureau of Investigation in the past may have been inclined to place emphasis on the end rather than on the means. Methods and means used at times may have been unlawful. That condition, however, does not exist in the Bureau of Investigation at the present time.'

Denying as entirely 'unwarranted and unfounded' allegations that the Bureau during his tenure had violated individual rights and engaged in political surveillance, Stone concluded by affirming:

The Bureau of Investigation under my instructions and direction has been confining its activities to the investigations of matters constituting a violation of the federal statutes which it is charged by law with investigating. It has consistently adhered to the limitations of its authority fixed by statute for I could conceive of nothing more despicable nor demoralizing than to have public funds of this country used for the purpose of shadowing people who are engaged in

115

legitimate practices in accordance with the constitution of this country and in accordance with the law of this country . . . The Bureau of Investigation today is composed of personnel of a very high character and type and it warrants and merits the respect and support of all law-abiding citizens.

Stone's confidence was based partly on faith — faith that Hoover had loyally carried out all of his specific directives and faith that Hoover had not lied about doing so. Impressed by Hoover's industriousness and success in recruiting higher-quality agents (several his fraternity brothers) and imposing more rigorous standards for performance, the attorney general was fully convinced that Hoover had obeyed his commands. That he appointed Hoover permanent Director only three months before his own anticipated departure to sit on the Supreme Court confirms his high opinion of Hoover's loyalty and acumen.

But Stone's trust was misplaced. Although Hoover had reformed the operations of the Bureau and thereby improved the quality of its performance, he had not abandoned the Bureau's surveillance of radical activity. As is documented in a memo sent to Acting Assistant Attorney General William Donovan in October 1924 (Donovan, a flamboyant World War I superhero, was another of Stone's young protégés), Hoover was not resigned to the new situation at all. Conceding that the 'activities of Communists and other ultra-radicals have not up to the present time constituted a violation of the Federal statutes,' and thus 'theoretically' the Bureau had 'no right to investigate such activities,' he nevertheless suggested that continued investigation of such people might be in order because they might *at some future time* be guilty of violating federal laws.

Determined to continue such surveillance, yet wary of the obvious risks involved — risks not only to himself but to his already-cherished Bureau — Hoover shrewdly contrived a way to circumvent Stone's explicit ban. Cautiously in 1924, and more boldly in later years, he organized a subterfuge to ensure that the Bureau could continue to monitor

'Communists and other ultra-radicals' and also (given his all-encompassing fear of dissent) civil libertarian groups such as the ACLU itself.

A search of the Bureau's files dating from 1924 to the end of the decade reveals an unbroken stream of reports about radical activities. Many of these reports were based on information provided by individual citizens, fraternal organizations (such as the American Legion and the American Defense Society), local and state police, and other federal investigators (from Customs, Immigration, and the Department of State, among others). Hoover had this unsolicited information incorporated into Bureau files, although the suppliers, duly thanked and urged to continue such submissions, were ceremoniously advised that because the forwarded information recorded no violation of federal law, the Bureau could not initiate an investigation.

Hoover's willingness to make use of private spies and informers and other federal investigative agencies in this way did not mean, however, that he confined his agents' intervention to receiving information. On the contrary, under his command Bureau agents continued to monitor radical groups by collecting their publications, attending their meetings, and clipping press accounts of their activities. Still, monitoring the press, auditing meetings, and accepting reports on radical activities from other sources technically did not violate Stone's prohibitions, as the Bureau was not actually conducting its own *investigation*. Hoover walked a fine line, but his journey did not end there.

Indeed, at the very time when his tenure as Director had been most in danger – that is, during his seven-month probationary period in 1924 when Assistant Attorney General Donovan was acting as his overseer at Stone's direction – he had begun to devise ingenious procedures to circumvent Stone's order. One such procedure is detailed in orders concerning the Chicago field office's surveillance of the Workers party (for a time in the early 1920s the Communist party went by that name). On 9 May 1924, the very day Stone requested Burns's resignation as Director, Hoover advised the head of the Bureau's Chicago field office, James Rooney, that henceforth reports submitted by the agent assigned responsibility for investigating the Workers party were to be worded to suggest that they had not been obtained from his own investigation but from a 'confidential informant.' Then, following Stone's order prohibiting Bureau investigations of political activities, Hoover on 31 May wrote to Rooney that this 'confidential informant' (i.e. Bureau agent) should be 'kept at Chicago and his work is not to be confined to the field of activity previously covered [the Workers party]. In other words it should be understood that he should be used as an informant on the regular lines of Bureau work.'

Hoover's confused directive seemingly reflected his unwillingness to abandon the proscribed investigative function. But appearances deceive. Rooney fully understood, and his own cryptic response acknowledging Hoover's instructions stated: 'In connection therewith I respectfully beg to advise that you may rest assured that your instructions in this matter will be followed out.' Thereafter the Chicago field office continued to submit to Hoover detailed reports of Workers party activities disguised as information received from 'confidential informants.'

In essence, then, Hoover had designed a system whereby the Bureau could continue to investigate radical activities, and safely, by making it appear that the results had been received from 'a very reliable and confidential source,' 'a very confidential and delicate source,' 'a delicate and confidential source,' and 'a very confidential source' – all phrases abounding in Bureau reports after 24 May.

From one such 'confidential' source, for example, Hoover learned that the ACLU branch in Los Angeles had transferred its account from one bank to another, and the amount of its weekly deposits. Another report, based on information received from a 'confidential informant,' apprised Hoover of a 'special meeting of the Executive Committee' of the same branch. Advised that the branch had persuaded Federal Judge Benjamin Bledsoe to speak at an 'Open Forum' sponsored by the ACLU, Hoover authorized his agents to inform Judge Bledsoe 'confidentially' about the 'character' of the ACLU, which they did, leading Bledsoe to withdraw his acceptance.

Hoover then acceded to Bledsoe's request for a 'summary of the history, activities and personnel' of the ACLU. Upon receiving the Bureau's summary – 'prepared and confidentially transmitted to the Judge' – Bledsoe issued a statement, published by the *Los Angeles Times*, explaining his reasons for declining the invitation and condemning the ACLU.

Had Stone had more time to get to know his subaltern, he might have gotten wind of what was going on. But Stone had his own overriding concerns, and thus his departure from the Department of Justice removed for the present any obstacle to Hoover's designs, and any prospect that the Director would abandon his antiradical campaign. For Stone was succeeded by an amiable nonentity, Coolidge's card-playing friend John Garibaldi Sargent, who saw even less evil than Stone had seen before him.

Initially successful in circumventing Stone's ban, Hoover soon devised additional procedures to ensure continued monitoring of radical activities. Los Angeles field office reports to Hoover on the IWW and the ACLU reveal how this was done. The substance of these reports, dated 26 and 28 March 1925, ostensibly had been received by an informer employed by the Los Angeles police department, but in fact Special Agent Arthur Hopkins had worked closely with the Los Angeles police on this matter 'and assist[ed] in directing all the operatives furnishing the data upon which these reports are based, and that to all effects is the same as though it had been originally gathered and reported by this office.'

Concurrently with this ongoing investigation of liberal and radical groups, Hoover also took steps to ensure that his agents collected – again without risk of discovery – information about 'obscene and indecent' activities – his own term. On 24 March 1925, acting on his own authority, he created a separate OBSCENE File[4] – an action that ensured that such sensitive information as was collected would be centrally and secretly maintained. The Director advised the heads of Bureau field offices that 'any obscene

119

matter of any nature whatsoever' was henceforth to be mailed in a sealed envelope on which was clearly marked 'in large type or letters the word 'OBSCENE', in order that the nature of the contents may be noted at a glance.' Such captioned documents were to be maintained separate from the Bureau's main filing systems in field offices and in the FBI Laboratory at Bureau headquarters.

Hoover carefully restricted access to this material – both to avoid discovery and, ever the Puritan, to protect the morals of his agents. This file was 'not [to] be exhibited to anyone outside [the FBI] unless specifically authorized by [his future aid Clyde] Tolson or myself.' And whenever 'obscene material which may arouse the curiosity of employees' was being held in field offices, it was to be maintained 'in either the gun vault or the SAC's safe. At no time should it be kept in a place which is readily accessible to other employees, such as the stock room or mail room.' It was not to be 'shown to other personnel in the office who have no need to observe it,' and there was to be 'no undue curiosity about such filth.'

When first established, the Obscene File contained, principally, printed pornographic literature, the publication of which might in extreme cases be adjudged a federal offense. By 1946 'obscene and indecent' submissions included as well 'stag' motion picture films, free-hand drawings, comic strip cartoons, playing cards, and photographs. FBI agents were directed to collect such information, 'even though no Federal violation exists, . . . in order to increase the effectiveness of the Obscene Files.' While deploring the 'general practice of such commercial exploiters to disseminate their products among school children and adults with perverted minds,' Hoover cited other beneficial results:

Each obscene literature investigation possesses potential publicity value because of the very nature of the investigation. Every Special Agent in Charge should closely follow obscene matter investigations in order that consideration may be given to obtaining proper publicity in appropriate cases. Where it is contemplated that publicity will result from the Bureau's investigation of an obscene matter case, it is the responsibility of the Special Agent in Charge to make certain that the Bureau is notified in advance of any contemplated arrest, arraignment, or other development prior to the time that any publicity is released.

The Obscene File, moreover, was not the repository of various types of pornographic materials alone; nor was its use confined to obtaining 'proper publicity whenever the FBI brought obscenity cases to trial. Having precluded discovery of the fact that his Bureau compiled information about illicit sexual activities, Hoover could safely use this file to further his policy objectives.[5]

When creating the Obscene File, Hoover recognized the value of gossip, which could be used either to discredit his adversaries or to curry favor with his ostensible superiors (whether in the White House, Justice Department, or Congress). In addition, he created this file to serve deeply felt moralistic convictions about sin and improper behavior and to fulfill a self-appointed mission as guardian of the nation's morals. Agents were required to collect information on any immoral conduct, and not simply violations of the Mann Act (although this measure provided the authority for the Bureau's early entrance into the field of sexual misconduct). Inevitably, given Hoover's obsessive interest in such derogatory information (and misinformation), such evidence of immoral conduct did not moulder unused in Bureau files. The Director circumspectly exploited this resource, even exchanging information about alleged personal misconduct with favored gossip columnists.[6]

Hoover did make one mistake at the beginning that might have cost him dearly had Stone been alert to his young protégé's designs rather than to his flattery. Hoover had been friendly for some time with an agent named George Ruch. The two men had been colleagues from 1918 until 28 July 1924, when Ruch, whose wages had risen only from four dollars to eight dollars a day, departed the Bureau in search of a better living. Like many former Bureau employees, he eventually moved to Pittsburgh, where, in the wake of the labor-management bloodletting of 1922, he had no difficulty gaining employment as a detective for steel companies and the Pennsylvania Railroad.

One of Edgar's first acts after Stone cancelled the requirement that all personnel matters be cleared with an assistant attorney general was to hire Ruch as assistant director at a salary of $5,200 a year. The appointment was announced in January 1925, and a storm of public criticism followed. Ruch, it appears, was qualified by neither temperament nor ability to fill the post. Stone moved in to save his man from himself, and the appointment was rescinded.

Hoover made no such mistake in the case of his friend Frank Baughman, although, to be sure, Frank was too young for consideration for promotion in view of Hoover's own youth. Frank was kept on, but only as a special agent expert in the analysis of firearms. It is likely that by this time Frank also *carried* a firearm, as the matter of personal safety was more than ever on Edgar's mind and later boon companions Clyde Tolson and Guy Hottel were reputed to have been regularly armed.

The casual coming and going between Annie's dinner table and the Fox theater on F Street had to come to an end, and Frank and Edgar thereafter saw each other mostly at work. (Frank probably by this time was seeking greater personal independence anyway.) Edgar requisitioned the first of a series of government-owned limousines, a bullet-proof Pierce Arrow, together with a black driver named Ferguson. And members of the family recall that shortly after that he stopped relying on the Fifth Precinct altogether. Always extremely security conscious, he sought ways to protect the home premises himself, using the ample resources of the Bureau.

However, there was one problem that even the nation's top cop could not solve: how to throw a protective perimeter around a semidetached house? Soon Edgar was discussing with his mother the merits of moving. Later their automotive house-hunting expeditions would become a Sunday routine. But for the present Edgar was too delighted by his success to make an issue of Annie's obstinate refusal.

Notes to Chapter Five

1. Ultimately, Daugherty balked the court that tried him for conspiracy to defraud the government by refusing to produce evidentiary material in the Bureau's files.

2. Edgar had carefully prepared for the encounter: there can be no doubt about his determination to succeed. The Bureau had already demonstrated its ability to influence events, and, as Adolf Berle observed (*Power* [New York: Harcourt, Brace & World, 1967], p. 40), 'the naked and entirely natural fact of the power instinct must be bracketed with the desire to overcome, and to be protected against, chaos.' Edgar's personal needs demanded that he succeed.

3. This marked a substantial salary increase − $1,500 − over Hoover's salary as acting director. Prior to that temporary appointment, Hoover had earned the standard civil service salary of $5,000 a year. Hoover's next major salary increase occurred in 1936 when Congress approved a special resolution, discreetly promoted by Hoover, increasing his salary to $10,000 a year, a princely sum in Depression-era America.

4. At this time, Hoover also began to compile a 'confidential' file in his own office containing 'various and sundry items inadvisable to be included in the general files of the Bureau.' Included in this file were extremely sensitive policy documents and dossiers reporting derogatory information on prominent personalities (including presidents, cabinet officers, congressmen and, much later, a First Lady).

5. To cite a later but pertinent example of its use: in January 1954, during the course of a criminal investigation, FBI agents in St. Louis wiretapped a conversation between John Vitale (whom they described as 'an Italian hoodlum') and an associate in Detroit. At the time, Vitale was seeking legal counsel for a forthcoming parole hearing. Vitale's Detroit associate recommended Herbert K. Hyde, whom he described as 'getting more powerful all the time' now that Hyde was the 'General Trial Attorney for General Services Administration.' Conceding that Hyde's job was not all that

123

impressive, Vitale's Detroit associate hastened to explain that Hyde has 'a good looking wife — he says that IKE [President Dwight Eisenhower] has been trying to get into her pants' and further that Hyde 'is scheduled to get a judgeship.'

Because it was reporting a rumored illicit sexual affair, the St. Louis office transmitted the transcript of this portion of Vitale's intercepted conversation to FBI headquarters under the 'Obscene File' procedure. Since this submission involved the alleged sexual indiscretion of an incumbent president, it was forwarded to Hoover's media and congressional liaison, Assistant Director Louis Nichols, to be maintained in his office file. Briefed on this intelligence, Hoover had his aides follow the matter closely, FBI files were checked for any references to Hyde; Hyde's employment in the General Services Administration was verified; and a 'separate [ten-page] memorandum' on him was prepared. (SAC, St. Louis, to FBI Director, 29 January 1954; OBSCENE Letter, partial transcript from wiretap of Vitale, 29 January 1954; Memo, Price to Rosen, 2 February 1954; ten-page report withheld in entirety; all in Dwight Eisenhower Folder, Nichols O&C.)

6. The case of the Hollywood comedian Charles Chaplin best illustrates Hoover's self-anointed role as moral guardian and stern Puritan. Learning of Hollywood actress Joan Barry's charge that Chaplin had fathered her yet-unborn child, Hoover ordered agents to conduct an intensive investigation of Chaplin's sex life that extended to bugging Chaplin's hotel room. The investigation lasted four months, and Hoover persuaded Justice Department officials to indict Chaplin for violating the Mann Act. (In the ensuing trial, Chaplin was exonerated, as Barry's accusation proved to be without foundation; a blood test of the newborn confirmed that Chaplin could not have been the father.) In addition, Hoover exchanged information with the Hollywood gossip columnists Hedda Hopper and Louella Parsons; he both welcomed and incorporated into the FBI's 1,900-page file on Chaplin unsubstantiated gossip provided by Hopper and Parsons and, in turn, leaked to them information on Chaplin's personal and political activities. (Hoover leaked this information under a Do Not File procedure; no permanent retrievable record of these transactions was created, allowing him to deny, without fear of contradiction, having done so.) See *New York Times*, 22 January 1986; David Robinson, *Chaplin: His Life and Art* (New York: McGraw-Hill, 1985), pp. 520–24, 750–56.

CHAPTER SIX

(1925–1933)
OPPORTUNITY

HOOVER BECAME Director of the Bureau of Investigation at a crucial time in its history, a time when its competence and integrity were seriously questioned. Many conservative Americans still believed that the federal government had no business getting involved in police work, except, that is, to deal with such crimes against the state as treason or assaults on the Treasury or mails, and many liberals felt that the Bureau was by its very nature a threat to civil liberties and democratic government. The scandals of the early 1920s had heightened these fears, raising questions not only about the commitment of federal detectives to the rule of law but also about whether a federal investigative agency, whose personnel owed their positions to the incumbent administration (the Bureau was not included in the Civil Service), would inevitably act as a partisan secret police force – and thus a threat to a democratic society.

At the outset, therefore, Hoover was determined to alter the Bureau's image, an undertaking for which, paradoxically, he proved in his confident rectitude ideally suited. For from the beginning he identified the Bureau with himself, regarded its reputation as a reflection on himself, and demanded of its agents the same puritanical standards of conduct that he demanded of himself. However conventional and unexamined, these standards – avoidance of partisanship, high professional qualifications, and, more important, religious piety, abstinence from alcohol, absolute loyalty, devotion to duty, and physical and moral purity – were fervently shared by millions of Americans. And as Hoover had already discovered in connection with his stereotypical antiradicalism, his strength – and now the Bureau's – came from the identity of his values with those of his vast although still inchoate national constituency.

Hoover had an innate feel for publicity amounting to genius, but at this juncture, sensitive to the antigovernmental mood of the 1920s, he did not try to exercise it. Fearing centralized power, the American public had responded favorably to the presidential candidacies of Warren Harding and Calvin Coolidge because both offered a low profile. Hoover, moreover, was still a virtual nonentity on the national scene, and for the moment he was content to be one. His appointment had gone unnoticed in most newspapers and magazines, and those organs of communication that had noticed it more often than not had gotten the story wrong, frequently identifying him as the new head of the Secret Service. The *Christian Science Monitor*, for instance, gave the appointment a mere one-column inch, noting on 22 December 1924 that 'J. E. Hoover, who has been acting director of the Justice Department's investigation bureau since the retirement of William J. Burns, has been appointed director of the bureau by Harlan F. Stone, Attorney General.' A brief second paragraph stated: 'Mr. Hoover has been a member of the department's force of secret agents for several years and served under Mr. Burns as assistant director.'

Metropolitan dailies across the country gave the event roughly the same amount of play, if they gave it any play at all, and the news services sent out the announcement as a filler item. The fullest coverage of the appointment appeared in the *Daily Worker* of New York, the chief organ of the Communist Party of the United States. On 22 December 1924, in a story running four one-column inches on the front page, it reported:

Despite the protestations of Attorney General Stone, that the vacancy caused by the dismissal of William J. Burns from his position as chief investigator of the department of justice would not be filled, the expected has happened.

After public excitement over the Teapot Dome graft scandal and the corruption exposed in the department of justice died down, the promises made by the government prior to the election were conveniently forgotten. Now that the excitement is over, we find J. Edgar Hoover slipping his feet in Burns' shoes.

The new attorney general promised after his appointment, that the bureau of investigation would not be used for spying on unions and radical organizations. But it is a well known fact among newspaper men in Washington that agents of the department of justice have been active recently, trying to engage men and women to do espionage work, in trade unions and political parties of the workers.

Although the *Daily Worker*'s was a voice crying in the wilderness, Stone nevertheless was smarting from criticisms of partisan federal law enforcement and of his controversial decision to prosecute Senator Wheeler, criticisms emanating from Harvard Law School and other bastions of scholarly opinion. Scheduled to appear before the Senate Judiciary Committee on 28 January 1925 for hearings on his confirmation to the Supreme Court, Stone seized the earliest opportunity to defend himself, although not by addressing the issue of the proper role of a federal investigative agency in a democratic society. In a public address on 24 January, Stone claimed that lax enforcement of the prohibitionist Volstead Act could seriously undermine the foundations of the Republic. 'Every time a citizen in this country violates the Volstead Act,' the attorney general argued, 'it is a sign that some law-enforcement official, somewhere along the line, has been corrupted; and corruption in the law-enforcing agencies of the government is a direct path to national disaster. The solidarity of the republic is at stake.' Commenting on the difficulties he confronted, Stone observed that he offended someone no matter what decision he made:

If I recommend the preparation of evidence for a grand jury indictment, I am subject to criticism, and if I feel, on the other hand, that evidence does not warrant a grand jury action, I am also criticized. However, I go right along offending some and pleasing others, as the dictates of my conscience guide, and thus assure myself of the sleep that comes with an easy conscience.

The persona of the hapless and unfairly maligned public servant damned for doing his duty seems not to have caused Stone the slightest embarrassment — and this role was readily adopted by his subaltern when confronting similar criticisms.

Three days later, emboldened by his mentor, Hoover was extolling his administrative reforms in the *Pittsburgh Press*. In an interview datelined 27 January 1925, the Director claimed to have already changed the character of the Bureau by firing some staff members and hiring others. 'The new agents are required to be either lawyers or accountants,' the story said, quoting Hoover's observation that 'Indictments are easy to get . . . Convictions are a different matter.'

Hoover then cited statistics, a practice that later became familiar to congressional appropriations committees. 'In the last six months of 1924, we obtained sentences totaling 443 years, four months and 289 days. Roughly, that is 174 years more than obtained in the same six months of the year preceding.'

'A system of close supervision of all offices has been put into effect,' the story concluded. 'There are now 40 such offices throughout the United States where formerly there were 52. These are subject to constant unannounced visits from inspectors and their work is continually checked up. A unified filing and reporting system has been installed in all offices. Hoover believes any district agent can now be transferred from one office to another and by use of the reports found in his new office can carry on the work without the loss of half a day.'

Other interview articles followed in which Hoover reassured a trusting public. 'I want the public to look upon the Bureau of Investigation of the Department of Justice as a group of gentlemen,' he said in a story in the March

1925 issue of *National Magazine*, 'and if the men here engaged can't conduct themselves in office as such, I will dismiss them.'

'I will never submit to an agent in this bureau spying into the affairs of a member of Congress or deliberately lying,' he continued. 'The badge of authority in the Bureau does not make a czar; the men here must treat the public justly.'

And in his Machiavellian way, Hoover meant what he said. He had, with brutal speed, reformed the Bureau in his own image, firing and reassigning the ruffians and prosecuting the occasional criminal. Gaston Means, for instance, left the Bureau with a four-year prison sentence and a $20,000 fine. Relying on his experience at the Library of Congress, the new Director *did* institute a uniform and efficient filing system, and he *did* consolidate the federal government's disparate fingerprint holdings in the Bureau's new Identification Division, thereby increasing the scope of his operations and the reach of his power. In short, he demonstrated at the outset the administrative genius and aggressiveness that would see him through to the end. But he also demonstrated the priggishness and pettiness that won him the sobriquet 'Queen Bee.'

Hoover's conviction of his own righteousness and his insistence on compliance with his personal idiosyncrasies is graphically captured in his first manual of instructions, which he prepared immediately after becoming Director. Unlike later manuals, which were prepared with assistance, this one exudes Hoover's vigorous authoritarianism, his exaggerated sense of his own importance, his intolerance of individuality, and his extreme narrowness of vision.

The manual's first instruction was that FBI employees 'shall be subject to call for duty at all times,' shall be 'expected to give due regard to their personal appearance and presentability,' and shall 'patronize hotels of the better class' – that is, not brothels. Agents were to 'exercise the utmost care to prevent the loss or destruction of their commission cards and badges' or pay the penalty of 'suspension or dismissal from the service.'

Agents were not to use the words 'Department of Justice'

or 'Bureau of Investigation' on 'visiting or personal cards from which official connection with the Government might be inferred' and were required to present any recommendations they might have through 'official channels.' Every employee was forbidden 'to furnish to the press, either directly or indirectly, any information whatsoever,' or 'to disclose in writing or orally any information obtained by him in his official capacity to an unauthorized person.' Furthermore, agents were to 'transmit to the Bureau clippings from any publications which relate to the Bureau, its personnel or activities.' Thus Hoover alone determined what Bureau information would be released, leaked, or suppressed.

Hoover stipulated that heads of the FBI field offices (special agents in charge, or SACs) were to have 'exclusive jurisdiction over their districts with the exception of agents on special assignments and Bureau Accountants' but could, 'where the exigencies of a case, emergencies or economy and common sense' required, enter another district provided they then advised the responsible SAC 'immediately.' SACs were obliged to 'obtain authority from the Bureau before leaving their headquarters, except in cases of emergency, when subsequent approval will be sufficient.'

Committed to achieving for the Bureau a spotless reputation, Hoover forbade all employees to use intoxicating beverages 'whether on official duty or otherwise,' to 'give testimonials or letters of commendation without the prior approval of the Bureau,' or to 'express either verbally or in writing to any person [information] bearing upon the efficiency or standing of any employee in the service of the Bureau.' Agents were also forbidden to accept any rewards or gratuities, and their supervisors were to report on 'the conduct of all employees of the Bureau of Investigation while on official duty and after official hours while they are in your territory.' Supervisors were to submit for each employee an annual report on his marital status (Hoover disapproved of divorce), memberships in societies and fraternal organizations, legal residence, and education, including degrees attained. All Bureau employees were to report directly to Hoover 'whenever cognizant' of another agent's 'use of intoxicating liquors, the neglect of duties as well as other indiscretions.'

Moreover, to ensure that Bureau employees were and remained properly qualified, Hoover in February 1925 instituted a system whereby 'the quality and quantity' of each agent's work was regularly and precisely evaluated every six months. SACs were to fill out Personal Efficiency Record forms evaluating twenty categories (accuracy, aggressiveness, dependability, health, industry, initiative, judgment, speed, knowledge, leadership, loyalty, office work, promptness, resourcefulness, tact, teamwork, personal appearance, executive ability, habits, and attitude toward work) on a scale of one to 100. The form also contained a space for SACs to write personal appraisals.

The exaggerated emphasis on detail captures Hoover's administrative style. Decisions emanated exclusively from the top; agents and SACs were personally responsible to the Director. All important communications from field offices to headquarters were addressed to the Director; all major policy directives were sent under the signature of the Director; and senior officials reported directly to the Director, wherefore the Director was soon aptly called 'The Boss.'

Hoover's insistence on discipline closely dovetailed with his strategies to keep the tiger outside the gates. He did not hesitate to punish any employee who failed to cater to his siege mentality. Indeed, he so arranged matters at the Bureau that employees who resisted his authority had no recourse at all. In keeping with the original requirements that Bureau appointments 'be based on merit,' promotions 'be made on proved ability,' and the Bureau itself 'be responsible only to the Attorney General,' he steadfastly opposed all attempts to bring the Bureau within the Civil Service. There would be only one judge of an agent's conduct, and that judge would be J. Edgar Hoover.

Hoover's stringent rules, not surprisingly, tended to instill fear and discourage initiative. Concerned as much with personal behavior as with job performance, Hoover's first manual (which devoted 131 pages to administration and comportment and only 38 to the actual conduct of investigations) struck many employees as a Bureau etiquette guide à la Emily Post. Disenchanted former agents wrote derisively about the pettiness or futility of Hoover's directives — whether 'no left turns,' a dress style that permitted the easy identification of agents, no 'wet palms,' or no 'pointy heads' — and they had good reason. For Hoover was obsessed, obsessed with a mythical FBI that became the mirror of the man. The image did not please all agents, or all Americans either. But it most assuredly did facilitate control.

According to Anthony Marro, who covered the Bureau at a later date for the *New York Times* and *Newsday*, 'The Seat of Government [SOG, a reference to FBI headquarters in Washington] people lived in a world of their own' and, in the view of many field agents, 'were far removed from the realities of the street. I think that they often were more interested in telling Hoover what he wanted to hear than in dealing with serious and complicated criminal problems.'

But despite this tension between agents in the field and officials at headquarters, Marro emphasized, 'the organization had high morale,' especially later when Hoover's sophisticated public relations machine began to roll. 'It enjoyed a very positive public image, a presumption of competence. There was cynicism, yes, but also esprit, especially in the field. Not every agent was a lawyer or accountant . . . These people [at the SOG] were recruited "out of the swamps." The Bureau would recruit them as clerks, get 'em some kind of degree.'[1]

In short, Hoover found raw material, mostly from the South and West, and molded it into loyal subordinates to staff his SOG. The men in the field were the real cops and, according to Marro, 'the field hated Washington,' especially Washington's periodic unannounced inspections. Hoover's immediate circle of aides, Marro added, were known as 'the Gandy dancers,' in honor of Helen Gandy, a wraithlike, grim-faced spinster from New Jersey who had begun work at the Department in 1918 and was Hoover's secretary and administrative assistant from the day of his appointment until the day of his death. 'By reputation,' Marro recalled, 'she was tough and firm and fiercely loyal to Hoover. I only saw her in person once,' he said. 'She shooed me away when I tried to talk with her. But that was later.'

Meanwhile opportunity was knocking at the door. In June 1925 the Supreme Court unanimously upheld the constitutionality of the Dyer Act of 1919, involving the Bureau in policing interstate traffic in stolen automobiles. Although as a practical matter stolen cars were recovered, when they were recovered, mostly by local police, the Bureau had been acting as a conduit for information and thereby taking credit for recovering property in virtually every case in which it was tangentially involved. The Court's ruling thus ensured that Hoover could continue to use statistics on Dyer Act cases to demonstrate the greatly improved efficiency of his Bureau.

At the same time there was a widespread perception in the country that crime was on the increase and, indeed, becoming a national scandal. This was due partly to the near-universal disregard of the Volstead Act, partly to a longstanding blindness to the endemic problem of crime in America, and partly to the increase of organized crime on an interstate scale occasioned by the requirements of bootlegging. In addition, the war, the uncertain peace, and a devil-take-the-hindmost attitude toward the regulation of business activity had all bred a flagrant cynicism among disaffected citizens that many conservative activists found alarming. The country seemed to many to have become a continental Sodom and Gomorrah, and increasingly these Americans looked to the federal government for relief.

To be sure, the automobile itself was probably the biggest factor behind the changes that were disturbing the peace of middle Americans. The vastly greater mobility that it afforded – to robbers, kidnappers, bootleggers, unmarried lovers, and everyone else – *had* created a host of new problems for local law enforcement agencies. But those agencies had cars of their own, and telephones. The breakdown of law and order was greatly exaggerated, both by individual Americans and by most of the nation's press — and unfairly attributed by some to the hated aliens in their midst. Still, many anxious observers had come to feel that the federal government had a legitimate role to play, if only in coordinating fingerprints and information.

Antiradicalism continued to be a flag of convenience for the Bureau throughout the 1920s, but Burns had spoiled it so far as congressional appropriators were concerned. So Hoover welcomed the windfall of Dyer Act cases as a means of stimulating increased Bureau budgets. (Volstead Act violations did not become his concern until 1930, when the Treasury Department's prohibition enforcement unit was transferred to the Department of Justice, and then only peripherally.) Although he had failed earlier to instigate a peacetime sedition law, Hoover could look forward realistically to an increased federal role in other areas, given the steady drumbeat from middle America.

Finally, the strands of national malaise came together in 1927 when an ad hoc group of conservative businessmen and former public officials, including Franklin D. Roosevelt, held its first meeting in Washington. Organized in 1925 by Mark Prentice, a businessman who had the distinction of having accompanied Benito Mussolini on his triumphal march on Rome in 1922 and who, incidentally, believed that aliens accounted for the great majority of violent crimes in America, the National Crime Commission, as it styled itself, included among its members Elbert Henry Gary, the chairman of the United States Steel Corporation during the bloody strike of 1919, Richard Washburn Child, a former ambassador to Italy and close friend of Mussolini, two generals, a Who's Who of captains of industry, and several educators.

Founded in the boardroom at U.S. Steel, the Commission generated a good deal of publicity but failed to enlist broad support. As Dean John H. Wigmore of the Northwestern University Law School observed after noting that the commission conspicuously lacked members with an expert knowledge of the law, 'We confess to doubt about this type of Commission, however composed, being able to accomplish much practically . . . National Commissions on problems lying within State constitutional powers are an anomaly and a novelty in our history; and our people are not accustomed to heed them.'

Paradoxically, it was the liberal activist Franklin Roosevelt who sided with the autocrats in the matter of federal intervention — when he became president. His conservative predecessors, Calvin Coolidge and Herbert Hoover, especially the latter, wanted no larger federal role in crime prevention. Until the Cold War years, conservatives consistently opposed federal regulation of both business and personal activities, fearing any centralization of power in the federal government. So the year 1927 passed without any further action, and Edgar perforce adhered to Stone's initial instruction to keep a low profile. But he was preparing himself to reach for power.

Meanwhile Frank Baughman had married, and Hoover was in need of a new right hand who had a gun and would travel. On 2 April 1928 he hired Clyde Tolson, the Iowa farm boy who had been an aide to Secretary of War Newton Baker. Not yet twenty-eight, clean-cut and athletic and, according to one former agent who spoke not for attribution, 'with icewater in his veins,' Tolson was right out of central casting as the macho troubleshooter to replace Frank.[2] Moreover, he had studied law at George Washington and thus was a member of the club.

Hoover assigned Tolson first to the Washington field office and then, following normal procedures, to a regional office, in Boston. But Clyde was soon recalled to the Seat of Government, where he celebrated his first anniversary on the payroll as an inspector, one of three. He and Hoover, both younger sons, in the meantime had come to know each other on a first-name basis — he as Clyde or sometimes, playfully, 'Junior,' and Hoover as 'Speed,' perhaps occasionally 'Eddie,' and finally 'The Boss.'

Tolson, unlike Hoover, was not a complete stranger to women, but, unlike Frank, he appreciated what an encumbrance a wife would be. Personally devoted to Hoover, willing to subordinate his ambitions to those of The

135

Boss, he soon established his indispensability by his unquestioned loyalty to Hoover's and the Bureau's interests. For a time, Hoover, Tolson, and Baughman were inseparable companions, occasionally dining at Annie's table, but after his marriage Frank gradually withdrew from that scene. Tolson was the new favorite and, less than three years after his enlistment at the Bureau, was assistant director as well.

Much has been made of Hoover's and Tolson's relationship. The two bachelors were constantly seen together, working, dining, or relaxing, at the Bureau, at Harvey's Restaurant or the Mayflower Hotel on Connecticut Avenue, where they ate lunch and often dinner together every weekday, or traveling on leisurely 'inspection tours' in southern climes. But there is no evidence that they were lovers. Hoover's extreme sensitivity to rumors of the kind can be read as suggesting that he was a closet homosexual, which may have been the case. But Tolson was reputed by several of his associates to be strongly heterosexual, and both men, not to mention all of their associates, conducted their lives in a very conventional way. The speculation invaded the Bureau itself, where one agent was reported to have said of Hoover, 'If he isn't queer, then he's weird,' but like James I of England and *his* favorites, Hoover and his several bodyguards were obsessed with the administrative responsibilities of running the Seat of Government. The strange likelihood is that Hoover never knew sexual desire at all.

By the time of Clyde's arrival, Margaret was gone from the Hoover household, but not forgotten. After returning to 413 Seward Square to live in 1926, she completed normal school while working summers at the Library of Congress as a cataloguer. Graduating in 1928, she secured a permanent appointment at the Library and, notwithstanding a terrible fight with her father in which he declared that 'a criminal court of law is the last place for a woman to appear,' and in which her Uncle Edgar took her side, she enrolled as a night student at George Washington's law school.

A year later she met a recent law graduate from George-town named Paul Fennell and fell in love — not for the first time either (her father had broken up one romance with a boy from California, and Uncle Edgar had had to pick up those pieces too, which he did in an exceedingly gentle manner). Paul was a Roman Catholic, and although Annie was sympathetic to that persuasion (a priest attended at her funeral), Dickerson had a fit. He gave Margaret a book entitled *Mixed Marriage*, she recalled, and delivered himself of a terrifying jeremiad. But she and Paul were married all the same, and she and Dick were eventually reconciled.

By then the Crash had come and gone and the Great Depression was deepening. Paul could not find work in Washington, so after the nuptials the couple moved to his boyhood home in Burlington, Vermont, where he eventually became state's attorney for Chittenden County and she produced five lively and brainy children.

Thus Edgar was more than ever alone, although also more than ever involved with his Bureau. He had weathered one storm in 1929, when a former agent named Joe Bayliss wrote to Attorney General William D. Mitchell accusing the Director of every possible act of misfeasance and malfeasance. (Hoover, getting wind of the trouble through his own channels, went straight to the attorney general and refuted the accusations. Whether because of his audacity or because by then he was performing political intelligence missions for the White House,[3] the matter came to naught.) Dangers seemed to increase whenever the Bureau's prospects brightened, and following the appointment of the presidential Wickersham Commission to investigate the national crime situation in 1930, Tolson called in an auxiliary to deal with the near-hysterical Director. It was a mistake that nearly cost Tolson his position.

The attributes that Hoover admired most in men were athleticism, toughness, virility, loyalty, and, perhaps in deference to his mother, piety. Clyde Tolson came as close as anyone to fulfilling Hoover's dream. Confident of his masculinity yet haunted by the insecurity bred of childhood poverty, Tolson was prepared to sacrifice everything to the

137

goal of keeping the Director on his side, even to be the Director's front man and take the heat for his lies — when they were discovered, that is. Tolson was the perfect foil for Hoover — steady, steely, a hands-on manager who handled discipline in the office and, above all, was willing to be a monk like Hoover himself.

But briefly, another man, more charismatic than Tolson and unblushingly sensual — a womanizer, in fact — nearly monopolized the Director's attentions. His arrival and departure were described by a Bureau veteran-turned-author: 'at one juncture . . . Tolson threatened to leave. Instead, he brought in an ex-football player with whom he had gone to college as a sort of third man accompanying them [Hoover and Tolson] on their outings and trips. The man remained on the payroll for twenty years, yet he is an 'unperson' never mentioned in FBI lore.'

The 'unperson' was Guy Hottel, who had been Tolson's roommate when the two were students at George Washington. A Mormon[4] who had grown up in the hills of Virginia, Hottel as a boy had demonstrated no special qualities other than a natural bravado. But his star ascended rapidly after he reached George Washington, where he heaped honors on himself as a tackle on the football team and, according to one colleague at the Bureau, played one too many scrimmages without a helmet. A superb all-round athlete, broad-shouldered and handsome, with fair, pellucid skin and a leonine brow, he was a charmer and an incorrigible roustabout, 'the sort of guy,' another agent recalled, 'who, when he figured you'd been in the telephone booth long enough, would drag you out.' Married four times in the course of his life, he was still married to his first wife, Adele, herself a beauty of no mean distinction, when he met Hoover.

Hottel had been brought in by Tolson to be a troubleshooter, but Hoover shortly adopted the burly young man to replace Tolson as his unofficial bodyguard. Thereafter the three traveled together, whether to lunch at the Mayflower or dinner at Harvey's, to the race track, or on alleged inspection tours to the velvet places of California

138

and Florida, where Hoover posed for photographs with his arm around the favorite's shoulders. Hottel seems not to have minded the invasion of his privacy in the least but, on the contrary, to have admired the audacity with which Hoover arranged to leave every luxury hotel they visited without paying a bill. However, Tolson minded very much. As another former agent testified, 'Tolson had good reason to resent Guy Hottel.'

But Hoover by this time had a much more serious problem on his hands than the trouble in his movable ménage à trois. President Hoover had easily turned the tide against the Democrats' Roman Catholic presidential candidate, Al Smith, in 1928, but by 1930 the Crash and the deteriorating economy were threatening his re-election. Moreover, in that year the respected Wickersham Commission finally reported that crime had indeed become a national problem, thereby upping the ante in Edgar's power game. The directorship was beginning to look like a plum rather than a cross to bear, and in the aftermath of Franklin Roosevelt's sweeping victory in the 1932 presidential election, patronage-minded Democrats began discussing the merits of Hoover's removal. Edgar's political intelligence missions for the Hoover White House were not then public knowledge, nor were they more than suspected by the Democrats. But because the young Director was a Republican appointee and because his position was not protected under Civil Service, he was a prime target for replacement in the inevitable turnover following the Democrats' return to power after a hiatus of twelve years.

It is not clear whether he acted on his own authority or whether President Hoover alerted him to the prospect of Hoover's possible replacement by a patronage appointee, but, in any event, a concerned Supreme Court Justice Harlan Stone interceded on behalf of his worried protégé, writing to Roosevelt adviser Felix Frankfurter in April 1933 to praise his administration of the Bureau.

The Director also put out lines to conservative congressional Democrats as insurance against Roosevelt's imminent house-cleaning. At the same time he practiced some patronage of his own, dismissing a number of long-time agents and replacing them with southern Democrats, so that by the time of Roosevelt's inauguration in March 1933, more than a hundred new Democrats were on the payroll. In the meantime he had muscled into the widely publicized Lindbergh kidnapping case, then being investigated by the New York and New Jersey police.

Nevertheless, it appeared that all of Hoover's efforts were in vain. In February 1933 Roosevelt announced his choice for attorney general, and he was none other than Thomas Walsh, the crusading senator from Montana who had been a member of the Senate Judiciary subcommittee investigating the Palmer raids and who, together with his fellow senator from Montana, Burton Wheeler, had promoted the Senate investigation of Justice Department corruption under Harry Daugherty.

Worse, Walsh had defended his junior colleague at the latter's conflict-of-interest trial in Montana. And worst of all, correctly suspecting that the indictment against Wheeler had been arranged to punish him for his role in challenging Interior Secretary Albert Fall's fraudulent disposition of government-owned oil leases at Teapot Dome and Attorney General Daugherty's refusal to investigate allegations of that scandal, Walsh had learned from a sympathetic hotel telephone operator of the federal prosecutor's nightly briefings of Director Hoover on the progress of the trial. Given this history, Walsh was undoubtedly the worst candidate from Hoover's standpoint that Roosevelt could have named.

But Hoover left no stone unturned in his struggle for survival at the Bureau. In January 1933 he appealed to his contacts in local and state police organizations to lobby the Democratic congressional membership to support his reappointment, and, as it turned out, these efforts were not in vain. One such, championed by Fred McDuff, president of the Alabama Sheriffs' and Peace Officers' Association, brought home to Hoover the gravity of the problem. McDuff's entreaty had elicited varied responses from the members of Alabama's congressional delegation. Some commended Hoover's candidacy; others were politely evasive. The most troubling responses, however, came from Alabama's two Democratic senators. Taking care not to commit himself, Lister Hill characterized the association's appeal for Hoover as a 'fine tribute' and promised to 'bring it to the attention of the proper parties in the event a change is contemplated in the Bureau of Investigation.' Hugo Black, on the other hand, was almost abrupt in his refusal to go along with the flagrant lobbying. 'I assume that Mr. John Edgar Hoover is a Republican,' he responded, 'and holds his office as a result of Republican patronage. His position is political[5] and in all probability the new Attorney General will name a new Director of the United States Bureau of Investigation in line with the usual policy that is followed by political parties, both Democratic and Republican.'

Then, on 28 February, Attorney General-designate Walsh announced his intention to reorganize the Department of Justice, adding that this would probably entail 'an almost completely new personnel.' For the purpose of dispensing patronage posts, as opposed to those that he planned to award on merit, the attorney general-designate had already invited aboard the very Homer Cummings who, as Democratic national chairman, had in 1919 prevailed on President Wilson to name A. Mitchell Palmer to head the Justice Department over the opposition of Palmer's predecessor, Thomas W. Gregory. Writing to Cummings on 22 February, Walsh invited him to accept appointment to the post of administrative assistant to handle all 'patronage matters, appointments of judges, district attorneys, marshals and other officers of like character.' Walsh stressed that Cummings's 'experience as a practitioner in the conduct of important lawsuits, as well as your familiarity with the country at large,' could help ensure 'the success of the new administration, and particularly to have it start off favorably regarded by the country on account of the personnel of the men appointed to executive positions.' Advising Cummings of his planned departure from Washington for a week, Walsh proposed that they meet after the inauguration to review the whole matter.

The inauguration took place as scheduled on 4 March, and Homer Cummings was there. However, Thomas Walsh was not. Recently remarried, he had gone with his wife on a brief wedding trip to North Carolina and there died of a massive myocardial infarction on 2 March. Hoover, realizing that the suspicion of foul play might dog him for the rest of his life, rushed senior Bureau officials to North Carolina to accompany Mrs. Walsh and the body of her husband on the train trip back to Washington and personally met Mrs. Walsh when the train arrived in the capital. In addition, he made sure that a thoroughly documented medical examination was made.

Walsh's death was doubly fortunate for Hoover. For, as attorney general, Walsh would have been in a position to learn that his own earlier roles in the Senate investigation into the Palmer raids and Burton Wheeler's discovery of Justice Department collusion in the Teapot Dome swindle had been carefully monitored by Hoover.

On 19 April 1922, for example, a Bureau agent in Seattle reported to Hoover about Walsh's alleged 'radical activities.' These activities included Walsh's having sent copies of the Senate report on the Palmer raids to 'such local radicals as George F. Vanderveer, attorney for the I.W.W., and to Attorney Ralph Pierce of the Central Labor Council.' The Seattle agent promised to continue to investigate the matter.

Walsh's FBI file also contained a more incriminating letter dated 26 February 1924 to Attorney General Daugherty from a friend urging an investigation into Walsh's dissolution of his law partnership in Montana. Such an investigation, Daugherty's friend urged, 'would throw light on Senator Walsh, that would be of great interest and benefit to the country,' emphasizing that if some of the allegations 'are true, Senator Walsh needs investigating as well as, or worse, than others.' After reading the letter and at Daugherty's direction, Bureau Chief William Burns assured his friend that he had read the letter 'with a great deal of interest' inasmuch as he was 'very anxious to get all the information possible along the lines stated in your letter.' The resulting inquiry proved fruitless, and thus the strategy to implicate both Walsh and Wheeler in alleged wrongdoing failed.

Walsh would have discovered other things as well, all of them quite sufficient grounds for Hoover's dismissal, if indeed new grounds had been needed. But that was not to be. The senator's sudden and untimely death had removed from the scene the one man with the stature and interest to blow the whistle. Then, as fate would have it, President Roosevelt named Homer Cummings to replace him.

Cummings, more the politician than the lawyer (although he was both), did not share Walsh's concern about Hoover's Bureau activities in the early 1920s. On the contrary, he was rather unscrupulously ambitious himself. Moreover, outgoing President Hoover, exploiting the occasion of the inaugural parade, urged Roosevelt to reappoint Hoover. The Director's other influential allies included White House aides Edwin Watson and Stephen Early, both of whom perhaps wanted a man at the Bureau who knew which side his bread was buttered on.

There remained, however, one last obstacle to Hoover's appointment. James Farley, Roosevelt's campaign manager and appointee to head the key patronage post of postmaster general, was then actively promoting the candidacy of a New York City private detective named Val O'Farrell. Hoover, ever alert to such dangers, had discovered this almost immediately and taken steps to nip the challenge in the bud.

On 1 May 1933 Cummings advised Hoover of a meeting he had had with John Hogan, a friend of O'Farrell, on 29 April. Hogan had then claimed to have learned of O'Farrell's candidacy for a position in the Department of Justice, for which he was currently under investigation. Cummings inquired about O'Farrell and whether the Bureau had investigated him.

Hoover denied having investigated O'Farrell 'in this regard' but admitted to having learned 'approximately six weeks ago' that O'Farrell 'was a candidate for the Directorship of the Bureau of Investigation.' Hoover then shared with Cummings the derogatory information that the Bureau had obtained on O'Farrell to the effect that 'O'Farrell had

143

while employed by the New York Police Department been charged with bribery and with making false affidavit, and that he was last year in the personal bodyguard of Dutch Schultz [a notorious hoodlum] known as Public Enemy No. One in New York City.' Hoover assured Cummings that 'these two pieces of information had been verified, but that outside this no investigation had been made of O'Farrell.'

Hoover once again dissembled, for in fact he had launched an intensive investigation of O'Farrell, and his agents were already trying to determine how successful O'Farrell had been in advancing his candidacy for the Bureau post. Under the pretext of answering a newspaper advertisement for detectives who spoke several languages, they had even insinuated themselves into the O'Farrell Detective Agency's offices and there tried to determine the relationship between the agency and various radicals. They had also clipped stories, dating from 1919 and 1920, about an O'Farrell bankruptcy suit and a suit charging collusion by an artist whose wife had employed the O'Farrell agency during a divorce proceeding. On 30 March 1933, following a Bureau investigation of the more serious allegations – an investigation that went far beyond public records and included a confidential source whose nature cannot be determined because the FBI withheld a page and a half of this report so as not to reveal a 'confidential source or reveal confidential information furnished only by the confidential source' – Hoover prepared a 'blind memo' on plain white paper for distribution to interested parties, including the attorney general.

But Hoover's efforts did not stop there. On 1 April 1933, again on the Director's order, an agent reported 'his efforts to determine the names of the Congressmen and Senators who Val O'Farrell recently approached.' O'Farrell had been in Washington on 19 March, the agent reported, adding that he was 'unable to ascertain the names of the Congressmen or Senators or any other persons whom [O'Farrell] contacted while there.' The agent continued that Farley had 'visited New York on March 5th or 6th, shortly after [Roosevelt's] inauguration, and was in company with some politicians from Memphis and gave a dinner at the Pennsylvania Hotel, where he was stopping, which Val O'Farrell attended and there were a number of politicians present whose names are unknown at this time.'

Cummings had meanwhile apprised Hoover of additional information provided by Hogan. Hogan claimed to have learned that another New York City detective, George Eustace, who had an office adjoining O'Farrell's, had admitted that he had followed Mrs. James Farley 'in particular with reference to her visits to night clubs and speakeasies,' attempted to get 'a line on all cabinet officers and in particular Mrs. Cummings,' and tried to establish that Cummings had been friendly with Mr. and Mrs. George Mara and 'had been very intimate' with Mrs. Mara. Vehemently denying this allegation, Cummings told Hoover that he had learned from Hogan that President Hoover's former secretary, Lawrence Richey, was directing an organization headquartered in the Shoreham Hotel in Washington and was 'assembling information that could be used against the private and official lives of public officials connected with the Democratic administration.'

Thus briefed, Hoover promised Cummings that an 'appropriate investigation will be made' of Hogan's various allegations. Thenceforward, having assumed the duties of chief of the Roosevelt administration's secret police, he had Homer Cummings hooked.

On 29 July 1933 Cummings asked Hoover to continue as Director.

Notes to Chapter Six

1. Marro later elaborated, 'The "out of the swamps" quote was not my own. That was a quote from a long-time agent in New York. . . . I don't have it [the quote] handy, but the full quote was something to the effect: "They recruit them out of the swamps, bring them into the Bureau as clerks, get them a degree from some eighth-rate night school, and ten years later they're part of the

clique that's running the Bureau.'' His point was that headquarters in particular seemed to be made up of a large number of small-town Southerners — many of whom had started by pushing a mail cart through the Justice Department corridors while getting an accounting or law degree from a night school — who had little understanding of the complexities of urban crime.'

2. In a 7 June 1931 profile in his hometown newspaper, *The Cedar Rapids Gazette*, Tolson was described as 'a tall good-looking young man with the kind of piercing black eyes you read about in detective yarns.' The mythologizing had already begun.

3. A representative case, although more graphically documented than most, arose two years later when a newsletter written and distributed by George Menhinick and titled *Wall Street Forecast* dismissed Presdent Hoover's optimistic predictions of economic recovery as grandstanding and stressed the gravity of the country's economic problems. In an effort to silence Menhinick, Republican National Committee treasurer Joseph P. Nutt complained to presidential secretary Theodore Joslin in October 1931. Joslin forwarded the letter to Attorney General Mitchell, who, in turn, sent it to Director Hoover. Hoover immediately dispatched five agents to Menhinick's home in Syracuse, New York, to interview the naysayer. If the purpose was to intimidate, the effort succeeded, as one of the agents reported back to Hoover that he had found Menhinick 'thoroughly scared' and not likely to 'resume the dissemination of any information concerning the banks or other financial institutions.' The Director then apprised his superiors of the results of his efforts.

Eager to ingratiate himself with the Hoover administration, the Director assisted in a number of ways — some solicited, others volunteered. For instance, he forwarded to the White House detailed reports on individuals and organizations that had criticized the president and his policies, as well as information about the unsavory associates of the author of a book critical of the president. He repeated this assistance in 1945. Briefing then-former president Hoover on a forthcomng book financed by a California Communist, the Director emphasized that the book could be enjoined prior to publication, and promised to provide photostatic copies of the manuscript as it evolved. See Kenneth O'Reilly, *Hoover and the Un-Americans: The FBI, HUAC, and the Red Menace* (Philadelphia: Temple University Press, 1983), pp. 19–21; Donald Lisio, *The President and Protest: Hoover, Conspiracy, and the Bonus Riot* (Columbia: University of Missouri Press, 1974), pp. 240–41, 246–48, 250; Richard Norton Smith, *An Uncommon Man: the Triumph of Herbert Hoover* (New York: Simon & Schuster, 1984), pp. 27–28, 348.

4. Hottel may have been the first of the Bureau's Mormons, who eventually became a considerable presence in Bureau ranks. Like the Masons, a semisecret society, the Mormons, also known as the Church of Jesus Christ of Latter-Day Saints, do not permit women to share sacred rites with men. Likewise politically conservative, they rely on loyalty and rituals, rather than on theology, to hold the fraternity together. As Robert Lindsay observed in 1986 ('The Mormons', *New York Times Magazine*, 12 January 1986, pp. 24, 38, 40), 'Some of these rituals are similar to rites of the Masonic Lodge, to which many of the early Mormons belonged.' Lindsay quotes a Mormon philosopher, Sterling M. McMurrin: 'Mormonism is not simply a commitment to a theology or a church practice, but a social-cultural order.' Peggy Fletcher, publisher of *Sunstone*, a journal of liberal Mormon opinion, also quoted by Lindsay, describes Mormonism as 'unambiguous, simple and straightforward when life is full of ambiguity and chaos.'

5. Hugo Black was right: Hoover's position was political, or had become political, and that fact had already begun to affect the Director's actions. As A. A. Berle observed, 'The vital distinction between political officers and civil servants . . . depends on whether they enter or are absent from the dialogue of responsibility. Functionaries, mere transmitters of power decisions, ordinarily do not, indeed are not expected to, carry on any part of the dialogue process. Newsmen do not ask them questions. . . . But if, by chance, or circumstances, or capacity, the civil servant does form policy or make decisions, he is promptly drawn into the dialogue, whether he chooses to be or not.'

CHAPTER SEVEN

(1933–1935)
'CRUSADE AGAINST CRIME'

HOOVER'S REAPPOINTMENT as director of the nation's foremost detective agency received widespread publicity, but so self-effacing had his performance under the Republicans been that he was greeted almost as a new face. For the most part the press simply noted that the director-designate of the renamed Division of Investigation was a career civil servant who had served as a special assistant to the attorney general under A. Mitchell Palmer and as assistant director of the old Bureau under William J. Burns and thereafter had worked his way up.

Nevertheless, Hoover's nine-year exercise in restraint and quiet empire building had paid off. Unnoticed by the general public, he had gained an influential if narrow constituency in the nation's police and judicial establishments, in such powerful lobbies as the National Association of Manufacturers and the veterans' organizations, in the directorates of major corporations, among both publishers and writers in what the late A. J. Liebling of the *New Yorker* used to call the fourth estate – the nation's press ('Freedom of the press is guaranteed only to those who own one.') – and, not least, among the elected denizens of Capitol Hill, approximately half of whom were fellow Masons.

Of several dozen letters of congratulation that Hoover received from personal friends, almost all were either from spokesmen for powerful fraternal or corporate organizations – two from officials of the Pennsylvania Railroad and one from a Carnegie Steel Company executive, among them – or from senators or congressmen, most of them quite senior members from rural states. The letters reflect the particular care that Hoover had taken a year earlier to cultivate support among the southerners who were the New Deal's right flank. But perhaps the most telling, considering his later elevation to the chief judgeship of the Supreme Court, was a handwritten note from Associate Justice Stone, posted from his summer home at Isle-en-Haut, Maine, on 8 August 1933. Expressing his pleasure over Hoover's appointment, Stone contentedly recalled having 'had a hand in setting you on your present path' and continued, 'I believe you have been giving an example of what can be accomplished in law enforcement by clean methods. If this new venture has the success which I believe it will the country should be better informed about the methods which have prevailed in the bureau under your direction. You are in a position now to give an object lesson to the whole country.'

Stone's suggestion that Hoover publicize the Bureau's exploits was unnecessary — Hoover was already doing so — and clearly the justice was not aware of Hoover's success in monitoring radical activities. Not alone among Hoover's many superiors, Stone had flattered himself that he could manage his servant, that his own power and prestige were sufficient to ensure the subordinate's obedience. In short, Stone made the mistake of regarding Hoover as a functionary rather than as another and abler politician.

Hoover's handwritten reply combined impetuosity and shrewdness, not to mention his characteristic obsequiousness toward someone in a position of higher authority:

I have always viewed with considerable pride the fact that I was appointed Director of the Bureau of Investigation by you, and this in effect has always meant a great deal to me, officially and personally. I am not indulging in fulsome praise when I state that you are recognized throughout the country as one of the most able men who has [sic] ever held the office of Attorney General of the United States, and that reputation has followed you to the present high position which you hold. Viewed as scrupulously honest, fearless and liberal by the entire country, naturally the contact which any one has had with you carries to him a certain

149

degree of this high standard which you have attained in the minds of the people. Therefore, I know that much of the confidence and praise which the Bureau of Investigation received was largely due to the fact that it was while you were Attorney General that you brought about the reorganization of and restoring of confidence in the Bureau of Investigation . . .

I shall certainly try with the new duties and responsibilities which have been placed upon me to measure up to the standards which you have set as my goal in 1924, so that I may continue to have your confidence, faith and support. . . . I shall certainly see that under my administration of the new Division of Investigation, while of course some mistakes may be made, they will be the mistakes that involve honesty, integrity or clean administration.

Hoover's self-confidence was equally apparent in the story the *Star* ran in tandem with the announcement of his reappointment. Based on an interview conducted by Rex Collier, the first (from 1929) although not foremost of the Director's free publicists, it foreshadowed the exquisite deference that Hoover showed throughout the 1930s toward the aspirations of his new boss, Homer Cummings:

With the selection of J. Edgar Hoover as director of the soon-to-be-created United States Division of Investigation, Attorney General Cummings yesterday completed organization of his 'supreme command' for the Government's Nation-wide war on kidnappers and other racketeers.

Hoover, 38-year-old Washingtonian, whose development of the Bureau of Investigation into a world-famous detective agency won him promotion to the important new anti-crime post, will collaborate with Joseph B. Keenan, special assistant to the Attorney General, in a relentless drive on gang terrorism.

Plans for the crusade, the scope of which will exceed anything ever before attempted by Federal authorities, have in view the spreading of a co-ordinated web of Federal, State and local detective forces from which few criminals may hope to escape.

Other favorable articles followed, notably the first of a series of twenty-four color stories on the Bureau written for *American Magazine* between 1933 and 1940 by a Midwestern feature writer named Courtney Ryley Cooper, probably the most important of all of Hoover's publicists during the crucial 1930s and eventually, as ghost writer, the voice of Hoover himself. But, at the same time, several discordant notes sounded.

On 22 August the *Washington Daily News* published a frank harbinger of trouble, reporting Tennessee Democratic Senator Kenneth McKellar's opposition to Hoover's appointment to head the Division of Investigation. Noting McKellar's refusal to release the text of his letter of protest, the *Daily News* quoted the powerful southern Democrat as having opposed the appointment as 'vigorously as I know how.' The newspaper proceeded to detail the basis for McKellar's opposition:

Some months ago, while the Republican regime was still in power, the office of Senator McKellar, of whom [*sic*] there was no more severe critic of the G.O.P. and President Hoover, was ransacked. Apparently nothing was taken. Neither then nor now has the Senator commented on reports commonly heard about the Senate Office Building at that time that Justice Department agents had visited his office. He only remarks that about the time his office was ransacked, investigations of high public [Republican] officials were being demanded.

McKellar is the ranking Democrat on the Senate Appropriations Committee. This winter, the succeeding year's expenses for J. Edgar Hoover's division, and for Hoover's salary, will have to be appropriated for. McKellar is famous for his memory, and for his interest in the details of appropriations.

151

These charges that J. Edgar Hoover's Bureau had operated as the intelligence arm of the Hoover White House were repeated on 22 September in the *Passaic* [New Jersey] *News Herald*:

The wise boys of the administration will offer you small bets that many of the more important hold-overs in public office will be out of jobs before Congress returns.

Two men in particular are being sniped at by the Democratic politicians. One is J. Edgar Hoover, director of the Bureau of Investigation . . . Hoover was appointed head of the reorganized Bureau of Investigation despite the fact that Postmaster General Jim Farley was gunning for him. The head sleuth has been in the Bureau since 1917 [*sic*]. Some Democrats insist he did a lot of undercover work for Herbert Hoover that was largely political.

Finally, on 5 November, the *Washington Post* simply reported that Hoover was slated to go.

But these rumors were false alarms. The ambitious Director moved quickly to rebut allegations that he had served the political interests of the defeated Republican president. He also strove to ingratiate himself with Cummings, who, whether he found Hoover's explanations convincing or not, recognized that Hoover's obsessive interest in retaining the directorship made him a useful instrument to advance his own, and the president's, political goals. Indeed, the attorney general and the Director were soon working hand in glove to ready the last details of Cummings's anticrime crusade. Cummings, in fact, gave every evidence of trusting his subordinate to go along with what was transparently a highly political publicity campaign.

Thus girded by a common ambition, the New Deal's politically advantageous anticrime crusade was ready to begin. It had been several months in the making. Cummings from the outset had seen his office as a pulpit from which to sell the New Deal. Alarmed by the breakdown of democratic self-government in Europe — first in Russia, then in Italy, and now in Germany with Hitler's ascent to the chancellorship in January 1933 — and shaken by the kind of instability at home that had foreshadowed totalitarian regimes elsewhere, Americans, Cummings believed, above all wanted reassurance. And it was his immodest belief, notwithstanding the president's ringing declaration in his inaugural address that 'the only thing we have to fear is fear itself,' that he was the one destined to provide it.

A politician with flair, Cummings was determined to be an activist attorney general. A Connecticut Yankee standing well over six feet tall, a dapper dresser who wore straw boaters and Fedoras and pince-nez, he, like Roosevelt, saw the crime problem as a clear opportunity. Building on some of the insights afforded by the Wickersham Commission's investigation, he defined the problem in admittedly simplistic terms — as a war between good guys and bad guys — and then proposed to solve it, to the everlasting credit of the administration.

However, unlike the authors of the Wickersham Commission report, who favored a campaign to arouse public opinion in support of *local* law enforcement, Cummings intended to use the issue of crime to involve the federal government directly in the areas of law enforcement that traditionally had been the responsibility of state and local governments (and traditionally had been badly managed by them)[1] — specifically through an extension of the legal authority of the Justice Department's new Division of Investigation. And FDR agreed. In July 1933, therefore, the president announced that he was transferring to the Division of Investigation the obsolescent Prohibition Enforcement Unit,[2] which had been assigned to the Justice Department (although not to the Bureau) in 1930, following the early departures of six Treasury Department directors in twelve years.

All of these plans were Cummings's. Hoover's quest for political power, although implicit in his character and already foreshadowed by his discreet empire building, still had not gone beyond A. A. Berle's second degree — that is, he enjoyed power but without being seen. In the ensuing months he would amply demonstrate his readiness to enter the field of political combat. But it was Cummings and Cummings alone who began the Division's public relations blitz.

Cummings's first priority was to extend his authority in order to justify retaining the force of revenuers, as the prohibition men were still called, and this he did in a couple of ways. First, at his direction, Justice Department lawyers drew up a so-called Twelve-Point Program — twelve bills for consideration by Congress at its spring 1934 session. These were designed to augment the barely enlarged federal law enforcement authority that had been granted by Congress in the New Deal's epochal first 'Hundred Days.' To this slightly broadened authority, Cummings proposed to add authority over bank robbery, racketeering, and certain catchall crimes that would expand federal jurisdiction in an unprecedented way.

Second, to support the Justice Department's case for the Twelve-Point Program, Cummings designed an ambitious anticrime public relations campaign. The essence of the campaign was the idea, well planted in the consciousness of the nation through the new medium of radio, that serious crimes were a 'declaration of war' against society and a moral affront to the conscience of the nation (a bank robbery in Kansas, for example, could wipe out the savings of an entire town). One purpose of the campaign was to arouse public opinion, long lulled by the romantic portrayal of criminals as heroes in popular culture. But the main purpose was to promote the idea of a 'super police force,' which Roosevelt had endorsed in his speech in July, a force armed with the new powers contained in the Twelve-Point Program.

The crusade began in August 1933, with Cummings declaring in a speech to the Daughters of the American Revolution: 'We are now engaged in a war that threatens the safety of our country — a war with the organized forces of crime.' Portraying the crisis as the outcome of a

154

conspiracy unprecedented in the history of the nation, he rationalized his call for a federal police with an argument paraphrased by a contemporary critic as follows:

> Crime, which was increasing to vast proportions, was no longer a local phenomenon but was conducted by interstate gangs who operated across State lines. Moreover, modern means of transportation had given criminals tremendous advantages in eluding capture [i.e., by moving from jurisdiction to jurisdiction] . . . On the other hand, State prosecution was breaking down. The police of the great cities were hopelessly corrupt. The rural system of crime control which was lodged in the sheriff and the constable was unsuited to modern conditions. If the elements of an offense were not all committed in a single State, such criminals might sometimes escape prosecution altogether.

Taking as his model a local campaign of the blue-ribbon Chicago Crime Commission in the early 1920s, Cummings publicized a 'Public Enemies' list containing the names of the nation's ten most-wanted criminals. Most of those he chose, small-time operators to a man, had already been identified by the Bureau in connection with a crime wave then going on in the Middle West, and all of them subsequently became legendary in the annals of crime.

The most dangerous was Charles 'Pretty Boy' Floyd, a twenty-five-year-old desperado who, together with others, had perpetrated the so-called Kansas City Massacre, in which the fugitive mail robber Frank Nash and four of his police captors, one of them a Division man, had been gunned down in an apparent attempt to free Nash. George 'Machine Gun' Kelly, the kidnapper of a wealthy Oklahoma oilman, Charles Urschel, had been sought ever since Urschel's release in early 1933, when, in collaboration with Hoover's agents, he had successfully identified his abductor. Lester Gillis, alias 'Baby Face Nelson,' an escapee from prison, was wanted for murder. The Barker-Karpis gang, led by Kate 'Ma' Barker and Alvin 'Old Creepy' Karpis, had robbed and terrorized the southern Midwest for more than a year, as had Clyde Barrow and Bonnie Parker, of *Bonnie and Clyde* fame.

The eventual number-one spot on the attorney general's list of most-wanted criminals, however, was reserved for a comparative nonentity, John Dillinger, who had held up several midwestern banks after his parole from prison in April 1933 but at no time, then or later, committed a known capital offense. (Dillinger was put on the list only after he fled across a state line in a stolen automobile, thereby committing a Dyer Act offense.) He seems, on the contrary, to have been chosen solely for his star quality. Youthful and brash, a well-known womanizer, he jeered at local and state policemen every time he eluded their traps.

During its early months the crusade against crime was largely a war of words – many of them spoken by Cummings, but with Hoover following up in speeches written for him by Rex Collier and, later, Courtney Ryley Cooper. The Division's pursuit of its most-wanted criminals at this time tended to be synchronized with pending congressional action, the conspicuous exception being kidnapping in which the victim had been transported across a state line. In that case the so-called Lindbergh Law, enacted in March 1932 in the wake of the kidnapping of the infant Charles Augustus Lindbergh, Jr., applied. But it granted federal jurisdiction only in cases in which the victim was *known* to have been transported across a state line and therefore did not empower the federal government to enter the then-unsolved Lindbergh case itself, although Hoover's Division of Investigation played an energetic advisory role.

Jurisdiction did exist, however, in the Urschel case. Hoover's agents, working night and day, traced the abductor to a small farm in Texas owned by Machine Gun Kelly's in-laws. The Division's brilliant detective work was widely publicized, and the chase ended with Kelly's apprehension on 26 September 1933. Taken alive by the government men, Kelly reportedly shouted, 'Don't shoot, G-Men,' thereby imparting his own high visibility to the department's public relations campaign.

Cummings had won his first battle in the war against crime

and had a test case of the Division's effectiveness to present to Congress. But although his purpose had been to promote himself as the leader of the forces of good against the forces of evil, and thereby to symbolize in himself the regenerative strength of the New Deal, ironically it was Hoover who emerged as the public hero. In a United News Service dispatch reporting Kelly's capture, the *Pittsburgh Post-Gazette* described it as the 'Federal Government's ultimatum to the underworld that kidnapping is an "extremely unsafe" business' and attributed the challenge to Hoover. The news story continued:

His eyes heavy from loss of sleep, the 38 year old director of the Government's man-hunters was at his desk as usual all day cleaning up details of the case.

'Kelly's capture means something to the underworld that the average person doesn't understand,' Hoover said in an exclusive interview with the United News.

'The criminal fears death more than anything else. At heart they are all rats — dirty, yellow rats. A gangster will kill you, oh sure, if he has a machine gun and you are absolutely helpless. They like to think they are above the law. But they actually operate most of the time with one eye on the electric chair.'

Deploring 'sentimentality' in the treatment of criminals, especially leniency by parole officers, Hoover, in his emerging new persona, affected the punchy delivery of a prosecuting attorney while taking the hard line of the cop on the beat, both of which stances would have been unseemly in an attorney general.[3] Thus, while Cummings continued to take the high road in the Crusade Against Crime, seeking to enlist the support of a bipartisan coalition of New Deal activists and conservative hard-liners, Hoover went straight to the masses.

Still, more successes in that season were not to be. The remains of an infant boy were discovered near the Lindbergh home in northern New Jersey, but despite the remorseless activity of police in New York and New Jersey, not to

157

mention their indefatigable advisers in the Division of Investigation, the perplexing Lindbergh case, a national *cause célèbre*, remained unsolved. And the other cases on the attorney general's list were beyond the Division's jurisdictional reach. Thus, while Cummings continued his Crusade — and, to be sure, Hoover increased his load of speeches to veterans' groups, business associations, and the like — the Director got his house in order in preparation for the battles that would follow anticipated congressional approval of the Twelve-Point Program.

Directly below himself in the chain of command, Hoover installed the so-called Big Five. Harold Nathan, fifty-three, assistant director in charge of investigations, was a native New Yorker and fellow Kappa Alpha who had entered the Bureau on 31 March 1917 and been named assistant director by Hoover on 1 May 1925. Clyde Tolson, thirty-three, assistant director in charge of personnel and administration, had occupied that position since 26 January 1931. Hugh H. Clegg, thirty-four, one of the Division's three inspectors (who made spot checks in the field and reported on them directly to Hoover) had charge of investigations and violations of federal law. A native Mississippian, he had graduated from Millsaps College. Like Hoover and Tolson, he was a George Washington University law graduate and a member of Kappa Alpha.

James S. Egan, forty-three, inspector in charge of accounting and preparation of accounting evidence for prosecutions, was a native of Omaha, Nebraska, who had joined the Bureau on 6 June 1922 and been named inspector by Hoover in 1927. Finally, John J. Edwards, forty, the inspector in charge of fingerprints and the technical lab, was a native of Coal Creek, Tennessee. A fellow Kappa Alpha and graduate of the George Washington University law school, he had been recruited by Hoover on 10 November 1931 and promoted to inspector on 16 December 1932.

Guy Hottel at this time was still Hoover's personal bodyguard but was in line for promotion to SAC of the Washington field office, pending further testing of his erratic character. Frank Baughman, the nominal head of ballistics investigations, had been so downgraded that he was shortly put in charge of drawing up the specifications for the Director's new bulletproof car.

At this time the Division had only 266 special agents and 60 accountants nationwide, not including the force of prohibition men, fewer than had been on the payroll when Hoover took charge. But most of the men in the Division were young and ready to exchange the sedentary work of investigation for the hazards of the war on crime. The most conspicuous exception was Hoover himself, who continued to direct the Bureau's affairs from the safety of his office in Washington.

By the turn of the year, the attorney general's crusade had enjoyed sufficient success to enlist the open support of the president. In his annual address to Congress, on 3 January 1934, Roosevelt termed crime a threat to 'our security.' Its depredations, he said, 'call on the strong arm of Government for their immediate suppression; they call also on the country for an aroused public opinion.'

Taking advantage of the snowball effect of the continuing Dillinger news story, Cummings then made his own play to the stands, admonishing the Investigation Division's agents to 'Shoot to Kill − then count ten.' Although the federal police were still hamstrung by jurisdictional restraints, the propaganda campaign was now in full swing.

However, Hoover as yet had no propaganda machine of his own. The prodigious Crime Records Division, though already in existence, had not yet become the publicity mill that would consume more than half of the later Bureau's energies. Except for a small group of speechwriters and his conservative claque in the Washington press corps, Hoover was still as much on his own as he had been with Stone.

Then, on 14 February 1934, Henry Suydam, the Washington bureau chief of the *Brooklyn Eagle* and a personal friend of the president, called on Tolson to discuss a writing project he proposed to undertake for *Forum* magazine. Tolson thereupon advised the Director that the editor of *Forum*, Henry Goddard Leach, was 'particularly desirous of using a story indicating the success of the

Division of Investigation in handling kidnapping cases and, to a limited extent, explaining the functions and organizations of the Division.' In effect, Hoover was being invited to become Berle's power holder of the third degree – one of those who 'by force of personality, by idealist motivation, by personal capacity, or from ambition, assume as much power as they can, intending to hold and extend it.' Hoover directed Tolson to cooperate.

Suydam's article appeared in April and lavished praise on both Hoover and the Division of Investigation. In response, the Director, who had granted Suydam a single interview, wrote to thank the reporter for his story and directed Tolson to place Suydam's name 'on the list of persons to receive various releases and documents issued by the Division.[4] I would [also] suggest that a copy of the article be forwarded to the Attorney General.'

The upshot of Hoover's self-promotion was that Attorney General Cummings, after reading the article, hired Suydam as a special assistant to handle the department's press relations and, incidentally, those of the Division of Investigation. Hoover was instructed to supply the urbane New Yorker with whatever materials he required to publicize the department's achievements.

Suydam was Cummings's man and although Hoover succeeded in winning Suydam's favor, the Director nevertheless continued to conduct his own public relations operation, such as it was. Suydam did project Hoover onto the national scene[5] and put the Director in touch with the country's leading radio and movie producers, notably Jack Warner and Samuel Goldwyn. But Hoover was unwilling to delegate entire responsibility for public relations to so obvious an outsider.

Instead, that year he recruited a young man who was destined to become, with the single exception of Hoover himself, the most influential figure in the history of the Bureau. Louis B. Nichols, subsequently known at the Bureau as 'L.B.,' or, less respectfully, 'Nick the Greek,' a twenty-nine-year-old Greek American from the northern Midwest, had graduated from Kalamazoo College and

Washington University law school. While working as a public relations officer for the Young Men's Christian Association and attending law school, he chanced to hear 'K-7,' one of the promotional soaps based on the Bureau and, after receiving his law degree, presented himself at the Seat of Government in Washington.

Hoover seems to have immediately recognized a man of his own stamp and hired Nichols forthwith to promote the Bureau.[6] Nor were the Director's sensitive antennae dysfunctional. 'Known at headquarters as a man who believed himself capable of selling anyone anything,' Nichols was the only person at the Bureau who could challenge Hoover or persuade him to reconsider his decisions. (On his retirement in 1957 after reaching the age of fifty, required for a pension, Nichols went to work for Louis S. Rosentiel, the ultraconservative head of Schenley Industries, at a salary reported to be $100,000 a year, and persuaded his new boss to found and endow, initially with a gift of one million dollars, the J. Edgar Hoover Foundation at Valley Forge, to promulgate the values of the Director and inculcate in American youth, later flown in each week for the purpose, the importance of 'Americanism.')

Nichols was placed on the payroll just in time to orchestrate the highly publicized manhunt for Alvin Karpis. However, the action had already shifted in March to Capitol Hill, where the Congress had begun its consideration of the attorney general's Twelve-Point Program. Cummings and Hoover came armed to the teeth with statistics and other data, although from the outset it was clear that the resistance shown by the previous Congress to enactment of the Lindbergh Bill had withered under the glare of Cummings's publicity. The national consensus that the G-Men should be allowed to carry firearms, for instance, and be granted the power of arrest was all but irresistible, and only the bravest and most principled proponent of states' rights dared to question it, so gravely had the Great Depression and the New Deal undercut congressional suspicion of expanding federal responsibilities.

The debate continued for three months and revolved

around an idea first tossed onto the table by Roosevelt himself when he was a member of the Wickersham Commission – the need for an American Scotland Yard, an American national police. Critics sought to point out that Scotland Yard was in fact only the investigative unit of the London metropolitan police minus the separate police force of the City of London and that it investigated elsewhere in Britain only at the express invitation of local police. But, again, these were voices crying in the wilderness, the more so after another of Hoover's unseasoned agents was killed in a shootout with gangsters in rural Little Bohemia, Wisconsin, during an unsuccessful attempt to capture John Dillinger, by then Public Enemy Number One.[7]

In May Congress passed six of the Justice Department's twelve bills. In June it passed three more. Hoover's agents as a result were granted full powers to arrest and carry firearms (of any kind), and the Division's jurisdiction was enormously expanded. A fugitive felon bill was passed, and the Lindbergh Law was amended to provide for constructive flight across a state line (and thus for federal jurisdiction) after one week.

Signing the legislation, the president declared: 'Federal men are constantly facing machine gun fire in the pursuit of gangsters, and gangster extermination cannot be made completely effective so long as a substantial part of the public looks with tolerance upon known criminals . . . or applauds efforts to romanticize crime.' The criminals, according to the war theory of crime, had declared war on America, and now America had declared war on them. The fighting could begin.

On 22 July John Dillinger was killed. Melvin Purvis, Chicago SAC and, incidentally, also a Kappa Alpha, had assured Dillinger's current mistress, Anna Sage, the famous 'woman in red,' that if she would betray the bandit by accompanying him to the Biograph Theater in a red dress, he would try to stall a deportation proceeding against her. As Dillinger left the theater, he was gunned down by a small army of Chicago police and government men. (Purvis was subsequently forced out of the Bureau, apparently for having the temerity to take the credit for the kill, and Miss Sage was deported.)

On 20 September Bruno Richard Hauptmann, a thirty-three-year-old German-born carpenter who had fought for the Kaiser during the war, was arrested in New York and charged with the Lindbergh kidnapping after he paid for gas with a marked Treasury Bill, a part of the ransom money. (The New York police commissioner subsequently condemned Hoover for trying to take the credit when Hoover and his men, as it turned out, had played only a minor role in facilitating the apprehension.)[8]

On 22 October Pretty Boy Floyd, who had dispatched three more special agents since the Kansas City Massacre, was apprehended and 'shot to rags,' as Ambrose Bierce would have said. Two months later 'Ma' Barker and her son Fred died in a hail of bullets as they tried to elude special agents closing in on their hideout in Florida, and in early 1935 Clyde Barrow was killed by a Texas posse as he fled from Hoover's men.

Thus in less than a year the attorney general could claim, with some justice, that his new federal police had checked the nation's crime wave. Only it was no longer *his* federal police. For by the beginning of 1935, Cummings's Crusade Against Crime had become a popular crusade, so popular, in fact, that, in the words of one analyst, 'it had taken on a life of its own.' And the hero of the piece was no longer Homer Cummings, but the young, neatly packaged supercop, J. Edgar Hoover.

In the meantime, though, Cummings's government by melodrama had moved mountains. In November 1934 Congress promptly granted his request for 200 additional agents, and the next year agreed to double the budget of the renamed Federal Bureau of Investigation, whose new name suggested its growing autonomy. In December 1934 Cummings, addressing his own Conference on Crime, had called for a 'West Point' of law enforcement, and the following July he presided at the foundation of the National Police Academy, an FBI-administered training school in Washington for police brought in from all over the country.

163

In all of these developments Hoover had taken a strong hand, providing ideas, plans, and always statistics to bolster Bureau budget requests. And Cummings, preoccupied as he was with numerous legislative battles, happily left the store in Hoover's hands.

So for the time being there was enough credit to go around. Cummings still regarded Hoover as his subaltern – a view Hoover took pains to reinforce – and in any case the attorney general soon had his hands full defending the constitutionality of New Deal legislation and then, in 1937, handling Roosevelt's Supreme Court-packing scheme.

Another major victory for 'law and order' was added in April 1935 when Warner Brothers released the feature film *G-Men*, starring a galvanizing young Irish-American actor named James Cagney as an FBI agent. At a stroke the tough, clean-cut, close-cropped Cagney became the prototype of the government policeman, so much so that Hoover began issuing new regulations requiring his agents to lose weight, cut their hair, improve their dress, and in general sharpen their image. Special agents were instructed to keep appearances in mind when interviewing candidates for employment, inasmuch as the 'impressions made by Special Agents on the public have a great deal to do with developing cooperation on the part of the public.[9]

The same month that Cagney's G-Man appeared on the screen, Courtney Ryley Cooper's *Ten Thousand Public Enemies* was published. The first of many mass-market books about the Bureau, it drew on the careful mythologizing Cooper had already done on the Bureau's behalf in several popular magazine articles. The Cooper myth in essence was a melodrama involving villains preying on unoffending, ordinary Americans, fearless young G-Men using an array of ingenious weapons and arcane technologies, and their lieutenants reporting through a flawless command structure to the supercop at the top, 'the most feared man the underworld has ever known' – J. Edgar Hoover.

By portraying crime as an epidemic disease that at any

moment might steal into any home in America, Cooper appealed to the morbid anxieties of his readers. 'The dreamy-eyed manicurist who files away so enthusiastically at your nails,' he wrote, 'may be thinking only of closing time, when she can hurry to meet the man whose 'moll' she will eventually become . . . it is almost certain that the very instruments which shape your fingernails have performed the same service for men who have known the cell block and the mess hall of prisons.'

From its very inception this G-Man myth was designed to enable the administration to manipulate public opinion – to 'arouse' public opinion, in the president's word. And the cynical manipulation was justified precisely on the ground that only an aroused public opinion could turn the tide against crime. Moreover, so successful had the myth-making been that Hoover, who had covertly assisted Cooper in his popular writings, put the reporter on the Bureau payroll. Serving as Hoover's ghostwriter, Cooper then authored a series of Hoover byline articles, published in *American Weekly* and other popular magazines, extolling the Bureau's success in the war on crime.

For the moment Hoover was in the catbird seat, nicely symbolized by a new office on Pennsylvania Avenue overlooking the Capitol. For in 1934, after nearly ten years in makeshift third-floor quarters in the Justice Department's old building on K Street (one of several Justice Department buildings), the entire department had moved into a new red-tile-roofed stone home of its own at the east end of the just-completed Federal Triangle.

'The Director's office,' Jack Alexander wrote in a 1937 *New Yorker* profile of Hoover, 'is a large, stately room, carpeted in cherry red. From the doorway to the desk, which is at the opposite end of the room, is a walk of thirty or thirty-five feet. A few paces to the rear of the Director, as he sits down at his desk, are two tall brass standards, topped by brass eagles and clingingly embraced by American flags . . . In the anteroom where visitors wait to be admitted to the Director's presence the most compelling decorative object is a startling white plastic facsimile of John Dillinger's death mask. It stares, empty-eyed, from under the glass of an exhibit case.'

In stark contrast was the little second-floor front bedroom on Seward Square which was the Director's office at home and to which he brought a briefcase full of work every night. There he kept the trinkets and mementoes collected in his childhood, empty dance programs, movie ticket stubs, and cheap statuettes of naked warriors and bathing sirens – his own version of the publishing tycoon's little sled 'Rosebud' in Orson Welles's film *Citizen Kane*. He and Annie had husbanded their money over the years, so that there was no question that they could afford a more comfortable house. And the neighborhood had become run down, heralding an influx of blacks, so that the lilywhite suburbs of northwest Washington beyond Rock Creek Park looked better than ever. But Annie still refused to move.

How many times, he thought, had Ferguson driven them out to Connecticut Avenue to look at houses for sale? And how many times had she found something wrong? A step down to the living room. Too shady a garden. Always little things, but insurmountable all the same. She was old now, seventy-five, set in her ways. Well, he would just have to put up with the situation until she died.

The thought must have stung him. Ferguson had died the year before – in 1934. And Lillian's husband, Fred, had just died – his brother-in-law. They said it was pneumonia. He and Annie had missed the funeral. In truth, he hadn't much cared. But Annie was another matter. She was his mother, his home. She entertained for him, laid on the Sunday after-church receptions, made dinner for him and Clyde. How could he live without her?

He didn't know.

Notes to Chapter Seven

1. The previous administration's position had been stated by Attorney General Mitchell before Congress in 1932: 'You are never

going to correct the crime situation in this country by having Washington jump in . . . Unless we can stimulate public opinion to get the right kind of men in our local governments, and to see that they do their duty and clean up those conditions, they will not be cleaned up.' Quoted in Max Lowenthal, *The Federal Bureau of Investigation* (New York: William Sloan, 1950), p. 414.

2. Congress had repealed the Eighteenth Amendment in February 1933, subject to ratification by two-thirds of the states, which was completed in December.

3. In fact the new 'hard cop' persona was almost entirely sham, as Hoover had never even been trained to fire a handgun.

4. This is the first recorded example of Hoover's longstanding practice of selectively releasing news to the press. Friends were favored, foes frozen out.

5. He was following the advice of Fulton Oursler, later senior editor of the *Reader's Digest*, to 'make G-Men heroes.' Quoted (from newsman James Early) in Kenneth O'Reilly, 'A New Deal for the FBI: The Roosevelt Administration, Crime Control, and National Security,' *Journal of American History*, 69 (1982): 643.

6. He also ultimately came to regard Nichols as a surrogate son, and Nichols reciprocated by naming *his* son after Hoover.

7. The killing outraged Hoover, who had come to regard the Division as an extension of himself. Unlike the Kansas City Massacre, in which a Bureau man had been trapped with local police, the Little Bohemia incident was seen as a direct attack on the Division, which had planned and orchestrated the bungled raid. From then on Hoover's pursuit of Dillinger was remorseless.

8. The young German's subsequent trial, according to documents in the FBI's file on the case obtained by Hauptmann's widow and son nearly fifty years after his execution, glossed over improprieties so serious as to cast some doubt on his guilt.

9. Denying any intent 'in any way to infringe upon [sic] the[ir] personal liberties,' Hoover nevertheless demanded that 'the personal conduct of the employees of this Bureau be of such character as to warrant no criticism from any of the other officials of the Department or any private citizen.' – SACs were to 'report promptly to the Director at Washington any activities which in their estimation, may be prejudicial to the degree of confidence and respect which this Bureau is seeking to establish.' (SAC Letter no. 386, 5 August 1924, FBI 66-04-x71.)

CHAPTER EIGHT

(1935–1940)
G-MAN

CIRCUMSTANCE more than anything else had placed Hoover in his new position of autonomous power. At the same time it placed the forty-year-old Director in jeopardy, for as a federal agency head in Franklin Roosevelt's administration, he was fair game not only for his old enemies on the left but also for the anti-New Deal irreconcilables, both Republicans and Democrats, on the right.

Moreover, he was sorely beleaguered at home, where his sole companion, the only personal anchor he had known in his life, Annie, had become ill with cancer. Edgar may not have known the nature of her complaint – other members of the family were not told – but the progress of the disease eventually obliged him to hire a nurse, and thereafter he could hardly have denied that his mother was dying.

At first they both behaved as if nothing was wrong. Annie went about her business at home in her usual compulsive manner, and Edgar, although increasingly attentive despite the growing pressures of his office, allowed himself two extended holidays with Tolson and Hottel, in 1936 – one to Miami in February for the races at Hialeah and the other to the Colorado Rockies in September.[1] But time clearly was running out, and thereafter he stayed closer to home. The demands of his office likewise were growing meteorically, especially as he had every intention of securing his hold on an increasingly powerful (and coveted) post.

Hoover's and Cummings's press agency had paid off, but mostly for Edgar. Honors poured in, beginning in 1937, when the National Institute of Social Scientists awarded him its gold medal for 'distinguished service to humanity.' One of four recipients that year, he shared the honor, at a dinner attended by about 300 guests at New York's Waldorf-Astoria Hotel, with James Rowland Angell, the president of Yale, Wesley Clair Mitchell, professor of economics at Columbia, and Mary Louise Curtis Bok, the founder and president of the Curtis Institute of Music.

Unable to attend the celebration because of her illness, Annie wired her congratulations to New York: 'My thoughts are with you tonight Edgar and I am proud and happy that you are my son.' The parental approbation must have seemed doubly sweet, considering that the previous year Dick had resigned in disgust from the Steamboat Inspection Service and retired to his hardscrabble farm in Glendale and that Lillian, now a widow, was living in near penury in her ruined colonial in Lanham. Only Edgar had made good in the end, and in the meantime he had made even better.

For Hoover had also emerged as something of a social lion, seen with celebrities at New York's Stork Club and with the very rich at Palm Beach. And on these excursions outside Washington, there was handsome Clyde Tolson, off to his right and a few steps behind, and, in front, the redoubtable Guy Hottel, his gun barely concealed under a double-breasted blue blazer perfectly tailored to his awesome physique – all of them dressed to kill.

The movie *G-Men* had marked the beginning of a new era for Hoover. No longer the creature of Homer Cummings but the creation of Courtney Ryley Cooper and Hollywood, the top cop laid down even stricter Bureau regulations to ensure the smooth maintenance of the G-Man myth (and to establish his own authority and indispensability). First, no news story emanating from the Bureau was to appear except over the Director's signature. Second, no credit could be accepted for the Bureau's work except by the Director, who might then share it with others not named. Third, only the Director could speak for the Bureau about matters of policy and ongoing cases, especially announcements of captures and kills. Fourth, to avoid conflicting accounts and any possible embarrassment to the Bureau, all speeches by agents to any public group 'which contain editorializing, predictions or comment on national problems or policies' were to be submitted for prior review and approval. Nor were agents to recommend to local and state police officials any books not listed in the bibliography prepared at FBI headquarters and issued under Hoover's imprimatur. Within a tightly centralized bureaucracy, then, there was to be a virtual cult of personality. Everything sprang from the brow of the Director. As Hoover would have it, in the words of Ralph Waldo Emerson, reputedly his favorite philosopher, 'An institution is the lengthened shadow of one man.'[2]

But not everyone was fooled by the Bureau's imagery, least of all the stalwart conservatives who defended states' rights and deplored the expanded federal powers ushered in by Roosevelt's New Deal. As a fellow traveling beneficiary of Roosevelt's grandstanding leadership style, Hoover galled precisely those conservatives who deplored the New Deal's assault on regionalism and laissez-faire doctrines. Deeply suspicious of centralized power, many thoughtful Americans found the whole G-Man pose preposterous. Greatly troubled by the rank manipulations going on, they saw in J. Edgar Hoover and his free-wheeling police the very thing they had dreaded in the Bureau from the start. According to this view, Hoover, despite his own conservative bias, was a menace and had to be stopped.

At the other extreme, articulating the view of liberal criminologists, Justin Miller, the chairman of the attorney general's Advisory Committee on Crime, condemned the Director's lack of professionalism. Commenting acerbically on Hoover's frequent public pronouncements on such subjects as arrest, probation, parole, and the work of prosecutors, Miller doubted that the Director's program 'will accomplish as much good as it will harm,' adding, 'I am satisfied that the people have been stirred sufficiently, so far as their baser emotional reactions are concerned, as to the importance of hunting down and killing outlaws and that it is time for emphasis to be given to the deeper implications involved in the problem of crime control.' Miller urged the 'importance of preventive and curative measures,' remarking that 'I have never heard Mr. Hoover reveal much acquaintance or understanding [of such measures] and I have heard him on several occasions reveal an intolerance and ignorance which cannot but provoke resentment and antagonism from those who are concerned with those phases of the problem.'

Fearing the impact of such criticisms, Hoover had his agents monitor all public commentary on his directorship. Apprised thereby of one ominous development, he alerted the attorney general to 'some information which I have just received from a thoroughly reliable source.' According to Hoover's source, Emil Hurja, an assistant to Postmaster General James Farley and presidential political intelligence agent, and several of his friends 'were going to get that "bastard" Hoover.' The Director also reported 'that they had already picked the man for Hoover's job and that Hoover will not last in his job much longer . . . that Hoover was 'shooting off his mouth' too much concerning politics and the corruption therein . . . [and Hurja] and a friend had discussed the matter with the President, who had concurred with them in their views.'

Hoover soon encountered a more immediate threat when, in March, the Senate Appropriations Committee, acting on an amendment to the House bill proposed by the committee's conservative chairman, Kenneth McKellar, [3] reduced the Bureau's authorization by $225,000, cutting by less than a fourth the Bureau's proposed budget increase. The measure seemed innocent enough to most observers, but to Hoover it smacked of hostility, and he fought it — successfully.

But after provisionally reversing the House's action and restoring the Budget Bureau's original recommendation, McKellar's subcommittee summoned the Director in April to defend his budget increase. There, McKellar ridiculed the Director's crime statistics,[4] derided his heroics, and taunted him with never having made an arrest. Using material obviously obtained from other federal investigating agencies, the senator accused Hoover of having stolen the show in the Lindbergh case when it was the Treasury men who had really traced Hauptmann. McKellar then proceeded to grill Hoover about his self-serving versions of other recent and famous cases. Perhaps most ominous of all, he implied that Hoover and the Bureau were wasting the taxpayer's money on publicity.

Hoover weathered the storm, but he wasted no time preparing for the next. The next month Alvin Karpis was apprehended in New Orleans in a much-publicized encounter, with Hoover flown in for the pinch. Before the month was over, two other, less notorious kidnappers were also smoked out, and Hoover again made the arrests. The spectacle of the by-then forty-one-year-old Director personally pursuing armed felons struck skeptical observers as ludicrous, especially as the heroics appeared so obviously staged, but the stories made great copy and the heroics went on.

Identifying Hoover's press agentry with that of other New Deal agencies, conservatives renewed their assault in June, after the Senate had restored the threatened $225,000. The opening gun was a long profile on the Director appearing on the front page of the *Chicago Tribune's* Sunday magazine for 21 June 1936. Written by the *Tribune's* Washington bureau chief, Walter Trohan, and entitled 'Chief of the G-Men — Record of His Career,' it displayed all the elements of a high-level conspiracy:

> For subtle mixture of fact and fancy the career of J. Edgar Hoover, No. 1 G-man by virtue of his turgescent official title, . . . is a fascinating study in the molding of a myth.
>
> In less than three years a tide of printer's ink, accompanied by a roar of sound films and radio programs, has given heroic stature to a relatively obscure bureaucrat, the son and grandson of undistinguished toilers in the federal red tape vineyards. Behind the precipitous rise were years of preparation, for Mr. Hoover, like the cautious conspirator, did not disclose himself to a startled public until he was certain he could command its attention.

Trohan dwelt on the other federal investigators' assessment of Hoover and his Bureau as 'a Keystone cop and . . . callow drug store cowboys with twitchy trigger fingers and a love of the limelight.' Representing the Director as a creature of the hated New Deal, Trohan depicted him as especially skilled 'in the political arena – his position alone bespeaks that. Further, the number of southerners in the ranks of G-men, a movement which took place shortly before the New Deal came into office and at a time when Democratic senators and representatives were preparing for the committee chairmanships they now hold, gives evidence that the director knows how to court favor.'

The Bureau had expanded its staff from 358 agents to 603, Trohan observed, reversing both its nonpublic role and its limited size in the 1920s; both trends were tied directly to the New Deal:

For the first nine years in his office Hoover proceeded quietly, without any search for public acclaim. He was more careful in the selection of agents than his predecessors and subjected them to stringent examination based on qualifications devised by himself . . . In those days D.J. [Department of Justice] men were bird dogs for local police; they pointed to the criminal, let local police make arrests, and disappeared. The public demand for an end to kidnaping which followed the Lindbergh outrage brought a radical change in the department. Congress made kidnaping across state lines a federal offense and about the same time gave the bureau jurisdiction over national bank robberies. With these acts came the authority to make arrests and carry weapons. The chatter of machine guns and popping of pistols that felled four agents and eight desperadoes in two years followed. Over the air and on the screen the fire was repeated, and out of the welter of dramatic gore Hoover emerged as the leading criminal chaser of all time.

Trohan emphasized the fraudulence of this image making, quoting from the record a colloquy between Senator McKellar and Hoover in which the latter tried doggedly but unpersuasively to defend his contention that the Bureau had solved the Lindbergh case. In this exposition, Trohan concluded, 'Mr. Hoover gave no credit to treasury men who listed the [Treasury] notes and directed the early investigation so important to the solution of the case.'[5]

For the first time a newsman had really gotten a fix on Hoover, but the Director, ever mindful of his position,[6] moved adroitly to neutralize Trohan's attack. In a personal and confidential memorandum to the attorney general enclosing a copy of Trohan's caustic piece, Hoover disclosed that the reporter had:

  procured his information largely from governmental
  sources, and mentioned in particular the Post Office
  Department; a Mr. Woody attached to the United
  States Secret Service at the White House; Elmer Irey,
  Chief of the Intelligence Division of the Bureau of
  Internal Revenue of the United States Treasury
  Department; and Colonel Starling of the United States
  Secret Service, attached to the White House.

Hoover itemized the alleged libels of the aforementioned public officials, speculated about the motives for their hostility, and deemed 'most reprehensible' their willingness to furnish Trohan 'with some of the misinformation . . . obvious inaccuracies and misstatement[s] of fact' that were publicized in the article. No federal employee, he insisted, had a right to abet these efforts to constrain the FBI or to impugn his leadership.

Meanwhile the hypersensitive Director had dealt with a second public attack by Justin Miller. In yet another personal and confidential memorandum to Cummings, he complained about a resolution adopted by the National Probation Association condemning his remarks on parole and probation. Noting that editorial comments on this resolution assumed that Miller (who was vice president of the association) was speaking for the attorney general in view of his status as special assistant to the attorney general and chairman of the Advisory Committee on Crime, Hoover expressed his willingness to answer 'the ill-advised and unfounded statements of the National Probation Association' but, quickly shifting to the high road, protested that:

I could not very well do so without making some criticism of Mr. Miller, and irrespective of his criticisms of the Bureau and of myself, I did not consider it to be in the interest of Departmental harmony or in the interest of law enforcement to engage in personal criticism of another official of the Department, and one who is attached to your office . . . I . . . felt constrained to bring this matter to your attention, because if the Federal Bureau of Investigation has accomplished one thing under your leadership it has been the creation of a respect upon the part of not only a great portion of our adult population, but certainly a major portion of our juvenile population, for law enforcement and for the so-called 'G-Men,' and everything which tears down or shakes that respect, in my mind, is subversive and vicious.'

Hoover's adept appeal to administration unity, especially in the context of conservative denunciations of the Bureau's expanded role, succeeded. Cummings duly chastised Miller, who capitulated in a graceful letter of apology. But Miller was merely the first target among the hostiles, and Hoover kept his wagon train drawn up in a tight circle. Soon apprised by his informants in the other departments of further unfriendly activity, he again alerted Cummings to the efforts of Secret Service agent G. L. Boatwright. The Secret Service operative, Hoover reported, had launched an investigation of the FBI and Hoover's directorship with the objective of obtaining 'as much information as possible in order to bring about [my] removal from office' and to effect the appointment of W. H. Moran (then head of Secret Service) as FBI director. This source confirmed, he added,

175

other information which I have forwarded to you recently, indicating that certain governmental agencies of the present administration are engaging in conducting an investigation of my administration of the Bureau. I do think that the time has come when either these activities should be put to an end or that they should be brought out into the open. It certainly is not conducive to the best interests of this Bureau, or of law enforcement, or the morale of the service, for representatives of other governmental agencies . . . to carry on such investigations. I would strongly suggest that communication be had with some responsible official of the Treasury Department to determine exactly what these activities are. You have not, so far as I know, been informed of any investigation which was to be conducted . . ., and I think such actions are highly reprehensible unless you have been advised of them.

Hoover was clearly taking a chance in suggesting that Cummings was being outflanked — especially if the attorney general had knowledge of the Treasury's investigation — but, as Hoover saw it, he had no choice. He either had to nip the insurgency in the bud or the problem of credibility would become his, something no prominent bureaucrat could hope to survive. For Hoover had already learned that a group of conservative southern Democrats (McKellar, Joseph Robinson of Arkansas, and Ed Smith of South Carolina) 'were going to have Mr. Hoover fired.' Seizing the initiative, he had alerted a friendly newsman and given out the story that he then told Cummings 'will probably be given some publicity within the next twenty-four hours.'

True to his word, the next day's *Washington Herald* carried the story under the headline 'SECRET SERVICE PROBING G-MEN'. Beginning on the front page and running more than two column feet, the story detailed the activities that Hoover had described to Cummings. Then, ingeniously, the *Herald* reported that these 'other investigative organizations of the Government have "ganged up" on the

G-Men in anticipation of hearings before the Byrd committee of the Senate on costs of Government agencies.' Referring to a select committee on government operations chaired by Harry Byrd of Virginia, the story attributed the actions of these other investigative organizations to fears that 'their activities may be merged with those of the Department of Justice,' leading them to start collecting 'anti-G-men material in the hope of wiping out that organization first.' Committed to promoting Hoover's cause, the *Herald* sought to force Cummings's hand:

> Hoover is known to have offered his resignation to the Attorney General half a dozen times in the past year and a half because of indignation concerning administration of the Department . . . Each time he has been dissuaded and has agreed to keep on at least until he has developed protection for his men from political patronage raids.

Hoover may not have been a smart cop, as his detractors in the field maintained, but he was a brilliant bureaucrat and his countersubversion worked. Each time he had won a point he had pressed Cummings a little harder. Now the *Herald* article inescapably implied that Cummings was undermining law enforcement by allowing the Treasury investigation to go on. But still, Hamlet-like, Cummings hesitated. The attorney general had communicated with Treasury Secretary Henry Morgenthau by this time, and been reassured with courteous denials. He had also been in touch with the presidential press secretary, Stephen Early, at the White House. But still he heard nothing but denials, apparently all the way up to the top. Clearly only one man could put a stop to the snooping, and that man was the president, Morgenthau's close personal friend and Farley's long-time political ally in New York.

Within the week, Hoover gave the screw another turn, advising Cummings that he had learned of a proposed grant to the Works Project Administration (WPA) to investigate the FBI. This was not idle rumor, Hoover emphasized, as he had 'now received confidential information to the effect that a request for $250,000 . . . went to the Works Project Administration from the Treasury Department . . . to study the activities and statistics of the Federal Bureau of Investigation . . . the letters for the President's signature are being presently prepared,' he continued, 'the request for the allotment having been approved by both the Budget Bureau and the Projects Control Division of the Works Project Administration. It has not, however, so far as I have been able to ascertain, been forwarded to the President for his signature, though it is intended it will go forth very shortly.'

Refusing to identify his source, Hoover charged that there could be no doubt that 'there are certain governmental agencies engaged in a very definite effort to discredit the work of this Bureau. The surprising and, indeed, amazing aspect of this situation to me is that any governmental agency such as the Secret Service, which has now been established beyond a scintilla of doubt as being engaged in the conduct of investigation of this Bureau, and this above referred to order, could all [sic] be initiating the same without the approval or condoning of such actions by persons in high places.'

Whether Hoover was implying that the president had initiated the investigation or that Secretary Morgenthau had is not clear. 'The Fox,' as FDR was sometimes called, occasionally resorted to oblique methods and on those occasions naturally sought to cover his tracks. But Morgenthau had his own reasons for wanting Hoover out, over and above interdepartmental rivalry. For Morgenthau's early concern for the fate of Europe's Jews was already a matter of record, and Hoover was opposed to relaxing immigration restrictions to let Jews in. Moreover, the Bureau was suspected of having established liaison with the Gestapo, through the international police organization Interpol, headquartered in Paris and at the time dominated by the Gestapo. Rumors circulated that Hoover had 'fingered' European Jews seeking admittance to the United States by confiding immigration data to the Gestapo via Interpol.

Whether this was true or not, Hoover was certainly hostile toward emigrating Jews from Europe and excessively concerned with 'possible Communist or other leftist connections of the sponsors.'

Hoover's aggressive posturing once again succeeded, in part because of his earlier successes in establishing his indispensability as the feared and efficient G-Man. The imbroglio ended as inconspicuously as it had begun, with Morgenthau this time apologizing to Cummings. Professing that he had been 'deeply shocked' by press reports about the Secret Service investigation of the FBI, the Treasury secretary expressed his disapproval, conveyed his determination to prevent any recurrence, and assured Cummings that 'suitable disciplinary measures will be taken.'

Morgenthau then made his letter to Cummings public and announced the demotion of two of his men, held responsible for the investigation. But Hoover was still not satisfied. He had learned that former Assistant Attorney General William Donovan, who was believed to have designs on the Director's post and had superb qualifications, was a member of the cabal. In a final personal and confidential memorandum to Cummings, he cited intelligence of still further intrigue against the Bureau and brazenly complained:

> sufficient impression has not been made upon the operatives of the United States Secret Service that they should attend strictly to their own business . . . When the recent situation was brought to a close by the action of the Secretary of the Treasury in announcing that he intended to demote Mr. Murphy and Mr. Boatwright, you suggested to me that you thought it would be highly desirable that I indicate to the personnel of this Bureau that they be most circumspect in any statements which they might make at any time relative to the Secret Service; that we be particularly careful in not commenting upon or criticizing that organization. Those instructions have been carried out and will be adhered to, but it certainly seems to me that the same

policy should be adhered to by the United States Secret Service . . . I must state that I am strongly inclined to the view that there is a lack of sincerity upon the part of Treasury officials in this matter.'

Thereafter nothing further was heard of the newspaper report, and there the matter died. The third and last concerted attempt by powerful officials of Roosevelt's inner circle to remove Hoover from office had been contained.[7]

In the meantime, on 1 July 1936, Hoover had created the new post of assistant to the director for Clyde. Clyde may have been less charismatic than Guy Hottel, but he was the indispensable number-two man in the Bureau, and Hoover, his nerves in a more or less permanent state of excitement, could not risk doing without Clyde. Besides, Clyde was first baseman on the Bureau baseball team, and a good one too. And as Hoover's nephew Fred Robinette later recalled, 'The Director liked to recruit athletes,' even though he was purely a spectator himself. (The Bureau's ball team, in fact, won the championship of the government agency league in 1936.)

Under the new regime, Tolson was the sole disciplinarian, although Hoover occasionally overruled him. Tolson was also in charge of personnel, making assignments, sometimes at Hoover's direction. He was, in short, the Major's captain in a distinctly militaristic chain of command.

Hoover thereafter spent most of his day simply keeping informed, a heroic task in itself. Every SAC was required to send a one-page memo to the Director's desk each morning, as were supervisors handling important cases. Newspaper clippings from the local and national papers were also regularly forwarded.

Hoover stayed behind his closed office door about half of each day, meticulously handling these details. 'Everything had to be perfection,' one former agent remembered. 'A letter did not leave the office with errors in it.' Hoover's attention to detail was calculated to eliminate any possibility of embarrassment to the Bureau. For example, he chastised agents for the frequency of errors in their reports (citing such minor ones as incorrect dates and incomplete or incorrect

180

titles) and for their frequent use of the phrase 'interrogated vigorously' (because 'persons outside the Bureau may gain the impression that some form of duress' had been used).[8] When interviewing individuals during White Slave Traffic Act investigations, he said, 'precautions should be taken to prevent being involved in a situation resulting in embarrassment to the Agent or the Bureau.' SACs and supervisors were advised that they were personally responsible for 'preventing and deterring' any 'incidents or misconduct of Bureau personnel' under their supervision.

Hoover's insistence on perfection applied particularly to any correspondence or press release issued over his name. Unable to read every communication addressed to him or the large volume of mail sent out over his signature, the Director demanded that other officials 'properly perform their functions in the handling' of this mail. To ensure that this was done and, in the event of error, to allow those who were derelict in their responsibilities to be penalized, Hoover insisted that those who read the mail and prepared the response initial the correspondence to signify 'that they have actually read and analyzed the same and in initialling it, vouch for it thoroughly.' FBI officials, furthermore, minutely reviewed, 'on a word-by-word basis,' the Director's congressional testimony to catch and correct any errors of fact, misstatements, malapropisms, misspellings, and grammatical mistakes before the *Congressional Record* was printed.

The overall responsibility for burnishing the Director's image reposed in Louis Nichols, who, as head of the Crime Records Division, managed the Bureau's active public relations center. Nichols was remembered as 'never close to anything but his work.'

Guy Hottel's role was as yet indistinct, although it was generally supposed that he was Hoover's troubleshooter. Hottel made the arrangements for outings and told the Director what security would be needed. 'Hoover probably looked on Guy as good physical support,' one agent recalled, 'as opposed to Tolson, who was good mental support. Guy was feisty. He loved life in general. There was never a question as to where his next wife or next Cadillac was coming from.'

'But he was a terrible roustabout and sometimes got himself into trouble. He might show up with a black eye that he'd got in a poker game the night before. And he sometimes got himself in the doghouse [with Hoover]. After one escapade he was sent over to the Identification Division in some insignificant position. But he couldn't be put down – he was wired in. On one occasion he was asked to come forward by his new superior. He stayed seated and said, "I am forward." And Hoover always seemed to forgive him.'

In the new, enlarged Bureau, Hoover emerged as the unquestioned leader. In addition to staying abreast of intelligence and deciding policy matters, he devoted hours of each day to ceremonial matters, ever alert to the need to equate himself and the Bureau in the public mind. The Identification Division by this time had become part of Washington's tourist trail (together with the Bureau of Engraving and the Washington Monument), and the Boss often took time personally to greet provincial notables or contingents from boys' clubs or men's voluntary fraternal groups. Photographs would be taken of these audiences, often described by grateful visitors in effusive thank-you notes as the greatest experiences of their lives, and sent to each visitor or member, all at taxpayers' expense. These sessions, known at the Bureau as 'grip and grins' in acknowledgment of the ceremonial handshake and set smile, were the equivalent of Lyndon Johnson's 'pressing the flesh' as a means of increasing constituent support.

At the same time, Hoover increased his outreach efforts through the media and personal appearances. Sponsoring organizations for the latter were carefully chosen for conservative orthodoxy, the better to brighten Hoover's image as a champion of patriotic 'Americanism.' Indeed, his self-aggrandizement – although it was technically always for the Bureau and the cause of law enforcement – was so flagrant as to seem foolhardy to those who did not know him.

The Boss, however, was not content merely to exploit

public appearances before conservative organizations. He also established covert relationships with them. One such, dating from the World War I period, enlisted the National Republic Organization (NRO). This brotherhood, Hoover advised his SACs, had been created 'as a means of furnishing information on subversive organizations to newspapers, schools, civic organizations, and other groups.' The FBI had maintained a 'very close relationship' with executives of this organization 'over a period of years,' he reported, and SACs were to prevent any public knowledge of this (adding that NRO officials had agreed to his stipulation that they 'make no reference to the FBI . . . [or] convey any impression that [the] organization cooperates with the FBI'). Accordingly, SACs who received any inquiries about the NRO were to respond that 'this is a private organization and has no official connection in any way, shape or form with the Bureau.'

Meanwhile, Hoover's constant publicity seeking had let yet another detractor, Sanford Bates, director of the Justice Department's Bureau of Prisons, to lodge a complaint with the attorney general. Bates objected to a forthcoming Hoover-authored *American Magazine* article on the wife of Machine Gun Kelly, which he had learned of from an advertising blurb. Recognizing the futility of protesting 'against this use of Department records' and 'exploitation of prisoners who are in the custody and control' of his bureau, Bates protested heatedly against the use of his agency's correspondence, which had been submitted to the FBI to assist it at the time of Kelly's arrest. The Prison Bureau 'had no expectation that this correspondence would be used to embellish magazine articles,' he said.[9]

That same month Hoover stirred up another hornets' nest by muscling in on the Harry Brunette arrest in New York City. Brunette, a twenty-five-year-old unaffiliated bank robber from New Jersey, was wanted, technically, for kidnapping a New Jersey state trooper and was holed up with his wife, still a teenager, in an apartment on West 102nd Street in Manhattan.

183

As reported by Jack Alexander in his *New Yorker* profile of Hoover:

Five minutes before midnight, Brunette was seen entering the house. One of the G-men telephoned Hoover, who was waiting in a room at the St. Moritz [Hotel]. Hoover took a taxicab to the scene and decided upon an immediate raid.

A *Newsweek* report on the arrest took the story from there:

A sharp clatter of gunfire echoed through the placid neighborhood. Federal men in the hall [outside the Brunettes' apartment] were firing through the door; somebody was shooting back. As the battle raged, an army of police arrived. Later, a tear-gas bomb set fire to the apartment and brought fire engines screaming to the scene . . . For 35 minutes, the shooting continued. Then a lull. 'Give up, or we'll shoot,' shouted a G-man — as if they had been throwing spitballs up to then. A young woman, the wife of Harry Brunette, staggered out, shot in the thigh. Then came the unharmed Brunette.

Thereafter, as Alexander put it in the *New Yorker*:

[Police] Commissioner Valentine [of New York] made public property of the long-gathering feud between the police and the G-men by denouncing the raid as melodramatic and implying that it had been made for publicity purposes. The police, Valentine said, had captured many criminals who were more desperate than Brunette, and with much less fanfare. Hoover remarked of the Valentine blast, 'Kindergarten stuff,' and said that, after all, the taxpayers had got their money's worth.

Nothing could stop the juggernaut of the Bureau's publicity campaign except the strong arm of the president or the attorney general, and in 1938, just before leaving office in the aftermath of the Supreme Court packing debacle, Cummings attempted to do just that. Hoover was so little daunted by this direct order to curtail the Bureau's publicity campaign that he shortly arranged with Walter Winchell to put the manacles on Louis 'Lepke' Buchalter of Murder Incorporated himself. Winchell, professing to represent the federal government in the person of his friend J. Edgar Hoover, promised Lepke that he could avoid capital punishment if he would turn himself in to Hoover. A rendezvous of all three men was thereupon arranged in an automobile in Manhattan, and Hoover made the pinch, promptly reported by Winchell. Lepke was tried for murder on state charges and executed.

The ostensible point of all the pyrotechnics was to enlist public support for law enforcement, but there was another string to the Director's bow. Nor was it in all likelihood, even in the heyday of the New Deal, a mean factor in his success. That factor was antiradicalism.

Hoover intensified his activity in this field in 1936, shortly after the clash with the Secret Service. On 27 January he reminded Cummings of their recent conversation concerning Secretary of War George Dern's request to reestablish a division within the FBI to 'conduct appropriate investigations into so-called subversive activities.' Appending to his letter a copy of a recent newspaper article entitled 'Spies Are Active in America,' Hoover commented that Cummings might want 'to consider the same in reaching a final decision relative to the request of the Secretary of War.'

Cummings did not authorize the recreation of the old GID. In 1934, however, under a still-secret presidential directive, Hoover had been authorized to conduct a limited investigation of the activities of American Nazis and American Nazi sympathizers. Over the next two years, recognizing the Director's usefulness and willingness to serve, Roosevelt and White House aides had requested FBI reports on numerous right-wing agitators, specifically members of Nazi-type fringe organizations like the Silver

Shirts, the Knights of the White Camelia, and the Coughlinite Christian Front. Hoover readily complied and later, following the outbreak of World War II in 1939, regularly forwarded to the Roosevelt White House reports on a host of the president's right-wing critics, including Gerald L. K. Smith, James True, Joseph McWilliams, Lawrence Dennis, Gerald Winrod, and William Dudley Pelley — and eventually including such prominent and respectable conservative critics of the president's foreign policy as former Republican President Herbert Hoover, Senators Gerald Nye and Burton Wheeler, Charles Lindbergh, and the America First Committee.

In the 1930s, however, the president did not share the Director's obsession with the 'subversive' threat, especially that from American leftists. Nor did administration officials contemplate giving the ambitious Director a warrant to investigate so inexact a category as 'subversive activities.' Their requests that Hoover monitor the administration's right-wing critics nevertheless allowed Hoover to curry favor and afforded him an opportunity to monitor the left as well.

In one case, directed to investigate a right-wing organization, Hoover turned the tables 180 degrees. Disturbed by a series of articles published in the right-wing *American Citizen* criticizing the Immigration and Naturalization Service for failing to deport alleged alien Communists, INS Commissioner Edward Cahill had requested an FBI investigation 'to ascertain the identity of the backers of this newspaper.' Cahill contended that the *American Citizen* 'was bringing all government departments into disrepute for the political purpose of discrediting and defeating the present administration . . . [and] that certain large corporations, among which is the Pacific Gas and Electric Company, were contributing large sums of money towards the support of "The American Citizen." '

Hoover responded to higher authority by emphasizing that 'there apparently was no Federal law violated herein which would give this Bureau investigative jurisdiction in the matter and therefore no action could be taken in the premises.' But despite his reservations, he complied, or appeared to, and in his report to Cummings listed the name and address of the newspaper's publisher and its corporate and individual sponsors. He then disarmingly described the paper's purposes as opposing 'the subversive activities of the "Western Worker" and other communistic publications so that the public may be informed as to the actions of these communists' and as disclosing 'to the public the identity of the leaders responsible for these communistic activities and the present labor trouble and also [making] an effort to correct the spirit of unrest and class hatred that is created thereby.'

Hoover was not alone in fearing the internal security threat posed by the American left, although his objectives were more ambitious than those of the president (himself considered a radical in some quarters), who authorized the Director, following a 24 August 1936 meeting at the White House, to begin monitoring Communist activities.

Roosevelt began that meeting, according to Hoover's memo to the files, by expressing interest in 'discussing the question of the subversive activities in the United States, particularly Fascism and Communism,' and by citing reports he had recently received on the activities of the Soviet consular official Constantine Oumansky and the 'definite indication' of foreign espionage in the United States. The president also reportedly said that 'some [domestic] organizations would probably attempt to cripple our war effort [in an emergency] through sabotage.'

Although Roosevelt had earlier expressed concern about foreign-directed espionage and sabotage activities in general, Hoover responded to this invitation by recounting the efforts of Communists in particular to control important trade unions (the West Coast Longshoremen, the United Mine Workers, the Newspaper Guild), 'activities which have recently occurred with [sic] Governmental service inspired by Communists,' and by citing the Communist International's directive that American Communists 'vote for President Roosevelt and against [Republican presidential candidate Alfred] Landon because of the fact that Governor Landon is opposed to class warfare.' In considerably less detail and with less animus, the Director then described the attempts of the Catholic priest Charles L. Coughlin to persuade the retired army general Smedley Butler to 'lead an expedition to Mexico' and those of other right-wing activists to persuade Butler to lead an anti-New Deal coup.

The president reiterated his concern 'about the movements of the Communists and of Fascism in the United States' and added that although the Secret Service had assured him 'they had informants in every Communist group,' their efforts were confined to 'getting any information upon plots upon his life, whereas what he was interested in was obtaining a broad picture of the general movement and its activities as it may affect the economic and political life of the country as a whole.'

When Hoover responded that no government agency was acquiring 'general intelligence information' on this subject, Roosevelt asked whether Hoover had any suggestions. Leaping at the opportunity, Hoover observed that the FBI's appropriation statute (of 1916) contained a provision authorizing the Bureau to investigate 'any matters referred to it by the Department of State and that if the State Department should ask for us to conduct such an investigation we could do so.'

Intrigued by Hoover's suggestion, Roosevelt nevertheless shrank from 'hav[ing] a formal request come through the State Department because of the many leaks therein.' Instead, he proposed a meeting of himself, Hoover, and Secretary of State Cordell Hull on 25 August, 'at which time the matter could be further discussed and an oral request could be made of me [Hoover] by the Secretary of State for investigation so as to avoid any possibility of any leak.'

Hoover, Roosevelt, and Hull duly met on 25 August, at which time Roosevelt advised Hull (in Hoover's words) of 'his concern relative to Communist activities in this country, as well as Fascist activities.' (It is not clear that Roosevelt referred to fascist activities as an afterthought; more than likely, this phrasing reflects Hoover's own set of priorities.) Expressing an interest in 'a survey' of these activities, Roosevelt remarked that this could be done 'if the Secretary of State requested the Department to conduct the inquiry, as under the Appropriation Act this Bureau would have authority to make such investigation if asked to do so by the Secretary of State.' Hull, quite willing to accommodate the president, inquired whether he should make this request 'in writing.' Roosevelt shook his head, preferring that 'the matter . . . be handled quite confidentially and that . . . the President, the Secretary of State and I [Hoover] should be the ones aware of this request.' Roosevelt then directed Hoover to brief Attorney General Cummings on the matter on his return to the capital and instructed Hull to 'talk over the techniques to be followed in this particular aspect, with the Attorney General.'

If Roosevelt intended to have the secretary of state and attorney general monitor an operation limited to an investigation of foreign direction of domestic political activities, he was sadly mistaken. His requirement of secrecy flew in the face of these intentions. For, having since 1924 disregarded former attorney general Stone's ban against political surveillance, Hoover now welcomed Roosevelt's initiative as providing formal presidential authorization for the broad-scale antisubversive investigations already being conducted by the FBI. Immediately after this conference and before briefing Cummings, Hoover ordered his senior aides to begin planning an enlarged surveillance program that would focus on domestic political radicals and trade union activities.

In particular, he ordered Assistant Director Edward Tamm to list the 'general classifications' of this program, which Tamm, a future federal judge, did as follows: 'Maritime Industry, Government affairs, steel industry, coal industry, newspaper field, clothing, garment and fur industry, general strike activities, Armed Forces, educational institutions, general activities – Communist and Affiliated Organizations, Fascisti, Anti-Fascisti movements, and activities in Organized Labor organizations.'

Hoover lauded Tamm's proposal as a 'good beginning' and on 5 September 1936 ordered all FBI field offices 'to obtain from all possible sources information concerning subversive activities being conducted in the United States by Communists, Fascisti, and representatives or advocates of other organizations or groups advocating the overthrow or replacement of the Government of the United States by illegal means.'

Then, on 10 September, Hoover belatedly briefed Cummings on the president's request, erroneously telling him that his meeting with Roosevelt and Hull had taken place on 1 September (apparently to avoid being asked why he had not briefed the attorney general sooner). Moreover, when informing Cummings of the president's request, Hoover misrepresented it as directing the FBI to investigate 'subversive activities in this country [whatever their origins], including communism and fascism.' A too trusting Cummings thereupon 'verbally directed' Hoover to proceed with the investigation, advising him to handle it 'in a most discreet and confidential manner' and to coordinate information, 'as the President suggested,' with military and naval intelligence and the State Department.

Although Roosevelt had requested a limited survey of foreign-directed movements, Hoover initiated a broad, intensive investigation of domestic radical activities that extended to spying on the nation's college campuses. A subsequent presidential request provided an opportunity for Hoover to extract unlimited presidential authority for the FBI's unending investigations of 'subversive activities.' In October 1938 Roosevelt directed Cummings to chair an executive committee 'to inquire into the so-called espionage situation.' Cummings immediately sought Hoover's advice. Hoover unhesitatingly outlined the 'present purposes and scope' of espionage investigations conducted by the FBI, the Military Intelligence Division (MID), and the Office of Naval Intelligence (ONI), as well as suggestions 'for expansion and such further coordination as may be effected.' The FBI, Hoover reported, was presently collecting 'through investigative activity and other contact . . . information dealing with various forms of activities of either a *subversive* or a so-called intelligence type' (emphasis added).

Hoover also described the general categories of information collected, leaving no doubt that the FBI was extensively monitoring radical political and trade union activities. Then, urging an expanded FBI investigative role, he recommended that this be 'covered' under 'present provisions in the annual appropriations bill of the Federal Bureau of Investigation.' In the past, he observed, the FBI had conducted investigations 'for the State Department of matters which do not in themselves constitute a specific violation of a Federal Criminal Statute, such as subversive activities. Consequently, *this provision is believed to be sufficiently broad to cover any expansion of the present intelligence and counter-espionage work which it may be deemed necessary to carry on'* (emphasis added).

Hoover specifically warned against seeking 'special legislation' for this purpose, as this 'would draw attention to the fact that it was proposed to develop a special counter-espionage drive of any great magnitude.' Instead, he recommended instituting this expansion 'with the utmost degree of secrecy' to avoid any criticisms or objections 'by either ill-informed persons or individuals having some ulterior motive.'

Another president might have regarded Hoover's memo as ample grounds to dismiss him, but not Roosevelt, who, like Harlan Stone, felt supremely confident of his ability to control him. After reviewing Hoover's report, Roosevelt met with the Director on 2 November and advised him of his approval of 'the plan which I [Hoover] had prepared and which had been sent to him by the Attorney General, except that he had not been able to grant the entire amount of money' – $300,000 – that Hoover had said the FBI needed to 'handle counter-espionage activities.' (Roosevelt approved only $150,000.)[10]

Hoover's successes in obtaining broad discretionary authority to investigate dissident activities eventually proved troublesome, but not because either the president or the attorney general reconsidered the Director's use of this secret authorization to investigate perfectly lawful dissent. On the contrary, all three men were simply too clever by half.

Unwilling to have it become known that he had authorized the FBI to investigate domestic political activities, Roosevelt agreed to the strategy that Hoover had suggested in the first place, whereby these 'investigations' were triggered by the language of the FBI appropriations statute (enacted in wartime and long forgotten), empowering it to conduct investigations requested by the secretary of state.

This triggering requirement first troubled Hoover in 1939, when he learned of a State Department plan to establish an interdepartmental committee chaired by the under secretary of state to coordinate domestic intelligence investigations. On 16 March 1939, in a memorandum to Frank Murphy (Cummings's successor as attorney general), Hoover described the FBI's current 'espionage, counter-espionage, and sabotage' investigations as being 'of a nature not within the specific provisions of prevailing statutes' and thus as requiring the State Department's 'specific authorization.' Fearing that State's establishment of this interdepartmental committee would allow other federal agencies to conduct domestic investigations, Hoover recommended that instead of having the authority to investigate, these agencies should be required to forward all information 'relating to espionage and subversive activities' to the FBI. Such a change, Hoover argued in a calculated appeal to Murphy's commitment to civil liberties, would avoid the confusion and violation of individual rights that had occurred during World War I.

Hoover's clever civil libertarian argument persuaded Murphy, who urged Roosevelt to dissolve State's interdepartmental committee system. All investigations involving 'espionage, counter-espionage, and sabotage matters,' Murphy said, should be confined to the FBI and the military and naval intelligence services.

Uncritically accepting Murphy's recommendation, Roosevelt on 26 June issued a secret presidential directive specifying that all such investigations were to be 'controlled and handled' by the FBI, MID, and ONI. Roosevelt's order forbade any other federal investigative agency to conduct such investigations and also instructed the heads of all federal investigative agencies to report to the FBI 'any data, information, or material that may come to their notice bearing directly or indirectly on espionage, counterespionage, or sabotage.' Chalk one up for the Director.

The care with which Hoover orchestrated these extensions of FBI authority, all of them effected either orally or through secret executive directives, makes clear that he understood the implications of both his own and the president's actions, was taking care to protect himself in the event of public disclosure of the Bureau's antiradical activities, and was fully cognizant of the opportunity afforded by such secret authorizations to extend the FBI's reach beyond the scope envisioned by the president.[11]

In addition, Hoover had begun transacting antiradical business covertly with leading conservative congressmen. Congress's official interest in antiradical activity went back to the World War I period, when a Senate committee chaired by Lee S. Overman (D.-N.C.) began a probe of German war propaganda and ended up by investigating American Communists. Similarly, in 1930, discreetly pressured by Hoover among others, the House established the so-called Fish Committee (named for its chairman Hamilton Fish, a conservative Republican from upstate New York) to investigate Communist subversion. Finally, in May 1938, appealing to both antiradical and antifascist sentiments, the House established the Special Committee on Un-American Activities – the so-called Dies Committee (named for its chairman, Martin Dies, D.-Tex.).

In the last instance at least, Hoover leaked selected confidential information from FBI files to members of the committee to enable them to publicize the Red Menace. But he refused to allow the committee itself, or its counsel, to define the terms of this assistance, for the committee posed two potential challenges to his tenuous power as Director of the FBI. In the first place, foreseeing that Congressman Dies would try to use the committee to discredit the Roosevelt administration, and by extension the Bureau's conduct of counterespionage investigations, Hoover feared the backlash resulting from too close cooperation. In the second, he distrusted Dies's implicit challenge to the FBI's monopoly in the internal security field. So the wily Director resolved to keep his distance.

Although determined that the FBI's resources should in no way come under the control of the committee, Hoover nonetheless communicated to committee members the impression that he could not cooperate because the Bureau lacked 'control over the files of the FBI, which were part of the Department of Justice records and it was necessary to have approval of the Attorney General's office before making them available to anyone.' And although willing to comply when ordered by higher authority, he still took care to ensure that the FBI not 'give publicity to such requests,' while at the same time he sought to ensure that the FBI's assistance was strictly limited. It was a perfect arrangement. By complying with certain committee members' requests on a selective basis while taking the position that the Bureau could not cooperate directly with Congress, Hoover succeeded at this critical juncture in avoiding any change in policy allowing congressional committees to gain direct, uncontrolled access to FBI files. Thus he was free to leak and thereby publicize such information as he wanted publicized without having to subject the contents of the files themselves to scrutiny, a very advantageous tradeoff indeed.[12]

To be sure, he also willingly, 'circumspectly,' and covertly assisted committee members and staff in selecting qualified staff members and investigators. In 1939 (and again in 1941) he had FBI officials brief committee officials on the backgrounds of individuals under consideration for staff appointments. By doing so, he curried favor with the committee and secured the appointment of sympathetic staff, thus ensuring that the committee would not challenge the FBI or act in ways inimical to the Bureau.

Hoover's punitiveness toward radicals and toward Mann Act offenders, expressed in a highly publicized series of vice raids at this time, may have been overcompensation for the loss of his mother, and the consequent fear of a loss of control. Annie died on 22 February 1938, having been an invalid for about two years, and so stricken was her son that Attorney General Cummings was moved to write him a very personal letter of condolence. So bereft was Edgar, in fact, that even a new brick house on Thirtieth Place in northwest Washington, which he bought in 1939 half-built, was no consolation. He was devastated and could not show it, and he apparently reacted by becoming more judgmental and punitive than ever.

More alarmingly, his long-muted personal crusade against radicals took a violent turn. In February 1940, acting on what was probably his most serious miscalculation up to that time, he ordered his agents in Detroit and Milwaukee to participate in simultaneous arrests of radicals accused of having enlisted volunteers for the International Abraham Lincoln Brigade, which had fought for the defeated Spanish Loyalists against Francisco Franco in the Spanish Civil War. Liberals were outraged, and this time the outrage did not stop with editorials.

Notes to Chapter Eight

1. Hoover's companions may have been brought along for security, but the evidence of the Director's photograph albums suggests that he was chummy with them as well. He is pictured in Miami not only with his arm around Hottel but again with his arm around Tolson, and he and Tolson are pictured together in Colorado in a corny, schoolboyish mock-snowball fight.

2. According to Assistant Director William Sullivan, eventually one of the disaffected, that adage was heard at the Bureau at least once a day. But apparently Hoover never read Emerson's Essay on Self-Reliance,' in particular the maxim 'He who would be a man must be a nonconformist.'

3. McKellar, a Democrat from Tennessee, had been after Hoover for more than five years. He first did battle with the Director at an Appropriations subcommittee hearing in 1931 when he tried, unsuccessfully, to force Hoover to disclose secret data obtained in an unauthorized investigation of a Tennessee judge. Again in 1934 McKellar tried to force Hoover to disclose

information about the Bureau. When told that such disclosure would be 'unwise,' the senator replied, 'I think the idea of a Cheka [the forerunner of the Soviet KGB] in this country is something that ought not to exist.' Again, at the Appropriations subcommittee hearings in 1935, McKellar warned: 'We are getting to have a tremendous secret service organization . . . [Such organizations] are frequently used as a means of doing great wrong, and I have my doubts about secret service systems in a republican form of government like ours. I have been astounded at the tremendous growth and the use of large sums of money for the "secret service," as it is called, of the Department of Justice.' (Quoted in Max Lowenthal, *The Federal Bureau of Investigation* [New York: William Sloan, 1950], p. 333.)

4. The Wickersham Commission had also criticized the Bureau's method of compiling crime statistics as inherently defective and cautioned against continuing the practice in 'any bureau or agency which is engaged in administering the criminal law.' It stated: 'A serious abuse exists in compiling them as a basis for requesting appropriations or for justifying the existence of or urging expanded powers and equipment for the agency in question rather than for the purposes which criminal statistics are designed to further.' (Lowenthal, *Federal Bureau of Investigation,* p. 388.) A Brookings Institution expert who studied the federal detective agencies for Senator Harry Byrd's Government Operations Committee cited one example of this abuse: 'The Director of the Bureau of Investigation referred in March 1936 to the "armed forces of crime which number more than 3 million active participants." Three months later he stated that "the criminal standing army of America" numbered 500,000, "a whole half-million of armed thugs, murderers, thieves, firebugs, assassins, robbers, and hold-up men." About six months afterward he gave the total criminal population as 3,500,000 and the number of crimes as 1,500,000. Five months later he stated that 4,300,000 persons were engaged by day and by night in the commission of felonies and estimated that 1,333,526 major felonies were committed in the United States during the year 1936.' (Ibid., p. 395.)

5. Trohan ultimately abandoned this hard-hitting examination of Hoover's public relations activities. As anti-Communism transformed American conservatism during the Cold War years, Trohan became an ardent supporter of Hoover's FBI.

6. Hoover kept in his office a framed homily entitled 'The Penalty of Leadership,' which read in part: 'In every field of human

endeavor, he that is first must perpetually live in the white light of publicity . . . When a man's work becomes a standard for the whole world, it also becomes a target for the shafts of the envious few.' (*Current Biography*, 1940, p. 401.) To grandiosity, he had now annexed a more appealing trait of the authoritarian personality: courageous self-reliance. His need to repress anarchy on the outside was matched by his need to deny dependence in himself. As Berle observes: 'Power . . . is personal. Its possessor upholds it in the presence of a field of responsibility. Inevitably, the love or hate, the support or opposition developed through myriad tiny power organisms constituting the field [of responsibility] reacts on him . . . The greater the power, the wider the field of responsibility, the more intense is the impact on the personality of the man. It may not be true, as Lord Acton says, that power corrupts. Yet it certainly penetrates the emotional life of the power holder. For one thing, he is invariably at the center of this particular state [the field of responsibility] — large or small, as the case may be. He is not merely 'expressing himself.' He is putting on an act. In this drama, he must always be the star. News items about him assume more importance to him than the weightiest dispatch about events. The effect on the structure of his personality depends on his tensile strength, on his capacity to endure this kind of strain.' (A. A. Berle, *Power* [New York: Harcourt, Brace & World, 1967], p. 121).

7. Hoover's intelligence system had enabled him to learn of the plans of his adversaries in the Treasury Department, highlighting both his ability to monitor developments throughout the executive branch and his interest in doing so. The extent of his spying on his ostensible superiors in government is suggested by his success, in the fall of 1940, in obtaining copies of the private correspondence between Secretary of Agriculture Henry Wallace (at the time President Roosevelt's vice presidential running mate) and Nicholas Roerich and others associated with the popular but controversial mystic. Briefed on the president's concern that the letters might be used 'to the detriment of Mr. Wallace and the President,' Hoover discreetly secured and forwarded to Roosevelt copies of 'this material' (and retained a copy in his own office file).

Wallace had begun corresponding with Roerich in 1933, conveying his attraction to mysticism and the occult. Written in cryptic language (including code names), Wallace's letters were potentially explosive. Should they fall into the hands of his political adversaries, they could be used to question his emotional stability.

In 1940 this dire possibility was contained; in March 1948, in contrast, it became a reality when the syndicated Hearst columnist Westbrook Pegler published excerpts from them. Wallace, then the presidential candidate of the radical Progressive party, paid a heavy political price for this disclosure. Although Hoover's role in effecting this publicity remains unclear, his possession of the letters suggests that he could have been the source. (Confidential Memo, Hoover, 30 January 1941, Sumner Welles folder, Folder no. 157, Hoover O&C; Henry A. Wallace-Nicholas Roerich Letters folder, Folder no. 152, Hoover O&C.) Hoover's extant office file contains derogatory personal and political information on Ambassador to the Soviet Union Charles Bohlen, Ambassador to the United Nations Henry Cabot Lodge, Supreme Court Justice Felix Frankfurter, Attorney General Frank Murphy, a Truman administration subcabinet official whose name has been deleted, White House Secretary Arthur Vandenberg, Jr., and Under Secretary of State Sumner Welles.

8. Whenever agents detained a woman for questioning or transported one to another place, they were to ensure that 'a matron shall be in attendance upon her at all times.' (Bureau Bulletin no. 5, 1st ser. 1940, 1 February 1940, FBI 66-03-289.)

9. In fact, this article (like other articles published by *American Magazine* under Hoover's byline) had been written by Courtney Ryley Cooper, whose melodramatic style attracted Hoover. The Director ordered his staff to render every assistance to Cooper, including furnishing FBI files and checking the completed manuscript for accuracy. In return, Hoover willingly serviced Cooper's numerous requests for assistance for his own books and articles on the crime theme, a most lucrative arrangement for the free-lance writer.

10. When approving Hoover's plan. Roosevelt knew that the FBI was already investigating dissident activities. For not only had Hoover's report listed the general categories of FBI investigations, but throughout 1938 Hoover had regularly forwarded, indirectly through the attorney general or directly through presidential secretary Marvin McIntyre, Bureau reports describing the political activities of right-wing and left-wing political activists. (Confidential Memo, Hoover, 7 November 1938, Franklin D. Roosevelt folder, Folder no. 136, Hoover O&C; U.S. Senate, Select Committee on Intelligence Activities, *Hearings on Intelligence Activities,* vol. 6: *Federal Bureau of Investigation,* pp. 563-67. A sampling of some of Hoover's reports on dissident activities filed in the PSF: Justice,

Hoover folder at the Franklin Roosevelt Library, Hyde Park, New York include: Personal Attention Letter, Hoover to McIntyre, 17 June 1938; Letter, Cummings to Roosevelt, 25 May 1938; Letter, Cummings to Roosevelt, 2 July 1938; Memo, Nathan to Cummings, 1 March 1938; Memo, Hoover to Cummings, 12 April 1938; Letter, Cummings to Roosevelt, 27 January 1938.

11. He also protected the Bureau's activities in this field by lying; witness Jack Alexander's *New Yorker* profile, which coincided with the inception of this ongoing antiradical investigation program: 'Remembering his sturdy service in Palmer's radical-baiting orgy, the pinks and some liberals shudder in apprehension lest another purge be launched. One hears in Washington that Hoover has secret dossiers on all left-wingers and is just awaiting a chance to clap them in concentration camps. Hoover pooh-poohs such stories. In discussing them, he points out that the Sedition Act has long since been repealed and that it is now anyone's privilege to advocate overthrow of the government so long as no overt act is committed He doesn't believe that the law should be so broad-minded, but says that as long as it is, he considers it no business of his to gather evidence on agitators, and insists that he has not done so.' ('The Director II', *New Yorker*, 5 October 1937, p. 22.)

12. This arrangement appears to have satisfied most members of the committee, the ambitious and publicity-seeking Dies being the notable exception. In the words of committee member J. Parnell Thomas: 'If all the Governmental departments cooperated with the Congressmen irregardless [*sic*] of their partisan affiliation, as John Edgar Hoover did, no one would have anything at all to complain about.' In 1938 Thomas asked the Bureau for a list of Communists employed by the government. Hoover, while responding for the record that the Bureau had no such list, apparently complied. Chairman Dies subsequently claimed that the Justice Department was investigating 2,850 known Communists in government. The FBI had compiled the list, the *Chicago Tribune* subsequently reported, but the Justice Department had suppressed it and had rebuked Director Hoover. (Kenneth O'Reilly, 'A New Deal for the FBI: The Roosevelt Administration, Crime Control, and National Security,' *Journal of American History* 69 [1982]:652.)

CHAPTER NINE

(1940–1945)

WARFARE ON THE HOME FRONT

THE PERIOD of World War II witnessed the Bureau's greatest expansion — from 898 agents in 1940 to 4,886 in 1945 — and entailed a major adjustment within the agency itself. It also provided Hoover with his greatest opportunity and, in the nature of things, the most persistent threats to his continued power. For the war undermined the resistance of many conservatives to a federal police force while heightening liberal suspicions about the FBI's expansion. It provoked the Bureau's ideological bedfellows into increasingly virulent attacks on radicals while stirring memories of the GID and the Palmer raids. In addition, Hoover had to refine his strategy for dealing with rivals in both Congress (not only the potential usurper HUAC, but key congressmen who remained serious about their oversight responsibilities and were troubled by Hoover's increasing success in immunizing the Bureau from external scrutiny) and the other intelligence agencies (which also sought to expand their authority).

The magnitude of this task required Hoover to abandon the ad hoc arrangements through which he had cemented his position. Employing his administrative genius, his shrewd assessments of all these challenges, and his confident assertion of his power, and always relying on his enormous provincial constituency, he steadily consolidated his tenure at the Bureau, so that by 1945 he was fully prepared to lead the postwar purge of American leftists that misleadingly traveled under the banner of 'McCarthyism.' However, his progress was not unopposed.

The 'Smear' Campaign

Hoover's controversial leadership of the FBI's highly publicized vice raids and the publicity provoked when FBI agents swooped into Detroit and Milwaukee to arrest radical activists who had recruited volunteers for the Abraham Lincoln Brigade precipitated a furor of protest in early 1940, followed by public demands, primarily from liberals and most notably from Nebraska Senator George Norris, for an investigation of the FBI and consideration of Hoover's dismissal.

Hoover responded by disparaging the honesty and loyalty of his critics and portraying liberal and radical demands for an investigation of the FBI as part of a conspiratorial 'smear' campaign. His thin-skinned public response (masking his more aggressive private response) surfaced during a January 1940 inquiry of a House Appropriations subcommittee.

The occasion for the hearing had nothing to do with the February raids but a great deal to do with Hoover's stewardship of the Bureau. The central issue involved a proposal to bring the FBI under Civil Service procedures, thereby reducing the Director's autonomy and ability to impose tight discipline on his agents. Incensed by this challenge to his absolute authority, Hoover misrepresented the proposal as endangering the very existence of the Bureau. Responding to a question from Congressman Louis Rabaut, a conservative Republican from Detroit, as to why there was no Civil Service at the FBI, Hoover retorted that 'the work of the Bureau is of such a character that I think the [unhampered] selection of its personnel is most vital to its proper and efficient and economical functioning.' Members of law enforcement agencies, he declared, 'cannot be properly selected through a mere stereotyped examination.'

Hoover did not hesitate to raise false issues to sustain his position and recapitulated for the congressmen a complaint he had made to a presidential committee studying Civil Service questions – that the Civil Service Commission, which had been authorized by law to recruit clerks for the Bureau's fingerprint division, had furnished a list of persons

201

'who were physically deformed,' psychotic, 'radical,' or disqualified by virtue of chronic ill health. Sputtering with indignation, he concluded that the commission had recruited misfits and that he had refused to accept them.

Congressman Robert Ramspeck (D.-Ga.), the chairman of the House Civil Service Committee, immediately challenged Hoover's testimony. Except for the fingerprint classifiers, Ramspeck pointed out, Hoover had a free hand, and even in this case the Civil Service Commission had agreed to allow the FBI to conduct its own character investigations.

Not condescending to answer Ramspeck's clarification directly, Hoover addressed to the full House of Representatives a letter in which he repeated his emotional charges:

> I do not want the Bureau bogged down with misfits and incompetents or by persons possessing communistic beliefs . . . I would be recreant to the trust imposed upon me if I did not protest to the utmost of my ability against the red tape, cumbersome and inept methods of appointment which have been clearly shown in the Bureau's experience with the Civil Service Commission.

After the dispute had aired again in the House Appropriations subcommittee hearings, a clearly troubled Congressman Ramspeck called attention to Hoover's deceptions. Recapitulating the Director's transparent strategy during testimony the previous year regarding a proposal to bring the FBI entirely within the Civil Service system, Ramspeck noted that Hoover had then charged the commission 'with sending white applicants to colored doctors for physical examination.' That statement, he said, was totally false 'because the Commission has no doctors' and was made 'off the record to prejudice that Committee, which was composed primarily of men from the South.'

Before adjourning, the Appropriations subcommittee summarized the findings of the president's committee, calling attention to a Brookings Institution report ranking the Bureau sixth of the seven major federal law enforcement agencies in its performance rating. The subcommittee report further cited the testimony of Elmer Irey, coordinator of the Treasury Department's investigative forces and an old Hoover enemy from the Lindbergh kidnapping days. After observing that other federal investigative agencies had been operating successfully under Civil Service for years, Irey made a spirited defense of the principle of civil service:

> The competitive Civil Service procedure is a democratic method of selecting personnel for the public service. It is a system based on merit, . . . provides freedom from political and personal pressure; the security of tenure assures impartial discharge of duties; the opportunity for promotion based upon merit is a safeguard against unwarranted advancement of unworthy employees; and the investigative service benefits because of the limited turnover of personnel.

Hoover haughtily dismissed these challenges, and preserved the Bureau's Civil Service exemption. But just as he overcame this challenge, he provoked the more serious one arising from the reaction to the February raids.

At first criticism focused on the methods FBI agents used in Detroit and Milwaukee when arresting twelve radical activists for having recruited volunteers for the Spanish Loyalist cause. Commenting on the long delay between the recruitment (in 1937) and the arrests (1940), not to mention the Bureau's having rounded up the recruiters in the middle of the night (demonstrated by press photographs of the prisoners handcuffed and chained together), the liberal and radical press insisted that Hoover's 'Gestapo' tactics proved the need for tighter congressional controls over the FBI.

In a particularly bitter denunciation, the *New Republic* likened the FBI's methods to those of the Soviet secret police. Shifting the focus directly onto Hoover's leadership, the magazine commented: 'The glamor that surrounds [Hoover] conceals the growth of a power inconsistent with our conception of democratic institutions.' In a similar vein, the *Milwaukee Journal* described Hoover's FBI as creating the impression 'of a "Gestapo" that can haul citizens off to prison and court in ignominy, imposing any kind of conditions the captors wish without accountability.'

On 26 February Senator Norris introduced the *New Republic* editorial into the *Congressional Record*. Then, in follow-up speeches on 27 April and 7 May, the liberal Republican from Nebraska sarcastically described Hoover as 'the greatest publicity hound on the American continent,' adding ominously that unless Hoover's publicity stunts were stopped, 'there will be a spy behind every stump and a detective in every closet in our land.'

The controversy precipitated by these arrests was compounded later that month by a huge FBI vice raid in Miami, personally led by Hoover. The latter raid, combined with revelations that the Bureau had responded to requests for assistance from the Florida attorney general, provoked a fresh round of criticism, this time from conservatives. The conservative editor and publisher of the *New York Daily News,* renewed old complaints that such investigations provided a 'convenient instrument to blackmail' and condemned Hoover's meddling in the private lives of citizens. Vito Marcantonio, the radical congressman from New York City, characterized Hoover as a 'Stork Club detective' in a speech to which the *Daily News* gave prominent play. Again radicals and conservatives made common cause against Hoover.

Hoover could not ignore these criticisms, and, unable to deny the charges, he chose again to characterize them as part of an orchestrated 'smear' campaign. Then he moved quickly to contain the damage. He focused his efforts on his most serious adversaries: Patterson and Norris.

To Hoover, Patterson's attack smacked of spite, given the persistence of the captain's opposition to the Director's active promotion of vice investigations. Hoover demanded that his aides summarize whatever information the FBI had compiled on Patterson, which he maintained in his office for appropriate use.

Senator Norris's insistence on an investigation of

Hoover's stewardship of the FBI was a more disturbing matter still. The veteran senator, who had participated in the Senate investigations of Bureau activities in the early 1920s, enjoyed marked credibility with educated Americans and the liberal press. And he did not lack the courage of his convictions. In May he declared:

> Mr. Hoover has an organization, maintained at public expense, writing speeches for him to make or for anyone else to make who will take the speeches. When he makes a speech a copy is sent to practically every newspaper in the United States.
>
> No organization that I know of meets in Washington without having some person appear before it to tell what a great organization the FBI is. The greatest man of all, who stands at the head of it, never made a mistake, never made a blunder. In his hands lie the future and the perpetuity of our institutions and our Government.

Later that month the senator observed:

> Unless we do something to stop this furor of adulation and praise as being omnipotent, we shall have an organization − the organization of the FBI − which, instead of protecting our people from the civil acts of criminals, will itself in the end direct the Government by tyrannical force, as the history of the world shows has always been the case when secret police and secret detectives have been snooping around the homes of honest men.

Senator Wheeler, no longer the Progressive firebrand of the early 1920s but still a man of undoubted principle, soon joined the debate:

> I do not care how good a man is, how able he is, he cannot be placed in a detective service without being affected mentally, and becoming of the snooping detective type.

. . . Those who have been seeing things around the corner all these years, who have attacked every liberal Senator and gone through his office . . . raided the office of the senior Senator La Follette . . . They have had files upon this Senator and that Senator.

Who builds up the files? A lot of cheap, two-by-four detectives . . . It was 'flatfoots' of that kind who were in that Department during the Daugherty Administration, and some of them are still there. Mr. Hoover was there.[1]

Hoover was by no means idle while all this fuss was going on. Having cultivated a member of Senator Norris's staff, the Director was able to keep close tabs on the senator's activities. From this source Hoover learned on 3 April that 'the office of Senator Norris has received a large volume of mail. A large number of complaints are of [Bureau] mishandling [of] cases and violations of civil rights alleged in this mail, although there is also a volume of mail favorable to the Bureau.' Underscoring how closely Hoover was able to monitor Norris's activities, the report continued that the 'office of Senator Norris was not particularly interested in the allegations concerning the Director being in Florida [directing the Miami vice investigation and] . . . was not particularly concerned about wire tapping allegations . . . [but]) is somewhat aggravated because Attorney General Jackson has made a blanket denial of allegations [regarding the FBI's role in the Lincoln Brigade case] without investigation . . . The office of Senator Norris believes Bureau agents used chains and violated civil rights [in that case] . . . Senator Norris's office would not insist upon a Congressional investigation . . . [but recommends] that when the Attorney General finally replies to Senator Norris he admit human frailty and occasional error . . . and state in general effect that from this lesson much has been learned and the Department will be careful in the future.'

Hoover meanwhile had moved to ensure both the attorney general's and the White House's support.

Exploiting his contacts with Assistant Secretary of State Adolf Berle,[2] he learned of Berle's desire 'to take some action in defense of the Bureau and to indicate [Berle's] conviction that the charges made against the Bureau were unfounded.' Hoover had his number-two aide, Assistant Director Tamm, brief Berle on the facts of the case, including the claim that Max Lowenthal, a liberal maverick who had served on Wheeler's congressional staff and was then employed by an executive agency, was responsible for the dissemination of anti-Bureau accusations. Trying to be reassuring, Berle observed that Lowenthal, while often acting as a runner for White House aide Thomas Corcoran, also acted on his own. Berle promised 'to speak to the President about this whole matter.'

Hoover was unwilling to rely solely on Berle's intercession, however. On his own initiative he had already attempted to pressure Attorney General Jackson into coming to his defense. Immediately after Norris's first public criticism of the FBI's role in the Lincoln Brigade raids, he had written to the attorney general to convey his concern about the 'recent attacks upon the Bureau.' When Jackson did not respond, he had then instructed Tamm to approach the attorney general personally and, specifically, to call to his attention a Hearst wire service report that the criticisms were part of a 'smear Hoover movement' mounted by Roosevelt administration officials seeking to effect Hoover's removal.[3]

Tamm thereupon apprised Jackson's aide Ugo Carusi of the Director's concern about the story — 'an attempt on the part of Mr. Thomas Corcoran to make the FBI free of J. Edgar Hoover for political uses during the next year' — and of his inability to comment to reporters on what was going on as he did not know the facts. 'The newspapers . . . are assuming that the story is correct,' Tamm added ominously, 'because no one has commented upon it.'

Hoover, remaining behind his closed office doors throughout most of these proceedings, was kept constantly informed by such memos and carefully directed the negotiations of his aides. He had told Tamm what to say.

Briefed by Carusi, Jackson later that day invited Tamm to meet with him. At that meeting Tamm urged Jackson to comment publicly, citing in addition to the Hearst article Senator Norris's call for an investigation into the Bureau's handling of the arrests of the Lincoln Brigade recruiters. Agreeing that some action was needed, Jackson promised to respond publicly to Norris's letter.

Jackson, however, failed to do so immediately. Tamm again interceded to demand some public response. At first pleading a busy schedule but promising to complete work on a draft before nightfall, the attorney general revealed the real basis for his hesitancy: his own doubts about Hoover. 'He had been very dubious of Mr. Hoover's policies in operating the Bureau when he became Attorney General,' Jackson reportedly admitted, a view 'prompted in no small degree by statements made to him from time to time by former Attorney General Frank Murphy.' On one occasion, Jackson commented, Murphy had informed him that 'the Bureau had an investigative file upon Tommy Corcoran, one on Mr. Jackson and most of the governmental officials in Washington;[4] that the Bureau kept Tommy Corcoran under surveillance and that the Bureau maintained taps upon the telephone of some of the more prominent government officials.'

Tamm categorically denied these charges, insisting that the FBI's only investigations of government officials involved appointments. Jackson disarmed, reportedly 'then stated that although he had considerable doubt in his mind concerning Mr. Hoover and the policies of the Bureau, his recent discussion with Mr. Hoover had considerably clarified this matter. Jackson agreed to issue a public letter,' and the ensuing response was carefully crafted after consultation with Tamm and Assistant Attorney General Gordon Dean.

The seriousness of the crisis had led Hoover to take drastic action. Seeking to force Jackson's hand, he authorized Tamm to inform the attorney general of his willingness to resign 'at once' should Jackson have 'any question as to the Director's administration of the Bureau.' While Hoover had no intention of resigning, he recognized, astute student of

208

politics that he was, that such a threat would pressure the attorney general to come to his defense in public. Thus, he had Tamm emphasize that because the public reaction to stories of a rift between the attorney general and the Director had been 'so bad, particularly in view of the complete silence of the Department, . . . you [Hoover] did not desire to cause [Jackson] any embarrassment whatsoever . . . [and] would submit your resignation at once to him if he had any doubt or question as to your policies or program and that you would do it primarily to prevent the causing of any embarrassment.' As Hoover fully expected, Jackson declined the offer, reaffirming his desire that Hoover continue as Director.

Checked by Hoover's ploy as well as his own belated recognition of the Director's mass following, Jackson released his letter to the press the next day. In it, he reaffirmed his and the Director's solemn commitment to civil liberties. In language intended to disarm Hoover's critics and to undercut demands for an independent investigation of the FBI, Jackson claimed that on becoming attorney general he had reviewed Hoover's and the FBI's activities and that both he and Hoover had agreed to 'confine' FBI investigations to violations of federal statutes, collecting 'evidence in cases in which the United States is or may be a party' and servicing orders of the courts. Signaling that he considered the matter closed, Jackson concluded, 'In carrying out the program I have been asked and promised the continued and efficient service of Mr. Hoover.'

The executive department thereby capitulated – Jackson, like Murphy, was shortly named an associate justice of the Supreme Court – but the public debate continued. There, too, however, Hoover had his agents working. Under his direction the Bureau monitored not only the public pronouncements of leading citizens (for example, Columbia University anthropologist Franz Boaz), but the private concerns of members of Congress, including those who might help in mounting Hoover's counterattack. Of the latter, four were particularly forthcoming: Senators Robert R. Reynolds (D.-N.C.), Alexander Wiley (R.-Wisc.), Pat

McCarran (D.-Nev.), and Styles Bridges (R.-N.H.). Declaring on the floor of the Senate that 'we are not going to forget all these benefits which have been rendered by the [Bureau] men, and to quibble in a fashion that at least might be termed ungrateful as to whether they have observed all of the rules prescribed by those whose concern appears to be more with the rights of criminals than with the protection of our citizens,' Senator Reynolds continued in Hoover's behalf:

I say again that of all times in the history of our Nation we were never more in need of a man of his character, ability, courage, and experience than now . . . Mr. J. Edgar Hoover has always been open and aboveboard.

In a similar vein Senator Wiley assured his colleagues:

The character of the FBI Director on the basis of his record . . . and [his] known integrity would prevent any misuse of his powers . . . The history of his organization is that it has made the civil rights we possess more secure in America than they were before his organization came into being; that it has made life safer; that it has made it better for us.

Hoover's most important recruits, however, were the powerful conservative Democrat from Nevada, a senior member of the Senate Judiciary Committee (and eventually chairman of the Senate Internal Security Subcommittee), and the ultraconservative anti-New Dealer from New Hampshire.

Failing in an attempt to contact Hoover himself on 30 May, McCarran accepted an invitation to talk with Supervisor Hugh Clegg, to whom he denounced Norris's and Wheeler's criticisms and declared that Hoover 'has some friends in the Senate who would like to defend his organization.' 'If Mr. Hoover has been wrong, then it ought to be brought out,' McCarran asserted; 'if Mr. Hoover has not been wrong, Mr. Hoover ought to defend himself and furnish information to his friends in the Senate who would be glad to defend him.'

Assured of McCarran's reliability (following a check of the Bureau's dossier on the affable but opportunistic Nevada politician), Hoover ordered that the necessary information be provided. This was done within the week. Thus was the first link in the so-called McCarthyite dragnet forged.

Nor was McCarran alone. In words that the Director could easily have written, Bridges assumed the offensive, querying:

> What is the source and what is the purpose of this widespread and incessant attack upon the FBI? . . . the purpose . . . is to destroy another American citadel of faith and decency. Also, let us not forget that the first step in the demoralization of a nation is the undermining of its law enforcement agencies . . . The radical forces, the false liberals, and the 'pinks' throughout the country are up in arms against Mr. Hoover and the FBI.

Bridges did not confine his assistance to delivering speeches of praise and defense. In close collaboration with the Director, he sought to coordinate his efforts with those of the Bureau itself. When Hoover, for instance, meeting with Bridges on 9 October 1943, lamented that FBI agents were not receiving fair recognition for the 'very important war work which they are doing,' Bridges willingly agreed not only to 'make a speech on the floor of the Senate commending the Director and the FBI' but also to 'collaborate with the appropriate [FBI] officials with regard to just what exactly the contents of the speech should be.'

Then, on 24 July 1944, Bridges contacted Hoover's office to express renewed concern over 'the Communist situation' and his continued belief that the Bureau 'is the only one to handle this matter.' Pointing out to the Director that he 'could be of decided help to the Bureau if he changed over [his membership on] one of his sub-committees on Army and Navy Appropriations to the sub-committee on State and

211

Justice Appropriations,' the senator wondered 'whether the Bureau would like him to seek this transfer.'

Hoover immediately saw the advantages of the transfer, and with the reorganization of the Senate following the 1944 congressional elections, Bridges secured the desired reassignment. Thereafter the Director provided Bridges with 'some "ammunition" as to statistics and details' to restore the approximately $3 million cut from the FBI budget by the House Appropriations Committee, which monies were promptly restored.

Meanwhile the so-called smear campaign had fizzled out in a pathetic reprise. From the same informer on Norris's staff, Hoover had learned on 2 December 1940 that Senator Norris 'was engaged in preparing material for [another] blast at the Bureau.' Norris reportedly was reviewing the annual reports of the attorney general dating from 1911 and 'was taking careful steps to prevent anyone knowing what he was working on.' Hoover's 'reliable source on the Hill' pledged to 'check into the matter further' and the next day reported back on the intensity of Norris's research effort and 'particular interest in documents covering the period from 1918 to 1922.' (Referring to the Bureau's red-raiders of 1919 and 1920, Norris had already declared that 'all, without exception, [were] agents under the control and supervision of Mr. Hoover.')

Thus briefed, Hoover ordered a check with the Senate Document Room to identify the particular list of documents sought by Norris's office. Through discreet contacts on 18 and 30 December, the 'attached list of documents' was assembled, and Hoover learned that 'it is believed that this material is being obtained by Max Lowenthal for the purpose of preparing a tirade against the Bureau.'

And there, anticlimactically, that story ends. Lowenthal did obtain documentary proof of Hoover's intimate involvement in Palmer's red raids, published in 1950 in his book *The Federal Bureau of Investigation*. But exactly why Senator Norris decided to acquiesce in Hoover's repeated and untruthful denials remains unclear. What is clear is that the most serious congressional challenge to Hoover's continuance as Director had come to naught.

However, the press attacks on Hoover and his inflated image and prerogatives continued. To contain the challenge, Hoover assumed the offensive himself, adopting the same antiradical subterfuge earlier employed by William Burns in 1924 and regularly by Hoover thereafter. Appealing to the prejudices of his conservative constituency, Hoover dismissed criticisms of the FBI's conduct as 'smear' tactics inspired by Communists and Communist 'propagandists.' Addressing the American Legion's annual convention in Boston in September, barely three months after the fall of France to Nazi Germany, he publicly outlined this line of defense:

> That the FBI was feared by the forces it was pitted against was attested by the campaign of vilification and hate that was directed against it by Communists, their fellow travelers and mouthpieces. Falsehood after falsehood was spread, in high places and low, with the hope that a public esteem won by deeds and not words would be weakened.
>
> . . . The Communists and the alien propagandists will continue to direct their vituperations against law enforcement because they realize their cause is hopeless unless law enforcement can be weakened and discredited.

Clearly referring to the liberal institutions of higher learning in the neighborhood, he cautioned his audience:

> Intellectual freedom is American. Intellectual license and debauchery is un-American. In righteous indignation it is time to drive the debauchers of America out in the open . . .
>   If their motivations are sincere, but due to ignorance, they have no right to instruct in the mental and spiritual development of America's youth. And if they espouse foreign causes, then they should be stopped from

further debauching . . . American educational forces must come to grips in a unified manner with the needs of the hour.

Two weeks later, as Japanese troops advanced in French Indochina, Hoover reiterated his call to arms in a speech to the FBI's National Academy:

That there is a Fifth Column which has already started to march is an acknowledged reality. That it menaces America is an established fact. That it must be met is the common resolve of every red-blooded citizen. A Fifth Column of destruction, following in the wake of confusion, weakening the sinews and paralyzing it with fear can be met only by the nation-wide offensive of all law enforcement.

The metaphor of subversion as the insidious attack of an infectious disease remained staple Hoover rhetoric thereafter. The precise identity of the 'stalker,' the 'debaucher,' the 'violator' of our 'civil liberties' may have been intentionally obscured, but Hoover's message to his fellow germ-phobic antiradicals was abundantly clear:

Regardless of the good work you do, there still remains a group of persons who go around the country like a pack of mongrels, yapping ill-advised, badly conceived ideas. Animated by personal motives . . . they carry their knapsacks of lies, nostrums and subversive propaganda, seeking to blind the eyes of America while they scuttle the forces that stand between them and success in debauching the land we love. The record is clear. There are those who hold that the Government of the United States can be overthrown. But to succeed they must first conquer American law enforcement.

The mixed metaphors and labored figures of speech, not to mention the timely fudging of the identity of the 'enemy within,' did not obscure the basic message, which was that only the authorized and anointed enforcers of law stood between the American people and a monstrous force intent on constitutional rapine and plunder. To undermine the law enforcer therefore was to yield to the plunderer. 'We must awaken!' Hoover declaimed in a speech at the University of the South at Sewanee, Tennessee. 'Youth must take America tight to its heart – and love America for its Americanism.' The alternative at the time these words were spoken – only days after Nazi Germany launched its invasion of the Soviet Union – was to yield to that other kind of invasion that weakens from within, 'poisons,' 'violates': America's only coherent radicalism, Communism and its unwitting allies.

Brush fires continued for another year – Francis Biddle, Attorney General Jackson's successor, apparently intended to dismiss Hoover but did not, and the surprise Japanese attack on Pearl Harbor prompted charges of Bureau incompetence – but in the end Hoover prevailed. Always forewarned, always forearmed, he fought his enemies tooth and nail and won.

Expanding the Bureau's Surveillance Activity

To a man of Hoover's ambition, the securing of his position was by no means an end in itself. With the eruption of warfare in Europe and the prospect of eventual U.S. involvement, a world of opportunity opened. He readily seized this chance to extend his grasp and neutralize his rivals, of whom the most visible in 1940 was Martin Dies, the conservative Democratic chairman of the Special House Committee on Un-American Activities.

The effort to expand the Bureau's authority came first. The secrecy required by the outbreak of the European war, and President Roosevelt's eagerness to defuse criticisms of his administration's nonneutral foreign policy, soon gave Hoover an opportunity to reach out with presidential approval, especially in the area of wiretapping policy.

Congress had specifically banned wiretapping in 1934

215

when it enacted section 605 of the Communications Act, forbidding any person to 'intercept any [wire and radio] communication and divulge or publish the existence, contents, substance, purport, effect, or meaning of such intercepted communication to any person.' Despite this ban, the Justice Department had continued to wiretap, adopting the position that the term 'any person' did not apply to federal investigative agents — a construction struck down by the Supreme Court on 20 December 1937 in the case of *Nardone* v. *United States*.

Hoover had at the time consulted Assistant Attorney General Alexander Holtzoff about 'the significance to the Bureau of the Supreme Court decision.' Responding, Holtzoff denied that the ruling was significant; the Communications Act banned interception *and* divulgence — hence, interception alone was not a violation. The act's restriction, he said, applied only to interstate phone calls. Acting on this assurance and Holtzoff's promise that the department would not prosecute FBI agents engaged in wiretapping, Hoover reaffirmed his standing policy: 'no phone tapping without my approval and as previously we will not authorize any except in extraordinary cases and then not to obtain evidence but only for collateral leads.'

In a second *Nardone* ruling, however, handed down on 11 December 1939, the Supreme Court extended its earlier ban on wiretap evidence to include the 'derivative use' of intercepted conversations (that is, information obtained from wiretapping could not be used during prosecution, and any evidence based on taps tainted the case and would necessitate throwing out the indictment). Delivering the majority opinion, Justice Owen Roberts argued that 'taken at face value the phrase "no person" comprehends federal agents . . . It is urged that a construction be given the section which would exclude federal agents since it is improbable Congress intended to hamper and impede the activities of the government in the detection and punishment of crime. The answer is that . . . Congress may have thought it less important that some offenders should go unwhipped than that officers should resort to methods deemed inconsistent with ethical standards and destructive of personal liberty.'

Although Holtzoff clung to his earlier position that the 'Federal Communications Act penalizes the divulging or publication of information obtained through the interception of interstate messages and that consequently the Bureau was under no legal or implied prohibition from utilizing telephone taps for investigative purposes only in cases of major importance,' Hoover was unwilling to risk continued FBI wiretapping on this basis. Sensitive to popular fears of government power, he sought, as always, to avoid public discussion. Unwilling to advocate legislation to authorize wiretapping by federal law enforcement officers as too controversial, he instead recommended that 'if the Department saw fit to indorse [sic] some type of wiretapping it should only be done after some outstanding lawyers, with liberal reputations, were consulted as to the type of legislation to be drafted.' When the department decided that Congress would not so act, Attorney General Jackson, on Hoover's recommendation, publicly announced that FBI wiretapping and other policy would conform to the recent rulings of the Supreme Court; that is: 'Wire tapping, entrapment, or the use of any other improper, illegal, or unethical tactics will not be tolerated by the Bureau.'

Jackson's ban did not long remain in force, however. In this case, the initiative came from the president. Worried that 'certain other nations have been engaged in the organization of propaganda or so-called "fifth columns" in other countries and in preparation for sabotage, as well as in active sabotage,' Roosevelt on 21 May 1940 issued a secret wiretapping directive. In it, he authorized the attorney general to approve on a case-by-case basis wiretapping of the 'conversation or other communications of persons suspected of *subversive* activities against the Government of the United States, including suspected spies. You are requested furthermore to limit these investigations so conducted to a minimum and to limit them insofar as possible to aliens' (emphasis added).

If Roosevelt intended thereby to limit FBI wiretapping

217

and to ensure that any tapping would be subject to the prior approval of the attorney general, his concern for secrecy (like that of the attorney general) foreordained that his objectives would not be met. Describing the procedures to be followed under this new policy, Jackson advised Hoover, as Hoover noted for the record, that 'he would have no detailed record kept concerning the cases in which wiretapping would be utilized. It was agreeable to him [Jackson] that I [Hoover] would maintain a memorandum book in my immediate office, listing the time, places, and cases in which this procedure is to be utilized.'

Jackson's decision not to maintain any record of his approval of specific FBI wiretaps finally opened the floodgates for Hoover. In effect, only if briefed about them by Hoover would subsequent attorneys general become aware of ongoing FBI wiretaps. Furthermore, since no attorney general maintained a record of approved wiretaps, Hoover could now authorize taps on his own authority and continue taps indefinitely whenever he judged they provided useful information.

Having his own priorities, and unwilling to accede to either the department's or the White House's political line, Hoover could now proceed safely – the president's secret directive had provided an unanticipated opening, and the attorney general's attendant decision to minimize the risk of discovery invited the highly politicized Director to advance his own political line.

Nor was his success in extending the FBI's investigative activities by circumventing the oversight role of the attorney general, his ostensible superior, confined to the use of wiretaps. In the equally unconstitutional area of preventive detention policy, Hoover charted an even bolder course.

On 2 September 1939, immediately following the German invasion of Poland, Hoover, acting on his own authority, had ordered all SACs to prepare reports on persons of 'German, Italian, and *Communist* sympathies' (emphasis added) and others 'whose interest may be directed primarily to the interest of some other nation than the United States.' The names of these persons were to be incorporated in a code-named Custodial Detention index composed of 'both aliens and citizens of the United States, on whom there is information available that their presence at liberty in this country in time of war or national emergency would be dangerous to the public peace and the safety of the United States Government.' Aware that this preventive detention program lacked any statutory authority and thus would provoke demands for his dismissal were it to become known, Hoover stipulated that the program 'should be entirely confidential and . . . [that the] color of authority under which these matters are handled is, of course, the Registration Act and, if necessary, inquiries as to the reason for the investigation should be answered by reference to the Registration Act requiring agents of foreign principals to register with the State Department.'

As the Registration Act in no sense envisaged empowering the government to spy on American citizens, Hoover's unilateral program entailed the abrupt abrogation of the constitutional rights of every American citizen affected by it. Lacking any statutory authority, however, his program could not become operational without at least the approval of the attorney general.

Belatedly, then, in June 1940, Hoover sought Attorney General Jackson's policy guidance in respect to 'a suspect list of individuals [sic] whose arrest might be considered necessary in the event the United States becomes involved in war.' And Jackson, undisturbed by the lack of any statutory authority and apparently unaware of Hoover's ambitious investigative plans, which involved mostly left-wing activists, concurred in the need to prepare a Custodial Detention index. Still, the attorney general directed the head of the department's Neutrality Laws Unit to review the names of the individuals whom the FBI proposed to list on its index.

Hoover had not anticipated Jackson's insistence on a supervisory role and immediately protested that this requirement might compromise the FBI's confidential sources and adversely affect its 'counter-espionage activities.' Urging that the departmental personnel assigned

219

to conduct these reviews 'be selected with a great deal of care,' he insisted that the department forgo prosecuting any individuals listed in the Custodial Detention index, as this might publicly expose FBI informers (and, incidentally, reveal whom the Bureau was investigating).

After five months of difficult negotiations, Jackson reached a compromise with Hoover permitting departmental review while meeting Hoover's objections. Under this agreement, the department would not prosecute any individual if this 'might interfere with sound investigative techniques' and would not disclose the identity of the FBI's confidential informers without Hoover's 'prior approval.'

In addition, Jackson had decided not to seek formal legislative authority for Hoover's preventive detention program. To surmount this problem, the attorney general outlined the following strategy: Following the outbreak of war and the issuance of a presidential proclamation, the attorney general would authorize warrants to arrest those alien enemies whose names were listed on the index while a specially established departmental committee would consider prosecuting listed American citizens under the Smith Act of 1940 'or some other appropriate statute.'

Francis Biddle, Jackson's successor as attorney general, did not share this indifference to whether or not the Custodial Detention program had statutory authority. Reviewing the operation of this program during the early war years, after the specter of the Fifth Column had failed to materialize, Biddle concluded on 6 July 1943 that 'these individual danger classifications . . . serve no useful purpose.' The Department's Alien Control Unit, responsible for detaining alien enemies, Biddle added, had found these classification procedures to be useless. Moreover, in a damning attack on his predecessor's policy, he emphasized: 'There is no statutory authorization or other present justification for keeping a "custodial detention" list of *citizens* [emphasis added]. The Department fulfills its proper functions by investigating the activities of persons who may have violated the law. It is not aided in this work by classifying persons as to dangerousness.' Biddle thereupon ordered Hoover to cease using such classifications and to include a card in the files of any individual given a custodial detention classification stipulating, 'This classification is unreliable. It is hereby cancelled, and should not be used as a determination of dangerousness or of any other fact.'

But Biddle's order did not resolve the matter, so independent had Hoover become and so convinced of the correctness of his own assessment of the 'subversive' threat. Unwilling to abandon an investigation-detention program and emboldened by having devised procedures that successfully averted discovery, the Director technically complied with Biddle's order — but only by changing the name of the program. Since the attorney general had banned a 'custodial detention' program, Hoover, on 14 August 1943, advised SACs that henceforth the 'character of investigations of individuals (other than alien enemies) who may be dangerous or potentially dangerous to the public safety or internal security of the United States shall be "Security Matter" and not "Custodial Detention." The phraseology, "Custodial Detention," shall no longer be used to designate the character of the investigation, nor shall it be used for any purpose in reports or other communications.' And to ensure that Biddle could not discover that he had circumvented his order by renaming the program, Hoover stipulated 'the fact that the Security Index and Security Index cards are prepared and maintained should be considered as strictly confidential, and should at no time be mentioned or alluded to in investigative reports, or discussed with agencies or individuals outside the Bureau other than duly qualified field representatives of the Office of Naval Intelligence and the Military Intelligence Service, and then only on a strictly confidential basis.'

As this concealment order suggests, Hoover's genius in anticipating problems of external oversight prevented higher authorities from discovering his ambitious political agenda and use of illegal investigative activities. By instituting a series of secret report-writing and filing procedures, Hoover in effect sequestered from authorized inspection all sensitive Bureau data.

Normally documents sent to FBI headquarters or maintained in field offices were indexed and recorded in a central records system, and each document was serialized — that is, numbered consecutively in individual case files (see the source notes in this book). Adherence to this practice, however, would inevitably render Hoover's authorization of illegal or politically motivated investigations vulnerable to court-ordered discovery motions, congressional subpoena, or requests from ostensibly superior Justice Department officials for particular case files. Therefore in 1940–1942 the Director, when launching a massive domestic surveillance program, devised a series of separate filing and reporting procedures. Especially sensitive documents were no longer to be indexed or recorded in the FBI's central records system but were to be maintained in the office files of Hoover's senior aides. Neither indexed nor recorded in the central records system, these documents theoretically did not exist. They could either be safely destroyed or allow Hoover and his aides to claim, in response to any demands for all documents pertaining to a specific investigation, that all relevant documents included in the FBI's 'central records system' had been produced.

Hoover first instituted this practice on 11 April 1940 when instructing other FBI officials how to prepare memoranda that were not to be filed in the FBI's central records system and, in some cases, were not to be maintained permanently. Such memoranda were to be prepared 'without carbon copies' on colored paper (first blue and then pink; in contrast, memoranda that were to be indexed and filed were prepared on white paper) containing the following notation on the bottom of the page: 'This Memorandum is for Administrative Purposes — To Be Destroyed After Action is Taken and Not Sent to Files.'

Spelling out the criteria for preparing and filing such memoranda, Hoover on 1 March 1942 advised that color-coded memoranda were to be used to report information 'solely for the benefit of the Director which will possibly be seen by the Director and other officials and eventually be returned to the dictator [of the memorandum] to be destroyed or *retained in the Director's office*' (emphasis added).

Similar procedures were to be employed when reporting information that could 'lead to subsequent embarrassment' (because obtained without a search warrant or otherwise illegally). Field offices were to submit such information on 'a separate unnumbered sheet of paper' attached to the agent's formal report without any reference to the attachment. To minimize the risk of the discovery of this requirement, Hoover's order was not conveyed in writing to FBI field offices but was instead transmitted either during 'retraining classes' attended by FBI agents or 'telephonically communicated to the individual Agents in Charge.'

Then, having decided that information about radical political activities (subscription and membership lists and correspondence) could only be obtained through break-ins of the offices of these organizations or the residences of their key officials, Hoover in 1942 further refined these procedures. Because 'black bag jobs' (the Bureau's term for break-ins) were 'clearly illegal' and thus authorization could not be obtained 'from outside the Bureau' (i.e., the attorney general), Hoover devised the 'Do Not File' reporting procedure.

Under this procedure, the SAC prepared a memorandum requesting approval to use this technique. In this memo, the SAC was required to 'completely justify the need for the technique and at the same time assure that it can be safely used without any danger of embarrassment to the Bureau.' Submitted to Hoover or Tolson 'for approval,' the memo was subsequently 'filed in the Assistant Director's office under a "Do Not File" procedure.' SACs prepared similar unrecorded ('informal') memoranda recording Hoover's approval, which were, in turn, maintained in their office safes 'until the next semi-annual inspection by Bureau inspectors, at which time [they were] destroyed.'

Ironically, having successfully prevented discovery of the scope of the FBI's investigations of radical political activities, including the use of illegal investigative techniques,

Hoover became the target of criticisms voiced by Congressman Dies among others that the Bureau was not devoting sufficient attention to confronting the serious German and Soviet espionage threats to American security. In a nationwide radio address of May 1940, for example, Dies claimed that the House Select Committee on Un-American Activities had access to 'a wealth of information on alien agents, including plans, names, and their headquarters.'

With consummate skill Hoover turned this potential embarrassment to his advantage. Briefing the attorney general on the congressman's speech, he urged Jackson to ask Dies to forward his information to the Bureau. Because Dies's charges were publicly made, Hoover argued, 'unless we make some approach to him requesting that he let us have any pertinent information, he may later claim to have had information upon which the Department should have acted and that he was never contacted for it after he had announced that he had such extensive information such as plans, names, and headquarters of subversive groups.'

Having persuaded the president to issue the public directive of September 1939 authorizing the Bureau alone to coordinate information relating to investigations involving national defense matters and 'take charge of investigations' involving violations of the espionage, sabotage, and neutrality laws, Hoover was determined to limit the Dies Committee's role in investigating 'subversive activities.' His motives were partly personal – he resented both the congressman's efforts to steal the limelight and his implied criticism of the FBI's handling of internal security investigations – and partly political. For although the rivals had a common ideological commitment to antiradicalism, they no longer shared a loyalty to the Roosevelt administration.

Dies had first been elected to Congress in 1930, at the age of twenty-nine, and had supported Roosevelt enthusiastically throughout the president's first term. But after the Supreme Court-packing affair, he joined his fellow Texan, Vice

224

President John Nance Garner, in a march toward the right. By 1940 Dies had turned vigorously against the New Deal, a realignment that Hoover may well privately have shared but was unwilling to assist, dependent as he was on the president's support and fearing as he did Dies's challenge to his authority as the chief red-hunter.

Under Hoover's supervision, therefore, FBI agents monitored the activities of the committee in Washington and of its members in their districts. The agents were instructed to obtain information on the committee's efforts to publicize its accomplishments, especially its claims to having uncovered information about subversive activities either not known to federal agencies or not shared with the committee by the Department of Justice and the FBI.

Then denying that there was any substance to the committee's assertions once they were made, Hoover sought the department's assistance to make Dies submit his information to the Bureau, to question his claimed achievements, and even to consider inviting him to present his evidence to a federal grand jury as the best means of establishing the emptiness of his claims. With this in mind, Hoover submitted to the attorney general a detailed memorandum on the congressman's specific criticisms of the administration, another to the effect that the Republicans were considering drafting Dies to run as their vice presidential candidate on the 1940 ticket, and yet another to the effect that Dies might campaign on behalf of the Republicans. Dies's 'great delusions of personal grandeur,' Hoover darkly warned, could lead him to plan 'a public hearing of spectacular dimensions for the purpose of advancing his designation [sic] as head of the Federal Bureau of Investigation.'

Hoover undoubtedly gave credence to Dies's claims to having the names of Communists employed by the federal government (since both the committee and the Bureau had obtained this information from break-ins at the offices of radical organizations). But here again he regarded Dies's assertions simply as intrusions on his own authority, especially after Congress in the summer of 1940 appropriated

$100,000 to enable the Bureau to investigate all federal employees who were 'members of "subversive" organizations'[5] and report their names to Congress. Playing both sides of the street, Hoover protested to the attorney general over the committee's irresponsibility in citing exact numbers of Communists employed by the federal government, while at the same time, through the Bureau's informers on the committee's staff, he vainly tried to obtain the committee's lists.

Worried that the committee could undercut the Bureau's authority in the internal security field, Hoover orchestrated an elaborate behind-the-scenes press campaign to discredit it and its chairman as irresponsible and demagogic. Using his own and the Bureau's contacts with selected 'friendly' reporters and editors, the Director leaked damaging information about Dies and the committee. Briefed by his aides on the pros and cons of complying with requests for information to be used in articles and editorials criticizing Dies, Hoover ordered that the FBI 'do so at once,' and on at least one occasion personally furnished derogatory information to editorial writer Jack Carley of the *Memphis Commercial Appeal*.

Thereafter, and for the duration of World War II, Hoover demanded that his agents closely monitor the activities of the Dies Committee and at one time he even considered planting an informer in the committee, an idea he finally rejected as too risky.

Hoover and the Other Intelligence Agencies

As the man in charge of America's domestic security in World War II, Hoover was responsible not only for coordinating the intelligence gathered by all federal intelligence agencies but also for preventing enemy spying and acts of sabotage. In this latter capacity — which applied, incidentally, to the entire Western Hemisphere under a secret wartime presidential directive of June 1940 — Hoover was extremely successful. There was little spying and virtually

226

no sabotage at home after the United States entered the war, mostly owing to the speed with which Hoover's men rounded up German and Japanese agents after the attack on Pearl Harbor. German spying in the fascist enclaves of Hispanic America was successfully contained. Moreover, when a German U-boat put ashore a team of eight saboteurs on the South Shore of Long Island in June 1942, Hoover had them all in jail within forty-eight hours.

But Hoover's Bureau was reluctant to cooperate with other intelligence agencies, especially if that cooperation could curb the Director's goal of establishing the Bureau's monopoly in the internal security field. Although sharing the antiradical biases of his counterparts in these other agencies, Hoover for strategic reasons sought to limit their domestic intelligence role. His principal loyalty was to the FBI and himself, and he tended to define the national interest accordingly.

Hoover's transactions with the other intelligence agencies dated from the end of World War I, during his tenure as special assistant to the attorney general. At that time, as previously discussed, he had cooperated intimately with Immigration officials to plan and effect the arrests of alien radicals for deportation under the 1918 Immigration Act. This cooperation was mutually reinforcing. For with the formal end of hostilities, Hoover lacked any statutory authority to investigate American radical activists, and the Immigration Bureau, whose deportation responsibilities repaired that deficiency, had no intelligence force of its own. It therefore behooved the young prosecutor to cooperate in planning and executing the so-called Palmer raids.

At the same time, however, Hoover's relations with the military intelligence agencies were vexed. With the end of the war, Attorney General Palmer severed the Bureau's connection with the American Protective League (APL), announcing that Justice Department officials were to have no official dealings with any private organization. Unwilling to abandon the field and convinced that radical activists threatened the national security, APL officials then volunteered their services to and were welcomed by military

227

intelligence agents, notably Colonel Marlborough Churchill, the head of MID, in the development of a contingency plan, War Plans White, devised to deal with an expected postwar uprising of labor and radicals.

Hoover's abiding concern about the possible intrusion of military and naval intelligence agencies into the field of domestic surveillance was not without cause. On the one hand, the FBI's surveillance of radical activists, reinstituted on a massive scale during the late 1930s and acquiring momentum throughout the World War II and Cold War years, was Hoover's ticket to fame and fortune; domestic political surveillance expanded the FBI's authority and won Hoover a powerful constituency among American conservatives. On the other hand, any activities that threatened to curb the Bureau's authority and operations (whether judicial or congressional oversight or the encroachment by other federal intelligence agencies) alarmed him.

Hoover had acted to expand the FBI's investigative role, and in the process to obtain external authority to monitor dissident political movements and activists, even prior to U.S. involvement in World War II. First, the Director had Roosevelt's authorization of 25 August 1936. This was not the total victory Hoover sought, for under this arrangement, he was required to coordinate the Bureau's investigative activities with both the State Department and the military intelligence agencies, all of which had an interest in limiting the FBI's role. Second, Hoover had Roosevelt's authorization of 2 November 1938, granting the Bureau $150,000 in discretionary funds to expand its domestic intelligence operations. And, finally, he had the grant of exclusive authority to coordinate domestic intelligence that FDR communicated to him secretly on 26 June 1939.

Roosevelt's 26 June order assigned primary responsibility for domestic intelligence investigations to the FBI, but it left unresolved the scope of the military and naval intelligence services' investigative activities. With the outbreak of World War II, a further problem surfaced, concerning the activities of local police and private citizens' groups. On 6 September

228

1939 Hoover apprised Attorney General Murphy of a decision of the New York City Police Department to create 'a special sabotage squad' of fifty detectives and a plan to augment this squad in the 'rather near future to comprise 150 men.' Creation of this squad, Hoover observed, had resulted in considerable publicity in the New York City newspapers 'and consequently much information in the hands of private citizens concerning sabotage and saboteurs will be transmitted to the New York City Police Department rather than to the FBI.' Emphasizing the need for efficiency and the danger of the recurrence of vigilante-type activities, he urgently recommended that President Roosevelt issue 'a statement or request addressed to all police officials in the United States and instructing them to turn over to the nearest representative of the Federal Bureau of Investigation any information obtained pertaining to espionage, counterespionage, sabotage, subversive activities and neutrality regulations.'

Impressed by Hoover's civil liberties argument, Murphy that same day persuaded the president to issue a draft statement prepared by Hoover. Roosevelt's statement authorized the FBI to 'take charge of investigative work in matters relating to espionage, sabotage, and violations of the neutrality regulations.' To ensure that this task would be handled in a 'comprehensive and effective manner on a national basis,' all local police officials were directed 'promptly to turn over to the nearest representative of the Federal Bureau of Investigation any information obtained by them relating to espionage, sabotage, subversive activities, and violations of the neutrality laws.'

In a press conference publicizing Roosevelt's statement, Attorney General Murphy emphasized his and the president's concerns for efficiency and for averting vigilante-type activities. Murphy's prepared statement stressed that 'foreign agents and those engaged in espionage' would no longer have a safe haven for their activities, as there 'will be no repetition of the confusion and laxity and indifference of twenty years ago.' Many new FBI offices had been opened, Murphy continued, and concluded by praising the professionalism of FBI agents and declaring that 'if you want this work done in a reasonable and responsible way it must not turn into a witch hunt. We must do no wrong to any man.'

Hoover immediately exploited the president's statement by sending a copy of it to all law enforcement officials 'in order that if you have not already been advised of the President's desires in the handling of cases of the type above enumerated, you may be informed concerning the Federal Government's program.' Hoover thereupon requested their cooperation in 'immediately notifying the nearest representative of the Federal Bureau of Investigation of any information received relating to cases in the above classifications.'

Roosevelt's September 1939 statement not only pre-empted local police investigations of 'subversive' activities; it also provided the first and only presidential authorization for the FBI's collection of information on dissident political activities. Heretofore, lacking any legislative charter, the FBI could conduct investigations only when Congress enacted legislation criminalizing particular activities. Roosevelt's statement, however, although it apparently only reaffirmed the FBI's legislatively mandated authority to investigate violations of the espionage, sabotage, and neutrality laws and did not explicitly authorize FBI investigations of dissident political activities (or, as Hoover generally described them, 'subversive activities') did provide a loophole.

The president authorized the FBI to be the recipient of 'any information relating to . . . subversive activities' acquired by local police officials. To be sure, the president had not authorized the FBI to investigate but only to receive information from local police officials pertaining to 'subversive activities.' But this statement provided a mandate for Hoover to maintain such information – and emboldened him to further expand the FBI's surveillance role.

There remained, however, the problem of delimiting the role of military and naval intelligence, particularly as these

230

services had defined their mission broadly during World War I and had continued during the 1920s and 1930s to investigate dissident political activities. Officials in these agencies, as in the FBI, might also attempt to exploit the war crisis to expand their authority. Nor was this possibility just hypothetical. For Hoover, this prospect assumed an ominous dimension in the fall of 1940 when American Legion officials, rebuffed by Attorney General Jackson when earlier offering their services to investigate 'subversive activities,' considered assisting either military intelligence or the Dies Committee. Again employing the rhetoric of a civil libertarian, Hoover persuaded Jackson to reconsider his rebuff and instead authorize the FBI to institute an American Legion Contact Program. Then he redoubled his efforts to restrain his military competitors.

During the 1930s military and naval intelligence officials had developed plans that spilled over into the domestic political surveillance field. The Attorney's MID, for example, developed an intelligence plan in 1936 for its Sixth Corps area (which covered Michigan, Illinois, and Wisconsin) calling for the collection and indexing of the names of members of several thousand suspect groups, ranging from the American Civil Liberties Union to pacifist student groups alleged to be Communist-dominated. The Army's sources of information included the FBI, the Treasury and Post Office departments, local police, and private intelligence bureaus employed by businessmen to keep track of organized labor.

Naval intelligence focused on these groups as well. In the mid-1930s William Puleston, director of ONI, authorized his agents to gather information on radicals, subversives, pacifists, and Communists through physical surveillance 'and other surreptitious methods.' The head of the Ninth Naval District and Great Lakes Training Station, John Downes, enlisted *Cleveland News* editor Dan Hanna and other prominent midwesterners in his reserve intelligence team. Downes also created an industrial intelligence service that infiltrated every firm under contract to the Navy to inform on suspected labor radicals, spies, or saboteurs who

231

might compromise the national defense by seeking to organize workers or strikes.

Concerned with 'subversive activities that undermine the loyalty and efficiency' of Army and Navy personnel and of civilians involved in military construction and maintenance, military and naval intelligence officials, lacking trained investigators of their own, had since 1938 turned to the FBI 'to conduct investigative activity in strictly civilian matters of a domestic character.' ONI, MID, and the FBI exchanged information of mutual interest; this arrangement was essentially voluntary, and without a formal delimitation agreement, ONI and MID might decide to expand their own capabilities.

Accordingly, acting on the authority of Roosevelt's 26 June 1939 directive, Hoover ordered his aides to develop a plan specifying the responsibilities of the FBI, ONI, and MID as the basis for such an agreement. Then, on 29 May 1940, relying on these recommendations, he submitted a proposal to the heads of the other intelligence agencies.

According to the terms of Hoover's proposal, during peacetime the FBI would 'handle all cases involving allegations of espionage, sabotage and such related matters as pertain to the activities of persons in the United States' not directly employed by the War and Navy departments 'who attempt to frustrate plans for national defense.'

Also, the FBI would conduct surveys of those industrial plants 'of essential interest' to the War and Navy departments and would 'keep in close touch with the activities and developments of Un-American[6] groups whose activities are aimed to frustrate or interfere with the national defense program.'

The FBI would share 'all information obtained during the course of its investigations which may be of interest to the armed services'; the three agencies would designate liaison officers 'to maintain contact with each other,' and regular weekly conferences would be held 'for the purpose of exchanging information of mutual interest, outlining programs and suggested future procedure in various categories for the individual agencies.'

In cooperation with MID, the FBI would prepare 'a program of internal security and protection to be followed in the event of domestic violence or other major internal strife,' while the War Department would have troops 'available to perform guard and police work in those situations which are beyond the control of the instructed municipal and state authorities.'

During wartime, the proposed agreement declared, 'in so far as it is possible and practical the War and Navy Departments should restrain [sic] from activities involving the investigation or prosecution of civilians.' The FBI was to have exclusive investigative responsibility for nonmilitary personnel, while the War and Navy departments 'will handle exclusively the entire censorship program with necessary administrative regulations permitting the immediate transmittal to the Federal Bureau of Investigation of any information developed through the censorship which will be of interest to the Federal Bureau of Investigation in connection with its espionage and counter-espionage work.'

Hoover's 29 May memorandum provided the basis for a delimitation agreement that the heads of the FBI, ONI, and MID approved on 5 June, defining their agencies' jurisdiction 'in the investigation of matters of interest to the national defense.' In accordance with Roosevelt's 26 June and 6 September 1939 directives, the FBI was assigned 'responsibility for all investigations' involving civilians on condition that it keep MID and ONI fully informed about developments relating to defense plants, vital utilities, critical points of transportation and communication, and 'cases of actual or strongly presumptive espionage or sabotage, including the names of individuals definitely known to be connected with subversive activities.'

In addition, the FBI was to 'act as the coordinating head of all civilian organizations furnishing information relating to subversive movements,' to 'assume responsibility for ascertaining the location, leadership, strength and organization of all civilian groups designed to combat "Fifth Column" activities,' and to inform MID and ONI fully of all 'information concerning these organizations and information received concerning their possession of arms.' ONI's and MID's investigative responsibilities were strictly limited to those cases involving individuals employed by the military services and civilians in the Canal Zone, Republic of Panama, the Philippines, Guam, and American Samoa.

Finally, the FBI was to investigate 'all cases in those categories directed from foreign countries . . . in which the State, War or Navy Departments specifically request investigation of a designated group or set of circumstances.' Hoover and his counterparts (Sherman Miles, the head of MID, and Walter Anderson, the head of ONI), however, agreed that this class of investigations had not been adequately defined and accordingly instituted 'a further study of [the foreign field category] matter.'

Notwithstanding its far-reaching provision of FBI authority, the 5 June 1940 delimitation agreement did not resolve the jurisdictional question to Hoover's satisfaction. In the first place, he remained concerned about a proposal Congressman Dies had made that the president 'should form a Home Defense Council to coordinate the work of the FBI, Military Intelligence, the Naval Intelligence, and the Dies Committee for the purpose of combating the so-called "Fifth Column" movement.' Dismissing this proposal as unnecessary in view of the steps the FBI had already taken under President Roosevelt's 6 September 1939 'order,' Hoover wrote to White House aide Edwin Watson and Attorney General Jackson to recommend that 'someone at a very early date should clear up any misunderstanding which the Dies statement may have created in the public's mind as to the need for a central coordinating agency for these matters.' To document his contention that matters were already working well, Hoover outlined in detail the FBI's effort to 'build up a system of internal security' and the excellent cooperation and coordination between the FBI, ONI, and MID.

Second, despite the positive tone of Hoover's report to the White House, the Director remained concerned about actions of ONI and MID that threatened to encroach on his monopoly in the internal security area, an anxiety compounded in January 1941 by proposed legislation (H.R. 2106 and S. 345) supported by the Navy Department that would 'authorize Naval Agents to assist civil authorities in the enforcement of law.' Seeking to enlist Jackson's aid to defeat the proposal, Hoover outlined to the attorney general his objections. The proposed bill, he said, did not 'confine the operations of Naval Agents to Naval establishments or personnel under the control of the Navy Department' and would thus authorize ONI officials to arrest 'any person alleged to be violating any statute pertaining to the National Defense.' If enacted, the bill would broaden the authority of ONI agents 'and would tend to duplicate the entire field covered by the Federal Bureau of Investigation in National Defense work.'

Stressing that the 'duplication of work' would be 'inefficient and expensive,' Hoover questioned the wisdom of granting naval or military agents the 'power of arrest in civilian fields.' Moreover, under the proposed statute, naval agents would have greater authority than the FBI, he pointed out, adding that the FBI could not seek warrants in 'National Defense' cases 'until these cases have been considered and specific authorization obtained in each instance' from the Department of Justice's Neutrality Laws Unit. In contrast, ONI agents, under the proposed legislation, 'will not be subject to this administrative regulation and restriction, and would therefore be in a position to function more quickly and more expeditiously in cases involving violations of statutes pertaining to the National Defense.'

Again, Hoover's objections prevailed. Jackson personally intervened with Secretary of the Navy Frank Knox, recommending that the 'bill should either be withdrawn or radically amended,' and the attorney general's opposition succeeded in undercutting congressional support for the proposal.

Hoover's discovery of the military's domestic surveillance interests — a source of constant contention among the services — combined with the unanticipated problems stemming from the creation of the Bureau's Special

Intelligence Service (SIS) on 21 June 1940 (established solely for the purpose of collecting economic, political, industrial, and financial information concerning the Latin American nations), led him on 7 February 1941 to propose a new delimitation agreement to replace the old one. Submitting to Attorney General Jackson a draft proposal covering both foreign and domestic intelligence investigations, the Director explained that its purpose was to 'cover [the subject] as completely and comprehensively as possible, and anticipate such difficulties as might arise in the future so that if this memorandum is approved by the President there would seem to be little or no reason for further controversies.' Under his proposal, the Director would chair the Inter-departmental Committee on Intelligence, established in 1939 to coordinate the intelligence activities of the FBI, ONI, and MID.

In support of this recommendation, Hoover noted that MID chief Miles had in the past called 'meetings on his own initiative, which led to certain complications.' Justifying the proposal's fine delineation of the FBI's exclusive responsibility in the domestic surveillance area and its strict limitation of ONI's and MID's domestic investigative roles, Hoover denied that the FBI sought 'any additional authority in intelligence work.' On the contrary, he claimed that 'if certain phases of intelligence work are to be handled, there should be no overlapping or duplication of effort, in order to insure greater efficiency and avoid complications, and for that reason one agency should be designated to do certain things and other agencies designated to handle matters in their particular fields.'

Hoover's revised delimitation agreement was not approved until 9 February 1942. By then the Japanese attack on Pearl Harbor, and actual U.S. involvement in World War II, favored issuance of the agreement, covering 'investigation of all activities coming under the categories of espionage, counterespionage, subversion and sabotage.' In the domestic area, the agreement guaranteed an FBI monopoly, as the FBI would conduct all investigations 'involving civilians in the United States' and keep MID and ONI fully informed of 'important developments . . . including the names of individuals definitely known to be connected with subversive activities.'

Hoover's success in seizing the field derived from the support he received from President Roosevelt, who for his own reasons welcomed the expansion of FBI surveillance activities. Roosevelt, moreover, was aware that FBI investigations ranged far afield and extended beyond investigating violations of federal statutes.

In fact, the president did not hesitate to use Hoover's FBI to advance his own policy interests. For example, on Roosevelt's order in July 1940, Assistant Secretary of State Berle contacted Hoover to relay a particularly sensitive request. *St. Louis Post-Dispatch* reporter Marquis Childs had warned the president that Republican former president Herbert Hoover and his personal secretary, Lawrence Richey, had 'addressed certain cablegrams to former Premier [Pierre] Laval of France.' Roosevelt demanded that the Director 'determine what messages, if any, of the type were sent by Mr. Hoover and Mr. Ritchey [sic] and what replies were received.' Hoover accordingly authorized a highly discreet investigation of 'trans-Atlantic communications,' which, however, 'failed to disclose that any such messages were sent.'

Roosevelt's interest in the former president's international communications stemmed from the latter's prominence as a critic of the Roosevelt administration's unneutral foreign policy and the possibility that the Republicans might obtain information from the former president's sources in the French government to be used in the forthcoming 1940 presidential campaign. The Herbert Hoover case, moreover, was not the only one in which Roosevelt turned to the Director to obtain political intelligence.[7]

Hoover had triumphed over all rivals in the domestic intelligence field. But unchecked though his domestic powers proved to be, he was firmly and repeatedly blocked in his efforts to take over William Donovan's responsibilities in intelligence overseas. 'Wild Bill,' the dashing and colorful New York lawyer with long experience in quasi-official intelligence work for J. P. Morgan and the Rockefellers among others, had been appointed by Roosevelt in 1941 to head the newly established Office of Coordinator of Information (OCI). Donovan's appointment marked a major institutional change in intelligence gathering in that it created an intelligence organization (albeit merely a coordinating one) directly responsible to the president. However, in June 1942 Roosevelt went a step further, transforming the OCI into the Office of Strategic Services (OSS) with power to *gather* intelligence overseas and conduct 'special' operations.

Heretofore such intelligence had been gathered by the Foreign Service and by MID and ONI, service agencies responsive to the State, War, and Navy departments respectively. Hoover had already, in one way or another, curbed any threat these agencies might pose to the Bureau's authority. But the OSS was an entirely new entity, a presidential agency, and one that threatened to become permanent in the event that the war ended in an uneasy peace. Hoover, who never in his life set foot overseas, now moved to stop Donovan.

Hoover's conflict with Donovan was both personal and bureaucratic and went back to his appointment as Director in December 1924. At that time Donovan was an assistant attorney general having the assigned responsibility to supervise Hoover's administration of the Bureau. Donovan's flamboyant administrative style irritated the newly appointed and insecure Director, and even after Donovan left the department in 1929, and before his appointment as head of OCI, he was the object of Hoover's close scrutiny.

Hoover was particularly interested in a rumor, uncovered in 1936, that Donovan and Senators McKellar, Ed Smith, and Joseph Robinson 'were going to have Mr. Hoover fired.' But his interest in Donovan peaked with the latter's appointment to head OCI. On Hoover's orders, the FBI monitored press reports of June 1941 (correct, as it turned out) that Donovan was to be appointed head 'of a new secret intelligence service' that would work closely with Army and Navy intelligence.

This spying on other federal agencies was unnecessary. For prior to the formal announcement of his appointment, Donovan sought a meeting with Hoover to allay 'any fears [Hoover] might have of his proceeding, in his capacity as Coordinator of the various Intelligence services, along the lines suggested in the press.' Unsuccessful in arranging an appointment with Hoover himself, Donovan met instead with Assistant Director Tamm, whom he assured that he had not wanted the appointment to OCI, preferring military service, and had accepted only 'upon the President's promise that Donovan could later handle troops if he would set up the coordinating agency.' The new office would 'not in any way . . . interfere with the functions of the Bureau, ONI and Military Intelligence,' would function primarily 'in the economic field,' and would simply coordinate information acquired by the various intelligence agencies, though in certain circumstances it might have to request information, and would be an independent agency funded through the president. The 'agency was to be a service agency – "a laundry" – through which the material of the various agencies would be ironed out and distributed to the persons interested in it.' Donovan intended to establish 'an advisory group which would function at all times in shaping policies for his coordinating agency' and 'wanted the FBI to be represented on this advisory group.'

President Roosevelt also sought to ensure Hoover's full cooperation, designating his son James as liaison between the OCI and the FBI. Hoover assured James Roosevelt that the FBI 'would do anything and everything possible to assist and cooperate with Col. Donovan and his organization in carrying on the duties assigned to them by the President.'

But such was not to be. Distrustful of Donovan and wary of his designs on the FBI's authority, Hoover had the Bureau shadow Donovan's operation closely. And thereby apprised of the rumor that Donovan might employ former FBI agent Leon Turrou,[8] who had been fired from the Bureau 'with prejudice' for selling an unauthorized account of his Bureau-work to a newspaper, the Director personally lobbied Donovan to forbid the Turrou appointment. At the same time, Hoover's aides monitored critical radio and press commentary on the OCI and on Donovan's administration and 'carelessness' in selecting personnel.

Although he did not dare accept the offer of an FBI informer to obtain 'every scrap of information concerning Colonel Donovan's office,' Hoover willingly exploited the informer's contacts with high-level administration officials to promote himself. To this end, advising the contact to emphasize that the 'FBI is manned with professional investigators with years of experience and proper background in the handling of intelligence work,' Assistant Director Tamm urged him to point out that 'it would be a mistake to . . . assign [the new intelligence functions] to untried and untested agencies which are manned for the most part with inexperienced personnel.' Likewise, through another contact, this one employed by Donovan's office, Hoover was able to make his case about the OCI's 'lack of coordination' in the conduct of its operations with an influential, high-level official.

Hoover was particularly sensitive to recurring rumors that Donovan was 'a logical successor to the present Director of the Federal Bureau of Investigation.' In response he had his aides investigate the rumors and report any information the Bureau had on Donovan and his direction of the OCI. Hoover's agents were unable to establish Donovan's connection 'with the source of these [news] stories,' although the FBI file search uncovered allegations that Donovan had been associated with 'German activities' and with 'Communist elements' (this evidence consisted of unsupported statements, and a list of clients and associates from Donovan's legal practice). The FBI's investigation, however, did uncover numerous allegations about Donovan's administrative incompetence as head of the OCI. Hoover accordingly retained this information (mostly misinformation in fact), doubtless to be used in the event that Donovan became involved in an attempt to unseat him.

As World War II wound down, Hoover confronted the possibility that its end would result in a retrenchment of the

Bureau's role at home and overseas. President Roosevelt's postwar intelligence plans were particularly worrisome, notably the president's request, on 31 October 1944, that Donovan formulate 'a plan for an intelligence service for the postwar period which would be in over-all supervision of all agencies of the Gov't. as to intelligence matters.'

Donovan on 18 November 1944 accordingly submitted a formal proposal for a postwar central intelligence service. Declaring that 'the problems of peace' required access to quality intelligence, he recommended vesting control over intelligence in the president and establishing a 'central authority reporting directly' to the President 'with responsibility to frame intelligence objectives and to collect and coordinate the intelligence material required by the Executive Branch in planning and carrying out national policy and strategy.' This central authority would leave the handling of operational intelligence 'within the existing agencies concerned' and ostensibly would not 'conflict with or limit necessary intelligence functions within the Army, Navy, Department of State and other agencies.' Donovan further recommended that Roosevelt decide whether the plan should be implemented 'by executive or legislative action.' In any case urging action 'at once,' he emphasized that 'we have now in the Government the trained and specialized personnel needed for the task. This talent should not be dispersed.'

Furnished with a copy of Donovan's proposal by one of his contacts, Hoover immediately demanded that his aides prepare a detailed critique of 'its objectionable features as well as errors of omission.' He then saw to it that Donovan's proposal was leaked to a sympathetic news source, *Chicago Tribune* reporter Willard Edwards. For his own reasons, Edwards was most accommodating. The ultraconservative *Chicago Tribune* ran a sensational front-page article to the effect that Donovan had recommended that President Roosevelt create a 'super spy system for the postwar New Deal.' The negative publicity succeeded in deterring Roosevelt from acting on the Donovan proposal before the end of the war.

In the interval, Hoover lobbied the heads of military and naval intelligence (who had similar objections to the plan to centralize intelligence activities) and, following Roosevelt's death in April 1945 and Harry Truman's accession to the presidency, he prodded Attorney General Biddle and Biddle's successor, Tom Clark, also to reject the proposal.

A consensus was reached with MID and ONI that the OSS had fulfilled a need for 'an evaluation and analysis unit' but that an intelligence organization should in the future be 'established, controlled and operating at the security level and by professional security-minded and trained people.' The needed analysis and evaluation unit could be established under the sponsorship of the Joint Committee on Intelligence, 'where it would be effective and not dominated by any one group.' MID, ONI, and FBI representatives finally agreed that 'there should be a worldwide intelligence organization,' composed of personnel drawn from military and naval intelligence, the State Department, and the FBI, 'without a superstructure imposed upon it and operating in defined fields,' and that an analysis and evaluation unit should also be established 'at a place where it could function efficiently and effectively without being subject to the domination of existing agencies, particularly the State Department.'

Hoover's lobbying effort was remarkably successful. Briefed on Biddle's meeting on 1 May with President Truman, Hoover learned of Truman's dissatisfaction with Donovan's plan and belief that 'the FBI through its Legal Attaches was working highly satisfactorily with the Military and Naval Intelligence Agencies in the U.S. and South America, and following the war, intelligence coverage should be arranged but that it should not be the Donovan plan.' Truman doubted that Donovan should handle such a program, not being 'convinced as to Donovan's loyalty to President Roosevelt.'

Learning that Truman had invited FBI agent Morton Chiles to the White House, Hoover had his aides orally brief Chiles so that during his meeting with the president he could discuss the merits 'of the Bureau's participation in World-Wide Intelligence' and the deficiencies of the Donovan plan. Hoover's intensive behind-the-scenes lobbying effort ultimately succeeded — following the Japanese surrender on 2 September 1945, Truman ordered the disbanding of the OSS as of 1 October of that year.[9]

Throughout this period, Hoover scrutinized press commentary on the Donovan plan. He dismissed one favorable news story by the *Baltimore Sun* reporter Frank Kent with contempt — 'He must be on Donovan's payroll' — and another, by the UPI reporter Revel Moore, as 'obviously inspired.' And when Donovan himself published an article in the 30 September 1946 issue of *Life* recommending anew the creation of a centralized intelligence agency with an independent budget and director, Hoover had the article ruthlessly analyzed by his aides.

Having torpedoed the Donovan plan, Hoover nevertheless failed in his more ambitious efforts to expand the FBI's postwar role to include foreign intelligence or at least to continue the FBI's SIS program. The close of World War II ended whatever need there was for an FBI role in Central and South America to counter German espionage activities, and responsibility for acquiring information about foreign economic and political developments had all along been vested in the Department of State and the Foreign Service. Like other World War II-created agencies, the FBI's SIS was phased out with the end of the war.

Hoover had won every battle but one, and that one alone he had lost to the President.[10]

The American Legion Contact Program

Hoover's efforts to broaden his authority while securing a firmer base at the Seat of Government had until World War II been restricted by the limits that Congress imposed on the Bureau's annual budget, give or take a few hundred thousand dollars in discretionary funds from the White House. Accordingly, when seizing the initiative to build up the Bureau in 1940, the Director welcomed the assistance of reliable citizens' groups to extend his access to information about 'subversive activities.' Pre-eminent among the fraternal organizations with which Hoover established and maintained so-called contact programs was the American Legion. However, he also established collaborative relations with the American Bar Association, B'nai B'rith, the Boy Scouts, the United States Chamber of Commerce, Kiwanis International, the Knights of Columbus, Optimists International, Rotary International, and the Veterans of Foreign Wars, among other fraternal orders, not to mention the Daughters of the American Revolution. In this way Hoover could establish the FBI as an autonomous organization operating with its own network of informers throughout every town and city in the United States.

The origins of this massive spying effort date from June 1940, before United States military intervention in World War II and the Roosevelt administration's policy shift toward belligerency. That month American Legion officers met with Attorney General Jackson and proposed that he authorize the 11,000 Legion posts to investigate 'subversive activities' in their geographic areas and report their 'findings to local law enforcement agencies.' Jackson declined their offer of help, counseling the Legion to refrain from any investigations and instead to seek to reduce 'mob violence and hysteria.'

Angered by the attorney general's brush-off, Legion officials proposed to offer their services elsewhere, to the Dies Committee or to military intelligence. Learning of these plans on the eve of the Legion's national convention, New York SAC B. Edwin Sackett contacted Hoover to urge reconsideration of the Legion's earlier offer. Otherwise, Sackett warned, the FBI could 'lose' Legion support. Sackett recommended that Hoover offer an alternative plan, convene a special conference with Legion commanders, and 'through this conference develop reliable informants, outline the type of information the Bureau desires, and also tell the Commanders when possible we need them as confidential informants[11] in certain situations, particularly stressing the need of informants in various plants.'

'Thoroughly sympathetic with the Legion,' Hoover endorsed Sackett's recommendation. The Director, however, was unwilling to bypass the attorney general, whose opposition to the Legion plan was on the record, and thus ordered Sackett to refine his proposal so that it could be cleared with Jackson. Hoover promised to secure Jackson's approval by 19 November: Legion officers were scheduled to meet that day to approve their own program, and Sackett planned to attend their meeting to brief them on his proposed alternative.

Hoover briefed Jackson about the Legion plans and Sackett's alternative proposal that same day, 18 November, emphasizing the Legion's resentment over Jackson's dismissal of their offer and their intention therefore to approve a 'broad program'

> whereby each American Legion camp will designate members of its group to investigate all information received concerning espionage, sabotage, subversive activities, un-American activities and all other matters related in any manner to the national defense. The American Legion members will report their investigative activity to the local and state police agencies, ignoring the Federal Bureau of Investigation entirely.

Emphasizing the 'potential damage' invited whenever 'inexperienced men' conducted investigations and the adverse effect it would have on the FBI's carefully planned 'national defense' programs, Hoover claimed that the FBI's alternative would

> obtain for the Department of Justice the support of the American Legion and at the same time keep the membership of that organization so occupied that there will be no attempt on the part of the members to carry on actual investigative activity.

Jackson reluctantly acquiesced, remarking that 'personally' he 'would much rather not do this but apparently something must be done.' When giving his approval, however, he understood that American Legionnaires were to be employed for two limited purposes. Legionnaires of German, Italian, French, and Russian descent would keep the FBI apprised of the activities of their respective ethnic groups, while Legionnaires employed at key defense plants would be used as informers. Legionnaires were not to conduct investigations but merely to report what they had learned from everyday activities.

Unknown to the attorney general, Hoover immediately exploited this opportunity to ensure 'the vital need of the Bureau to know conditions in various localities throughout the country.' Legionnaires were asked to provide information about 'communities where groups or settlements of persons of foreign extraction or possible un-American sympathies are located.' The Director stressed the importance of learning 'the identity of the leaders of these groups, the locations of their meeting places, the identity and scope of operation of their social clubs, societies, language schools, etc.; whether persons are sent into the communities to spread propaganda; to raise funds for various purposes or for the purpose of agitating such foreign extraction groups.'

The contact program was based on the Bureau's and the Legion's ideological affinity. The Director emphasized to his agents that

> because of the fact that the American Legion membership has proven its courage and patriotism we are desirous of utilizing them to assist the FBI in safeguarding our internal security. Legion members of every nationality reside in every community . . . are level-headed, possess good judgment and are desirous of being helpful.

Thereafter Hoover relied on his Legion sources to monitor radical dissent. However, in contrast to the Bureau's arrangement with the APL, which was limited to the duration of World War I, Hoover turned the American Legion Contact Program into an ongoing affair in which, unknown to the attorney general, the more reliable Legion contacts were recruited to serve as 'Confidential National Defense Informants.'

Legion contacts evidently provided little information of prosecutive value (internal FBI memoranda described the program as having only public relations value). But through the Legion's extensive contacts with conservative publicists and congressmen, Hoover was able to enhance his own and the Bureau's authority. Moreover, the program enabled Hoover to recruit thousands of 'confidential informants' to expand the FBI's monitoring of American dissidents.

Given the riskiness of his unilateral action, particularly in view of Jackson's reluctant approval, granted only to limit the Legion's activities, the Director impressed on his aides the need to cooperate closely with Legion officers to ensure that only the 'most productive and best' Legion posts and the more 'reliable' Legionnaires were recruited.[12] He further demanded that SACs develop intensive nationwide coverage, ensure that information from Legion informers be received regularly, and make absolutely sure that the utilization of Legionnaires as 'sources of information[13] be kept strictly confidential and that no publicity whatsoever result.'

Hoover's interest did not fade with the program's formal establishment. Thereafter he closely monitored his SACs' contacts with American Legion officers and each field office's recruitment of Legion informers. He demanded immediate action from dilatory offices. Repeatedly emphasizing the need for 'intensive coverage,' he threatened (and administered) discipline whenever any SAC failed to respond quickly. At the same time he impressed on his agents the program's positive benefits:

Although I appreciate the fact that it is undesirable as a general policy to rely upon outside groups to render assistance to the FBI, I believe that the members of the

American Legion are substantial, patriotic citizens, whose assistance should be used to the utmost. Due to the great volume of work which this Bureau is required to handle at the present time, and due to the existing delinquency of such work, it would be advisable for each Special Agent in Charge to explore the possibility of utilizing the services of the American Legion to greater advantage.

The scope of the program is documented by statistics on the number of contacts, interviews with proposed informers, and recruited informers. By 20 August 1941 some 813 American Legion department and district officers and 8,847 Legion post commanders and local officers were contacted. These Legion officers in turn identified 46,864 potential informers, of whom FBI agents eventually interviewed 32,918. The supervisor administering this phase of the program estimated that when the planning was completed, 43,000 informers (both 'sources of information' and 'confidential informants') would have been recruited from the Legion's 11,700 posts nationwide.

Hoover, however, was still not satisfied. He learned in September 1941 that many Legion post commanders had been excluded from the recommended list under the accepted procedure of obtaining names of 'reliable' Legionnaires from Legion officers; ignorant of the Bureau's American Legion Contact Program, these commanders had begun cooperating with the military intelligence agencies. He therefore ordered each SAC to secure from the Legion department commander in his region a list of all Legion posts that had been contacted. The SACs were then to ascertain — at once — whether uncontacted post commanders were interested in cooperating with the FBI. In consequence, by October 1943 approximately 60,000 Legionnaires had been recruited as informers.

The end of World War II ostensibly ended the reason for the program. Still, Hoover remained committed to it, inasmuch as the Legion had great value as 'a vast pool of information which should be used to the fullest extent by the Bureau, both in security matters and other matters coming within the jurisdiction of the Bureau.' Accordingly, on 13 February 1945 he approved a recommendation that SACs review their American Legion files 'with the thought of having as much coverage as possible in the postwar period through American Legion Contacts in general investigative as well as in National Defense matters.'

The program continued until 1966, when the anti-Communist dynamic was so thoroughly spent as to make further continuance simply a burden. But in the meantime Hoover had parlayed the program, in conjunction with his other secret operations, into a latter-day Inquisition.

Notes to Chapter Nine

1. Ironically, Wheeler's efforts to unseat Hoover were unproductive partly for the reason that Hoover's arch-rival for the Bureau's directorship, William Donovan, had supported Harlan Stone's decision to prosecute Wheeler in 1924 and thereby earned Wheeler's implacable opposition.

2. Berle's subsequent scholarly ruminations on the nature of power were based on first-hand experience.

3. The Director almost certainly planted the story, written by Hoover loyalists David Lawrence, Hugh Johnson, Kent Hunter, and William Hutchinson.

4. Within a month after Murphy was named attorney general in late December 1938, Hoover opened a secret file on him containing derogatory information about Murphy's political beliefs and personal life and kept the file open even after Murphy had moved on to the Supreme Court. (Attorney General Frank Murphy folder, Folder no. 118, Hoover O&C.)

5. This authority had been granted under the provisions of the 1939 Hatch Act, which prohibited federal employees' 'membership in any political party which advocates the overthrow of our constitutional form of government.' The act also led to the creation of the first attorney general's list of subversive organizations, membership in which likewise was grounds for dismissal from government service.

6. The problem with this term was that no one, least of all Hoover, had satisfactorily defined what was 'American.'

7. Furthermore, Roosevelt did not hesitate to turn to Hoover for assistance in personal matters – in 1941, for example, to contain a possible scandal involving Kermit Roosevelt (Franklin's cousin and the son of former president Theodore Roosevelt). At the time involved in a steamy affair with a masseuse, Kermit required hospitalization as a result of his excessive drinking and his having contracted a serious venereal disease. It was hoped that the FBI could locate the missing Kermit, tail his mistress during his subsequent hospitalization, and possibly sever their scandalous relationship. (Kermit Roosevelt folder, Nichols O&C.)

8. Turrou resigned from the Bureau and then sold his exposé memoirs (detailing his role in breaking a German espionage ring) to the *New York Post* in 1938. Incensed at this action, Hoover revised FBI records to list Turrou as having been fired 'with prejudice.' Turrou subsequently published a popular book, *How to Be a G-Man*, again to Hoover's distress.

9. Truman soon concluded, however, that a coordinating body was after all needed to coordinate, plan, evaluate, and disseminate intelligence. So by executive directive on 22 January 1946, he established the Central Intelligence Group (CIG). Hesitant to challenge the autonomy of the existing intelligence services, the president at first avoided creating a central intelligence agency; the CIG's budget and staff, moreover, were drawn from the separate services. Truman eventually abandoned this arrangement and in 1947 recommended legislation creating the CIA.

10. The Roosevelt administration's near-total unwillingness to challenge the Director's empire building or to restrain his investigative zeal had decidedly ironic results. For the subjects of the FBI's intensest interest were not just American Communists and non-Communist radicals but respected liberals as well, including the president's wife. To cite one example: in January 1942 FBI agents broke into the New York office of the American Youth Congress (AYC) and photocopied Mrs. Roosevelt's correspondence with AYC officials. (Because of their sensitivity, the duplicate copies made of this correspondence were hand-delivered to Hoover's office by the head of the FBI's New York office, whereupon the Director ordered that they be 'carefully reviewed & analyzed.' All too well aware of the furor the burglary would arouse if it became known, Hoover had the resulting report prepared under the 'blue memorandum' procedure, and Assistant

Director Louis Nichols maintained the two copies in his office.) (American Youth Congress folder, Nichols O&C.)

The report of another break-in, at the headquarters of the International Students Service (ISS) in December 1942, informed Hoover that 'Mrs. Roosevelt was always on hand to use her personal influence on those who threatened to oppose openly the Great Power line' and cited her lobbying of the Lithuanian delegate to cease condemning 'Russian aggression and atrocities in Lithuania' and to sacrifice the delegate's 'particular interest "for the larger common good of the Assembly." ' Mrs. Roosevelt was also described as having a 'sincere interest in youth and [realizing] the political value of the International Student Assembly [sponsored by the ISS] both in winning the war and influencing the terms of the peace,' while the ISS was described as acquiescing in 'practically every demand or suggestion of the Russian delegation.' Hoover responded viscerally and bitterly to this report: 'This is nauseating.' (Memo, Ladd to Hoover, 1 December 1942, Miscellaneous A-Z folder, Nichols O&C.)

The Director's interest in Mrs. Roosevelt's political activities surfaced anew later that year following a report that was ostensibly the result of an FBI 'survey concerning foreign inspired agitation among the Negroes in this country.' The Savannah and Birmingham field offices, inspired by the political definition of subversion that informed the Bureau's surveillance activities, had obtained information 'concerning other causes of agitation than those which are possibly foreign inspired' and cited rumors 'concerning the formation of Eleanor or Eleanor Roosevelt Clubs among the Negroes.' Assistant Director D. Milton Ladd briefed Hoover on this conspiracy:

'Such incidents as Negro maids allegedly demanding their own terms for working and at the same time stating they were members of an Eleanor Roosevelt Club are typical of the rumors reported to the Savannah Field Division. No substantiating information, however, has been received concerning these rumors. However, it is stated that complaints are received that the cause of the agitation among the Negroes in this area is largely attributed to the encouragement given Negroes by Mrs. Roosevelt. The Birmingham Field Division has received a report . . . that attempts in that area are being made to form Eleanor Clubs by a strange white man and a large Negro organizer traveling in an automobile. The unverified information indicates that only female domestics are desired for membership. The alleged slogan of the club is "A

White Woman in the Kitchen by Christmas'' inferring [*sic*] that Negroes work only part of the day. Similar clubs are claimed to be in operation in other cities in Alabama.'

Despite the absence of any legal authority and the flimsy nature of the evidence, Hoover ordered his aides to run down these rumors. He soon learned, from another informer in New Orleans, that 'practically every negro knows of these [Eleanor] Clubs and that they are places to patronize. ' 'As you know,' Ladd assured Hoover when submitting this report, 'the Bureau has made many inquiries in an effort to obtain specific information concerning the existence of such Clubs, which inquiries have met with negative results.' An undaunted Ladd promised to press this informer to 'furnish more specific information concerning his allegation relative to the existence of the "Eleanor Clubs." ' (Memo, Ladd to Hoover, 11 September 1942, FBI 62-116758; Memo, Ladd to Tamm, 21 October 1942, FBI 62-116758.)

Fearful of Mrs. Roosevelt's influence, Hoover did not confine his monitoring of the First Lady to her political activities. By far the most sensitive file he maintained on the First Lady related to her alleged wartime affair with Joseph Lash. Cautious bureaucrat that he was when it came to individuals of national stature, Hoover did not dare investigate the First Lady directly; rather, he sought information on her political activities by focusing on other individuals and organizations with which she was associated. In the case of Joseph Lash, Hoover obtained this information from MID officials. Because of its explosive character, he maintained it in a secret dossier, captioned under Lash's name, in his office.

MID's willingness to share this derogatory personal information stemmed from a succession of events: Mrs. Roosevelt's inadvertent discovery in April 1943 that military intelligence agents had had her under surveillance during a visit that March to Chicago; her subsequent protest to White House aide Harry Hopkins and General of the Army George Marshall; and, finally, Marshall's resultant order to destroy all military domestic surveillance files. Rather than destroy the documents pertaining to Mrs. Roosevelt, military intelligence officials turned them over to Hoover's aides.

Unknown to Mrs. Roosevelt, she had become the subject of investigative interest to conservative military intelligence agents in February 1943 because of her association with Lash, at the time stationed as an army trainee at Chanute Field (near Urbana, Illinois). Military intelligence agents had (1) beginning on 14 February monitored and read his personal correspondence with

Mrs. Roosevelt and his wife-to-be, Trude Pratt; (2) on 15 February intercepted Lash's telephone conversation with Mrs. Roosevelt; (3) monitored his 5-7 March meetings with Mrs. Roosevelt in the Urbana-Lincoln Hotel; (4) bugged his 12-14 March meetings with Trude Pratt in the same, recording their sexual activities as well as entering their hotel room in their absence to read Pratt's personal papers; and (5) bugged Mrs. Roosevelt's Blackstone Hotel room in Chicago, recording her meeting of 27-28 March with Lash.

When offering the documents relating to this surveillance to Hoover's aides, military intelligence officials claimed that Lash and Mrs. Roosevelt had been having an affair that President Roosevelt inadvertently discovered. According to Hoover's military intelligence sources, White House aide Harry Hopkins had discovered that a military counterintelligence unit had bugged Mrs. Roosevelt's hotel room in Chicago and when the president thereupon learned of his wife's affair with Lash, he had ordered the 'dismemberment of counterintelligence corps, G-2' and further that 'anyone who knew about this case should be immediately relieved of his duties and sent to the South Pacific for action against the Japs until they were killed.' (Joseph Lash, *Love Eleanor: Eleanor Roosevelt and Her Friends* [Garden City, N.Y.: Doubleday, 1982], p. 461; Joseph Lash folder, Folder no. 103, Hoover O&C.)

The most that can be said for this account is that it was erroneous in every respect, excepting Hopkins's discovery of the spying. Hoover, however, never doubted its accuracy and accordingly maintained the surveillance documents and the summary report in his office, ensuring both that his interest in such misinformation could not be discovered and that, when it was safe to do so, he could make political use of it.

Such an opportunity presented itself in 1953, with the election of a Republican administration with its own stake in discrediting the former First Lady. Thus, in January 1953 Assistant Director Louis Nichols briefed two key Eisenhower campaign aides, George Murphy and Francis Alstock, on Mrs. Roosevelt's 'affair' with Lash in order to strengthen the president-elect's resolve not to reappoint Mrs. Roosevelt to the U.S. delegation to the United Nations. So long as Mrs. Roosevelt was a member of the delegation, Alstock reasoned in response to this briefing, 'she would not become the object of any Congressional investigation, but that sooner or later there was going to be an investigation of her affair with Joe Lash.' Then, in February 1954, Hoover had Nichols brief the president on this alleged affair in view of the fact that 'Joe Lash is working for the *New York Post* which has been exceedingly critical of the President as well as of us.' (Memo, Nichols to Hoover, 8 January 1953, Dwight Eisenhower folder, Nichols O&C; Memo, Nichols to Hoover, 2 February 1954, Joseph Lash folder, Folder no. 103, Hoover O&C.)

11. 'Confidential informants' were individuals whom the FBI recruited as informers and whose surveillance activities were targeted and controlled by FBI 'handlers.'

12. Sackett obtained from Homer Chaillaux, director of the Legion's National Americanism Commission, the names of national and state Legion officers. Contacted by SACs, these officers in turn identified Legionnaires in their areas who were reliable and could be 'safely contacted' for possible recruitment as informers.

13. In contrast to 'confidential informants,' 'sources of information' were individuals who (1) provided information to the FBI whether or not they had been solicited or encouraged, (2) were not paid, and (3) were not directly controlled by the Bureau. Legion 'sources of information' were considered for recruitment as 'confidential informants' if, upon review of information and an interview with FBI agents, they were judged to have provided valuable assistance and to be reliable.

CHAPTER TEN

(1945–1950)

VICTORY, AUTONOMY, AND 'THE CAUSE'[1]

BY THE END OF WORLD WAR II, the United States had won its victory and Hoover his. The Director had established the Bureau's dominance in the domestic intelligence field, in part by demonstrating his usefulness to the president and impressing three consecutive attorneys general with the political power of his far-flung constituency. Having also forged a covert alliance with conservatives in the media and Congress, he had now assured himself a degree of autonomy with which to pursue radicals in the postwar era. Indeed, the only major strategic goal denied him at this time was the desired role in overseas intelligence operations.[2]

Hoover's wartime success in carving out an FBI monopoly in internal security investigations over the opposition of the State Department and the military intelligence agencies ironically doomed any chance that the FBI would assume OSS's international intelligence responsibilities. President Truman's influential aide and White House liaison to Hoover, General Harry Vaughan, recalled the crucial showdown in an interview in the early 1970s.

> By 1945 Hoover had already established his position in terms of power and importance . . . Hoover was so successful with the FBI nationally that he wanted to take over foreign duties . . . Truman created the Central Intelligence Agency to great protest from Hoover, who wanted to take it over as an auxiliary of his organization . . . Hoover was very provoked by that, and he tried to argue with the President, . . [but

the president] said no, and when Hoover persisted, he said, 'You're getting out of bounds.'

The Director meanwhile had become all but indistinguishable from his public persona, so removed was he by work from family and friends. Consumed by his passion to further the Bureau's power, his private life was dreary and lonely. His brother Dick had died in October 1944, still struggling to make a go of his hardscrabble farm, and his sister Lillian, by then a dependent of her children in Lanham, was an invalid suffering from Parkinson's disease. Dick's son, Bus, just out of the Navy, was exploring the Shenandoah Valley in search of a new and larger farm, for, as Dick had foreseen, the acreage in Glendale, although arid, was a speculator's gold mine. Lillian's son, Fred, who had joined the Bureau as a special agent in 1942, was serving in North Carolina. In 1945 he requested and was granted a compassionate transfer to Washington, where, sadly, he tangled with Guy Hottel, by then the head of the Washington field office, and eventually found himself out on the street. (Hottel himself, of course, was ultimately cashiered, although in his case as in many others a racing commission sinecure was arranged.)

In the absence of close friends, Hoover's social relationships outside were casual get-togethers with some of his neighbors on Thirtieth Place, who welcomed his proximity for the security it gave. Of these, the most important in the years to come was Lyndon Johnson, elected to the Senate in 1948, who lived diagonally across the street toward the end of the quiet cul-de-sac. None of these contacts resulted in a close friendship. The only constant in the Director's life was Tolson, who rode to work with him every morning, lunched with him (and occasionally Hottel) every midday, and more often than not dined with him at night.

Hoover's normal evening routine, once he had established bachelor's quarters on Thirtieth Place, was one drink – usually Jack Daniels Black Label – enjoyed on a back verandah overlooking his brick-walled (and eventually

Astro-turfed) rear garden, dinner alone or with Tolson, served by a cook-housekeeper, Annie Fields, who lived in (in the basement), Bureau homework or occasional light reading (he professed to like mysteries), and eventually moderate exercise on an exercise machine in his bedroom before going to bed in the nude. Although a bachelor very much in the news, he was the capital's most notorious non-party-goer.

In the morning he ordinarily enjoyed a leisurely breakfast — more leisurely, as time went on, and more frequently shared with a neighbor or two, especially Harry Duncan, a fast-food-chain millionaire and right-wing Republican whose garden backed onto Hoover's own — before his chauffeur, James Crawford (later Tom Moten), arrived with the car. Then the two proceeded south on Connecticut Avenue and west to Massachusetts and Wisconsin Avenues, where Tolson joined them for the ride downtown. In good weather Hoover, who never lost his enthusiasm for walking, had Crawford drop him and Tolson near the White House, whence they continued on foot to the Federal Triangle several blocks further along Pennsylvania Avenue toward the Capitol. It was a life without surprises, except at the Bureau.

Consolidating the Gains

During the war Hoover had mounted an unprecedented recruitment drive, quintupling the Bureau's size and transforming the character of FBI personnel. Since its creation in 1908, the Bureau had been staffed with white Protestants, many of them from the South. Beginning in 1940, however, Hoover dispatched recruiters to New York City, whose sizable Catholic population at the end of the Depression, while relatively well educated and just as stoutly anti-Communist as the hard-shell Baptists, was still disproportionately underemployed.[3]

Catholic girls had earlier been recruited in the city because, as one former agent recalled, they had good stenographic and typing skills and dressed and acted demurely. Thereafter it was only a matter of time before their brothers and cousins attending St. John's and Fordham applied. At first the ethnic recruitment was slow, notwithstanding the brilliant projection of the G-Man persona by the Irish American actor James Cagney. According to the same agent, 'The Irish and Italians, who were Catholic and therefore okay,[4] nevertheless had all the wrong image and style – long hair, a flip manner, a givenness to acting streetwise. The Jews at CCNY [City College of New York] were all wrong for another reason – they weren't reliably anti-Communist. And blacks were recruited only when the pressure was put on much later.'

So Catholics were ultimately preferred. Hoover reportedly favored Irish Catholic youths, finding them generally clean-cut and good-looking and earnest about their religion. He actively sought them out and later, after Notre Dame and Marquette granted him honorary degrees, recruited heavily at those universities.

For the present, however, in the uncertainties of 1945, Hoover was determined mainly to keep what he had, and that entailed resisting the natural postwar tendency to scale down domestic intelligence operations. He resisted with everything he had, using anti-Communism – or'the cause' – as his engine. He enjoyed for the purpose the support of two immensely powerful institutional allies – the media and conservative congressmen.

Hoover's sophisticated press agentry had originated in the 1930s, when, first in tandem with Attorney General Cummings and then on his own, he promoted the image of the G-Man by carefully courting prominent journalists. But by 1945 he was no longer content with exploiting opportunities as they presented themselves. Instead, capitalizing on the change in public attitudes toward federal authority and giving free rein to his own preference for efficiency and order, he fine-tuned what had begun as a reactive public relations campaign into a continuous program combining both self- and agency-promotion. The culmination of this was the launching of the now well-known list of 'Ten Most Wanted' criminals (as opposed to 'Public Enemies') in 1950.

As part of this promotional effort, Hoover divided reporters, newspapers, and prominent citizens into two groups: those who were 'not to be contacted' and those listed as 'special correspondents.' The latter were to be favored with assistance, the form and extent of which was determined by him and his senior aides. The FBI's media operations evolved into an ongoing and highly orchestrated campaign that went into high gear whenever developments threatened either to undermine public support or, by raising questions about FBI operations, to precipitate an inquiry into Hoover's leadership of the Bureau. Two such crises were the Pearl Harbor debacle of December 1941 and the so-called smear campaign of 1940–1941. A third, to be discussed below, was the Judith Coplon case of 1949–1950.

A second public relations front was opened in the still-new field of radio. Instigating on 16 April 1945 the production of a nationwide weekly radio serial, 'This Is Your FBI,' Hoover carefully instructed his SACs on its promotion. SACs were to grant interviews to key local stations. Forwarded a list of thirteen questions prepared by the national network – along with the approved answers – SACs were to use these materials not only for radio interviews but also in their responses to press inquiries concerning the radio program.

The questions and answers consisted of unrelieved puffery intended to promote a Bureau image of high professionalism, confident authority, and efficiency and an image of Hoover as a dedicated leader and incorruptible public servant. The proposed response to the planted question 'What are the three most important requirements for an FBI agent?' was that an agent 'first of all must possess an unblemished character and reputation. Prior to appointment every member of the FBI undergoes a searching character and fitness investigation which goes back to the date of his childhood [sic]. Secondly, he must have the courage of his convictions to carry him through the most trying of experiences, and thirdly, he must have the necessary physical and educational requirements.'

SACs were then to emphasize Hoover's central role in the

fulfillment of the FBI's mission. The proper response to the question 'How should a citizen contact the FBI?' was that the number of the local FBI field office was listed on the first page of every phone book, but: 'A citizen, in cases of emergency, can always communicate with Mr. Hoover in Washington.' The correct response to a question relating to FBI cooperation with local and state police officials emphasized the need to assure citizens of full protection, but, 'As Mr. Hoover has frequently pointed out we have no need, nor do we want any semblance, of a National Police Force in the United States. We can best preserve our internal security by proper cooperation among all law enforcement agencies.'

If asked whether the FBI endorsed the serial 'This Is Your FBI,' SACs were to respond affirmatively, stating that 'Mr. Hoover [in a stunning reversal] was happy to make the facilities of the FBI available in the preparation of this program as a public service. It has always been his view that the tax payers of America are entitled to know how our Bureau functions, and the new program in effect will be the FBI's report to the Nation.'

Anticipating that 'This Is Your FBI' would continue for 'an extended period' (it did, until 1953), Hoover demanded that all FBI employees recommend 'material to be used as a basis for future programs.' SACs were to consult with their agents and submit a list within fifteen days. Such submissions, Hoover counseled, should include only cases resulting in 'successful prosecutive action.' White slavery or sex crimes 'are not suitable,' he added, but 'outstanding investigative techniques,' the 'effectiveness of the Bureau's methods and facilities,' the breadth of the 'Bureau's activities and the investigative skill and ingenuity of the agent personnel' were to be emphasized. The Director also stressed that in each case subjects should have been apprehended by FBI personnel and cases 'preferably should be somewhat dramatic in nature,' and that composite cases should be prepared incorporating the 'most dramatic and interesting elements.'

Hoover soon briefed SACs on one field office's imaginative use of the series. The office in question had cooperated with a Boys' Club in holding an 'FBI Night' and, as part of this program, made arrangements with the local radio station to dedicate that week's installment of 'This Is Your FBI' to the meeting. As a result, Hoover noted approvingly, 'the radio station announced the boys' club program on every newscast for two days before the meeting. Local newspapers gave the meeting splendid publicity.' Hoover promised whatever assistance was needed by any field office desiring to 'cooperate with a police-sponsored boys' club or other youth group in such a meeting.'

In developing these tie-ins, Hoover enjoyed the cooperation of the serial's corporate sponsor, the Equitable Life Assurance Society. In time, Hoover approved a plan to hold youth meetings in conjunction with the radio broadcast, and a trial youth meeting was held in Syracuse, New York. Following the 'definite success' of the Syracuse program, Hoover then spelled out how other SACs were to conduct similar programs, demanding full cooperation with the insurance company's local representatives and 'careful planning and detailed preparation,' and prohibiting any 'departure from the attached outline of procedure.' The planned demonstration, he ordered, 'should include an exhibit, an explanation of the uses of the .38 caliber revolver, the magnum revolver, the Thompson machine gun, the shotgun, the rifle, and the gas gun [all of them tourist attractions proved out at the Bureau in Washington]. It will also be satisfactory to display gas grenades.' Hoover emphasized that the 'principal purposes of these youth programs are to combat juvenile delinquency by furnishing entertainment of a wholesome and educational nature and to promote constructive friendliness between teen-age youngsters and law enforcement generally.' To that end the Director also required SACs' 'appearances before civic groups and law enforcement organizations.'

Hoover was not content to rely on the media's interest in the area that was his highest priority: the need to educate the public to the threat posed by the Communist party and by 'the support which the Party receives from "Liberal" sources and from its connections in the labor unions.'

Accordingly, in February 1946 he authorized a covert propaganda campaign for which his aides prepared 'educational material which can be released through available channels so that in the event of an emergency we will have an informed public opinion.' Working thereafter closely with conservative congressmen and reporters — selected on the basis of their ideological affinity and willingness to preserve the confidentiality of their source — Hoover succeeded in furthering this decidedly political objective.

Keenly interested in promoting the FBI's image in every known medium, Hoover also assisted Twentieth Century-Fox in 1948 in producing the feature film *The Street With No Name*. When the film was completed and its release imminent, Hoover moved quickly to implement his assurance to the studio's executives that the Bureau would help promote the film, in part by supplying 'a list of office contacts and friends to preview the picture.' Should SACs be contacted by representatives of Twentieth Century-Fox, they were to 'invite friendly representatives of the press, law enforcement and public officials, and other Bureau contacts to attend the preliminary screening' in their city. Unable to furnish equipment for lobby displays, Hoover advised the SACs that the movie company would 'prepare a layout of pictures, posters, etc., based upon material furnished Fox by the Bureau which would be made available to local exhibitors' of the film.

Immediately after the release of *The Street With No Name,* Hoover reopened consideration of whether the FBI should do a film with Metro Goldwyn-Mayer, a proposal that had been held in abeyance for more than a year because of the Twentieth Century-Fox project. Hoover's unlikely confidante Morris Ernst (Ernst, a New York attorney long associated with the ACLU, was Hoover's mole in the liberal community) urged going ahead, with his partner Harold Stern as Bureau-MGM go-between.

Ordered by Hoover to meet with Stern, Assistant Director Nichols reported back that 'the time has come when we should make a decision as to whether we should or should not make another picture.' Nichols recommended that the

FBI 'keep a picture in the process of development at all times, which would mean the release of a feature picture approximately every two years. Each feature picture of course is seen by millions of people, particularly if it is a good one.' Conceding the demands on his own time required to develop such a film, and the difficulties in working with Goldwyn, Nichols argued nevertheless that the 'only problem is, Do we have the time to devote to it? I think this is an incidental one because in the last analysis, How can we afford not to take the time to do a job for the Bureau that a feature picture would do?' Should Hoover concur, Nichols emphasized the need to conclude 'an ironclad agreement in writing with Goldwyn so that we may be protected at every step of the way.'

Hoover did not share Nichols's enthusiasm; his experience with Fox had shown that he could not fully control the product. The Director was interested in 'a really good picture on the Bureau – I don't consider the last one [*The Street With No Name*] as a class "A" one' – but added, 'we *can't* do it because we are not equipped for it. Our *whole* public relations has been in the doldrums for the last 9 months. We must get the *essential* things working properly first[5] before embarking on such a project as this.' Accordingly, he wrote to Ernst declining the latter's offer of his good offices.

Undaunted, Ernst recontracted Hoover a year later urging 'that another movie be made on your material.' Arguing that the earlier movies were 'good entertainment' and proved that FBI agents were 'good craftsmen and that they could perform miracles,' Ernst thought that the 'important affirmative feature of another movie, which might be based on the life of an FBI agent, would be to clarify in the public mind some of these issues, presently confused, such as wiretapping, gossip in your files, etc.' Ernst emphasized that if Hoover wanted, he could 'get some company which we [Ernst's law firm] represent, in a position where they would do a picture not only for entertainment but to include, implicit in the picture, the answer to the question of the FBI's smear campaign without taking the defensive.'

Although again unresponsive to Ernst's repeated entreaties because the proposed film would not advance the anti-Communist cause, Hoover had not abandoned his interest in the movies. In the 1950s he authorized Nichols to assist Hollywood's production of a number of militantly anti-Communist films that served a dual educational purpose: extolling the virtues of the Bureau and emphasizing the sinister nature of the Communist internal security threat. These included the 1951 film *I Was a Communist for the FBI;* the 1952 films *My Son John, Walk East on Beacon,* and *Big Jim McClain*; and the 1959 film *The FBI Story*.[6]

Hoover early recognized the potential of television. Thus, when the persistent Ernst contacted Nichols to determine whether the FBI would be interested in developing a television series, Nichols responded that the FBI was 'carrying on at the present time preliminary discussions with the Equitable Life Assurance Society.' In that case, Ernst noted, should Equitable decide not to sponsor a Bureau program, he knew 'some people who would,' adding that 'it would be purely an institutional advertising project and that he did not want to say anything as to identities at the moment.' Hoover agreed to 'keep this in mind.' (Nothing materialized from these discussions until September 1965, when ABC began a fairly popular series, *The FBI,* which lasted until September 1974. This time Hoover closely monitored the development of the series, vetoing the rumored consideration of Hollywood star Rock Hudson to play an agent because of reports of Hudson's homosexuality.)

In all of these endeavors Hoover's thinking was dominated by one overriding concern: control. Thus when declining a friendly invitation to address the annual meeting of the American Society of Newspaper Editors in April 1948, he advised Tolson and Nichols that 'I think it would be unwise for me to speak. If I spoke on the record it would have to be in generalities & that is no good. If I spoke off the record I would be pestered afterwards for quotes just as happened in the [Marquis] Childs interview. I did that solely for background & yet we have now been forced into

264

quotation. It is too hazardous & too annoying.' Instead, he concentrated his speaking efforts on veterans and other reliably acquiescent groups.

But, all in all, Hoover preferred less public tactics, and he had the FBI's Crime Records Division leak information selectively to favored reporters and congressmen.

At the same time he relied on the other function of the FBI's vast grapevine – *collecting* information – to keep him abreast of any potential threat to his reputation and carefully crafted image as superefficient G-Man. Rumors that he was a homosexual especially piqued his interest. Because these allegations impugned his integrity and thereby detracted from his lofty reputation, he demanded that his aides run any such rumor down and then intimidate his detractors. Having successfully turned the FBI into his own personal instrument, by the 1940s Hoover unhesitatingly employed its resources for personal reasons.

During the course of an FBI interview in 1944, for instance, a prominent New Yorker reported having heard 'a rumor to the effect that Mr. Hoover was a "queer." ' The agents present vigorously defended Hoover's character and, according to their account, claimed to have convinced this New Yorker that 'the rumors concerning Mr. Hoover's morals was [*sic*] undoubtedly baseless.' Their report was immediately delivered to Hoover, who exploded on reading it: 'I never heard of this obvious degenerate. Only one with a depraved mind could have such thoughts.'

Because rumors of Hoover's homosexuality circulated widely, all FBI personnel were required to be alert to them – regardless of the context. Indeed, agents and SACs were chastised if they failed to do so. During a regular weekly conference of FBI supervisors, New York SAC E. E. Conroy 'very forcefully' cited two instances in which supervisors had been derelict in not having 'immediately called' to his attention 'scandalous and scurrilous remarks' about the Director.

One of the supervisors sought a meeting with Conroy the next day, having concluded that the SAC's comments had been directed at him. The supervisor admitted that an agent had informed him that someone had described Hoover as a 'fairy.' The source of this remark was a house guest of the agent, and the supervisor had attempted to obtain this guest's Detroit address but had dropped the matter on the ground that the remark was 'nebulous' and that to pursue it would 'just cause rumor.' Conroy duly reported this incident to Hoover 'for appropriate action.'

The SAC in Detroit was thereupon ordered to have a 'competent' agent interview the individual in question, who doubted having made the remark attributed to him, but admitted to having possibly heard it at a cocktail party in Washington. Describing this individual as 'scared to death' that 'we are going to investigate him' (with reason, as the interviewing agent had warned him that if he admitted calling Hoover a homosexual he 'might take care of him right there on the spot'), the Detroit SAC concluded that the individual 'will not repeat such a statement in the future.'

The matter did not rest there, however. Because the supervisor had delayed reporting this allegation, he was formally reprimanded. Letters were included in both the New York agent's and his supervisor's personnel files: the agent's letter commended him for having 'fulfilled his obligation' in reporting this matter to his supervisor, whereas the supervisor's letter found him to have been 'derelict' for having considered the matter 'nebulous' and failing to 'refer this to the Bureau.'

The supervisor had learned an important lesson; henceforth agents and SACs were quick to respond on learning of any such rumor, no matter how innocent or nebulous. And they were quick to report their actions to Hoover. A report of Louisville SAC M. W. McFarlin describing his success in obtaining a signed confession from the source of another of these rumors conveys this sense of duty: 'so long as there is a Federal Bureau of Investigation . . . those associated with you will exert every means in their power to protect you from malicious lying attacks and throw the lies down the throats of those who utter them.'

And when Cleveland SAC L. V. Boardman learned that a woman attending a bridge party held by the aunt of an

FBI agent had stated that 'the Director was a homosexual and kept a large group of boys around him,' he summoned the woman to his office and severely chastised her, pointing out that 'he personally resented such a malicious and unfounded statement.' The terrified woman claimed not to have repeated the story at any time except on this one occasion and promised to advise her friends at a future meeting of the bridge club that her allegation 'was not founded on fact and that she was deeply sorry that she had made it and it should not have been made at all.' She also promised to tell Boardman 'when this had been done.' Concluding his report to Hoover on this matter, Boardman repeated that he had 'chastised her most vigorously' and ensured that she 'understood the untruth of her statements and the serious nature of her action in having made them.'

Learning of another incident in which a Washington beauty parlor operator and one of her beauticians had claimed that 'all of the bookies in Washington turned in money to the Director and paid him off' and that 'the Director was a sissy, liked men and was a queer,' Hoover immediately dispatched two agents 'to take this scandal monger & liar on.'

Hoover's agents aggressively confronted his detractor, warning her and the beautician that 'such statements' would not be 'countenanced' and threatening to have both called before a grand jury where they and their accuser (an FBI clerk who heard the remark while having her hair done in the shop) 'will be given an opportunity to testify . . . as to exactly what they did or didn't say.' This intimidation succeeded, and Hoover was subsequently assured that both women fully realized the seriousness of their accusations and would never 'be guilty of such statements again.' For that reason no 'further action' was taken, since 'nothing will be gained by further pursuit of the matter.' Hoover commended the FBI clerk 'for her loyalty to the Director and the Bureau.'

No holds were barred, however, in those cases in which rumors were widely circulated. One such occurred in January 1948 when Hoover learned from the International

News Service reporter Martha Kearney that Lawrence Spivak, publisher of *American Mercury,* had commissioned the *New York Times* reporter Anthony Leviero to do a "smear" article' on the Director. (Smearing was the magazine's specialty.) Kearney claimed to have read Spivak's letter to Leviero commissioning 'a highly critical "smear" article in the nature of a profile relating to [Hoover] personally rather than to the Bureau as an organization.' Leviero was instructed to 'charge you [Hoover] with perversion; . . . that you personally "steal glory" by claiming personal credit for accomplishments of the local police, of other Government departments, and "within your own Department"; . . . that you "play politics" and that while constantly disclaiming that there is any political consideration in your policies, you are, nevertheless, a most successful politician.'

Thus forewarned, Hoover immediately sought to contain any possible damage. Tolson, for one, belligerently accosted Spivak in Harvey's Restaurant to inquire how his 'smear article' on Hoover was coming. Spivak denied having commissioned a smear article. Nichols concurrently asked *Reader's Digest* senior editor Paul Palmer, a former partner of Spivak's on the *American Mercury,* to approach Spivak about the proposed Hoover article. Palmer did so, reporting back that Spivak had not commissioned a smear article and 'had no intention of doing anything which would hurt the FBI or which would hurt the Director personally.' The reference to Hoover's homosexuality was without basis, as 'the matter of perversion was so completely libelous that a man would be a fool even if he had evidence to print anything on it.'

Palmer's intercession prompted Spivak to ask Leviero about the source of the rumor. Leviero denied that it had come from him. Leviero then contacted Nichols, denying as well ever having intended to write a smear article and expressing his serious reservation about writing the profile at all. On the basis of this interview and his conclusion that Leviero would not willingly jeopardize his position with the *New York Times,* Nichols promised to help the *Times* reporter should he decide to write the article. At Hoover's direction, Nichols also spoke personally with Spivak.

Spivak began the interview by expressing his dismay over his confrontation with Tolson. He then denied having commissioned a smear article, showed Nichols his correspondence with Leviero to prove it, and requested a personal meeting 'to let Mr. Hoover know that he does not operate' that way. He intended to publish 'an objective piece and nothing else' and 'would check each fact and triple check it and if there was anything that was the least bit derogatory he would check it with Mr. Hoover personally.' Inquiring as to the source of Hoover's information, Spivak wondered if 'it was a Communist-inspired plot as the Communists are out to get him as they have been out to get the Director.' Nichols, while refusing to disclose the FBI's source, singled out the 'element of perversion' as the thing that 'infuriated us' and promised to brief Hoover on their meeting.

Assured by Nichols that Spivak had impressed him in their meeting as 'very jittery,' 'considerably upset,' and yet sincere, Hoover decided to accept Spivak's explanation and considered the 'incident closed.' Nichols so advised Spivak, who, in a revealing comment, characterized the incident as 'a wonderful demonstration of a free country, [adding] that had this occurred in any other country he would have been shot by now.' The *Mercury* never ran a profile article on Hoover.

These cases were not exceptional; on the contrary, they demonstrate how Hoover successfully intimidated all who dared to question his character and power and how he relied on a vast network of influential editors, congressmen, and prominent citizens to assist him. Predictably, in keeping with his own troubled sexuality and constricted personality, his responses were invariably vindictive — and all the more so when the suspected offenders were homosexual themselves.

The Congressional Liaison Program

A main part of Hoover's effort to contain any challenge to his authority was always to be well informed and, as one means to achieve this, he enlisted the support of fellow conservatives in Congress. For Hoover, Congress could be a potential problem (given its oversight and appropriation powers) or a helpful ally. To ensure that it was the latter, he devised an efficient congressional liaison program. Originally despatched by Hugh Clegg, responsibility for this task later devolved on the assistant director heading the Crime Records Division (Louis Nichols, then Cartha DeLoach, then Thomas Bishop). Contacts were to be maintained with key congressional staff aides and sympathetic congressmen, and Hoover was to be briefed on all matters of interest. This program began informally and in time evolved into a highly professional operation.

In March 1943 Clarence Cannon, the chairman of the House Appropriations Committee, had asked Hoover to assign Supervisor Clegg on a temporary basis 'for a period of three or four months,' to 'help organize and initiate the work' of the staff of the House Appropriations Committee. Clegg had served thereafter as the committee's temporary chief of staff and proved so valuable that Cannon pressed him to remain beyond the term agreed to – perhaps on a permanent basis. Clegg declined, pleading his overriding obligation to the Bureau. Instead, he recommended that Cannon retain another FBI chief clerk whom Clegg described as 'thoroughly familiar with budget activities' and who could 'continue in charge of the Staff if the Committee desired.' A compromise was soon reached whereby Clegg, for 'brief and temporary periods,' assisted the Appropriations Committee staff.

Hoover's willingness to accede to the committee's unusual request was, of course, self-serving. Although the Appropriations Committee might thereby have secured the services of a skilled investigator and administrator, Hoover in return had ensured that the Appropriations Committee would look favorably on Bureau budget requests. Moreover, unknown to Cannon, Clegg used his Capitol Hill employment to monitor the operations of other federal agencies subject to Appropriations Committee oversight and to assess the attitudes of committee members toward the

Bureau's extraordinary service and their interest, if any, in sustaining the relationship.

In this way the temporary arrangement was systematized and made permanent. Hoover agreed to assign three FBI agents each year to the staff of the committee, to serve staggered tours of duty for three years. The agent beginning his third year was 'in charge of the investigators' for the committee and thereafter returned to the FBI.

(When Congressman George Mahon succeeded to the chair in 1965, he requested continuance of this arrangement 'in the same way.' Hoover agreed 'to continue the same system if it is of assistance to the Committee.' Thenceforward Mahon contacted Hoover regularly to ask him either to replace an agent whose tenure on the committee was coming to an end or to extend the tenure of certain agents assigned to the staff whose services he particularly valued.[7])

Hoover's appearances before the House Appropriations Committee in consequence were extremely gala affairs. Committee members used each occasion to lavish praise on the Director, to expedite his appropriation requests, and to secure from public disclosure any information about FBI activities that conflicted with the FBI's carefully manufactured public image. Indeed, Appropriations Subcommittee Chairman John Rooney once conceded to NBC correspondent Garrick Utley that Hoover had told him in confidence of the FBI's compilation of derogatory information on the civil rights leader Martin Luther King, Jr., and that he had also been informed of the FBI's wiretapping and bugging of King. Asked by Utley whether reporting information obtained from the use of these methods was 'proper,' Rooney responded unhesitatingly, 'Why not?'

Hoover's interest in containing any challenge to his authority also led him to keep close tabs on members of Congress to determine which would support the FBI's interests and which might not. Such background information kept Hoover's sophisticated congressional liaison operation running efficiently, as well as letting the

Director know whom the FBI could leak information to without risk of being exposed.

On Hoover's order, his aides compiled dossiers on every member of Congress and every congressional candidate. When confronted later by public claims that the Bureau maintained files on members of Congress, he denied these charges – and technically he was right, for Hoover had devised a system whereby his agents compiled 'summary memoranda' on all congressmen based on information already contained in FBI files. After completing the summary memorandum, agents were to destroy all the documents in the FBI's central records system upon which it was based. 'Summary memoranda' were not files – thus Hoover could truthfully deny that the FBI had files on members of Congress.

Hoover began this practice on an informal basis in the 1920s, and refined it gradually over the years. At first, files on individual congressmen were based on information FBI agents had garnered from clipping the papers, following congressional hearings, and tapping their contacts on Capitol Hill. Information so collected included attitudes on issues affecting Hoover, possible criminal activities, and allegations of 'immoral' and 'subversive' practices.

Hoover eventually systematized this program in the 1950s, after deciding to increase the FBI's personal contacts with members of Congress. One aspect of this strategy was to send congratulatory letters, over his signature, to recently elected congressmen who were deemed friendly. Hoover's aides thus had to compile information about nonincumbent candidates for election as well.

To ensure that the FBI's maintenance of 'summary memoranda' on all members of Congress could not be discovered, Hoover ordered that they be maintained separately from the FBI's central records system, under lock and key, and with no additional copies or portions of the memoranda to be created. Access to the files was tightly controlled; only senior Bureau officials and supervisors might call the Administrative Review Unit if they were 'preparing memoranda concerning the Member or some matter about which he has inquired or a communication to the Member and the supervisor wants to know what the FBI's relationship has been with a Member in the past.'

By reviewing these memoranda, Hoover and his aides could determine what 'kind of relationship would be proper with the candidate if elected to the office which he sought. If he was not elected, the memorandum was destroyed as having no value.' Hoover demanded that these summary memoranda be revised and updated regularly, with reference cards 'on former Members filed alphabetically in an inactive section in the Administrative Review Unit where they are retained for six years (a Senator's term) in the event they may be reelected. If not reelected after six years, the cards are destroyed.'[8]

Public Education Campaign

In addition to being a main source of support, Congress was a primary mechanism for disseminating Bureau information, although not the only one. (Hoover also used the secret informer networks provided by the various conservative business and fraternal organizations to sow propaganda and 'educate' the public about the dangers of Communism, as well as churches and clergymen, various self-appointed accusers, and even entrepreneurs who assembled blacklists for sale to corporations and other interested parties.) In the immediate postwar period, however, the main vehicle for thus influencing public opinion was the House Committee on Un-American Activities (HUAC). Reviled by liberals throughout the postwar era (rechristened the House Committee on Internal Security, it was not dissolved until 1975) for its flagrant grandstanding and unsubstantiated charges, in fact HUAC owed its influence less to its own efforts than to the covert assistance rendered by Hoover's FBI – and to the enthusiastic support accorded it by the conservative press.

The Special Committee chaired by Martin Dies had been on the verge of expiring in December 1944 after its embattled chairman declined to run for re-election. At the beginning of the new Congress in 1945, however, Congressman John Rankin of Mississippi, a reactionary and unapologetically ethnocentric Democrat who once called Walter Winchell 'a slimemongering kike,' introduced an amendment to House rules to make the Dies Committee a standing committee of Congress. Rankin's amendment carried on a rollcall vote, and thereafter the Mississippi congressman and his conservative Republican cohorts Karl Mundt, J. Parnell Thomas, and (after 1947) Richard Nixon carried the ball.

'The extreme privilege of free press and free speech,' Mundt warned in 1946, would not prevent the committee from exposing persons 'engaged in actions which are un-American even though their activities are legal.' A year later Hoover publicly concurred, without adding, however, that the Bureau was the source of many of the committee's charges.

Hoover's willingness to cooperate with HUAC masked a change of mind. There were two reasons for this: first, Dies's removal from the scene[9] and the willingness thereafter of key HUAC members and staff to cooperate with the Bureau; and, second, the reorganized committee's provision of a forum for laundering information that the FBI could not use for prosecutive purposes, either because there was no violation of law or because the information was illegally obtained (by burglarizing or wiretapping the offices of the American Youth Congress, the Washington Committee for Democratic Action, the American Peace Mobilization, the Communist party, and other radical organizations).

Hoover was unwilling, however, to depend simply on the resources of HUAC, and he sought alternative avenues for obtaining and disseminating information. Another ally in this education program was the American Legion. Although the wartime Legion 'contact program' had officially ended (and had not been designed to disseminate propaganda), Hoover's discontinuance order had not terminated the use of Legionnaires but merely the annual drive to recruit new Legion informers. He made this limited restriction clear in his instructions to his agents:

274

Those American Legion contacts presently listed in [field office] indices who may be of informational value to the Bureau at this time should be appropriately indexed as Confidential Informants, Sources of Information, or Contacts. When this has been done, the American Legion Contact Index may be destroyed.

These instructions are not to be taken as indicating that it is no longer necessary to maintain a close relationship with the American Legion. Rather, it is more vital than ever at this time to retain the continued support and active cooperation of this ever-increasingly important organization.

Thereafter, employing Assistant Director Cartha DeLoach's dual responsibilities (as head of the FBI's Crime Records Division and the Legion's Public Relations Division), Hoover could rely on the Legion to champion the theme of the Red Menace. The Legion's value, moreover, encouraged Hoover to circumvent the ostensible supervisory authority of the attorney general and the White House. So independent had his FBI become that when deciding to reinstitute the American Legion Contact Program in July 1950, after the outbreak of the Korean War, the Director concluded that 'it was not necessary to contact the [Justice] Department prior to starting this program. The [FBI Executives] Conference felt that the initial step should be personal contact by [FBI Inspector and liaison with the Legion] Lee Pennington with the National Commander of the American Legion.'

Thus raised like Lazarus from the dead, the American Legion program was made part of Hoover's more general campaign to influence public opinion by releasing 'educational materials' through 'available channels.' One of these channels involved leaks to friendly reporters. Begun on an informal basis in the 1940s, Hoover's media campaign had by the 1960s evolved into an efficient, formal, code-named Mass Media Program. Nor was Hoover content to rely solely on reporters.

In February 1951 he instituted another educational

campaign, code-named the Responsibilities Program. Under this program, state governors and other 'reliable' public personalities and organizations (e.g., the Red Cross, the Library of Congress, police departments, and former Republican President Herbert Hoover) were recruited to help educate public opinion.

When instituting the Responsibilities Program,[10] Hoover rationalized his decision to leak information to selected outsiders on the grounds that

> the Bureau is responsible for the internal security of the country as a whole and [considering] that public utilities, public organizations and semi-public organizations are serving large portions of the people, it is plain that we have an obligation for the protection of the facilities when we have information of a subversive nature affecting them.

The Director also relied on friendly individuals. Father John Cronin, the assistant director of the National Catholic Welfare Conference (NCWC), was one of his willing collaborators. Assigned the responsibility in 1945 of preparing a secret report for the Catholic bishops on Communism in the United States, Cronin sought Hoover's assistance, and particularly FBI reports describing Communist influence in the trade union movement. Hoover eagerly provided this assistance, with the result that Cronin's report helped strengthen anti-Communist attitudes within the Church hierarchy. Thereafter, and more important, his acquired knowledge and access to the FBI made him a valuable resource for other anti-Communist activists, as the following episodes show.

In December 1945 the board of directors of the U.S. Chamber of Commerce decided to mount an anti-Communist propaganda campaign and appointed Francis Matthews to chair a committee to prepare a report on 'the menace of Socialism in Europe, and its effect upon this country.' Matthews immediately contacted NCWC General Secretary Howard Carroll, who referred him to Cronin. Cronin readily agreed to write the report.

In it, in addition to stressing the seriousness of the internal Communist menace, Cronin claimed that 'there are reasons to believe that Soviet armies may be on the march in but a few weeks. Christianity through much of the world is threatened. Within the nation, the Communist fifth column is functioning smoothly, especially within the ranks of government and atomic scientists.'

Cronin's forty-page report, which publicly identified Matthews as its author, was titled 'Communist Infiltration in the United States' and was widely distributed, receiving extensive publicity as well – the Chambers had approved an initial printing of 400,000 copies. This highly inflammatory diatribe condemned the Communist infiltration of the nation's public and private institutions and urged that 'because Communist loyalty is primarily given to a foreign power, Communists *and* their followers should be excluded from government service. Congress should appropriate adequate funds for a stringent but fair loyalty test.'

Hoover's covert use of Cronin was by no means limited to propagandizing the Red Menace theme through an internal report to the Catholic bishops and a widely circulated Chamber of Commerce report. In the process, Cronin had acquired a reputation as an authority on the domestic Communist problem and was soon tutoring an eager pupil, the recently elected congressman from California, Richard Nixon.

Hoover sought out still other potential allies in his anti-Communist crusade, notably Austin Canfield, a prominent American Bar Association officer and chairman of an ABA committee 'to study Communist tactics, strategy, and objectives, particularly as they relate to the obstruction of proper court procedure and law enforcement.' Committed to purging local and state bar associations, and the profession as a whole, of Communist and pro-Communist lawyers, Canfield's committee investigated 'certain organizations which use their members to defend Communists in court and in hearings before Congressional inquiry committees.' By this, Canfield meant the National Lawyers Guild (NLG), a left-wing lawyers' group that had consistently defended radicals.

In early 1951 Hoover authorized Assistant Director Nichols to provide Canfield with four blind memoranda listing the subversive activities of Guild officers — Canfield had earlier contacted Hoover's office to request this information. Recontacting Nichols in January 1952, the ABA officer complained that 'the National Lawyers Guild is whooping it up and they [Canfield's committee] have to decide whether to take them on or not.' Canfield was encouraged to continue on the premise that 'he would probably have trouble as long as the National Lawyers Guild remained in operation.' Hoover further authorized leaking the latest FBI report on the NLG to service Canfield's desire to 'get basic facts [on the Guild's review of the Smith Act trial of Communist officials in California] and there will be a special meeting of his Committee in an attempt to move the American Bar Association into action against the National Lawyers Guild.'[11]

In the end the requirements of Hoover's public education campaign laid a heavy burden on his agents. Hoover's recruitment practices ensured that most agents shared his obsession with the Red Menace and would thus go along with a punitive attack on radicals. But despite a shared ideology, many agents, in time, became cynical, less from civil libertarian sympathies than from disdain for the overregulation of Bureau activities and the massive misallocation of Bureau resources. Even so, most remained unwilling to forego the prestige and perquisites of Bureau employment.

William Sullivan, who joined the Bureau in 1940 and rose to become an assistant director before his abrupt dismissal in October 1971, was one who eventually denounced Hoover's often petty and vindictive rules and regulations. Above all, he disliked the cult of personality that underlay the entire organization.

They laid it on so heavily. I'll never forget the first time [Hoover] came to our class . . . I went out to get a drink of water and I saw men, agents, lined up along the walls, and I said to one 'What's going on?' He said, 'You know from the schedule that the Director is due to speak in your class in the next five minutes. We're forming a guard for him along the corridors.' You know, I went back in my room and it just disgusted me, it really did.

Sullivan recalled the advice of a fellow agent. 'Remember we've got an unusual man heading the Bureau in J. Edgar Hoover,' this agent declared, and went on to describe the Director's conceit, vanity, penuriousness, and love of receiving gifts and other tokens of esteem. 'Write on his birthday and at Christmas and every other day, always write flattering letters to him. You may not like this [but] if you don't do this when everyone else is doing it you're going to stand out like a sore thumb.'

Sullivan dutifully followed this advice. When he eventually arrived at the Seat of Government, summoned by the Director himself, he discovered how right the agent had been.

Everyone was writing him [Hoover] these damn flowery letters. He must have had file cabinet after file cabinet full of this stuff. [He did.] I remember an assistant director called me one day. 'Say,' he said, 'the Boss just came back from the Appropriations Committee.' I said, 'Yes.' He said, 'You know,' and he mentioned a certain Assistant Director's name, 'he's got a flattering letter in, telling the Boss what a marvelous job he must have done up there on the Hill. I'm calling you because I'm writing one now, right now, and every assistant director is going to write him one.

M. Wesley Swearingen, a veteran agent who retired in 1977 after twenty-seven years of service including heading the Chicago break-in squad, wrote to the authors:

[Hoover] instilled loyalty and unquestioning obedience through fear. The fear or threat of punishment was begun on the first day of a new agent's class and mounted throughout one's career . . .

Relations between the field and the Bureau were best stated by SAC Guy Bannister in Chicago at the time I was an agent there. Hoover or one of his goons wrote a letter to all field offices asking for suggestions or recommendations on a particular subject . . . Bannister wrote to Hoover . . . 'The Bureau divorced itself from the field many years ago and has been living in a state of adultery ever since.' The shit hit the fan. Instant rumors had it that Bannister was being transferred forthwith to El Paso. When Bannister heard the rumor he called Johnny Mohr, assistant director [in charge] of the Administrative Division. Bannister said, 'What's this I hear about being transferred to El Paso?' Mohr [then] said, 'You're not going to El Paso, you're going to Honolulu.' Bannister replied, 'That's what you think. I just retired.'

Hoover never talked about the agents who quit. He discussed only those who were in ten years, twenty years, twenty-five years, thirty years, etc. When I was in Chicago in the fifties, agents were resigning on the average of one or two a week. I quit in 1960 in total disgust with the FBI. Eleven months later I went back to the FBI as a retread. I had decided that being a prostitute for Hoover offered good security and an excellent retirement at the age of fifty. I retired on my fiftieth birthday, May 20, 1977. You would be amazed at how many left on their fiftieth birthday.

Cartha DeLoach, another former assistant director, had a less harsh view of the Director and his methods, although, to be sure, the genial Georgian who headed the Crime Records Division was a Hoover favorite. 'Basically,' DeLoach said, 'he was an insecure individual and that caused him to be harsh to personnel. That might have been caused by his very frugal rearing . . . He wanted to maintain what he had, both from a financial standpoint and from a professional one . . . But Mr. Hoover was the engine that pulled the train. Everyone understood that and everyone respected him for it.'

The Purge Begins

The continued exercise of Hoover's power from the beginning of the postwar era was contingent on a public perception that spies and their unwitting dupes seriously threatened the nation's internal security – that, in the charged rhetoric of the McCarthyites, there existed Communists everywhere, 'Communists in the State Department,' and Communists in other sensitive agencies of government, the media, educational institutions, and business. Attorney General J. Howard McGrath eloquently expressed this soon-to-be accepted view when he warned: 'There are today many Communists in America. They are everywhere – in factories, offices, butcher stores, on street corners, in private businesses. And each carries in himself the germ of death for society.'

Although red hunting had long since become Hoover's second nature, the wartime alliance with the Soviet Union and the emphasis on accommodation had temporarily undercut the appeal of anti-Communism. The deterioration in U.S.-Soviet relations after 1945, however – with the adoption of the containment policy and the institution of a federal employee loyalty program in 1947 – soon created fertile ground.

Hoover's first opportunity to equate Soviet expansionism with internal subversion presented itself in August 1945 when a disgruntled ex-radical, Elizabeth Bentley, walked into the FBI's New Haven field office and confessed to having been a courier for a Communist espionage ring during the war. World War II had ended only days earlier, and as victory was due at least as much to the efforts of the Russians as to those of the Americans and their British ally, Miss Bentley's story at first offered limited prospects for political mileage – the more so as she could provide no documentation to support her sweeping allegations.

Undaunted, she unburdened her heart to two agents, who duly recorded her story. During the war, at the instigation of her lover, Jacob Golos, a Soviet NKVD agent, she said, she had become involved with a number of American Communists holding second-level appointments in the federal government. Exploiting their official status, these domestic Communists had photocopied thousands of government documents, which she had delivered to Golos. In these transactions she had come across other American couriers and now she named names. According to her story, the death of her lover, by releasing her from her infatuation, had caused her to see the error of her ways.

For more than two months, Hoover sought ways to capitalize on Bentley's allegations. And for more than two months he held back. His hesitancy stemmed from distrust of her histrionics, the absence of hard evidence, and the potential for embarrassment inherent in the proposition that a Soviet spy ring had operated domestically for years without his knowledge. But Bentley's accusations conformed with Hoover's own suspicions about the federal employees she had named, who, because of their involvement in radical politics, had earlier come to his attention. So, freed by the end of the wartime alliance and seizing the opportunity provided by the Truman administration's hard-line policy toward the Soviets, between November 1945 and March 1946 the Director sent a flurry of reports to the White House (and to sympathetic cabinet officers). There, being unsubstantiated, they moldered for some time.

In the meantime, in the summer of 1945, Hoover became embroiled in another affair, one that offered a better prospect for advancing the anti-Communist cause. The *Amerasia* case was an object lesson in Hoover's extralegal methods of judicial and political prosecution.

The case arose when an analyst for the Office of Strategic Services (OSS), Kenneth Wells, noticed that an article in the 26 January 1945 issue of *Amerasia,* a periodical on Far Eastern affairs, was an almost verbatim copy of an 11

December 1944 report he himself had prepared on Thailand. Wells called the coincidence to the attention of his superiors, and an investigation of the apparent leak was begun, including an OSS burglary of the New York offices of *Amerasia* on 11 March 1945. The OSS agents thereupon discovered and photocopied reams of classified State, Navy, and OSS documents and the next day reported their findings to the Department of State. State Department officials, because of the seriousness of the matter, referred the case to the FBI on 14 March.

After an intensive investigation, the Bureau determined that Philip Jaffe, the editor of *Amerasia,* had probably obtained the documents from Emanuel Larsen, a State Department employee, and Andrew Roth, a lieutenant assigned to the Far Eastern section of ONI. Following a conference between State, Navy, and FBI representatives on 18 April, the FBI broadened its investigation to determine whether Jaffe had other sources in the State and Navy departments and had sought documents for use by the Soviet government. (Jaffe's alleged Communist associations and Marxist orientation underlay this surmise.)

In its ensuing investigation the FBI monitored the activities of Jaffe and *Amerasia* co-editor Kate Mitchell and learned that they had been in contact with Larsen, Roth, and Foreign Service officer John Stewart Service, who had recently returned from China. The Bureau also discovered that a free-lance reporter, Mark Gayn, had had access to the documents as well. In the course of making these discoveries, FBI agents kept Jaffe and Mitchell under surveillance, broke into, bugged, and tapped the offices of *Amerasia,* broke into the apartments of Gayn and Larsen, bugged Jaffe's hotel room in Washington while he was on a visit to the capital, and tapped the home telephones of Larsen and Jaffe. Unable to establish that the pilfered documents were being delivered to the Soviets, the FBI learned that Lieutenant Roth was just about to be transferred to Honolulu. For that reason Hoover recommended on 28 May that the case be considered for prosecution.

Although aware of the Bureau's illegal investigative methods, Special Assistant to the Attorney General James McInerney supported prosecution. McInerney judged that there would be 'sufficient evidence' against all of the suspects (Jaffe, Mitchell, Larsen, Roth, Gayn, and Service) 'following the apprehensions since the arrests should be so made as to make possible searches of the premises of the subjects incidental to arrest.'

The arrests accordingly were timed to occur 'while Jaffe and Mitchell were at the offices of *Amerasia,* Larsen was at his home and Gayn was at his home [earlier FBI break-ins having established that classified documents were maintained at these locations], in order that agents could conduct a search of these premises.' This plan entailed a risk that the FBI's and the OSS's illegal investigative activities might be disclosed during trial, thereby preventing conviction, but the risk was accepted.

Briefed on the Justice Department's decision to arrest the subjects, Secretary of the Navy James Forrestal demurred, fearing the adverse effects of the case on U.S.-Soviet relations at the time of the San Francisco Conference and the drafting of the United Nations Charter. President Truman, however, overrode Forrestal's objections, enthusiastically adding that he wanted to 'use this case as an example to other persons in the Government Service who may be divulging confidential information.'[12] Indeed, so strong were his feelings that on 2 June the president personally ordered the FBI to proceed with the case as soon as possible and asked Inspector Myron Gurnea to advise the White House of any resistance the FBI might encounter from other agencies.

On 6 June FBI agents raided the *Amerasia* offices, arrested Jaffe and Mitchell, and seized 1,700 classified State, Navy, OSS, and Office of War Information documents. Other agents simultaneously arrested Gayn, Roth, Larsen, and Service. The warrants for their arrests accused all six individuals of 'conspiring to violate the Federal Espionage Statutes through theft of highly confidential documents' — Service, Roth, and Larsen for having delivered classified documents and Jaffe, Mitchell, and Gayn for having obtained them.

But on 21 June, fearing that it could not convict under the Espionage Act, as no incriminating evidence had been uncovered during the prearrest investigation, the Justice Department decided to seek the indictment of the six for unauthorized possession of government documents. On 30 July Justice Department officials Robert Hitchcock and James McInerney (the head of the department's Internal Security Section) secured the indictment of Jaffe, Larsen, and Roth — the grand jury voted 20-0 not to indict Service, 14-6 not to indict Gayn, and 17-3 not to indict Mitchell. Service had admitted to meeting Jaffe, but maintained that he was sharing information with Jaffe as with any other reporter; Gayn claimed that he had used the documents only for background for articles he was writing on the Far East; while Mitchell could not be held as culpable as her boss, Jaffe.

Arraigned on 30 August, Jaffe, Larsen, and Roth all pleaded not guilty. Then, prior to the start of the trial, Larsen inadvertently learned, through the janitor of his apartment building, of the FBI's prearrest break-in at his apartment. On 28 September his attorney filed a motion to quash the Larsen indictment.

Faced with the possibility that the case against the other defendants would be lost at trial and, worse, that Jaffe too might soon learn of the unauthorized break-in at Larsen's apartment, Justice Department lawyers quickly arranged a deal whereby Jaffe agreed to plead guilty and pay a fine of $2,500 and to pay Larsen's fine of $500 after the latter pleaded no contest. Moreover, because the department had no case against Roth without the testimony of Jaffe and Larsen (FBI agents had seized classified documents from Larsen's apartment and at *Amerasia's* office but had found none in Roth's possession at the time of his arrest), on 15 February 1946 the department dropped the case against Roth. Thus, what began as a sensational espionage case ended in the legal exoneration of Service, Mitchell, Gayn, and Roth and small fines for Jaffe and Larsen.

The disposition of the cases infuriated Hoover, who objected both to the settlement and to the implication (not verifiable at the time) that the FBI's illegal investigative activities had foreclosed prosecution. For him, the *Amerasia* case had become a challenge to the FBI's integrity as well as a test of the administration's commitment to an effective internal security program. Thus, while Truman had seen the case as an opportunity to discourage others from leaking government documents, Hoover had become convinced that the FBI had uncovered an espionage operation and had then become the victim of a liberal-engineered cover-up.

Hoover did not view the FBI's illegal investigation as posing either an ethical or a constitutional problem. The government, in his mind, had no obligation to the court or to the defense to disclose that it had illegally obtained evidence prior to the arrests of the defendants. As internal FBI documents show, although Hoover's aides made a distinction between admissible and inadmissible evidence and therefore questioned the wisdom of a government prosecution, the Director himself believed that there was sufficient admissible evidence to justify risking prosecution.

Hoover's position rested on somewhat tortured reasoning – specifically, the argument that the Larsen break-in occurred in an apartment from which Larsen had moved and that the Bureau agents who installed the bug in Larsen's second apartment in the same building (before he moved in) had been admitted by a janitor, who used his pass key – hence no break-in. Thus, according to Hoover's logic, the documents seized at the time of Larsen's arrest technically were admissible, as they had not been obtained through a break-in. Moreover, as the janitor had not known of the FBI's entry into Larsen's first apartment, the burden of proving that evidence leading to the arrest had been illegally obtained would rest heavily on the defense. Hoover also argued that as his agents had not seized documents during the break-ins but had simply noted their existence, the government technically could contend that the evidence to be presented in trial was legally obtained.

Hoover took this position in pressing for prosecution in

1945 and in defending the FBI's role when the case resurfaced as a political issue (first during a 1946 House inquiry led by Congressman Samuel Hobbs of Alabama into the Justice Department's handling of the case and then again in 1950 during a Senate inquiry led by Millard Tydings of Maryland into Senator Joseph McCarthy's charges of Communist influence in the State Department). Yet the FBI's own analysis of the law and relevant court cases, prepared by the Bureau's legal counsel, concluded that 'the evidence was tainted and that there is [sic] no definite cases available to substantiate that the evidence secured is admissible.' In short, Hoover's position was not based on law but on politics.

At first, the Director's principal concern was to counter suspicions about the FBI's role. Thus, briefed by Assistant Director Ladd and Inspector Gurnea that Justice Department officials Lamar Caudle and James McInerney had advised Congressman George Dondero on 4 December 1945 that they had opposed arguing in court against Larsen's motion to quash the indictment, 'as it would divulge confidential methods used by the FBI and in so doing jeopardize other Communist cases that were pending,' Hoover protested to Attorney General Tom Clark[13] on 6 December. 'At no time,' Hoover complained, had the department taken up this matter with the Bureau or himself. Pretending injury, he asserted that the FBI 'is prepared at all times to proceed vigorously with such prosecution as might be approved by the Department' and denied any concern 'relative to the divulging of any confidential methods used by the Bureau.'

While conceding that the matter was mooted by the department's acceptance of a plea bargain, Hoover nevertheless added disingenuously that 'at no time did any Agents of the Bureau obtain by improper or illegal means any documents whatsoever in connection with the Larsen aspect of the case or any other aspect of it.' 'All of the documents,' he insisted, 'were obtained as an incident to a lawful arrest upon a duly issued warrant.' Unwilling to accept a subordinate position, Hoover demanded that in

287

future whenever criticisms were directed against the FBI, 'we be advised so that the true facts may be obtained and all branches of the Department fully informed, thus avoiding different positions being taken.'

Hoover, then, reluctantly acceded to the department's disposition of the case in 1945; he had no alternative, given the climate of public opinion. But when the matter resurfaced in May 1950, by which time the Cold War had catapulted him into national prominence as the protector of the nation's security, he was emboldened to act more aggressively. The occasion grew out of a speech by Senator McCarthy charging that at the time of Service's arrest in the *Amerasia* case Hoover had publicly declared, 'This is a 100 per cent air-tight case of espionage.' Justice and State Department officials immediately denied McCarthy's assertion. Asked by Deputy Under Secretary of State John Peurifoy whether Hoover had made such a statement, Assistant to the Attorney General Peyton Ford replied unequivocally, 'Hoover did not make the statement which has been attributed to him.' Ford's and Peurifoy's letters were thereupon released to the press.

Enraged by the coverage given to the matter, Hoover wrote Peurifoy to inquire why the Director of the FBI had not been contacted prior to the release of the letters. Observing that the FBI 'does not make decisions as to prosecutive action' – that was the province of the Justice Department – Hoover added, 'Had I been queried at the time of the arrests in the *Amerasia* case, I certainly would have been most emphatic in stating that the arrests were thoroughly justified upon the basis of the findings of the Criminal Division of the Department and on the evidence obtained.'

Protesting again to Attorney General J. Howard McGrath, Clark's successor, Hoover deplored 'the use of my name by either the Department of State or by Mr. Peyton Ford, and I most certainly protest such use of my name, particularly when that use does not accurately reflect my views.' After recapitulating the FBI's role and regretting that the case had not been presented in court, he objected vehemently to blaming 'the Federal Bureau of Investigation through such "official" rumors that the Department had to temporize in its dealings with the [*Amerasia*] defendants because of illegal entries on the part of Agents of this Bureau.' Outraged by this slight to the Bureau, he self-righteously concluded that 'in the event I had been asked at the time the arrests were made whether I thought we had an airtight case, I would have stated that I thought we had. Further, if I were asked today, I would have to so state.'

By 1950, it would appear, Hoover could both dissemble about the FBI's role in the case and exploit other information he had uncovered in another sensitive investigation to blackmail the Truman administration into defending that role in the forthcoming Tydings Committee hearings. For the public account of 1950 bore slight resemblance to the history of the case itself.

What had actually happened was this: hearing that charges against the three indicted in the *Amerasia* case were to be dropped, Hoover briefed Attorney General Clark on 20 August 1945 on information intended to impugn Service's loyalty. (At the time Service had not been indicted and remained a State Department employee assigned to General Douglas MacArthur's staff in Japan.) The FBI, Hoover informed Clark then, had received information 'through various sources indicating that John Service's political sympathies are with the Chinese Communists.' Hoover then recounted the 'inadmissible' and 'admissible' evidence that the FBI had acquired during its prearrest investigation, which he said established Service's 'close relationship' with the other defendants and confirmed that Service had given Jaffe classified State Department documents.

Never resigned to the Bureau's failure to effect Service's indictment in 1945, Hoover now, in 1950, was determined to convict Service of espionage in a setting in which he would be powerless to defend himself.

Hoover's interest in Service also stemmed from resentment over the efforts of three former advisers to President Roosevelt — Washington attorney and lobbyist Thomas Corcoran, State Department Counselor Benjamin

Cohen, and White House aide Lauchlin Currie — to prevent Service's indictment. Liberal activists who had played a major role in drafting New Deal legislation and shepherding it through Congress, Corcoran, Cohen, and Currie had traveled different routes during the 1940s but continued to consult one another and shared a friendship with and concern for Service. Ironically, Hoover had learned in 1945 of their various efforts to defend Service as a result of a particularly sensitive request by the Truman White House — and one that had no bearing on the *Amerasia* case at all.

Having acceded to the presidency by the accident of Roosevelt's death, Truman not surprisingly wished to modify the administrative operations of the White House and to assure himself of the loyalty of high-level staff aides in the White House and other federal departments. He turned to Hoover for covert assistance, delegating responsibility for this extremely sensitive operation to his chief administrative assistant, Edwin McKim, and naval aide James K. Vardaman.

On 21 August 1945 Vardaman met with Assistant Director Gordon Nease to discuss future operations under the FBI's already ongoing 'White House survey' and to request that the FBI 'secure all information possible on White House employees.' The impetus for the survey had been the president's fury over a series of leaks involving telegrams that presidential emissary Harry Hopkins had sent to the White House from Moscow between 26 May and 7 June. (Hopkins's daily reports on his meetings with Soviet Prime Minister Joseph Stalin had been picked up by the syndicated columnist Drew Pearson, among others.) Wishing to stop the leaks, Vardaman 'requested that the FBI investigate suspected White House aides, wiretap Treasury Department aide Edward Pritchard, and study the operation of the White House with the objective of offering recommendations to improve its efficiency.'

Commenting on the wiretap phase of this survey, Vardaman warned Nease that 'intercepts of the phone conversations of those employees would be of extreme value [but] . . . if it became known that we were investigating these

Beginnings

Hoover was a fearful child who clung to his mother and had phobias about snakes and germs. His origins in southeast Washington were modest but his mother's expectations for him were great, and he did not disappoint them. A studious pupil in grade school, he was valedictorian of his high school class and commander of Cadet Company A in President Wilson's first inaugural parade. An honors student at George Washington University evening law school, he joined the Justice Department in 1917 at the age of 22.

Hoover at four. Courtesy of the
National Archives (65-H-111-2).

The Director grew up in this semidetached frame house a 413 Seward Square, three blocks east of the Library of Congress on Capitol Hill. Courtesy of the National Archives (65-H-340).

Dickerson Naylor Hoover, Sr., with his wife, Annie, and younger son, John Edgar. Courtesy of the National Archives (65-H-297-7A).

Hoover's high school yearbook biography. Courtesy of the J. Edgar Hoover Foundation.

CLASS OFFICERS

Lawrence McCeney Jones..President
Hazel Deborah Spear..Vice-President
John Harrison Stokes, Jr..Treasurer
Esther Belt..Secretary
John Edgar Hoover..Valedictorian
Claud Elwyn Babcock..Historian
Thomas O'Connell..Poet

Hoover, center in back row, in his 1913 Central High School yearbook, *The Brecky*. Courtesy of the J. Edgar Hoover Foundation.

Hoover at center, flanked by four companions. Courtesy of the National Archives (65-H-334).

Dickerson Naylor Hoover, Sr., shortly before his death in 1922. Courtesy of the National Archives (65-H-297-5).

Annie Scheitlin Hoover, shortly before he death in 1938. Courtesy of the National Archives (65-H-297-6).

The Inner Circle

The young Bureau of Investigation Director shortly after
his appointment in 1924. Courtesy of the National
Archives (65-H-369-1).

*Like James I of England, Hoover had a succession of male favorites,
beginning with Frank Baughman, whom he recruited for the Justice
Department in 1919 and took with him to the Bureau in 1921.
Hoover's special relationship with Clyde Tolson, like Hoover a lifelong bachelor, was temporarily upset by the arrival on the scene of
Guy Hottel, a handsome ex-college football player and notorious
roustabout who tested Hoover's normally inconsiderable patience.
Hoover made Hottel head of the Washington field office but ousted
him from the Bureau in the 1950s. Clyde Tolson, Hoover's deputy
chief and constant travelling companion from the 1930s on, shared
ample leisure time with the Director on Bureau trips. The one woman
with a life commitment to Hoover besides his mother, Helen Gandy,
the Director's executive secretary for nearly fifty years, eventually
decided who could and could not enter the Boss's office.*

Baughman inscribed this portrait "To 'Speed' Hoover with kind regards, Thomas Frank Baughman." Courtesy of the J. Edgar Hoover Foundation.

Clyde Tolson signed this photograph "To my best friend 'Speed' with affectionate regards." Courtesy of the J. Edgar Hoover Foundation.

Hoover with Guy Hottel. Courtesy of the J. Edgar Hoover Foundation.

Tolson and the Director on an Atlantic City convention excursion in 1941. Courtesy of the National Archives (65-H-592-2).

Hype

Hoover exercises his famous bulldog persona. Courtesy of AP/Wide
World and the National Archives (65-H-1187-1).

*The image of Hoover that was projected by the Bureau's Crime Rec-
ords Division was almost entirely manufactured. In reality a determined recluse who never carried a gun, the Boss by the 1930s presented himself as a quasi-playboy and a friend of celebrities and the
very rich. He routinely garnered support for the Bureau by releasing
promotional shots to the press.*

Hoover fingerprints Vice President John Nance Garner. In the 1930s, fingerprinting celebrities was one of the Bureau's most successful promo devices. Courtesy of the National Archives (65-H-376-1).

Hoover, center at left, hefts a firearm with "Amos and Andy." Courtesy of the National Archives (65-H-104-1).

Hoover received the 1939 Christmas card on right from the proprietors of the Del Mar (California) Racetrack, Bing Crosby, Pat O'Brien, and Bill Quigley. Courtesy of the National Archives (65-H-488).

Hoover and Tolson celebrate New Year's Eve 1935 at the Stork Club in New York. Courtesy of UPI/Bettmann Newsphotos and the National Archives (65-H-182-1).

GReeTINGS TO FROM DEL MAR

Pat O'Brien

Bill Quigley

Hoover with Marilyn Monroe and Milton
Berle. Courtesy of the National Archives
(65-H-1250).

The Director with Shirley Temple.
Courtesy of the J. Edgar Hoover
Foundation.

Hoover with the cast of
the film *The Greatest
Show on Earth*.
Courtesy of the National
Archives (65-H-1086-3).

Crusader

Hoover (center) testifies before the Senate Internal Security Subcommittee on the Harry Dexter White case on November 17, 1953. Tolson is on the left and Lou Nichols on the right. Courtesy of UPI/Bettman Newsphotos and the National Archives (65-H-1178-1).

Strengthened by a series of emergency presidential directives during World War II, Hoover emerged from the war prepared to do battle with the hated Old Left. The "cause" of anti-Communism preoccupied him for the rest of his life, almost to the exclusion of organized crime. Despite his forceful denials, Hoover authorized selective leaks of Bureau documents to HUAC, Senator Joseph McCarthy, and the Senate Internal Security Subcommittee on many occasions. He was most cooperative with both Presidents Nixon and Johnson in providing purely political intelligence. Until his death in office at the age of 77, Hoover remained impregnable.

Hoover and Tolson relax with Senator Joseph McCarthy (left) and another fellow guest at the Hotel del Charro in California. Courtesy of the National Archives (65-H-1414-1).

Hoover with President John Kennedy, left, and Attorney General Robert Kennedy, right. Courtesy of AP/Wide World and the National Archives (65-H-1676-1)

Hoover with President
Richard Nixon.
Courtesy of UPI/
Bettman Newsphotos
and the National
Archives (65-H-2821).

Hoover with President
Lyndon Johnson.
Courtesy of the National
Archives (65-H-2204).

The Director toward life's end. Courtesy of the
National Archives (65-H-2925).

people, it would be incumbent upon both the President and him to deny that any such investigation had been ordered.'

Meanwhile, McKim had met Inspector Myron Gurnea (ironically, the official responsible for coordinating the Bureau's *Amerasia* investigation) on 2 June to praise Hoover 'for the hell-of-a-swell job' the FBI had done in wiretapping Pritchard, an assistant to Treasury Secretary Fred Vinson. (The tap had been installed when White House aides learned that Pritchard took a 'dim view' of Truman's abilities and of the 'numbskulls' Truman had appointed to his administration. This tap subsequently yielded a discreet collusion between Supreme Court Justice Felix Frankfurter and columnist Drew Pearson.)

Commenting that he had hesitated to show Truman the log based on the wiretap 'until they were on the boat and out in the river,' McKim characterized Pritchard's conversations as having been 'treasonable' (to President Truman, not the United States). When Gurnea inquired whether Truman had read the log, McKim said that he had, and had pronounced it 'the damndest thing I have ever read.' McKim quickly added that 'we are taking corrective action' and 'want to keep that tap on.'

Gurnea immediately pointed out that the tap was not on Frankfurter but on Pritchard, to which McKim replied that 'that was quite all right, and that they [he and the President] desired that it be continued.' McKim requested that the FBI 'currently advise him of any conversations such as the one of reference,' 'of any other sources' that Pearson had in the administration, and about Thomas Corcoran's activities. Finally, he requested taps on both Pearson and Corcoran. Alluding to Corcoran's influence at the Justice Department, McKim remarked caustically that Corcoran for all practical purposes 'has been Attorney General.'

Hoover approved the tap on Corcoran, although not on Pearson, after Gurnea advised him that in his conversation with McKim, 'nothing was said in any way, shape or form as to the consequences should this [wiretap on Corcoran] ever become known. It was understood that it was highly confidential.' Records of subsequent conversations between

Nease (who personally delivered the Corcoran and Pritchard wiretap reports to the White House) and White House aide Harry Vaughan preserve Vaughan's warning that 'if the [wiretap on Corcoran] should ever become known it would be our [the Bureau's] baby and that Vaughan [*sic*] would deny any knowledge.'

Through this wiretap on Corcoran, then, Hoover had inadvertently discovered the lobbyist's behind-the-scenes role in influencing the Justice Department's handling of the *Amerasia* case. On 10 June, four days after Service's arrest, Hoover had learned of Corcoran's determination to assist Service and of Cohen's and Currie's interest in Service's exoneration. Far more important, Hoover had learned of Corcoran's use of his influence at the Justice Department to foreclose Service's indictment, including direct contacts with such high-level officials as Attorney General Clark, Assistant Attorney General McGranery (who had supervisory responsibility for presenting the case to the grand jury), and McInerney (one of the Justice Department officials directly involved in presenting the case to the grand jury).

Bureau reports record the following story. Corcoran opposed having Service testify before the grand jury or accede to any joint defense strategy suggesting that the case was a political witch hunt. Indifferent to the fate of the other defendants, Corcoran was jealously protective of Service and was determined to see that Service's career in the State Department was not harmed. (At the time, McInerney was seeking to persuade Service to appear before the grand jury to make a statement that would clear his name, as the department had nothing on him. But good lawyer that he was, Corcoran had serious misgivings about the risks involved whenever inexperienced witnesses appear before grand juries.)

Thereafter Corcoran relented and, after first securing a pledge from Assistant Attorney General McGranery to 'take care' of the Service matter, urged Service to testify. Corcoran had also cleared this arrangement with Attorney General Clark and had been assured that Service would not be harmed or required to appear as a witness in any trial involving the other *Amerasia* defendants. Corcoran's misgivings had been disarmed by assurances that Justice Department officials presenting the case would not be 'antagonistic.' He had also learned that McInerney's only reason for insisting on Service's testimony was that 'they didn't want any doubt about this because of the FBI.' Service 'puts up a hell of a fine appearance,' McInerney had assured Corcoran, and his appearance before the grand jury was 'the best way of clearing it up.'

Fully informed of Corcoran's activities – and of the collaboration of Currie, Cohen, McGranery, and McInerney – Hoover was apparently poised to retaliate. But for the moment he could not act on this intelligence. For the Corcoran tap had been installed on his own authority and with the understanding that the White House would deny any knowledge of it. Moreover, Hoover had not sought or obtained Attorney General Clark's approval for the tap, as was required for all FBI wiretaps under President Roosevelt's May 1940 wiretapping directive.[14]

But Hoover did not have to wait long for an opportunity to try to redress the miscarriage that he, and a number of conservative congressmen, thought had occurred. As early as 1946 a House Judiciary subcommittee chaired by Samuel Hobbs of Alabama conducted a closed investigation of the case. Informed of the OSS and FBI break-ins and wiretaps, the subcommittee nevertheless agreed to Hoover's pleas to suppress the evidence of official misconduct and in its final report portrayed the case as demonstrating the inadequacy of the State Department's procedures for handling classified documents and the need for a federal employee loyalty program.

The *Amerasia* case did not go away, however. The intensification of the Cold War heightened popular anxieties about internal security, and a fresh opportunity to exploit the case presented itself in February 1950 following Senator McCarthy's highly publicized charges that month identifying eighty-one cases of 'known Communists' in the State Department and the establishment by the Senate of the so-called Tydings Committee to investigate McCarthy's charges. John Stewart Service was one of McCarthy's eighty-one cases, and this led, in turn, to a revival of interest in the *Amerasia* case. In view of the altered political landscape, Hoover moved beyond the containment effort of 1946 to promote a broad public airing of the department's disposition of the case in 1945 and of the behind-the-scenes role of Thomas Corcoran.

In this effort, Hoover's aides worked closely with the conservative reporters George Sokolsky and Frederick Woltman, who were themselves seeking to revive public interest in the *Amerasia* case, and with Republican Senator Henry Cabot Lodge, Jr., and minority staff counsel Robert Morris of the Tydings Committee. Because of the sensitivity of the Corcoran tap, and the fact that it was not known outside the White House and the FBI, Hoover could not widely disseminate anything from the log, although he did use tap information to pressure Justice Department officials during often tense negotiations in July 1950. Thus, when briefing his conservative collaborators on this matter, Hoover had to exact their agreement to handle this information discreetly. For this reason and not for any want of interest on the Director's part, Corcoran's role in circumventing Service's indictment in 1945 never became a political issue.

But although Hoover was unable to use the Corcoran wiretap to advance the cause, he had other means to do so. On the one hand, working in tandem with the Truman administration, Hoover utilized the Smith Act's ban against advocating revolutionary ideas to effect prosecution of the leadership of the Communist party in 1948-1949. On the other hand, in this case acting contrary to the administration's political interests, he secretly assisted members of HUAC in publicizing the pervasiveness of the Communist threat.

Prosecution of the top leadership of the American Communist party under the Smith Act offered two attractions for Hoover: imprisoning the party's leadership could effectively cripple the organization and render it ineffective, and trial proceedings could be used to demonstrate the seriousness of the Communist subversive threat, thereby educating public opinion.

Under Hoover's close direction and persistent admonishment, FBI agents had since World War I closely monitored the activities of Communist party members and leaders. These investigations intensified during the political economic crisis of the Great Depression and did not abate despite the forging of the wartime alliance with the Soviet Union (instead, Hoover authorized a massive campaign of break-ins, wiretaps, and bugs to obtain information about the party's secret strategy and decisions). With the onset of the Cold War, Hoover exploited fully this new opportunity to move from the mere collection of information to the use of this information to prosecute the 'top functionaries' of the Communist party.

Although the Truman administration had its own reason for considering indicting the Communist party leadership under the Smith Act − a desire to disarm Republican criticism, in a presidential election year, of the Democrats' alleged softness toward Communism − the impetus to the decision to present the case to a federal grand jury was Hoover's persistence. In January 1948 the Director recommended to Attorney General Tom Clark prosecution of the 'important officials and functionaries' of the Communist party on the premise that it could 'result in a judicial precedent' that the Communist party 'as an organization is illegal' and further that 'the patriotism of Communists is not directed toward the United States but towards the Soviet Union and world Communism.'

At first Clark demurred, having concluded that the Smith Act was 'directed at the individual rather than the group or party' and that Communist party leaders 'have each denied that they have the aim or purpose to overthrow the Government by force or violence.'

Undaunted, Hoover continued to pressure the attorney general to reverse this public position and forwarded to Clark over the next two months a massive 'brief' of approximately 2,000 pages containing approximately 900 exhibits intended 'to establish the illegal status of the

Communist Party of the United States of America.' This brief, Hoover argued, 'relates to the Party rather than to its members and officers' and did not present 'detailed and complete evidence of specific violations of Federal law within the Statute of Limitations on the part of an individual officer or member of the Party.'

Hoover's brief did not move Clark to action. Not sharing Hoover's sense of urgency, the attorney general did not even forward the brief to U.S. Attorney John McGohey until April. He then instructed McGohey to study the brief and determine whether a sufficient case had been made to justify seeking an indictment from the grand jury. McGohey proceeded deliberately at first, but his strategy was effectively annulled by Hoover's intensive lobbying efforts. And, despite the fact that neither the attorney general nor his principal deputy, Peyton Ford, was briefed on McGohey's hurried decision to seek the indictment of the Communist party's national leadership under the Smith Act, they were unwilling to countermand this decision. Clark, briefed on 18 June, requested only that the forthcoming indictments (which were to be handed down in four days) be sealed for a month — until after the conclusion of the Democratic National Convention, which was scheduled to end on 20 July — to avoid creating the impression that the indictments had been brought for political purposes. Such an impression was likely, in view of the fact that he had publicly claimed before HUAC in February that the Communist party leadership could not be prosecuted under the Smith Act and had opposed (with the president) legislation proposed by Republican congressional leaders (Karl Mundt, Richard Nixon, and Homer Ferguson) to outlaw the Communist party. Highlighting Hoover's power as well as the Truman administration's subservience to the Director on this issue, Hoover was the catalyst for the decision to indict the Communist Party leadership.

In the ensuing trial, which dominated national news for most of 1949, the Justice Department (relying on FBI reports and informers) documented its case both by quoting from Communist party publications and by equating the party leadership's changing positions on domestic and foreign policy issues with those of the Soviet Union. Prosecution was successful; the Supreme Court in 1951 upheld both the constitutionality of the Smith Act and the conviction of the party leaders, and the case served a useful educational purpose.[15]

Yet prosecution under the Smith Act offered only limited prospects for advancing the cause. For one thing, court rulings on the admissibility of evidence and the adversarial nature of judicial proceedings, whereby defense attorneys could challenge the government's evidence and seek to impugn the credibility of FBI informers, rendered a prosecution strategy of limited value. HUAC provided a better forum, and one which Hoover fully exploited when assisting the committee in its two most highly publicized postwar hearings: the so-called Hiss-Chambers case in 1948 and the equally widely publicized hearings into Communist influence in Hollywood in 1947 and 1950.

HUAC originally had not intended to focus in the summer of 1948 on Chambers's allegations about Alger Hiss. The committee, like its Senate counterpart (chaired by Republican Senator Homer Ferguson), initially focused on the allegations of Elizabeth Bentley that she had acted as a courier for a Soviet espionage ring in wartime Washington. Interviewed by FBI agents in November 1945, Bentley had then charged that a group of former Treasury Department employees headed by Nathan Silvermaster were part of a Soviet-directed infiltration operation and, in passing, named other government employees as engaged in communistic activities, including Harry Dexter White and Alger Hiss. Hoover, as noted above, bombarded members of the Truman administration with reports based on Bentley's allegations, which, because unsupported by other corroborative evidence, were ignored. In 1947, however, the Justice Department unsuccessfully sought to indict the Treasury Department employees named by Bentley. The convened grand jury found Bentley's allegations incredible, but her grand jury testimony had then been leaked to the conservative reporter Frederick Woltman. In a series of dramatic articles portraying Bentley as the 'Red Spy Queen,' Woltman publicized the story of a Communist espionage operation, which was immediately seized upon by HUAC and the Senate subcommittee. Because Bentley's resulting public testimony also lacked credibility – leading many to criticize HUAC's hearings as a partisan anti-New Deal ploy – the beleaguered committee sought corroboration, subpoenaing another, but more credible ex-Communist, Whittaker Chambers, at the time a senior editor of *Time*.

Chambers's highly publicized charges, in which he named Hiss as well as seven other former New Dealers as members of a Communist cell that had sought to promote Communist influence in Washington during the 1930s, were made in an intense partisan atmosphere, causing President Truman impulsively to dismiss HUAC's hearings as a 'red herring' designed to divert public attention from the 'reactionary' record of the Republican-controlled 80th Congress. Truman thereby made the committee's charges an issue in the 1948 presidential and congressional elections, forcing the conservative congressmen to substantiate Chambers's allegations. In this effort, they found Hoover more than ever willing to help.

Foremost among these committee members was Congressman Richard Nixon, an ambitious freshman representative from California who had been assigned to the unprestigious committee in 1947. Lacking any particular knowledge of Communism, Nixon had sought the assistance of another freshman congressman, Charles Kersten, who had introduced him to Father John Cronin, the author of the U.S. Chamber of Commerce report on domestic Communism. Using information he had obtained from confidential FBI documents, Cronin briefed Nixon 'about certain Communists in atomic espionage rings and in the State Department.' Cronin specifically named Alger Hiss as one of these disloyal federal employees. Thus, when Chambers publicly accused Hiss of having been a member of a prewar Communist cell, and Hiss publicly denied the charge – in the process questioning HUAC's partisan purposes – Nixon turned to Cronin for assistance. Acting as an intermediary between Hoover's FBI and Nixon, Cronin then furnished Nixon with invaluable assistance in making the case for Hiss's Communist past, and thereby rescuing the committee's reputation. Cronin subsequently admitted:

> Ed Hummer was one of the FBI agents I had worked with. He could have got in serious trouble for what he did, since the Justice Department was sitting on the results of the Bureau's investigation into Hiss – the car, the typewriter, etc. But Ed would call me every day, and tell me what they had turned up; and I told Dick, who then knew just where to look for things and what he would find.[16]

It was not the case, however, that a zealous agent had acted surreptitiously and on his own to assist the young California congressman. Having by then established his reliability, Nixon enjoyed the express support of senior FBI officials and, although not in actual contact with the Director at that time, worked closely with Hoover's congressional liaison, Louis Nichols. Surviving FBI documents do not fully disclose the nature of Hoover's assistance during HUAC's 1948 hearings, but two FBI memoranda of December 1948 hint at the closeness of the relationship. One, dated 9 December, reports a conversation between Nixon and two former FBI agents (Patrick Coyne and Robert King) in which Nixon 'voluntarily stated during the course of the evening that he had worked very close [sic] with the Bureau and with Nichols during the past year on [the Hiss-Chambers] matter.' The other, dated 2 December, briefed Hoover and Tolson on a phone call Nichols had received in the middle of the previous night from Nixon.

On the evening of 1 December, Nixon and HUAC counsel Robert Stripling visited Whittaker Chambers at his Maryland farm, at which time Chambers told them that he possessed potentially explosive evidence damaging to Hiss that would be of interest to the Committee. Nixon's decision to visit Chambers had been occasioned by two conflicting reports that day — a news story asserting that a sitting grand jury would not indict Hiss for perjury for having denied Chambers's charges before HUAC in August, and the cryptic comment of an investigator for Chambers's attorneys that Chambers had recently turned over documents damaging to Hiss.

In his 2 December memorandum, Nichols reported that Nixon had called 'late last night on a strictly personal and highly confidential basis' about his conversation with Chambers, that Chambers 'did not tell the FBI everything he knew,' and that Chambers 'still has other documents and material that substantiate and vindicate his position which have up to this time not become publicly known.' HUAC intended to subpoena these documents for hearings scheduled for 18 December, and Nixon had called 'merely to apprise the Bureau so that the FBI would not be caught off base.' HUAC would handle 'the matter so that there will be no criticism to the FBI,' but Nixon requested that 'we do nothing about the information which he has just furnished as he feels the statute of limitations has run.' The FBI should 'not tell the Attorney General that we were told of this information as the Attorney General would try to make it impossible for the Committee to get the documents. He also asked that the Bureau not look for the documents themselves.'

In addition to the documents described in these December 1948 memoranda, Nixon shortly came to possess others that demonstrate incontestably his close covert relationship with Hoover's FBI, a relationship that both he and Hoover went to great pains to hide.

Among the documents that Chambers subsequently claimed to have obtained from his sources in the government bureaucracy during the 1930s was a four-page memorandum in the handwriting of Harry Dexter White, who was then at the Treasury Department. Chambers did not give this memorandum to HUAC investigators on 2 December (in response to a committee subpoena for all documents in his possession). Instead, on 3 December his attorney, Richard Cleveland, gave the White memorandum to the FBI and only to the FBI. Nixon, however, immediately obtained a copy,

300

which he used when questioning Chambers during an executive session hearing of a HUAC subcommittee on 28 December.

This was not the only case of the Bureau's providing Nixon with documentary assistance. Five days after Hiss's conviction for perjury (for denying espionage charges before a grand jury), on 26 January 1950, Nixon addressed the House of Representatives to praise HUAC's role in uncovering the evidence leading to Hiss's conviction (and, inter alia, to condemn the dereliction of the Truman administration in failing to pursue evidence of Hiss's involvement in a Communist conspiracy). In his speech, Nixon recounted in detail the Justice Department's strategy in presenting the Hiss case to the grand jury in late 1948 – in such detail, in fact, as to betray his sources at the Bureau. Moreover, he proceeded to quote from a classified FBI report of 25 November 1945 that could only have been obtained from his sources at the FBI.[17]

Hoover, it would appear, had more than a little to do with Nixon's instant celebrity. But the Director's assistance was by no means confined to helping the redoubtable Nixon, having earlier been lavished on HUAC members and staff initiating hearings into Communist influence in Hollywood.

Recognizing the national exposure that could be had for the taking by convening hearings involving the motion picture industry, Congressman J. Parnell Thomas, the chairman of the committee, had traveled to Los Angeles in May 1947. There he contacted the head of the FBI's field office, Richard Hood, to request his public testimony before the committee. Ordered by Hoover to inform Thomas that 'he obviously could not appear before the Committee in open session because to do so would spotlight the things we are trying to do with respect to keeping in touch with the Communist situation,' Hood was nevertheless instructed to convey the Director's desire to 'cooperate.' Should Thomas insist on a closed session, Hood would be permitted to appear but 'should be very careful and discreet in answering any inquiries.' Thomas was also to be informed that the Director 'could not make available information from our

301

files,' but in the event that 'any individuals in the motion picture industry had been the subject of publicity which is available to anyone, there would be no objection to pointing out such instances to the members of the Committee.'

Almost immediately Hoover relaxed his ban on leaking information from FBI files to the committee. Briefing the Director on a subsequent meeting between himself, Thomas, and committee counsel Robert Stripling, Hood reported that the 'Committee was exceedingly friendly' and that Thomas had emphasized that 'the Committee was cooperating with the Bureau and the Bureau with the Committee, that the Committee had given the Bureau access to its files and was appreciative of what the Bureau had been able to do to help [with other HUAC investigations, notably those involving Eugene Dennis and Gerhart Eisler].' In view of the committee's limited resources, however, Thomas felt 'severely handicapped by lack of any information' when questioning prospective witnesses and therefore requested information about nine named Hollywood personalities as well as 'any data we can furnish on the Communist infiltration of the motion picture industry which could be helpful to decide whether they should put an investigator out there for the next month or so and plan on holding hearings in Los Angeles on June 16th.' Thomas further emphasized that the committee understood 'the confidential character of [FBI] files,' respected it, and did 'not want information the disclosure of which would in any way embarrass the Bureau.' Nevertheless, the HUAC chairman argued, 'there was [sic] background data to be furnished which would not hurt the Bureau but would further Mr. Hoover's premise that the way to fight Communists was to expose them.'

Hood and Nichols considered how the FBI might best service Thomas's request, discussing 'various possibilities such as furnishing the names of known anti-Communists who have some basis for knowledge of Communist activities, the known Communist front groups and officers concerning whom the Committee might investigate.' Fully briefed on Hood's meeting with the committee and the Nichols-Hood recommendations, Hoover enthusiastically instructed his aides: 'Expedite. I want Hood to extend *every* assistance to this Committee' (emphasis in original).

Thereafter Hood searched high and low for relevant information in the Los Angeles office's files while Hoover's aides at headquarters compiled additional information, subject to the Director's sole condition that 'the disclosure of such data will not in any way embarrass the Bureau' (i.e., reveal that the FBI was the source of the information). Among other things, Hoover's aides compiled and provided HUAC with two lists – one identifying those Hollywood artists who were or had been members of organizations characterized as Communist-controlled or Communist-influenced and the other identifying non-Communists who 'may possess information of value re infiltration and would probably be cooperative and friendly witnesses.' Also provided was a memorandum summarizing FBI information on 'Communist activities in Hollywood.'

Hoover had his aides convey these three documents to Stripling on 13 May, with 'express instructions' that the committee ensure confidentiality about his assistance. In particular, the Bureau material contained a summary memorandum on the nine Hollywood personalities about whom Thomas had requested background information and profiles of thirty-two individuals who were described as 'cooperative and friendly witnesses' or who could give information about Communist influence in the motion picture and radio industries.

The names of twenty-eight of the thirty-two 'friendly' witnesses were deleted when the documents were released. The four whose names were not withheld were Ronald Reagan and Robert Montgomery (whom the FBI described as 'both past presidents of the Screen Actors Guild'), Emmett Lavery (described as 'president, Screen Writers Guild, who has previously testified before [California State Senator Jack] Tenny [*sic*: actually Tenney] Committee [on Un-American Activities]'), and Upton Close (described as a 'Radio Commentator and writer').

When recommending that HUAC invite Reagan as a

'friendly witness,' Hoover did so advisedly. From 1941 he had appraised Reagan as someone 'who might be of assistance to the Bureau,' and from November 1943 the actor had periodically furnished the Los Angeles field office with information about radical political activities in the film industry. Because of this covert assistance, Hoover had approved the Los Angeles office's recruitment of Reagan as a 'confidential informant.'

Reagan's willingness to inform on radical activities in the film industry proved particularly helpful, as, on 12 April, one month before Thomas's request for Hoover's assistance, the actor had briefed his FBI contact on the two cliques in the Screen Actors Guild that 'follow the Communist Party line' on all policy questions and had then proceeded to identify by name the actors and actresses who were members of each clique. Although Reagan did not name these individuals during his public testimony before HUAC, he did name them in executive session and worked closely with HUAC counsel to ensure that his public testimony would conform to the committee's expectations and would not violate the committee's agreement with Hoover.

The eventual outcome of these hearings was the blacklisting by the film industry of uncooperative witnesses and the premature termination of their careers.

While the Hollywood hearings progressed, another highly publicized case came to light. This one involved Judith Coplon, an employee in the Justice Department's alien registration section. On 4 March 1949 Coplon was arrested as she was about to deliver twenty-eight FBI documents to Valentine Gubitchev, a member of the Soviet Union's United Nations staff. Indicted for unauthorized possession of classified government documents, Coplon was tried in the Federal District Court in Washington, D.C.

The trial, the first of two in her case, was not an unalloyed success for Hoover. During testimony, Archibald Palmer, Coplon's attorney, demanded the production as evidence of the full text of the twenty-eight FBI documents found in the defendant's handbag at the time of her arrest. The

304

government opposed the motion at Hoover's insistence, citing 'national security' grounds. Ruling that the government could not seek to convict Coplon of a national security offense without producing in an adversary proceeding the documentary evidence to support its charge, Judge Albert Reeves ordered the release of all twenty-eight documents.

For good reason, Hoover adamantly opposed their production. He told Attorney General Clark that he would rather see the 'Coplon case go by default' than have the Justice Department permit the defense (and therefore the public) access to the contents of FBI documents. Resorting to alarmist language, he expressed fears 'for the future not only of the Bureau but of the Department and its effectiveness to discharge its responsibilities in the more important field of internal security.' In an effort to convince Clark and to exploit President Truman's commitment to executive privilege (most recently manifested in his refusal to release the loyalty reports on federal employees), the Director disingenuously worried about the reputations of 'individuals on whom information is contained in investigative reports who are placed in the difficult position, for all practical purposes, of having charges made against them without having an opportunity to answer.' He then warned that 'if the present actions of Defense Attorney Palmer are permitted to continue there will be an unprecedented outburst of criticism not only of the FBI but of the Department and yourself [Clark].'

Failing to persuade Clark to drop the case rather than honor the judge's order, Hoover directed his liaison to the White House, Ralph Roach, to show White House aide John Steelman a copy of his communication to the attorney general, 'pointing out my position & date of it & stressing that had A.G. [attorney general] acted as I suggested all of this furor would have been avoided.' Roach was ordered not to leave a copy of Hoover's memo with Steelman.

Roach met Steelman and learned that the Coplon case had been discussed at a special conference in the president's office on 10 June, at which time the attorney general had

305

advised the president of Hoover's recommendation. But, Clark added, the army and naval intelligence officials with whom he had discussed the case stressed the importance of winning a conviction at all costs.

Clark's presentation, according to Steelman, was not calculated to elicit a decision from the president but instead to advise Truman of his own decision to proceed. Impressed by Hoover's arguments, and particularly their emphasis on individual rights, Steelman added that had the president 'been properly approached and apprised of the facts as set forth in your [Hoover's] memorandum, he would have concluded the trial if it necessitated further disclosure of FBI reports.' Such an action, Steelman continued, would have been 'in accord with the Presidential order [opposing] disclosure [to congressional committees] of such reports in loyalty investigations.' Conceding that nothing could be done at present, Steelman promised to 'follow this matter closely at the White House, and . . . keep the Bureau informed of any developments which may arise there.'

Hoover, of course, had not opposed the release of the Bureau's reports because of any concern over internal security or the privacy rights of innocent individuals. The potential furor to which he referred stemmed from the fact that release of the reports would embarrass the FBI – disclosing, as they in fact later did, the political basis of FBI investigations and the extent of FBI wiretapping; fifteen of the twenty-eight reports contained information acquired through wiretaps.

For Hoover, then, the Coplon case was at best a learning experience. On the one hand, it dramatized the vulnerability of FBI documents to court-ordered discovery motions. On the other, it demonstrated that Justice Department employees not only could secure FBI documents for espionage purposes, but, as alarmingly, could leak them to reporters and columnists. To avoid these demonstrated dangers, Hoover instituted two new procedures to govern the preparation and filing of FBI reports.

On 9 July he ordered that henceforth agents preparing reports were not to include 'facts and information which are considered of a nature not expedient to disseminate, or which would cause embarrassment to the Bureau, if distributed.' Such information instead was to be reported on 'administrative pages at the conclusion of the report, which will be detached before distribution.' Whenever reports having administrative pages were 'distributed to any agency outside the Bureau,' Hoover specified, 'the administrative pages should be detached.'

The Director then listed examples of the kinds of information to be reported on administrative pages. One example was information that would reveal the FBI's collection of noncriminal derogatory personal information – for instance: 'An anonymous complaint alleges A . . . is a member of the Communist Party and further that A is a man of loose morals, a heavy drinker living with a known prostitute. On the basis of other information in the files a case is opened. The allegation of Communist Party membership should be included in the investigative section while the allegation concerning loose morals should be included in the administrative section.' Or: 'During the legal search in a white slave traffic act investigation there is found an address book containing data identifying prominent public officials. Unless the names appearing therein are material to the investigation, this type of information should be placed in the administrative section.'[18]

Hoover's July directive supplemented another record procedure he had instituted on 29 June. According to that procedure, reports recording either the FBI's use of 'highly confidential' sources (i.e., illegal investigative techniques, such as wiretaps, bugs, break-ins, or opening of letters) or 'most secretive sources, such as Governors, secretaries to high officials who may be discussing such officials and their attitude,' were not to be included in the FBI's main case files, where they were vulnerable to court-ordered discovery motions, congressional subpoenas, or requests from the Justice Department. Such reports were to be 'communicated to the Bureau by letter, which will be forwarded to the Director under personal and confidential cover. The communication should be sealed in an envelope bearing the code word "June" and then placed in an envelope addressed to the Director "Personal and Confidential." ' When received at FBI headquarters, 'June Mail' was to be kept in a 'separate confidential file maintained under lock and key.' Copies of such letters were to be kept 'in a confidential file by the Special Agent in Charge and this file, too, shall be retained under lock and key.'

Additional embarrassing developments in the Coplon case prompted further refinement of the June Mail procedure. In December 1949, during pretrial hearings for Coplon's second trial, this one held in New York City, it was disclosed that FBI agents had dissembled about FBI wiretapping practices and had recently destroyed wiretap records. At Coplon's earlier trial, and in response to the disclosure of extensive FBI wiretapping activities, her attorney had sought a hearing to ascertain whether his client's phone had been tapped, thus resulting in the prosecution's obtaining tainted information leading to her arrest. With FBI agents in attendance, the U.S. attorney prosecuting the case had then characterized the defense motion as a 'fishing expedition,' declaring that there was no evidence of FBI wiretapping of Coplon. On that occasion, the presiding judge had denied defense counsel's request.

At Coplon's second trial, for intent to deliver classified documents to an agent of a foreign power, the presiding judge, Sylvester Ryan, ordered a hearing to determine whether her phone had been tapped. The ensuing inquiry established that, yes, her phone had been tapped, both before and after her arrest (there was a possibility that even privileged conversations with her attorneys had been intercepted), that the agent who had originally denied any knowledge of wiretapping Coplon had regularly received reports based on these wiretaps, and finally that Hoover had ordered the Coplon wiretap logs destroyed 'in view of the imminence of her trial.'

These disclosures came at a time when Hoover was already deeply concerned about the apparent strategy of Coplon's attorney in her New York trial, Abraham Pomerantz. Pomerantz had subpoenaed the records of the New York and Washington telephone companies and had sought to interrogate FBI agents about their tapping of Coplon. Reacting to this new danger, Hoover had telephone company representatives alerted to Pomerantz's strategy, declaring to his aides that should the attorney succeed, 'all wiretapping is through.'

Hoover then instituted still other procedures, calculated to avert this dire possibility. On the one hand, every supervisor, SAC, and agent who might in future be assigned to a particular case, and thus become vulnerable to subpoena, was ordered not 'to engage in any searches, physical surveillances, interviews with subjects or other types of work which may make him a competent witness in the event . . . it should be decided to prosecute. Thus, the Agents who might in these instances be competent witnesses would have no specific testifiable knowledge of the existence of a technical surveillance [wiretap] in that particular case.'

All wiretap logs, on the other hand, and all 'administrative correspondence' relating to wiretaps (such as field office requests and headquarters authorization memoranda) were to be captioned 'June' to ensure that they were 'retained and filed separate and apart from the main file room in a confidential office' under 'lock and key.' Only one copy of a wiretap log was to be permanently retained, and special care was to be given to the selection of agents who monitored wiretaps or prepared wiretap logs. Reports submitted under the June caption were 'not to be opened in the file room' but were to be sent to Hoover's aides at FBI headquarters. Finally, to minimize the risk that these orders could be discovered, instructions were 'telephonically issued' to all SACs stipulating that all 'microphone surveillance[s] which involved trespass were to be considered June mail.' Furthermore, all instructions regarding June matters were to be 'transmitted orally.'[19]

To house the 'June'-coded documents, Hoover ordered the creation of a Special File Room, a secure locked area at FBI headquarters. Only agents having a need to know could secure access to the documents stored in this room. Other illegally obtained documents stored there included the fruits of the mail-opening programs that Hoover had authorized in the 1940s and the photocopies of letters the FBI had received from the CIA's mail-opening program, HTLINGUAL.[20]

In addition, certain do-not-file-type documents were maintained by senior FBI officials in their offices (Hoover maintained two sets of such files in his office, Tolson another in his, and Nichols a confidential file in his). To ensure that these office files could not be publicly compromised, in March 1953 Hoover ordered their regular destruction — every sixty days for those maintained by FBI supervisors and every six months for those maintained by FBI assistant directors.[21]

The Coplon case, which had contributed to the refinement of these carefully crafted concealment practices, was itself an unmitigated disaster for Hoover. Apprised of the FBI's wiretapping and then its destruction of wiretap logs, the courts ordered that Coplon be retried. Unwilling either to answer questions about FBI procedures or to drop the case, Hoover persuaded subsequent attorneys general to hold the case in abeyance, so that prosecution of Coplon was formally dropped only in 1967. Thus the espionage defendant against whom the government had its strongest case went unpunished.

His Enemy Grows Older: The Dewey Campaign, the NLG, and the Collapse of the Old Left

Hoover's successful 'educational campaign' was not won without a struggle. Rivals continued to scheme against him, and his critics, most notably Max Lowenthal, were fired with enthusiasm by the belief (correct, as it turned out) that Hoover was secretly abetting HUAC and, after 1951, the Senate Internal Security Subcommittee (SISS), chaired by the Director's old friend from Nevada, Pat McCarran.[22]

President Truman's March 1948 executive order had in theory prohibited congressional access to the Bureau's files, but Hoover secretly leaked FBI information on a selective basis to conservative congressmen and other anti-Communist activists – all the time denying that he was doing so. All requests from HUAC and SISS were 'individually considered and information is furnished where the best interests of the Bureau would be served.' Indeed, Hoover's public testimony before HUAC in 1947, applauding the committee's exposure practices and hyping the theme of the Red Menace, masked the real nature of his covert relationship with HUAC – helpful but on the Director's terms. By 1947, moreover, Hoover had become a star on the right-wing lecture circuit, haranguing DAR and American Legion audiences with ghostwritten speeches on the Red Menace.

For a brief moment, it appeared that this relationship would be severed. In December 1948, fresh from his upset victory over Republican presidential candidate Thomas Dewey and still smarting from HUAC's partisan attacks on his administration's internal security record, Truman resolved to confront HUAC head on. Having decided to recommend HUAC's dissolution in his State of the Union address of January 1949, the president directed Attorney General Clark to prepare a resolution that the House Democratic leadership could introduce in January when the rules for the organization of the House were adopted. But by then, as a result of Alger Hiss's indictment for perjury on 15 December, Truman had abandoned his plan.

Then, the following June, after the embarrassing series of disclosures of FBI malpractices in the Coplon case, Clifford Durr, the president of the National Lawyers Guild, petitioned Truman to create a blue-ribbon commission to investigate the FBI. The president was by no means indifferent to Durr's proposal, as privately his own aides were encouraging him to do something about the Bureau. But, looking to anticipated Republican gains in the 1950 congressional elections, he equivocated. Meanwhile, the NLG plea had found its way back to Hoover.

The next month Hoover was informed that Nichols had learned from one of his press contacts that 'the President had made up his mind to let the Director go' but had been

311

advised not to do 'anything rash' in view of Hoover's tremendous popularity. The president had been warned that if he 'did anything which would cause the Director to leave, it would reflect adversely on the elections in 1950 and 1952. The President stated he guessed this was so.'

Nevertheless, Hoover remained troubled. Truman's evasiveness about the Coplon trial revelations when grilled by reporters during a June press conference and his refusal to defend Hoover outright had particularly alarmed the Director. Then, the *Washington News,* in an 18 June 1949 editorial, concluded that 'it's beginning to look as if Truman Administration would welcome the resignation of J. Edgar Hoover, and chance to put one of its own men in charge of FBI.' The *News* doubted that Hoover would resign, criticized Attorney General Clark for permitting the public release of FBI documents in the Coplon trial, and speculated whether Clark would seek a showdown with Hoover. Should the attorney general seek to force Hoover to quit, the *News* opined, neither Congress nor the public would go along, and Hoover's 'partisans in Congress' would draft legislation to 'make FBI independent agency.'

Syndicated Hearst columnists Fulton Lewis and Constantine Brown also contacted Nichols after Truman's press conference. Lewis criticized the president's failure to come to Hoover's defense, while Brown inquired about 'a rumor that the Director was about to resign, that Clark was trying to force the Director out by his attitude and by his tactics in letting the [Coplon] reports go into evidence.' Brown added that Drew Pearson had heard similar rumors. Nichols immediately sought to dispel Brown's concern that 'the Director was resigning. I told him while we could not make any comment for him not to get too excited about it.'

Whether or not Truman and Clark were actually seeking to force Hoover to resign, the Director had no intention of stepping down. Confident of his support in Congress and the media, Hoover went on the offensive, working closely with conservative reporters (notably UPI Washington bureau chief Lyle Wilson) to prevent the establishment of a presidential commission and then leaking derogatory

312

information about the NLG to create the impression that any criticism of Hoover and the FBI was a subversive effort to undermine the nation's internal security.

Ironically, a year earlier Hoover had himself sought to effect Truman's forced retirement from national politics. Sharing the conventional wisdom that the Republican presidential nominee, New York governor Thomas Dewey, would win the election and eager to retain the FBI directorship, Hoover, despite his misgivings about a Dewey presidency,[23] covertly assisted the Republican candidate during both the primary and final election campaigns.

Hoover first became seriously concerned about Dewey in October 1942, following Dewey's nomination as the New York Republican gubernatorial candidate. The Director then demanded that his aides review FBI files and prepare a summary memorandum on Dewey, to 'be filed for future reference.'

The FBI failed to amass any significant derogatory information on Dewey, a failure particularly disappointing for Hoover when, two years later, Dewey won the Republican presidential nomination and an alarmed New York SAC, E. E. Conroy, informed Hoover that Dewey, if elected, might not continue him as Director. Ordered to investigate this rumor, Conroy contacted one of Dewey's associates and reported back that, contrary to his earlier report, 'Dewey would reappoint you as Director of the FBI because of your recognized ability and the fact that Dewey always surrounded himself with men of ability.'

Yet Conroy's original briefing had already moved Hoover into action, and from other sources the Director had received more ominous reports on Dewey's plans. One, attributed to a Republican committeeman, stated that 'if Dewey were elected President, the Director would be replaced.' Hoover demanded that these conflicting reports be investigated with 'extreme care and caution' and ordered a concerted effort to learn 'the Republican Party's political aims, particularly with respect to the entire Department of Justice.' Hoover's agents, after an intensive inquiry, then discreetly sought to ascertain the views of those close to the Republican nominee and prepared a lengthy summary memorandum outlining in particular Dewey's views on crime and law enforcement.

The matter did not end with Dewey's defeat in the November elections. On 15 December Conroy advised the Director that an intercepted conversation disclosed that 'Governor Dewey had planned to remove the Director from office if Governor Dewey were elected President.' Two months later, Hoover learned additional disquieting information that the FBI's 'confidential informant' Ronald Reagan had provided to an agent of the Los Angeles field office. Reagan had reported that 'while he was not present personally, several of his friends were present during a private and "off the record" conversation with DEWEY in Los Angeles when he was here on his campaign tour.' At this time, Dewey allegedly stated that 'when he was elected President there would not be enough jails in the country to hold the people he was going to put into them, and that JOHN EDGAR HOOVER of the FBI was going to be one of the first.'

Circumstance again appears to have been crucial to Hoover's survival at the Bureau, for, however much he may have distrusted Hoover's politics and priorities, President Truman by early 1949 was unwilling to challenge the powerful Director. Left to its own devices, the NLG responded to Truman's inaction by culling the court records in the Coplon case and preparing its own detailed report on FBI improprieties.

Through his extensive informer system, Hoover almost immediately learned of this plan and the imminent release of the damning NLG report. Thereupon he ordered an intensive search of FBI files on the Guild. A 300-page report was quickly compiled, charging the Guild with being a Communist front organization. On completion of the report, portions were leaked to sympathetic reporters and to HUAC (which in turn released them under the committee's imprimatur in a 50-page booklet titled 'Report on the National Lawyers Guild: Legal Bulwark of the Communist Party').

Still the NLG pressed on, informed on by the Bureau spies

and accused by Hoover loyalists in the press and in Congress. When the newsman I. F. Stone attempted to advise Durr on ways to maximize the effect of the pending Guild report's disclosures, FBI agents intercepted the call and reported its content to the Justice Department and White House.

Finally the NLG report was ready for release, and a press conference was planned for 23 January 1950. Much of the information amassed was published later that year in Max Lowenthal's book and amounted to a bill of particulars covering more than twenty-five years of official abuse.

But an official investigation of the FBI was not to be. On 22 January, the day before the planned conference, Richard Nixon publicly demanded a HUAC investigation of the Guild. Hoover then urged its inclusion in the attorney general's subversive organizations list. Thrown utterly on the defensive, spied on, burglarized, tapped, the NLG all but disintegrated within the next few years. It was but one of many victims of Hoover's by then awesome power and ability to employ the Bureau to silence his own and the FBI's critics.

Notes to Chapter Ten

1. *Note to chapter title:* The term 'the cause' was articulated by Hoover's aide Louis Nichols. Commenting ruefully in the summer of 1953 on the possible adverse political fallout of McCarthy's methods as chairman of the Senate Government Operations Committee, Nichols expressed his fear that 'the cause had suffered.' (Memo, Nichols to Tolson, 23 July 1953, Miscellaneous A-Z folder, Nichols O&C.)

2. Hoover may have failed in this respect, but not for lack of trying. The Director remained alert to any prospect that other officials might obtain this authority. In November 1945 he learned, through the good services of Senator Styles Bridges, of the ambitions of former MID official Alfred McCormack. An erstwhile corporation lawyer, McCormack had served in military intelligence during World War II and had recently been appointed to head the

State Department's Office of Research and Intelligence. This newly created office was to provide unified, government-wide intelligence about foreign countries, and State Department officials intended that it be the successor to the disbanded OSS. Opposed by the military services and the FBI which feared an encroachment on their authority, McCormack's office soon became the object of critical scrutiny by conservative congressmen.

Bridges, as part of this containment effort, alerted Hoover to a letter from a former MID official to President Truman questioning the loyalty of McCormack's wartime associates in MID and claiming that McCormack had sought to purge information about their subversive backgrounds from their FBI files. A House Military Affairs subcommittee soon publicized these charges in a public hearing, which was abruptly terminated when McCormack requested an opportunity to answer them. Then, in April 1946, the House Appropriations Committee voted against funding the newly created Office of Research and Intelligence, leading McCormack to resign in protest. Bridges's helpful briefing of Hoover about these charges, the month before McCormack's appointment and the creation of this new office were publicly announced, enabled the Director and the heads of the military intelligence services to concert with their conservative allies in Congress to suffocate the baby aborning. (Memo, Carson to Ladd, 9 November 1945, FBI 62-116758; *New York Times*, 23 December 1945, p. 5; 21 March 1946, p. 12; 26 March 1946, p. 24; 27 March 1946, p. 10;10 April 1946, p. 21; 24 April 1946, p. 4; 25 April 1946, p. 8.)

3. Ideological considerations apparently determined Hoover's changed recruitment efforts. The example of future Supreme Court Justice Potter Stewart's candidacy to become an FBI agent in 1941 provides a case in point. Protestant in religion and the son of a prominent Ohio Republican — his father was a long-time mayor of Cincinnati and later served on the Ohio State Supreme Court — Potter Stewart's interest in becoming an agent would seem to have been a boon for Hoover's FBI. A graduate of Yale College (where he was Phi Beta Kappa) and Yale Law School (where he was a top student), Stewart initially sought appointment as an FBI agent rather than enter what proved to be a highly successful career in corporate law and public life. The resulting applicant investigation turned up information that Stewart had been a member of an isolationist college organization while a student at Yale, the Committee of College Men for Defense First, and that

316

his mother was apparently a member of the Peace League (an isolationist group) and the League of Women Voters (whose local Cincinnati chapter had supported the highly publicized investigation of the munitions industry conducted by the so-called Nye Committee of the Senate). Upon learning this, Hoover ordered the head of the Cincinnati field office to ascertain without delay whether Stewart's mother was the same person listed as a member of the Peace League and further demanded that 'particular care be given to the possibility that the applicant or his family may be engaged in any subversive activities.' Although the resulting investigation uncovered 'no evidence of subversive activities on part of applicant's mother nor on part of any member of family,' Stewart was not appointed an FBI agent. (Letter, Hoover to SAC, Cincinnati, 3 May 1941; Report, Cincinnati Field Office, 12 June 1941; Telegram, Stewart to Hoover, 6 July 1941; and Letter, Hoover to Stewart, 7 July 1941; all in FBI 67-198330.)

4. Not all Irish Americans were reliably anti-Communist, of course, but as Father Andrew Greeley has pointed out, most of their clergy were, in those days of the 'immigrant church.'

5. This was a reference to the 'educational' campaign about the Red Menace that Hoover had formally authorized in February 1946.

6. Hoover's interest in promoting movies that glorified his role as Director and the FBI's supposed efficiency in combating The Red Menace led him to conclude a contract with New York agent-producer Louis de Rochemont in July 1951 under which the FBI Director assigned the rights to make a motion picture based on his ghostwritten May 1951 *Reader's Digest* article, 'Crime of The Century,' on the Rosenberg case. Under the provisions of the agreement, de Rochemont undertook to pay Hoover $15,000 'within ninety (90) days after the first general release of the motion picture.' But apparently Hoover had second thoughts about the arrangement, especially the possibility that it might become known that he was profiting from his position as Director. Accordingly, on 30 December 1952 — approximately a year and a half later — he wrote de Rochemont specifying that he considered his present letter an amendment to their 1951 contract 'in that I do not desire to accept any payment for the said motion picture rights conveyed therein.' (Letter, de Rochemont to Hoover, 13 July 1951; and enclosed copy of signed contract; Letter, de Rochemont to Hoover, 31 August 1951; Personal Letter, Hoover to de Rochemont, 30 December 1952; all in Louis de Rochemont Crime of the Century

folder, Folder no. 56, Hoover O&C.) No such inhibition prevented his sharing with other Bureau officials the proceeds of his ghostwritten book *Masters of Deceit*. For reasons unknown, the film was never made.

7. In September 1970 Hoover briefed White House aide Egil Krogh on this arrangement, at a time when the White House, in concert with the FBI, sought an appropriations increase to hire an additional 1,000 FBI agents. The FBI, Hoover disclosed, maintained 'a staff of our own men who are assigned to the appropriations committee for three years and then they rotate, to carry on any investigations the chairman may order in any of the government agencies. Mr. Krogh said this sort of cements good relations. I said yes, we have had excellent relations with the committee and, of course, I have always gotten along well with [Appropriations Subcommittee Chairman] John Rooney, as well as the chairmen on back.' (Memo, Hoover to Tolson, Mohr, Bishop, and Callahan, 30 September 1970, Tolson File, vol. 5.)

8. Learning of this program inadvertently on 26 October 1972, through a wire service story reporting that an agent in Ohio had contacted a newspaper to request information on a congressional candidate, Acting Director L. Patrick Gray immediately ordered its termination.

9. Dies returned to Congress in 1953 but failed to regain a seat on the controversial committee.

10. The Bureau memorandum describing this program in addition listed the following congressional committees as having been 'furnished information' by the FBI: Joint Committee on Atomic Energy, Senate Appropriations Committee, Senate Armed Services Committee, Preparedness Subcommittee to the Armed Services Committee, Senate and House Judiciary Committees, Senate Committee on Labor and Public Welfare, Subcommittee on Labor Management Relations of the Senate Committee on Labor and Public Welfare, Senate Foreign Relations Committee, Senate Subcommittee on Internal Security, House Committee on Un-American Activities, and 'Senate Permanent Investigations Committee (McCarthy) up until the late summer [1953] when the Committee appointed former Special Agent [Francis] Carr as Staff Director.' Under this massive but covert program, the FBI 'volunteers information regarding subjects who are on the [FBI's] Security Index to the Governor of a state, or to a responsible local official . . . when the subject is employed in a public utility . . . or in a public or semi-public organization [including college

318

professors and primary and secondary school teachers]. In each instance the Bureau specifically passes upon the information to be disseminated; the dissemination is oral; and the field is required to furnish a statement regarding the reliability and discretion of the individual to whom the information is to be given before authority is granted.' (Memo, Executives' Conference to Hoover, 14 October 1953, FBI 66-7588(?); Memo, Executives' Conference to Hoover, 30 April 1951, FBI 62-93875 – Not Recorded.)

11. Hoover's interest in discrediting the Guild stemmed from that organization's prominence in questioning the FBI's activities in the wake of the Judith Coplon case, discussed hereafter, although the Guild's left-liberal orientation had much earlier made it an object of his scrutiny, as were individual lawyers holding radical political views. As early as 1936 Hoover had authorized his aides to provide officials of the National Conference of Bar Examiners with information on the organizational ties and political beliefs of applicants to practice law. Headquartered in Chicago, the Conference assisted local and state bar associations by investigating the character and fitness of applicants for admission to the bar. Hoover began this covert assistance in response to a request from Will Shaforth, the secretary of the conference, for information about foreign lawyers applying for admission to the bar. In time, the Director expanded the program to encompass all applicants, stipulating that this assistance be kept 'strictly confidential.' Not surprisingly, the secret FBI reports detailed information on the applicants' criticisms of Supreme Court decisions, support for labor unions and civil rights causes, and participation in functions sponsored by the NLG. Originally, Hoover had sought the attorney general's authorization before providing this assistance. In 1954 the Director ceased seeking approval on a case-by-case basis, after obtaining Attorney General Herbert Brownell's blanket authorization to provide such information to the conference. Similar information was also supplied to local bar associations in Washington and New York. (*New York Times*, 15 June 1985, p. 30.)

12. Truman's concern about leaks led him to request FBI wiretaps of columnist Drew Pearson, Treasury Department official Edward Pritchard, and Washington lobbyist Thomas Corcoran, discussed later in this chapter.

13. Clark had succeeded Biddle as attorney general in June 1945.

14. Clark first authorized a wiretap on Corcoran five months later, on 15 November 1945, when briefing Hoover on the White

House's concern over Corcoran's lobbying activities with certain members of the federal bureaucracy. The ostensible purpose then was to ensure that 'such activities did not interfere with the proper administration of government.' (Strictly Confidential Memo, Hoover for the File, 15 November 1945, White House Correspondence, 1945 CO Technical Coverage folder, Folder no. 1, Hoover O&C.)

15. Later, in 1956, second-level party officials who had changed their defense strategy and retained as legal counsel attorneys with no radical taint, won acquittal in a case tried in Cleveland. Seeking to counteract the effect of this exoneration, Hoover in highly publicized testimony before the Senate Appropriations Committee darkly warned of a new Communist strategy that included 'legal maneuvers – acquiring eminent counsel to defend the Party and its leaders – and the use of petitions, forums, mass meetings, and radio broadcasts.' (Percival Bailey, 'The Case of the National Lawyers Guild, 1939–1958,' in Athan G. Theoharis (ed.), *Beyond the Hiss Case,* pp. 159–60.)

16. In his memoirs, Nixon confirms Cronin's account of the FBI's covert assistance: 'Because of Truman's [March 1948] executive order [prohibiting federal officials from honoring congressional subpoenas for FBI loyalty files], we [HUAC] were not able to get any direct help from J. Edgar Hoover or the FBI. However, we had some informal contacts with a lower-level agent that proved helpful in our investigations.' (*RN: The Memoirs of Richard Nixon* [New York: Grosset & Dunlap, 1978], p. 58.)

17. When the Harry Dexter White case resurfaced in November 1953, Hoover's aides learned that the Hearst newspapers intended to publish the FBI memorandum of 25 November 1945. Ordered to ascertain how the Hearst papers, and other conservative activists, had obtained a copy of this memo, Nichols, when reporting his findings in this matter, invariably referred to the memo as either the 'so-called Nixon memo' or the 'Nixon memo.' (Memo, Nichols to Tolson, 12 November 1953, FBI 61-7582.)

18. Hoover later modified the Administrative Pages procedure. Potentially embarrassing information, he ordered, 'should be set out in a cover letter transmitting the report.' While emphasizing that cover letters were to be used infrequently, Hoover nevertheless reiterated that they should 'include information which, if placed in a report, might cause embarrassment.' (Strictly Confidential Bureau Bulletin no. 16, ser. 1951, 20 April 1951, FBI 66-03-1119.)

19. In January 1969 Hoover ordered an internal study to

determine whether the June code word should continue to be used for 'intra-Bureau correspondence relating to highly sensitive techniques' such as wiretaps. *True* magazine's publication of a Drew Pearson/Jack Anderson article, 'The Last Days of J. Edgar Hoover,' had threatened to compromise the 'security of our code word "JUNE." ' When discussing the FBI's bugging of Fred Black (discussed in Chapter 14), Pearson and Anderson described one FBI report on this surveillance as 'so hush-hush that they even used a code word for "secret" and stamped the report "June." ' Pearson's and Anderson's discovery, Hoover complained, had resulted from recent developments, 'such as publication of our technical surveillances [wiretaps] through judicial proceedings.' Although the Director's aides were divided over whether the 'June' procedure should be continued, Hoover decided against any change, viewing the case for continued secrecy to protect 'sources illegal in nature' as conclusive. (Memo, Wannall to Sullivan, 17 January 1969, FBI 66-1372-49; Memo, Caspar to Mohr, 30 January 1969, FBI 66-1372-50; Memo, Brennan to Sullivan, 19 May 1970, FBI 66-1372-51; SAC Letter no. 70-29, 26 May 1970, FBI 66-04-3741.)

20. Hoover had earlier devised another discreet reporting procedure, 'Personal and Confidential' letters, and had extended it in 1940 to include any intraheadquarters correspondence that, owing to its sensitivity, should not be serialized in the Bureau's central records system. His order stipulating that this correspondence should not be serialized empowered his aides to destroy it without risk of discovery, no record of the correspondence having ever been made.

Hoover further refined this procedure after deciding that some of these memoranda might warrant preservation, or were no longer sufficiently sensitive to require their destruction. In 1949 he directed that a pink memorandum was to be 'reviewed every six months for the purpose of determining whether or not it should be sent to the files.' Each such memorandum was to be returned to its author after serving its informational purpose, and if after six months such memoranda 'are of no further value to the Bureau they should be destroyed.' Whenever such memoranda emanated from Hoover's office, however, 'as they have served their purpose, [they] should be returned to me [Hoover] instead of being maintained in the official's files to whom the memorandum is directed.' (Memo, Executives' Conference to Hoover, 24 December 1948; Memo, Hoover to Tolson et al., 5 January 1949; both in FBI 62-116758.)

21. In most cases – the exceptions being Hoover's Official and Confidential File, Nichols's Official and Confidential File, and a portion of Tolson's Personal File – these office files *were* destroyed. Documents recording the destruction of other documents, describing the general contents of destroyed files, and explaining why certain files were created or destroyed offer stunning insights into how Hoover operated and how he succeeded in preventing discovery of his abuses of power.

22. Other beneficiaries of Hoover's leaks and other assistance included Congressmen John J. Rooney (D.-N.Y.), George Mahon (D.-Tex.), Clarence Cannon (D.-Mo.), Richard Nixon (R.-Cal.), Karl Mundt (R.-S.D.), Gerald Ford (R.-Mich.), F. Edward Hebert (D.-La.), Francis Walter (D.-Pa.), John Kerr (D.-N.C.), Karl Stefan (R.-Neb.), John Rankin (D.-Miss.), Howard Smith (D.-Va.), and Edward Cox (D.-Ga.); and Senators Joseph McCarthy (R.-Wis.), Homer Ferguson (R.-Mich), Thomas Dodd (D -Conn.), Strom Thurmond (R.-S.C.), Pat McCarran (D-Nev.), Everett Dirksen (R.-Ill.), Barry Goldwater (R.-Ariz.), Bourke Hickenlooper (R.-Iowa), Styles Bridges (R.-N.H), Gerald Nye (R.-N.D.), and James Eastland (D.-Miss.). In one case, during the height of the Vietnam War, Hoover had his aides write the speech that Congressman Smith delivered in the House attacking as subversive the anti-Vietnam War movement.

23. Hoover's misgivings dated from the 1930s, at a time when Dewey was seeking to make a name for himself as an assistant U.S. attorney in New York through a highly publicized campaign against crime. Distrustful of Dewey's success in monopolizing the news and his implicit criticisms of the Bureau's crime-fighting record, Hoover kept Dewey at arms' length.

CHAPTER ELEVEN

(1950–1955)

RINGMASTER

JUSTIFYING HIS OPPOSITION to the public release of information from FBI files in testimony before a Senate committee in 1950, Hoover cited 'fundamental principles of common decency' and 'basic American rights of fair play'. 'I would not want to be a party to any action which would "smear" innocent individuals for the rest of their lives,' he proclaimed – a principle in striking contrast, he well knew, to the publicity-seeking red baiting of HUAC, for instance, and such politically ambitious red-hunters as Congressman Richard Nixon and Senator Joseph McCarthy. Above all, Hoover insisted, the FBI must remain a nonpartisan fact-finding organization sensitive to individual rights and resistant to the abuse of its information-gathering powers for political reasons.

Hoover's declamation was good public relations. But it was far from the truth. In fact, as part of the 'educational' campaign he had launched in February 1946, derogatory information from FBI files had been disseminated to favored reporters and congressmen for years, and the effect of this leaking had been to intensify public fears of the Red Menace and smear innocent individuals for the rest of their lives.

The Director's absolute control over access to information in FBI files underpinned his success in promoting a second Red Scare while projecting an image of utter fairness and political impartiality. Indeed, little in the way of incriminating evidence survived Hoover's secret records-destruction process, although what remains, by accident, leaves no doubt about his duplicity and abuse of his power.

Early in his tenure Hoover realized the importance of

ensuring secrecy if he was to shape the image of the Bureau to suit his designs. By immunizing Bureau activities and his own conduct from outside scrutiny, he not only could deceive with impunity but also conduct operations that otherwise would be tantamount to political suicide. This success was not foreordained, however. As Director, he operated within certain theoretical limits. As the investigative division of the Department of Justice, his FBI was technically subject to the oversight of the attorney general and, ultimately, the White House. As a federal agency dependent on congressional authorization for its budget, the FBI was accountable to Congress, and its files were liable to congressional subpoena. As a law enforcement agency preparing cases for trial, its conduct and its records were subject to the review authority of the courts. And, finally, under provisions of the Federal Records Act, Bureau records of historical value had to be preserved for public access, and the National Archives was empowered to ensure that result.

Hoover's administrative ingenuity minimized these potential checks on his freedom of action. The control of his executive, legislative, and judicial overseers he evaded by secrecy and legerdemain; that of the Archives, by a firm demonstration of power. Arguing that any research into FBI records could compromise the Bureau's law enforcement and countersubversive responsibilities, he flatly refused to turn over *any* FBI records to the National Archives. Instead, he negotiated an agreement whereby the Bureau need only seek Archives approval before destroying any class of records – and without Archives officials' review of the records to be destroyed.

This arrangement, however, created a major administrative burden, given the volume of records generated over the years by Hoover's agents. In order to lessen the load, Hoover in 1944 requested Archives approval to destroy 'superfluous' FBI records relating to White Slave Traffic Act investigations of 1912 to 1919. Because these records documented the illicit sexual activities of a broad cross-section of the American public, the Archives rejected Hoover's request, citing their rich research value to historians and sociologists and asking Hoover to turn the records over to them for preservation, to be made available for outside review subject to the Director's 'explicit approval.'

Concluding that turning over such sensitive records to the Archives 'could be suicidal,' Hoover withdrew the destruction request. Instead, all 'superfluous' records were to be microfilmed to alleviate the space problem. Supervisor Robert Cartwright summarized the rationale for this decision: 'There is, undoubtedly, considerable information of a very personal nature and potentially derogatory to the character of persons still living [in the White Slave Traffic case files].' And because the vast majority of these cases did not result in prosecution, should such material 'perchance, become, even in part, public property, we should be in an embarrassing position without even the defense of an indictment or authorized complaint.' Thereafter, from 1950, under Hoover's order, no FBI records were to be transferred to the custody of the Archives, or any other agency, and any 'portions thereof pertinent for retention because of historic or archive value [would] remain in our custody.'

There remained, however, the problem of containing any possible threat from the new Eisenhower White House. Eisenhower's election brought about the first partisan transfer of executive power in twenty years. In December 1952 Hoover ordered his aides to check FBI files for information on the president-elect's key White House aides – Thomas Stephens, H. Douglas Weaver, and William T. Pfeiffer – and Eisenhower's choice as chairman of the Republican National Committee, Wesley Roberts. Earlier, following Eisenhower's nomination at the Republican convention, comparable checks had been made on the nominee's principal campaign advisers, Leonard Hall, Wayne Hood, Wesley Roberts, and Robert Humphreys.

Hoover's interest in the backgrounds of Eisenhower's advisers stemmed in part from his concern about the adequacy of Eisenhower's appreciation of the Communist menace (at the time of his nomination and election, most of Eisenhower's positions on national issues were unknown).[1] His doubts intensified following a meeting on

325

31 December 1952 between aide Louis Nichols and Ogden Reid, the publisher of the *New York Herald Tribune* and an adviser to the president-elect. Reporting his pre-election warning to Eisenhower 'about being taken in by Communists and . . . about secret Communists' and his advice that Eisenhower 'at the very beginning [of his administration] . . . bring about a security awareness on the part of his top administration,' Reid cited as evidence of the problem the cases of Lee Pressman, Lauchlin Currie, Frank Coe, and Harry Dexter White (all Roosevelt and Truman appointees identified by HUAC as Communist agents). According to Reid, Eisenhower expressed 'surprise' upon learning of these details, obviously had not heard of these cases, and also was 'somewhat shocked to think that there were professional people such as lawyers, doctors, clergymen and college professors who were Communists.'

'Top administrators' had failed in the recent past, Reid continued, 'to take seriously the manifestations of subversive activities and [had been] entirely too trusting.' Reportedly agreeing with Reid's observation, Eisenhower then requested assistance 'on getting the facts together' and also suggested that Reid arrange to have Hoover 'meet with him and his top people [and Reid inferred from this that he meant the cabinet] for one hour on January 20 [1953] or shortly thereafter to give them a briefing in general terms on the meaning of intelligence information, the difficulties of obtaining intelligence information, and give some picture of the influence of concealed members of the [Communist] party both in the government and in civilian life.' Worried about Eisenhower's 'inclination to be naive on concealed members of the Party,' Reid suggested that in this briefing Hoover 'mention a couple of shocking cases that have occurred; persons in either Government or civilian life.' Concluding his report on this meeting with Reid, Nichols recommended that Hoover discuss the 'Robert Oppenheimer case and how he blocked the production of the H-Bomb for several years,' adding that there 'is no question as to Reid's sincerity in fighting Communism in my mind and in his loyalty to the Bureau.'

Hoover had serious reservations about the proposed briefing, fearing that the FBI might be placed 'in an undesirable position for its long range good.' The principal risk, he felt, was that the FBI might be held responsible in the event of any future disclosure of 'Communists in Government.' Furthermore, a precedent could be created threatening the Bureau's hardwon independence by making it subject to the direction of the White House. Still, Hoover directed Nichols to 'get started *at once*' drafting a memo in response to the proposal 'in case [Eisenhower] goes through with it.' A lengthy memo, with accompanying copies of relevant documents, was completed, and following the scheduled briefing of the cabinet and key White House aides, Hoover forwarded a copy to Assistant to the President Sherman Adams.

Thereafter Hoover had his aides closely monitor the decisions of the recently elected president. In this, he relied on the volunteered assistance of prominent conservatives, with whom the Bureau had extensive contacts. Some of them were appointed as White House aides or subcabinet officials (Milt Hill, Joseph Beeb, and John Henshaw); others had access to the president because of their role in the campaign (Francis Alstock and George Murphy); and still others were considered media allies (e.g., syndicated Hearst columnist and radio commentator Fulton Lewis, Jr., to whom Eisenhower had expressed 'appreciation for the assistance Fulton gave our campaign'). These contacts ensured that Hoover was fully informed on developments within the White House, who had or was losing influence, and the priorities governing administration appointments and policy.

So committed were Alstock and Murphy to furthering Hoover's interests that they proposed that 'the Bureau should have its man at the White House.' They even advised how this could be done: 'through [former National Committeeman from Oregon and then Oregon Governor] Ralph Cake, and [prominent Republican businessmen Edward] Birmingham and [Robert] Burroughs, if we had any desire merely to give them the name of the individual we wanted and they would take him over at the White House after January 20 and become an important position.'

Whether Murphy and Alstock succeeded in installing an FBI man in the White House is not known. A follow-up memo reporting Nichols's 27 January 1953 conversation with Alstock suggests that they did. Alstock then confided that Stan Rumbaugh, an assistant to Under Secretary of Commerce Walter Williams, 'wanted a contact in the Bureau to whom he could come for advice and guidance.' Alstock referred Rumbaugh to Nichols, adding that the latter, if unable to handle any request of Rumbaugh's, would 'take it up with the Director or put [Rumbaugh] in touch with the Director.' Alstock assured Nichols that 'Rumbaugh is thoroughly briefed on the left-wing issue, the need of giving the Bureau what it needs in the way of support, etc.'

Not that Hoover needed to plant his own spies in the Eisenhower administration to ensure support for his anti-Communist crusade. In fact, the president shared the Director's rabid anti-Communism. Where they differed (and here Eisenhower departed from his more extreme right-wing advisers as well) was over the realism and political costs of pursuing an unremitting war against Communism at home and abroad. These differences are dramatically illustrated in the debate within the administration on how to respond to the crisis precipitated by the fall of the French garrison at Dien Bien Phu (Vietnam) on 7 May 1954.

Deliberating how best to offset this French loss, Eisenhower's National Security Council (NSC) in mid-May 1954 debated whether to commit U.S. troops to military conflict. Leery about the political costs of such a decision (in view of the reaction to Truman's unilateral decision of June 1950 to commit U.S. troops in the Korean conflict), the NSC weighed a proposal to introduce a congressional resolution granting Eisenhower full authority for such a commitment. Attorney General Herbert Brownell felt compelled to brief Hoover in confidence on this pending decision, given the possibility that the FBI's surveillance role would have to be expanded. The FBI was fully capable of managing such 'a very heavy' responsibility, Hoover assured Brownell, 'as soon as Congressional action is taken.' The

Director recommended that the matter should be 'thoroughly considered and that if the decision was to go ahead as indicated, that I trusted it would be upon an all-out basis and not with the intolerable restrictions such as had been imposed upon our armed forces in Korea.' As it turned out, Eisenhower's political caution, in view of the unwillingness of the Democratic congressional leadership to provide a blank-check authorization, led to the rejection of this military option in 1954. Hoover could only have been dismayed by this apparent pusillanimity.

Hoover nevertheless was more than willing to promote one of the newly elected Republican administration's partisan efforts. Having won control of the presidency and the Congress in 1952 in part by exploiting popular doubts about the Democrats' commitment to an effective internal security program, Republican strategists in 1953-1954 sought to sustain these doubts. Attempting, unsuccessfully as it turned out, to work in tandem with Senator McCarthy, the Eisenhower White House concurrently sought to establish its superior anti-Communist credentials, particularly by highlighting the inadequacies of former President Truman's internal security practices, in striking contrast to its own more hard-headed and realistic approach.

The most dramatic of these partisan efforts involved a 6 November 1953 speech of Attorney General Brownell to a Chicago businessmen's group attacking Truman's handling of the Harry Dexter White matter. A high-level Treasury Department official, White had been nominated by Truman in early 1946 for appointment as executive director of the International Monetary Fund. Although Hoover had then sent the president a series of reports (based on the unsubstantiated allegations of Elizabeth Bentley) questioning White's loyalty, Truman chose to support the nomination anyway.

Briefed on the background to Truman's decision and the attendant disregard of 'evidence' of White's disloyalty, Brownell in his 1953 speech cited the White case as demonstrating the contrast between the Eisenhower administration's and the Truman administration's records on internal security issues, and the greater attentiveness of the Republicans to FBI reports.

Embittered by the criticisms of his administration's internal security record leveled by the McCarthyites since 1950, Truman immediately denounced Brownell's implicit suggestion that the Democratic administration had sanctioned disloyalty. Appearing on national television to rebut the attorney general's highly publicized speech, Truman claimed to have consulted FBI reports and to have effected an arrangement with Hoover to allow White's nomination to go forward so that the FBI could continue to monitor any subversive activities on White's part. Truman concluded his televised denunciation by accusing the Eisenhower Administration of McCarthyism.

Truman's rebuttal threatened to undermine Republican politics. It could not go unanswered, and Brownell enlisted Hoover's support through the forum provided by the Senate Internal Security Subcommittee. Arrangements for a joint appearance were carefully worked out between Brownell and the Republican-led SISS, Brownell later claiming that Hoover had 'volunteered' to appear with him. In this forum, Brownell carefully detailed the series of FBI reports challenging White's loyalty that Hoover had forwarded to the Truman White House between November 1945 and March 1946 and then proceeded to declassify the reports. Hoover not only confirmed Brownell's account of these submissions but, in addition, denied that he had made any arrangement of the kind Truman had described. In the *coup de grace,* Hoover also contended that White's new appointment had in effect undermined the FBI's investigation into the Bentley allegations of a Communist espionage cell operating in the Treasury and State departments.

Hoover, however, was not content merely to appear in public to support Brownell's partisan tactic. He also welcomed the opportunity provided by the public hearing to settle another score, this one involving the Truman administration's decision to abort prosecution of the *Amerasia* defendants and its implicit attribution of this action to the FBI's illegal investigative activities.

330

Preparing for his scheduled appearance before the Senate subcommittee, Hoover planned to capitalize on the doubts raised by the McCarthyites over the failure of the Truman administration to secure John Service's indictment during the *Amerasia* inquiry and to publicize Thomas Corcoran's behind-the-scenes role in preventing it. Hoover had been unable to use this information during the Tydings Committee hearings in 1950 because it had been obtained through an illegal wiretap of Corcoran's office phone. Disclosing that the FBI had tapped the phone of a prominent Washington attorney and former high-level aide to President Roosevelt could have been politically explosive — the more so as the tap, although installed in June 1945 at President Truman's request, was not officially authorized. At that time, as previously mentioned, White House aide Harry Vaughan had warned that if the FBI's wiretap of Corcoran 'should ever become known it would be our [the FBI's] baby,' as the White House 'would deny any knowledge.'

Hoover was now willing to go public with this information pertaining to Corcoran's role, but only if he could document that the FBI had been acting under presidential orders. Accordingly, on 8 November 1953 (the day after Truman's rebuttal, when arrangements were being formulated to answer the former president), he ordered Nichols to search the FBI files for any records documenting that Vaughan had received reports based on the Corcoran wiretap in 1945. Nichols's search proved unsuccessful — the assistant director was forced to report back that 'there are no such letters which I can recall or find.' The only communications he had been able to uncover from the Corcoran wiretap pertained to the period from 1947 to 1948, and none contained information involving the Corcoran matter.[2] The absence of such a record persuaded Hoover to abandon this course of action.

Although willing to assist the Eisenhower administration under certain circumstances, in this instance Hoover remained steadfastly committed to advancing his own policy goals. This independence explains his interest in allegations about Eisenhower's possible misconduct. The hint of scandal

– picked up, incidentally, from a wiretap of John Vitale, 'an Italian hoodlum' who was the subject of a criminal investigation – particularly intrigued the Director. In a tapped conversation with an associate in Detroit, Vitale solicited the assistance of a good lawyer for a pending parole board hearing – that is, a lawyer having political clout. The associate recommended Herbert K. Hyde, whom he described as a trial attorney for the General Services Administration who was 'getting powerful all the time.' Conceding that Hyde's job title was unimpressive, he explained that Hyde had 'got a good looking wife – he says that IKE has been trying to get into her pants' and that Hyde 'is scheduled to get a judgeship.' Suitably impressed, Vitale commented, 'Ain't that a dandy?'

Because of the allegation of a presidential affair, a copy of this section of the wiretap transcript was immediately forwarded to Hoover. The Director, in turn, had his aides seek information about Hyde. All FBI files were thoroughly checked, Hyde's employment with the GSA was verified, and a ten-page 'separate memorandum' on Hyde was assembled for Hoover's attention. Just what information about Hyde had been uncovered cannot be ascertained, as the FBI has withheld this memorandum in its entirety.

Allegations about Eisenhower's illicit sexual activities only whetted Hoover's appetite, and the Director was soon alerted to another, more credible affair. On 13 May 1955 Don Surine, a staff aide to Senator Joseph McCarthy, contacted Nichols 'in confidence' to report 'scuttlebut [sic]' that in 1944 Eisenhower had written to General George Marshall to ask whether a divorce might affect his future career in the Army. This inquiry, Surine continued, 'occurred at a time when General Eisenhower was allegedly having an affair with Kay Summersby, the British WAC. General Marshal[l] is reported to have squelched the idea of the divorce and to have engaged in maneuvering which broke up the affair with Kay Summersby.' The syndicated columnist Drew Pearson had a photocopy of Eisenhower's letter to Marshall, Surine added.

Surine was not innocently passing on a widespread, if

unprinted, rumor. By 1955 Senator McCarthy had become the president's bitter political adversary and welcomed any information that could damage Eisenhower's reputation. Following up on this report, Surine recontacted Nichols four months later to 'confidentially advise that Kay Summersby, a former WAC Staff Officer assigned to President Eisenhower in Europe, has been staying at the [Washington] Shoreham Hotel for the last 30 to 45 days under an assumed name.' Briefed immediately on this report, Hoover ordered Nichols, 'See if we can discreetly get the name.'

An exhaustive effort was made to verify the allegation. Nichols 'discreetly contacted' Surine to learn the latter's 'confidential source.' Surine identified his source and added that he 'did not reveal interest of FBI in matter.' (Nichols assured Hoover that Surine had been told that 'interest in this stems from personal curiosity and has no connection with the FBI.')

At the same time, Hoover's aides reviewed FBI files for any information on Summersby, advising the Director that she had been married twice; had been divorced by her first husband in 1943 on the grounds of adultery; had served as Eisenhower's confidential secretary, aide, and driver during World War II; had been sexually attacked by a black man while stationed at WAC officers quarters in California after the war (her assailant had been tried and convicted of intent to rape); and was presently married to Reginald Morgan, a Wall Street broker.

Finally, and most significantly, Hoover had his agents attempt to run down the story. The Washington field office was first ordered to make a 'discreet check through contacts at Shoreham [Hotel].' This check proved unfruitful, as 'no individual is registered there under the name of Kay Morgan, Mrs. Reginald H. Morgan, or Kay McCarthy (maiden name). Other variances [of names] were checked with negative results.' The New York field office was thereupon enlisted and made two 'pretext' telephone calls to Mrs. Morgan's New York residence. 'Conversation was carried on under pretext to some extent and Mrs. Morgan was most pleasant. There was no information received which would indicate whether she had recently been in Washington or not,' Hoover was advised in the resultant report on this comprehensive, if ultimately unsuccessful inquiry. 'All checks mentioned above,' the New York office assured him, 'were made with complete secrecy and it is felt that no interest has been aroused on the part of outsiders concerning this matter.'

Stymied in his quest for derogatory information on the president, the Director moved to consolidate his position with the very congressional committees from which he had taken such pains to distinguish himself in his Senate testimony in 1950. For by that year the cumulative impact of the 'loss' of China, the successful test of a Soviet atom bomb, HUAC's highly publicized investigations, and the convictions of Alger Hiss and William Remington had so aroused public opinion that the Director was emboldened to assist – surreptitiously and on his own terms – the efforts of congressional investigators to find scapegoats.

Only one serious obstacle remained in the inquisitor's path: Max Lowenthal's forthcoming critical study of the FBI, *The Federal Bureau of Investigation*. Working for more than a decade, Lowenthal had compiled a formidable indictment, and the Director knew it. Thus Hoover was determined either to prevent publication of the book or to discredit it and its author beforehand.

Alerted on 28 August 1950 by a *Publisher's Weekly* forecast, Hoover first attempted to prevent publication by asking his old friend Morris Ernst to intercede with Lowenthal's publisher. Ernst, however, was reluctant 'to contact the publishers [William Sloane Associates] as he is fearful that they might seize upon any contact and issue a statement that the Director, through his attorney, had approached them on the book.' Undaunted, Hoover tried to persuade Ernst to call it 'to their [Sloane's] attention that the book was filled with distortions, half-truths and incomplete details as well as false statements.' He had Nichols approach Ernst directly, preferring to operate behind the scenes, and authorized his aide to advise Ernst that although the Director was 'perfectly willing to leave everything to [Ernst's] judgment,' nevertheless some action must be taken to discourage the publisher.

Unwilling to act himself, Ernst suggested a more devious course and inquired whether 'somebody at the Library of Congress might not write to [Sloane] merely indicating that they know a book is coming out through advertisements, and then asking if the publisher knows that they have indexed a writing under a similar title and that considerable confusion on the public might occur unless the title is changed. If not the Library of Congress, I am about persuaded that the FBI itself should write to the publisher but in doing so, make clear that even the change of the title should not be construed as putting a blessing on the book in any form, etc.'

As it was not Hoover's style to operate openly, he finally sought to blacken Lowenthal's reputation by exploiting the FBI's other resources, primarily the local contacts of FBI field offices and the members and staff of HUAC. HUAC staff members visited Lowenthal twice, in late August and early September, as well as his publisher. On 15 September, in response to a committee subpoena, Lowenthal testified in executive session and was grilled on his past 'subversive' associations, particularly his membership in the National Lawyers Guild. Then, immediately following publication of his book on 21 September, HUAC released Lowenthal's testimony to the press, the next thing in the popular mind to a formal indictment.[3]

About the same time, on 6 September, Hoover briefed all SACs on the impending publication of Lowenthal's book, noting that 'book salesmen of [Sloane] are endeavoring to secure advance orders at a reduced price and there is some indication they are attempting to sell copies of this book to Chiefs of Police and other law enforcement officials.' 'It is well known,' the Director added, 'that Max Lowenthal has been exceedingly active in the past ten years in his attempts to discredit the FBI.'

As evidence of Lowenthal's base motives, Hoover submitted to the SACs a copy of a speech delivered on 1 September by the conservative Republican congressman

George Dondero, a speech that the FBI had helped prepare and that stressed Lowenthal's 'subversive' background. Hoover expressed his hope that Dondero's speech would be prominently covered by the press, lamenting that the *New York Times* and the *New York Herald Tribune* had made 'no mention of Max Lowenthal.'

Deeming this omission 'significant,' Hoover advised SACs that the 'Bureau has had the opportunity of reviewing the book. It is filled with distortions, misrepresentations, erroneous conclusions, and outright falsehoods.' Nevertheless, Hoover feared that Lowenthal's book might impress 'the uninformed individual' owing to his extensive 'quotes from numerous editorials, Congressional debates, public hearings, etc.' Emphasizing that the FBI 'does not desire to dignify the book with any comment,' Hoover told the SACs that 'should any question arise regarding the book from law enforcement officials and friendly sources, there is no objection to your informally advising them of the true character of the book.'

The Director's overriding concern, evidenced by his feigned indifference, was to avoid a public showdown. Nothing, however, was left to chance. Under the careful direction of the Crime Records Division, critical reviews were prepared and planted with sympathetic reporters and other public opinion leaders (including syndicated columnists Walter Winchell, Fulton Lewis, Jr., and George Sokolsky; reporters Walter Trohan and Frederick Woltman; and Georgetown University dean Edmund Walsh), and derogatory information on Lowenthal and his publisher was assembled and leaked. (Nichols suggested that an NBC news commentator, whose name the Bureau withheld on personal privacy grounds, report the thrust of the press response to Lowenthal's book as showing 'how stooges do the Communists' work.') FBI agents in turn visited booksellers around the country, pressuring them not to stock the book.

Finally, to contain any damage 'in view of the Lowenthal book,' Hoover also arranged, through *Reader's Digest* senior editor Fulton Oursler, the expeditious publication of an article praising FBI practices by no less a civil libertarian

336

than Morris Ernst. Published in the December 1950 issue of the *Digest,* Ernst's 'Why I No Longer Fear the FBI' was actually a threeway collaboration of Ernst, Oursler, and Louis Nichols of the Bureau's Crime Records Division.'

In the event, not altogether surprisingly, Lowenthal's book did not sell. It proved to be a gold mine for later writers, but for the remainder of Hoover's life it was all but ignored by the general public.

Meanwhile, Hoover's invisible witch-hunting campaign, using guilt by association and far-reaching innuendo, was alive and well. Subpoenaed by Hoover's congressional allies, educators, actors, scientists, federal employees, even politicians were duly exposed as dangerous subversives, as witness the case of Trinity College professor Odell Shepherd, a former lieutenant governor of Connecticut, who was branded for his earlier left-wing views.

In reality, politics, not subversion, determined Hoover's monitoring of the activities of dissident Americans, a conclusion dramatically confirmed by the FBI's file on the renowned physicist Albert Einstein.[4]

From its inception, the FBI's investigation of Einstein was based on the physicist's political activities. A summary memorandum on Einstein reports: 'Investigation of Einstein [was] instituted 1950 based upon information that he was affiliated with over 30 Communist-front organizations. Investigation reflected he sponsored entry into U.S. of numerous individuals with pro-Communist backgrounds . . . Extensive investigation in U.S. showed Einstein affiliated or his name extensively associated with literally hundreds of pro-Communist groups. No evidence of C.P. [Communist party] membership developed.' Such as it was, the 'evidence,' duly recorded and retained for future reference, included the fact that the physicist publicly advocated pacifism, civil rights, and racial equality; supported the Hollywood Ten (blacklisted filmmakers), Progressive party presidential candidate Henry Wallace, the Scottsboro Eight (black youths arrested in Scottsboro, Alabama, on a dubious rape charge), and William McGee (a black youth arrested in Mississippi who, Einstein believed, had been framed on a rape charge); was a friend of Charles Chaplin, Paul Robeson, and Frank Lloyd Wright; advocated the abolition of HUAC; sponsored a testimonial dinner for the black radical W. E. B. DuBois; and published articles in the *Bulletin of the Atomic Scientists* advocating world government and a more humanistic, less militaristic foreign policy.

Undaunted, Hoover had his agents continue to seek evidence confirming Einstein's disloyalty. The resulting intensive investigations failed to link Einstein to atomic espionage or any federal crime. At the same time, Hoover's agents readily recorded the wildest accusations, among them the charge that during his years in Germany Einstein had 'collaborated internationally' with Communists and had allowed his office in Berlin to be used as a mail drop for Soviet couriers. A vain effort was made to corroborate such allegations, even though the sources should have been rejected as incredible – in fact, the basis for one allegation was that Einstein and his alleged Communist traveling companion had created a stir as passengers on a trans-Atlantic ship crossing to the United States in the 1930s by refusing to stand during a rendition of the German national anthem.

The Einstein report – 'suitable for dissemination, containing all the pertinent data' – ran to 1,160 pages. The 'pertinent data' included a number of extraordinary allegations – among others, that Einstein 'is experimenting with a ray which will help to destroy armed opposition – aircraft, tanks, and armored cars. He hopes that with it a dozen men could defeat 500. Through it 500 could rule a nation.'

Another Bureau informer accused Einstein of having framed Bruno Hauptmann, the convicted kidnapper of Charles Lindbergh's son. Still another claimed to have met Einstein in his suite at the Ambassador Hotel Los Angeles and to have been told that 'if I wanted to get ahead in Hollywood I had better play ball with him, that through Einstein they were getting control of every studio, and that if I didn't be sensible I might be through in Hollywood.' This last charge was given sufficient credence that a follow-up Bureau investigation was ordered, but the resulting twenty-page report established only that Einstein had never rented a suite at the Ambassador Hotel.

Hoover's obsessive anti-Communism ensured that even allegations of this kind were seriously entertained. Furthermore, the Director was not content to rely on the press and HUAC as forums for public exposure. In March 1951 he agreed to service the requests of his old friend Senator Pat McCarran, who in December 1950 had become chairman of the newly formed SISS, as another means of promoting the anti-Communist cause.[5] But of all the adventurers who entered the field of anti-Communism in search of glory, none was quite the equal of Senator Joseph R. McCarthy, the ex-Marine and amateur boxer from Wisconsin who traded upon his outspoken anti-Communism to win the chairmanship of the Permanent Subcommittee on Investigations in 1953 and thereafter subsumed the entire anti-Communist movement under his name.

Hoover's relationship with McCarthy began on a friendly basis in 1947, the year McCarthy arrived in Washington as a Republican senator-elect from Wisconsin. Hoover had always admired tough, combative men, and within a few months of McCarthy's arrival in Washington, the thirty-seven-year-old bachelor legislator and the Director were seen dining together at Harvey's and frequenting the nearby Bowie racetrack, where the senator was a favored guest in Hoover's private box. Their friendship was in part political, as they shared the brand of conservatism that regards radicalism as in its very nature subversive.

That McCarthy quickly captured Hoover's attention is attested by the Director's invitation to the younger man to address the graduating class of the FBI National Academy in February 1948, an honor usually reserved for established notables whose politics and loyalty to the Bureau were above reproach. Hoover also sought to promote McCarthy's stature in Wisconsin, and accepted an invitation in April 1949 to appear on a radio interview show that McCarthy directed to his Wisconsin constituents. Careful arrangements were made in advance about the specific content of the show, and Hoover's aides helped prepare the script of both McCarthy's questions and the Director's answers. And in November of that year, during a McCarthy visit to Phoenix, Arizona, the local SAC both entertained the senator at a dinner party and furnished him with transportation throughout his week-long stay.

In the most exceptional instance of extraordinary courtesy, Hoover on 28 November 1950 telegraphed the head of the FBI's Honolulu office, Joseph Logue, to inform him that Jean Kerr, McCarthy's administrative assistant (and future wife), was vacationing at the Royal Hawaiian Hotel. Logue was ordered to 'contact her and extend every possible courtesy during her visit.' In a follow-up telegram of 7 December, Hoover demanded a report on the specific measures taken to comply with his earlier directive.

He got an earful. For that evening, as Logue was escorting Miss Kerr around Honolulu, she fell and broke her hip while leaving a private party. Logue drove her back to her hotel and called a doctor, then drove her to the hospital, where an operation was performed. He thereupon briefed Assistant Director Ladd on these developments, observing that Hoover 'would possibly desire to assure Senator McCarthy that Miss Kerr was receiving the best medical care, and that every consideration possible was being extended by the Honolulu Office of the FBI.' The office would 'assure [Kerr] of every comfort' during her hospital stay, Logue promised, including 'daily' visits, and he would submit up-to-date reports to Hoover 'as to her condition.'

Thereafter, Logue reported regularly on Miss Kerr's condition, emphasizing that 'every attention and courtesy' was being extended. When McCarthy inquired about the reputation of Miss Kerr's doctor, Ladd contacted Logue, who, in turn, described the doctor, Warren White, as 'one of the eminent bone doctors in the country.' The senator 'was very appreciative' when apprised of this information.

Because Miss Kerr was hospitalized in a nursing home on Christmas day, Logue and a number of other Bureau agents celebrated the holiday with her, exchanging gifts and ensuring, as Logue reported, that the 'attendants at nursing

home arranged most pleasantly Christmas atmosphere.'
Logue also 'looked into the matter of insurance with a view
toward compensation for the medical expenses involved.'

Several weeks later, in an urgent radiogram to Hoover,
Logue reported that Miss Kerr was leaving Honolulu on 19
January and would require 'wheelchair and ambulance
service during [her] layover in Los Angeles,' a courtesy that
the Los Angeles office was happy to provide. The same
courtesy was arranged at Hoover's direction for her change
of planes in New York preparatory to her return to
Washington.[6]

In fact, the Bureau's crucial, if indirect, assistance to
McCarthy had begun before March of that year. On 9
February 1950 the senator catapulted himself into national
prominence with a speech before a Republican women's club
in Wheeling, West Virginia, in which he claimed to possess
a list of 205 'card-carrying Communists' in the State
Department. (In subsequent speeches that month he charged
variously that there were first 57, then 81, Communists in
the department.) When planning the Wheeling speech,
McCarthy's staff contacted *Washington Times-Herald*
reporter George Waters, who eagerly accepted a paid
assignment to draft the senator's speech. Unable to write
the speech alone because he lacked the requisite background,
Waters secured the assistance of fellow *Times-Herald*
reporter Ed Nellor and *Chicago Tribune* reporter Willard
Edwards. The final product, mostly written by Nellor, was
pieced together by Waters.

So impressed was McCarthy by this assistance that he
hired Waters as his press secretary and invited Nellor to
become his speechwriter. Nellor declined, having accepted
a more lucrative offer to join the staff of *Look Magazine,*
until the magazine's editors agreed to keep him on the
payroll, while assigning him to McCarthy on a full-time
basis. This extraordinary arrangement was made through
the good offices of Republican National Committeeman
Arthur Summerfield, who saw in publicizing McCarthy the
means to undermine public confidence in the beleaguered
Truman administration.

341

Nor was this the only case of such support for McCarthy at that time. Something akin to a support system was in the making. Following another, highly publicized, speech on 21 February, this one to the Senate itself, that body's Democratic leadership had set up a special committee, chaired by Millard Tydings of Maryland, to investigate McCarthy's now-81 cases of 'known Communists in the State Department.' To counter the Democrats' strategy of discrediting the Republicans' partisan anti-Communism by discrediting McCarthy, and wishing in any case to enable McCarthy to document his sensational charges, a larger group of conservative newsmen[7] volunteered their services, the fruits of their earlier research, and (as it turned out) their access to information from FBI files to McCarthy. Orchestrated by J. B. Matthews, the former staff director of HUAC, this cabal wrote McCarthy's speeches using information obtained from their FBI contacts.

Former Assistant Director William Sullivan, in his book on the Bureau, claims that immediately after delivering his Senate speech on 20 February, McCarthy telephoned Hoover to request his assistance in documenting his allegations – and that the Director ordered his aides to search FBI files for anything that would help McCarthy defend himself against the Tydings Committee.[8] If anything, Sullivan's account is understated.

Hoover's first action on McCarthy's behalf was to improve the quality of the senator's staff. Prior to the Wheeling speech, McCarthy had little interest in, and even less knowledge of, the Communist issue. Thrust unexpectedly into the limelight, and forced in the hostile forum of the Tydings Committee to sustain his charge that the Truman administration was indifferent to the State Department's employment of 'known Communists,' he needed to repair this deficiency. Accordingly, several days after the creation of the committee, Hoover recommended that McCarthy appoint former FBI agent Don Surine to his staff as an investigator. (Hoover had fired Surine for his involvement with a prostitute during a White Slave Traffic Act investigation but valued Surine's abilities and militant anti-Communism.)

Surine's value to McCarthy went beyond his own abilities; he afforded McCarthy access to his extensive contacts at the FBI. In addition, Surine has admitted that he and McCarthy met secretly and repeatedly with Hoover and Tolson over lunch to exchange information. This covert assistance enabled McCarthy to withstand the challenges posed by the Tydings Committee, most notably by providing him with material relevant to his widely publicized charges against Owen Lattimore and, following release of the committee's final report dismissing McCarthy's charges as without basis, by supporting his contention that the committee's investigation was a 'whitewash.'

Lattimore, a professor at Johns Hopkins University, had been a member of the Institute of Pacific Relations, a wartime think tank that advocated accommodation with the Chinese Communists on the ground that they were the next wave of an ongoing Chinese revolution. When presenting his case before the Tydings Committee, McCarthy accused Lattimore of being the 'top Russian espionage agent in this country' (a charge he soon had to abandon, as he had not a shred of evidence to support it), and when Tydings, in accordance with his mandate, directed his select committee to investigate this charge, Lattimore was called to testify. Seeking corroboration for McCarthy's sweeping contention, Surine contacted his sources at the Bureau.

FBI records document how Hoover and McCarthy concerted on a strategy by which the Director could assist the senator without risk of exposure. The method employed was underhanded and complicated and requires discussion in some detail.

Following release of the majority report of the Tydings Committee, which concluded that there was no basis for McCarthy's charges, McCarthy retaliated, as noted above, by dismissing the report as a 'whitewash.' In support of his position, he discussed the case of one of the eighty-one State Department employees, Edward Posniak, whom he mysteriously identified as Mr. X.

Claiming to quote from an 'FBI secret report,' McCarthy advanced 'a complete and airtight case proving that one of

343

the important officials in the State Department is a Communist.' The senator presented four affidavits in support of his charge, pointing out that these had not been included in Posniak's loyalty file, which the Tydings Committee had reviewed. This, the senator claimed, was proof that the files had been 'raped.'

McCarthy's ability to quote from the FBI's classified loyalty report profoundly upset Attorney General J. Howard McGrath, who demanded that Hoover investigate 'the source from which such FBI reports were obtained by Senator McCarthy.' There was an apparent violation of federal laws, McGrath declared, 'dealing with the theft, embezzlement, and unlawful removal of Government documents.' Hoover should report back 'at the earliest possible moment' whether the reports that McCarthy had cited were 'in fact . . . official FBI reports and whether or not there is material contained in this exhibit which is not contained in the original and official reports of the Bureau.'

Hoover could not ignore McGrath's directive; at the same time, to convey the sense that the FBI had investigated the matter thoroughly and was itself not McCarthy's source, the Director, in carefully chosen words, two days later advised McGrath that the 'FBI secret report' cited by McCarthy 'is not, of course, an official FBI report.' Although it bore the heading 'United States Civil Service Commission – Report of Investigation,' Hoover added, it 'is not an official document of the Civil Service Commission either.' McCarthy's exhibit instead was 'a summary of material actually contained in the Bureau's loyalty reports' on Edward Posniak, except that the official FBI report contained additional information, which he detailed. Thus apprised, McGrath demanded 'a complete investigation . . . , particularly since the reports of the Bureau have been compromised and misrepresented.'

As part of this follow-up investigation, FBI agents interviewed McCarthy. The senator, however, refused to identify his source (as did members of his staff). The inquiry then shifted to the Civil Service Commission, the agency identified in McCarthy's document, and to conservative staff members of the Loyalty Review Board who were known to have been impatient with the board's concern for constitutional rights. But nothing came of this inquiry either, and eventually Hoover notified McGrath that the Bureau had been unable to identify McCarthy's source.

Hoover had dissembled. In close cooperation with Surine, he and his aides had devised a procedure to finesse any threat of exposure of the FBI's assistance to McCarthy. This arrangement was inadvertently disclosed in a report on a meeting between Surine and an agent assigned to the Washington field office. At that time Surine had requested a copy of the Bureau's summary on Owen Lattimore, 'inasmuch as Senator McCarthy, in the future, would not make any further allegations without being able to support such allegations by an investigative report.' To disarm any objections that this additional assistance could compromise the FBI, Surine stated that he 'could attribute the information contained therein to another government investigating agency, explaining that "this is what happened in the Posniak Case." '

'If he had the LATTIMORE summary report,' Surine explained, 'it would be handled in the same fashion as was done in the Posniak Case': namely, 'he would insert the information appearing in the Bureau report in the form of a summary of information appearing in the CSC [Civil Service Commission] investigative files, thus making it appear that his office had secured a CSC file rather than a Bureau file.'

Washington SAC Guy Hottel relayed Surine's request, emphasizing that Surine 'did not specifically ask' his FBI contact to 'secure a copy of this report, nor did he indicate that he could obtain this report from his Bureau acquaintances. He likewise did not indicate that Senator MCCARTHY was aware of the practice evidently adopted by [Surine] in the Posniak Case or in making such an informal request for a Bureau report.' Hottel promised Hoover that the Washington office would continue to maintain contact with Surine and to receive such 'correspondence as Surine voluntarily makes available' (apparently a quid pro quo arrangement), adding that the agent had told Surine that the FBI's summary report on Lattimore 'would not be made available to him.'

It does not follow, however, that Surine was denied the requested Lattimore information. In a confidential follow-up report, Hottel admitted that 'information appearing in FBI reports in the Posniak case was obtained [from the Bureau] and inserted in the form of a Civil Service Commission summary of information, thus making it appear that Senator MCCARTHY's office had secured access to Civil Service Commission investigative files rather than FBI files.' This report further recorded Surine's promise to handle the FBI summary report on Lattimore 'in the same fashion as was done in the Posniak case, explaining that [Surine] had inserted the information in the FBI report in the form of a summary of information appearing in the Civil Service Commission Investigative Files, thus making it appear that his office had secured a Civil Service Commission file rather than an FBI file.'

Because the summary report on the Surine interview would have to be forwarded to McGrath (in view of his order that the FBI ascertain how McCarthy had obtained classified government documents), Hoover was faced with the unpleasant prospect of having to confess the Bureau's outrageous deception. Unable to handle such an ordeal, he had the report amended so that the full 'interview of Don Surine would not be included in this report.'

After reading the doctored summary, which left unanswered the initial question of McCarthy's source, Deputy Attorney General Peyton Ford demanded that the FBI interview Surine. During the interview, Surine denied knowing anything 'concerning the so-called investigative report in the Posniak case, and [stated] that any questions are to be referred to the Senator.' When the interviewing agent pointed out that the Bureau had 'reliable information' of his 'knowledge of the matter,' Surine amended his statement to refuse comment. Briefed on this matter, Hoover learned of McCarthy's concern 'at the prospect of

Surine being interviewed,' and concurred: 'This is not being included in the details [of this interview] because of Surine's stipulation that only his formal refusal to comment be disseminated beyond the Bureau.'

Hoover's clandestine support of McCarthy, extending from March 1950 to July 1953, was intended to further the cause, McCarthy having become by 1950 the visible symbol of anti-Communism and the target of liberal attack. Not personal friendship but shared political objectives shaped Hoover's decision to help McCarthy so long as this could be done safely — for example, by doctoring documents to prevent their being traced back to the Bureau. Hoover's assistance was manifold, including making supportive speeches, monitoring McCarthy's critics, and offering direct assistance (including 'name checks for the committee through liaison with Mr. Nichols') and counsel, the latter in an effort (unsuccessful as it turned out) to impress on the senator the need to proceed cautiously and conduct thorough investigations before making public charges.

On 12 March 1953, McCarthy and committee counsel Roy Cohn met with Hoover 'to discuss confidentially' whether the committee should investigate 'the activities of J. Robert Oppenheimer.' After outlining the 'number of problems to consider before embarking upon this project,' Hoover warned the senator of the possible resentment of SISS and the Joint Committee on Atomic Energy should McCarthy's committee take 'on this investigation unless he first cleared with them.' McCarthy agreed that this jurisdictional matter would have to be resolved.

In addition, Hoover pointed out, Oppenheimer 'has been one around whom the scientists of the country have usually rallied whenever there has been any question raised about the loyalty and integrity of scientists.' In view of Oppenheimer's work in the development of the atomic bomb as well as his wide and extensive associations within the United States and abroad, Hoover advised, 'whatever the Senator's Committee did concerning Oppenheimer should be done with a great deal of preliminary spade work so that if and when the Committee moved into the open it would

347

have substantive facts upon which to predicate its actions.'
McCarthy promised to follow this advice.

Wary of the senator's habit of shooting from the hip and
answering questions later, Hoover assumed the role of
political consultant, committed for a time to safeguarding
the senator's credibility. Periodically he counselled
McCarthy to investigate matters more thoroughly before
making public charges. And in time he also assisted
McCarthy directly, whenever this could be done without
compromising the FBI's reputation. The extent of this
personal cooperation is illuminated by the Director's
response to McCarthy's request for assistance in defeating
President Eisenhower's nomination of Charles Bohlen to be
U.S. ambassador to the Soviet Union.

A former member of the U.S. delegation to the Yalta
Conference, which shaped the face of postwar Europe,
Bohlen continued thereafter to defend that conference's
controversial agreements, even doing so during his
confirmation hearings. Bohlen's defense of Yalta disturbed
many conservative Republican senators, who since 1949 had
campaigned against the Yalta Conference and had
demanded the purging of 'Yalta men' from the State
Department. Committed to defeating Bohlen's
confirmation, they questioned his qualifications in light of
his position on Yalta and other foreign policy issues. The
more rabid opponents also tried to impugn Bohlen's
character and sought evidence to confirm rumors of the
ambassadorial nominee's homosexuality.

McCarthy led this effort. Attempting to capitalize on his
pipeline to Hoover, the senator phoned the Director on the
day Secretary of State Dulles was to testify before the Senate
Foreign Relations Committee in support of Bohlen's
confirmation. Put through to Hoover, McCarthy confided
that the Bohlen nomination suggested that despite
Eisenhower's election, the situation in the State Department
remained unchanged and 'everything was running about the
same as it was a year ago.' McCarthy then asked Hoover
to 'tell him in complete confidence just how bad Bohlen
actually was.'

348

Hoover replied that 'this, of course, was very hard to evaluate; that we made the [security clearance] investigation and that the request for the investigation was not received by us until after Bohlen was named for the appointment.'

Advising Hoover of his intention to oppose Bohlen's nomination, McCarthy 'wondered if [Hoover] had any public source information such as from the Daily Worker which he could use.'

Hoover admitted that the FBI had investigated Bohlen 'from the security and morals angle' but said that 'frankly most of the material we got was from the State Department. I indicated we did not go into the analysis of political speeches, and so forth, as that was supposed to be handled by the State Department.'

Briefed on the allegations of Bohlen's homosexuality and other derogatory comments made by individuals whom the FBI had interviewed during the Bohlen investigation, McCarthy, who had charged before that the State Department harbored homosexuals as well as Communists, asked whether Hoover thought Bohlen was a homosexual.

Hoover confided that he 'did not know,' because this 'was a very hard thing to prove and the only way you could prove it was either by admission or by arrest and forfeiture of collateral.' Hoover added that the FBI had been unable to uncover such hard evidence in Bohlen's case 'at all as far as we know, but it is a fact, and I believed very well known, that [Bohlen] is associating with individuals of that type.' Re-emphasizing the difficulty of proving 'a charge of homosexuality,' Hoover admitted that the FBI 'had no evidence to show any overt act,' and yet commented that 'Bohlen had certainly used bad judgment in associating with homosexuals.'

The senator lamented that such associations could not be cited during Senate debate, observing that 'it was so easy to accuse a person of such acts but difficult to prove.' Hoover agreed, adding that homosexuality 'was often a charge used by persons who wanted to smear someone.'[9] In the absence of hard evidence, this planned strategy fizzled, and Bohlen was subsequently confirmed.

Hoover's solicitude toward McCarthy extended even to personal matters, so that the Director became in effect McCarthy's in-house counsel. Indeed, Hoover even advised McCarthy on how to deal with personal attacks – including, in one case, charges that the senator was himself a homosexual.

On 16 January 1952 Senator Carl Hayden forwarded to Attorney General McGrath a letter allegedly written the previous December by Lieutenant David Sayer (then assigned to an Army unit stationed in New York City) to Senator William Benton (D.-Conn.). In August 1951 Benton had introduced a resolution calling for an investigation of McCarthy's activities to determine whether the senator should be expelled from the Senate. The resolution in turn had prompted a Senate investigation in the course of which a Senate investigator had contacted the FBI for any 'derogatory information' about McCarthy. Hoover had refused the request and instructed his aides: 'We must meticulously refrain from furnishing any information.'

Sayer's letter charged that while he was visiting in Washington he had been picked up by McCarthy at the Wardman Park Hotel and that the senator had taken him to his room, 'gotten him drunk and had committed an act of sodomy on him.' Inasmuch as the Truman administration was seeking to discredit McCarthy, on learning of this letter Attorney General McGrath immediately demanded an FBI investigation. Now forced to act, Hoover just as swiftly contacted McCarthy, as 'the decent thing was to let him know what allegations had been made and what we proposed to do.'

McCarthy expressed his appreciation for Hoover's solicitude, adding that he suspected that 'one of the most likely reasons for the allegation' was to allow Drew Pearson 'to say that the FBI is investigating Senator McCarthy.'[10] Accordingly, McCarthy requested that the FBI 'investigation be very circumspect as he would like to be sure there is no possible leak from here so he will know that Drew Pearson is at the other end of it.' Hoover assured McCarthy that 'the only place [Pearson] could find out would be from either the Attorney General or myself and that it would be handled very, very tightly at this end.'

Interviewed by FBI agents, Sayer denied having written the letter (an FBI analysis of his handwriting confirmed that Sayer had not signed it). Hoover had also contacted MID head Major General A. R. Bolling to request permission to interview other Army personnel, emphasizing the need to ensure that the investigation not 'break in some column.' The interviews were duly undertaken and the conclusion reached that Sayer was a homosexual and that his homosexual friends had written the letter, signing his name to discredit Senator McCarthy 'for his attack upon those [homosexuals] who are supposed to be in the Government.' Hoover reported the results of this investigation to McGrath, Bolling (who advised Hoover of his intention to discharge Sayer immediately), and Senator Hayden.

Pearson meanwhile had concluded that the story was too hot to handle, but he passed along his information to another McCarthy critic, *Las Vegas Sun* editor and publisher Hank Greenspun, who used it the following fall. At that time, during a statewide radio address in Las Vegas supporting the re-election of incumbent Republican Senator George Malone, McCarthy called Greenspun an 'ex-Communist' (he had meant to say 'ex-convict'). Greenspun, who happened to be in the audience, thereupon loudly rejoined that McCarthy was 'the most vicious type of demagogue,' stormed the stage, and seized the microphone from the senator, who retreated in stunned disbelief. Lambasting him for the remaining twenty-seven minutes of McCarthy's radio time, Greenspun compared McCarthy's voting record on foreign policy issues to the record of the *Daily Worker*.

Two weeks later Greenspun published in his signed column, 'Where I Stand,' an exposé of McCarthy's sexual activities and associations. In particular he cited McCarthy's liaison with Charles Davis, whom the editor described as a former Communist and confessed homosexual; he reported that one of McCarthy's administrative assistants, Ed Babcock, had been picked up by Washington police 'while working for McCarthy and charged with the offense of solicitation for a lewd and lascivious purpose' and been fined for this homosexual offense; and he likewise reported that McCarthy's administrative assistant, Don Surine, had been fired by the FBI for having had sexual relations with a prostitute while investigating her under a White Slave Traffic Act inquiry. Most seriously, Greenspun charged that while attending the Wisconsin Republican Convention, 'McCarthy spent the night with William McMahon, formerly an official of the Milwaukee County Young Republicans, in a Wausau hotel room, at which time, McCarthy and McMahon engaged in illicit acts with each other.' 'It is common talk among homosexuals in Milwaukee who rendezvous at the White Horse Inn,' Greenspun concluded, 'that Sen. Joe McCarthy has often engaged in homosexual activities.'

Sent two copies of Greenspun's page-one column, Hoover tersely ordered that 'no dissemination be made of this material.' Later, when McCarthy sought his advice on whether to sue Greenspun for libel, Hoover counseled against that course of action, as 'any suit instituted would probably make the matter privileged and it would be carried throughout the country, whereas the original article by Greenspun has only had a very narrow circulation.'

Hoover urged McCarthy instead to consider 'having Senator [William] Jenner's Committee [on Internal Security] call Greenspun before it to inquire into his activities' and advised McCarthy of Greenspun's 'past associations' not only in the 'criminal field but to some extent in the subversive field.' Sketching a possible scenario, Hoover emphasized that while appearing before SISS and under oath, Greenspun 'might be questioned concerning the basis [of] the allegations made in the libelous article printed about Senator McCarthy and whether it was part of a Communist plot to smear the personal character of the Senator.'

McCarthy liked Hoover's suggestion, remarking that 'this was an angle he had not considered but thought it was well worth while exploring.' Apparently, McCarthy did contact Jenner but found that the SISS chairman had other priorities[11] and was unwilling to consider the proposal unless McCarthy could make a case against Greenspun. An undaunted McCarthy thereupon recontacted Hoover's office, in July 1953, to request 'any public information which could be made available' about Greenspun, claiming to have learned that Greenspun had been convicted of smuggling. Following a thorough check of FBI files, Hoover forwarded to McCarthy a copy of the Bureau's information.

Significantly, McCarthy was not able to contact Hoover directly in July because, unknown to the senator, Hoover had decided to sever their relationship. Denied the benefit of the Director's counsel, McCarthy unwisely initiated legal action against Greenspun. The catalyst was the Greenspun column of 8 January 1954, in which the editor asserted inter alia that McCarthy's unfounded allegations impugning the loyalty of federal employees might ultimately threaten his life. Convinced that this column justified prosecutive action, McCarthy wrote to Hoover on 13 January, claiming that Greenspun was 'either threatening or advising murder.'

Hoover on this occasion observed routine procedure and referred McCarthy's letter to the Department of Justice, asking whether Greenspun's column violated federal law. Assistant Attorney General Warren Olney III responded that it 'is difficult to interpret this article so as to read a threat to murder or advice to murder into it. It seems to be more in the nature of prophecy.' Federal criminal statutes generally did not cover threats, Olney added, and Greenspun's article did not come under the two that did. Hoover relayed Olney's conclusion personally to McCarthy, but without comment.[12]

The contrast between Hoover's willingness to offer McCarthy counsel in May 1953 and his perfunctory referral of McCarthy's letter to the Justice Department in January 1954 marks the crucial change that had occurred in their relationship. Unknown to McCarthy and his aides at the time, Hoover had long since decided to terminate the relationship, having concluded that the senator's recklessness could imperil his own and the FBI's image of lofty impartiality. Hoover had been attracted to McCarthy in the first place by the opportunity the flamboyant senator afforded to advance the anti-Communist cause. But McCarthy's excesses as well as his inclination to betray his covert link with the Bureau ultimately led the Director to ally with the Eisenhower administration, with which McCarthy by the summer of 1953 was in indirect (later to become direct) conflict.

The breach had been in the making for months. McCarthy had not foreseen this, counting on Hoover's continued support now that the Republicans had captured the presidency and control of Congress in the 1952 elections, elevating himself to the chairmanship of the Senate Government Operations Committee and its Permanent Investigations Subcommittee. Following the Republican sweep of the 1952 elections, an obviously elated McCarthy had confidently 'anticipated closer cooperation with and more extended use of the FBI and its facilities following the beginning of the new Congress.' Discussing the matter with Guy Hottel at the Washington field office, McCarthy had observed that 'in the past it was not always to one's advantage to be seen talking to or associating with MCCARTHY.' But all this would be changed 'now with his re-election and the new Congress.' McCarthy planned to 'confer' with Hoover 'in the not too distant future relative to obtaining suggestions for prospective investigative personnel for his investigative committee.'

McCarthy did meet with Hoover, on 28 November 1952, seeking his advice on prospective staff and on strategy. The senator also raised the matter of access to FBI files. According to Hoover's summary of this meeting, McCarthy reiterated his concern about the quality of his staff 'and asked that I give some thought to recommending to him a number of competent investigators that he might consider for appointment.' Whatever his misgivings at the time, Hoover immediately ordered Tolson 'to have this given prompt attention.'

At a follow-up meeting on 12 January McCarthy urged the Director 'to feel free at any time to contact him whenever [Hoover] saw any activity of any member' of the Permanent Investigations Subcommittee staff that the Director thought was not 'in the best interests of good administration.' McCarthy also solicited Hoover's advice on 'the over-all plans which [McCarthy] has for carrying on the work of his subcommittee,' about which McCarthy 'will, no doubt, be in contact with us from time to time.'

McCarthy's staff problems nonetheless continued, problems arising mainly from his disorganized administrative style, his uncritical loyalty to his appointees, and their serious personal shortcomings. Indeed, the subcommittee's impact was steadily imperiled by personality conflicts as well as incompetence. The subcommittee would pick up an issue, only to drop it and begin another inquiry, which in turn was soon abandoned. The confusion was hardly conducive to advancing the cause.

Shortly after assuming the chairmanship of the Permanent Investigations Subcommittee, McCarthy announced an investigation into possible 'mismanagement, subversion, and kickbacks' among Voice of America (VOA) employees. After holding executive session hearings, the senator starkly advised the assembled press that the subcommittee had acquired evidence that VOA employees 'are doing a rather effective job of sabotaging Dulles's and Eisenhower's foreign policy program.'

Convening public hearings, McCarthy's subcommittee began by raising questions about the selection of sites for VOA transmitters. The hearings then abruptly shifted focus to the materials used in preparing VOA broadcasts and the books included in the overseas libraries maintained by the United States Information Agency (USIA). In another abrupt shift, the subcommittee then dropped this issue to focus on the question of trade by Greek shipowners with the People's Republic of China. Then, just as suddenly, subcommittee staff counsel Roy Cohn and his handsome young subordinate G. David Schine embarked on a tour of Europe prominently billed as an investigation of USIA's overseas libraries. Given the extensive publicizing, the lack of preparation, and the unclear purpose of the mission, the sweeping charges of subversion threatened to embarrass not only McCarthy and his subcommittee, but the entire

Republican party, including the Eisenhower administration.

McCarthy too had come to question the effectiveness of his staff and had concluded that major adjustments in the subcommittee's operation were needed, in particular easing out chief counsel Francis Flanagan. Through his contacts with the American Legion, Hoover soon learned that McCarthy intended to appoint former Dies Committee counsel J. B. Matthews as his subcommittee's director of research and another ex-radical and current research analyst for the Legion's Washington office, Karl Baarslag, as a research assistant. McCarthy had not first cleared these appointments with Hoover, although the senator belatedly briefed Nichols on his plans to ease out Flanagan and to appoint Matthews staff director, indicating his intention 'to call the Director' on this matter, praising Matthews's 'dominant personality and [observing that he] will be able to control the situation so far as the Committee [*sic*] is concerned, and he knows this will be highly pleasing to the Director.'

Nichols 'quite frankly' communicated Hoover's opposition. The Director could not forget some of Matthew's activities 'during the days of the Dies Committee when we were fighting with our backs to the wall, and further that there had been instances wherein we had contacted Matthews and shortly thereafter seen items in the papers.' When McCarthy protested that he had been led to believe that Matthews 'was close to the Bureau and the Bureau held Matthews in high regard,' Nichols conceded that the FBI hierarchy had 'never expressed ourselves on the point, that naturally we would subordinate our feelings on those fighting Communism but that he, McCarthy, should be cautious about Matthews issuing press releases, as during his period on the Dies Committee he was issuing them with great frequency.' Reporting McCarthy's intention to be 'very cautious' and his distress at learning of Hoover's unfavorable reaction, Nichols urged the Director to give Matthews 'a chance,' counseling that the FBI 'keep our guard up but at the same time, see if he has changed his ways.' A skeptical Hoover commented, 'Let me see what we have on Matthews first.'

356

Hoover's reservations were quite warranted, as it turned out. For just before joining the Permanent Investigations Subcommittee staff, Matthews published an article in the *American Mercury* entitled 'Reds and Our Churches' in which he claimed that 'the largest single group supporting the Communist apparatus in the United States today is composed of Protestant clergymen.' The irresponsible nature of his charge combined with McCarthy's failure to consult other subcommittee members before making the Matthews appointment precipitated a crisis. Democratic committee members and influential Protestant leaders denounced Matthews. At first unwilling to force Matthews's resignation, McCarthy eventually had no alternative.

In an effort to repair the damage and ensure the quality of the subcommittee's personnel, the senator then decided to appoint Frank Carr to replace Matthews. McCarthy aides Jean Kerr and Roy Cohn, following a meeting with Hoover, had assured the senator that the appointment had been cleared with the Director (at the time Carr was an FBI supervisor in the New York office and a trusted confidant of Kerr and Cohn). But, ironically, the Carr appointment proved to be McCarthy's most serious mistake.

On 23 July, while consulting with Nichols on other matters, McCarthy voiced his satisfaction at having Carr on his staff. Expressing his pleasure that 'the Director finally approved,' McCarthy admitted that he 'had deliberately not [directly] contacted the Director as he wanted to be in the position of saying that he had not been in touch with the Director.' He reiterated that Kerr and Cohn had assured him that 'the Director approved Carr.'

Nichols immediately disabused McCarthy of this belief, stating that Hoover had in fact 'told Jean Kerr & Cohn [he] was opposed' to the Carr appointment. Reminding McCarthy of his conversation with Hoover 'some weeks ago,' Nichols recalled the Director's position: 'we would not give Carr a leave of absence, we would not release him, we would not ask him to go to the Committee, we would not approve his going to the Committee, [but] obviously if Carr resigned and wanted to go with the Committee this was his

357

position.' Hoover 'would neither approve nor disapprove' and, out of deference to the senator, 'would not make any public protest.' Hoover opposed the Carr appointment, Nichols explained, because 'it now placed a very tight restriction upon the Bureau, that we would have to lean over backwards because if at any time the Committee came up with something having an FBI angle, the charge would be made that Carr was a pipeline and that it would have been so much better to have had an outsider.' The senator stated that he understood this but hoped that Hoover 'will not be angry.'

McCarthy's political error in appointing a current FBI employee to a key staff position forced Hoover to draw the line – more in sorrow than in anger. A Bureau memo of 15 October 1953 describes the altered relationship: 'We have furnished information to the Senate Permanent Investigating Committee (McCarthy) up until the late summer [1953] when the Committee appointed former Special Agent Carr as Staff Director. Since then no information has been furnished to this committee.' Yet Hoover and McCarthy (who knew nothing of Hoover's ban) vacationed together the next month in La Jolla, California.

According to Allan Witwer, who managed the Hotel del Charro at La Jolla for eight years in the 1950s, Hoover and Tolson took extended holidays there each year. Aptly named (*el charro is* Mexican for 'cowboy'), the hotel was owned by Clint Murchison, a wealthy Texas entrepreneur who heaped notoriety on himself in a proxy battle for the Pennsylvania Railroad. Guests included Secretary of Health, Education and Welfare Oveta Culp Hobby, Vice President Richard Nixon, John Connolly of Texas, and such Hollywood luminaries as Clark Gable and Elizabeth Taylor. Also included in this seamless microcosm of American society were Johnny Drew, henchman of the late Al Capone in Chicago, and Carlos Marcello of the New Jersey Mafia.

There were two rules at the Del Charro, each proved by one exception. No Jews were allowed (a ban that extended to Cohn and Schine), and nobody paid a bill (Hoover's bill, running between $3,000 and $4,000 annually for accommodations booked from mid-June to early September, was regularly paid by a Murchison-controlled corporation). The exception in each case was Barry Goldwater, who was a Jew (turned Episcopalian) and who paid his bill.

Twelve miles from the hotel was the Del Mar Racetrack, built by Bing Crosby, bought into by Bob Hope, and heavily frequented by Hoover, who, according to Witwer, placed $100 bets there ('He had inside information, after all'). The track eventually became Murchison's, purchased through a dummy corporation, Boys Incorporated, which was supposed to spend all profits to build Boys Clubs. None, reportedly, was ever actually built.

That summer Hoover and Tolson checked into the Del Charro in their usual way. A group of Bureau agents had inspected the premises two days beforehand, planning security. On their arrival, Hoover and Tolson were booked into Bungalow Number One, a comfortable hacienda-style cottage with a kitchen, living room, and two bedrooms. These and Hoover's and Tolson's poolside cabana were checked for electronic bugs, and both locations were scouted so that patrols could be mapped. The agents remained for the duration of the Director's stay.

Each morning the Director and his companion, Tolson in the lead scenting danger, emerged from their bungalow, went to the lobby, then proceeded to the pool, where they ate breakfast in the privacy of their cabana. Thereafter they retired for a nap before leaving for the track. Returning in the evening, they had dinner beside the pool – 'flaming torches and steaks cooked by your cabana,' Witwer recalled – and perhaps a nightcap with their hosts before retiring to bed. 'Once or twice a week,' Witwer said, 'they would go to the Scripps Clinic for tests and observation' – their annual medical check-up.

'You had to be there to feel the power of this man,' Witwer continued. 'Hoover had more power at that time than the President of the United States. But one man he didn't faze at all was Texas oil man Sid Richardson. Richardson would say, and did so at a particular party with Senator Goldwater, "Edgar, get your ass over here and get me some more chili." And Hoover did.' As Witwer said, 'It was an intimate hotel.'

It was into this select company that Senator McCarthy barged in August 1953, accompanied by his young epigone Cohn. The visit was McCarthy's first (he returned only once, in 1954),[13] so he was unaware of the regulation against Jews. Cohn was told to leave.

At that time, Witwer remembered, 'There was quite a thing in the papers about a feud between Hoover and McCarthy.' But that seemed doubtful to Witwer. 'They weren't feuding, but were the best of friends – their arms around each other and all that sort of thing.'

According to Witwer, 'McCarthy was virtually on Murchison's payroll,' a paid entertainer. 'McCarthy was just a good-time Joe – very uncouth. He'd get drunk and jump in the pool, sometimes naked. He urinated outside his cabana, flew everywhere in Murchison's plane.'

According to a Murchison lieutenant, Witwer said, Murchison didn't seem to mind. ' "He's going to get those homos out of the State Department," he'd say.' Nor were Murchison and his wife, Virginia, in a strong position to stand in judgment about the excess drinking.

Hoover, who, according to Witwer, stayed perfectly sober, may not have been personally disgusted by McCarthy, as a strong aura of affection continued to surround the pair, but the Director's ban remained. Nor could McCarthy charm or cajole Hoover into lowering it.

Denied direct assistance, McCarthy that fall and winter sought to circumvent the ban by hiring several former FBI agents and relying on their knowledge of FBI investigations. But this practice only enraged Hoover more, and he instructed Nichols in February 1954 that 'we should indicate to Cohn our concern over the more and more instances where they are . . . crossing wires in our current investigations . . . It is becoming more and more obvious that they are hiring ex-agents solely for the purpose of getting information acquired by such employees while in FBI service. We are not responsible for Cohn acting precipitously – that is his choice but in doing so he is wrecking our internal security coverage and he should recognize it.'

Hoover's protest was relayed to Cohn, but without success. Hoover and Tolson feared that by hiring ex-agents, McCarthy might 'get access to our complete security set up, as well as knowledge of individual cases and informants.' Hoover cited this as his reason for having originally opposed Carr's appointment, commenting that 'ex-agents trying to make good on committee job[s] are not going to drop a curtain on their past knowledge of Bureau cases, informants, etc.'

Hoover's double-whammy — refusing to leak information from FBI files and discouraging ex-agents from joining McCarthy's staff — proved fatal. Denied information he had readily obtained when he dominated the national scene from 1950 to 1953, McCarthy was cut off at the very time he was most in need of such assistance — the spring and summer of 1954, when the Eisenhower administration, the media, and leading Republican senators initiated efforts to discredit the embattled senator.

The irony is that while Hoover was materially responsible for McCarthy's rise to prominence, he was as responsible for McCarthy's demise. Motivated by his twin desires to sustain the cause and to minimize any fallout to the Bureau, Hoover finally adopted a hands-off policy toward McCarthy. By July 1953 he had concluded, however reluctantly, that McCarthy was a hopeless cause, and his conclusion was swiftly reinforced.

For that same month the Director learned that 'a group of Catholics in the United States led by Cardinal Spellman is at odds with the Vatican on various foreign issues.' In particular, Hoover's source described Spellman's followers 'as a "conspiracy" working to undermine the Eisenhower Administration and to eventually bring about the election of McCarthy as President.' (In August Spellman publicly praised McCarthy's campaign against Communism, stating that McCarthy 'is against Communism and he has done and is doing something about it. He is making Americans aware of the dangers of Communism.') McCarthy was allegedly receiving the support of many wealthy Catholics, including 'prominent individuals such as ex-Ambassador Joseph P. Kennedy, and . . . the "conspiracy" group is sending to McCarthy all sorts of individuals, which included émigrés who are passing out fabricated information.'

Assured that this information was 'reliable' and was not 'anti-Catholic,' Hoover decided to brief Attorney General Brownell on this 'alleged conspiracy to undermine the Eisenhower Administration,' after having first ordered a review of FBI files for any 'derogatory' information on the source. In the ensuing meeting, Hoover began by telling Brownell that the FBI's informer claimed to have reported this information to presidential adviser C. D. Jackson and to have discussed 'some aspects of this matter' with Brownell. The FBI had pressed the informer 'concerning the reliability of his information' and had been assured that 'although his statements might sound "wild" he was convinced he was right.' The informer had denied being anti-Catholic, Hoover continued, and a 'review' of FBI files 'has failed to disclose any derogatory information' on him. Hoover closed his report with the comment that the FBI 'is not taking any further action concerning the alleged "conspiracy." '

Having decided to cast his lot with the president, Hoover restricted his cooperation to the Senate subcommittee to cases in which the targets were liberals and the FBI's assistance could not be traced. But he made no attempt to rescue McCarthy.

By 1955 McCarthy and Eisenhower had broken completely. Beginning with the Fort Monmouth investigation in the late fall of 1953 and the related Army-McCarthy hearings in the summer of 1954, McCarthy questioned Eisenhower's commitment to an effective internal security program. Forced to choose sides, conservative journalists and politicians, who had rallied behind McCarthy when his targets were Truman and New Deal liberals, deserted the Wisconsin senator. As the rift between McCarthy and Eisenhower widened, the senator's erstwhile allies turned on him. Led by Republican Senator Ralph Flanders, these new anti-McCarthyites championed a resolution calling upon the Senate to censure McCarthy.

The Senate vote to censure McCarthy on 2 December 1954 extended this rupture. Alone and battered, embittered by his abandonment, McCarthy lashed out at the president – going so far, during a public hearing of the Permanent Investigations Subcommittee in December 1954, as to apologize for having supported Eisenhower in the 1952 campaign in the 'mistaken' belief that an Eisenhower administration would pursue 'a vigorous, forceful drive against Communists in government.'

By then McCarthy had worn out his welcome at the White House and was the only committee chairman not invited to official dinners for Senate leaders. So the Wisconsin Senator retaliated, in 1955 introducing a resolution criticizing President Eisenhower's decision to attend a summit conference with Soviet leaders in Geneva and commissioning a poll of Republican leaders to determine his own chances of defeating Eisenhower's renomination at the 1956 Republican Convention.

But these were the actions of a desperate man. Shunned by nearly everyone except Jean Kerr, by then his wife, McCarthy drank more and more heavily and behaved more and more recklessly. Hospitalized for hepatitis, which an old antagonist, the *New Yorker* reporter Richard Rovere, described as cirrhosis of the liver, he died on 2 May 1957 at the age of forty-seven. Hoover, fifteen years his senior, outlived him by fifteen more, and continued his own, covert anti-Communist crusade by employing other, more dependable proxies.[14]

Notes to Chapter Eleven

1. Eisenhower's commitment to the anti-Communist cause continued to concern Hoover after the inauguration. Advised in March 1953 that the president was receiving 'strong pressures against the investigation in education [recently initiated by the Senate Internal Security Subcommittee] and some people are trying

to get the President to make a statement against Congressional Committee investigations,' Hoover was relieved to learn that White House aide Wilton Persons had 'been able to avoid this.' (Memo, Nichols to Tolson, 7 March 1953, FBI 61-2582-1885.)

2. Hoover's unprecedented public foray into partisan politics infuriated one of his principal sources of support: southern Democrats in Congress. In January 1954 a number of influential southern Democrats – including Mississippi Congressmen Jamie Whitten and William Winstead and Mississippi Senator James Eastland – communicated their displeasure. Whitten singled out Hoover's appearance before the SISS and warned, 'When the Democrats regain control of Cong[ress] that efforts would be made, on part of Democrats, to remove Director from his position.' Hoover's justification of his action as involuntary (the obligation to honor a congressional subpoena and testify fully to the facts; pressure from Attorney General Brownell) did not convince these congressmen: They observed that the Director 'has avoided appearing on Capitol Hill on many occasions in the past and that he could have avoided that particular appearance.' Later that spring Hoover learned that 'certain [southern Democratic] Senators are determined if and when the Democrats get back in power to make every effort to remove the Director.'

Southern Democrats did not carry through on this threat after the Democrats regained control of Congress in 1954, in part because the decision to retain or dismiss Hoover was not theirs to make and Eisenhower had every reason to keep Hoover on board. Nonetheless, in 1958, cognizant of Hoover's sensitivity to their criticisms, southern Democrats sought to pressure the Director either to scale down FBI investigations in civil rights matters (in the aftermath of passage of the Civil Rights Act of 1957) or to have such investigations conducted by the Civil Rights Division of the Justice Department. Senator Olin Johnston's aide, H. L. Edwards, assumed a leading role in this subtle campaign, reminding one of Hoover's aides that 'many of the Southern Senators have not forgotten the Director's testimony in the Harry Dexter White case, . . . that at the time of the White matter, . . . the feeling was so great that definite steps had been taken to attempt to have the Director removed from his job.' This earlier incident, Edwards counseled, 'coupled with the present unrest in the South on civil rights matters has made many reasonable people take an unreasonable attitude.'

Edwards's warning did not have its desired effect. Hoover

rejected the suggestion that he lobby Congress to create a separate civil rights investigative division in the Department of Justice. The Director's refusal, however, doomed congressional approval of the FBI's pending request for special appropriations to fund additional 'super grades' for FBI agents. (Memo, Holloman to Hoover, 3 February 1954, Director folder, Nichols O&C; Memo, Tracy to Hoover, 1 April 1954; Memo, Nease to Tolson, 22 January 1958, J. Edgar Hoover (Directorship) folder, Folder no. 85, Hoover O&C.)

3. Hoover did not allow the matter to rest here. Following the creation of HUAC's Senate counterpart, SISS, Hoover directed his aides to raise with the subcommittee's staff 'the possibilities of the Committee looking into the matter of Communist infiltration into the book publishing business' in order to 'counteract the left-wing element in the publishing business, which has been the source of attacks on the Bureau . . . particularly the Max Lowenthal book, William A Sloan [sic] Associates, Merle Miller's "The Sure Thing" and others.' Because of the press of other matters (the Institute of Pacific Relations hearings, investigations of Communist infiltration of federal agencies and the United Nations), the subcommittee did not act on this recommendation immediately. When it found time to do so, in February 1953, Hoover decided against providing assistance: 'A year ago we had more time. Now we haven't.' (Memo, Nichols to Tolson, 27 February 1953, FBI 62-88217-943.)

4. Herbert Mitgang and Natalie Robins have offered insights into the scope of Hoover's surveillance interests and their political character, disclosing that the FBI prepared dossiers recounting the political activities and subversive thoughts of the nation's most prominent writers. These included: Sinclair Lewis, Carl Sandburg, Pearl Buck, William Faulkner, Ernest Hemingway, John Steinbeck, Theodore Dreiser, W. H. Auden, John Dos Passos, Thomas Wolfe, Nelson Algren, Truman Capote, Thornton Wilder, Robert Sherwood, Kay Boyle, Tennessee Williams, Archibald MacLeish, Edna St. Vincent Millay, William Carlos Williams, and a host of others. (Herbert Mitgang, 'Annals of Government: Policing America's writers, *New Yorker, 5* October 1987 pp. 47-90; Natalie Robins, 'Hoover and American Lit: The Defiling of Writers, *The Nation*, 10 October 1987, pp. 367-72.)

5. Hoover initially cooperated with the subcommittee on a 'personal basis.' In March 1951, however, Attorney General J. Howard McGrath authorized the Director to establish a formal

liaison relationship with it, advising McCarran that he was 'delegating the complete responsibility to the Director to do whatever the Director felt should be done.' Quickly seizing this opportunity, Hoover effected an arrangement whereby the FBI serviced the subcommittee's requests for name checks on prospective witnesses and information on targeted organizations and, in addition, provided portions of FBI files, exhibits, and summary memoranda 'with appropriate leads and suggested clues.' Hoover's sole condition when rendering this assistance was that the subcommittee 'concern itself primarily with matters of current internal security significance, . . . that the Senator [McCarran] wanted to use this Committee not only to strengthen internal security for the good of the United States but to help the Bureau in every possible manner.' Having concluded that the 'goal of the Committee and the FBI was the same' Hoover fully exploited this informal but covert liaison both to direct the scope and nature of the subcommittee's 'educational' efforts and to determine what information from FBI files could be safely released. When the Eisenhower administration came to power in 1953, Hoover at first hesitated to continue assisting the subcommittee. He had Nichols advise McCarran's Republican successor as chairman, William Jenner, that continuance of this 'cooperation' required the approval of the new attorney general, Herbert Brownell, but at the same time emphasize that the FBI intended to maintain our friendly relationship and if we could be of service to him personally that we would do so.' As it turned out, there was no need to return to the original 'personal basis' relationship; Brownell unhesitatingly authorized continuance of this cooperation.

6. Somehow Jack Anderson, syndicated columnist and radio commentator Drew Pearson's investigator, learned of the FBI's assistance to Miss Kerr, and on 27 April he contacted Nichols to report what he had learned − that on her trip to Hawaii Miss Kerr had carried a letter signed by Hoover introducing her to Logue and requesting that 'the local office extend services to her.'

Denying that Miss Kerr had been given such a letter, Nichols told Anderson that the FBI's Honolulu field office had merely been advised of her visit and told to extend whatever courtesies were normally shown to members of Congress and their administrative assistants. When Anderson then asked how Kerr had broken her hip, Nichols admitted that she had fallen during a visit to a private residence with Logue, emphasizing that 'this was also after office hours' and that that was 'all there was to it.'

Anderson then disclosed that he was seeking 'to determine whether this [story] was true because if it was then it was evidence of a connection between the Bureau and Senator McCarthy.'

Nichols denied any such connection and, when asked if the FBI was working with McCarthy, replied that 'we steered a middle of the road course with everybody and merely did our duty.' Concluding his report to Hoover, Nichols wrote that Pearson did not intend to use this story on his radio program or in his column but 'was merely inquiring for his information,' to which Hoover appended: 'This fellow Anderson & his ilk have minds that are lower than the regurgitated filth of vultures.'

7. These included Hearst reporter Howard Rushmore and columnists George Sokolsky and Westbrook Pegler; *Chicago Tribune* reporters Willard Edwards and Walter Trohan; and Scripps-Howard reporters Frederick Woltman and Tony Smith. Later, *Washington Times-Herald* executive Garvin Tankersley also assisted McCarthy.

8. 'During the Eisenhower years.' Sullivan maintained, 'the FBI kept Joe McCarthy in business. Senator McCarthy stated publicly that there were Communists working for the State Department. We gave McCarthy all we had, but all we had were fragments, nothing could prove his allegations. For a while, though, the allegations were enough to keep McCarthy in the headlines.' In the same vein, Sullivan wrote that Hoover 'had us preparing material for [McCarthy] regularly, kept furnishing it to him while [Hoover] publicly denied that we were helping him.' (*The Bureau: My Thirty Years in Hoover's FBI* [New York: Norton, 1979], pp. 45, 267; see also Ovid Demaris, *The Director* [New York: Harper & Row, 1975], p. 167.)

9. During this same conversation Hoover and McCarthy also agreed on the menace presented by the Ford Foundation's funding academic studies of state and federal loyalty investigations. When McCarthy indicated that he intended 'to look into' this funding, Hoover commented that 'there were a lot of bad persons in the Ford Foundation and I was greatly puzzled about this whole thing.'

10. McCarthy, known in some circles as Tailgunner Joe, an allusion to his military service in World War II, was right in suspecting that Pearson was interested in a homosexual angle. The columnist had already reported the arrest of a McCarthy staff aide for a homosexual act and, furthermore, had compiled a file on this topic, replete with affidavits from individuals claiming to have

had homosexual relations with McCarthy. Pearson never published this material.

11. In 1953 the Jenner Committee focused on the problem of 'subversive' influence in federal agencies. SISS did not initiate an investigation of the news media until 1955. By that time, as a result of the Democrats' success in the 1954 elections, Jenner had been replaced as chairman by Pat McCarran (no fan of McCarthy), and the influential Nevada editor was not interrogated.

12. In a simultaneous 13 January letter to the Post Office Department, McCarthy had inquired whether the Greenspun article violated any postal regulations and whether it might justify denying the *Las Vegas Sun* second-class mailing privileges. The Department ruled that this one-time action did not justify a denial of second-class privileges but nevertheless referred the matter to the U.S. attorney in Las Vegas. When McCarthy called the department on 5 March to inquire about its action, he was advised of this referral. Stating that he 'preferred to have the whole matter handled in the Post Office Department,' he added that he did 'not want the criminal prosecution.' By then, however, matters were beyond the Post Office's control. The U.S. attorney requested and on 2 April received approval from the Justice Department for authority to seek Greenspun's indictment. Greenspun was indicted on 8 April for having deposited 874 copies of the 8 January 1954 *Sun*, 'which contained nonmailable matter of an indecent character tending to incite murder or assassination.' Greenspun's trial was delayed until April 1955, at which point the editor won acquittal. (*New York Times*, 9 April 1954, p. 14; 10 April 1954, p. 8; 31 August 1954, p. 7; 22 December 1954, p. 14; 5 January 1955, p. 18; 17 February 1955, p. 13; 16 April 1955, p. 8; 19 April 1955, p. 25.)

13. By then Hoover's relations with McCarthy had become so distant that the Director rejected a CBS request for a newsreel shot of himself 'talking informally' with McCarthy in view of the fact that they would be vacationing together at Del Charro. Hoover stated that he had 'no plans for a conference with the Senator.' (Memo, Nichols to Hoover re: Senator Joseph McCarthy, undated, but 23 August 1954, FBI 94-37708-024.)

14. Guy Hottel meanwhile had been prematurely retired from the Bureau, perhaps a burnt offering to atone for the sins of the Washington field office, the nefarious activities of which had become common knowledge in official Washington.

CHAPTER TWELVE

(1955–1960)
DEFENDING THE FAITH

WITH McCARTHY out of the picture, the Director's principal conduits for stigmatizing the left were the always-reliable SISS and HUAC as well as various 'contacts' in the news media. Backed by a team of ghostwriters employed by his Crime Records Division, Hoover played a self-anointed role as defender of the faith. Virtually untouchable, he no longer feared any challenge to his own or the Bureau's authority, although he still responded vindictively to those whose criticisms or politics he abhorred. He was a celebrity, a hero, the guarantor of virtue and the purity of youth. His FBI was an American institution, incorruptible, superprofessional, the safeguard of the nation. Showered with honorary degrees by leading universities, he traveled from coast to coast delivering speeches filled with uplift and barely concealed political freight.

The old guard of the New Deal was in full retreat. Eisenhower had been effectively checked, and his attorneys general, first Herbert Brownell and then, from 1957, William Rogers, granted the Director near-absolute rule. Beyond that, the Eisenhower White House, as had its predecessors, eagerly turned to Hoover for dirt on its critics. (In Congress a conservative coalition of Republicans and southern Democrats, many of them Hoover allies, acquiesced.) At sixty, Hoover was still ten years from mandatory retirement and, like himself, his enemies had grown older. No liberal at this time ventured to call for his removal. In the repressive climate of the 1950s, no national politician could afford to challenge Hoover's leadership of the FBI without suffering an inevitable attack on his patriotism or charges of subversive proclivities.

To be sure, the conditions favoring Hoover's political dominance were beginning to change, and the nation faced new problems overseas and at home. The Eisenhower administration had negotiated a stand-off truce in Korea in the fall of 1953, but before that winter was over it confronted the strategic impasse of the siege of Dien Bien Phu and the collapse of French military power in all of Southeast Asia. (Britain withdrew from the area two years later.) Revolutionary developments in Cuba, the Congo, Central America, and the Middle East as well as Southeast Asia threatened to unravel the anti-communist consensus on which internal security policy and thus Hoover's autonomy were based. Moreover, the administration's duplicitous relations with its British and French allies in the Middle East led in 1956 to their desperate and humiliating Suez adventure and then to French reassessment (under DeGaulle) of the desirability of deferring to American leadership. Last, beginning with the Geneva summit conference of July 1955, at which the president sought to reduce U.S.-Soviet tensions, a new phase of the Cold War appeared with an attendant muting of the fear of Communism, the very stuff on which Hooverism, misnamed McCarthyism, had flourished.

At home, the Supreme Court, in *Brown* v. *Board of Education*, in 1954 struck down as unconstitutional an earlier Court's separate-but-equal ruling, thereby requiring public school desegregation to ensure black children the equal protection of the laws and, not surprisingly, inaugurating a protracted and divisive civil rights struggle in the South.[1] At the same time, in a series of controversial civil liberties rulings – *Yates v. U.S.* (1957), *Cole v. Young* (1956), *Jencks v. U.S.* (1957), *Communist Party v. Subversive Activities Control Board* (1956), *Watkins v. U.S.* (1957) – the Supreme Court reaffirmed the rights of Americans to engage in radical political activities without fear of prosecution and directly challenged the constitutionality of some of the tactics that Hoover's FBI, and other federal loyalty agencies, had employed in the Cold War antiradical crusade.

Disturbed by the impact of these Court decisions, which

found Eisenhower's Court appointees (Warren, Harlan, and Brennan) often ruling with the majority, Hoover willingly furthered the president's belated objective of ensuring that future Court nominees would hold sound law enforcement positions. A far more cautious president in 1957 nominated a safely conservative jurist, Charles Whittaker, to replace the retiring Stanley Reed. Aware of the president's preference for selecting candidates from current federal district and court of appeals judges, in May 1958 Hoover directed his aides to compile a list of qualified ones. Potter Stewart, then serving on the Circuit Court of Appeals in Cincinnati, was on this list. On Harold Burton's retirement in October 1958, Hoover ordered the FBI's Cincinnati office to furnish 'promptly any available information' on Stewart, 'with particular reference to whether he is conservative or liberal . . .' Advised of Stewart's conservative standing (based on his reputation as an attorney and his appeals court decisions), diligence, and 'clear appreciation of the problems of law enforcement,' and the fact that he 'has not rendered any opinions which can be construed as anti-law enforcement or anti-Bureau,' Hoover immediately relayed this information to Attorney General William Rogers. The next day, 7 October, Eisenhower announced that Stewart was being nominated to the Supreme Court. This was neither the first nor the last time Hoover successfully influenced the composition of the Court, in the process helping to limit the possibility of the Court's restraining his and the Bureau's operations.

Moreover, fulminations on the right had hobbled the Democratic opposition to the resurgent Cold War conservatism. Management had lately won two signal victories over a recently invigorated organized labor movement with congressional enactment in 1947 of the Taft-Hartley Act (which among other provisions outlawed the union shop and required union executives to file non-Communist affidavits with the National Labor Relations Board) and in 1954 of the Communist Control Act, which denied the privileges of the NLRB to 'Communist-infiltrated' unions. After conducting their own purge of

Communist activists, labor leaders partially regrouped when the AFL and CIO merged in 1955.

National industrial policy had also been skewed by anti-Communism. The private sector's triumph over the public was marked by the deregulation in the early 1950s of the railroad industry, creating large windfall profits for lucky or enterprising stockholders as it ridded itself of its unprofitable passenger routes. Other legislation established the Highway Trust Fund (authorizing the use of federal gasoline taxes for interstate highway construction, which urbanologist Lewis Mumford predicted before a Senate committee would mean the destruction of every inner city in the land), thereby setting the stage for wholesale abandonment of urban housing, the effluence called suburban sprawl and what economist John Kenneth Galbraith at the end of the decade, in *The Affluent Society*, called 'private affluence and public squalor.'

During the Eisenhower era momentous decisions were made, and were made with barely a whisper from the demoralized left. Nor were liberal Democrats willing to challenge the conservative status quo, numbed as they were by Adlai Stevenson's two crushing defeats in the 1952 and 1956 presidential elections. Even labor took a political holiday in the 1956 campaign, refusing to endorse either candidate.

Ironically, despite the Director's success in promoting the image of the fearless G-Man confronting and containing hoodlums and spies, organized crime functioned without effective federal restraint. Hoover steadfastly denied that the Mafia existed – until 1957, when New York state police, alerted by the sudden appearance of a phalanx of black limousines, discovered a meeting of crime family chieftains in the small upstate village of Apalachin. An embarrassed Hoover then granted the existence of the so-called Cosa Nostra and launched a code-named Top Hoodlum program, belatedly employing the same illegal techniques he had earlier employed in his war against Communism.

Still, whatever the long-range implications of the triumph of the right, for the moment nothing disturbed the Director's

372

peace. For the first time in his career he was above the fray, a paragon to an enormous constituency, an inspiration to many, a law unto himself. After years of tireless effort, he was ready and willing to relax.

Assured of the Eisenhower administration's political correctness and lack of interest in challenging his sway, Hoover by the mid-1950s had scaled down his activities. Describing this more laid-back style, Cartha DeLoach, who succeeded Louis Nichols as head of the Crime Records Division on the latter's retirement from the Bureau in 1957, reported that in the late 1950s and early 1960s, 'Hoover showed a gradual change of habits . . . He began to enjoy life more. He was in his office from nine until twelve, then out to lunch at the Mayflower Grill. He returned to the office at one-fifteen, but his door would be closed till three [while he napped]. Then he was in until a quarter to five.'

Posted outside his door at all times was the redoubtable Miss Gandy, her stern face recalling Cerberus at the Gate. Eventually, according to one former agent, Miss Gandy determined what went to the Director's desk and what did not, and 'that wasn't right.'

Hoover and Tolson also took longer vacations. Allan Witwer recalls at least one summer when the pair were in residence at the Del Charro off and on from mid-June until early September. In the office and elsewhere, the two were nearly inseparable. 'Tolson slavishly dedicated his life to Mr. Hoover,' DeLoach recalled of this time. 'There was a genuine love that Clyde Tolson had for Mr. Hoover . . . [However,] there were moments in his last years when he had some misgivings . . . Tolson was a very shy individual but he liked girls,' told good jokes, and was 'as sharp an individual as I have ever known,' DeLoach continued. 'He had a clean desk all the time. His only failing was his slavishness. I never saw Tolson disagree with Mr. Hoover. He used to say, "The Boss says this, and this is the way we're going to do it." ' In fact, although Tolson may not have challenged Hoover's orders openly, his unquestioned loyalty made him a totally reliable assistant, to whom all major policy memoranda were first routed, and Hoover inevitably acceded to Tolson's recommendations. Indeed, after Tolson suffered a series of strokes in the 1960s and could no longer perform to the best of his abilities, Hoover became more intemperate, seeking confrontations where he would have compromised a few years earlier.

The breakfasts with assorted neighbors, including an adolescent boy next door, became an almost daily routine while the Director was in Washington, with Annie Fields, dressed in a gray uniform, doing the honors in the kitchen. Hoover indulged his taste for collecting (his collections included the calendar with the famous nude photograph of Marilyn Monroe), adding numerous statuettes to the decor in his living room. The display cases were installed by agents at Bureau expense. Other services followed.

According to a *New York Times* report based on a General Services Administration investigation undertaken after Hoover's death:

No dollar estimate was placed on the value of these goods and services, but they included construction of a front portico on Mr. Hoover's home and the building of a fishpond [in the rear garden], equipped with a water pump and outdoor lights . . .

F.B.I. workers constructed shelves, telephone stands and an 'Oriental fruit bowl' for their director, and serviced and repaired home appliances, air conditioners, stereo equipment, tape recorders, television sets and electric wiring . . . They also painted his house each year while he was traveling on his annual vacation, and built a deck at the rear of the home. . . .

. . . They also maintained his yard, replaced sod twice a year, installed artificial turf, and planted and removed shrubbery. They built a red-wood garden fence, a flagstone court and sidewalks, and a power window with sliding glass doors . . .

Clocks were reset, metal polished, wallpaper retouched, firewood provided and furniture rearranged, according to the [GSA] report. Employees were on call night and day for this work.

When Bureau goods and services did not suffice, Hoover resorted to two other sources — his wealthy patrons and the entire personnel of the FBI. An inventory probated with his will itemized shares in Texas oil wells and other stocks acquired either by gift or on the advice of insiders. Gifts from Bureau colleagues were routine. As former Assistant Director Sullivan recalled shortly after the Director's death:

> Hoover was always hitting us for gifts, and we'd have to buy him extremely expensive gifts. His anniversary with the Justice Department, his anniversary with the Bureau, Thanksgiving Day, Christmas Day, his birthday, we were always pitching in on a collection for a gift. They handled it very cleverly. It would always come out of Tolson's office . . .
>
> We used to collect from the supervisors, but they got very angry. One supervisor absolutely refused to contribute. He said, 'The only time you need to come to me for a contribution is when you have to buy flowers for his funeral . . .' We kicked in his share because they kept a count. For example, I used to have one hundred and thirty-three men working for me in the Domestic Intelligence Division, and if you took up a collection of two dollars each, they'd add it up and make damn sure it totaled two hundred and sixty-six dollars.

By this time Hoover had almost no contact with his family. Dick's death had dried up communication with that branch, even though Margaret Fennell had returned to Prince George's County in 1952, earned undergraduate and graduate degrees at the University of Maryland, and become the principal of a public school. On 5 July 1956 Lillian died at Lanham, having suffered from Parkinson's disease for more than twenty years (family members recall that Hoover and Tolson arrived late for her funeral and left early), and thereafter communication with that branch withered too.

Destitute of family or close friends, Hoover compelled Tolson's company almost every night. Sometimes they dined at Hoover's house, sometimes at Tolson's, sometimes out. But neither was often alone after five.

In contrast to this sad domestic routine, Hoover's public life was pure celebration. The comfortable arrangement made with the House Appropriations subcommittee, which had responsibility for the FBI's budget, had evolved in 1943 into something of a confraternity, a trend that culminated in the elevation of Hoover's longtime ally John Rooney to the chair in 1949 (the Senate for years had abdicated its responsibility and gone along with the House subcommittee's recommendations). As former Attorney General Ramsey Clark later observed, the conservative Roman Catholic from New York 'was a terrible restraint on a good Department of Justice.' Indeed, the congressman knew more about the abuses going on at the Bureau than did either presidents or attorneys general, and cared less.

The laboriously rehearsed annual appropriations hearings, moreover, bore a strong resemblance to the court of an absolute monarch, with congressmen assuming the courtiers' parts:

> We are delighted that you have dealt so successfully with the Communist menace. I do not know what we would have done in this country if it had not been for the FBI. Your foresightedness and efforts certainly reflect upon you and the personnel of your agency who have been persistent in combatting those elements that would undermine or threaten our internal security. In the absence of your Bureau, the goal sought by these subversive elements could have well been achieved in this Nation. (1957)

> Mr. Director, it is always gratifying to have you appear before us as a witness, someone who is as forthright as you are . . . At the same time, someone who has the most comprehensive grasp of the statements that you make to us of any witness with whom I have any knowledge or with whom I have had any experience. (1966)

Mr. Director, it is a real privilege to listen to your testimony. It is always an outstanding presentation. The fact that you disclose in your budget the accomplishment of the FBI and also candidly report the problems in crime enforcement [*sic*] and espionage is always worthwhile ... The high regard that the American people have for the FBI and its integrity and the job it is doing is certainly a credit to your leadership and your associates' dedicated efforts. (1968)

The respect that Hoover enjoyed in high places was not wholly due to affection or gratitude. As Andrew Greeley has said of John Cardinal Cody, archbishop of Chicago, so might it be said of Hoover that he 'suffered from what is clinically known as an anti-social character defect, a little understood syndrome, not uncharacteristic of many of those who rise to high power, in which the person and possibly an overwhelming mother figure are the only "real" persons in the world. Everyone else is a pawn and a potential enemy to be manipulated and has no personal rights or dignity or even basic humanity.' In fact, Hoover's enemies were still legion, and his real friends few. But most men of probity understood the nature of his power and avoided provoking him.

The sources of Hoover's power were the files; his ability to avert critical scrutiny and independent knowledge of his administration of the FBI; services rendered to VIPs; information given to politicians about their opponents and to high-ranking corporate officials about militant labor unionism; and his cozy relationship with key reporters, editors, and syndicated columnists. Nevertheless, many prominent Americans willfully denied what he was doing. William Rogers, for example, as attorney general gave verbal authorization to install microphones, even when break-ins were needed to do so, instead of requiring his written authorization on a case-by-case basis. On one occasion, Rogers utterly discounted rumors that the Director employed FBI files for political ends:

I think that's an overpublicized concept. I don't know many persons who are fearful about disclosures of their files. You have fear of your FBI file? It never occurred to me. I can't think of anybody in my acquaintanceship who's been worried about his FBI file. Certainly the idea that Congress supported Hoover and the FBI so wholeheartedly was because they feared disclosure of their files is nonsense.'

Rogers's confidence was not shared by members of Congress, however. As noted in the Introduction, Emmanuel Celler, for a generation the chairman of the House Judiciary Committee, gave voice to the widespread conviction that 'the source of [Hoover's] power derived from the fact that he was the head of an agency that in turn had tremendous power, power of surveillance, power of control over the lives and destinies of every man in the nation. He had a dossier on every member of Congress and every member of the Senate . . . He held in the palm of his hand the reputation of many people, and a good many of the members of the House [Rooney among them][2] and the Senate and the officials had a lot of skeletons in their closet. A lot of these men were not pure and righteous; they probably committed wrongs too, and it fed Hoover. It fed his tapping of their telephones and stuff like that. That's what made him so feared and made him loom large in the eyes of the public.'

While Celler, as we have seen, could not document his suspicions, he was not far off the mark. Eschewing 'files,' Hoover had had his aides prepare 'summary memoranda' on *all* members of Congress, detailing derogatory information about their 'subversive activities' and 'immoral conduct' − and in a way that allowed the Director to deny what he was doing. Furthermore, Hoover did not hesitate to use this information. In testimony before the House Intelligence Committee in 1975, a former FBI agent described how this was done. Puzzled as to why Hoover maintained such information on congressmen, the agent had approached Assistant Director Cartha DeLoach. DeLoach, the agent recounted, had explained:

378

'You fellows have been in the Bureau for more than 10 years, so I guess I can talk to you off the record.' He said, 'The other night we picked up a situation where this Senator was seen drunk, in a hit-and-run accident, and some good-looking broad was with him.' He said, 'We got the information, reported it in a memorandum' and DeLoach — and this is an exact quote — he said, 'By noon of the next day the good Senator was aware that we had the information and we never had any trouble with him on appropriations since.'

Former Assistant Director William Sullivan more starkly described how Hoover dealt with members of Congress. During an interview with *Los Angeles Times* reporter Jack Nelson, Sullivan characterized Hoover as a 'master blackmailer. The moment he would get something on a senator he would send one of the errand boys up and advise the senator that we're in the course of an investigation and by chance happened to come up with this data on your daughter. But we wanted you to know this — we realized you'd want to know it. Well, Jesus, what does that tell the senator? From that time on, the senator's right in his pocket.'[3]

Having covered all members of Congress, Hoover did not have to blackmail them directly — it was sufficient that they feared he was capable of doing so. He did, however, employ the Bureau's vast resources whenever he concluded that a congressman's activities threatened his own political agenda — as in the case of Congressman Don Edwards, a California Democrat who in the 1980s headed the Civil and Constitutional Rights Subcommittee of the House Judiciary Committee and who himself was an FBI agent briefly during the early 1940s. Elected to Congress the same year John Kennedy won the presidency, Edwards on taking his seat 'made critical comments about the Bureau' to his House colleagues and in 1965 drafted a resolution calling for the abolition of HUAC. Alerted by Federal Judge Edward Tamm (a former FBI assistant director) to Edwards's plan to introduce the HUAC resolution, Hoover ordered a search of FBI files for information about the congressman and had DeLoach, by then the Bureau's liaison with Congress, apprise HUAC staff director Francis McNamara of Edwards's intention. Already concerned about 'an intensive drive' to abolish HUAC or reduce its appropriations, Hoover instructed DeLoach to contact three or four former FBI agents who were currently members of Congress to 'get to Edwards and try to pull his fangs.' DeLoach not only did this (approaching Republican Congressman H. Allen Smith) but personally sent Edwards two handwritten notes on unwatermarked plain paper ('informal' memoranda, another Hoover-authorized device for disowning Bureau knowledge or responsibility). Edwards described both notes as 'abusive,' instructing him not to 'go public' and inviting him to meet with DeLoach. The first note failed to silence the congressman, but the second one succeeded, as Edwards candidly admitted.[4]

Yet Hoover's success stemmed less from his capacity to intimidate than from his ability to assure himself favorable press coverage. In this effort, the Director could rely on a stable of reporters willing to profit from a confidential relationship whereby, in return for agreeing not to disclose the FBI's covert assistance, they were leaked carefully selected FBI documents. From this covert assistance successful careers were made. One favored reporter, Don Whitehead, reaped a personal fortune enabling him to retire early and thereafter obtain FBI assistance for a lucrative free-lance writing career.

A feature writer for the Associated Press wire service since 1931, Whitehead had written a highly favorable series of articles on Hoover in 1954. Recontacting Hoover's press liaison Louis Nichols in 1955 seeking assistance for a proposed article 'on the fight against Communism and what the Communists are now doing,' Whitehead received an unanticipated response. From the reporter's writings, Hoover had concluded that Whitehead 'has clearly established his reliability,' and he now was willing to grant the AP reporter privileged access to FBI files to write a history of the Bureau. Before finally deciding to launch this 'special project,' Hoover ordered a 'Special Inquiry type investigation' of Whitehead's background, to be handled 'on a very discreet basis' and without contacting AP, his present employer. The ensuing intensive investigation convinced Hoover that Whitehead could be trusted to write a proper history, and arrangements were made, beginning on 1 November 1955, to allow Whitehead access to carefully selected FBI files through a specially established office in the Bureau.

Whitehead accepted with alacrity both the offer and the conditions attached to it, among them his agreement to allow Hoover's aides to review the copy before publication (the Bureau ultimately insisted on certain changes in the manuscript). Hoover personally monitored Whitehead's research and writing, at one time conveying his 'pleasure with the first four chapters.' On completion of the manuscript, moreover, Hoover had Nichols accompany Whitehead 'to New York to discuss same with [Whitehead's publisher] Bennett Cerf.' The Director insisted that Nichols secure an agreement giving the FBI a voice in planning the publicity for the book to ensure that it was 'dignified and [was] passed upon by the Bureau.'

Whitehead's book, *The FBI Story* (1956), eulogized Hoover and the Bureau, extolling in particular their successful battle against the Communist menace. Eager to boost sales and distribution, Hoover had the Bureau itself purchase copies through the FBI Recreation Association. His efforts were not in vain: *The FBI Story* became a best seller and was later made into a popular movie of the same name.

Capitalizing on Whitehead's success, the Domestic Intelligence Division, under Sullivan, and the Crime Records Division, in Nichols's swansong, undertook to prepare under Hoover's own byline a personal memoir of the crusade against the Red Menace. Published by Henry Holt and Company, a publishing house owned by Clint Murchison, *Masters of Deceit* (1958) sold 250,000 copies in hardback and two million in softcover. According to Sullivan, whose account remains undisputed, although the book was prepared entirely by the Bureau, Hoover 'put many thousands of dollars . . . into his own pocket, and so did Tolson, and so did Lou Nichols.' Still, the book only added to Hoover's *réclame*.[5]

Under Eisenhower the traditional American spirit of fair play yielded to a sophisticated indulgence: give the McCarthyite witch-hunters enough rope and they will hang themselves. But, in fact, the real witch-hunters operated without oversight, without accountability, without the public's knowledge. Moreover, their assault on the rights of law-abiding Americans did not stop with leaked dossiers, planted news stories, and whispering campaigns.[6]

An ardent anti-Communist throughout his career, Hoover until the 1950s had nevertheless been relatively restrained in his battle against the left, feeling compelled to obtain either executive authorization or enactment of antisubversive legislation. Although he had not hesitated to act without authority, he had done so stealthily and then only when secured against any threat of discovery. But in the Eisenhower administration the Director found kindred spirits who shared his commitment to an unrelenting crusade against Communism and a willingness to countenance far-reaching intrusions on constitutional rights – so long as they need not directly authorize the illegal activities.

Disturbed by the Communist party's potential to commit 'espionage and subversion' (as dramatized by the Rosenberg case) President Eisenhower on 8 March 1956 convened a meeting of the National Security Council to address the threat. (Attending, among others, were Hoover, Attorney General Brownell, Vice President Nixon, Secretary of State Dulles, and Secretary of Defense Charles Wilson.) During this meeting, Hoover briefed those present on the scope of the FBI's surveillance of the Communist party, including a report on the Bureau's use of such illegal investigative techniques as break-ins, bugs, mail opening, and wiretaps. Hoover added that in the interest of protecting the national security, the FBI was seeking to 'infiltrate,

382

penetrate, disorganize and disrupt' the Communist party.

Encountering no criticism following this disclosure of the FBI's illegal activities and future plans, Hoover on his own authority (and without the prior authorization of either the attorney general or the president) in August 1956 launched the code-named COINTELPRO-Communist Party to 'harass, disrupt and discredit' the party by targeting key officials and members and non-Communist radical activists as well.

Hoover's decision to inaugurate this program of harassment stemmed from his deep concerns about the impact on FBI investigations of a series of Supreme Court decisions limiting the Justice Department's ability to prosecute American Communists. In response, Hoover shifted from developing information for prosecutive purposes to the use of more aggressive tactics to contain radical activists. In time he expanded this program from the Communist party (1956) to the Socialist Workers party (1961), to the Ku Klux Klan and white supremacist groups (1964), to black nationalist groups (1965), and finally to the New Left (1968). Under these COINTELPROs, agents were authorized to use subterfuge, plant agents provocateurs, leak derogatory information to the press, and employ other disruptive tactics to destabilize the operations of the targeted groups. Similar tactics (ranging from efforts to break up marriages to provoking violence among rival black street gangs) were employed against prominent individuals (Martin Luther King, Jr., Leonard Boudin) and other organizations (National Committee to Abolish HUAC, Southern Christian Leadership Conference) whose political influence alarmed the Director.

In a 12 October 1961 letter to selected field offices, Hoover revealed the political motivation behind his decision to initiate the COINTELPROs. As justification for targeting the Socialist Workers party, for example, he observed that the party

has, over the past several years, been openly espousing its line on a local and national basis through running

383

candidates for public office and strongly directing and/or supporting such causes as Castro's Cuba and integration problems arising in the South . . . a disruption program along similar lines [to COINTELPRO-CPUSA] could be initiated against the SWP on a very selective basis. One of the purposes of this program would be to alert the public to the fact that the SWP is not just another Socialist group but follows the revolutionary principles of Marx, Lenin and Engels as interpreted by Leon Trotsky.

. . . this program is not intended to be a 'crash' program. Only carefully thought-out operations with the widest possible effect and benefit to the nation should be submitted. It may be desirable to expand the program after the effects have been evaluated.

All of these disruption-harassment programs were instituted unilaterally. However, at times Hoover did brief Eisenhower and Johnson administration officials about the FBI's counterintelligence activities involving the Communist party and the Ku Klux Klan, in carefully worded reports implying that the FBI was merely cooperating with local police officials or was seeking to contain the activities of foreign agents, the accepted meaning of counterintelligence. (During congressional testimony in 1975, former attorney general Nicholas Katzenbach aptly characterized Hoover's selective and misleading briefings as invariably using 'terms of art, or euphemisms, without informing the Attorney General that they were terms of art.')

Hoover's selective and incomplete briefings, however, did not lead either presidents or their attorneys general to demand fuller information. A tacit agreement had been reached: Hoover was accorded broad latitude to conduct sensitive operations — operations that no attorney general could approve because of the necessary resort to illegal methods — on the assumption that these investigations were limited to suspected foreign agents and their American operatives. Attorneys General Brownell and Rogers thus may not have been informed about the COINTELPROs.

384

Hoover saw no need to brief them, having been encouraged to believe that they wished the FBI to monitor and destabilize 'subversive' activists without creating any written record. This indifference to legality, and to their oversight responsibilities, informed Brownell's and Roger's microphone surveillance policy as well, and also their willful ignorance of FBI wiretapping authority.

In March 1955 (at a time when Congress was considering legislation to rescind the 1934 Federal Communications Act's ban against wiretapping), Hoover advised Brownell that FBI wiretapping had been based on President Roosevelt's May 1940 directive and on a July 1946 directive from President Truman. Should the attorney general feel that these directives provided insufficient authority, Hoover continued, he 'may want to present the matter to President Eisenhower to determine whether he holds the same view with respect to the Department of Justice with respect to wiretapping.' Responding later that month, Brownell assured Hoover that no such presidential briefing was required, inasmuch as 'I personally explained to the President, the Cabinet, the National Security Council and the Senate and House Judiciary Committees during 1954 the present policy and procedures on wiretaps, at which time I referred specifically to the authorization letter to the Attorney General from President F. D. Roosevelt.'

Brownell's response reveals his ignorance of the Truman directive – and his reluctance to press Hoover for further details. Not surprisingly, the Director did not repair Brownell's ignorance, in part because Hoover had craftily drafted the July 1946 directive himself, wording it to imply that Truman's approval had been sought merely to reaffirm Roosevelt's earlier directive. By selective editing, Hoover had secured Truman's unknowing authorization to extend FBI wiretapping to cover 'subversive activities.'[7]

Meanwhile assistance to congressional investigating committees continued, with the Justice Department's authorization in the case of SISS, although not in the case of HUAC. The Bureau's transactions with the Senate subcommittee continued uninterrupted until the subcommittee's death in 1978, the subcommittee dutifully accepting the Director's guidance.[8] In contrast, the FBI's *sub rosa* transactions with HUAC shifted wildly from hot to cold according to the vagaries of Hoover's moods and his relations with its chairman, whether Harold Velde, Francis Walter, or Richard Ichord.

After the Republicans' success in the 1952 presidential and congressional elections, the newly elevated chairman of HUAC, former FBI agent Harold Velde, resolved to exploit his post to the fullest. Velde's ambition and hunger for publicity disturbed Hoover. The Director's wariness was compounded when, in July 1953, Thomas Beale was appointed chief clerk of the committee. Deeming Beale unreliable (because unfriendly toward the Bureau), Hoover henceforth limited FBI assistance to providing the committee with the addresses of potential witnesses, having decided that 'close liaison was not in the best interests of the Bureau.' FBI field offices were to sever 'liaison' with representatives of the committee but were to accept 'information, if volunteered.'

Independently of this reduction in FBI assistance, former FBI agent and committee counsel Louis Russell (who since 1947 – unknown to senior committee staff and committee members – had surreptitiously provided Nichols with information about the committee's activities) was fired as a result of a personality conflict with other senior committee staff. Russell's dismissal substantially reduced Hoover's ability to monitor the committee's activities, although his other sources on the committee (Raphael [Ray] Nixon, William A. Wheeler, Earl Fuoss, and Don Appell) continued to provide 'information on a confidential basis concerning areas in which the HUAC plans to conduct hearings' and concerning 'the identity of potential witnesses.'

Briefed on how his aides monitored HUAC hearings, Hoover inquired 'to what extent do we seek information from files of HUAC?' Assistant Director Alan Belmont responded that the FBI reviewed the files daily in connection with its investigations of the loyalty of federal employees. In addition, Belmont said, the Bureau acquired information

386

about the committee's hearings through a confidential relationship between the Washington field office, the Los Angeles office, and committee staff members Nixon and Wheeler. Through this 'confidential relationship,' Hoover learned about 'the planned future hearings of the Committee as well as the identity of individuals to be subpoenaed' and received 'transcripts' of Executive Session and other testimony 'in instances where such testimony has not been voluntarily furnished to the Bureau's representative.'

Through his spies on the committee then, Hoover was apprised of its activities, and any possibility that it might encroach on the FBI's interests. For example, from committee investigator (and former FBI agent) Earl Fuoss, Hoover learned of Fuoss's plans to inform the head of the FBI's Miami office about 'his activities in order that he [Fuoss] will not interfere with any activities of our office.' Hoover thereupon directed the Miami SAC not to 'furnish any information to Fuoss, but should receive any information volunteered and promptly inform the Bureau.'

Fuoss did contact the Miami SAC, offering to 'cooperate fully' in any matters he undertook and to 'furnish the names and identities of potential witnesses to the FBI well in advance of the time they are to appear as witnesses.' As a former FBI agent, Fuoss acknowledged the confidentiality of FBI files and promised to 'do nothing that would cause any embarrassment to the Bureau in any way whatsoever.'

Cooperation improved, paradoxically, when the Democrats regained the chair. Following the 1954 elections, the new committee chairman, Francis Walter, Hoover's coeval at George Washington Law School, met with Nichols to propose the re-examination of FBI regulations limiting assistance to the committee. Current regulations, Walter emphasized, denied him 'guidance' from the FBI; accordingly, he wondered if this might not be given 'on a personal and confidential basis, as we should know by now that he could maintain a confidence.' Walter also asked Nichols 'who the people were on his staff and who they were before the staff hired them, [so] he could put a stop to [matters that undermined cooperation between the committee and the FBI] when he became Chairman.' Nichols refused to modify the FBI's regulations, but nevertheless assured Walter that 'if at any time we could be of help, we would certainly do whatever was possible.'

Walter recontacted Nichols three days later and promised to respect 'the proper relationship' between the committee and the executive branch (there was nothing proper about it), and particularly not to seek information 'surreptitiously' from executive agencies. Acknowledging the importance of maintaining 'the security of security agencies,' Walter described HUAC's purpose as 'to alert the public and to point to the need for legislation;' 'he hoped that there could be developed cooperation between the committee and the executive agencies; that we are all working toward a common end, but that he deplored and condemned competitive actions among committees.'

Acting on these assurances, and having confidence in Walter, Hoover authorized resumption of the unofficial relationship he had established with HUAC Chairman Thomas in 1947. Hoover also had Nichols brief Walter about Committee Chief Clerk Beale 'in confidence' – Beale, in Hoover's view, was a fly in the ointment.[9]

Nichols broached the Beale matter with Walter the next month, whereupon Walter assured Nichols that Beale was not influential. In any case, he said 'he [Walter] could not be in a position of firing all the Republicans; that in his opinion Beale was the lesser evil.' Walter then reported his intention to focus on 'Communist infiltration among lawyers' and the 'financial setup of front organizations,' adding 'that if there was anything that the Committee could do for us or any area that they could go into or any records they could get with their subpoena power, we had but to give him confidentially the nod.' Nichols assured Walters that 'we would certainly keep this in mind.'

Hoover's willingness thereafter to provide informal reciprocal assistance to Walter varied according to the quality and amount of Walter's shared intelligence, and to the recentness and enormity of the congressman's indiscretions – in short, according to Hoover's estimation

388

of Walter's overall value. When, for instance, the committee refused to allow the use of HUAC executive-session testimony in presenting a case for the perjury indictment of Harvey Matusow, a recanting FBI informer, Hoover concluded, 'I think we should discontinue trying to deal with Walter as this instance shows a lack of forthrightness . . . and cooperation.'

Walter compounded the trouble on another occasion by inadvertently admitting during a CBS nationwide radio interview that HUAC checked its witnesses by obtaining a 'report from the FBI and its judgment as to whether a witness is responsible, trustworthy, reliable and honest.'[10] Apologizing to Nichols in the noisy aftermath, Walter regretted 'that he had made this error and would not make it again.' Angered but seeking to pressure Walter to amend his ways, Hoover directed Nichols to 'tell Walter & indicate if his staff are going to act that way there is not much use of us contacting him & having our motives misrepresented by an underling.' Thereafter, when committee counsel Don Appell requested an FBI list of all district secretaries of the United Electrical Workers union, Hoover refused, observing that the Bureau's 'past contact with the Committee' necessitated that 'we must be most cautious in order to safeguard our actions with HUAC from being misrepresented at some future date.'

Still, Hoover remained singlemindedly loyal to the cause, even though the public was finally losing interest. Sharing the Committee's political objectives, he did not hesitate to help Walter when the latter expressed his concern in late August 1955 over 'a general decline of public interest in subversion.' To rekindle this interest, the congressman had approached Nichols for information on 'one or two situations which the Committee might develop and which would bring up to date the current knowledge of domestic Communist activities.' Assuring Walter that 'naturally we would like to help him,' Nichols promised to 'do some exploring' and report back.

After consulting with Hoover, Nichols urged Walter to hold hearings at which 'two or three witnesses' well versed in Communist activities around the world would offer testimony on 'Communist strategy and tactics in a manner which would clearly prove what we all know; namely, that Communists come out of the same mold and that the activities in Spain, China or Europe vary only in a matter of degree and approach.' Nichols also urged Walter to 'develop the Marxist Leninist theoretical tactics to show the strategy and tactics of highlighting the basic Communist premise that 'We Will Build Communism with Non-Communist Hands' and in this way highlight the secret Party member and the individual who does the Communist bidding and then give widespread distribution to a well-founded report.'

Walter found this advice 'excellent' and requested further suggestions and ways to implement them. He also expressed an interest in 'get[ting] into one or two [other] areas wherein the field has not previously been worked over so that there would be a freshness to the approach.'

On Hoover's orders, FBI files were then reviewed 'to determine if we can come up with something which could be used by the Committee and which would not, of course, jeopardize any current Bureau investigations. This review involves an analysis of many files, and the results of this research will be set out in an appropriate memorandum as soon as it is completed.'[11]

Hoover's equivocal responses to HUAC's requests did not mean that he opposed in the least assisting the committee's efforts to advance the cause. He insisted only that the FBI's cooperation be on his own terms and conditioned on the committee's approaching him hat-in-hand and with appropriate deference.

In June 1956, for example, although he had earlier withheld information on a prominent official of the Fund for the Republic, Nichols furnished committee aide Karl Baarslag with background information on two recipients of Fund support – Theodore Draper and Alan Westin – on the understanding that Baarslag 'would treat everything we discuss with him with utmost confidence.' Indirectly relaying advice to the committee through American Legion officials,

Hoover also persuaded Walter to postpone the committee's planned hearings on the Fund in order to 'present better hearings than were originally scheduled.' And when the committee resumed its hearings on the Fund in December, Hoover followed them with intense interest.

Encouraged by Hoover's helpfulness, Walter met with the Director on 2 May 1956. Walter began the interview by announcing the appointment of former SISS counsel Richard Arens as HUAC's staff director. He then brought up the real reason for having sought this meeting – to request Hoover's assistance on a matter of importance to the committee. Walter asked Hoover to furnish HUAC with 'the identities' of FBI informers who had been publicly compromised by having testified during Smith Act trials, denaturalization hearings, or SACB hearings 'so that the Committee might consider calling such ex-informants and building hearings about such information as they may have already disclosed in judicial or administrative proceedings.'

Hoover was noncommittal. Following the meeting, however, he ordered his aides to prepare 'a list of names of such informants with whom we are thoroughly through and who are of no value to the Government so that we may forward the same to Congressman Walter.' It is not clear whether Hoover thereupon surreptitiously gave this list to Walter. He did, however, advise Attorney General Brownell of Walter's request, adding that the FBI could not pinpoint when an informer had been 'used.'

When Arens later recontacted Hoover's office to complain about the 'dearth of information and a dearth of good projects' that the committee had to work on and asked for the names of three or four FBI informers who had left the Communist party so that the committee could use them as friendly witnesses in future hearings, Hoover at first hesitated. But although he decided that it did 'not appear that the Government's fight against communism would appear to benefit' from providing the names of FBI informers, he did approve an alternative proposal to give Arens the names of individuals who had defected from the Communist party but had refused to cooperate with the FBI.

391

Hoover reasoned that these individuals might 'cooperate' with the committee rather than suffer the glare of 'publicity and embarrassment'; no FBI informer would be lost; and such assistance might result in the committee's uncovering information of 'value' that would otherwise be unavailable to the FBI. Such a list was prepared and given to Arens.

Finally, in July 1956, a formal liaison program was established between the FBI and HUAC, modeled on the program the Bureau had worked out earlier with SISS. What had been a rocky relationship, in which FBI assistance varied according to Hoover's reactions to committee initiatives, thereafter became a comparatively smooth collaboration intended to further the cause. Working closely and on a personal basis with committee counsel, Nichols (and then DeLoach) selectively assisted the committee – providing addresses and current employment of prospective witnesses, background information on a rather extensive list of individuals (e.g., alleged Communist teachers and movie actors), the names of financial contributors to the Communist party (to be used in 'exposing the "angels" of the Communist Party') and advice on possible 'friendly' witnesses and alleged experts for future hearings (specifically on 'international communist fronts'), as well as editing and correcting errors in committee reports.

Notwithstanding the declining interest in the Communist issue in the nation as a whole, Hoover continued to promote the committee's various anti-Communist political efforts. Like the committee's staff members, the Director was concerned over the liberal drift in national politics, particularly in the aftermath of the Democrats' sweeping successes in the 1958 congressional elections (picking up forty-eight seats in the House and fifteen in the Senate). From DeLoach's recent meeting with Arens, Hoover learned that HUAC's staff director feared that the election of 'many liberal members' had swung the Congress 'approximately 15% to the left.' Walter, Arens assured DeLoach, 'is doing a great deal of maneuvering behind the scenes in order to arrange for conservative committee members who think and feel the way he does about internal security.'

Hoover willingly abetted Walter's efforts to blunt the liberal trend and the hesitant moves of prominent liberals to undermine the dogmatic anti-Communism of the late 1940s and early 1950s. Meeting with the Director on 10 February 1959, the HUAC chairman cited the refusal of college administrators, specifically at Bryn Mawr, to require a loyalty oath as a condition for student loans and requested Hoover's assistance in an undertaking to solicit statements from 'one or more outstanding educators in the country' that loyalty oaths did not infringe on academic freedom. Hoover dissuaded Walter from his contacting former Harvard president James Conant, observing that Conant 'had more or less condoned the employment of professors who might have communist backgrounds,' but agreed to furnish a list of sympathetic 'outstanding educators in the country.' The next week he forwarded to Walter 'biographical data concerning 14 educators who would appear to warrant your consideration.'

Hoover's ideological identification with HUAC reached its zenith in 1960 in the midst of the furor occasioned when University of California-Berkeley students demonstrated against committee hearings in the Bay area. Briefed on the demonstration, which resulted in the forced dispersal of the protesting students, Hoover ordered intensified FBI 'coverage of activities in schools & colleges as trend seems to be not only in U.S. but elsewhere to inflame youth.' Directing the FBI's San Francisco office to submit a detailed report on 'riotous demonstrations at House Committee on Un-American Activities hearings on the part of communists and their sympathizers,' Hoover demanded that the FBI 'continue to intensify coverage of such activities.'

After preparing a formal report, entitled 'Communist Target — Youth,' charging that the demonstrators had been Communist-led, the Director sought to encourage conservative activists to defend the committee. Answering one of the favorable letters he received after dissemination of the report, Hoover explained, 'The communist movement relentlessly seeks areas of controversy and with practiced methods agitates to turn these situations to its advantage

393

. . . This report emphatically does not cast doubt on the purposes or loyalty of American Youth. It is intended rather as urgent encouragement to young people to learn the true nature of this evil conspiracy, and, armed with that knowledge, resist effectively wherever its influence threatens.'

On the other hand, when Hoover received a critical response to his statement, FBI agents were ordered to search FBI files for derogatory information on the correspondent, and the FBI Laboratory went so far as to try to identify the writers of anonymous letters. Learning that *Harper's Magazine* was considering reprinting a *Des Moines Register* editorial calling for the abolition of HUAC, Hoover authorized dissemination of derogatory information on the editors of the magazine. This was in fact done after *Harper's* reprinted the editorial in its October 1960 issue.

Hoover's small triumphs, however, were becoming irrelevant. The emerging issues in the nation's political dialogue were no longer domestic Communism, the need for secrecy for national security reasons, or homosexuals in the State Department, but organized crime, equal rights for black Americans, and the need to challenge executive claims to secrecy and inherent national security powers. The relaxation of Cold War tensions, in the aftermath of Eisenhower's efforts to promote détente with the Soviets, including the 1955 Geneva summit conference and the 1959 Khrushchev visit to the United States, combined with a delayed reaction to the president's commitment to shore up an anti-Communist government in South Vietnam (in violation of the Geneva Armistice Agreement of 1954 ending the colonial war in former French Indochina), reshaped the political agenda in ways that Hoover could neither accommodate nor change.

After Apalachin, Attorney General Rogers, recognizing if not altogether understanding the Director's longstanding reluctance to become involved in policing organized crime, set up a Special Group on Organized Crime, a Justice Department trouble-shooting operation under the direction of Milton R. Wessel, a former assistant U.S. attorney.[12]

Meanwhile the Senate was conducting its own investigation of organized crime through the medium of the Select Committee on Improper Activities in the Labor and Management Field, chaired by Senator John McClellan (D.-Ark.). During the course of this investigation, McClellan's chief counsel, Robert Kennedy, exposed Teamster President David Beck's (and his successor, James Hoffa's) associations with underworld figures. Indeed, Kennedy, who had served briefly — in his twenties, before abruptly resigning — as minority counsel to Senator McCarthy's Permanent Investigations Subcommittee and later as majority counsel to the same subcommittee under McClellan, was making a name for himself, much to Hoover's chagrin.

In the civil rights field, Hoover found himself in an even more serious bind, as his most important supporters in the South — members of Congress[13] and officers of the state police — were segregationist almost to a man. In addition, many of the Bureau's own agents were white southerners opposed to desegregation. Finally, there was Hoover himself. He did not sympathize with the demands of those seeking racial justice and equality. His attitude was perhaps best expressed when, ordered to begin integrating the Bureau in 1961, he selected for his first black special agents his elevator operator, Sam Noisette, and his driver, James Crawford.

Notes to Chapter Twelve

1. Disturbed by the implication of the *Brown* ruling and by a renewed challenge to segregation in the South in the aftermath of the Montgomery, Alabama, bus boycott of 1955 — engineered by a young Baptist minister, the Reverend Martin Luther King, Jr. — Hoover in the spring of 1956 sent President Eisenhower a series of reports detailing Communist influence in the civil rights movement. At the president's invitation, Hoover briefed the cabinet on the southern racial situation, emphasizing the Communists' role in lobbying for civil rights. (Athan Theoharis, *Spying on Americans* [Philadelphia: Temple University Press, 1978], p. 135.)

2. On the other hand, Hoover gave Rooney whatever derogatory information the FBI had on two of the congressman's challengers, Peter Eikenberry and Allard K. Lowenstein, who opposed him in the Democratic primary in Rooney's Brooklyn district.

3. Indeed, this very operation was conducted in the case of Democratic Congressman Henry Reuss, using information the FBI had learned about the congressman's daughter, a student at Swarthmore College. In this case, however, Hoover did not have Reuss in his pocket.

4. Years later Edwards discovered among the contents of his FBI file, which he had obtained under the Freedom of Information Act, how Hoover had orchestrated this effort to contain his challenge to HUAC's continued tenure and, further, the Director's response to an Associated Press report of 1970 (erroneous, as it turned out) that Edwards would not seek re-election. Hoover had added to the routing slip attached to the AP story: 'Good riddance.' (Don Edwards interview, 4 February 1985.)

5. DeLoach recalled that Tolson, who generally acted as Hoover's front man in order to ensure the Director deniability, took the heat for this abuse of office too. The Director, supposedly innocent of any knowledge of the matter, nevertheless kept his share. (DeLoach interview, 9 April 1985.)

6. One force calculated to chill political debate at this time was the loyalty oath required by public agencies and private industry. At the height of the furor an estimated 20 percent of middle management in the American *private* sector was required to swear loyalty as a condition of its employment. The state of Indiana went so far as to require loyalty oaths of those seeking a license to wrestle in the state. (Ralph S. Brown, Jr., *Loyalty and Security: Employment Tests in the United States* [New Haven: Yale University Press, 1958], pp. 92-163.)

7. Hoover achieved this by drafting a letter in July 1946, which Attorney General Tom Clark sent over his own signature, ostensibly seeking Truman's approval for a reaffirmation of President Roosevelt's wiretapping policy. Hoover's draft began by quoting from the final authorization paragraph of Roosevelt's directive. The Director, however, had dropped the final sentence of that paragraph, which limited FBI wiretapping to 'national defense' investigations: 'You are requested then to limit the investigations so conducted to a minimum and to limit them insofar as possible to aliens.' This intentional deletion allowed Hoover to represent Roosevelt's directive as having permitted wiretapping during

investigations of 'subversive activities.' (Memo, Roosevelt to Jackson, 21 May 1940, and letter, Clark to Truman, 17 July 1946, both in Stephen Spingarn Papers, National Defense-Internal Security, Truman Library, Independence, Mo.; Demaris, *The Director, p.* 123.)

8. The one exception occurred in May 1953. Disturbed because the FBI was doing 'a great deal of work for the Committee for which it received no credit and, in fact, for which the Committee took credit,' Hoover considered 'the advisability of completely discontinuing supplying of any information' to it. Hoover was persuaded instead to 'put the brakes on & make certain we carefully screen all requests' in view of the Eisenhower administration's willingness to honor congressional requests for information. (Memo, FBI Executives' Conference to Tolson, 8 May 1953, FBI 62-88217-1061.)

9. Learning that Beale 'has been carrying on an infight against [former Committee Chairman Harold] Velde and former Bureau Agents working for the House Committee on Un-American Activities,' Hoover had queried, 'What do we have on Beale?' He was informed that Beale 'has now succeeded in setting the stage for Ray Nixon to be fired and the possibility exists that he will also influence Walter against Fuoss . . . Both Fuoss and Nixon have been friendly disposed [sic] to the Bureau and have been helpful since they have been on the Committee. Nixon has been more helpful and has gone out of his way on occasions. We, of course, know about Beale and his anti-Bureau views which go back a number of years.' (Memo, Nichols to Tolson, 7 January 1955, FBI 61-7582-2602, and Memo, Jones to Nichols, 10 January 1955, FBI 61-7582-2601.)

10. Karl Mundt, a former ally of Hoover's on HUAC and later a member of the McCarthy Committee, had been guilty of a similar indiscretion when during an informal address to the Bonneville (Utah) Knife and Fork Club he inadvertently disclosed the Bureau practice of 'tipping off' congressional committees in security cases in which there was not enough evidence to obtain an indictment. Hoover privately advised Mundt to deny having made the statement, while he himself publicly dismissed the charges of Bureau assistance to conservative congressmen as 'an absolute lie.' (Kenneth O'Reilly, *Hoover and the Un-Americans: The FBI, HUAC, and the Red Menace* [Philadelphia: Temple University Press, 1983], p. 128.)

11. After considering the problem for two months, the Bureau's

Internal Security Division offered two recommendations. First, emphasizing the absence of any 'known single source document available for research by students or other individuals interested in the Communist movement which outlines the true nature of the aims and purposes of the International Communist movement,' it recommended that the Committee review the statements and publications of Soviet and American Communist party leaders (Stalin, Marx, Lenin, Foster, Browder, Dennis) to select 'statements showing that the Communist Party, if successful, would establish a Soviet-America patterned after the Government of the Soviet Union or the "people's democracies" behind the iron curtain rather than establishing a Socialist form of government.' Such a document would 'not furnish Representative Walter with large headlines of a sensational character,' the Internal Security Division staff conceded, but would be 'an outstanding achievement,' as HUAC could publish it in large quantities and at a low price to be purchased by 'patriotic organizations all over the country.'

Second, the staff urged the committee to obtain transcripts of completed Subversive Activities Control Board hearings. A review of these hearings 'would give Representative Walter a tremendous amount of information which could be utilized for executive session or public session hearings on various phases of the Communist menace. It is not believed that the testimony given at SACB hearings has been fully exploited as only a small amount of publicity resulted therefrom.'

Even though these suggestions lacked dramatic publicity value, Nichols reported them to Walter, and the committee eventually prepared a detailed document. Hoover carefully followed the favorable response the report received in the conservative press and personally assisted the effort to publicize the Communist menace by submitting a prepared statement on 'Communist activities in the United States.' (Memo, Baumgardner to Belmont, 22 October 1955, FBI 617582-2872.)

12. Wessel was soon frustrated by the Director's apparent hesitancy in enlisting in the war against organized crime. Hoover did, however, increase FBI investigative activities in the organized crime field, initiating a Top Hoodlum program that included the use of break-ins and bugs during FBI investigations of prominent crime bosses. Not aware of the Bureau's resort to these illegal techniques, and thus equally ignorant of Hoover's reluctance to prosecute crime leaders for fear that these illegal methods might be exposed, Justice Department officials unfairly denounced

Hoover's seeming passivity. Richard V. Ogilvie, who headed Wessel's midwestern office, expressed this frustration when commenting in the 1960s: 'Hoover was very cool to the whole idea of the Attorney General's Special Group. He ordered that the FBI files, containing the very information we needed on organized crime, were to be closed to us . . . Criticizing Hoover is a dangerous thing for anyone to do . . . But honesty compels me to say that some of Hoover's ideas are sadly behind the times.' (Quoted in Fred C. Cook, *The FBI Nobody Knows* [New York: Pyramid, 1965], p. 219.)

Hoover's reluctance, as we have seen, was not based on archaic notions or indifference. Unable to develop criminal informers to penetrate the Mafia, the FBI for the most part obtained information illegally. For this reason, Hoover resisted departmental efforts to obtain access to FBI files, fearing the adverse impact the resulting publicity might have on the Bureau's carefully wrought reputation as an agency respectful of legal and constitutional limitations.

13. Ironically, even southern segregationists began to doubt Hoover's reliability. Meeting Assistant Director Gordon Nease on 22 January 1958, H. L. Edwards, an administrative assistant to South Carolina Senator Olin Johnston, warned that 'the Bureau was rapidly losing prestige in the South; that while the South had always been one of the staunchest Bureau supporters, the civil rights question has people thinking in an unreasonable manner; and that some of their constituents are continuously getting to the Senator and blaming the Bureau for investigating civil rights matters which they feel are strictly of local concern, and that we are being made pawns of the NAACP.' Emphasizing his understanding that the FBI had the responsibility to investigate violations of civil rights laws, Edwards suggested that the 'Bureau's solution to the problem is for enough pressure to be brought to set up an investigative staff in the Civil Rights Division of the Department in order that the Bureau can keep away from such matters entirely.' Accordingly, he urged Nease 'to suggest to Mr. Hoover that he speak to his close friends along this line . . . [Edwards] fully realizes the potential danger in this for the Director, but he feels that it is a must.' Then, returning to the occasion for his meeting with Nease, the Senate Post Office and Civil Service Committee's consideration of additional 'super grades' for FBI agents, Edwards promised that 'if there is anything he could do to include the additional super grades in the current pay raise bill, he would do so and let me know. I told him that we did not want to push the matter under the

circumstances and that he should use his own good judgment, which he stated he would do.' Hoover recoiled at this crude attempt at blackmail. Rejecting as 'completely untenable' Edwards's suggestion that he lobby Congress to create a separate civil rights investigative division in the Department of Justice, Hoover observed that Johnston's attitude probably doomed the FBI's chances of securing the additional super grades. He then added, "It is amazing how utterly unobjective some individuals get. We have a job to do & we will do it.' (Memo, Nease to Tolson, 22 January 1958, J. Edgar Hoover [Directorship] folder, Folder no. 85, Hoover O & C.)

CHAPTER THIRTEEN

(1960–1963)
OUT OF SYNC

BY 1960 Hoover was incontestably *the* symbol of law and order in the United States, and had been for a number of years, but the relevance of his positions on major issues was no longer so clear. With John F. Kennedy's election to the presidency in November of that year, the country began to move away from the politics of antisubversion and instead address the problems of crime, race, and poverty through proposals to promote health, education, and welfare. As Arthur M. Schlesinger, Jr., the chronicler of the Thousand Days, flippantly put it somewhat later, 'Subversion was out. Organized crime was in. Hoover grudgingly went along.'

Hoover went along only to get along, however; his change of heart was mostly feigned. In 1961 he secretly authorized the extension of the COINTELPRO-Communist Party to the Socialist Workers party, renewed his efforts to sustain the anti-Communist consensus (including red-baiting the Fair Play for Cuba Committee and attempting to demonstrate Communist influence in other dissident movements), and intensified the FBI's monitoring of the civil rights movement, with particular attention to the charismatic Martin Luther King, Jr. Yet Hoover had to make some accommodation to the more liberal politics of the New Frontier because, to the surprise of many and the disappointment of more than a few, President-elect Kennedy swiftly reappointed the sixty-five-year-old Director. Distrustful of the veteran bureaucrat, yet – in part because of the narrowness of his own victory over Republican Richard M. Nixon – reluctant to dismiss him, Kennedy placed between them, in the position of attorney general, his brother Robert, with instructions to keep the powerful Director at bay.

Hoover despised the arrangement from the beginning. Accustomed to communicating directly with the White House, he was made to understand that he was accountable to a slight, boyish-looking thirty-five-year-old. Moreover, the attorney general, as the brother of the president as well as the president's erstwhile campaign director, could not be bypassed — without being informed. Accordingly, Hoover's practice of going over the attorney general's head and submitting reports to the White House, a practice dating from Franklin Roosevelt's time, had to be abandoned. Finally, Robert Kennedy acted early to secure his authority, in February 1961 apprising White House aides of his intention 'to keep abreast of any contacts between the White House staff and his Department.' White House aides were to 'go through the Attorney General first' before arranging 'any' meetings with Justice Department officials, including those in the FBI.

Ever the astute bureaucrat and realist, Hoover adapted quickly to this new scheme of things. While continuing to submit reports of ordinary interest to the president through his brother (notably on allegations of John Kennedy's sexual affairs), he also separately serviced sensitive White House requests.[1]

But Hoover had to adjust in more fundamental ways. Whereas previous attorneys general had requested audiences with the Director only on their own turf, young Kennedy was wont to drop in on the Director unannounced and in shirtsleeves. Worst of all, Hoover's liaison with the attorney general, Courtney Evans, an attractive and worldly young assistant director, had been chosen from the Bureau's ranks by the Kennedys themselves.

Nor did the Kennedys' developing attack on the nation's problems reassure the Director. To be sure, the narrowness of the president's victory — a margin of only 119,450 votes out of almost 69,000,000 cast — had compelled him to trim the sweeping legislative program that he had planned. Still, in his first months in office Kennedy made clear his intention to lobby for a liberal legislative agenda establishing his long-range goals.

Almost everything on the Kennedy agenda Hoover perceived as a threat — not only to the nation, as in the case of the president's alleged softness on domestic Communism, but to Hoover and the Bureau itself. The attorney general's declared war against organized crime, using the mechanism of a separate Justice Department Task Force, for instance, could only call attention to the past inaction of the Bureau. Robert Kennedy, furthermore, was determined to racially integrate the Bureau, which from Hoover's standpoint was a direct assault on its professionalism and integrity. And, finally, considering the warm patronage Hoover had received over the years from magnates in the nation's steel industry, he could have regarded President Kennedy's success in forcing a steel price rollback in the spring of 1961 only as incendiary and distasteful.[2] (Indeed, when ordered by the attorney general to interview three reporters who had filed stories on Bethlehem Steel President Edmund Merkin's admission to company stockholders that a price increase was not needed to cover the company's wage settlement, Hoover had his agents interview them in the middle of the night at their homes, creating the impression of a Gestapo knocking at the door, much to the embarrassment of the Kennedy administration.) In any case, the Kennedys were a new breed and increasingly popular, and therefore doubly to be feared.

Hoover recognized his vulnerability. But he still had several tricks up his sleeve, not least his ability to play on the fears of millions of Americans. Realizing that the Red Square had abated[3] but determined to hold on to his position, he modified his germ-phobic rhetoric to emphasize a generalized assault on American values. In a November 1963 speech delivered to the national convention of the Catholic Youth Organization in New York City, he declared:

Americans, in growing numbers, are developing a dangerously indulgent attitude toward crime, filth, and corruption. No one can deny that motion pictures are deliberately and defiantly pursuing an increasingly bold courtship with obscenity. No one can deny the role of the television industry in bringing lurid portrayals of violence and sadism into the living rooms — and even the nurseries — of our homes. No one can deny that sensual trash is moving closer and closer to children's books on the shelves of our newsstands and magazine stores.

Then, anticipating Jerry Falwell and other preachers of the twice-born right, he continued:

Here and abroad mortal enemies of freedom and deniers of God Himself conspire to undermine the fundamental forces which are the lifeline of our country's vitality and greatness, our most formidable weapons, in peace and war . . . These are America's great bulwarks. They are under savage attack today, just as they were so severely tested nearly 200 years ago at Bunker Hill and Valley Forge.

Hoover's skills as a propagandist were superb in large part because he saw himself as utterly sincere. The fact that he chose not to go to church, for instance, in no way inhibited his salvationist zeal. However, his best assurance of surviving the Kennedy challenge was to be found in his confidential files.

The Director maintained three sets of such files in his office: a so-called Official and Confidential File, a so-called Personal and Confidential File, and 'about a drawer and one half of Bureau files which were kept in [Hoover's] office under lock and key.' Asked in 1975 why the files in this last category were so maintained, Hoover's Executive Assistant Helen Gandy replied 'for safekeeping,' because they 'were highly confidential Bureau information.'

Of these three confidential files, only the Official and Confidential File is extant; presumably the third set has long since been reincorporated into the Bureau's central records system; and Miss Gandy destroyed the Personal and Confidential File immediately after Hoover's death and pursuant to his express order. This was not a personal file, however – that is, a file containing documents pertaining to Hoover's private life and correspondence.[4] So much is clear. For, although a destroyed file cannot be reconstructed, one of Hoover's memoranda in his Official and Confidential File, captioned 'Memorandum for Personal File,' generally describes the documents Hoover maintained in his Personal and Confidential File, and they definitely were not all personal.

In this memorandum, Hoover outlined the precautions he had taken to ensure against any possible leaks to the news media involving 'many of the memoranda I have sent back and forth.' Such memoranda were filed 'in a Personal and Confidential file in my office and not in the main Bureau [files] so the great mass of file clerks don't get access to that and even Supervisors in the Divisions don't get access to them unless it is a *case* they personally are handling' (emphasis added).

There is an additional reason to doubt the contention that Hoover's Personal and Confidential File contained only personal correspondence, tax records, memorabilia, and the like. For, included among the documents in Hoover's extant Official and Confidential File are eight folders containing official policy memoranda that were originally filed in the Personal and Confidential File. In 1971, for reasons unknown, Hoover transferred these highly sensitive memoranda from this file to his Official and Confidential File. In addition, other memoranda in Hoover's Official and Confidential File bear the notation that copies were maintained in the Personal File. A review of both the transferred documents and the multiple-copy documents confirms that extremely sensitive official policy documents were filed in Hoover's Personal and Confidential File.

One of the transferred documents is a memorandum describing the 'Do Not File' procedure for 'black bag jobs.' When created in July 1966, this extremely sensitive memorandum was filed in the Director's Personal and Confidential File. Pursuant to Hoover's November 1971 order, however, the 'Do Not File' memorandum was shifted to the Official and Confidential File. Had Hoover not ordered this transfer, the illegal FBI practice and record-destruction procedure described in it would never have come to light.

All of the other transferred documents involve sensitive official policy matters. They conform to a pattern suggesting that Hoover intentionally consigned to his Personal File documents that, if exposed to public attention, would definitely have jeopardized his tenure as Director and blackened the reputation of the Bureau.

Clearly, Hoover's Personal File was a formidable collection. And its destruction forever limits our understanding of how he operated, the scope and nature of the information he personally collected, and the uses he made of the FBI's vast resources. However, one *can* understand his operational style, uses of power, and at least one reason for his longevity as Director. For he inadvertently left behind his Official and Confidential File, a file that he himself characterized in October 1941 as containing 'various and sundry items believed inadvisable to be included in the general files of the Bureau. Among the material are certain items, such as confidential information on [phrase deleted], Communist infiltration into the Department of Justice, etc., which if they are to be of value, must be properly indexed and filed.

Hoover's description betrays not only his interest in having immediate access to information he deemed 'of value' but also his concern that this interest not become known. (At the same time it reveals his expansive conception of 'Communist infiltration,' as the suspected 'Communists' in the Justice Department were the prominent liberal New Dealers Charles Fahy, Thomas Emerson, Herbert Wechsler and Edward Prichard.) Sixty-four of the 164 folders in Hoover's Official and Confidential File contain derogatory personal information on two presidents, a First Lady, a cabinet member, and countless other prominent personalities. And by maintaining these documents in his office, Hoover and his senior aides could, whenever responding to a congressional, judicial, or executive inquiry, testify that a full search of the Bureau's central records system uncovered *no* files recording the Director's interest in derogatory information on presidents, members of Congress, or other prominent persons. Neither indexed nor recorded in the Bureau's central records system, Hoover's office file technically did not exist.

The thousands of pages in Hoover's Official and Confidential File memorialize the nature of Hoover's interests. Although the FBI, as of 1988, continued to withhold the vast majority of these documents, the index to the file, generally describing the targets and the information contained in Hoover's massive dossiers, permits a partial reconstruction of their contents. Thus, one folder containing two documents, totaling five pages, itemized information compiled on former Democratic presidential candidate Adlai Stevenson, Jr. The FBI withheld these pages in their entirety on 'unwarranted invasion of personal privacy' grounds, thereby indirectly disclosing the nature of the withheld information. A second folder, numbering 279 pages, withheld entirely on 'personal privacy,' 'national security,' and 'confidential source' grounds, contains 'summary memorandum of information Bufiles [Bureau files] and copies of correspondence from and to [name deleted] alleged to be homosexual. TOP SECRET MATERIAL CONTAINED.'

A third folder consists of twelve reports numbering sixty-seven pages – entirely withheld on 'personal privacy' grounds – based on information furnished by an informer. These reports on 'prominent persons' detailed 'Allegations that [name and title deleted] was a homosexual and Communists were using this to blackmail [name deleted] to place other Communists on the [name of office deleted] staff. During interviews information received which linked [name deleted] with [name deleted] as a homosexual.' A fourth folder, again totally withheld, contained 'personal background data relative to [name deleted but 'prominent person'] one time [name of position deleted], memo regarding his alleged homosexual tendencies. [Name deleted] association with [name deleted] was also reported to be a homosexual and news clippings relative to [name deleted].'

A fifth folder contains seventy-seven reports totaling 647

pages that had been compiled by the FBI and the Washington district of military intelligence on certain members of Congress and other prominent persons. Although all 647 pages have been withheld, the index identifies the information as having been compiled by military intelligence from 'informant reports,' agency checks, and interviews. '[Name deleted], a self-admitted homosexual, alleged to an informant of the military that former [name of congressman deleted] and other prominent persons had engaged in homosexual activities.'

As a result of the censorship of the entire contents of these folders, their significance remains unclear. We cannot understand why Hoover maintained this information in his office, how he used it, and who were the subjects of his interest. The volume of the information, however, and the fact that the seventy-seven reports were dated between 9 August 1950 and 24 April 1959 make clear that, as in the case of the military intelligence reports on the alleged Eleanor Roosevelt-Joseph Lash 'affair,' the Director not only valued this kind of information but kept it close at hand because of its potential usefulness.

The most revealing of the sixty-four folders containing derogatory information that Hoover kept in his Official and Confidential File contains twenty-four reports submitted to Hoover between 5 June 1958 and 22 October 1965 by the head of the Washington field office. These reports contain notations either that no other copy was made or that the copy was destroyed, ensuring that there was no extant, retrievable record of the Director's interest. (It is not clear whether only the head of the Washington field office submitted reports of this type to the Director, and then only for the period 1958-1965. This group of reports constitutes the entire *surviving* record of this type.)

These Washington field office reports were heavily censored before their release, but the general tenor of the information being reported is clear, as are the methods by which it was obtained. The index card for one folder, for instance, describes the folder's contents as containing 'derogatory' information concerning 'general immoral or criminal activities on the part of diplomats, Government employees, politicians, sport [sic] figures, socially prominent persons, Senators and Congressmen.'

Even the most heavily censored reports contain enough information to shed some light on the nature of FBI activities and Hoover's supervision of them. For example, the reports conclusively show that the Washington field office regularly obtained information through illegal investigative techniques (wiretaps, bugs, and break-ins) and informers (including high-level officials and secretaries) about potentially embarrassing sexual activities or drinking habits — that the wife of a prominent official 'was reported to have been among the higher priced "call girls" in New York' and that a former U.S. congressman and current Washington-based lobbyist was 'reportedly drinking excessively.' Other documents demonstrate that Hoover was keenly interested in and approved the collection of such information.

Reports were also filed on political developments in Washington. Thus Hoover was advised that a proposed bill to raise the per diem compensation for government employees to eighteen dollars would probably not pass during the current session of Congress; that the administrator of the Bureau of Security and Consular Affairs, Roderic O'Connor, would resign as of 1 January 1959; and that the U.S. ambassador to Canada, Livingston Merchant, would be returning to Washington to serve as assistant secretary of state for European affairs. Another report memorialized Republican congressman Robert Michel's criticism of the U.S. exhibits at the Brussels world's fair; another the surprise of high-level officials at the Department of Health, Education and Welfare at the appointment of Bertha S. Adkins as undersecretary of the department; and yet another the fact that twenty key Republican congressmen were 'delighted' to see the Sherman Adams 'mess' 'exposed.' (President Eisenhower's powerful administrative assistant had been forced to resign in September 1958 following revelations that he had accepted generous gifts from Boston industrialist Bernard Goldfine and had interceded on Goldfine's behalf before various federal regulatory agencies.)

Hoover also preserved in his office file a series of memoranda from the head of the Los Angeles field office, dated from 1 April to 27 April 1960, reporting on his contacts with local law enforcement officials and other information he had received on law enforcement matters – juvenile delinquency, wiretapping policy, relations with local police. There are extensive deletions in this folder too, again justified on personal privacy grounds, and the index to the folder identifies one of these deletions as pertaining to the discovery by the editor of *Confidential Magazine* that '2 mulatto prostitutes' who had been at a party with John Kennedy were 'worried about his sex activities.' The report on this matter, captioned 'confidential,' was censored in its entirety.[5]

Although this example might suggest that Hoover had only incidentally learned of allegations of John Kennedy's womanizing, in fact he was keenly interested in the subject. Among the 164 folders constituting Hoover's Official and Confidential File, no fewer than three contain reports on various Kennedy 'affairs': one captioned 'Senator John F. Kennedy,' a second captioned 'President John F. Kennedy' (these two folders duplicate the various allegations of Kennedy affairs), and a third, a massive 628-page file consisting of 256 documents, captioned 'Mrs. Paul Fejos, nee Inga Arvad-IS-ESP-G' (Internal Security-Espionage-Germany). Documents in this third folder pertained to Kennedy's wartime affair (at the time he was an ensign in the Office of Naval Intelligence) with 'another man's wife' between January and June 1942.

The folder contains not only numerous memoranda pertaining to the initiation of the FBI's surveillance of Fejos-Arvad, but also transcribed tapes from the FBI's bugging of her visit over two weekends with Kennedy in Charleston, South Carolina.

A columnist for the isolationist *Washington Times-Herald* and a Danish national who allegedly had earlier been in contact with Nazi officials, Arvad became the subject of an FBI investigation in January 1942, when the Roosevelt White House, ONI officials, and Hoover mistakenly suspected that she might be a German spy. In the course of this investigation, Hoover learned that Kennedy had been 'playing around,' and 'apparently been spending the night' with Arvad while on duty in Washington, D.C., in January; that after his transfer to Charleston, South Carolina, Arvad had visited him over two weekends in February, at which time, through an FBI bug, it was discovered that 'they engaged in sexual intercourse on a number of occasions in the hotel room'; and that Kennedy and Arvad were in periodic contact until June 1942. Despite the fact that the FBI closed its investigation of Arvad in 1945 'as no subversive activities were determined,' these records were not filed with those of other FBI espionage investigations. Instead, they were maintained in Louis Nichols's office file until 14 July 1960 following Kennedy's nomination as the Democratic presidential candidate, when Hoover ordered their transfer to his secret office file.

(When former Nixon aide Charles Colson admitted during a February 1975 appearance on NBC's 'Today' show that the FBI had furnished 'extensive' information to the Nixon White House in 1971 or 1972 concerning Kennedy's wartime affair with Arvad, FBI officials assured then-Attorney General Edward Levi that a 'complete review' of the Fejos-Arvad file 'fails to indicate any data concerning John F. Kennedy's affair with Mrs. Fejos in 1942 was ever disseminated by the FBI either orally or by memorandum to anyone at anytime [*sic*] including the White House in 1971 or 1972 as implied by Mr. Colson.' Despite this disclaimer, Colson clearly knew of the affair and, given Hoover's commitment to secrecy, it is not likely that the Director would have created a written record of having volunteered this information to any outsider. Hoover recorded such dissemination only if the request had come from a president or an attorney general, and then only to protect himself.)

Not all of the information that Hoover maintained on John Kennedy in his office file involved allegations of affairs. A substantial part involved political matters and had been compiled during the spring and summer of 1960, when it appeared that the then-Senator from Massachusetts might win the Democratic presidential nomination.[6] Indeed, on

13 July 1960 supervisor Milton Jones prepared a nine-page summary memorandum for Hoover listing the 'highlights of pertinent available data concerning Kennedy in view of strong possibility he will be Democratic candidate for President.'

In his memo, Jones assured Hoover that the 'Bureau and Director have enjoyed friendly relations with Senator Kennedy and his family for [a] number of years' and cited several instances of friendly transactions. Marginal underlining discloses those reported matters that interested the Director. These included observations that the senator held liberal views on civil rights and, more ominously, was allegedly soft on communism; had evolved 'away from the political influence of his father, further away from the conservative wing of the Catholic Church'; and had 'expressed opposition to loyalty oaths for students getting Federal scholarship loans'; a reference to 'allegations concerning immoral conduct on the part of Kennedy and hoodlum connections of Kennedy' was also marked. Hoover's interest was further piqued by reports that John Kennedy's brother Robert was an 'outspoken advoca[te] of a Federal Crime Commission.'

Jones then outlined the 'allegations of immoral activities on Senator Kennedy's part' that had been 'reported to the FBI over the years.' Rather than describe them 'in detail,' Jones listed the highlights:

> They include . . . data reflecting that Kennedy carried on an illicit relationship with another man's wife during World War II; that (probably in January 1960) Kennedy was 'compromised' with a woman in Las Vegas; and that Kennedy and Frank Sinatra have in the recent past been involved in parties in Palm Springs, Las Vegas and New York City. Regarding the Kennedy-Sinatra information, 'Confidential' magazine is said to have affidavits from two mulatto prostitutes in New York.[7]

Hoover's intense interest in the collection of derogatory information in general, and that on the Kennedys in particular, led to his post-election discovery, through a wiretap on Meyer Lansky installed during an antiracketeering investigation, of Lansky's claim that Robert Kennedy was 'carrying on an affair with an El Paso, Texas girl.' In view of Lansky's hoodlum background – and, more important, the fact that the FBI's acquisition of this information could not be questioned – Hoover dispatched Courtney Evans to apprise the attorney general of Lansky's allegation. Unimpressed by Hoover's source, Robert Kennedy categorically denied ever having been in El Paso and declared that there 'was no basis in fact for the allegation.' He nonetheless expressed appreciation for having been informed of the rumor and then reflected on the propensities of 'gossip mongers.': 'he was aware there had been several allegations concerning his possibly being involved with Marilyn Monroe. He said he had at least met Marilyn Monroe since she was a good friend of his sister, Pat Lawford, but these allegations just had a way of growing beyond any semblance of the truth.'

Rumors about the attorney general's affair with Monroe subsequently became the basis of allegations from right-wing activists that he had in fact been involved with her and was responsible for her death, allegations incriminating his older brother too. In his gossipy biography *Goddess: The Secret Lives of Marilyn Monroe,* a book based on personal interviews and published innuendo, Anthony Summers refines these allegations, claiming that both brothers had affairs with M.M. – John's dating from the 1950s, Robert's rather later. Because of John's omnivorous sexual appetite and Robert's genuine concern about Monroe's emotional state, Summers further contends, both brothers became indiscreet in their attentions to her. Finally, fearing scandal and alarmed by Monroe's obvious deterioration, Robert supposedly broke off their relationship, secretly flying to Monroe's home on 4 August 1963, the date she committed suicide. Then, in an account partaking of equal parts of fantasy and Chappaquidick, Summers claims that Kennedy enlisted his brother-in-law Peter Lawford and Director Hoover in an elaborate coverup, Lawford removing and destroying all correspondence between Robert and Marilyn, including Marilyn's suicide note, and Hoover enlisted to have his agents destroy all telephone company records of Robert's phone calls to Marilyn over the previous months.

Summers's account made good copy, especially as it tied in with an even darker tale of Bureau political blackmail, but no part of the story is substantiated by the FBI files Summers obtained. The heavily censored documents released to Summers do not even suggest an interest on Hoover's part in a Kennedy-Monroe connection — with two exceptions: an 8 July 1964 Hoover memo to Robert Kennedy reporting an allegation by right-wing author Frank Capell regarding a Monroe-Robert Kennedy affair, and a 13 March 1967 blind memo reporting a Bureau informant's unsubstantiated allegation that Robert was present at Monroe's death.

Had either Kennedy been involved in an affair with Marilyn Monroe and, furthermore, had Robert contacted Hoover to have the FBI retrieve telephone company records of his calls to Monroe, Hoover would have been apprised of the former situation and would have created a written record of such a sensitive request as the latter, both to protect himself and the Bureau and to increase his political leverage. Hoover's Official and Confidential File contains no memorandum recording such a request, which he would not have hesitated to use at three critical times: in 1964, when seeking to convince President Johnson of Kennedy's supposed disloyalty; in early 1966, when a Senate subcommittee chaired by Senator Edward Long initiated an inquiry into Justice Department wiretapping and bugging practices during Robert Kennedy's tenure as attorney general; and in the summer of 1966, when Hoover sought to enlist Johnson's assistance in containing the potential damage to his and the Bureau's reputation during the Fred Black case (discussed in detail in Chapter Fourteen).

In neither 1964 nor the summer of 1966 did Hoover brief President Johnson on the matter; nor did he exploit the opportunity to do so posed by an inquiry from the Long Subcommittee counsel, Bernard Fensterwald. In January

414

1966 Fensterwald asked 'whether or not former Attorney General Kennedy had ever requested the FBI to place a microphone on matters strictly pertaining to politics.' Advising Fensterwald that 'Kennedy had not had the nerve to do this,' Hoover's aides added that 'Hoover would have tendered his resignation immediately had Kennedy attempted to force the FBI to do such a reprehensible thing.' In view of the Long Subcommittee's and Hoover's shared interest in discrediting Kennedy's public protestations of his ignorance of the scope of FBI wiretapping and bugging practices, it is inconceivable that Hoover would not have availed himself of this opportunity to drop the Kennedy cover-up bombshell.

Hoover did not because he could not. Indeed, the only memo he maintained in his office on rumored indiscretions of the attorney general involved Robert's alleged El Paso romance. Hoover's massive office folder on John Kennedy, moreover, contains no reference to any affair between the president and Monroe – despite the frequent rumors about one. As far as J. Edgar Hoover was concerned, it is clear, there was no Kennedy-Monroe affair, and therefore no blackmailing the Kennedys on that score.

Nevertheless, the Director's curiosity about the Kennedys bordered on the obsessive and was altogether exceptional; there are no comparable Hoover office files for any other president. (Hoover's office file on Richard Nixon, for example, contains only documents relating to Nixon's failure to be appointed an FBI agent when he applied to the Bureau after graduating from Duke University Law School in 1937.)

In addition to documents reporting derogatory personal information about John Kennedy, Hoover also maintained in his office copies of numerous published pamphlets, news stories, and letters from right-wing activists accusing Kennedy of disloyalty. But why? Was Hoover so threatened by John Kennedy's election? Was he fearful that Kennedy might not keep him on as FBI Director, particularly after he reached the mandatory retirement age of seventy in 1965? Was he, like other radical conservatives, convinced that Kennedy was a subversive and thus that his presidency had to be neutralized to prevent him from reshaping national policy in the internal security area? Hoover's office files on Kennedy offer no definite answers to these questions. But given the scope and nature of information he could and did call upon – the FBI's case files on the president's father, Joseph, for example, reached the staggering number of 343 – the John Kennedy files hint strongly at the intention to blackmail.

Hoover's collection of information on John Kennedy dated from the senator's strong bid for the vice presidential nomination at the Democratic convention in 1956. In May 1957, for instance, Hoover was briefed on a 'rumor circulating in New York' that the *New York Times* Washington bureau chief, Arthur Krock, 'actually wrote Senator Kennedy's book *Profiles in Courage,* which was on the best seller list for more than a year . . . and which received the Pulitzer Prize.' Hoover's aide, Louis Nichols, had picked up this rumor from the Hearst syndicated columnist George Sokolsky, who also disclosed that a 'group of New York people were working on this trying to get it verified' with the intention of charging fraud on the day the Pulitzer was awarded. Although the rumor proved to be groundless, Hoover included this memo as one of the earliest entries in his Kennedy file.

The Director was soon alerted to another potentially damaging piece of information – namely, that Senator Kennedy, during a speaking engagement in Tucson, had attended church services with Gus Battaglia, an alleged 'top hoodlum.' Later that same year, 1958, this time at the direction of the Justice Department's Civil Rights Division, the FBI investigated whether Kennedy's recent speech on behalf of a Democratic congressional candidate in Michigan, carried over six radio stations and sponsored by a local automobile dealer, violated a federal law prohibiting private corporations from contributing to candidates for federal office. (In this case Hoover alerted Kennedy to the initiation of the investigation. Kennedy expressed his gratitude 'at being informed and greatly appreciated the Director's thinking of him.')

In March 1960 Hoover learned from one of the New Orleans field office's informers in the organized crime field that Joseph Fischetti and 'other unidentified hoodlums are financially supporting and actively endeavoring to secure the nomination for the Presidency as [D]emocratic candidate, Senator JOHN F. KENNEDY.' The informer's evidence to support this allegation was that Frank Sinatra 'is going to campaign for KENNEDY in several of the primaries . . . SINATRA is a nephew of JOE FISCHETTI. SINATRA is only booked to appear after clearance is obtained with FISCHETTI.' The informer decided to report this information, he claimed, after learning that Sinatra's assistance was intended to ensure that Fischetti 'and other hoodlums will have an entre [sic] to Kennedy.'

This informer further aroused Hoover's interest by declaring that during a visit to Miami, where Fischetti and Meyer Lansky operated:

He had occasion to overhear a conversation which indicated that Senator KENNEDY had been compromised with a woman in Las Vegas . . . [and that] when Senator KENNEDY was in Miami, Fla., an airline hostess . . . was sent to visit Sen. KENNEDY. [The FBI informer] stated that he learned this from an airline hostess whom . . . he declined to identify.

Thus apprised, Hoover ordered the New Orleans office to press its informer for evidence to support these allegations. The resulting discreet inquiry failed to substantiate them, as the New Orleans SAC learned only that there was no way to check the accuracy of this information. He reported that the FBI's informer believed the information to be correct and was concerned lest 'a pawn of the hoodlum element such as SINATRA have access to the White House.' Conceding that these allegations were 'to a great extent non-specific,' the New Orleans SAC claimed to have brought them to Hoover's attention 'in view of the prominence of Senator KENNEDY.' He promised Hoover to follow the matter 'closely to assure that any additional information received by [the informer] is made available.' Hoover did not brief Kennedy about these allegations.

These reports show only that Hoover was the recipient of information obtained by his agents during the course of legitimate criminal investigations; they raise questions about Kennedy's associations but do not confirm any intent on Hoover's part to blackmail or to use the FBI's resources as leverage to retain power. That Hoover *was* in fact so motivated is shown by another category of documents that the Director saw fit to retain in his secret office file – all pertaining to allegations about Kennedy's illicit sexual activities and supposed immorality.

The first of these allegations to come to Hoover's attention did so in 1959, when he received two letters from Mrs. Florence Kater and a compromising photograph allegedly of John Kennedy. Cartha DeLoach, at the time the head of the Crime Records Division, briefed Hoover on this material, describing the letters as containing 'allegations regarding personal immorality on the part of Jack Kennedy.' These allegations had received 'rather widespread distribution,' as Mrs. Kater had sent the letters and photograph to about thirty-five reporters. In her letter, Kater also claimed that Kennedy was seeking to intimidate her because of her discovery and photographing of his illicit sexual activities.

At the time, Kennedy was an influential Democratic senator and the Eisenhower administration was in power – and DeLoach was quick to remind Hoover that a Justice Department official 'some months ago' had 'received from a reliable source information reflecting on Senator Kennedy's sex life. You will recall that we have detailed and substantial information in Bufiles [Bureau files] reflecting that Kennedy carried on an immoral relationship with another man's wife [Inga Arvad] during World War II.' In this case Hoover rejected DeLoach's suggestion to bring 'to the attention of the attorney general [William Rogers] for his information' Kater's letters and the accompanying photo, inasmuch as they had 'apparently received widespread distribution.'

The Kater charges did not end in 1959. In April 1963 Kater wrote to Hoover, with copies to the major newspapers and magazines, claiming to have 'personal knowledge and proof that Miss Pamela Turnure, press secretary to Mrs. John F. Kennedy, had had an illicit sexual relationship with President John F. Kennedy.' Kater's allegation, and photographs supposedly showing Kennedy leaving Turnure's house at 1:00 A.M., were given front page publicity in the *Thunderbolt,* the official publication of the segregationist National States Rights Party. The Birmingham field office immediately forwarded copies of the article and accompanying photographs to Hoover for his attention.

After studying Kater's letter, Hoover decided not to share this material with Attorney General Kennedy and the Kennedy White House. Following publication of the *Thunderbolt* article, however, he sent copies of the periodical by 'courier service' to the president's special assistant, Kenneth O'Donnell, with the notation that another copy was being made available to the attorney general. With their publication, it became possible for Hoover to alert the attorney general and the White House to the story without revealing that he had been collecting and maintaining such information.

A 30 January 1961 report further documents the scope of Hoover's resources and of the FBI's exhaustive approach to derogatory information about President Kennedy. In this report, the FBI's Rome office forwarded to Hoover a copy of an interview with Alicia Purdom published in the Italian weekly *Le Ore* concerning her alleged relationship with John Kennedy in 1951. Purdom claimed that she had been engaged to Kennedy but that the marriage had been vetoed by the Kennedy family because she was a Polish-Jewish refugee. At Hoover's direction, a memo on the *Le Ore* story was sent to Attorney General Robert Kennedy. Hoover at the same time directed that other charges – that Kennedy was a sex pervert and that his wife had had an affair with a New York multimillionaire – be forwarded to the attorney general.

Then, in March and again in July 1962, Hoover learned

of allegations that the president had previously been married to Durie (Kerr) Malcolm. Hoover's responses to these briefings varied. In March, he did not advise the attorney general of the rumor but had his agents investigate it. In July, however, having learned that this allegation was being published, he concluded that it was advisable to forewarn Robert Kennedy.

The attorney general, refusing to be intimidated, acknowledged Hoover's report on the rumor 'being circulated about the first marriage of the President' and admitted knowledge of it but remarked that it was based on erroneous information contained in a Malcolm genealogy. The person who had compiled the genealogy, he continued, was deceased (as was Malcolm); the executor of Malcolm's estate had reviewed her papers, 'and all he found was a newspaper clipping saying the President had gone out with the girl.' Kennedy then added that his deceased older brother Joseph had dated Malcolm and that John had taken her out once.

Taken aback by the attorney general's frankness, Hoover lamely explained that his reason for reporting this information (which, on his order, his agents had painstakingly corroborated by consulting the genealogy) was simply to inform him that 'apparently some individual is sending [this story] out anonymously to people.' His only interest, he told Kennedy, was in ensuring that the attorney general 'be alert to this.'

The attorney general's composure and his request that the FBI monitor and report all rumors, did not dissuade Hoover from using derogatory information as leverage with the Kennedy administration. In the case of the Judith Campbell-Exner affair, Hoover acquired hard evidence that could not be dismissed as rumor. From a wiretap on a California organized crime boss, John Roselli, the FBI intercepted in August 1962 a series of telephone calls from Roselli to Chicago underworld leader Sam Giancana. Courtney Evans briefed Hoover on Roselli's background:

During our investigation of Roselli we picked up information connecting John Roselli with Judith

Campbell who we have determined has been in telephonic contact with Sam Giancana, Chicago gangster and with other underworld figures. In addition, she is the individual who has been in telephonic contact with Evelyn Lincoln, the President's secretary at the White House. The nature of the relationship between Campbell and Mrs. Lincoln is not known. However, one [name deleted], a private investigator of questionable reputation in Los Angeles, has alleged that Judith Campbell at one time had an affair with President Kennedy. The information concerning Campbell's contacts with the President's secretary has been furnished previously to the White House and the Attorney General.

Frank Sinatra had introduced Kennedy to Judith Campbell, an attractive divorcee from an upper-middle-class family, in Las Vegas in February 1960. According to Campbell, they did not have sexual relations until March 1960, when they stayed together in New York City's Plaza Hotel. Thereafter Campbell maintained at least frequent telephonic contact with Kennedy, as White House telephone logs record no fewer than seventy calls from her.

Whether Campbell and the president were having an ongoing affair or not, the Director's knowledge of Campbell's telephone calls to the White House and his personal confrontation of the president with that knowledge on 22 March 1962 only increased his leverage at the White House. Indeed, preparatory to that meeting with the president, Hoover had had his aides prepare a 'restatement of information relating to telephone calls made to the President's Secretary from Judith Campbell's Los Angeles residence' on 7, 10, 13, and 14 November 1961 and 14 February 1962. The restatement conceded ignorance as to the nature of Campbell's relationship with Mrs. Lincoln but reported that an FBI informer 'of questionable reputation' had claimed that 'Campbell [was] the girl who was "shacking up with John Kennedy in the East." '

The President could hardly have failed to be impressed

by the scope of the Director's investigative resources and sources of information — in this case an apparently legitimate wiretap on a powerful organized-crime figure and in the related cases from other evidently legitimate sources. In any event, on the strength of Hoover's briefing, Kennedy severed all contacts with both Judith Campbell and Frank Sinatra.

Hoover's subtle use of such information and misinformation as he could obtain helped dissuade the president from challenging the powerful Director. But, at the same time, it quickened his interest in effecting Hoover's retirement — mandatory once the Director reached the age of seventy in January 1965. Like so many other things on Kennedy's agenda, however, Hoover's retirement was contingent on the president's re-election,[8] which, with the passage of time, seemed increasingly likely, for several reasons.

Despite the resistance of a conservative Republican and southern Democratic coalition, President Kennedy had succeeded in generating public support for a number of broad-based liberal domestic programs, including tax reform, aid to depressed areas, urban redevelopment, aid to education, and free medical care for the elderly under Social Security. Perhaps most important, with urging from his brother Robert and the enthusiastic support of the nation's liberal and black communities, he had moved toward an activist role in the civil rights struggle, exemplified by his use of federal marshals in desegregation conflicts (used reluctantly by President Eisenhower before him) and by a White House proposal for new civil rights legislation. Partially sobered by his own brinkmanship in negotiations with Soviet Premier Nikita Khrushchev over removing Soviet missiles from Cuba, the youthful president shifted his emphasis to promoting improved U.S.-Soviet relations, leading to the 1963 treaty outlawing nuclear tests in the atmosphere. The ensuing relaxation of Cold War tensions enhanced the President's popularity and contributed as well to a more liberal political climate, and, after the murder of four young black children in a church bombing in Birmingham, Alabama, the nation appeared poised to break the resistance to integration in the South.

The evolving picture made Hoover seem increasingly anachronistic. The Director had enunciated the FBI's policy on federal civil rights violations in 1946, and a 1961 report of the Civil Rights Commission summarized his approach. The report laid out the background of the Bureau's foot-dragging performance, quoting in full Hoover's letter to the attorney general expressing his resolve to withdraw from the civil rights field altogether rather than continue on the present course. The Bureau, Hoover protested, was 'expending a considerable amount of manpower' investigating alleged crimes in the South 'in which there cannot conceivably be any violation of a Federal statute.' In such cases, he observed, the Bureau became burdened 'in the public mind and in the press with the responsibility' for their solution, and this adversely affected its image. Although Hoover did not 'condone the type of activities' involved in such cases, he felt that jurisdiction properly belonged 'in State Courts.' In conclusion, the Director argued that 'it is a mistake for the Department to accept for investigation so many of these cases in which . . . there is no possibility of federal prosecutive action and in which the Bureau and the Department are merely assessed in the public mind with a responsibility which is neither discharged nor executed.'

Hoover's anxiety about what he regarded as Kennedy's radical departures meanwhile led him to cement his relations with his old friend, the free-wheeling Lyndon Johnson.[9] Johnson, like Kennedy, was the subject of bureau reports of compromising activities, but in Johnson's case Hoover assumed a more protective stance, seeking to curry favor with the Texan by containing potentially damaging allegations.

The Director's professional interest in the former Senate majority leader dated from 1956, when he learned of voting irregularities in that year's Texas primary. This discovery was neither innocent nor calculated to exert leverage at that time, for in this instance as in another involving the powerful legislator, the Director was willing to service the political interests of the Eisenhower White House, which at that time found the Democratic majority leader extremely helpful in advancing the president's legislative program.

In the first instance, Hoover learned that the dominant faction in Laredo, known as the Independent Club, had controlled elections in the adjoining counties by systematically purchasing votes by paying poll taxes, the cost financed through a levy on the salaries of local government officials. Hoover reported this to the Justice Department, which declined to take action because the alleged abuse violated only state laws, which were not enforced. Still, Hoover urged his agents to 'follow' local developments. This too proved futile, however, because, as the FBI's informer explained, Senator Johnson 'considers Laredo his private county.' Should the FBI initiate any inquiry in Laredo, 'Johnson would immediately have that investigation stopped. [The informer] said that if an FBI Agent talked to any official of the Independent Party or checked any record at the Clerk's Office regarding alleged irregularities, that Mr. Johnson would be advised of this matter within six hours and would have the investigation stopped.'[10]

The freewheeling behavior that had characterized Johnson's checkered career did not change with his elevation to the vice presidency, although his relations with Hoover did. The vice president's continued dealings with a host of unsavory characters threatened to end his political life, and his vulnerability played directly into Hoover's hands. For the Director kept in his office file an ample stack of reports on Johnson's questionable activities and associations.

What precisely Hoover had on the vice president is still unknown, as the FBI withheld some of these reports (claiming that their release would violate Johnson's privacy rights) and heavily censored those that were released, again on personal privacy grounds. But it is clear that one of the latter concerns Johnson's publicized appearance, 'attended also by numerous prominent personages,' at the Carousel Motel in North Ocean City, Maryland, in October 1962. (Johnson's former aide Bobby Baker used the Carousel to

424

entertain prominent businessmen and congressmen, together with call girls.)[11]

In response to this report, alleging immoral activities and 'hoodlum interests,' Hoover demanded that the Bureau's source be contacted to ascertain the accuracy of the allegations. Thereupon 'appropriate discreet inquiries through logical sources' were conducted by the Baltimore field office, and Hoover was 'promptly advised' of information it had learned. But the information itself again was withheld from the authors.

Hoover also carefully followed the FBI's investigation into the mysterious death of Henry Marshall, an Agriculture Department official who had initiated an investigation resulting in the indictment of another Johnson associate, Texas businessman Billie Sol Estes, for manipulating federal farm support programs. Once again, the information Hoover obtained about Estes's activities and relations with Johnson is still unknown – the extensive documentation in Hoover's file was withheld in its entirety.

The Estes matter began to plague Johnson in 1962, when a story in a Pecos, Texas, weekly newspaper raised questions about the vice president's relations with Texas gubernatorial candidate John Connally and alleged that Johnson had lent Estes $5 million. Fearing serious, perhaps irreparable damage to his political career, the more so because CBS had picked up the local news story, Johnson immediately contacted Hoover to ask 'if the Bureau could talk to the editor of the weekly newspaper in Pecos, Texas.' Johnson identified the editor by name and said that 'people with that paper have played this [incriminating] tape to the [investigative reporter] for CBS.'

Keenly interested in being helpful, Hoover promised to 'get started on it right away.' Johnson and Hoover then discussed how best this could be done, the vice president inquiring 'what to do on these things except to call DeLoach.' 'That was the thing to do,' Hoover replied, and DeLoach apparently defanged the editor. Johnson also agreed that in the future 'he would have his assistant, Walter Jenkins, get in touch with Mr. DeLoach in such instances.'

Now assured of Hoover's support, and having devised secure means for safeguarding Hoover's assistance, Jenkins, on learning that Congressman Bill Cramer (R.-Fla.) was preparing impeachment proceedings based on the vice president's and Mrs. Johnson's alleged association with Estes in two grain storage operations in Texas, asked DeLoach to have the FBI 'interview Cramer immediately.' Emphasizing that Hoover 'would, of course, want to be of every possible assistance to the Vice President,' DeLoach recommended that 'in [sic] this particular occasion it might be better if we received the information from a third party rather than from the Vice President's office.' Because the request involved a member of Congress (Cramer) and a subsequent congressional inquiry might uncover Johnson's initiative, Jenkins agreed.

The next morning Thomas Corcoran, the lobbyist, contacted DeLoach to report having learned that Cramer planned to initiate impeachment proceedings against the vice president. DeLoach thereupon briefed Hoover, recommending that Cramer be 'immediately' interviewed as a 'legitimate responsibility in the current Estes investigation.' Hoover, however, perceiving the threat of a major congressional investigation, rejected the recommendation and instead ordered his aides to clear the matter with Attorney General Kennedy before approaching Cramer. While willing to be of discreet assistance to the vice president, Hoover had concluded that the FBI 'should *keep out of this completely*. We have already checked into the story told by Cramer & found it false; Cramer himself is a loud-mouth; Corcoran is the devious "Tommy." ' Jenkins was immediately advised of the Director's decision.

Undaunted, Jenkins recontacted DeLoach later that month to convey the vice president's request for a meeting to discuss an editorial in *Farm and Ranch Magazine*. At the ensuing meeting approved by Hoover, Johnson denounced 'the false allegations [about his financial relations with Billie Sol Estes] made in the editorial,' offered evidence to challenge the allegations, and requested that Hoover have 'FBI Agents interview the editor of this magazine, Mr. Tom

Anderson, to ascertain if Anderson had any basis for making such false allegations.' DeLoach assured Johnson that 'the Director would want this done immediately,' and the vice president expressed his 'appreciation.'

Hoover thereupon referred the matter to the FBI's General Investigative Division 'for appropriate action,' demanding that it report back to 'the Vice President's office the results of the interview.' At the same time, Hoover recognized President Kennedy's political interest in the matter and therefore briefed Attorney General Kennedy on Johnson's complaint and on the information the FBI had uncovered on the vice president's relationship with Estes.

Hoover's quiet helpfulness only encouraged Johnson to resort to the Bureau to silence his detractors, who, given his sleazy associates and wheeler-dealer style of operating, were legion. Accordingly, the vice president was soon back at Hoover's doorstep, and the services went on.

Then, just as Johnson appeared to have contained the Estes affair, details of his relationship with Bobby Baker surfaced again, but in a more ominous way. In October 1963 Hoover briefed Attorney General Kennedy on the matter of Ellen Rometsch, an East German alien resident and one of six women who were 'involved [with] and all tie[d] in with Bobby Baker.' Rometsch and these five alleged prostitutes, Hoover reported, frequented Baker's house in Washington, visited the Quorum Club (which Hoover described as having been 'formed by Bobby Baker, who was secretary of it, and . . . a kind of place where Senators and Congressmen go'), and had appeared at Baker's office numerous times. Hoover's briefing worried the attorney general, who expressed concern that should Senator John Williams (R.-Del.) learn of Rometsch's role and East German origin, he could exploit the 'security angle.' Hoover accordingly recommended that Rometsch be denied a visa to re-enter the United States. Kennedy agreed with this containment strategy and promised to brief the president. The accompanying FBI reports on the Rometsch case and its relationship to Johnson, if any, have been withheld in their entirety on claimed personal privacy grounds.

More than willing to assist the vice president, Hoover nevertheless by 1963 had recognized the need to keep the president fully informed about Johnson's associations, further intensifying the White House's political worries. By 1963 the vice president's problems were driving a wedge between him and senior White House aides, who welcomed this situation as an opportunity to drop Johnson or at least to disseminate rumors of a 'dump Johnson' strategy for 1964. The president, however, had not joined this effort and in fact told Ben Bradlee of *Newsweek* on 22 October 1963 that the idea 'was preposterous on the face of it,' as the Democrats needed to carry Texas to win. Such disclaimers, however, failed to convince the vice president, who confided his fears to Hoover.

The lack of trust itself might have become serious enough to tear up the ticket had not fate in the guise of an assassin altered the course of history. Concerned about a serious schism in the Texas Democratic party, the president and Johnson paid a good-will visit to Dallas on 22 November. And there, in a sequence of events that may never become clear, Kennedy was shot and killed while riding through the city in a motorcade. Johnson, who was riding in a car behind the president's, was sworn into office about an hour after Kennedy's death and, seizing his chance for greatness, promptly dedicated himself to shepherding the late president's legislative proposals into law.

Notes to Chapter Thirteen

1. Between 1961 and 1963, for instance, the president had the FBI investigate the sources of leaked classified information (including wiretapping *Newsweek* reporter Lloyd Norman and *New York Times* military correspondent Hanson Baldwin) and individuals lobbying for legislation to increase the sugar quota of the Dominican Republic (including wiretapping three Agriculture Department officials, the secretary to House Agriculture Committee Chairman Harold Cooley, and a lawyer registered as

a lobbyist for the Dominican Republic, and bugging Congressman Cooley's hotel room in New York City after the Bureau learned of his planned meeting with representatives of the Dominican government). At the time, the Kennedy administration was seeking to use economic pressure to force the Trujillo government to make desired political reforms, and thus sought the defeat of the proposed quota. (Athan Theoharis, *Spying* on *Americans* [Philadelphia: Temple University Press, 1978], pp. 167-69.) The resort to the Bureau for assistance seems not to have caused a qualm.

2. James M. McCarthy, a Chicago businessman, recalls the outrage that was felt within the business community:

'In June 1962 I was working for National Patent Development Corporation, a company that at that time held licenses for Soviet processes in which American firms were interested. One such company, National Steel, was considering the Soviet continuous-casting process. For that purpose, two of its executives arranged to visit the USSR. One was a Mr. Williams Hill, Vice President, Engineering . . .

'I met both of these gentlemen in Moscow in June . . . Among other things, Mr. Hill talked about President Kennedy's operation the previous April that forced the major steel companies to rescind a hike in prices they had planned. The President used the FBI in this operation, routing people out of bed, etc., to try and determine if there'd been any collusion on the part of the steel companies in raising the prices. Mr. Hill was irate about Kennedy's use of the FBI for this purpose, and said that when he was in Washington, he'd complained to Mr. Hoover. According to Hill, Mr. Hoover responded: "I have to do what Bobby Kennedy tells me to do." ' (Letter, James M. McCarthy to Cox, 20 September 1984).

3. The Director had not abandoned the cause of anti-Communism. Despite his earlier ambivalence about honoring some requests for assistance by HUAC members and staff, fearing that the committee might hamper FBI operations, he quickly rallied to HUAC's defense when alerted to the creation in 1960 of the National Committee to Abolish HUAC (NCAHUAC). Hoover ordered an 'expedited' investigation of NCAHUAC and its officials and preparation of detailed memoranda 'suitable for dissemination.' Then he ordered DeLoach to brief the FBI's 'sources at' the committee and his 'contacts' in the media about NCAHUAC's background and plans. Adopting the same aggressive tactics employed under the various COINTELPROs,

FBI officials thereafter used their contacts on college campuses to prevent NCAHUAC representatives from speaking and, in one case, arranged to station a 'friendly newspaperman' at the entrance to a Washington church where a NCAHUAC official was to speak, the theory being that this 'inquiring reporter's' request for names and addresses might dissuade those entering the church from attending the meeting. (Kenneth O'Reilly, *Hoover and the Un-Americans: The FBI, HUAC, and the Red Menace* [Philadelphia: Temple University Press, 1983], pp. 259-70.)

4. Conflicting accounts about Hoover's office files led the Department of Justice in July 1975 to direct the FBI to investigate whether 'any official files were removed from Mr. Hoover's office to his residence following his death and may have been subsequently removed from that address following the death of Clyde A. Tolson.' The 'inquiry' concluded that no 'official files' had been removed but that Helen Gandy *had* removed approximately thirty-five cabinet drawers of Hoover's 'personal correspondence,' which she then destroyed after ascertaining that they contained no official documents. Gandy admitted to having also removed two three-drawer cabinets and two two-drawer cabinets containing folders pertaining to Hoover's 'personal business affairs.' These cabinets – their contents intact – were preserved in the basement of Hoover's home until deposited at the Hoover Foundation at Valley Forge.

Gandy's testimony on the amount of material removed from Hoover's office was contradicted by the truck driver assigned to transport it. He remembered a total of '20 to 25 file cabinets,' maintained that these cabinets were full, and claimed that during transit one of the cabinets had opened, allowing him to observe 'light colored folders inside with the contents of each folder roughly one inch thick.' Addressing this discrepancy, the department concluded that the driver had a 'jumbled recollection of the facts due to the passage of over three years since Mr. Hoover's death,' basing its conclusion on the fact that all other individuals who were interviewed (including Hoover's housekeeper and caretaker as well as other FBI employees) disputed the larger number. In this instance, the inquiry report conceded, the discrepancy could not be resolved, as any records of the truck's trip(s) 'were destroyed [by the FBI] in the normal course of business.' (U.S. Senate Select Committee on Intelligence Activities, *Hearings* on *FBI, vol.* 6 [94th Cong., 1st sess., 1975], pp. 351-56; U.S. House Subcommittee on Government Information, Hearings on Inquiry into Destruction of Former FBI Director Hoover's Files and FBI Record Keeping [94th Cong., 1st sess., 1975], p. 101.)

5. In February 1962 the head of the FBI's Los Angeles field office personally advised Hoover of the current status of the Bureau's investigation of a group of prostitutes recently arrested by the Los Angeles Police Department. He reported having learned that one of the madams had sent 'prostitutes to [names deleted, but John Kennedy and Frank Sinatra], after which she received telephone calls from these two individuals to send other girls to their associates' and that this had occurred 'just prior to the opening day of the Democratic Convention in 1960.' When Courtney Evans, Hoover's liaison to Attorney General Robert Kennedy, later informed the attorney general of these 'allegations,' he reported back that Kennedy was 'most appreciative' of the briefing. (Memo, Evans to Belmont, 12 February 1962; Memo, General Investigative Division, 9 February 1962; Airtel, SAC Los Angeles, to Hoover, 7 February 1962, all in [name deleted] et al., White Slave Traffic Act folder, Folder no. 4, Hoover O & C.)

6. Hoover in fact had his aides monitor press reports on Kennedy's campaign closely and thus soon learned of the candidate's August 1960 comment that if elected president he intended to retain Hoover as Director and 'have the FBI maintain its present scope of operations.'

7. Jones's reference to Kennedy's wartime affair with Arvad triggered Hoover's order to have the Arvad folder transferred to his office file.

8. According to former attorney general Ramsey Clark, who served in the Justice Department under both Kennedy and Johnson, it was 'pretty clear that Kennedy would *not* have extended Hoover.' (Clark interview.)

9. Johnson had customarily checked with Hoover prior to appointing individuals to key positions on his Senate staff or his radio and television stations in Texas. Briefed, for example, on the FBI's derogatory political information on radio humorist John Henry Faulk, Johnson withdrew his offer to Faulk to head the public affairs division of his Texas Broadcasting Corporation. (Memo, Nichols to Tolson, 18 April 1955, FBI 100-181329-34; Memo, Jones to Nichols, 15 April 1955, FBI 100-181329-33; Memo, SAC New York to Hoover, 2 May 1955, FBI 100-181329-36; Memo, SAC New York to Hoover, 7 June 1955, FBI 100-181329-36; Interviews with John Henry Faulk [14 February 1984] and former Johnson press secretary George Reedy [29 October 1984].)

10. Hoover did, however, service another less risky Eisenhower administration request involving Johnson. In December 1956 Attorney General Brownell asked the Director whether the FBI had investigated Johnson's and his wife's acquisition of radio station KTBC in Austin, Texas, and in particular whether Elliott Roosevelt had a financial interest in the corporation. Since Brownell had not directly authorized an investigation of Johnson, Hoover merely checked FBI files and reported back that there was no record that the FBI had ever conducted an inquiry. Alerted to the possibility of impropriety on Johnson's part, Hoover soon learned of the Internal Revenue Service's interest in this matter. Briefed on the IRS 'inquiry,' Hoover discovered that 'it is possible that local [IRS] field auditors looked into either the corporation or the Johnsons' tax affairs and this fact would not be known at [IRS's] National Headquarters . . . In order to conduct such an inquiry discreetly, the request would have to come from the headquarters under some subterfuge, in view of the close political ties of all employees of the local Internal Revenue Service with persons of local political prominence. Such a discreet inquiry has not been made. Our contact is not available today and if a local discreet contact is desired, it can be initiated in the event it meets with your [Hoover's] approval, just as soon as the [FBI] liaison contact [with IRS] is available . . . even though headquarters, namely Washington, may initiate a discreet request, in view of the lack of centralized control on the part of Internal Revenue, it is quite probable any inquiry would get back to the Johnsons if it were made on the local level.' FBI agents did make a 'discreet check of our sources at Internal Revenue,' discovering that the IRS was not investigating the LBJ company. On learning this, Hoover agreed that 'no further inquiries are being made concerning this matter at this time.' He nevertheless noted and filed in his office a record of these allegations. (Senator Lyndon B. Johnson Folder, Folder no. 22, Hoover O & C.)

11. Baker was subsequently convicted of tax evasion and fraud in connection with alleged influence peddling.

CHAPTER FOURTEEN

(1964–1968)
YEARS OF CRISIS

ALTHOUGH HOOVER had willingly serviced the partisan and policy interests of every president since Herbert Hoover (inclusive), his services to President Johnson were unique in their scope and nature. For one thing, Johnson did not hesitate to turn to Hoover for information about his administration's critics (which information, for ideological as well as strategic reasons, Hoover generously gave); for another, Johnson, like Hoover, harbored an inordinate interest in derogatory personal information – and, like Hoover, insisted that his requests for such information and the FBI's submissions of it be kept strictly confidential. In that sense, the two men were made for each other.

Moreover, President Johnson, for all of his seeming assurance and legislative legerdemain – most of Kennedy's stalled domestic measures were enacted into law in less than a year – remained a very insecure man in a number of ways, of which most played directly into Hoover's hands. Not for the first time had an accident of history benefited the wily Director, although, to be sure, he was ready when his chance came.

One of Johnson's first concerns,[1] repeatedly raised in his various conversations with Assistant Director DeLoach, who swiftly succeeded Courtney Evans as Hoover's White House liaison, was the 'continued employment' of individuals associated with Robert Kennedy, who stayed on as attorney general until the summer of 1964 and was generally regarded as heir to the Kennedy legacy.[2] Hoover both catered to and sustained Johnson's fears – for his own reasons.

The Director first learned of this opportunity in January 1964, following DeLoach's briefing on a recent meeting with

Walter Jenkins concerning an individual described by Jenkins as 'strictly Bobby Kennedy's boy and [one] that Kennedy had been protecting . . . all along.' 'As a matter of "strict confidence,"' Jenkins advised, Johnson 'was not yet quite ready to take on Bobby, however, [name deleted but apparently Paul Corbin][3] would definitely be eased out in the near future when the time was right.' Hoover unhesitatingly queried: 'Have we furnished Jenkins a memo on [name deleted]?' On Hoover's order DeLoach furnished the memo to Jenkins that same day.

Then, on 10 February, Hoover learned about a recent conversation between Richard Held, the head of the Minneapolis field office, and U.S. Attorney Miles Lord. Describing Lord as 'a very good friend of the Minneapolis office, a staunch supporter of the FBI, and an ardent admirer of you [Hoover],' Held reported on Lord's recent visit 'with a group of individuals in the Justice Department whom [Lord] described as the "Kennedy crowd." ' These individuals had 'openly discussed how they were doing everything they could to stir up the "Bobby Baker mess," with the avowed purpose of trying to embarrass the President in every way possible' and 'hoped to create a situation whereby the President would be forced to pick the Attorney General, Robert Kennedy, as his running mate in order to assure his re-election.' According to Lord, 'prior to the assassination of President Kennedy, [this group] had intended to use the Baker issue as a means of freezing Mr. Johnson out as Vice President, . . . [and had] openly criticized you and the FBI, and indicated that they would like to break up the excellent relationship that exists between you and President Johnson.'

Held had failed to extract from Lord precise details of these criticisms or the identities of members of the group. Indeed, Lord had admitted that he 'had heard nothing that would directly connect the Attorney General with the reported plans of this group.' Inasmuch as these Justice Department officials were all close to the attorney general, however, Lord had concluded that 'they could possibly be repeating or expressing his views.' On the other hand, as

Lord was an acquaintance of Senator Hubert Humphrey and was 'indebted' to him for his present position, Held observed, the U.S. attorney might have simply repeated information picked up at Senator Humphrey's office in view of Humphrey's 'acknowledged interest himself in the possibility of becoming Vice President.' Nevertheless, because of the 'alleged remarks about [Hoover] and the Bureau,' Held had seen fit to communicate them to Hoover, 'as vague as they are.'

Vague though they were, Hoover immediately alerted Johnson to these allegations, shrewdly advising the president that Kennedy's assistants at the department were holding secret meetings to try to play up the Bobby Baker case 'in order to cause you embarrassment so that you'll have to take the Attorney General on the ticket.'

Ironically, in this instance Hoover's neglect to notify the attorney general did not go unnoticed. From his own sources in the White House, Kennedy soon learned about the Director's attempt to curry favor at his expense. Meeting with DeLoach on 6 March 1964, Edwin Guthman, Kennedy's press officer, began by complaining about Hoover's abrupt severing of his relations with the attorney general following President Kennedy's assassination. Guthman rejected DeLoach's explanation that Johnson and Hoover had been close friends for years, adding, according to DeLoach's account to Hoover, that Kennedy had 'received information indicating that you and I had furnished furnished either files or memoranda of a derogatory nature concerning White House employees close to the Attorney General, to the President' and 'had voluntarily done this in order to get the Attorney General's "friends" removed from office.' Disclosing his full knowledge of the affair, Guthman pinpointed Lord's role — namely, that he 'allegedly had overheard several of the Attorney General's closest aides conspiring to embarrass President Johnson by "blowing up" the Bobby Baker case' and 'also allegedly had overheard these same aides making derogatory remarks concerning [Hoover] and the FBI.' On returning to Minneapolis, Guthman continued, Lord had then briefed FBI personnel at the Minneapolis office on these alleged remarks, and 'you [Hoover] then prepared a letter to the President concerning this matter.' Guthman concluded that 'the "close aides" to the Attorney General apparently felt that there was a campaign on in the FBI to embarrass the Attorney General by "carrying tales" to the President.'

DeLoach brazenly denied these allegations, all of which were true, and, as he informed Hoover, pressed Guthman for his source in the White House (who had obviously read Hoover's report). Guthman refused to identify the individual so that he could be questioned about these rumors, admitting only that the attorney general had obtained this information 'from a source either in the White House or somewhere else' who was 'a rather substantial source.'

DeLoach withstood this challenge, for, as his memo to Hoover continued:

> Obviously there has been a bad leak either in the White House or at FBI Headquarters. With your permission, I showed Jenkins, and he showed the President, the letter from the SAC in Minneapolis, quoting U.S. Attorney Miles A. Lord concerning the statements he had obviously heard while at the Department of Justice derogatory to President Johnson and you. Jenkins told me that the President was shocked over this matter.
>
> The second allegation specifically concerns the two memoranda we furnished the President regarding [names deleted] after which both men were fired. These memoranda were specifically furnished at the direction of the President. Jenkins told me later in confidence, as I reported to you in blind memoranda, that the Attorney General was extremely shaken by the dismissals of [names deleted]. He obviously expected to use these men in the campaign for his Vice Presidency.[4]

Hoover immediately ordered DeLoach to inform Jenkins 'in strict confidence that these matters have been brought to our attention and that obviously there is a "leak" somewhere.' He himself would 'mention this to the President' at their forthcoming luncheon meeting.

Then, on 20 March, Hoover learned that Guthman had again raised this matter, and, further, that Deputy Attorney General Nicholas Katzenbach had also done so in his meetings with Courtney Evans (who continued as Hoover's liaison with Robert Kennedy and his staff). Surmising that Katzenbach's and Guthman's probing contacts 'must be predicated upon some inquiry from the Attorney General,' DeLoach added, 'Obviously neither Guthman, Katzenbach or the Attorney General desire [sic] to reveal [name deleted but apparently Richard Goodwin, a Kennedy loyalist who remained as a speechwriter for Johnson] as their source of information at the White House. They know that to confirm our suspicion in this regard would mean that the President would have proof that [name deleted] has not been loyal to him.'

Reacting to this information, Hoover ordered, 'If Guthman, Katzenbach or anyone else brings this up again they should be told I have instructed that if they seek any information to take it up with me as I am fed up on the malicious lies & calumnies they have circulated.' Hoover's boldness in denying that he had briefed the White House – he knew that Kennedy could not confront him without disclosing his source there – utterly defeated the attorney general's efforts to bring his ostensible subordinate into line. And at the same time Hoover had won favor with the president.

In return, Johnson the next month granted Hoover an 'indefinite' reprieve from the sentence Hoover dreaded most: retirement. On 8 May Johnson issued an executive order waiving mandatory retirement for Hoover at age seventy. But, although he was entirely willing to keep Hoover on as Director, Johnson's qualified extension required Hoover to continue to curry favor and, furthermore, reduced whatever leverage Hoover might have commanded from his Johnson dossier. As a result, Hoover, having been allowed to continue as Director at the sole discretion of the president, was in no position to resist Johnson's blatantly political request to assign a special FBI squad to monitor the 1964 Democratic National Convention in Atlantic City the following August.

Determined to ensure that a unified Democratic party would emerge from the convention, Johnson sought to contain the efforts of civil rights activists to force the convention to adopt a more militant civil rights plank and to challenge the credentials of the segregationist delegation from Mississippi. Because these divisions could harm his electoral prospects, Johnson sought to minimize them and this, in turn, required that he obtain advance information about the strategies of the activists. To effect this, Hoover dispatched a special thirty-man squad of FBI agents, under DeLoach's direction, to the convention for the period from 22 to 29 August, which, 'by means of informant coverage, by use of various confidential techniques [a wiretap on Martin Luther King, Jr.'s, hotel room and a bug installed in the local headquarters of the Student Nonviolent Coordinating Committee], by infiltration of key groups through use of undercover agents, and through utilization of agents using appropriate cover as reporters, . . . [kept] the White House fully apprised of all major developments.'

In the course of informing Johnson, DeLoach also persuaded White House aides Bill Moyers, Walter Jenkins, and Clifton Carter to 'make major changes in controlling admissions into the Convention Hall and thereby preclude infiltration of the illegal Mississippi Freedom Democratic Party (MFDP) delegates in large numbers into the space reserved for the regular Mississippi delegates. Through our counterintelligence efforts,' he reported to Hoover, 'Jenkins, et al., were able to advise the President in advance regarding major plans of the MFDP delegates. The White House considered this of prime importance.'

Throughout the convention, DeLoach's squad submitted daily reports to the White House on 'minute by minute developments.' These reports enabled Moyers and Jenkins to 'make spot decisions and to adjust convention plans to meet potential problems before serious trouble developed.' In addition, the squad alerted Johnson's aides to any

438

developments of possible interest to 'insure that there was nothing which would "embarrass the President." ' And DeLoach's squad brought with them to Atlantic City 'blind memoranda' on dissident groups and their leaders and thus were able to provide Jenkins with information about particular activists 'within 15 minutes of the request.' Jenkins, elated over this timely assistance, described it as of 'vital importance to their operation.'

Impressed by DeLoach's leadership and by the Johnson White House's enthusiastic appreciation, Hoover exultantly ordered that 'DeLoach should receive a meritorious award.' An agent who had served on DeLoach's squad later reported that 'it was obvious that DeLoach wanted to impress Jenkins and Moyers with the Bureau's ability to develop information which would be of interest to them.' Nor had DeLoach fallen short in this regard. Indeed, Jenkins personally called Hoover to report the president's opinion that 'the job the Bureau had done in Atlantic City was one of the finest the President had ever seen.' Moyers added his own private praise, effusively thanking DeLoach for the FBI's assistance. In reply, DeLoach pronounced it 'a pleasure and privilege to be able to be of assistance to the President, and all the boys that were with me felt honored in being selected for the assignment.' Pleased that 'everything worked out well' and that 'we were of assistance to you and Walter [Jenkins],' DeLoach assured Moyers that 'you know you have only to call on us when a similar situation arises.'

Hoover's intelligence service to Johnson was performed, of course, covertly — and, of course, illegally. But while willingly compromising the integrity of the FBI in order to curry favor with the president, Hoover had compromised Johnson too, as the president could no longer afford to challenge Hoover: the Director might retaliate by leaking the records of the Bureau's assistance. The leverage Hoover acquired thereby ensured his continued tenure as Director throughout Johnson's presidency. And this was starkly put to the test before the end of that year.

During a rare press conference with selected Washington newspaperwomen on 18 November 1964, Hoover gave vent to his strongly felt and decidedly controversial prejudices. First, he denounced the recently released report of the Warren Commission on President Kennedy's assassination for its criticism of the FBI's failure to fully brief the Secret Service on alleged presidential assassin Lee Harvey Oswald.[5] (Hoover's remarks dramatized his overreaction to any criticism of the FBI and his tendency to assume that, unlike other federal agencies, the FBI should be shielded from critical scrutiny.) He then savagely attacked Martin Luther King, Jr., on the same score. Dismissing King's charge that the FBI had failed to prosecute civil rights cases because most FBI agents stationed in the South were southerners, Hoover branded King 'the most notorious liar in the country.'

Responding the next day to Hoover's attack, King reiterated his interest in meeting with the Director to discuss civil rights matters and, in a carefully considered comment, attributed Hoover's uncalled-for personal attack to the fact that he 'has apparently faltered under the awesome burden, complexities and responsibilities of his office.' At the same time, leaders of the major civil rights organizations met with Johnson to express their support for King. (The president listened quietly to their protest, but gave no indication of his position.) And, in an editorial entitled 'Time to Retire,' the *New York Times* questioned the wisdom of President Johnson's 8 May executive order. Expressing concern over Hoover's inability to accept legitimate criticism and citing his recent intemperate comments, the *Times* concluded, 'Under the circumstances, it would be wise to let the mandatory provisions of the federal retirement law take effect on Mr. Hoover's 70th birthday.'

Then, in a 24 November speech in Chicago, the embattled Director exacerbated his problems with the civil rights and liberal communities. Defending the FBI's civil rights record, he denounced the criticisms of 'zealots or pressure groups' as having been 'spearheaded at times by Communists and moral degenerates.' Hoover's crude attempt to discredit his critics unleashed a storm of protest from civil rights leaders, who called for his resignation.

440

At this juncture, with Hoover's seventieth birthday five weeks away and his continued tenure as FBI Director resting only on Johnson's executive order, inevitably the question arose whether the president had reconsidered his decision of the previous May.

The issue surfaced during a 28 November press conference in connection with a remark by Hoover that he continued to command the president's support and had been assured that he could remain as Director for the remainder of Johnson's presidency. Johnson was intentionally vague when answering repeated inquiries. On the one hand, he characterized the public disagreement between Hoover and King as a difference between strong-minded individuals and defended their right to freedom of expression. On the other, he refused to confirm that Hoover had his assurance of indefinite tenure, urging reporters to consult the record surrounding the 8 May executive order.

Because that order had extended Hoover's tenure only for 'an indefinite period of time,' Johnson's press conference neither silenced the protests nor resolved the question of Hoover's continuing in office. Forced to respond to a *Newsweek* story, based on reliable White House sources, that the president did in fact plan to replace the Director, White House press secretary George Reedy denied that the president ever 'entertained any such idea' and had 'never heard of such a plan.' Reedy, however, did not substantiate Hoover's claim that he had an assurance of indefinite tenure.

A decidedly insecure Director resolved to take the offensive. First, on Hoover's behalf, Tolson wrote to *Newsweek,* branding its story 'a new low in reporting.' (The story had claimed not only that Johnson intended to replace Hoover, but also that Hoover had placed five agents on the staff of House Appropriations Subcommittee Chairman John Rooney). *Newsweek* in turn insisted that it had based its story on a 'most responsible White House source' and had learned from Justice Department officials about the agents on Rooney's staff.[6] Second, on 4 December Hoover granted a rare interview to proclaim that he felt 'fine' and was in 'better physical condition than I have been in years.

441

I intend to remain active because I don't like the rocking chair life. If I retired, I wouldn't enjoy life very much.' Hoover also defended his earlier comments about King and reiterated his determination to respond to any criticism of the FBI, as it was essential to retain public trust in the Bureau.

In the event, Hoover weathered the storm of November-December 1964 simply because he could continue to command Johnson's support. So long as Johnson failed to rescind his executive order, in part because he had come to rely on the intelligence services Hoover provided and in part because (in his own description) he preferred having 'Hoover inside the tent pissing out rather than outside pissing in,' Hoover's position was secure. And thus it remained throughout Johnson's tenure.

The stage had been set thereby for a new, more brutal attack on King. The assault began in November 1964 when DeLoach offered to Ben Bradlee of *Newsweek* copies of a purported FBI microphone surveillance transcript recording Dr. King's illicit sexual activities. The same information was offered to *Los Angeles Times* Washington bureau chief David Kraslow, with a further titillating description placing King in the midst of a sex orgy. *Chicago Daily News* reporter James McCartney was shown FBI photographs of King leaving a motel with a white woman, the implication being that King had had sexual relations with her. Others who were offered copies of transcripts, photographs, or recordings allegedly detailing King's illicit sexual activities included *New York Times* reporter John Herbers, *Chicago Daily News* columnist Mike Royko, *Atlanta Constitution* editors Ralph McGill and Eugene Patterson, and *Augusta* (Georgia) *Chronicle* reporter Lou Harris.

Hoover's war against King extended far beyond disseminating derogatory personal information, however. Having learned of King's planned meeting with Teamsters' president Jimmy Hoffa and interest in avoiding publicity about this meeting, Hoover ordered an aide 'to alert friendly news media of the meeting once the meeting date is learned so that arrangements can be made for appropriate press coverage of the planned meeting to expose and disrupt it.' Hoover was subsequently advised that the FBI had successfully alerted a *New York Daily News* reporter and a national columnist to the scheduled meeting and that 'in view of publicity in the New York Daily News regarding this proposed meeting, King and his aides had decided that it would be unwise to meet with Hoffa.' Friendly reporters were thereupon alerted to King's imminent trip to Washington so that they could quiz him about the canceled meeting. Advised that this 'counterintelligence aim to thwart King from receiving money from the Teamsters has been quite successful to date,' Hoover proclaimed this 'excellent.'

Like Hoover's office folder on John F. Kennedy, the Martin Luther King, Jr., folder was massive, numbering between 500 and 600 pages. An unspecified number of pages of King's files were withheld in their entirety under Court order of 31 January 1977, requiring the purging of FBI files of 'all known copies of the recorded tapes, and transcripts thereof, resulting from the FBI's microphone surveillance, between 1963 and 1968, of . . . Martin Luther King, Jr.; and all known copies of the tapes, transcripts and logs resulting from the FBI's wiretapping, between 1963 and 1968, of the [Southern Christian Leadership Conference's] offices in Atlanta, Georgia, and New York, New York, the home of Martin Luther King, Jr., and places of public accommodation occupied by Martin Luther King, Jr.' In effect, then, this withholding notice confirms that Hoover maintained in his office the tapes and transcripts produced by the FBI's tapping and bugging of King.

But even purged, Hoover's office file on King records the intensity of the Director's commitment to use the vast resources of the FBI to discredit King and 'remove King from the national picture.' On Hoover's order, for instance, DeLoach met with NAACP leader Roy Wilkins and attempted to persuade Wilkins to convene a meeting of prominent civil rights leaders for the stated purpose of briefing them on the FBI's civil rights activities. DeLoach could then brief them as well, 'on a highly confidential basis,' on the 'security background of King and [phrase deleted, but a reference to King's alleged illicit sexual activities]. The use of a tape, such as contemplated in [Assistant Director William Sullivan's] memorandum, together with a transcript for convenience in following the tape, should be most convincing.'

The tape in question was to be a composite made from the FBI's bugging of King's hotel rooms. Such a tape had been mailed to King's wife, Coretta, the previous month with an accompanying anonymous letter to King.[7] The letter, a copy of which Hoover maintained in his office file, called King 'a colossal fraud and an evil vicious one at that' and added that 'like all frauds your end is approaching.' Its crude but threatening conclusion warned:

The American public, the church organizations that have been helping − Protestant, Catholic and Jews will know you for what you are − an evil, abnormal beast. So will others who have backed you. You are done. King, there is only one thing left for you to do. You know what it is. You have just 34 days [a reference to the date when King was to be awarded the Nobel Peace Prize] in which to do [sic] (this exact number has been selected for a specific reason, it has definite practical significant [sic]). You are done. There is but one way out for you. You better take it before your filthy, abnormal, fraudulent self is bared to the nation.

Another containment effort had involved a December 1963 news story reporting *Time* magazine's selection of King as 'Man of the Year.' Hoover's specific strategy cannot be ascertained because of heavy deletions in the released FBI documents. But part of this effort involved working with sympathetic news media, as one of Hoover's aides queried whether Assistant Director Sullivan had 'decided yet if we can tell [name deleted], [title deleted] of Radio Free Europe, about the "script"? Marrie and I are ready to go.'

Finally, Hoover's handwritten comment on a 27 January 1964 memo from Sullivan pertaining to a proposed installation of a bug in King's hotel room in Milwaukee sums up the personal and political motives behind Hoover's campaign against King. The Milwaukee police, Sullivan had advised Hoover, had rented the room next to King's suite in order to provide security. In view of this, he said, the Milwaukee SAC felt that 'the likelihood of King's going ahead with any [phrase deleted but sexual] plans is greatly minimized.' Hoover, contemptuous of his aide's defeatism, wrote: 'I don't share the conjecture. King is a "tom cat" with obsessive degenerate sexual urges.'

Hoover's obsession with discrediting King continued even after the civil rights leader's murder. Thus, when the Director learned that Senate Republican minority leader Hugh Scott proposed to introduce a bill to strike a commemorative medal in honor of King, he directed that the senator (who was described as having 'always been very friendly' and having a 'cooperative attitude' toward the FBI 'over the years') be briefed 'on a most confidential basis as to the background of Martin Luther King. Obviously, Scott has been "hoodwinked" as to King's true background.'

Hoover's hatred of King, like his hatred of Dillinger thirty years earlier, seems to have grown beyond all reason and to have been deeply involved with the civil rights leader's supposed sexual prowess. According to several accounts, the Director had become obsessed with both men, in his later years constantly alluding to them in conversations in a kind of involuntary incantation, as if all of the world's evil had been reposed in their two vile bodies. The irrationality of his behavior by this time, in fact, recalls the description of the paranoid in *The Authoritarian Personality,* who, although he 'is beset by an overall hatred, . . . nevertheless tends to "pick" his enemy, to molest certain individuals who draw his attention upon themselves: he falls, as it were, negatively in love.'

Whether Hoover's growing intemperateness was an aspect of aging alone or of other factors as well is unclear, but many at the Bureau supposed that it had a good deal to do with the decline of Clyde Tolson. Beginning in the middle or late 1960s, Tolson suffered a series of minor strokes that hobbled his abilities and drained his strength. After each attack Hoover and his driver, Crawford, clandestinely transported the patient from the hospital to Hoover's home, where Annie Fields and they could look after his needs. And on each occasion Hoover insisted on Tolson's returning to work prematurely. The mechanism of denial, which had served the Director so steadfastly in his early life, was coming up against the hard truths of old age and impending death. (Unexpectedly, Tolson outlived Hoover by three years and inherited the bulk of Hoover's estate.)

Meanwhile the Johnson years were witnessing a succession of crises at the Bureau that seemed to grow out of the very duality of the Director's character. The main pillars of his celebrity — patriotism, antiradicalism, and the protection of innocent youth — began to split along the faults of an undeclared war (and a new skepticism about the received truths of the Cold War), a broad-based effort to finish the unfinished business of the New Deal, and a student revolt against paternalistic authority. The very success of the repression of the 1950s, while it hastened the drift toward power without accountability exemplified by the uncritical deference toward Hoover's FBI and the undeclared and eventually unacknowledged war in Southeast Asia, excited a passionate reaction. Although the antiwar movement and the closely allied student movement generated their own excesses, the passionate minority, like passionate minorities from the dawn of history, changed the course of human events. And Hoover, had he lived long enough, would finally have found himself on the losing side.

Because these changes occurred after 1965, they were particularly threatening to Hoover and determined his conduct during his last years in office. Having passed the mandatory retirement age of seventy on 1 January 1965 and thus lost the irresistible leverage with which he had once ensured his continuance in power, the Director became more and more embattled. Revelations of abuses or misconduct could force his retirement, he knew — especially in the more liberal climate of the 1960s, buoyed as it was by the Warren Court and the change in the composition of Congress.

Demands for secrecy and claims of national security no longer sufficed to deter popular protest or congressional action, as demonstrated by congressional approval of the Freedom of Information Act of 1966 and the burgeoning congressional opposition to the Vietnam War after 1965. No longer could Hoover rely on his conservative allies in Congress and the media to protect him from attack. Moreover, after 1965 a series of unanticipated events served to raise doubts about FBI procedures – and hence the Bureau's leadership.

Yet the Director still had his champions, and his declining years began auspiciously, with the incorporation on 10 June 1965 of the J. Edgar Hoover Foundation at Valley Forge, Pennsylvania. Its mission, as stated in its charter, was to 'safeguard the heritage and the freedom of the United States of America and to promote good citizenship through the appreciation of its form of government and to perpetuate the ideas and purposes to which the Honorable J. Edgar Hoover has dedicated his life.' It proposed to, and in fact still does at the amply endowed Freedoms Foundation campus at Valley Forge: 'conduct education programs; organize study groups; give lectures; establish scholarships and endow chairs . . . [and] circulate magazines and books and pamphlets.' One of the foundation's first disbursements, in the words of Louis Nichols, by then ensconced in a high-level Schenley Industries executive slot, gave '$5,000 to the National College of Defense Lawyers for the J. Edgar Hoover lectures on the protection of innocence.'

Hoover's detractors, however, were gathering strength and were soon galvanized by disclosures in the press that the FBI had been wiretapping and bugging extensively. That July Senator Edward V. Long (D.-Mo.), chairman of the Subcommittee on Administrative Practice and Procedure of the Senate Judiciary Committee, launched a crusade against government eavesdropping. The so-called Long Subcommittee had begun its investigation by focusing on the surveillance practices of the Internal Revenue Service (IRS) in 1964. In the course of its inquiries it had learned

447

that the IRS was spending large sums of money to purchase eavesdropping equipment and had asked the Post Office Department to install mail covers (a practice by which the names and addresses of the sender and recipient of letters are recorded). At that time the Long Subcommittee broadened its investigation to all federal intelligence agencies (including the FBI), requesting their responses to a detailed questionnaire 'in an effort to develop as many facts as possible' on the scope of federal surveillance practices.

Among the subcommittee's many questions were: Had the FBI ever surreptitiously installed or monitored a telephone tap? Had the FBI requested the assistance of (or assisted) another federal, local, or state agency in installing or monitoring a tap? How many times, if any, for the 1959–1964 period? Had the FBI purchased microphones (bugs) and closed circuit television equipment? And how many for 1959-1964? Had the FBI requested mail covers, and, if so, how many times and for what purpose? Last, the subcommittee demanded copies of all rules (both written and oral) governing the FBI's installation and use of wiretaps, bugs, and mail covers.

Had Hoover answered the subcommittee's questions truthfully, unknown to the subcommittee staff and to Chairman Long, he would have had to disclose the broad scope and political nature of the Bureau's surveillance practices. He would have had to reveal that the FBI had used wiretaps and bugs extensively during so-called intelligence (noncriminal) investigations; that the FBI had, on its own authority, instituted a series of mail intercept programs (that is, actually opening and photocopying the contents of letters); and that the FBI had extensively broken into offices and residences not only to install microphones but to secure the membership, subscription, and contributor lists of targeted individuals and organizations. Hoover would also have had to disclose the elaborate separate filing procedures devised since 1940 to prevent discovery of these FBI practices: the 'Do Not File' procedure for break-in requests and authorization memoranda; the 'June Mail' procedure for 'sources illegal in nature' and for information obtained from 'sensitive confidential' sources, 'such as Governors, secretaries to high officials who may be discussing such officials and their attitude'; the 'administrative pages' procedure, used when reporting 'facts and information which are considered of a nature not expedient to disseminate, or which could cause embarrassment to the Bureau, if distributed'; and the 'Special File Room' used to maintain particularly sensitive documents to avoid their inclusion in the case files of the FBI's central records system.

Not surprisingly, then, Hoover moved quickly to meet this threat to his directorship. The first problem he dealt with was the Long Subcommittee's inquiry into the FBI's mail cover practices. In order to blunt the inquiry and harmonize the responses of the various intelligence agencies to the 'problems raised' by the investigation, he persuaded President Johnson to assign to Attorney General Nicholas Katzenbach, who had succeeded Robert Kennedy on the latter's resignation in September 1964, the responsibility for coordinating the answers of the CIA and other intelligence agencies as well as the FBI.

In discussing strategy, Katzenbach, as yet unaware of the extent of the Bureau's illegal activities, advised Hoover not to answer any of the subcommittee's questions having 'national security implications.' Katzenbach intended to tell Senator Long and subcommittee counsel Bernard Fensterwald that the subcommittee was touching on 'extreme national security matters' and 'there could be exceptions to the answers given in the testimony when they touched on such sensitive security matters.' Committed to controlling 'this matter . . . at the committee level' (i.e., by outflanking the subcommittee) Hoover agreed that additional 'pressure would have to be applied,' given Fensterwald's zealousness. Katzenbach reported back that Vice President Humphrey 'had promised to talk to Long concerning Fensterwald,' and that he personally would confer with Long and would advise Hoover of the results of the meeting.

Hoover was unwilling to rely solely on the Johnson administration's political influence, and at the same time had DeLoach (by then the Director's liaison to Congress as well as to the White House) 'contact [Judiciary Committee Chairman James] Eastland in an effort to warn the Long Committee away from those areas which would be injurious to the national defense.' DeLoach's planned intercession with Eastland, a Mississippi Democrat of extreme conservative views, was 'of course' not mentioned to the attorney general.

No longer confident that his containment strategy would work, Hoover began to consider abandoning the sensitive investigative methods that he had for so long, and secretly, authorized. Before taking that crucial step, however, the Director personally contacted Eastland on 1 March 'in regard to the hearings before the Long Committee concerning mail covers, et cetera.' At the Director's suggestion, Eastland agreed 'to caution [Long] that this fellow Fensterwald must not get into the kind of questioning' involving FBI operations that he had pursued in his recent interrogation of the Post Office Department's Chief Inspector Henry Montague.

Meanwhile, Katzenbach, advised of Eastland's imminent meeting with Long, asked whether it might be best if he delayed his own meeting with Long until after Eastland's. Hoover replied that it would – that by delaying his meeting with Long, Katzenbach 'would probably tie it down once and for all' and thus the attorney general should first 'let Senator Eastland see what he can do.' 'Senator Eastland thoroughly understands the matter,' Hoover emphasized, and did 'not intend to have' the Long Subcommittee investigate FBI mail operations.

Katzenbach did not wait until Eastland met with Long. After talking with the Missouri senator that night, he informed Hoover that Long, who had apparently already been approached by Eastland, had agreed that the attorney general should 'personally and confidentially' review the list of former FBI agents the subcommittee proposed to call as witnesses and 'have any names involving national security deleted.' Katzenbach and Hoover then discussed the subcommittee's intention to investigate government wiretapping. Protesting that other government agencies wiretapped extensively and without the attorney general's authorization, Hoover opposed any legislation requiring prior court warrants to install taps 'because of the composition of some of our courts and the employees thereof.' Instead, he thought that the president should issue an executive order requiring the attorney general's prior approval for all wiretaps installed by federal agencies.

Then he returned to Katzenbach's arrangement with Long concerning the planned testimony of former FBI agents. Conceding that the 'Attorney General had made good headway with Senator Long,' he reiterated his (and Eastland's) 'lack of faith and confidence' in Fensterwald's willingness to clear all prospective witnesses with him. Katzenbach, who did not share Hoover's anxieties, emphasized that whoever had talked with Long – whether Eastland or Vice President Humphrey – had 'waked him up.'

Katzenbach's hunch was right. The Long Subcommittee shortly abandoned its inquiry into the FBI's mail cover operations. But it almost immediately considered investigating FBI wiretapping and microphone practices (a more serious matter because of the greater public interest in such activities). This threat continued to bedevil the Director until the end of the subcommittee's hearings.

Katzenbach had been invited to testify before the subcommittee but expected no problem with the inquiry into FBI wiretapping. Senator Eastland, for one, had assured the Director that 'Senator Long would not raise any questions about the FBI's operations in the matter of' wiretaps and microphones.

But despite this assurance, during the ensuing hearing subcommittee counsel Fensterwald queried Katzenbach about FBI wiretaps, and the attorney general, ignorant of all the facts, agreed to supply certain information to the subcommittee. Hoover duly ordered his aides to prepare a memorandum answering Fensterwald's questions, but commented ruefully that 'obviously Senator Long did not keep his promise to Senator Eastland' to focus on practices of the Internal Revenue Service and not involve the FBI. In view of the 'growing delicacy in this whole field,' Hoover advised his aides he was increasingly reluctant 'to approve requests for [wiretaps] until the atmosphere has been clarified'; future requests for taps and bugs should be 'most circumspect,' while ongoing taps and bugs should be discontinued if 'not really productive.'

To avoid any future surprises, Hoover had Supervisor Milton Jones monitor the subcommittee's activities and immediately learned that Long 'has been taking testimony in connection with mail covers, wiretapping and various snooping devices on the part of Federal agencies.' Stressing that the Senator 'cannot be trusted,' Hoover observed that although 'the FBI has not become involved in the hearings our name has been mentioned quite prominently on several occasions.' At that point a forewarned Hoover contacted Long directly, then briefed Katzenbach on Long's promise 'that he does not intend to call and will not call anyone from the Department in connection with the hearings he has gone into.' Both Hoover and Katzenbach determined to 'keep watch on the situation.'

Thereafter the irrepressible subcommittee kept coming back to the FBI's wiretapping and bugging operations – the more eagerly because the press gave great play to reports of FBI wiretapping. And Hoover, although satisfied with the FBI's lobbying efforts, worried that such an inquiry, if it should occur, might disclose some of his most controversial activities, and in particular the Bureau's relentless electronic surveillance of Dr. King. Accordingly, he reserved 'final decision' on discontinuing all FBI bugging of King's hotel rooms 'until DeLoach sees Long.' Two weeks later, Hoover officially discontinued the bugging.

Meanwhile, Hoover learned from DeLoach's meeting with the subcommittee chairman that Long was sympathetic to the FBI's position but that 'unfortunately a number of people were bringing pressure on him to look into the FBI's activities in connection with the usage of electronic devices.' In order to get around this essentially public relations problem, as he saw it, DeLoach advised Long, as he reported to Hoover, to 'issue a statement reflecting that he had held lengthy conferences with top FBI officials and was now completely satisfied, after looking into FBI operations, that the FBI had never participated in uncontrolled usage of wiretaps or microphones and that FBI usage of such devices had been completely justified in all instances.' Long, who was himself under investigation for alleged ties to organized crime, agreed to this proposal but added that 'he frankly did not know how to word such a release.' DeLoach assured him that he 'would be glad to prepare the release for him on a strictly confidential basis.'

DeLoach duly prepared a release 'written from the viewpoint of the Senator and his Committee.' The release, he assured Hoover, 'indicates they have taken a long, hard look at the FBI and have found nothing out of order — but that they will continue looking over our procedures and techniques from time to time in the future.' This approach was 'essential if the statement is to have the desired effect,' for any differently worded 'statement reflecting a stronger pro-FBI position might not only prove ineffective in thwarting those persons who are exerting pressure on the Subcommittee for a probe of our operations, but it could also bring criticism and additional pressure on Senator Long.'

The FBI statement that Senator Long was to release as the subcommittee's finding asserted that the staff and chairman 'have not only conferred at length with top officials of the FBI, but . . . have conducted exhaustive research into the activities, procedures, and techniques of this agency.' The subcommittee had found that FBI wiretapping and bugging operations had been 'under strict Justice Department control at all times,' had been subject to a 'rigid system of checks and balances,' and were 'strictly limited' to the 'most important and serious crimes either affecting the internal security of our Nation or involving heinous threats to human life.' 'Investigation made by my staff,' the statement concluded, 'reflected no independent or unauthorized installation of electronic devices by individual FBI Agents or by FBI offices in the field. We have

453

carefully examined Mr. J. Edgar Hoover's rules in this regard and have found no instances of violation.'

Long, of course, could not risk issuing the statement for fear of inevitable leaks from the subcommittee staff challenging its baseless assertions. So Hoover, disturbed by the senator's indecision, had DeLoach meet again with the subcommittee chairman and counsel.

At the outset of this meeting, DeLoach asked Long 'point blank whether or not he intended to hold hearings concerning the FBI at any time in the future.' Long denied that he did, whereupon DeLoach demanded that the senator 'give us a commitment that he would in no way embarrass the FBI.' Long agreed, but then Fensterwald interrupted to request that either DeLoach or Assistant Director James Gale appear before the Long Subcommittee 'and make a simple statement to the effect that the FBI used wiretaps only in cases involving national security and kidnapping and extortion, where human life is involved, and used microphones only in those cases involving heinous crimes and Cosa Nostra matters.' Unable to give such assurances under oath, DeLoach feinted, arguing that 'to put an FBI witness on the stand would be to open a Pandora's box, in so far as our enemies in the press were concerned [and] that such an appearance as only a token witness would cause more criticism than the release of the statement in question would ever cause.' Long assured DeLoach that 'he had no plans whatsoever for calling FBI witnesses'; Fensterwald, however, wanted to invite one former FBI witness. DeLoach immediately characterized this former agent as 'a first class s.o.b., a liar, and a man who had volunteered as a witness only to get a public forum.' Unwilling to challenge DeLoach, Fensterwald agreed not to call the witness.

Appraising the results of the meeting, DeLoach assured Hoover: 'While we have neutralized the threat of being embarrassed by the Long Subcommittee, we have not yet eliminated certain dangers which might be created as a result of newspaper pressure on Long. We therefore must keep on top of this situation at all times.'

Hoover accordingly took a couple of precautions of his

own to defend his administration of the Bureau. First, he ordered his aides to search the Bureau files and prepare a 'summary of information' on each member of the Long Subcommittee and on Fensterwald.[8] Second, he drafted a statement for use in case he was required to testify before the subcommittee.

Purporting to survey the history of FBI wiretapping and bugging, the draft testimony implied that eavesdropping techniques had always been both tightly controlled and conducted only with the specific knowledge and authorization of the attorney general and the president. Confronting what had by then emerged as a controversial issue in *Black v. U.S.*, a recent Supreme Court case, Hoover sought particularly to document that FBI electronic surveillance practices during the Kennedy years had been conducted with the specific knowledge and consent of the attorney general. The closing paragraph captures Hoover's strategy of foisting responsibility on the Kennedys:

> In conclusion, let me reiterate that official records of the Federal Bureau of Investigation . . . make it indelibly clear that the FBI used microphones, as well as wiretaps, during Robert Kennedy's administration of the Justice Department with Mr. Kennedy's knowledge and approval. The record is equally clear that we have used these devices on a very limited and strictly controlled basis – solely for intelligence purposes – in matters involving major considerations of national security and safety.

Fortunately for Hoover, he never had to defend that statement in public, since, largely as a result of his own efforts, the Long Subcommittee threat collapsed. However, he soon encountered a more serious problem in the form of the Black case.

Fred B. Black was an influential Washington lobbyist who represented a number of Las Vegas businessmen and other private contractors interested in exploiting his high-level government contacts. In May 1964 Black was convicted of having evaded personal income taxes in 1956, 1957, and 1958. Petitioning the U.S. Supreme Court two years later, he sought a rehearing based on information that the FBI had bugged his Washington hotel room. In response, the solicitor general conceded that Black's privileged conversations had been bugged during an unrelated criminal investigation. The Supreme Court therefore directed the Justice Department to present a brief outing the legal authority for the installation of that bug.

The ruling created a serious problem for Hoover – and not simply because a legal rationale had to be developed for an apparent violation of Black's Fourth Amendment rights. The real problem was that the attorney general had not authorized the bugging of Black's hotel room. Hoover alone had approved the Washington field office's request to conduct 'appropriate surveys at [Black's hotel room and office in Washington] and, if considered feasible and secure, to install a misur [microphone surveillance] at one or both of these locations.'

Hoover's action in the Black investigation was not unprecedented. Convinced that microphones provided essential information, yet aware that installing bugs by trespass was unconstitutional, he had on his own authority authorized FBI bugging since 1938.

Thereafter the Director had trod a narrow path. Not until October 1951 did he apprise his ostensible superior, the attorney general, of this practice, although in June 1950 he considered requesting Attorney General J. Howard McGrath's approval in the matter. (The Director decided not to, having concluded that 'to raise this issue with the Attorney General might result, when trespass was involved, in the loss of this investigative technique so vital to the fulfillment of the Bureau's responsibilities,' since it 'was extremely doubtful that the Attorney General, as the principal Federal law enforcement official, would grant such authority.') Reassessing this policy in October 1951, when briefing McGrath on FBI wiretapping in the light of questions posed by the Judith Coplon case,[9] Hoover spelled out the problems entailed in FBI bugging practices. 'As you are aware,' he reported to McGrath,

> this Bureau has also employed the use of microphone installation on a highly restrictive basis, chiefly to obtain intelligence information. The information obtained from microphones . . . is not admissible in evidence . . .
>
> As you know, in a number of instances it has not been possible to install microphones without trespass. In such instances the information received therefrom is of an intelligence nature only. Here again, as in the case of wiretaps, experience has shown us that intelligence information highly pertinent to the defense and welfare of this nation is derived through the use of microphones.

Whether or not McGrath knew about the FBI's past bugging practices, Hoover's memorandum meant that he could no longer plead ignorance — the more so because the Director specifically requested McGrath's 'definite opinion' whether the FBI should continue to break in to install microphones 'or whether we should cease the use of microphone surveillance entirely in view of the issues being raised.' McGrath responded on 6 February 1952:

> The use of microphone surveillance which does not involve a trespass would seem to be permissible under the present state of the law . . . Such surveillances as involve trespass are in the area of the Fourth Amendment, and evidence so obtained and from leads so obtained is inadmissible.
>
> . . . please be advised that I cannot authorize the installation of a microphone involving a trespass under existing law.

Thus informed in writing that the FBI was installing microphones in violation of the Constitution, McGrath shrank from lending his authority to the practice. Loath at the same time to forbid the practice, he closed his eyes to it, insisting only that the department be briefed on such use when particular cases were referred for possible prosecution. (In other words, McGrath wanted only to be informed of any potential legal problem and the attendant possibility of embarrassment so that the department might make an informed judgment not to undertake prosecution.) His 6 February memorandum meant, in effect, that thereafter any FBI bugging operation would contravene the attorney general's written opinion that the practice was unconstitutional.

McGrath's curious ruling led Hoover to advise SACs that 'authorization will not be granted to install any microphone surveillance involving trespass.' To get around this requirement, however, SACs were immediately encouraged to devise means of installing microphones without an agent's having to commit trespass (whether by installing spike microphones in the walls of adjoining rooms or apartments or, more questionably, by securing entry through the assistance of friendly custodians). SACs were also advised that 'if the contemplated installation is of such importance and value that it is desired despite the fact that one or more of the requirements for legal microphone surveillances cannot be followed,' they must obtain the Director's 'specific authorization in each and every instance to make such an installation.'

In an effort to obtain approval of this evasion of McGrath's distinction between legal and illegal microphones from James McGranery, McGrath's successor as attorney general, Hoover in April 1952 submitted certain 'hypothetical situations' to test whether, for each case, the department would conclude that 'trespass was involved.' The department's current interpretation 'regarding the use of microphones without trespass,' Hoover argued, was 'so highly restricted' and the 'instances in which we could install microphones without trespass are so few that we have been stripped of this medium of gathering intelligence.' Unwilling to accept McGrath's restrictive ruling, Hoover hoped to pressure an insecure McGranery (whose confirmation had been narrowly won through the Director's behind-the-scenes maneuvering) to relax McGrath's declaration that the practice was unconstitutional.

Resurrecting the 'national security' ploy and claiming that the Bureau had 'a definite obligation to obtain and furnish such intelligence [obtainable only through bugs] to responsible officials,' such that 'if we did not do so, we would be derelict in our duties,' Hoover now argued that the need to protect the nation from 'subversive elements' and 'foreign invasion' required the use of 'all possible means, consistent with good judgment.' He further emphasized that tight restrictions on the use of 'investigative techniques in the face of such grave responsibilities could be considered detrimental to the best interests of this nation . . . The Bureau as the responsible agency should be permitted to utilize any reasonable means at its disposal as long as such activity is properly supervised.'

Under this reasoning, the attorney general, having the responsibility for the security of the country, would have to 'give complete backing to the Bureau in the use of this technique [microphones installed by means of trespass].'

To ensure this support, Hoover met with McGranery to seek a reconsideration of McGrath's earlier ruling. In the past, the Director emphasized, the FBI had installed microphones 'on a very limited basis' and 'only in cases which directly affected the internal security of the United States.' McGrath's ruling had forced him to discontinue 'some of the microphone installations which had been established, where it had been necessary to commit technical trespass.'

McGranery too was unwilling to accept the risks darkly outlined by Hoover, but under pressure he orally authorized FBI bugging 'in any case where elements were at work against the security of the United States.' In instances where Hoover concluded that microphones should be installed, even though trespass might be committed, McGranery 'would leave it to my judgment as to the steps to take. I told the Attorney General that this authority would only be used in extreme cases and only in cases involving the internal security of the United States.'

Unwilling to exercise his oversight responsibility, McGranery had in effect given the green light to Hoover to use microphones whenever he saw fit. Nevertheless, as McGranery had not given his authorization in writing, McGrath's written ruling that the practice was unconstitutional remained in force. For the time being, Hoover had to accept that. But, committed to continued use of the technique and wishing to obtain an explicit written authorization for it, he moved quickly to exploit the newly elected Eisenhower administration's greater political commitment to anti-Communism.

On Hoover's orders, in early 1953 his aides met with officials of the Justice Department's internal security section to seek 'a less restrictive interpretation of the law pertaining to microphone surveillances.' This strategy triumphed: the Department agreed 'upon a new legal approach under which a microphone installed through trespass would not be seen as the result of an illegal entry,' because the entry was 'not for the purpose of a search and seizure, and thus, not within the proscriptions of the Fourth Amendment.'

While welcoming this altogether permissive interpretation, Hoover still sought formal Justice Department approval for the practice. At a meeting with department officials in July, Assistant Director L. V. Boardman proposed that the attorney general approve each bug in advance. Justifying the need for the change, Boardman warned that if anything went wrong and an FBI break-in to install a bug was disclosed, 'it would precipitate considerable adverse publicity in the press and result in embarrassment publicly, both to the Bureau and the Department.'

Justice Department officials did not respond immediately. Restive over the delay, Hoover directed Belmont and Boardman to meet with Assistant Attorney General Warren Olney III (the head of the internal security section) and Nichols to meet with Deputy Attorney General William Rogers.

In his meeting with Rogers, Nichols complained that McGrath's February 1952 memorandum and the department's 'rather narrow definition of trespassing' had

deprived the FBI of 'the coverage that we felt was needed.'
Nichols then added, 'for [Rogers's] personal and
confidential information, there had been a few instances
wherein we had on our own utilized microphone
surveillances.' The FBI, he entreated, needed 'some backing
of the Department to utilize microphone surveillances where
the intelligence to be gained was a necessary adjunct to
security matters and important investigations, in instances
when prosecution is not contemplated.'

Rogers registered no protest whatever to the FBI's
confessed independence, nor did he insist that FBI policy
conform to the requirements of the Fourth Amendment.
Instead, he agreed that 'the Department's order should back
the Bureau' and 'should be sufficiently general to cover all
situations.' Rogers further proposed that in situations not
covered by the ruling, the Bureau might best conform to
current wiretap policy, requiring the advance approval of
the attorney general on a case-by-case basis.

Nichols readily agreed with this proposal, but urged that
the department also 'give an over-all policy to cover all
needs.' Rogers again assented. He asked Hoover to 'think
about how best this could be handled' and give him 'on an
informal basis on plain paper a draft of what we needed.'
Rogers promised to consult with Olney and Attorney
General Brownell 'and try to get the matter adjusted.'

Boardman's and Belmont's meeting with Olney was
equally successful. Olney agreed that 'microphone coverage
is necessary in security cases,' that any cases going to
prosecution 'must be carefully evaluated if a microphone
has been used,' that the 'Department will broaden its
interpretation of what constitutes trespass in the installation
of microphones,' that the 'Department would back the
Bureau in the use of microphones in security cases,' and that
the 'Attorney General should furnish a memorandum to the
Bureau' covering these points.

To 'assist the Department,' Boardman agreed to 'furnish
an informal draft of a proposed memorandum covering
these points from which the Attorney General's
memorandum will be drafted.' Olney also proposed that the

461

procedure already used for wiretapping should be adopted for bugging — that is, that the attorney general approve each installation in advance. The assistant attorney general doubted, however, that 'the Attorney General could authorize a microphone where trespass is clearly indicated.'

Briefed on the department's willingness to allow him to define the FBI's microphone surveillance authority, Hoover ordered his aides to 'prepare an informal draft to assist the Department in preparing the Attorney General's memorandum to the Bureau.'

The FBI's draft was submitted to Rogers on 14 April, and Hoover was duly apprised that Rogers had 'stated it looked perfectly satisfactory to him, that he would talk to the Attorney General and then to Olney.' Rogers had serious reservations about the earlier suggestion 'of having the Attorney General clear microphone surveillances on the ground that time was of the essence and he thought the Attorney General would be in a much better position to defend the Bureau in the event there should be a technical trespass if he had not heretofore approved it.' Not sharing this hesitancy, Hoover preferred that the FBI 'submit requests to AG (attorney general) as we do wire taps.'

Rogers remained unwilling to have the attorney general assume responsibility for directly monitoring FBI bugging. Expressing his own agreement with an earlier FBI draft, the deputy attorney general favored a general authorization procedure.

Not surprisingly, Brownell too preferred issuing a generally worded policy directive to assuming direct responsibility for monitoring FBI uses of this technique. The attorney general's secret directive to Hoover asserted that:

> the national interest requires that microphone surveillance be utilized by the Federal Bureau of Investigation. This use need not be limited to the development of evidence for prosecution. The FBI has an intelligence function in connection with internal security matters equally as important as the duty of developing evidence for presentation to the courts and

the national security requires that the FBI be able to use microphone surveillance for the proper discharge of such functions. The Department of Justice approves the use of microphone surveillance by the FBI under these circumstances and for these purposes.

Commenting specifically on the Supreme Court's recent decision in *Irvine* v. *California* (denouncing as unconstitutional the gross violation of personal privacy rights perpetrated when local police installed a microphone in a bedroom during a gambling investigation), Brownell urged that such installations be avoided during internal security cases 'wherever possible. It may appear, however, that important intelligence or evidence relating to matters connected with national security can only be obtained by the installation of a microphone in such a location. It is my opinion that under such circumstances the installation is proper and is not prohibited by the Supreme Court's decision in the *Irvine* case.'

Then, seeking to provide a constitutional rationale for this practice (as well as formally rejecting the reasoning underpinning McGrath's February 1952 memorandum), Brownell concluded in language both opaque and permissive:

not infrequently the question of trespass arises in connection with the installation of a microphone. The question of whether a trespass is actually involved and the second question of the effect of such trespass must necessarily be resolved according to the circumstances of each case. The Department in resolving the problems which may arise in connection with the use of microphone surveillance will review the circumstances in each case in the light of the practical necessities of investigation and of the national interest which must be protected. It is my opinion that the Department should adopt that interpretation which will permit microphone coverage by the FBI in a manner most conducive to the national interest. I recognize that for the FBI to fulfill its important intelligence function, considerations of internal security and the national safety are paramount and, therefore, may compel the unrestricted use of this technique in the national interest.

Technically, Hoover was Brownell's subordinate. However, the attorney general's reluctance to assume supervisory responsibility over FBI policy in an area as fraught with constitutional questions as authorizing FBI break-ins to facilitate the installation of bugs demonstrates how independent Hoover had become. For not only had the Director's draft served as the basis for Brownell's May 1954 directive, but Assistant Attorney General Warren Olney, who wrote the final directive signed by Brownell, first cleared it with Hoover. Analyzing this draft, the Director concluded that the 'Attorney General is giving us the go ahead on microphones whether or not there is trespass at the same time suggesting that discretion be used in certain cases.'

The lid was off. Brownell's refusal to require his explicit consent before each installation emboldened Hoover to expand FBI uses of bugs and to brief the attorney general and responsible Justice Department officials only selectively and after the fact.[10] Rationalizing this policy of selective briefing, Assistant Director James Gale candidly wrote that 'the Department completely lacks security, leaks confidential information to the press and has demonstrated a propensity for going forward and advising the courts wherever they have knowledge of the existence of microphone coverage regardless of whether or not this coverage had any bearing on the case under consideration.' To advise the department of FBI microphone coverage, Gale added, 'could result only in the Department running to the courts with resultant adverse publicity to the Bureau which could give rise . . . to a demand for a Congressional inquiry of the Bureau.'

Furthermore, although Hoover's sole rationale when lobbying Justice Department officials to rescind McGrath's earlier ruling had been the importance of obtaining intelligence in 'internal security' cases, an emphasis employed as well in the Brownell directive, the Director subsequently interpreted the directive's vague language as permitting the installation of bugs during criminal investigations.

But these guidelines applied only during the Eisenhower administration. John F. Kennedy's election to the presidency and Robert Kennedy's appointment as attorney general required Hoover to reassess this strategy. Kennedy's predecessors (Brownell and Rogers) had intentionally avoided being briefed about FBI microphone surveillances, in effect delegating this responsibility to Hoover. Because Hoover suspected that Robert Kennedy might be either more assertive of his authority or less willing to defer uncritically, he did not directly attempt to ascertain Kennedy's views on the constitutionality of FBI microphone surveillance practices and whether he might require his prior approval for each installation. Rather, Hoover sought to slip the question past Kennedy as a mere reaffirmation of established policy.

Hoover's craftiness succeeded in part because the attorney general was equally insensitive to constitutional issues. Robert Kennedy was convinced of the value of wiretaps for obtaining information to be used in criminal prosecutions and apparently had no qualms about the impact of their use on privacy rights. Desirous of using information so obtained for prosecutive purposes, he had drafted legislation to amend the ban against wiretapping contained in Section 605 of the Federal Communications Act of 1934.

In preparing him for his forthcoming testimony on this proposal before the Senate Judiciary Subcommittee on Constitutional Rights, officials of the Justice Department and the FBI met in Deputy Attorney General Byron White's office to 'formulate a position' for Kennedy to use in his prepared statement and to develop his responses to expected questions about the various bills already introduced to legalize wiretapping. In the course of their discussion, these officials recognized that the attorney general would have to be prepared to answer questions about microphones.

Accordingly, they agreed to invite 'any pertinent observations' regarding microphone surveillance policy from any division of the department.

Briefing Hoover, Assistant Director Courtney Evans (who had attended the meeting) recommended reiterating the FBI's views on microphone surveillances, 'since this type of coverage is important not only in security-type investigations but also in connection with our investigations of leading racketeers and hoodlums.' Hoover directed his aides to draft 'a suggested memorandum in this regard.'

In his memo to White, Hoover claimed to be offering the FBI's views on microphone surveillance for the attorney general's consideration in preparation for his Senate testimony. FBI microphone surveillance policy was based on Brownell's May 1954 directive authorizing 'the use of microphone surveillance with or without trespass,' Hoover maintained, and then quoted selectively from the Brownell directive. The quotation, however, consisted of a single sentence from that lengthy document − in which Brownell asserted that 'considerations of internal security and the national safety are paramount and, therefore, may compel the unrestricted use of this technique microphones (with or without trespass) in the national interest.'

This distorted summary of Brownell's actual authorization was calculated to mislead Kennedy. Hoover then continued:

> In light of this policy, in the internal security field, we are utilizing microphone surveillance on a restricted basis even though trespass is necessary to assist in uncovering the activities of Soviet intelligence agents and Communist Party leaders. In the interests of national safety, microphone surveillances are also utilized on a restricted basis, even though trespass is necessary, in uncovering major criminal activities. We are using such coverage in connection with our investigations of the clandestine activities of top hoodlums and organized crime. From an intelligence

standpoint, this investigative technique has produced results unobtainable through other means.

Conceding that there was 'no Federal legislation at the present time' regulating the use of bugs, Hoover argued that 'the passage of any restrictive legislation in this field would be a definite loss to our investigative operations, both in the internal security field and in our fight against the criminal element. This is especially true in the case of organized crime where we have too few weapons at our command, to give up the valuable technique of microphones.'

Kennedy found Hoover's arguments persuasive, in part because he shared the Director's view on the overriding advantages of electronic surveillance. Accordingly, during his Senate testimony, he opposed any legislation that would change microphone surveillance practices and confined his support to legislation that would remove the ban against wiretapping. In the process, however, he failed to examine the accuracy of Hoover's rendition of Brownell's authorization or to consider whether as attorney general he should formulate his own guidelines and, in particular, require his advance approval for each FBI bug.

This carelessness led Kennedy to approve Hoover's further request to expedite FBI bugging activities. Briefed on a meeting in the attorney general's office at which departmental strategy to fight organized crime had been discussed, Hoover learned that Kennedy had indirectly raised the possibility of 'utilizing "electronic devices" similar to those being utilized in espionage cases.' Kennedy had been advised by Assistant Director Evans that this had been fully considered but that there were certain problems, whereupon Kennedy, taking the hint, had dropped the matter. Evans doubted that Kennedy 'has any comprehension as to the difference between a technical surveillance [wiretap] and a microphone surveillance' and sought Hoover's approval to brief Kennedy on the FBI's 'strong objections to the (generall utilization of any telephone taps and the limitations of microphone surveillances.' Having concluded that 'this is a field which should be closely controlled by the Bureau,'

Hoover agreed that a personal discussion with Kennedy would enable the FBI to 'forestall any precipitous action by the Department.'

The FBI was already using bugs during criminal investigations 'in all instances where this was technically feasible and where valuable information might be expected,' Evans subsequently advised Kennedy. The use of bugs, he continued, did not pose the same legal problems as wiretaps because the ban incorporated in the Federal Communications Act of 1934 applied only to wire interceptions.

As a result of this briefing, Evans reported, Kennedy came to understand why telephone taps 'should be restricted to national-defense type cases' and was pleased that the FBI had 'been using microphone surveillances where those objections do not apply wherever possible in organized crime matters.' Referring to his approval of 'several' wiretap authorization requests in 'security-type investigations since he took office,' Kennedy reportedly admitted to having kept no record and thus not knowing 'what surveillances were currently in operation.' The attorney general therefore requested a list of such wiretaps, adding that it should 'be brought over to him personally and that he would look it over and immediately return it because he realized the importance of having these records maintained under the special security conditions which only the FBI had.' The list was submitted to Kennedy and was then returned to the 'Bureau's file.'

Kennedy's deference, his interest in FBI wiretapping practices, and his tacit approval of FBI resort to bugs emboldened the Director to solicit the attorney general's blanket authorization for FBI bugging activities. This proposal was formally presented the next month as a request for assistance in the FBI's investigations of organized crime in New York City. Specifically, Hoover had drafted a letter, which Kennedy signed on 17 August 1961, in response to a written request from the New York Telephone Company that it be furnished with a letter 'on each occasion when a special telephone line is leased by the FBI.' Such leased lines had been used in the past during wiretap operations and were to be used as well 'in connection with microphone surveillances.' Thereafter, whenever requesting leasing lines from the telephone company in New York and elsewhere, Hoover cited Kennedy's 17 August letter as his authority – without, however, briefing Kennedy on each of these requests.'

In effect, then, Hoover had defined FBI microphone surveillance policy himself. His success in doing so sprang from the reluctance of Attorneys General McGranery, Brownell, Rogers, and Kennedy to exercise their authority and to insist on being fully informed about the FBI's practices. Aware of the legal questions posed by resort to this technique, these attorneys general preferred being uninformed to exercising their lawful authority, willingly granting Hoover a blank check. The Director, in turn, welcomed this indefinite waiver of accountability and, in time, came to regard it as his right.

Attorney General Katzenbach in 1965 became the first to challenge Hoover's unquestioned authority. Having learned that the FBI was wiretapping and bugging individuals (most notably Martin Luther King, Jr.) without his prior knowledge and consent, Katzenbach decided to tighten existing administrative procedures governing both wiretaps and bugs. Accordingly, on 30 March he instituted new guidelines – to wit, that a wiretap, when first authorized, was to be limited to a six-month lifespan, after which time a written request for re-authorization had to be submitted for the attorney general's approval. Every bug was to be subject to the same procedure, for the first time requiring the attorney general's prior approval, which, again, was to stay in force for only six months, after which time reauthorization would be required.[11]

Greatly concerned both by Katzenbach's assertion of his authority and by the 'present atmosphere,' which had resulted in 'congressional and public alarm and opposition to any activities which could in any way be termed an invasion of privacy,' Hoover informed Katzenbach of his intention to 'further cut down on wiretaps.' He would not

469

request 'authority for any additional wiretaps' and would 'discontinue completely the use' of bugs. This cutback, he complained, would adversely affect the FBI's ability to protect the nation 'against subversion and the rising crime rate.' But so be it.

Because Hoover's cutback went beyond Katzenbach's intended restrictions, Katzenbach redefined the guidelines for future FBI wiretapping and bugging practices. 'Wiretaps and microphones involving trespass,' he wrote, were not to be 'used without my authorization' except in emergency cases, when approval could be obtained after the fact. Such uses were to be 'confined to the gathering of intelligence in national security matters, and I will continue to approve all such requests in the future as I have in the past. I see no need to curtail any such activities in the national security field.' Recognizing that these restrictions could hamper coverage in the organized crime field, he nevertheless urged Hoover to redouble FBI efforts to develop intelligence through other means.

Katzenbach's decision to issue these new guidelines foreshadowed his response to the Supreme Court's order in the Fred Black case. The attorney general first learned of the FBI's bugging of Black in August 1965, and then only accidentally. Having asked Hoover whether any evidence in the case against Bobby Baker had been tainted, he discovered that the FBI had intercepted some of Baker's conversations from two bugs that it had installed in Black's office and hotel room in 1963. (Hoover noted on his copy of the memo advising Katzenbach of these bugs: 'Due to the highly confidential nature of such installations the Department was not previously advised regarding the installations on Black.')

When preparing to answer the Court, Katzenbach was already skeptical of Hoover's claim that former Attorney General Kennedy had known about FBI bugging activities. Writing to Katzenbach on 5 January 1966, Hoover had challenged then-Senator Kennedy's public protestations of ignorance of the FBI's use of microphones during investigations of organized crime. Hoover trotted out a number of cases in which, he asserted, Kennedy *had* been informed. His sole reason for briefing Katzenbach, the Director insisted, was to clarify that former Attorney General Kennedy and other department representatives 'were fully cognizant of the FBI's use of microphones, in conjunction with leased telephone lines, in our investigations directed against the leadership of organized crime during recent years.'

An unconvinced Katzenbach focused on Hoover's asseition that the former attorney general had known of 'the use of electronic devices in conjunction with local telephone lines in investigations of organized crime.' Katzenbach then recounted a recent conversation in which Kennedy had told him that 'he was unaware that any use was being made in the organized crime field of electronic devices of questionable legality.' From his own conversations with Hoover, Katzenbach added, he had learned that Kennedy 'was not familiar with the particular location of any such devices and that, unlike telephone taps, specific installations were not discussed with or approved by the Attorney General. In these circumstances, I can readily appreciate the possibility of a misunderstanding between Attorney General Kennedy and the Bureau as to his appreciation of the full extent of the use of electronic devices by the Bureau.' Having concluded that FBI bugging practices 'were in any event justified' on the basis of Hoover's 'understandings' with attorneys general prior to 1961, Katzenbach intended to 'stand behind [his predecessors'] actions.' In view of his own directive that any FBI bugging have his prior 'specific approval,' the attorney general observed, 'any misunderstandings which may have occurred in the past would seem to be academic. I doubt that any purpose would be served by airing any such differences as may exist between the Bureau and former Attorney General Kennedy.'

Katzenbach's suspicions were further aroused by Hoover's protest over the department's decision to advise the Supreme Court that the FBI had bugged Black's Washington hotel room and office in 1963. Hoover conceded that the FBI, as an investigative agency, would 'defer to the Department insofar as reaching a decision as to what information, if any, should be volunteered to the Court by the Department relative to the microphone coverage on Black.' Nevertheless, he protested that it would be 'extremely poor timing' to disclose the FBI's bugging of Black in view of two other pending cases against individuals who had been the targets of FBI bugs (one of whom was Bobby Baker). Such a disclosure, Hoover argued, 'would result in widespread publicity and would undoubtedly trigger a great deal of unwarranted criticism against the Bureau and the Department.' Furthermore, Black's rights were not affected, since the intercepted conversations had not been disseminated outside the FBI and were not available to government prosecutors. Hoover also protested that the solicitor general's proposed petition was 'drawn in extremely broad fashion and unnecessarily volunteered information concerning highly confidential [i.e., microphone] coverage not only in Washington, D.C., but in two other cities.' Last, Hoover specifically challenged the petition's assertion that department attorneys had only recently learned of the FBI bug on Black, pointing out that this had been known to the department as early as August 1965.

The Director's opposition notwithstanding, the department advised the Court that Black's hotel room and office had been bugged. Immediately, Hoover objected to the language of the department's brief. He reiterated his earlier claims that it unnecessarily revealed the FBI's bugging of Black 'in cities other than Washington,' which was the issue at trial (department attorneys agreed to revise this section of the brief) and that it erred in asserting that department attorneys had only recently learned about the bug in Black's suite, thus 'unnecessarily reflecting upon the Bureau.' Moreover, behind the scenes, he ordered his aides to search for evidence documenting that former Attorney General Kennedy had been briefed about the Black bug. But he had not been, and Hoover was forced to revise his strategy of implicating Kennedy.

Already upset, Hoover became even more incensed on learning how Katzenbach intended to handle the Court brief.

For the attorney general had decided to state, in a footnote in the revised petition, that incidents such as the bugging of Black 'will not recur' and, further, that 'although longstanding policies of the Department of Justice had required the specific authorization of the Attorney General in each instance for the interception of wire communications, until recently such authorization was not required with respect to the use of other types of listening devices. However, since early 1965 the use of listening devices in circumstances such as those described in this memorandum has been strictly confined to the collection of intelligence importantly affecting the national security and may be undertaken only pursuant to the express written authorization of the Attorney General in each instance as has been the case with wire communications.'

Hoover objected 'vehemently' to the implication that the Bureau 'was operating independently when we employed listening devices,' claiming that Kennedy had authorized the FBI to use microphones. The Director threatened to 'very definitely make it known publicly that former Attorney General Robert Kennedy had given general authorization for the use of microphones if this became necessary because of any public misconception caused by this footnote.'

Seeking to accommodate Hoover (and moved in part by his threat to disclose Kennedy's general authorization), Katzenbach reluctantly agreed to reword the footnote: 'Present Departmental policy which has been in effect since 1965 confines the use of listening devices such as those herein involved and also the interception of wire communications to the collection of intelligence affecting the national security. It also requires in each instance a specific authorization by the Attorney General. This policy superseded the broader Departmental authorization which had been in effect for a number of years.' Briefed on Gale's successful efforts to secure a statement to the effect that the department had in the past generally authorized bugging activities, thereby avoiding the 'impression that the Bureau was operating on its own initiative,' Hoover praised Gale for having 'handled this masterfully.'

473

Katzenbach, however, soon had second thoughts about making this admission, and Assistant Attorney General Mitchell Rogovin was dispatched to advise Gale that the footnote would be dropped altogether. How did the Department intend to handle the matter in the event of press inquiries? Gale asked. Along the lines of the footnote, Rogovin responded. In that case, the footnote should be kept, as 'oral statements have a way of being sleazily handled so as to give the wrong impression,' Gale observed. 'If there was any confusion on the part of the press, the FBI very definitely was going to correct the record by giving detailed information as to our Departmental authority insofar as microphones were concerned, and we have had this authority from Attorney General Robert Kennedy well documented.'

Concluding that Katzenbach was 'trying to wiggle out' of his agreement, Hoover ordered his aides to line up 'our ammunition concerning Bobby Kennedy's authorization of microphones, for subsequent release to the press in the event the footnote is not put in writing and the Department attempts to double-cross us by putting out any ambiguous statements reflecting that we were installing these microphones on our own initiative.'

Apparently Hoover's hard-ball approach worked, as later that day Katzenbach, although resolved to delete the footnote, decided to 'answer all press inquiries with 'no comment,' that this is a pending matter in court.' Hoover hoped that the no-comment procedure would be strictly followed, but was prepared, in the event of leaks to the press, 'definitely' to take 'appropriate steps to correct the record.'

Ordered to follow the matter closely, the FBI's Special Investigative Division and Crime Records Division prepared a statement concerning 'Kennedy's approval of microphones in the event it becomes necessary to use it because of any 'leaks' by the Department.' This 'blank, undated statement by 'an FBI spokesman'' categorically charged that Kennedy knew and approved 'the FBI's use of electronic devices in crime and racketeering cases.' Hoover forwarded this statement to Crime Records Division head Robert Wick for 'possible future use' with the further understanding that his 'specific approval will be needed *at the time it is given out.*'

Distressed by press reaction to the department's answer to the Court, Hoover once again protested to Katzenbach over the revised version of the department's brief. The reworked footnote should not have been dropped, the Director claimed, at the same time condemning the brief's admission that department attorneys preparing the Black case had not known of the FBI bug (although that would appear to have been obvious). This 'may be technically accurate,' Hoover conceded, but it 'was not at all revealing,' since the press had emphasized 'that what the Bureau did in the Black case in the use of microphones was unknown to the Department at all times.' Reminding Katzenbach of their earlier conversation concerning Robert Kennedy's claim to having 'had no knowledge that the Bureau was using microphones,' Hoover submitted a number of memoranda presumably indicating Kennedy's knowledge of FBI bugging practices. And, finally, commenting on Kennedy's recent press statement that he had not known of the Black bugging, Hoover did not dispute 'that statement as made,' but deplored its implication that the former attorney general 'was never advised that the Bureau was using microphone installations notwithstanding the specific approval by him of this.' The brief gave the impression, 'picked up by all of the press,' that the FBI was entirely responsible for bugging Black 'and that the Department of Justice was ignorant and completely without knowledge that microphone surveillances were being used.'

In a vain attempt to placate the Director, Katzenbach agreed that Hoover was right to be concerned about the 'problem of authorization for the use of microphone surveillance involving trespass.' This was not at issue in the Black case, since the evidence leading to Black's conviction had not been tainted and thus the interception had not affected Black's trial. Nevertheless, Katzenbach said, he had to inform the Court of the bugging, although he regretted the 'embarrassment' caused by its disclosure. Katzenbach did not doubt 'the good faith or integrity of the Bureau' on the question of authorization and had been willing to express this publicly in the proposed footnote. Katzenbach nevertheless challenged Hoover's criticism of the department's failure to include the footnote in the petition filed with the Court, observing that no objection had been raised to this decision at the time. He also defended the footnote's statement that no department attorney knew of the Black bugging during the preparation and trial of the case. Katzenbach pointed out that Black was convicted on 5 May 1964 and that Hoover had not briefed anyone in the department on the FBI's bugging of Black until August 1965. In short, Hoover had no legitimate objection to the brief that the department had filed with the Supreme Court.

Unwilling to back down and convinced that Katzenbach would not admit publicly that the department had authorized FBI bugging practices (because he was 'obviously determined to do anything at all in order to protect Bobby Kennedy'), Hoover answered Katzenbach's memo on 3 June, pointing out its 'inaccuracies, innuendos and distorted views.' The question of authorization was indeed highly relevant, he said. Press accounts had conveyed 'the impression that the Bureau utilized microphones without authorization.' He continued that FBI bugging had been based on Brownell's directive of 1954 as continued by Rogers and Kennedy – until Katzenbach changed the policy to require the attorney general's prior authorization. Referring in passing to Brownell's and Rogers's authorization, Hoover stressed that Kennedy was fully knowledgeable and, specifically, was aware that the FBI installed bugs through trespass. Returning once again to the proposed footnote, Hoover contended that its deletion 'created a false and erroneous impression that the Bureau was operating microphones without Departmental authority and the vast majority of the press has printed this erroneous impression.'

On 13 June 1966 Hoover's complaint was made moot by the Supreme Court's response to Solicitor General Thurgood Marshall's petition. The Court ordered a 'response from the Government . . . toward the kind of apparatus used by the Government; the person or persons who authorized its installation; the statute or Executive Order relied upon; the date or dates of installation; whether there is in existence a recording of conversations heard; when the information concerning [Black] came into the hands of any attorney for the Government and to which ones, as well as what use was made of the information in the case against [Black].'

Most of these questions were technical and factual and posed no policy problem – and clearly they were germane to the case. The Court's demand for information about authorization and knowledge, however, went to the heart of Hoover's conflict with Katzenbach, ensuring that the matter could no longer be skirted and also that Hoover would be infuriated by the department's response.

Acting as Katzenbach's liaison, Deputy Attorney General Ramsey Clark attempted to handle this delicate mission. He asked Hoover that same day to designate an FBI official to cooperate with Assistant Attorney General Rogovin in preparing 'our reply.'

Hoover answered abruptly that in view of the FBI's 'recent experience with Rogovin and his efforts to twist oral discussions had with him to the Bureau's detriment,' the FBI would only respond in writing and would not directly work with Rogovin 'at this time.' And in a memo to Katzenbach, the Director again belabored the question of 'the installation of the microphone in this matter,' charging that it 'was made with general Departmental authorization under former Attorney General Robert F. Kennedy.'

Then, commenting on the Court's request for statutory or executive authorization for FBI bugging, Hoover cited President Roosevelt's May 1940 wiretapping directive and Brownell's May 1954 bugging directive, claiming that this authority had been 'reaffirmed' by Attorney General Rogers and 'continued during Mr. Kennedy's tenure as Attorney General' until changed by Katzenbach's March 1965 order. The FBI's liaison with Attorney General Kennedy, Courtney Evans, Hoover told Katzenbach, 'had often briefed Mr. Kennedy concerning the Black investigation.' On one occasion, Hoover claimed, Evans had furnished Kennedy with 'information which could only have come from a microphone.' Kennedy could 'well have inferred the usage of microphones as a result of this information furnished to him by Mr. Evans.'

Hoover's brazen attempt to pressure Katzenbach to defend the FBI's interests at the expense of the department's failed. Unwilling to accept Hoover's claims at face value, Katzenbach with brilliant insight pressed Hoover for specific answers and documentation supporting his assertions, particularly his assertion that Attorneys General Brownell and Rogers had not required their prior authorization for installing bugs. When had this authorization occurred? Was the confirmation oral or written? Why had Hoover not referred to McGrath's February 1952 memo? Why was Black bugged, since he 'was the subject of legal proceedings?' Why had Hoover not 'promptly' advised the Department that Black's conversations with his lawyer had been intercepted?

Katzenbach's questions posed grave problems for Hoover, for the Director's claimed authority was quite groundless. Researching the background of the Brownell directive, Hoover's aides came across former Assistant Attorney General Olney's memorandum recommending the attorney general's prior approval for the installation of microphones. 'Olney's views did not correspond with the decision subsequently expressed by Rogers and the Attorney General's memorandum of May 20, 1954,' Gale observed as justification for a decision not to refer to 'Olney in our current response to the Department.' 'There is no point in giving the Department Olney's name,' Gale advised Hoover, 'as he is antagonistic toward the Bureau and he might well confuse the issue further with misleading statements if he were contacted by the Department.'

Because Hoover knew that he could not satisfactorily answer Katzenbach's questions about the Bureau's coverage of Black, he fell back again on the argument that Kennedy must have known of the Black bug. Responding to Hoover's demand to know why he had not been briefed at the beginning of the dispute over McGrath's February 1952 memorandum, given Katzenbach's citation of this memorandum in his letter, Gale answered that it had been superseded by Brownell's directive of 1954. The Director's aides unhesitantly reverted to what had become Hoover's last line of defense: 'as the Director has noted, Katzenbach is indeed "digging into antiquity" in his desire to protect former Attorney General Kennedy on the question of authorization of microphones . . . (and) has raised a completely extraneous issue. The main and central issue in the Black microphone is and has been the authorization of the use of microphones by Attorney General Kennedy.'

As he still in fact had no evidence to show that Kennedy knew about or had authorized the Black microphone (let alone FBI microphone installations in general), Hoover decided as a last resort to emphasize Kennedy's 'unique, close and informal relationship' with Courtney Evans. Because of this 'unique' relationship, he now claimed, Evans 'apparently frequently failed to reduce his conversations in writing until events occurred which required the submission of such memoranda.' Katzenbach's purpose, he suggested, was 'to draw this matter away from Kennedy and confuse it with extraneous and irrelevant issues which took place during the regimes of former Attorneys General, such as McGrath.' Hoover concluded his letter to the attorney general by sharply placing Kennedy's supposed authorization 'back in focus with the current problem, i.e., the Black case' and by putting the 'responsibility where it belongs on Attorney General Kennedy.'

When responding to Katzenbach's questions, Hoover followed this line of argument. Unable to cite specific documents recording Brownell's and Rogers's blanket authorization, the Director referred repeatedly to 'discussions' the FBI had with Rogers in 1954. Kennedy had continued the blanket authorization practice in 1961, Hoover then claimed, alluding to his 'unique, close and informal relationship' with Evans and to his having listened to tapes of FBI bugs during his visits to FBI field offices. He also referred to Evans's briefings of Kennedy on the Black investigation and to his having furnished Kennedy with information that could only have been obtained from a microphone. 'In our opinion,' Hoover declared categorically, 'this constituted notification to the Department in the Black case.' Hoover concluded his case by pointing to Kennedy's insistence that the FBI fully utilize all of its resources, including microphones, when investigating whether Teamster President James Hoffa might have had a mole in the Justice Department. That directive, he insisted, set the 'guidelines' for FBI bugging of subjects of a criminal investigation.

Hoover's obvious animus toward Kennedy, as well as his failure to cite documents supporting his claims, failed to disarm officials of the department. But meanwhile Hoover had ordered his top troubleshooter Cartha DeLoach to monitor the department's second response to the Supreme Court. DeLoach soon learned that Katzenbach intended to advise the Court either that 'permission to place a listening device was given by a duly constituted authority' or that 'the Director of the FBI authorized the listening device.' DeLoach warned Katzenbach's representative, Deputy Attorney General Clark, that the FBI 'of course, would object to both versions and particularly the latter one.' The assistant director, playing hardball, 'hoped it would not be necessary for us to request an audience before the Supreme Court or to necessarily put out the absolute truth in a formal press release.'

Clark's briefing accurately foreshadowed Katzenbach's proposed response to the Court, which he communicated to Hoover beforehand for the Director's 'consideration and comment.' Katzenbach intended to have Solicitor General Marshall advise the Court that

the director of the Federal Bureau of Investigation has general authority to act for the Department of Justice in conducting investigations or gathering intelligence with respect to matters within the Department's jurisdiction. Specific authorization by the Attorney General has been required for the interception of wire communications since 1940, but no similar procedure existed until 1965 with respect to the use of devices such as those involved in the instant case. Oral and written communications within the Department of Justice reflect that under departmental practice put into effect more than a decade prior to 1965, the Director of the Federal Bureau of Investigation was given authority to approve installation of devices such as that in question for intelligence purposes whenever justified by considerations of internal security and national safety. The Director approved installation of the device involved in the instant case.

At issue was nothing less than who had authorized the illegal bugging of Fred Black. Not surprisingly, Hoover was outraged by the draft and insisted on revisions to the effect that former Attorneys General Brownell, Rogers, and Kennedy had all authorized FBI microphone installations during criminal investigations. It was Caliban delivering an ultimatum to Prospero.

Designated as Katzenbach's emissary, Clark attempted again to work out the differences over the proposed response. Neither Brownell nor Rogers, Clark explained, had ever authorized microphones 'outside of the internal security area'; they 'were completely unaware of trespass being involved in the usage of any microphones' and had refused 'to go along with the Director's suggested language.' In view of this, Clark said, Katzenbach had decided not to insert the demanded revision and particularly not to accede to his insistence on adding that Kennedy had verbally authorized the Black installation. Katzenbach had also found Evans (who had meanwhile resigned from the Bureau) to be 'quite vague about any conversations he had with former Attorney General Kennedy concerning the Black case.'

Hoover more than rose to this occasion. First, he had DeLoach contact Rogers to secure his support, since Brownell, who was out of the country, was willing to defer to his fellow Republican. By shrewdly appealing to Rogers's partisan loyalties and by misrepresenting Katzenbach's position as an attempt to defend Kennedy, DeLoach soon brought Rogers around to Hoover's side.

Requesting a personal meeting with the former attorney

general, DeLoach then explained that he wanted to show him 'various communications relative to this matter.' Clearly sympathetic, Rogers agreed to the meeting, saying that 'he, of course, did not want to do anything which would cause embarrassment to the Director and the FBI,' although he 'wondered why it was necessary to go back to 1954,' since Black had been bugged in 1963. When DeLoach claimed to have extensive documentation reflecting Rogers's 'agreement with our use of microphones in criminal cases,' Rogers pleaded 'a hazy recollection in such matters,' reiterating his desire that there be no reference to pre-1960 developments. DeLoach agreed, saying that 'it was obvious that Katzenbach was attempting to state that FBI usage of microphones began with the Republicans and that Bobby Kennedy merely inherited the situation.' Rogers opined that 'this was absolutely true and all the more reason why he and Brownell should not be brought into the matter.' Were he and Brownell left out of the brief entirely, Rogers emphasized, they would both 'merely give "no comments" if they were queried by reporters after the brief had been presented to the Supreme Court.'

Briefed on DeLoach's initial contact with Rogers, Hoover directed his aide to prepare a counterproposal to the effect that 'the brief merely cover the period of the Kennedy and Katzenbach administrations and not go back beyond 1960.' There would be no retreat from Hoover's original position that he had obtained such bugging authority from Brownell and Rogers; such a narrowing, however, would 'defeat Katzenbach's purpose of bringing the Republicans into this matter' and would also 'adequately protect the FBI and at the same time point out that authority was definitely given by Kennedy and Katzenbach.'

In his meeting with Rogers, DeLoach emphasized that the FBI 'more or less had its back against the wall' owing to Kennedy's and Katzenbach's refusals 'to admit the truth.' Showing Rogers the department's proposed response to the Supreme Court and the FBI's counterproposal, DeLoach stressed that it was Katzenbach's idea and not Hoover's 'to express in the original brief the intimation that microphone

authority was initiated a decade ago by the Republicans.'
'The reasons were perfectly obvious,' DeLoach observed,
'i.e., to blame someone other than Bobby Kennedy for usage
of microphones.' DeLoach's misrepresentation of
Katzenbach's position and his groundless claim to have
evidence that Kennedy had known of the bugging and had
even authorized the FBI to install bugs during criminal
investigations elicited the desired response.

'Greatly surprised' and appalled at Katzenbach's 'brazen
effrontery,' Rogers could not understand 'why Katzenbach
and Kennedy had attempted to lie their way out of
responsibility.' Rogers at once called Katzenbach's office
to arrange a meeting, promising to brief Hoover
'immediately following his meeting.' Then, examining the
limited documentation that DeLoach had brought with him,
Rogers agreed to 'stand back of any memorandum in Bureau
files which quoted him' (there was none, but Rogers had
no way of knowing that). How would Rogers handle any
press inquiries 'regarding the language Katzenbach proposed
to send to the Supreme Court?' DeLoach asked. Rogers
promised to 'make "no comment" to the press if it was
clearly indicated that it would embarrass the FBI' and added
that should Katzenbach 'deliberately' attempt to embarrass
him and Brownell, he would 'fall back on' Brownell's 1954
directive. Such a position 'would certainly not harm the FBI
in any manner.' DeLoach thanked Rogers, later assuring
Hoover that 'we could count on him.'

Thus assured of Rogers's support, DeLoach approached
Clark. During the course of their conversation, Katzenbach
telephoned Clark, after which the deputy attorney general
reportedly told DeLoach, 'You obviously did a good day's
work yesterday. The "ancient history" will undoubtedly be
removed from the brief.' (Clark's demeanor, DeLoach
exulted later, made it 'quite apparent that Rogers had called
Katzenbach in some anger and had laid the law down to
him.')[12] All the FBI wanted in this matter, DeLoach
insisted, was the 'truth,' and it 'was not going to be made
the 'goat' in this case.' Hoover was 'perfectly willing to lay
the evidence before Senator Long's committee and thereafter

stand on the record.' ('Clark made no reply,' DeLoach reported, 'but I am certain he got the point.')

DeLoach's reference to Senator Long was not an idle or a spur-of-the-moment threat. At the time when the department was considering whether to tell the Supreme Court that Black's hotel room had been bugged, Hoover 'confidentially' briefed Long on the FBI's bugging of Black and the department's intended brief. Long agreed that 'this was a most unfortunate development in that columnists like Drew Pearson, Fred Graham of the New York Times, and Dave Kraslow of the Los Angeles Times, together with liberals on his committee, and the anti-FBI groups, would again raise a hue and cry for the Long Committee to hold hearings on the FBI.' He had been successful in averting such hearings, Long pointed out, because he could claim that the FBI 'only used these devices in organized crime and security cases,' and although the 'case on Black potentially involved organized crime . . . it would be difficult to get this over to the public.' Long appreciated being briefed 'prior to the motion being filed because otherwise some reporters could have really caught him off guard,' and he reiterated 'that he had no desire to hurt the FBI or hold hearings on the FBI and he would figure out something with respect to handling his critics.'

Thus assured of Long's loyalty, Hoover contacted the senator one month later. Again sympathetic, Long promised to put Katzenbach 'on notice that the Attorney General's reply to the Supreme Court had better be absolutely factual or else hearings would be held.' Sending such a letter the next day, Long anributed his interest in the Black case to the publicity it had received, and warned against any 'deliberate attempt . . . to shield or defend any parties.' His subcommittee had a mandate to see 'that responsibility for such actions is properly fixed,' and although hearings 'in regard to the Justice Department,' had not 'definitely' been set, the subcommittee 'will certainly be interested in the reply of your Department to the Supreme Court in regard to the questions raised concerning various wiretapping (sic) activities. No doubt we will want to schedule hearings at some later date so that the Congress may have perhaps further details in the matter than might be filed with the Supreme Court.'

Before sending his letter, Long chanced to meet Katzenbach at a White House signing ceremony. There the senator told the attorney general (as the senator confided to DeLoach) of his interest in the Black case and admitted to having already written him about the matter. 'Unless the Department's reply to the Supreme Court was handled in a proper manner,' Long said he emphasized, 'it might be necessary to call both the Director and the Attorney General for public hearings.' According to Long's report, the attorney general responded, 'Oh my God, not that! Let's don't bring all this stuff out.' Then, claiming to have told Katzenbach that 'he would take no action until he saw' the attorney general's reply to the Supreme Court, Long confided that he had no intention 'whatsoever' of calling the director or the attorney general but concluded that 'his conversation this morning and his letter would certainly put the "fear of God" in the Attorney General.' Long promised to 'follow this matter closely.'

Long's conversation and letter had the desired effect. When responding to the letter, with a copy to Hoover, Katzenbach expressed his willingness 'to discuss the matter with you at any mutually convenient time.'

Hoover at the same time sought to enlist the support of the Johnson White House — in this case by appealing to the president's animosity toward Robert Kennedy. Briefing Special Assistant to the President Marvin Watson on the department's response to the Supreme Court, Hoover called attention to Katzenbach's comment that Kennedy had denied approving FBI bugging during criminal investigations. Katzenbach had then been told that Kennedy 'was either lying or had a very convenient lack of memory,' and Hoover had then offered examples of Kennedy's authorization. Watson might be interested in this documentation, Hoover concluded, for review by the president 'in the event he is questioned at any time concerning the matter.' Thereafter Hoover periodically briefed Watson on the dispute, representing the issue as an attempt by Katzenbach 'to absolve' Kennedy of any responsibility for authorizing the 'use of wiretaps and microphones with trespass.'

Hoover's shrewd appeal to Johnson's anti-Kennedy prejudices had the desired effect. In response, the president urged Hoover 'to bring 'the facts' concerning Kennedy's authorization of wire tapping [sic] before a Congressional Committee' and recommended 'someone like [Congressman] John Rooney, or perhaps another committee.' Hoover thanked Johnson and agreed to consider his suggestion. Or at least so DeLoach advised Watson, who assured him that 'the President was most anxious to see that the Director not get hurt in connection with this matter. He wants to put Kennedy in his place.'

Given this background, Clark not surprisingly was eager to accommodate Hoover's demand for revisions in the department's response to the Court. First, Clark agreed to delete some of the specific references to the Director and explained that 'if the title of "Director" appears too many times in leading statements, possibly newsmen will tend to overemphasize the Director's role.' It was understood that this change was 'simply utilization of better phraseology insofar as newspaper consumption is concerned.' Second, and more important, Clark agreed to Rogers's demand that the reference to Departmental authorization use the vague phrase 'for some years' and not cite the 1950s. Clark then addressed the 'crux of the problem,' Hoover's insistence on insertion of a statement that 'no information [was] obtained by means of the listening device, other than that verbally given to the Attorney General on a frequent basis during the course of the Black investigation.' Katzenbach would not agree to this language, but recognized that 'it is now the responsibility of the Department to prepare a new draft and send it over to the FBI.'

Rather difficult negotiations ensued over the next week, closing only when Solicitor General Thurgood Marshall formally presented the department's response to the Court's order. The content and phraseology of the response suggest that Hoover had been the final arbiter of its language.

And that, in fact, was the case. Representing Hoover in these negotiations, DeLoach had not hesitated to threaten Clark with the Director's 'most anxious' desire that Senator Long initiate inquiries concerning this matter. DeLoach emphasized, 'that the FBI had nothing to fear, yet would have considerable evidence to present in behalf of this case,' adding that the Director's sole concern 'was simply to have the facts spelled out in the form of truth.' By mutual agreement, as a result, Hoover was to review all proposed changes and deletions.

But Katzenbach had still refused to accede to all of Hoover's demands. For one thing, he rejected the Director's request to delete the phrase 'There is, however, no specific statute or executive order expressly authorizing the installation of a listening device such as that involved in this case.' Katzenbach also refused to grant Hoover's request to include language to the effect that Kennedy had been 'verbally' briefed on the Black microphone. Both Kennedy and Evans disputed the Director on this point, and there was no written record confirming Hoover's contention. Finally, Katzenbach refused to append to the brief the specific list of documents Hoover recommended; the Director's list was incomplete, and other sensitive documents could not be publicly disclosed.

As a result, the formal departmental response to the Court accurately reflected the fact that Hoover had acted on his own authority because attorneys general since McGranery had been unwilling to accept responsibility for monitoring FBI bugging activities:

Under Departmental practice in effect for a period of years prior to 1963, and continuing into 1965, the Director of the Federal Bureau of Investigation was given authority to approve the installation of devices such as that in question for intelligence (and not evidentiary) purposes when required in the interest of internal security and national safety, including organized crime, kidnappings, and matters wherein human life might be at stake. Acting on the basis of the aforementioned Departmental authorization, the Director approved installation of a device involved in the instant case.

Katzenbach's insistence on exercising his authority as Hoover's superior had provoked a tense confrontation with the insecure but powerful Director. And the Director did not forgive. As Katzenbach candidly admitted during the 1975 congressional testimony, his unwillingness to knuckle under to Hoover when preparing the department's response to the Court's order in the *Black* case had made him 'dramatically aware of the lengths to which the Bureau would go in trying to justify its authority. My correspondence with Mr. Hoover at that time unavoidably became a bitter one, and it persuaded me that I could no longer effectively serve as Attorney General because of Mr. Hoover's obvious resentment toward me.' Katzenbach subsequently resigned to accept appointment as Deputy Under Secretary of State.

Katzenbach's steadfastness, however, was at least partly vindicated. Having failed to secure the attorney general's total acquiescence in his demands and therefore threatened by the prospect that another congressional committee might inquire into FBI investigative activities more zealously than had the outmaneuvered Long Subcommittee, Hoover feared for his job. Furthermore, Katzenbach's insistence on being fully briefed and on authorizing any FBI microphone surveillance installations demonstrated that Hoover could no longer rely on the blind acquiescence of the attorney general.

Hoover therefore decided to abandon these practices. Already in February 1965, in response to the Long Subcommittee's planned inquiry into FBI surveillance activities, he had considered 'discontinuing all techniques – technical coverage [wiretaps], microphones, trash covers, mail covers etc. While it might handicap us I doubt they are as valuable as some believe & none warrant[s] the FBI being used to justify them.' Now he instituted this ban. Furthermore, following Katzenbach's March 1965 order requiring his written authorization and reauthorization for all FBI wiretaps and bugs, Hoover had cut back by one-half the Bureau's wiretaps and virtually abandoned its use of bugs. The *Black* case then redoubled the Director's fears, particularly as the bug in that case had been installed by an illegal entry.

Accordingly, in July 1966, Hoover formally ordered both that 'no more such techniques [black bag jobs] must be used' (i.e., that the FBI should refrain from staging break-ins to obtain the correspondence and the membership and subscription lists of targeted 'subversive' individuals and organizations) and that FBI mail-opening programs were to be terminated. The Director had also concluded that existing records procedures were inadequate, for he then ordered FBI officials 'to avoid maintenance of records which might at some time prove embarrassing, in that it shows cognizance on their (FBI officials') part of an illegal entry.'

Nevertheless, Hoover's orders supposedly terminating FBI break-ins and mail openings were not clear, whether because of his ambivalence about abandoning these illegal practices or his concern over the possible discovery of his earlier authorization. He issued no written directive terminating FBI mail openings, and despite his July 1966 order that resort to break-ins should cease, he continued to receive requests to authorize such activities (as had been required under the 'Do Not File' procedure). Moreover, in striking contrast to his usual reaction when disobeyed, he was now surprisingly tolerant of efforts at noncompliance. In a Strictly Confidential 6 January 1967 memo to Tolson and DeLoach, he commented:

I note that requests are still being made by Bureau officials for the use of 'black bag' techniques. I have previously indicated that I do not intend to approve any such requests in the future, and, consequently, no such recommendations should be submitted for approval of such matters. This practice, which includes surreptitious entrances upon premises of any kind, will not meet with my approval in the future.

489

Hoover's 1966 directive may have been intended simply to replace a written authorization procedure with an oral one.[13] Alternatively, it is altogether conceivable, in view of the atmosphere of lawlessness Hoover had created within the Bureau,[14] that his senior aides and ambitious SACs, opposed to the Boss's restrictive order and belatedly acquired sense of caution, acted insubordinately and on their own. Whatever the case, the illegal investigative activities continued.

Hoover's caution probably isolated him from day-to-day operations of the Bureau, but his position for the time being was assured by his willingness to protect the one individual who could dismiss him as Director, President Lyndon Baines Johnson. Having volunteered his services since 1961 to contain possible threats to the then-vice president, after November 1963 Hoover turned the FBI into the domestic intelligence arm of the Johnson White House — and, in the wake of Johnson's decision to intervene in the Dominican Republic in 1965, a foreign intelligence arm as well.

In 1961 Dominican Republic strongman Raphael Trujillo was overthrown in a popular military coup, and in free elections held the next year the Social Democrat Juan Bosch won the presidency. Bosch's reformist policies led to a countercoup by disgruntled military officers in 1963. The new military government's incompetence and unpopularity soon precipitated another coup, on 24 April 1965, by a group of junior military officers committed to restoring democratic government under Bosch. Concerned about the spread of the rebellion and about the radical politics of the rebel leaders, President Johnson on 28 April ordered U.S. marines into the deteriorating military situation. Raw military power defeated the coup and restored order.

Having won a military victory, Johnson confronted a complex political problem. First, he needed to disarm opposition within the United States to this interventionist act, and, second, he needed to establish a new government in the Dominican Republic untainted by association with Trujillo, yet not aligned with the more militant Boschists.

As his original justification for sending in the marines, Johnson publicly insisted that although the first coup might have been led by Boschists, they had lost control to Castroites. In defense of this claim, the U.S. ambassador to the Dominican Republic, William Tapley Bennett, produced a list of seventy-seven alleged communists and communist sympathizers. Reporters who checked Bennett's list almost immediately discovered that those listed were not communists – and some had been in prison or out of the country when the revolt began, while still others were known anti-American nationalists with no communist associations.

To avert further embarrassment and ensure public acceptance of promised elections (to be held in 1966), Johnson needed better intelligence about the political situation in the Dominican Republic and about potential candidates whom the United States could support. To achieve these complementary objectives, he requested Hoover's assistance. In May 1965 the Director therefore dispatched fourteen FBI agents to the island to conduct security checks on potential members of the provisional government. Reporting back to Johnson the next month, Hoover described the situation as 'touch-and-go,' claiming that the Boschists were 'doing everything in their power' to thwart the president's efforts 'to bring order out of the chaos which exists there,' but that the FBI's fourteen agents were 'producing excellent results' in influencing the political situation. In response, Johnson asked Hoover to 'take the evidence coming in and prepare in writing the strongest case [you] can to prove that [Communist domination] when and if we have to.' Hoover said that he would 'have this done.'

While actively involved in investigating Dominican political leaders, Hoover also worked closely with National Security Adviser McGeorge Bundy, screening presidential candidates to ensure the selection of a 'strong man who is anticommunist.' Agreeing to 'get ourselves organized and not to let ourselves drift,' Hoover also undertook to talk to 'Dominican official [name deleted] pretty sharply and roughly to keep him in line' and to review other appointees to key executive positions in the provisional government.

Bundy, in turn, asked Hoover to run a check on his proposed [name deleted] nominee as U.S. ambassador to the Dominican Republic and to give his own 'opinion on it, as he, Bundy, knows the President values my opinion.' Hoover promised to do so.

Later that same month Special Assistant to the President Jack Valenti solicited Hoover's 'personal judgment' on 'a memoranda [sic] from McGeorge Bundy on the Dominican Republic.' Hoover again promised to take care of the request immediately and submitted his evaluation to Valenti the next day.

Then, with the victory in the delayed presidential election of Joaquin Balaguer, a former Trujillo associate whom the president deemed acceptable, Johnson called Hoover to request that the FBI's principal agent in the Dominican Republic, Clark D. Anderson, remain there 'until the inauguration is over.' Later, on Anderson's return, the president requested that Hoover bring him to the White House 'so the President can salute him and thank him as he thinks a good job was done and he wanted to personally tell him.'

Hoover's assistance to Johnson in the Dominican Republic may ultimately have determined the outcome there. However, it paled into insignificance in comparison with his helpfulness in the more complex and politically explosive Vietnam War crisis that followed Johnson's decision to escalate the U.S. military role there. The president's authorization of the bombing of North Vietnam and his subsequent commitment of U.S. troops in support of the South Vietnamese government precipitated opposition from radical activists and a small minority of liberal congressmen. And as U.S. involvement escalated, so did public opposition, with its legions centered on the college campuses. To sustain support for an increasingly costly policy and to discredit his critics, Johnson sought to revive Cold War passions (offering a 'domino theory' rationale for the U.S. commitment) and to raise public doubts about the loyalty of his critics. To achieve this latter objective, he turned once again to Hoover.

492

At first, the White House requested only FBI name checks on individuals who had written letters or telegrams criticizing the president's policy. Hoover dutifully complied and went one step further, submitting reports on the Committee for a SANE Nuclear Policy (an organization in the forefront of opposition to American intervention in the war) and on individuals and organizations that had demonstrated in opposition to the president's Vietnam policy. Then, in 1967, the White House, in an even more sensitive request, asked Hoover for file checks on seven liberal senators who had criticized the president's decision to resume the bombing of North Vietnam (which had been temporarily suspended). Hoover forwarded whatever derogatory information the FBI had on all seven senators in an attempt, as he said, to prove that 'the Communist Party and other organizations are continuing their efforts to force the United States to change its present policy toward Vietnam.'

The president by then had made a still more sensitive request, asking Hoover in February 1966 to monitor the Senate Foreign Relations Committee's forthcoming televised hearings on the administration's Vietnam policy and to prepare a memorandum determining whether Committee Chairman J. William Fulbright (D.-Ark.) and other Senate critics 'were receiving information from Communists.' Hoover immediately forwarded a memorandum 'which sets out the Communist Party line concerning some of the issues raised during the Senate Foreign Relations Committee hearings on U.S. policy in Vietnam.' The enclosed memorandum correlated Senators Fulbright's and Wayne Morse's statements with those of Communist leaders and Communist party publications. Hoover, however, could not confirm that the Communist party 'or any other subversive groups' had furnished materials to these senators and had thereby prompted their statements.

An undaunted White House soon escalated its demands. In March 1966, for example, the president asked Hoover to 'constantly keep abreast of the actions of representatives of (Soviet and Communist bloc officials) in making contacts with Senators and Congressmen and any citizens of a prominent nature.' Johnson confided that 'much of this protest concerning his foreign policy, particularly the hearings in the Senate, had been generated by (Communist officials).'

Eager to honor the president's request, Hoover had his aides prepare a sixty-seven-page chronological survey, based on FBI wiretaps, of the contacts of U.S. senators, representatives, and congressional staff members with Soviet bloc embassies during the period from I July 1965 to 17 March 1966. Hoover sent this report to the White House on 22 March 1966, submitted a follow-up report on 13 May, and thereafter, until January 1969, forwarded biweekly any additional information on congressional contacts with Communist officials acquired through the FBI's foreign embassy wiretaps.

The Director's assistance to the president went even beyond submitting reports supposedly documenting the subversive nature of antiwar dissent. On 27 April 1965 Central Intelligence Agency Director John McCone advised McGeorge Bundy that the Chinese and North Vietnamese believed that antiwar sentiment in the United States might force the country to withdraw troops from Vietnam. Bundy, in response, asked Hoover if the FBI could document the Communist role in developing opposition to the administration's Vietnam policy, and Hoover sent the requested information that same day. Hoover's evidence, however, consisted only of press clippings from conservative columnists attributing antiwar agitation to the Communists.

Meeting with Hoover on 28 April, Johnson thanked the Director for the clippings, reiterated his concern over antiwar criticism (claiming that 'no doubt' Communists were 'behind the disturbance'), and asked Hoover to 'brief at least two Senators and two Congressmen, preferably one of each Party, on the demonstrations so that they might in turn not only make speeches upon the floor of Congress but also publicly.' This also was done.

Hoover went even further, this time on his own, directing his aides to prepare a memorandum on the militantly antiwar student organization Students for a Democratic Society

(SDS) that could 'be used publicly by prominent officials of the Administration whom the President intends to send in various parts of the country on the Vietnam situation.' Hoover demanded that his aides prepare a 'good strong memorandum' drawn up with sufficient care that 'there will be nothing to uncover our informal coverage' of SDS. The requested memorandum was delivered to Bundy that same day.

As antiwar criticism on college campuses mounted, Hoover's FBI intensified investigations of college-based 'subversive activity,' particularly the teach-in movement and the so-called free universities. In March 1968 the Director authorized another investigative program, code-named VIDEM, to ascertain Communist influence in antiwar demonstrations. Under this program, field offices forwarded all information regarding demonstrations 'for immediate dissemination to the White House and other interested Government agencies.'

Meanwhile, on I June 1967, alerted to the possibility that a 'Peace Party' ticket might be formed for the 1968 election, Hoover approved a plan to disrupt this political campaign by 'effectively tabbing as communists or communist-backed the more hysterical opponents of the President on the Vietnam question in the midst of the presidential campaign [which] would be a real boon to Mr. Johnson.' Hoover also demanded that all FBI field offices forward information 'on a continuing basis' for 'prompt . . . dissemination to the news media . . . to discredit the New Left movement.' Field offices were to be alert to any information on the political associations, Communist links, and personal habits of New Left activists – Hoover specifically demanded that 'every avenue of possible embarrassment must be vigorously and enthusiastically explored.'

Equally intent on punishing the left and pleasing the president, Hoover also sought to exploit the Bureau's contacts with the American Legion. He launched this project by arranging a meeting between the president, DeLoach (the FBI's liaison not only to the White House but also to the Legion), and Legion National Commander Eldon James to

495

'talk about some highly secretive [*sic*] matters.' During this meeting, Johnson briefed James on the FBI's reports on subversive influence within the antiwar movement and requested 'the support of The American Legion in connection with his policies involving Vietnam.' Johnson asked that the Legion take 'a firmer stand in the near future' and 'take the initiative in having thousands of letters sent to Senator Fulbright,' probably the administration's most prominent critic.

Johnson likewise requested Hoover's help in monitoring the press. Periodically after 1965 the White House requested FBI name checks on its more prominent media critics, including NBC commentator David Brinkley, AP reporter and Vietnam correspondent Peter Arnett, *New York Times* reporter Harrison Salisbury, syndicated columnist Joseph Kraft, *Life* magazine Washington bureau chief Richard Stolley, *Chicago Daily News* Washington bureau chief Peter Lisagor, and *Washington Post* executive Ben Gilbert.

In the case of Lisagor, the president also insisted on learning the journalist's sources of 'classified Air Force material.' Complaining that Lisagor was 'tearing' him apart and 'getting information from someplace,' Johnson asked Hoover 'to find out what he is doing and where he is getting his information.' The FBI 'could not do that,' Hoover objected, for 'if it were found out it would bring considerable discredit not only on the FBI, but the President himself.' Since the FBI had given the White House 'everything we have' on Lisagor, Hoover recommended to his aides that they 'stand pat for a few days and not make any positive emphasis on investigating Lisagor' but just advise White House officials 'we have various lines out to get a line on Lisagor.'

Hoover did not sit idly by, however. Quite the contrary, through the Bureau's contacts in the Washington press corps, the Director attempted to identify Lisagor's sources. But the only information uncovered, through a *U.S. News and World Report* reporter, was that Lisagor was 'probably one of the most able 'diggers' for news among the

Washington press corps,' attended all background briefing conferences at the State Department and Capitol Hill, had 'a knack for picking out significant remarks made at such briefings,' and had 'excellent contacts high up in the State Department.'

The president's concern about leaks subsequently led him to seek Hoover's assistance in identifying those in his administration responsible for providing information to *Washington Post* reporter Philip Geyelin about his decision to escalate U.S. involvement in the Vietnam War. Hoover was able to identify three individuals in the administration who were the 'most loquacious people we have come across.' One of them, he said, claimed to know 'nothing about this at all but his reputation is that he has a few favorites in the press that he talks to'; the second has 'quite a wide acquaintanceship and is friendly' with Geyelin, and the third was also friendly with Geyelin and 'has opposed the acceleration of any war in Viet Nam.' Hoover added that the FBI was 'going over the files in the Pentagon at the present time.'

After identifying the officials who either had attended the National Security Council meeting in question or with whom he had discussed the planned escalation, Johnson demanded that all be interviewed. The FBI had already begun interviewing, and two days later Hoover reported on the result of the Bureau's investigation. Seventy-five people had been interviewed, and one person had been identified as a possible source of the leak. Conceding that the evidence was 'circumstantial,' but outlining the reasons for his suspicions, Hoover provided Johnson with all of the FBI's information on the suspect.

Hoover's meticulous helpfulness could not save Johnson's presidency, but it led Johnson in 1969 to apprise his Republican successor, Richard Nixon, of the Director's inestimable value. 'If it hadn't been for Edgar Hoover,' Johnson reportedly stated, he 'couldn't have carried out [his] responsibilities as Commander in Chief. Period. Dick, you will come to depend on Edgar. He is a pillar of strength in a city of weak men. You will rely on him time and time again

497

to maintain security. He's the only one you can put your complete trust in.'

Notes to Chapter Fourteen

1. Another fear — for his and his family's personal security — was communicated to Hoover personally on 29 November 1963, after which Hoover recorded that Johnson thought of him, the Director, as 'more than head of the FBI — I [Hoover] was his brother and personal friend; that he knew I did not want anything to happen to his family; that he has more confidence in me than anybody in town.' (President Lyndon B. Johnson folder, Folder no. 92, Hoover O&C.)

2. Hoover's and Johnson's shared interest in purging the Justice Department of Kennedy loyalists continued after the November 1964 presidential election. Meeting with Hoover shortly after his victory, Johnson inquired 'about the fact that the Department of Justice was reemploying a number of individuals who had worked on the [successful] Bobby Kennedy campaign' for election to the U.S. Senate that same year. Then, in a follow-up meeting with DeLoach, Johnson voiced his intention 'to raise hell' with Robert Kennedy's successor as attorney general, Nicholas Katzenbach, on this matter and demanded information on the number of such people who had been rehired. Hoover instructed DeLoach to 'find out discreetly' who they were and to provide this information to White House aides Bill Moyers or Jack Valenti 'verbally so that nothing will be written in this regard.' (Informal Blind Memo, DeLoach, 18 November 1964, FBI 77-51387-Not Recorded.)

3. A Kennedy loyalist on the staff of the Democratic National Committee, Corbin was fired from the staff because of his efforts to promote Robert Kennedy's vice presidential candidacy in the New Hampshire primary.

4. The Johnson White House's extensive use of the FBI, and concomitant desire that this practice not become known, soon led White House aide Marvin Watson to propose to DeLoach, on 1 March 1966, that whenever the president requested information 'concerning matters of extreme secrecy, the FBI should not respond in writing by formal memorandum' but employ a 'blind-type memorandum which bore no government watermarks or no letterhead signifying the source of the memorandum.' The Director

would honor this request, DeLoach subsequently advised Watson, but proposed a modified procedure. It was Hoover's understanding that communications 'in those cases involving extremely confidential matters' would be maintained by the White House in a 'secure place.' The requested information would be submitted in 'a blind memorandum which will contain the pertinent subject matter,' and this would be attached to Hoover's nondescript cover letter to the White House. The cover letter itself would 'not reveal the specific subject matter, but will merely indicate that a memorandum is attached. We will, of course, in our records here at [the FBI] indicate on the yellow [carbon copy] of the Director's letter the subject matter in the blind memorandum. This will give us a record for future reference purposes.' (President Lyndon B. Johnson folder, Folder no. 92, Hoover O&C.)

5. The Warren Commission concluded that the FBI had taken an 'unduly restrictive view of its role in preventive intelligence work prior to the assassination.' 'A more carefully coordinated treatment of the Oswald case by the F.B.I.,' it suggested, 'might have resulted in bringing Oswald's activities to the attention of the Secret Service.' Hoover was so incensed by these glancing criticisms that he severed his long-term cooperative relationship with the Chief Justice the next month, ordering the removal of Warren's name from his Special Correspondents list. In 1948 Hoover had authorized FBI agents to furnish requested information to then-Governor Earl Warren of California 'in strictest confidence and none of the information can be attributed to the FBI.' Following up on this order, Hoover emphasized in 1951 that 'whatever the Governor requests I want prompt attention accorded to it.' Hoover's assistance extended as well to providing personal services to Warren, including on several occasions offering a personal car and drivers. Responding to the requests of a concerned parent, Hoover also had FBI agents check into the backgrounds of Dan Dailey (in 1954) and Stuart Brien (in 1955), beaus of Warren's daughter Nina (Nina married Brien in 1955). (*New York Times*, 29 November 1985, p. 32; Earl Warren Folder, Nichols O&C.)

6. Technically Tolson was right on this point, as Hoover had placed only *three* FBI agents on the subcommittee's staff.

7. On 21 December, moreover, Hoover sent copies of a specially prepared two-page FBI report entitled 'Martin Luther King, Jr.: His Personal Conduct' to the White House, vice President Humphrey, Secretary of state Dean Rusk, Secretary of Defense Robert McNamara, and the heads of the CIA, USIA, and the four

military intelligence services. Hoover sent another report to Attorney General Nicholas Katzenbach claiming that King had a reputation as a heavy drinker.

8. Beyond identifying the various senators' attitudes toward the FBI (all were described as 'friendly'), this file check came up with derogatory personal information only on Senator Quentin Burdick and Fensterwald.

9. Following that case, defense attorneys in internal security cases filed discovery motions on the premise that evidence leading to their clients' arrest had been obtained through illegal wiretaps.

10. The number of microphones installed by the FBI increased from 52 in 1953 to 99 in 1954, 102 in 1955; it averaged 72.6 for the remaining five years of the Eisenhower administration. During Robert Kennedy's attorney generalship, FBI uses increased further to 85 in 1961, 100 in 1962, 83 in 1963, and 106 in 1964. And a May 1966 FBI memorandum reports that of a total of 738 microphone installations dunng the period 1960-1966, the 'Department and/or United States Attorneys were notified of 158.' These totals, if broken down between internal security and criminal cases, reveal that the Department was notified of the FBI's use of microphones in 57 of 239 internal security cases and 64 of 380 criminal cases.

11. Not wholly resigned to these 'restrictions and limitations,' Hoover attributed them to 'the recent activities of Senator Long's Committee.'

12. In his meeting with Katzenbach, Rogers claimed that he had reviewed FBI documents on this matter and that 'the FBI certainly had a strong case and was certainly authorized to use microphones under the orders of Attorney General Kennedy.' Protesting against Katzenbach's bringing himself and Brownell 'into this matter,' Rogers pointed out that the Black case 'had never been under any consideration by the Department during their administrations.' (Memo, Hoover to Tolson, DeLoach, and Gale, 27 July 1966, Tolson File, vol. 3.)

13. Two examples support this conclusion. In his February 1980 report to Attorney General Benjamin Civiletti, FBI Director William Webster wrote that a review of the Bureau's files 'did not identify any post-1966' break-ins involving the Socialist Workers Party. Webster conceded, however, that FBI files recorded that twenty-two FBI break-ins were conducted against radical organizations after 1 January 1966 (Webster did not specify how many of these twenty-two were conducted after Hoover's July 1966

500

order banning such practices) and further that between 1970 and 1975 five FBI break-ins were conducted. Webster claimed that four of these involved foreign counterintelligence investigations and one a domestic terrorist. Another (internal) FBI report conceded that 'it is unclear . . . whether this prohibition [Hoover's July 1966 ban] continued unaltered' and attributed this uncertainty to the fact that 'notwithstanding Hoover's note . . . an instruction went out from Headquarters to the Chicago and New York City Field Offices on January 25, 1968, instructing them to conduct a survey determining the feasibility of technical surveillance [wiretapping] on the Chicago National Headquarters and the New York regional headquarters of SDS [Students for a Democratic Society].' In conducting this survey, this FBI report continued, at least one break-in was conducted against SDS offices in mid-1968, with the results forwarded to FBI officials in Washington. And in August and November 1966, September 1967, and March, May, and June 1968, the New York SAC briefed Hoover on a number of FBI break-ins. (Report, Webster to Civiletti, 19 February 1980, pp. 17, 20-21; U.S. Senate, Select Committee on Intelligence Activities, Supplementary Detailed Staff Reports on Intelligence Activities and the Rights of Americans, book 3, p. 365; Marro, 'FBI Break-in Policy,' in Theoharis, Beyond the Hiss Case, p. 106; Memos, SAC New York to Hoover, 18 August and 9 November 1966; 14 September 1967; 28 March, 22 May, and 11 June 1968; all in FBI 62-117166-131 Bulky Enclosure Section 25.)

14. Hoover's response to the comment of an agent from the New York office, volunteered during an FBI training class, that break-ins were unconstitutional underscores this point. Assistant Director L. V. Boardman immediately briefed Hoover on this incident and initiated an internal investigation to ascertain whether the agent was a friend of any of the agents assigned to the New York break-in squad and whether 'his mental outlook might be present among other members of that squad.' The New York SAC, after first identifying the squad members, attempted to 'determine which of these men should be retained on this type of activity and which should be deleted.' (Memo, New York SAC to File, 10 May 1955, FBI 62-117166-131 Bulky Enclosure.)

CHAPTER FIFTEEN

(1969–1972)
ENDGAME

UNLIKE LYNDON JOHNSON, whose relationship with the Director was personal and not ideological (except perhaps in Cold War terms) Richard Nixon had forged a longstanding political alliance with Hoover during his tenure on HUAC in 1948. Indeed, so close were the two politically that when Nixon considered running for governor of California in 1962, following his personally devastating defeat in his 1960 bid for the presidency, he turned to Hoover, among other political advisers, for counsel on whether to seek the state office. (Hoover urged Nixon to run so that he might have a political base for a future presidential bid.)

Perhaps Nixon hesitated to consider using the FBI as the intelligence arm of the White House, but, if so, Hoover soon relieved him of his misgivings. In one of his first meetings with the newly elected president, the Director reported how presidents dating from Franklin Roosevelt had requested his assistance in monitoring their political opponents – including erroneously telling Nixon that President Johnson had ordered him to wiretap Nixon himself in the closing days of the 1968 presidential campaign.[1]

A succession of discreet errands followed. Perhaps the most improper was the Director's wholehearted collaboration in Nixon's efforts to change the personnel, and thus the liberal character, of the federal judiciary. Within limits, Hoover sought to assist the president, Attorney General John Mitchell, and, later, Chief Justice Warren Burger (appointed to the Court in May 1969) in creating a more conservative judiciary.

It all began on 9 May 1969, when *Life* magazine published

an article by William Lambert on Supreme Court Justice Abe Fortas. Lambert described how Fortas had done legal work for Louis Wolfson, a millionaire industrialist recently convicted of violating security laws. More important, he disclosed that in January 1966 the Supreme Court justice had received a $20,000 check from the Wolfson Foundation. This check, Fortas's former law associates claimed, was the justice's compensation for advising the Foundation on grants for charitable purposes. (Lambert had written to Fortas directly, but the judge had not himself referred to this fee or to having done consulting work for the Wolfson Foundation.) The *Life* reporter then recounted Wolfson's attempts to capitalize on his relationship with Fortas, Fortas's meetings with Wolfson in June 1966, after the industrialist had been indicted and convicted for securities violations, and Fortas's repayment of the money in December 1966.

Lambert's revelations when published on 4 May, created an explosive political issue. Conservative Republicans called for the justice's impeachment, while the nation's press and leading congressmen demanded additional inquiries. Fortas's difficulties were compounded when Wolfson surrendered to government investigators documents describing the basis for the $20,000 payment. Under the terms of the understanding, the Wolfson Foundation had agreed to pay Fortas an annual $20,000 retainer for the rest of his life or for as long as Fortas's widow was alive. The furor over the additional revelation increased demands for Fortas's resignation from Congress and the Nixon administration and within the Court. Bowing to the furor, the justice resigned on 15 May.

Fortas's forced resignation, however, had not been the result merely of an enterprising reporter's uncovering evidence of questionable conduct. Assistant Attorney General William Rehnquist had obtained an advance copy of Lambert's article, alerted Attorney General Mitchell to it, and pointed out that had Fortas helped Wolfson to avoid conviction, the justice could be prosecuted. Mitchell, in turn, had one of his aides alert every major news organization to the forthcoming *Life* article. In addition, the attorney general met personally with Chief Justice Earl Warren to outline the case against Fortas, warning that if Fortas resigned voluntarily, the criminal investigation of his conduct would 'die of its own weight,' but that an investigation would harm Fortas and by extension the Court.

The Justice Department's role, however, was not confined to forcing Fortas's resignation. On 2 June, if not earlier, Hoover learned from 'a reliable source' on an 'extremely confidential basis,' and at once reported to Mitchell, that 'in connection with the investigation involving former Supreme Court Associate Justice Abe Fortas, the Department furnished considerable information to William Lambert,[2] writer for *Life* magazine, which not only enabled Lambert to expose the Fortas tie-in with the Wolfson Foundation but additionally kept Lambert advised regarding the FBI interview with Louis Wolfson and the fact that he had furnished papers supporting Fortas's connection' with the Wolfson Foundation.

Mitchell professed ignorance of this assistance and advised Hoover that he too was concerned about 'leaks of information from this Department.' 'We have started an investigation within the Department,' he assured the Director, 'with the hope of ascertaining the source of such leaks,' and he invited Hoover to meet with him to discuss the problem.

Hoover's and Mitchell's exchange was intended to create a written record showing that lower-level Justice Department officials had leaked the story to Lambert and that Hoover and high-level officials in the Nixon administration had become aware of the situation only when the story broke on 4 May. But that was not the case. Both Hoover and Nixon were aware of Lambert's forthcoming article from late April at the latest. During a telephone conversation with Hoover on 23 April, Nixon brought up 'one other thing as he understands *Life is* coming out with an expose on Justice Fortas.' Hoover admitted knowing that *Life* had 'a story by Bill Lambert,' which he described as 'very strong.' Lambert was a good reporter, Hoover assured the president, 'so if he has the facts, and I understand he does, it ought to do something.' Responding to Nixon's question why Fortas would do 'such a silly thing,' Hoover enumerated Fortas's other transgressions and specifically the justice's collaboration with other investors to buy a building that was then rented to the government, which if 'not a violation of law, . . . is a tax dodge.' Hoover admitted having 'been checking . . . to find out what pressure, if any, has been brought to bear on GSA by Fortas or anybody in his behalf to get those buildings rented to the Government. I said if there is any indication, it is a conflict of interest and I am hoping to dig something up.' Warming to this revelation of possible misconduct, Nixon 'said he [Fortas] ought to be off of there [the Supreme Court].'

Fortas, to be sure, had earned his early retirement. However, Hoover and Nixon did not confine their behind-the-scenes efforts to create a more conservative Supreme Court to the Fortas case. On 15 April 1970 the new House Republican minority leader, Gerald Ford, in the midst of a heated congressional debate over Nixon's controversial and eventually futile nominations of Clement Haynsworth[3] and G. Harrold Carswell to the Supreme Court, introduced a resolution calling for a special congressional investigation of Supreme Court Justice William O. Douglas's fitness to continue to serve there. (As evidence of Douglas's alleged unfitness, Ford cited the publication in *Evergreen Review,* an avant-garde literary journal, which Ford characterized as erotic, of an article by Justice Douglas based on his recently published book *Points of Rebellion.)* Instead, on 21 April the Democratic chairman of the House Judiciary Committee, Emanuel Celler, appointed a special five-member subcommittee of the Judiciary Committee to investigate Ford's charges. By following established procedure governing impeachment inquiries, Celler adroitly neutralized Ford's stratagem of employing a far-ranging public inquiry to raise doubts about Douglas's character and judicial philosophy, the congressman having no evidence that Douglas had committed an impeachable offense.

Ford was undeterred. While denying that his call for

Douglas's impeachment had been coordinated in any way with the Nixon White House, he criticized the proposed five-member inquiry as a whitewash, demanded public hearings into his charges, and, when the subcommittee's report, issued in December, found his charges without merit, announced his intention to press for Douglas's impeachment anyway. In the end, this tactic also failed — Ford had not a crumb of substantial evidence documenting Douglas's unfitness, and, besides, the press and the congressional establishment dismissed his effort as inspired by opposition to Douglas's judicial philosophy.

Ford may have been acting on his own when he introduced the impeachment resolution on 15 April. His initiative, however, had been welcomed by the Nixon White House. Moreover, when it became obvious that Ford lacked evidence to sustain his charges, Nixon interceded and, counting on Hoover's vast resources, inquired whether the Director would provide Ford with whatever information the FBI had that could effect Douglas's impeachment. Hoover willingly obliged.

The occasion for Nixon's request was a telephone conversation he had with Hoover on 5 June. The focus of the conversation was the Supreme Court's recent rulings in obscenity cases, but Nixon abruptly shifted the discussion, as Hoover reported to his aides:

(Justice) Douglas had an article in one of those magazines (*Evergreen*). I said he did — a magazine that is pornographic. I said the attitude of (Justice) Douglas and Black is they won't look at a pornographic motion picture like 'I Am Curious — Yellow.' The President asked if he had Jerry Ford call me, would I fill him in on this; that he (Ford) is a good man. I told him I would.

And he did. But Hoover's willingness to assist Nixon, and Ford, proved unavailing. Lacking in this case the kind of evidence of questionable ethical conduct that had served to force Fortas's resignation, Hoover could only recycle information about Douglas's judicial philosophy.

In addition to Nixon's efforts to purge liberal members of the Supreme Court, Chief Justice Warren Burger sought Hoover's assistance in an effort to move the lower federal circuit and district courts in a more conservative direction. Acting as emissary for the Chief Justice, on 11 January 1971 Federal Judge Edward Tamm (the former assistant director and also number-three man in the Bureau at the time of his appointment to the federal judiciary in 1948) advised Hoover of Burger's forthcoming call 'in the next few days.' Hoover might want 'advance information' about the Chief Justice's interest, Tamm said.

Reminding the Director of the Chief Justice's role in securing legislation authorizing the appointment of court executives for each circuit court and in creating a school to train them at the University of Denver, Tamm reported that Burger wanted Hoover, 'now and from time to time' to recommend 'FBI men who are retiring or who are on the verge of retiring or are otherwise available' to attend this training school 'with all expenses paid and then become court executives.' Burger thought that 'men with FBI training would be admirably situated' to bring 'a sense of realism in these deliberations' and could 'influence these judges who are so completely inexperienced and unlearned in the practicalities of law enforcement . . . (and the agents) could be a tremendous force for keeping some of these stupid appellate opinions from coming out.' Deeming this 'wonderful if it could be done,' Hoover characterized the administration of the courts as 'the greatest weakness as it exists today but by having someone who will watch, no doubt a great deal could be done,' and, at the same time, the position would provide the opportunity 'for the man to ultimately become a judge.'

Hoover kept no record of his follow-up discussion with the Chief Justice on this proposal. But later that year Burger asked Hoover to expedite the processing of FBI field examinations for these court executives. Hoover assured Burger that he would 'get at it personally.'

Meanwhile the ante had also been steeply upped in the Nixon administration's transactions with its political opponents. The administration's unacknowledged authorization of U.S. bombing of neutral Cambodia in early 1969 (followed by its unacknowledged military incursion into that country in May 1970) set off a wave of student protests, in which four student demonstrators were shot to death at Kent State University in Ohio and two more at Jackson State University in Mississippi. The protests continued through 1970 and reached a crescendo the following spring with the indictment of Father Philip Berrigan and other antiwar Catholic clergy and then the leak to the *New York Times, Washington Post,* and other newspapers of top-secret government documents relating to the history of U.S. involvement in the Vietnam War — the so-called Pentagon Papers.

Eager to impress the Nixon White House with his helpfulness in this area as well, on 6 November 1969 Hoover instituted a new, more formal and efficient program 'to furnish high-level intelligence data in the security field to the President and the Attorney General on a continuing basis.' Code-named 'INLET,' this program provided 'information obtained in connection with our investigations which has the qualities of importance and timeliness necessary to secure the President's interest and to provide him with meaningful intelligence for his guidance.' SACs accordingly were ordered to furnish 'on a continuing basis intelligence items suitable' for such regular submissions to the White House and to 'be alert to flag specific items for this purpose.'

Leaving nothing to chance, Hoover spelled out the six categories to be covered in these regular submissions. Five of the categories captured both Hoover's and Nixon's obsessive interest in 'security related' cases or 'inside' information concerning demonstrations, disorders or other civil disruptions which is of more than local significance.' The sixth illuminates Hoover's resolve to advance Nixon's and Mitchell's political interests: 'Items with an unusual twist or concerning prominent personalities which may be of special interest to the President or the Attorney General.'

The institution of the Inlet program merely refined

Hoover's ongoing effort to promote Nixon's political objectives. From January 1969, Hoover had forwarded to the White House thousands of reports detailing the strategies, plans, and backgrounds of the president's various political adversaries. These reports described the activities of prominent personalities (syndicated columnist Joseph Kraft, CBS correspondent Daniel Schorr, actress Jane Fonda, New Left professors, Southern Christian Leadership Conference President Ralph Abernathy, Americans for Democratic Action Chairman Joseph Duffy, film producer Emil D'Antonio) and various dissident organizations (opponents of the administration's proposed antiballistic missile system, ecologists planning the 1970 Earth Day rally, the women's liberation movement, conferences on amnesty for absconded Vietnam veterans, and even the right-wing American Christian Action Council).[4] On 27 July 1970, moreover, Hoover acceded to White House aide Larry Higby's request and ordered the resumption of FBI reporting on the contacts of members of Congress and congressional staff with officials of Soviet and Soviet-bloc embassies.

Hoover's collusion soon involved him in a number of activities that both won the president's favor and compromised Nixon's ability to control the Director. The most sensitive of these involved a 25 November 1970 request from White House aide H. R. Haldeman.

Disturbed over the critical reporting of the Washington press corps and by the disappointing results of the 1970 congressional elections, Haldeman telephoned Hoover to relay a potentially explosive request from the president. Nixon had thought that the Director 'would have it pretty much at hand so there would be no specific investigation (needed), for a run down on the homosexuals known and suspected in the Washington press corps.' Haldeman specifically named one reporter (whose name was deleted from Hoover's report), adding that the president was also interested in 'some of the others rumored generally to be [homosexuals] and also whether we had any other stuff; that he, the President, has an interest in what, if anything else, we know.'

Hoover admitted that 'we have some of that material' and promised to 'get after that right away' and 'to send it over' to the White House before the end of the week. Within the hour he directed his key aides Richard Beaver, William Sullivan, and Thomas Bishop to handle this request. A detailed report, based on a search of FBI files, was promptly delivered to the White House.

In the meantime, in a June 1969 meeting with the Director, National Security Adviser Henry Kissinger had communicated the White House's concern 'about the disturbances which have arisen' during Governor Nelson Rockefeller's trip to Mexico and South America. Could the FBI, he wondered, investigate 'the sources of the disturbances and whether they were spontaneous and came from within the countries visited by Governor Rockefeller, or whether there was a pattern of conspiracy initiated from the outside of these countries that led to the disturbances?' Although the query more properly might have been addressed to the CIA and although the FBI might lack the resources to monitor foreign-based dissident activities, Hoover immediately demanded 'a memorandum on what we know about this' so that he could service the White House's interest.

The Nixon administration's obsession with domestic dissent and its unwillingness to rely exclusively on the CIA for information about foreign-based domestic protest activities provided a further opening for Hoover. In order to serve the White House better and at the specific request of the president, in September 1970 Hoover considered expanding the FBI's foreign liaison program (under which agents were stationed in specified foreign capitals to effect liaison with their police and intelligence services). Opposition from the Department of State at first delayed this expansion. Then Assistant Director William Sullivan counseled against the expansion in view of its costs. But Hoover refused to be balked; he demanded a review of the costs and feasibility of an expanded liaison program.

Aware of the Director's keen interest in going ahead, Assistant Directors W. Mark Felt and Richard Beaver disparaged Sullivan's arguments, first by claiming that the assistant director apparently was 'more on the side of CIA, State Department and Military Intelligence agencies, than the FBI' and then by emphasizing that he 'apparently does not realize that this is being considered at the specific request of the White House.' The FBI had disseminated 'over 200 items of interest' to the White House between January and June 1971, Felt pointed out, and Kissinger had sent the Director 'several warm letters of appreciation' and had personally thanked him 'for the very valuable material which the Bureau had been supplying to him for the last two years.' Without these reports, Kissinger doubted that 'he could have effectively performed his functions as he has been able to do.'

Increasingly insecure in his position yet encouraged by this opportunity, Hoover decided that expanding the FBI's foreign liaison program would cement his relations with the White House. So in September 1971 he authorized the expansion 'in accordance with the desires of the President and Dr. Kissinger' and informed Nixon, Kissinger, and Secretary of State William Rogers of his decision. He then arranged with Under Secretary of State John Irwin III how best to implement the FBI's expanded overseas role.

Hoover's helpfulness emboldened Nixon to ask the Director next to provide information for Vice President Spiro Agnew's speeches; by 1970 Agnew had emerged as point man for the administration. Happy to oblige, Hoover worked closely with Agnew and the vice president's assistant Kent Crane, who requested classified and other information on civil rights and student radical activities. When Agnew's vitriolic speeches then precipitated protests from liberal columnists and congressmen, Hoover urged the vice president to continue his attacks and, to ensure their effectiveness, increased his assistance. Apprised of Agnew's determination to escalate the war of words against student protestors and the liberal media, Hoover cooperated by providing FBI information in summary form on a regular basis and by updating this material 'every couple of months.'

Next learning that the vice president intended to 'start

511

destroying' [SCLC President Ralph] Abernathy's credibility because of Abernathy's speeches denouncing the administration, Hoover agreed to provide background information as well about the civil rights leader. True to his word, within twenty-four hours he forwarded to the vice president a lengthy memorandum detailing all the derogatory information the FBI had on Abernathy. Then, shifting the discussion ever so slightly from Abernathy, Hoover volunteered to Agnew the information the FBI had compiled about the late Martin Luther King's alleged sexual indiscretions, adding that he had 'told the (House) Appropriations Committee' about this information and that the Committee members had 'in turn, briefed some of their colleagues' in an effort to defeat a proposed congressional resolution to make a national holiday of King's birthday.

Encouraged by Agnew's successes in capturing media attention and in putting down liberal congressmen and his administration's television and newspaper critics, Nixon met with the Director the next month to seek his further assistance. A recent poll indicated that crime, not the Cambodian crisis, was the number-one public concern in America, Nixon observed. Yet while this necessitated action against organized crime, Congress refused 'to enact [even] one piece of legislation which had been recommended and suggested by the Administration on the matter of crime.' He planned to have Agnew 'make some speeches placing the responsibility directly on Congress for its failure to function in this field.'

Hoover heartily agreed with Nixon's view of the crime problem, adding that he thought the vice president 'should take a particularly strong position against Congress on inaction in this field.' Accordingly, he agreed to provide information that Agnew 'could use in speeches on organized crime,' and noted that he had 'already supplied the Vice President with material dealing with the violent activities on campuses and also activities of the Black Panthers' as well as a student protest over a presidential address at a Billy Graham Revival in Knoxville, Tennessee. Hoover thereupon ordered his aides to give 'immediate attention' to preparing the latest report on organized crime and other relevant material.

Nixon recontacted the Director later that month, this time to seek his assistance to rebut an article in the 24 June *Washington Post*. The FBI, the *Post* reported, had concluded that the Ohio National Guards' shooting of the four Kent State students was unjustified, that the lives of the guardsmen had not been endangered, and that the guardsmen could have taken less violent steps to control the situation. The FBI had reached no such conclusion, Hoover advised the president, adding that Assistant Attorney General Jerris Leonard may have made 'such a statement.' Nixon and Hoover agreed that 'the Guard had a lot of provocation,' while the president 'told his people he was going to have [the story] 'shot down' as he was not going to have this student business erupting as, basically, what do you expect the Guards to do.' On Nixon's order, Hoover arranged to have the news story 'knocked down' insofar as the FBI was concerned.'

Hoover was also more than willing to have the FBI enlisted in Nixon's controversial strategy of containing the Pentagon Papers 'crisis' – a crisis threatening the White House's control over information. Following the Supreme Court's ruling upholding the right of the *New York Times* to publish the Pentagon Papers, an unrepentant president pursued new avenues in his rage to prevent any recurrence of such leaks and to penalize those responsible for either leaking or publishing the Papers. Meeting with White House aides John Ehrlichman, H. R. Haldeman, and Charles Colson the day after this ruling was handed down, Nixon voiced his intention to go on the offensive. The lesson of the Court's decision, he argued, was that the press had 'won the constitutional right to profit (by) the publication of stolen documents under the First Amendment. This right is superior to the right of our soldiers to live.' The president vowed to convey this message to the public, and proposed to 'leak stuff out. This is the way we win.'

But by the next day, Nixon had reassessed this strategy of selected press leaks. Instead, he directed Ehrlichman,

Haldeman, and Colson to persuade the renamed HUAC (in 1971 known as the House Internal Security Committee) to conduct hearings publicizing the Pentagon Papers affair as a conspiracy harmful to the national security and to 'get the conspiracy smoked out through the papers.' Could the committee chairman, Richard Ichord, handle this task? Nixon asked. Were such an operation to succeed, careful preparation was needed, and this, in turn, required Hoover's 'cooperation' so that Daniel Ellsberg, the former government official responsible for the leak, could be 'tried in the papers' and convicted 'before a committee.' Assured of this cooperation, Nixon was particularly pleased that the 'FBI [was] going all out now.' But just to be sure, he ordered his aides to have 'our men push HUAC and the bureaucracy' – that is, the FBI, CIA, USIA, and Defense Department.

Following up on the president's order, Haldeman asked Hoover for 'a current progress report on the investigation of the Times' personnel participation in this obtaining of the stolen papers.' Nixon was primarily interested in the 'involvement of individuals,' Haldeman emphasized, and wanted a summary report on the current status of the FBI's investigation with follow-up weekly status reports.

Hoover promised to do this 'right away' and immediately ordered the preparation of a memorandum 'just as quickly as possible on the angles of the New York Times personnel who are involved in the Ellsberg case that may result in indictments or prosecution.' Thereafter, weekly reports were to be prepared 'on the progress we are making in the Ellsberg case as to those various angles like [New York Times reporter Neil] Sheehan and [Rand Corporation employee Anthony] Russo and anyone else.'

Assured of Hoover's support (although the FBI never uncovered hard evidence of a conspiracy), on 13 July White House aide Charles Colson contacted Bill Hecht, a key staff aide to Congressman Ichord. Hecht was 'enthusiastic over the prospect' of investigating the supposed miscreants, Colson advised Haldeman, 'and is in all respects a good Hill counterpart for the Hunt operation.' (White House consultant E. Howard Hunt's attempt to uncover derogatory information on Ellsberg included a break-in at the office of Ellsberg's psychiatrist.) The one fly in the ointment, Colson continued, was that Ichord, having decided to run for governor of Missouri, was 'very reluctant to start any sensational' hearings. To 'handle' this problem, Hecht had recommended that the president personally 'tell Ichord that this was a matter 'important to the national security.' In that case, Hecht suggested, 'Ichord would order the hearings immediately.' Before making such a contact, Colson proposed that the White House first assess 'how good our information is and how effective we think we can be in putting our case together.'

In the end Nixon never contacted Ichord and no further effort was made to employ the committee to publicize the supposed conspiracy, in part because of his doubts about Ichord, his belief that Senate Judiciary Committee Chairman Eastland was 'more dependable,' and his fear that congressional hearings could prove harmful 'due to HAK's [Henry Kissinger's] exposure.'

A further reason behind Nixon's abandonment of the conspiracy strategy was Hoover's inability to produce the desired information to ease the president's reservations. Acting on his own, however, the Director attempted to depict Ellsberg's role as part of a sinister plot. In this case he ordered a review of the Bureau's files on Ellsberg's attorney, Leonard Boudin. When evidence was uncovered of Boudin's 'sympathy for communist causes,' and his having served as counsel for 'an accused soviet espionage agent' and 'legal representative to the Castro Cuban Government in this country for a decade,' Hoover ordered this information leaked to Copley News Service Washington bureau chief Ray McHugh, who, in turn, filed a news story listing Boudin's subversive activities. Hoover thereupon sent copies of the story (which revealed Boudin 'in his proper light as a communist and Soviet apologist') to Haldeman, Attorney General Mitchell, and Deputy Attorney General Richard Kleindienst.

Hoover's most sensitive and politically explosive mission for the Nixon White House, however, was to wiretap four

515

members of the Washington press corps and thirteen administration officials employed on the White House staff, the National Security Council staff, and the State and Defense departments.[5] In early 1969, in one of his administration's riskiest actions, 'International English') Nixon authorized the bombing of North Vietnamese supply lines and positions in Cambodia. Fearing the inevitable public furor should his escalation of the war in Southeast Asia become known, Nixon took elaborate precautions to preserve the secrecy of the operation, including falsification of military reports (having the bombing raids listed as occurring over Vietnam) and offering misleading responses to congressional inquiries.

Somehow this containment effort failed, for on 8 May 1969, *New York Times* reporter William Beecher wrote that 'according to Nixon administration sources,' American B-52 bombers had raided several Vietcong and North Vietnamese supply dumps and base camps in Cambodia. The Cambodian government had not protested against these bombing raids, Beecher's story continued, but was cooperating with U.S. and South Vietnamese military officials.

That same day Kissinger and his key aide, Colonel Alexander Haig, contacted Hoover. Claiming to speak for the president, Kissinger demanded that the FBI 'make a major effort to find' Beecher's source (or sources). Kissinger and Haig also stressed that ' "they" do not want anything in writing' and that the investigation must be handled discreetly 'so no stories will get out.' This was 'so sensitive it demands handling on a need-to-know basis, with no record maintained,' Haig reiterated.

Although willing to assist the Nixon administration, Hoover did not comply with Haig's request that the FBI create no record, being concerned to protect himself and the Bureau in the event of discovery. But he had Assistant Director Sullivan maintain in his office the records of the White House's requests and of the wiretap logs (because of the 'extreme sensitivity of the request from the White House'), rather than file them with the FBI's other 'national security' wiretap records. Nor were other departmental wiretap authorization rules followed: the attorney general was not asked to authorize, and after ninety days reauthorize, all wiretaps, and the names of all those whose conversations were intercepted were not listed in the FBI's ELSUR Index.

Despite an intensive investigation, Hoover could not identify the leaker. He could only conjecture as to the source, advising Kissinger (after preliminary FBI inquiries) that national security aide Morton Halperin could have leaked this information, on the grounds that Halperin 'knew Beecher and that he (Hoover) considered (Halperin) a part of the Harvard clique and, of course, of the Kennedy era.' Kissinger thanked Hoover for this information and, as Hoover recorded, asked him to 'follow it up as far as we can take it and they will destroy whoever did this if we find him, no matter where he is.'

Hoover's failure to uncover the source of the leak did not end this massive wiretapping operation. The Halperin tap, for instance, was not terminated after Sullivan reported, two months later, 'Nothing has come to light that is of significance from the standpoint of the leak in question.' Indeed, Halperin's phone continued to be tapped even after he left the NSC staff and thus had no access to classified information. But this was because the purpose of this wiretapping program had shifted almost from its inception. For the wiretaps provided another benefit: information of political value to the Nixon administration.

After leaving the NSC staff, Halperin and another wiretapped NSC aide, Anthony Lake, joined the campaign staff of Democratic presidential aspirant Senator Edmund Muskie of Maine — and thereafter the taps on their phones uncovered valuable political intelligence. For example, on 22 December 1970, Hoover informed the White House that former President Johnson 'would not back Senator Muskie for the Presidency as he intends to stay out of politics.' Hoover likewise reported on proposed speeches and articles of the administration's critics, about Lake's intention 'to work with Senator Fulbright in opposing the war,' and about the sexual activities and personal problems of these officials and their families.

In at least one case, the Nixon White House acted on information acquired from these taps. Alerted by Hoover on 12 December 1969 to former Secretary of Defense Clark Clifford's preparation of an article for *Life* magazine criticizing Nixon's Vietnam policy, to be followed up by an interview in *Time* magazine and an appearance on 'Meet the Press,' White House aides moved quickly to 'counteract' Clifford's efforts 'in any number of ways.' Praising the White House staff for this initiative, White House counsel John Ehrlichman advised Haldeman, 'This is the kind of early warning we need more of – your game planners are now in an excellent position to map anticipatory action.' To which Haldeman responded, 'I agree with John's point. Let's get going.'

Nixon himself had in time come to recognize the political value of these wiretaps, and in doing so increased Hoover's leverage vis-à-vis the White House. Meeting with the Director on 13 May 1970, the president ordered that henceforth the reports based on these 'sensitive' wiretaps were to be 'handed' personally to White House Assistant Haldeman or, in his absence, given in a 'sealed' envelope to Haldeman's aide Lawrence Higby. Still willing to comply, Hoover ensured that there would be a tightly held written record of Nixon's instructions. Only one copy of this order was created (under the 'Do Not File' procedure), and this too was kept in Sullivan's office with the other records of the wiretap operation.

The existence of written records of the Bureau's political assistance to the Nixon White House in time became known to the president, who immediately recognized the danger should these records fall into the wrong hands. But he hesitated to take steps to secure them. For to do so might endanger his mole at the Bureau.

For the president, the problem surfaced in the summer of 1971. The occasion was a conflict within the FBI hierarchy between then-Assistant to the Director Sullivan and Hoover. Sullivan's relations with Hoover had seriously deteriorated (their widening rift eventually resulted in Sullivan's forced retirement in late September). Seeking to consolidate his position by garnering the support of the White House, to which he was Hoover's liaison, Sullivan in July approached Assistant Attorney General Robert Mardian to discuss the problem of potential 'abuses of the material.' As custodian of the wiretap records as well as the records reporting Kissinger's, Haig's, and Nixon's requests, Sullivan was in a unique position to judge their sensitivity and the likelihood that Hoover 'might use these tapes for the purpose of preserving his position as Director of the FBI.'

Impressed by Sullivan's bleak warning, Mardian flew to San Clemente to brief the vacationing president, who thereupon ordered Mardian to retrieve the records from Sullivan and to deliver them to the White House for safekeeping. (An internal FBI memorandum reveals not only why Hoover at the outset had sought to safeguard the records from discovery but also why the president was now so eager to obtain physical control over them: 'Knowledge of this coverage represents a potential source of tremendous embarrassment to the Bureau and political disaster for the Nixon administration. Copies of this material itself could be used for political blackmail and the ruination of Nixon, Mitchell, and others of this administration.')[6] The records were duly removed to the White House.

Sullivan's warning and the president's automatic response were both extremely daring, inasmuch as both broke faith with the Boss, but they are not surprising in view of the roles both men played in the formulation and abandonment of what came to be called the Huston Plan, a plan that had its origins in the president's efforts to discredit his antiwar critics.

On acceding to the presidency, Nixon, as previously noted, had sought an early end to the divisive Vietnam War through the increased use of American air power. At the same time, he recognized the political risks of this strategy, which was bound to intensify domestic opposition. Hoping to discredit, and thereby isolate, his critics, the newly

519

inaugurated president pressured the intelligence community, and primarily the CIA, to document foreign direction of antiwar dissent. Desiring as well to tap the FBI's vast resources, he, through National Security Adviser Kissinger, contacted Hoover, on 30 January 1969.

The president had asked the CIA to compile a report 'about the worldwide student unrest, its significance, the leadership, motivation, et cetera,' Kissinger stated on that occasion, adding that the president also sought Hoover's 'reflections on this problem and the relationship of what goes on abroad to what goes on in this country.' Nixon in particular was interested in learning 'who are these people, is (student dissent) organized, spontaneous, what motivates them, what is the connection between what is spontaneous and what is organized; that I (Hoover) know the concern, whether there is or is not a worldwide pattern to this.' Sharing Nixon's political objectives, Hoover unhesitatingly agreed to prepare the requested report within the week 'on a strictly confidential basis.'

Hoover's report, like that of the CIA, described Communist influence and participation in antiwar dissent. But neither the FBI nor the CIA could come up with the desired hard evidence that the dissent was directed from abroad. Therefore, the White House redefined foreign influence to include mere contact, advice, or association. Making the philosophical breakthrough, White House aide Tom Charles Huston, a twenty-eight-year-old Indiana wunderkind and former student leader of the ultra-conservative Young Americans for Freedom, advised Hoover, and the CIA as well, that 'foreign Communist support' should be 'liberally construed to include all activities by foreign Communists designed to encourage or assist revolutionary protest movements in the United States.' More important, Huston met with Sullivan, supposedly to emphasize the president's desire to learn in 'greater depth' details of New Left activities and particularly 'all information possibly related to foreign influences and the financing of the New Left.'

Thereafter, despite his wish to serve the president's

political interests, Hoover still could not produce the desired evidence, conceivably a punishable offense. For, unknown to the Director, the Nixon initiative had provided an opportunity to undermine his authority. This opportunity was not missed.

During the course of their frequent meetings, Huston and Sullivan struck up a friendship, Sullivan confiding to the imperious young White House aide that the FBI's inability to be more helpful stemmed from Hoover's restrictive orders limiting wiretapping and bugging and prohibiting break-ins and mail opening in the wake of the Fred Black case. Sullivan's portrait of an obstructive Director committed more to retaining his hold on the FBI than to advancing the national interest shortly catalyzed a Huston-Sullivan plan to circumvent the cantankerous old man. The specific events triggering what became the Huston Plan were Hoover's order to sever the FBI's relations with the CIA in the aftermath of the Thomas Riha affair[7] and the firestorm of campus protest following President Nixon's decision to order an American invasion of Cambodia.

Hoover's rash act in the former case seriously interfered with the CIA's presidentially mandated mission. But when CIA Director Richard Helms sought to restore the earlier working relationship and requested that Hoover have the FBI perform sensitive missions on the agency's behalf, Hoover curtly rebuffed him. Should the CIA director desire the FBI's assistance in monitoring domestic targets, Hoover declared sanctimoniously, he should first clear the matter with the attorney general.

Helms was clearly dismayed by Hoover's intransigence — the CIA director was altogether unwilling to go on record as requesting that the attorney general authorize the FBI to wiretap or open the mail of domestic political organizations. Helms, moreover, was not alone in his impatience with Hoover's more cautious approach, which dated from 1965. National Security Agency officials Louis Tordella and Marshall Carter had also attempted, in 1967, to persuade Hoover to relax his restrictions on FBI break-ins, their goal being to obtain information from foreign embassies essential to the NSA's code-breaking activities. Having at first relented, Hoover later reconsidered and informed Tordella and Carter that the FBI would provide the requested assistance only if specifically ordered to do so by either the president or the attorney general.

Thus, unless Hoover could be pressured into reversing his restrictive orders of 1965-1966 and allowing the FBI to proceed as it had before 1965, the objectives of CIA and NSA officials as well as the Nixon White House could not be realized. Hence the Sullivan-Huston effort. Working behind the scenes in June-July 1970, Sullivan and Huston devised a plan to bypass the Director by having Nixon appoint a special interagency committee composed of representatives of the various intelligence agencies — ostensibly to discuss how to improve coordination between the White House and those agencies. On 5 June Nixon agreed to this plan, appointing a special working committee composed of representatives from all the intelligence agencies and headed by the FBI's representative (namely Sullivan) with the assigned task of preparing a report listing needed improvements in intelligence gathering. The committee was not intended to be a fact-finding body, though. The purpose behind the proposal was to devise a means whereby Hoover's restrictive orders could be lifted, based on the knowledge that the Director would never rescind his restrictions on his own. The interagency committee was to provide the forum for achieving this end-run result.

The principal obstacle to the intriguers' success was Sullivan — or rather his dual status as one of Hoover's trusted aides and as a self-seeker at the White House. Because he served as Hoover's representative on the working committee, Sullivan had to report back to the Director on the committee's activities. However, his reports could not accurately reflect his central role in drafting its position paper. For this reason, Sullivan led Hoover to believe that the committee was simply responding to a presidential request for a report listing various recommendations, it being reserved to the president to accept or reject them.

Normally, such working committees would draft a preliminary report, which would then be reviewed by the responsible agency heads, who would then have the power to veto any proposal they found unacceptable. Sullivan's and Huston's stratagem to get around this obstacle was to limit the committee's role to listing a number of options, reserving to the president the right to decide which to approve and which to reject. Because the committee itself was not making recommendations, this method would deny Hoover any final veto.

The report drafted by the working committee formally recommended that the president consider lifting restraints that hampered 'intelligence collection activities.' If Nixon so ruled, it provided, he could authorize an increase in FBI wiretapping and bugging (rescinding Hoover's numerical limit), repeal Hoover's restriction on FBI mail openings and mail covers, modify Hoover's ban on break-ins to permit their selective use during FBI investigations of radical activists and organizations, and increase FBI coverage of campus activities by lowering the minimum age of FBI informers to eighteen (Hoover had recently raised the age to twenty-one). In addition, the report recommended that the president establish a permanent interagency committee subject to the direction of the White House and responsible for preparing periodic intelligence reports for the president.

In effect, these recommendations would repeal all of the restrictions that Hoover had imposed in 1965 and 1966. Furthermore, the interagency committee proposal would reduce the FBI's independence and make the Director more a creature of the White House. So at this point Sullivan, having succeeded in drafting a proposal that would undercut Hoover's orders, and having misled Hoover about his own role in the preparation of the report, confronted a difficult task: as Hoover's representative, he had now to brief the Director before formal submission of the working committee's report to the White House. The disloyal aide could only anticipate the Boss's bitter resentment.

In the event, Hoover was the last intelligence agency head briefed on the committee's report. Not until the heads of

NSA, CIA, and the Defense Intelligence Agency (DIA) had been approached and their approval obtained did Sullivan forward the report to Hoover. In his cover memo, he sought to defuse the Director's inevitable objections to the intrusions on his authority. The 'investigative restraints and limitations' section and the section proposing the creation of a permanent interagency committee, he blandly claimed, were 'in accordance with the President's request, with the pros and cons outlined and with no recommendations of any kind made by the committee.' Anticipating Hoover's opposition, he counseled the Director either to offer no objection, or to convey his objections 'verbally' to the President, or, as a last resort, to list his objections in writing. Hoover opted for the third suggestion and ordered Sullivan to itemize his objections to the report's investigative restraints section in the form of footnotes.

The basis of Hoover's objections was not the report's recommended use of what he called 'clearly illegal' activities but the risks involved in such use, especially in view of the Nixon administration's confrontational style. Fearing the threat to his tenure should such FBI activities become known, he abandoned his longstanding monopoly in the domestic security field and instead agreed to allow other intelligence agencies to conduct such operations. Commenting on the proposal to expand the use of wiretaps and bugs, he stated, in his footnoted objection, that he 'would not oppose other agencies seeking authority of the Attorney General for coverage required by them and thereafter instituting such coverage themselves.' But he would not do so himself. Other Hoover footnotes, characterizing mail openings and break-ins as illegal, emphasized the political risks entailed in their use. Information about mail-opening programs, he warned, 'would leak out of the Post Office to the press' and seriously damage the intelligence community.

Hoover's footnoted objections threatened to scuttle the whole effort. The Director's characterization of these techniques as illegal, combined with his agreement not to object should other intelligence agencies elect to employ them, highlighted what had been the major problem from the start: his refusal to have the FBI perform 'clearly illegal' investigations at the request of the other intelligence agencies. Furthermore, Hoover had created in the footnotes a written record of his objections to the employment of these techniques, further magnifying the risks to the other agencies, barred as they were by executive order and by statute from conducting internal security operations themselves.

On receiving a copy of Hoover's annotated objections, DIA Director General Donald Bennett and NSA Director Noel Gayler immediately protested to Huston. Either the interagency committee should reconvene to get Hoover to remove the footnotes, or they should be allowed to insert their own explanatory footnotes. But then they relented, agreeing with Huston that it was better to avoid confronting the obstreperous Director. Huston promised to convey their views in his cover memorandum to the president. Thereafter the final signing ceremony proceeded without difficulty.

Huston delivered on his promise. In his cover memo to the report, he began by emphasizing the various agencies' near-unanimity and eagerness to meet the president's requirements. Hoover alone was represented as obstructionist, and his footnoted objections as 'inconsistent,' 'frivolous' and excessively concerned with appearances. From the start, Huston reported, Hoover had attempted to 'divert the committee from operational problems and redirect its mandate to the preparation of another analysis of existing intelligence.' Then, changing gears, Huston granted that Hoover was a 'loyal trooper' who would accede to any decision of the president. As a means of ensuring this cooperation, Nixon should call Hoover in for 'a stroking session' to explain his decisions, thank the Director for his advice and past cooperation, and seek his future cooperation.

Keenly aware of the serious political risks of a plan envisaging that he directly authorize 'clearly illegal' investigative techniques, Nixon chose not to follow Huston's additional proposals that he first convene another meeting of the intelligence agency heads to announce his decision and then formalize his 'precise decisions' in an 'official memorandum.' Instead, Nixon had Haldeman instruct Huston that he had 'approved' the recommendations but was too busy to meet again with Hoover and the other intelligence agency heads. Nixon would not 'follow the procedure you outlined . . . regarding implementation [i.e., a review procedure to ensure compliance]. He would prefer that the thing simply be put into motion on the basis of this approval.'

Accordingly, on 23 July Huston sent an 'official memorandum' over his own signature authorizing the use of these 'clearly illegal' investigative activities – hence the designation of the program as the Huston Plan. Huston's memo simply reported that President Nixon had 'carefully studied' the draft proposal and had 'made the following decisions.' It did not explicitly say that the president had authorized the illegal activities. Indeed, this assurance of presidential deniability explains Nixon's attraction to the procedure. The president's maneuver, however, failed to take account of the administrative genius of the wily FBI Director, who instantly saw that he could not claim to be bound by direct presidential orders if the FBI's conduct of such 'clearly illegal' activities was ever discovered. Accordingly, on 27 July, he briefed Attorney General Mitchell on the plan. (Mitchell had not been involved in the deliberations leading to its formulation.)

While allowing that the plan was binding, Hoover announced his intention to create a written record that the FBI was following presidential orders. Observing that 'the President has directed the relaxation of four investigative restraints directly affecting the responsibility of the FBI,' he reiterated his own 'clear-cut and specific opposition to [their] lifting.' Hoover slyly agreed 'to implement the instructions of the White House at your direction. [But] of course, we would continue to seek your specific authorization, where appropriate, to utilize the various investigative techniques involved in individual cases.'

Hoover's determination to create a written record showing

both that the FBI was responding to a presidentially authorized directive and that for each use (of a break-in, mail opening, wiretap, or bug) the attorney general's approval had been sought and obtained utterly defeated Nixon's strategy of deniability. Thus, when Mitchell immediately contacted Nixon to advise him of Hoover's intention, the president decided forthwith to rescind the plan. He did so, he said, because:

> Mr. Mitchell explained to me that Mr. Hoover believed that although each of the intelligence gathering methods outlined in the Committee's recommendations had been utilized by one or more previous Administrations, their sensitivity would likely generate media criticism if they were employed. Mr. Mitchell further informed me that it was his opinion that the risk of disclosure of the possible illegal actions . . . was greater than the possible benefit to be derived. Based upon this conversation with Attorney General Mitchell, I decided to revoke the approval originally extended to the Committee's recommendations.

Nixon had been outmaneuvered, but he had no acceptable means of redress. He could not get rid of Hoover, for thereafter — and Nixon knew this from previous experience — the Director could arrange to publicize the White House pressure on him. The Huston Plan had backfired. Rather than forcing Hoover's acquiescence, it had permitted him to consolidate his position.

Secure for the moment on that front, the Director's continued tenure now came under attack on another front — a revived and more assertive liberalism. Abandoning their earlier passivity, Hoover's liberal critics were poised to capitalize on an apparently never-ending series of revelations of FBI misconduct and administrative pettiness.

The least dramatic of these revelations involved Hoover's handling of a personnel matter concerning Jack Shaw, an agent assigned to the New York field office and at the time enrolled in the John Jay College of Criminal Justice.

Responding to critical comments about the FBI made by one of his instructors, Shaw had written to the professor to defend the Bureau. In doing so, he granted that Hoover concentrated on 'dime-a-dozen' bank robberies to the neglect of organized crime and employed a 'sledge-hammer' public relations approach, but, he maintained, the Director ran a good Bureau. Because Shaw's letter had been typed by the New York office's secretarial pool, Hoover learned of its contents, and, briefed by New York SAC John Malone, he ordered Shaw's transfer to Butte, Montana, after a thirty-day suspension. Hoover hoped that Shaw would retire rather than accept the new assignment, adding,

> Ordinarily I would dismiss him but he is a veteran and you have to go through a long procedure and they have indicated dismissal would not be sustained because he didn't mail the letter. I said I wanted his transfer to Butte because I hope he will resign as I understand he has four children and the working conditions of the Butte office would be difficult for him in his circumstance.

Shaw's wife was dying of cancer; he could not consider a transfer to Butte. He advised his supervisor that 'if he is fired with prejudice, he will have to fight it and, if he is transferred, the condition of his family is such he will have to resign.' Informed of this response, Hoover ordered Malone to 'go ahead and suspend him for 30 days and then transfer him and we will be well rid of him.' When Shaw predictably resigned, Hoover ordered that his resignation be accepted 'with prejudice.'

Thanks to Hoover's petulance, the matter did not rest there. Shaw sued for reinstatement, and the attendant publicity came to the attention of Senator George McGovern, the liberal South Dakota Democrat, who publicly criticized Hoover's handling of the matter and demanded that Attorney General Mitchell investigate the dismissal. Contacted by Deputy Attorney General Richard

Kleindienst, Hoover drafted a reply defending the disposition of the case. Undaunted, McGovern continued his attack, citing an anonymous communication that he had received from ten FBI agents criticizing Hoover's administrative rules and procedures.

Stung by the criticisms and no longer restrained by Clyde Tolson, by then seriously disabled by his repeated strokes (although still obliged to appear at the Bureau), Hoover demanded a review of the Bureau's files for any derogatory information on McGovern. The resulting eighteen-page memorandum detailed McGovern's involvement in various alleged 'subversive' activities, culled from comments made by former college faculty associates and political adversaries in South Dakota. Among other things, he was accused of being 'a communist and at least pro-communist and one who attempted to 'tear down' the U.S. Government's position in domestic and foreign relations.'

Notwithstanding the fact that the FBI's information consisted entirely of unsupported allegations offered by McGovern's conservative associates, Hoover promptly sought Assistant Director D. J. Dalbey's recommendation as to how to handle McGovern. Far less emotionally involved, Dalbey counseled dropping the matter:

Although McGovern can be expected to take an occasional potshot at the Director, it seems to me that his present campaign based on the Shaw case is about ready to fade out . . . I would not want to do anything to fan the flames all over again at this time. If he wants to be President, he'll have to run on something other than a campaign against the Director. There is no act that would get political sympathy for McGovern quicker than the belief of other politicians that the Director had used the power at his disposal against McGovern. There is no gain here to justify the risk.

Hoover was persuaded to abandon his plan to disseminate the FBI's McGovern material. Shaw, in turn, decided to drop his suit and to accept damages of $13,000. (After

Hoover's death, he obtained employment in another agency of the Department of Justice.)

McGovern, not knowing the blackball plan, in time again challenged Hoover's fitness to head the FBI. This time he condemned Hoover's thinskinned reaction to the comments of a TWA pilot who had accused FBI agents of mishandling a highjacking. As had been his wont, Hoover responded vindictively, attempting to destroy the pilot's career by publicizing derogatory information obtained from the pilot's Air Force records. When this effort backfired, the Director peevishly decreed an FBI boycott of the airline and barred his agents from acting as air marshals on TWA flights, unsustainable orders that he was subsequently obliged to rescind.

But like the elephant who never forgets, Hoover sought to settle matters with TWA. Responding to the 'outrageous action' of the TWA pilot, who had compelled two FBI agents to leave a plane unless they surrendered their guns, he had his aides draft a letter of protest to the president of TWA with copies to the FAA and the Airline Pilots Association. Subsequently reviewing the draft presented to him, he deplored its 'rather "mouselike" contents' and peremptorily rewrote it himself. 'I want any correspondence with TWA to be curt and to the point,' he declared. 'The original letter drafted for my signature did not emphasize the angry and incensed actions of the Captain of the TWA plane at Chicago. In fact, it made no mention of the same. I had to change the salutation in that it was addressed to "Dear (name deleted but president of TWA)" and closed with 'Sincerely yours.' I want all correspondence going to TWA to be addressed either "Sir" or "Dear Sir" and closed "Very truly yours." Recalling the shabby treatment accorded the Bureau, Hoover insisted that the FBI 'be aggressively pertinent when we are communicating with that organization.'

Petulance also colored Hoover's responses to criticisms of a more powerful adversary, Democratic House majority leader Hale Boggs, Jr., of Louisiana. In a speech on the House floor on 5 April 1971, Boggs demanded that Attorney

General Mitchell dismiss Hoover on the grounds that the Bureau was using the 'tactics of the Soviet Union and Hitler's Gestapo.' Claiming that the FBI both wiretapped members of Congress and infiltrated college campuses,[8] Boggs argued that 'it's time for the Director no longer to be the Director.' The congressman promised to document his charges – but was unable to do so.

No longer sacrosanct, Hoover had become an inviting target for liberals, who for decades had chafed at his self-righteous posturing. In the more cynical climate of the 1970s, they now had the opportunity to knock him off his pedestal and possibly even effect his retirement. For they had recently acquired an unanticipated boon: documentary evidence of his abuses of power and the politicized nature of his Bureau's surveillance.

On 8 March 1971 a self-proclaimed Citizens Commission to Investigate the FBI had done the unthinkable. Breaking into the FBI's Media, Pennsylvania, resident agency in the middle of the night, it had obtained a rich cache. The thousand pages of seized FBI documents, brilliantly and selectively released to the press and key congressmen (the intruders were never caught), disclosed the scope of the FBI's illegal surveillance of dissident political groups (primarily antiwar and black activist), the extent of the FBI's monitoring of college-based activists and organizations (and its use of secretaries and administrators in this effort), its use of illegal investigative techniques, and, most important, its involvement in a concerted program to harass the New Left. Two of the seized documents were particularly damaging. One described the COINTELPRO–New Left (calculated to 'expose, disrupt, and otherwise neutralize' this radical movement); the other instructed agents to increase the number of interviews of New Left activists 'for plenty of reasons, chief of which are it will enhance the paranoia endemic in these circles and will further serve to get the point across that there is an FBI agent behind every mailbox.'

As the seized documents received wider publicity, they raised the question of why Congress had been so lax in its oversight of the Bureau. And when neither the Judiciary

Committee nor the Appropriations Committee followed up on the revelations of FBI abuses, an offshoot of the American Civil Liberties Union, the Committee for Public Justice (CPJ), assumed the initiative in launching a broad-based reassessment of Hoover's leadership. To that end, CPJ officials organized a conference on the FBI to be held at Princeton University in October 1971 under joint sponsorship with Princeton's Woodrow Wilson School of Public and International Affairs.

Alerted by his extensive sources and by the organizers' preconference publicity that Robert Sherrill, Vern Countryman, Fred Cook, Aryeh Neier, Thomas Emerson, Victor Navasky, and Frank Donner were scheduled to present papers, Hoover demanded that this 'group of anti-FBI bigots' be 'handle[d].' He further ordered his aides to prepare 'a detailed brochure type memorandum concerning the conference,' to include 'summary memoranda' on all those invited to attend and the members of the CPJ's executive committee, and to 'expedite' this project so that it was completed prior to the start of the conference.

The angry Director thereupon orchestrated a multifaceted operation having the twin purposes of discrediting the conference and countering any favorable publicity it might receive. In what was almost a reflex response, he directed his aides to brief Richard Ichord, chairman of the House Internal Security Committee, on the 'subversive affiliation' of CPJ officials and to provide more detailed information to committee counsel Donald Sanders (himself a former FBI agent). An accommodating Ichord pledged to be alert for 'an appropriate occasion . . . whereby he or some other member of the Committee could make use' of this information. Twice, on 28 October and 29 November, in speeches to the House Ichord used this information to question the loyalty of those attending and sponsoring the conference.

In a parallel step, Hoover had his aides draft and disseminate 'speeches to our friends on the Hill,' in this instance a stable of conservative activists led by New Jersey Republican John Hunt. An equally accommodating Hunt invited to his office six aides to conservative congressmen, Maryland Republican Congressman Lawrence Hogan (a former FBI agent), and Jay Parker of the Friends of the FBI for the purpose of conferring with Inspector David Bowers of the Crime Records Division on strategy. This group decided that Hunt was to request a ' "special order" of one hour for himself and other Members' to launch an attack on the conference.

Hunt thereupon contacted Hoover directly to request 'public source information concerning various individuals participating in the conference.' The New Jersey Republican promised to disseminate this information 'to the appropriate people without the FBI being identified with it.' Hoover ordered this done.

Securing the allotted time, Hunt, joined by Congressmen Floyd Spence (R.-S.C.), Joe Waggoner (D.-La.), William Colmer (D.-Miss.), William Dickinson (R.-Ala.), and Jerry Pettis (R.-Cal.), defended the FBI as an apolitical organization, criticized the papers presented at the conference (using as a guide the FBI's detailed critique), and linked the various participants to a liberal-subversive plot (based again on the FBI's summary memoranda on the participants and CPJ officials).

On Hoover's further order, his aides contacted 'some of our good friends in the news media such as Victor Riesel, Bob Allen, Ed O'Brien, Ray McHugh, etc.'[9] Crimes Records Division head Thomas Bishop thereupon asked McHugh, the Washington bureau chief of the Copley News Service, 'to write a column on this matter which would clearly reflect the biased nature' of the CPJ. When McHugh's column was published in the 24 October issue 'of all newspapers in the Copley chain,' Bishop then arranged to have it reprinted in the *Congressional Record* and sent a copy of the column together with 'background' information to Jack Cox, the administrative assistant to Congressman Barry Goldwater (R.-Cal.). The next day Goldwater dutifully delivered a short speech condemning the CPJ. Directly contacted by a syndicated conservative columnist for information to rebut the publicity generated by the conference, Hoover ordered Bishop to search FBI files for information on conference organizers Ramsey Clark, Burke Marshall, and Roger Wilkins and to help this columnist 'in any way we can.'

Although Hoover's behind-the-scenes efforts contained the potential damage of the Princeton conference, the rising chorus of criticism continued to trouble the Nixon administration. Already doubtful of Hoover's loyalty to the White House, Nixon's aides convened a high-level meeting in the Oval Office in October 1971 to discuss recent developments in the Hoover problem. Citing the declining morale within the Bureau (Sullivan had recently been fired, and DeLoach had resigned), John Ehrlichman and other White House aides urged the president to request Hoover's resignation. Attorney General Mitchell did not dissent from this recommendation but, emphasizing Hoover's mass following, pointed out that any attempt to replace him, especially if this involved a public confrontation, could be costly. Nixon then commented that, regrettably, Hoover himself had become the issue, so obsessed with retaining his office that he failed to think 'enough about the cause he wants to serve.'

Mitchell thereupon recommended that Nixon ask Hoover to announce his voluntary retirement at the time of his seventy-seventh birthday on 1 January 1972. Only Nixon could make such a request, Mitchell insisted; 'Hoover is not about to listen to anyone other than the President of the United States when it comes to this question.'

Nixon agreed to undertake this responsibility and invited Hoover for a breakfast meeting. Recalling later what happened, Nixon reported having pointed out, subtly and gently, that 'as an astute politician [Hoover] must recognize that the attacks were going to mount in number and intensity in the years ahead' and that it would be a tragedy if his career were to end under such sustained attack. Hoover reportedly answered, 'More than anything else, I want to see *you* re-elected in 1972. If you feel that my staying on as head of the Bureau hurts your chances for re-election, just let me know. As far as these present attacks are concerned, and the ones that are planned for the future, they don't make any difference to me. I think you know that the tougher the attacks get, the tougher I get.'

Hoover clearly did not intend to resign, and Nixon hesitated either to request or to demand his resignation, appreciating as he did the political pitfalls inherent in the situation. For, on the one hand, forcing Hoover's resignation would raise the delicate political question of his replacement and provide liberal Democrats with a forum for more intensive discussion of the FBI's proper role and the need for closer congressional oversight. And, on the other hand, Nixon could not be sure that Hoover would bow out gracefully and not leak information about the Nixon administration's more questionable activities on behalf of its objectives.

In effect, then, Nixon's political uses of the FBI left him no choice. They constituted a form of self-imposed blackmail — and Mardian's briefing three months earlier on the possible adverse consequences should the NSC wiretap logs maintained in Sullivan's office fall into Hoover's hands underscored the problem.

Nixon thought again about Hoover's dismissal. Instead, he decided, he says, to wait until after the presidential election. He could then safely request Hoover's resignation along with those of all other high-level officials in his administration — and then, after praising effusively Hoover's record of sacrifice and service, appoint a new Director. In any case, the Director left the Oval Office that day still the Director.

Yet Nixon had decided that the Director's usefulness had ended. Hoover soon found himself frozen out, his access to the White House and authority over the Bureau tightly circumscribed. In effect, he ceased to be The Boss. Whereas earlier he had regularly received calls from the White House and the attorney general seeking his assistance and counsel, after November 1971 he heard nothing of consequence from them. Senior FBI officials had also read the handwriting on the wall and, as well, questioned the Director's acumen and judgment.

As a result, Hoover's remaining months in office were occupied with perfunctory meetings with agents and officials for the purpose, befitting a low-level functionary but not a powerful Director, of compiling reports evaluating their past performance and future promise. For one who had dominated the Bureau since 1924 and national politics since 1945, Hoover ended his Directorship a lonely man, commanding neither the power nor the veneration he had exacted for so long. His last eight months in office found him a pathetic figure – and his death, from a heart attack in his sleep on 2 May 1972, precipitated an internal conflict between his loyalists and a new guard of G-Men who sought to capitalize more flexibly on the legacy he had made.

Notes to Chapter Fifteen

1. The reality was quite different, and Johnson's request more circumspect and indirect than elsewhere reported. Concerned that South Vietnamese officials were in contact with Nixon campaign officials in the hope of forcing a 'harder' line during ongoing U.S.-South Vietnamese negotiations with the North Vietnamese in Paris, on 29 October 1968 Johnson asked the FBI to wiretap the South Vietnamese embassy in Washington. Authorized by Attorney General Ramsey Clark, this wiretap was continued until 6 January 1969. The next day, 30 October. J. Bromley Smith. the executive secretary of the National Security Council, relayed the president's request that the FBI monitor the activities of Mrs. Anna Chennault. Johnson suspected that Chennault, a prominent Republican, was attempting to dissuade South Vietnamese officials "from attending the Pans peace negotiations until after the election since it would devolve to the credit of the Republican Party." Beginning that day, FBI agents followed Mrs. Chennault closely and reported on her travels in Washington, D.C., and New York (including visits to the South Vietnamese embassy). Hoover, however, decided against wiretapping Chennault, because it 'was widely known that she was involved in Republican political circles and, if it became known that the FBI was surveilling her this would put us in a most untenable and embarrassing position.' On 7 November, having

received daily reports on Chennault's travels, Smith ordered the termination of this physical surveillance. Then, on 13 November, Johnson asked Hoover to have the FBI check telephone toll call records in Albuquerque, New Mexico, to ascertain whether, on 2 November, Republican vice presidential candidate Spiro Agnew had telephoned Mrs. Chennault or the South Vietnamese embassy. The resulting check uncovered no such calls; the FBI also verified Agnew's arrival and departure times in Albuquerque during this campaign appearance. (U.S. Senate, Select Committee on Intelligence Activities, *Hearings on Intelligence Activities, Federal Bureau of Investigation, vol.* 6: pp. 164-65, 193, 195-96, 251-53, 483-84; Report, *Intelligence Activities and the Right of Americans,* book 2, p. 228 n.10; *Supplementary Detailed Staff Reports on Intelligence Activities and the Rights of Americans,* book 3, pp. 314-15.)

2. This was not the only occasion when the Nixon administration sought to enlist the services of this influential investigative reporter for a major national news magazine. A Republican in affiliation, Lambert was approached again in 1971 by the White House aide E. Howard Hunt, who sought to pass off a faked document to effect publication of a major *Life* expose of the 'true story behind the Diem coup,' the 'story' being President Kennedy's responsibility for Diem's assassination. Interested in this story, Lambert nonetheless insisted on authenticating the document, and as a result the proposed story was never published. (U.S. House, Committee on the Judiciary, *Hearings* on H. *Res. 803,* May-June 1974, book 7, pt. 2, pp. 1067-69.)

3. In the case of the Haynsworth nomination (as earlier in Potter Stewart's case), Hoover willingly complied with a request from Attorney General John Mitchell to conduct a perfunctory check in order to allow Nixon to announce when making the nomination that the FBI had conducted an investigation 'to fill the requirements of the Judiciary Committee.' Accordingly, after checking with the SAC in Columbia, South Carolina, Hoover that day assured Mitchell that Haynsworth was highly regarded as the foremost jurist in the area, was 'considered very conservative,' was 'well disposed toward law enforcement,' and was 'definitely in favor of law and order.' (Memo, Hoover to Tolson, DeLoach, and Gale, I July 1969, and Memo, Hoover to Mitchell, I July 1969, John Mitchell folder, Folder no. 115, Hoover O&C.)

4. The American Christian Action Council's opposition to 'Nixon's China trip' and support for a 'public school prayer'

amendment and demonstrations opposing school busing triggered Hoover's interest.

5. The four Washington reporters were *New York Times* reporters William Beecher and Hedrick Smith, *London Times* reporter Henry Brandon, and CBS correspondent Marvin Kalb. The seven NSC members were Morton Halperin, Anthony Lake, Winston Lord, Helmut Sonnenfeldt, Daniel Davidson, Richard Moose, and Richard Sneider. The three White House aides were William Safire, John Sears, and James McLane. The three State and Defense department employees were Richard Pedersen, William H. Sullivan, and Robert Pursley.

6. This was not the only instance in which Hoover conducted politically sensitive investigations for the Nixon White House and developed special filing procedures to safeguard the records. Disturbed by syndicated columnist Joseph Kraft's recent columns, the White House asked Hoover to have the FBI monitor Kraft's forthcoming trip to France to cover the negotiations between the U.S. and North Vietnamese governments. Hoover dispatched Sullivan to Paris to report on Kraft's contacts and activities (using physical surveillance of Kraft and a bug that a French security agency installed in Kraft's hotel room). Created under a Do Not File procedure, Sullivan's reports were maintained in his office until he delivered them to Mardian in July 1971. In response to another White House request, Hoover authorized a wiretap on Charles Radford II, a navy yeoman assigned as staff assistant to the Joint Chiefs of Staff. Although installed because of a suspicion that Radford might have been the source of a leak to syndicated columnist Jack Anderson, the wiretap instead disclosed a Pentagon scheme to obtain highly classified NSC documents. (Frozen out of information on Kissinger's trip to China, Pentagon officials had sought to spy on their intelligence counterparts.) Owing to their sensitivity, the Radford tap records were 'kept completely isolated from other FBI records, and there are no indices whatsoever relating to this project.' (Athan Theoharis, *Spying on Americans* (Philadelphia: Temple University Press, 1978), pp. 191, 194.)

7. Riha, a professor of modern Russian history at the University of Colorado, had mysteriously disappeared in 1969. The FBI apparently knew his whereabouts but refused to tell the police because it did not want to compromise its confidential sources. In 1970 an agent in the Bureau's Denver field office nevertheless passed on information about Riha's defection to a representative of the CIA. Learning of this, Hoover insisted on having the name

of the agent. When the CIA refused his demand, the Director petulantly severed further personal liaison between representatives of the Bureau and the CIA.

8. Boggs's carefully prepared speech, and a later speech of 22 April, were based in part on the FBI documents disseminated by the so-called Citizens Commission following their break-in the previous month into the FBI's agency in Media, Pennsylvania. Boggs had other knowledge of the FBI's questionable practices: that of an insider and obtained through frequent secret meetings with Hoover's congressional liaison Cartha DeLoach during the 1960s – when the southern congressman was considered a reliable confidante.

9. Sharing the biases of conservatives in general, Hoover deeply distrusted the liberal press, particularly the *New York Times* and the *Washington Post*. While claiming to read neither paper, he admitted to being 'happy' whenever they criticized the FBI – but 'if they ever praise us I would call a meeting of top executives to see what was the reason.' Reading the *Times* and the *Post* was 'just a waste of time,' Hoover continued, and he generally waited 'until I get downtown in the morning to buy a New York Daily News to find out what happened overnight as the other papers are distorted and slant the news as well as the editorials, so I do not buy any and do not pay any attention to them.' Despite this feigned indifference, the Director contacted Deputy Attorney General Richard Kleindienst to warn that 'there is developing throughout the news media arrangements whereby the Washington Post, the Washington Star, the New York Times, and the Los Angeles Times all exchange columns and editorials . . . I said we seem to be getting a situation which poisons the public mind and I don't think it is right.' (Memo, Hoover to Tolson, DeLoach, Rosen, Sullivan, and Bishop, 11 May 1970, Tolson File, vol. 4; Memo, Hoover to Tolson, Sullivan, Bishop, and Brennan, 7 January 1971, and Memo, Hoover to Tolson and Bishop, 13 April 1971, both Tolson File, vol. 5.)

AFTERWORD

DID HOOVER'S DEATH end the possibility, or at least likelihood, of FBI abuses? That seemed to many to be the case. After all, Congress had enacted legislation in 1968, in anticipation of the Director's retirement, limiting his successor's tenure to ten years and requiring Senate confirmation, and in the aftermath of Watergate and the Church and Pike committees' hearings, the congressional leadership (particularly the House Judiciary Committee) began to conduct a more careful scrutiny of FBI activities. Moreover, passage of the Freedom of Information Act in 1966 (with amendments in 1974) had ensured access to FBI files by reporters, academics, and activists and had correspondingly reduced the press's dependence on Bureau handouts. No longer could an FBI director, through spoon-fed leaks and ghost-written articles, control the image that was communicated to the American people.

Congressional findings of 1975–1976 – in particular those documenting that Hoover had willingly serviced politically inspired requests of the White House and that attorneys general either had no knowledge of the scope of his activities or had intentionally avoided monitoring his administration of the Bureau – gave rise to demands for enactment of a legislative charter to define how the Bureau would operate in the future. While Congress mulled over various proposals (and ultimately enacted none), in March 1976 Attorney General Edward Levi issued new guidelines to govern FBI 'domestic security' investigations.

Based on the premise that FBI investigations should be initiated only in cases in which there was evidence of violations of federal statutes, Levi's guidelines sought to curb the discretion that previous attorneys general and presidents had conferred on Hoover throughout his tenure. In effect, the new guidelines permitted the FBI to initiate 'preliminary' investigations of non-criminal activities but limit them to ninety days. 'Preliminary' investigations were to be confined to verifying or refuting allegations of criminal conduct. This limitation in practice ended the ongoing fishing expeditions that had allowed Hoover to acquire damaging personal information about dissident activists, members of Congress, and other prominent persons (on the ground that they might one day violate the law or that they had associations with proscribed organizations or individuals).

Levi also sought to ensure that future attorneys general would exercise their oversight responsibilities. His guidelines required that the Department of Justice annually review the 'results of full domestic intelligence investigations . . . [and] determine in writing whether continued investigation is warranted.' These requirements of a full briefing and creation of a written record of authorization were calculated to prevent resort by FBI officials to Do Not File procedures (to hide what the Bureau itself had termed 'clearly illegal' activities), to ensure that the attorney general saw that the laws were faithfully executed, and to circumscribe the ability of future directors to advance the political interests of the White House.

Imposed as they were by executive order and not by statute, however, Levi's restrictions could be rescinded whenever future presidents established different priorities. And within five years, with Ronald Reagan's election to the presidency, this occurred. Expressly committed to 'unleashing' the intelligence agencies, Reagan moved quickly to return the FBI to monitoring dissident political activities.

Acting cautiously at first, the president, by Executive Order 12333 of 4 December 1981, directed the Bureau to 'conduct within the United States, when requested by officials of the intelligence community designated by the President, activities to collect foreign intelligence or support of foreign collection requirements.' How were such 'foreign intelligence' activities defined? Seeking to disarm foreseeable criticism that simple political dissent would be the focus of such investigations, Reagan's order prohibited any investigation undertaken 'for the purpose of acquiring information concerning the domestic activities of United States persons.' But this prohibition was cleverly qualified to permit the acquisition and dissemination of: (1) 'information obtained in the course of a lawful foreign intelligence, counter intelligence, international narcotics or international terrorist investigation' if necessary to protect 'the safety of any persons or organizations, including those who are targets, victims or hostages of international terrorist organizations'; (2) 'incidentally obtained information that *may* indicate involvement in activities that *may* violate *Federal, state, local or foreign law*'; and (3) information 'necessary for administrative purposes' (emphasis added). Not surprisingly, then, among the targets of such 'foreign intelligence/counterintelligence' investigations were critics of the administration's Central American policy.

Emboldened by the absence of any sustained protest, on 7 March 1983, William French Smith, Reagan's first attorney general, exploiting a current fear of international terrorism, issued new FBI 'domestic security/terrorism' guidelines. Smith's executive order rescinded the two explicit limitations of the Levi guidelines – that forbidding indefinite monitoring of dissident political activities and that requiring that attorneys general authorize FBI investigative activities in writing. The distinction between preliminary and full investigations was thereby abandoned, as was the requirement that FBI investigations be predicated on a probable violation of statute standard. The FBI, instead, was empowered to conduct investigations 'when the facts or circumstances reasonably indicate that two or more persons are engaged in an enterprise [to further] political or social goals wholly or in part through activities that involve force or violence and a violation of the criminal laws of the United States' and to 'anticipate or prevent crime.' Under Smith's more permissive guidelines, the FBI could resume investigating individuals who 'advocate criminal activity or indicate an *apparent intent* to engage in crime, particularly crimes of violence' (emphasis added).

Abandoning as well the Levi requirements of tight Justice Department supervision, Smith invited FBI officials to employ their new authority broadly, using their own perceptions of need and with minimal supervision by senior Justice Department officials. To be sure, the FBI director or a designated FBI assistant director was authorized to initiate 'domestic security/terrorism' investigations only for a limited, 180-day period, but this time restriction too was rendered meaningless when Smith empowered the FBI director or assistant director to reauthorize investigations for additional 180-day periods.

At the same time, protecting the principle of presidential deniability, Smith eviscerated the attorney general's oversight role. FBI officials need 'notify' the Justice Department's Office of Intelligence Policy and Review only when initiating a 'domestic security/terrorism' investigation. Smith also dropped the requirement that the department must 'determine in writing whether continued investigation is warranted.' Instead, his guidelines stipulated that the attorney general 'may, as he deems necessary, request the FBI to prepare a report on the status of the investigation.' Neither the attorney general nor the Office of Intelligence Policy and Review was required to create a written record of its authorization − thereby inviting FBI officials to institute and continue investigations whenever they themselves deemed them warranted and, more ominously, to reinstitute the Do Not File[1] procedures that Hoover had earlier devised to prevent discovery or effective oversight by Congress or the courts.

In view of President Reagan's earlier activities as an FBI 'confidential informant' and his role in alerting Hoover to Thomas Dewey's hostility, no one should have been surprised that his administration promptly ended restrictions inhibiting FBI monitoring of dissident political activities.[2] But Reagan's givenness to allowing the government to use the full power of its resources to monitor domestic political dissent was not his alone; it reflected as well the priorities of American conservatives throughout the Cold War era.

Conservatives in America were no longer committed to checking centralized power by having FBI activities confined to investigating criminal conduct. They had abandoned their earlier concern that an ambitious and independent FBI director could abuse his power for purely political ends. Consumed by their obsession with the 'communist' threat, they either advocated or tolerated the case for secret government and viewed any dissent on the left as a threat to orderly government. Conservatives, who once deplored Franklin D. Roosevelt's alleged usurpation of states' rights and penchant for bureaucratic independence, now championed an imperial presidency and the suppression of lawful dissent. The odyssey of *Chicago Tribune* reporter Walter Trohan from Hoover critic of the 1930s to Hoover partisan of the Cold War years epitomized this profound shift — underscored in 1987, during the Iran-contra hearings, by revelations of CIA Director William Casey's plan to use the profits from secret arms sales to Iran and contributions from private citizens and foreign governments to establish an 'off-the-shelf, self-sustaining, stand alone' entity to conduct intelligence operations without any need to brief Congress or request appropriations. The Reagan administration's decision to have the National Security Council staff conduct covert operations in order to circumvent the requirements both of congressional oversight (mandated by the Intelligence Oversight Act of 1980) and of specific restrictions on U.S. military support for the contras (imposed by the Boland Amendment of 1984) also sheds light on why Hoover was able to amass and consolidate his power after 1945 — given the fact that his principal constituency was always the American right.

In the final analysis, then, Congress's failure to enact an FBI legislative charter left the way open for another director-adventurer who, by exploiting a crisis atmosphere and supported by conservative anti-Communists, could reinstitute yet another reactionary scare and a wholesale repression. The potential for abuse did not die with Hoover in 1972.

1. National Security Council staff member Oliver North disclosed, during the Iran-*contra* hearings, that senior NSC officials employed a do not log procedure to ensure that especially sensitive documents were not indexed in the NSC records system and thus could be safely destroyed.

2. The terms in which Reagan justified doing so were suggested by the *Los Angeles Times* syndicate on 1 October 1987, in an account of an interview with the president conducted by newsman Arnaud de Borchgrave for the *Washington Times*. 'Members of Congress 'and a great many in the media and the press,' he president was quoted as having said, 'might be willing agents of Soviet influence or dupes of communist disinformation efforts.' When Reagan then described the 'dupes' as 'willing idiots,' de Borchgrave reportedly added, 'useful idiots.' 'Yes,' the president replied. 'They were to engage in a campaign that would make anticommunism unfashionable. They have succeeded. There was once a Congress in which they had a committee that would investigate even one of their own members if it was believed that person had communist involvement or communist leanings. Well, they've done away with those committees. That shows the success of what the Soviets were able to do in this country, with making it unfashionable to be anti-communist.'